ALL ■ IN ■ ONE

PHR®/SPHR®
Professional in
Human Resources
Certification

EXAM GUIDE

ALL IN ONE

PHR®/SPHR®
Professional in
Human Resources
Certification

EXAM GUIDE

Dory Willer, PCC
William H. Truesdell, SPHR

Mc
Graw
Hill
Education

New York   Chicago   San Francisco
Athens   London   Madrid   Mexico City
Milan   New Delhi   Singapore   Sydney   Toronto

ABOUT THE AUTHORS

Dory Willer is a certified executive coach with over 30 years of experience as a senior HR executive, keynote speaker, and strategic planning facilitator. She has broad and diverse experience working for blue-chip and Fortune 100 companies, leaving her last corporate position as a Vice President of HR to open Beacon Quest Coaching based in the San Francisco Bay Area. Willer coaches senior and C-suite executives in leadership enhancement, performance improvement, and career renewal, helping her clients to unleash their full potential. Additionally, she facilitates strategic planning sessions that stretch paradigms, align behaviors with goals, and hold groups accountable to produce results. She was among the first graduating classes from Stanford's Executive HR Certification Program (Graduate School of Business 1994). Willer achieved the designation of SPHR more than 20 years ago. She holds a B.S. degree in behavioral science from the University of San Francisco and several advanced certifications in professional coaching.

William H. Truesdell is president of The Management Advantage, Inc., a personnel management consulting firm. He spent more than 20 years in management with American Telephone and Telegraph in HR and operations. Truesdell is an expert on the subjects of personnel practices, employee handbooks, equal opportunity, and performance management programs. He is past president of the Northern California Employment Round Table and former HR course instructor at the University of California, Berkeley extension program. Truesdell holds the SPHR certification and a B.S. in business administration from the California State University at Fresno.

About the Contributor and Technical Editor

Bill Kelly, SPHR-CA, is the owner of Kelly HR, an HR consulting services firm specializing in providing generalist HR consulting services and support for small business enterprises. Bill's experience includes over 40 years of professional-level HR responsibilities, including 22 years at Bechtel in San Francisco and, later, at Brown and Caldwell Environmental Engineers in Pleasant Hill, California. His credentials include experience in employee relations, state and federal legal compliance, staffing and recruitment, equal employment opportunity and affirmative action, compensation, benefits, training and development, health and safety, and government contract management. Bill also has 18 years of experience in HR consulting that includes providing HR services, support, and advice to a wide range of Northern California clients. He has 17 years of experience as an instructor for the University of California extension program teaching such courses as Management of Human Resources; Recruiting, Selection, and Placement; California Employment Law; and Professional HR Certification Preparation. Bill has taught the Professional PHR/SPHR Certification Preparation Course for more than 15 years and the California HR Certification Preparation Course for 7 years for the Society for Human Resource Management (SHRM) and the Northern California HR Association

(NCHRA). He played a key role in the development of California's HR certification credential; he was also the project manager for the team of California HR professionals who developed SHRM's first California Learning System in support of California certification. Bill's professional leadership also includes roles on the board of directors and as national vice president for the Society for Human Resource Management (SHRM); the board of directors and president for the HR Certification Institute (HRCI); state director for the California State Council of SHRM; the board of directors and president for the Northern California HR Association (NCHRA); and commissioner and chair for the Marin County Personnel Commission. Bill received his B.S. in political science from Spring Hill College in Mobile, Alabama, and undertook post-graduate studies in organizational management at the College of William and Mary in Williamsburg, Virginia, and the University of Virginia in Richmond, Virginia. Prior to HR, Bill had a military career achieving the rank of Major in the United States Army with tours of duty in the United States, Germany, Thailand, and Vietnam.

Cataloging-in-Publication Data is on file with the Library of Congress

McGraw-Hill Education books are available at special quantity discounts to use as premiums and sales promotions, or for use in corporate training programs. To contact a representative, please visit the Contact Us pages at www.mhprofessional.com.

PHR®/SPHR® Professional in Human Resources Certification All-in-One Exam Guide

1234567890   DOC DOC   10987654

ISBN: Book p/n 978-0-07-182376-0 and CD p/n 978-0-07-182381-4
of set 978-0-07-182520-7

MHID: Book p/n 0-07-182376-X and CD p/n 0-07-182381-6
of set 0-07-182520-7

Sponsoring Editor Meghan Manfre	**Technical Editor** Bill Kelly	**Production Supervisor** Jean Bodeaux
Editorial Supervisor Jody McKenzie	**Copy Editor** Nancy Rapoport	**Composition** Cenveo Publishing Services
Project Editor Howie Severson, Fortuitous Publishing	**Proofreader** Paul Tyler	**Art Director, Cover** Jeff Weeks
Acquisitions Coordinator Mary Demery	**Indexer** Jack Lewis	

To all HR professionals who constantly strive to do better.
—The authors

To my husband, Jeff, who is my very own personal cheerleader,
constantly supporting and nudging me to new levels of success.
—Dory

To my wife, Donna, for her tolerance and encouragement.
—Bill

CONTENTS AT A GLANCE

CONTENTS

ACKNOWLEDGMENTS

First and foremost, we'd like to thank Meghan Manfre and her extremely talented staff at McGraw-Hill Education for making this book happen. Meghan's expertise as an acquisitions editor for this project included a huge dose of patience, perseverance, and encouragement. She understands that "life happens" once one commits to a goal, and then best laid plans go awry.

We'd also like to provide a note of mahalo to our literary agent, Carole Jelen. Carole has known Dory professionally since 2007, and throughout the years, she has been encouraging Dory to write a book. Carole brought this project to Dory's doorstep in 2013, and it was her tenacious guidance that created wings for this project.

Additionally a special shout out goes to Dr. Larry Bienati, who is one heck of a progressive HR professional. Larry's initial consultations, from his perspective as a college professor teaching human resources, helped us develop our unique formatting for the book—all with the intent to help the reader pass their exam. We'd also like to send a bucket of gratitude to the professionals who contributed to our *In the Trenches* sections: Grant Bassett, Larry Bienati, Susan Chritton, Susan Farwell, Jim Foord, John Fox, Fredi Foye-Helms, Joel Garfinkle, Jane Henderson, Rob Hyde, and Christina Nishiyama. These folks have provided insight, expert sage advice, and awesome perspective based on their first-hand experience, which is priceless.

Finally, there is no way this book could have been started, much less completed, without the expert input and guidance of Bill Kelly, our technical editor and contributing author of the compensation and benefits chapter. In addition to Bill's treasure trove of advice about the HRCI exams, and his experience as a facilitator/teacher for HRCI exam study groups for eons, it has just been plain delightful and an honor to have his helping hand on this project.

And with a last note of acknowledgement from Dory to coauthor Bill Truesdell: When this project was presented to me and I sought out a coauthor, your name leaped out of my contact lists, and I am so glad you said "yes." Your incredible knowledge, ease of writing, and great sense of humor have kept me upright and focused in times when I was overwhelmed. Thank you for the fantastic professionalism you've brought to this book and the graceful "I can do that" attitude!

INTRODUCTION

Allow us to be the first to congratulate you on making the decision to sit for an HRCI certification exam and to strive to obtain your Professional in Human Resources (PHR) or Senior Professional in Human Resources (SPHR) certification! Professional certifications are a mark of distinction that sets you apart in the profession, and speaks volumes about your commitment to your craft. More than 140,000 of your colleagues around the globe have obtained the HRCI certifications, including us.

Human resources is most likely part of our DNA makeup; we've lived it and breathed it for many decades. Our purpose is to share with you some strategies and experience that will assist you when you sit for the certification exam(s). It is our intention that this book will provide the knowledge and concepts you are expected to have mastered as a PHR and SPHR candidate. It is our pleasure to share those things with you. You also bring your own professional experience to the process. As you combine your experience with the information included in this book, you will be better able to answer the situational-based and competency-based questions about human resource situations that you will find on the exam.

We want you to be successful. It is our belief that the HRCI professional certifications are important because the certifications endorse your knowledge and expertise to employers and clients. Having a professional certification has become increasingly important. It may be a requirement of your next job assignment or the promotion you are pining for within your organization. You may decide that these certifications are necessary qualifications for future HR professionals that you hire. In any event, we wish you the best professional regards and success in passing your exam and earning the prestigious designation of PHR and SPHR.

HRCI Certification vs. SHRM Certification

At the time of this writing, there is a great deal of buzz from both SHRM (Society of Human Resource Management) and HRCI (Human Resource Certification Institute) regarding SHRM's plans for developing new HR certifications. Regardless of what ultimately happens with the development of the SHRM certifications, HRCI says it will continue to work diligently with HR professionals in the same way it has since administering its pioneering certification back in 1976. HRCI will continue to confer its industry-recognized certifications for professional levels of achievement.

The year of 2015 is going to be a transition year for SHRM's new certification program. SHRM has represented that it will permit individuals who hold HRCI certifications to also apply for and receive certification in its new program, which will carry the designations of SHRM-CP (SHRM Certified Professional) and SHRM-SCP (SHRM Senior Certified Professional). In terms of categories of knowledge and responsibilities defined by SHRM for the planned exams, we will learn more as we move into the future and SHRM creates its own exam structure. Whatever happens, the HRCI exams will continue to be administered and HRCI will remain a leader as an established, honored, and respected certifying body for the HR profession.

How to Use This Book

This book covers the entire PHR and SPHR Body of Knowledge (BOK) as it has been divided into six functional topic areas of human resources. The organization of this book, however, does not follow the ordering of the functional areas as defined by HRCI. Instead, we've purposefully arranged the functional areas in such a way that we begin with those topics we've found students to have the most experience with and build up to those topics that we feel are more complex and may require additional time for study. Our ordering of the functional areas is as follows:

1. Risk management

2. Workforce planning and employment

3. Business management and strategy

4. Employee and labor relations

5. Human resources development

6. Compensation and benefits

Additionally, within each functional area, we have also organized the presentation of topics to follow this same logic. As you progress through the material, we hope you will do so with a feeling of accomplishment at mastering the information presented and thereby increase your drive and motivation to continue.

Following is a brief overview of the organization of this book and how we feel this organization will benefit you.

Chapter 1

In Chapter 1, we explain everything you need to know about PHR and SPHR exams and also discuss the different types of HRCI certifications. Additionally, you'll find information about the process of registering for the exams, the actual exam experience, and what the style and format of questions are on the exams.

Chapter 2

Chapter 2 provides a list of all the U.S. laws and regulations that you will need to know. We placed this information in a chapter rather than an appendix to emphasize the importance of reviewing these laws and regulations prior to diving into the functional areas. Understanding these laws should make it easier for you to grasp the reasoning behind the material that is presented in Chapters 4–9. You will find some questions on the certification exams that are directly related to these laws.

Chapter 3

This chapter lists the 23 additional knowledge items that HRCI has identified as core knowledge items. These items may have applications across more than one functional area. We spell each knowledge item out individually and show you how they link to other knowledge mastery requirements for the certification process.

Chapters 4 Through 9

Chapters 4 through 9 go into the specifics of each functional area and discuss what we believe is essential knowledge for the HRCI exams. These chapters are designed to be concise and yet to effectively communicate the information. Each chapter provides an overview, a list of laws that will be applicable to the topics covered, and court cases that apply to the subject area At the end of each chapter, there is a review section that briefly summarizes the salient points of the chapter.

In The Trenches

In these chapters, you will find contributions from experts in the field titled "In The Trenches," which contain valuable insight and sage advice from professionals about a specific topic in that functional area.

Notes

Specially called out *Notes* are part of each chapter, too. These are interesting tidbits of information that are relevant to the topic and point out helpful information.

Questions and Answers

At the end of Chapters 2 through 9, you will find a set of review questions and answers to help you test your knowledge and comprehension. Practice, practice, practice—it will pay off on exam day.

Appendixes

We have also included four appendixes to supplement the information you need to know.

Appendix A   Appendix A is a list of abbreviations. The HR field is notorious for abbreviations creating the jargon in HR language, and these abbreviations have flowed into the everyday business language of employers, employees, and the public at large. It is likely that you will see questions on the exams that include and reference these acronyms so please familiarize yourself with this list.

Appendix B   In Appendix B, we have listed all of the associated legal cases you should know and review prior to sitting for the exams. The cases are organized by functional area and include a brief synopsis of what each case addressed. A URL is provided so that you can review the case in more detail, and we do recommend that you spend time reviewing these cases.

Appendix C   Appendix C provides you with additional resources that we feel would be helpful for digging deeper into some of the topics: literature, books, and websites that you can reference for greater insight and expanded information.

Appendix D   Appendix D provides information for the accompanying CD-ROM and the two practice exams we've created. Each practice exam consists of 175 questions with answer explanations for each answer choice, both correct and incorrect. These two exams should help you prepare yourself for the real McCoy when sitting for an actual HRCI exam.

Glossary

A glossary of terms has been created for your ease of reference. Using the glossary will help you review the key terms covered in this book.

Index

In the very back of the book is an index that will guide you to the appropriate pages where a term is mentioned or discussed.

The Examination

The PHR and SPHR exams are not simple true/false or memory-recall exams. You will be sitting for a three-hour, 175+ question multiple-choice exam that may contain up to five different question types. There will be complex situational questions, formula-based questions, knowledge-based questions, interpretational questions, and specific technique questions. Knowing how to get the most out of each question is crucial.

Situational Questions

The situational questions will test your ability to identify the relevant content. These questions will be lengthy. Pay particular attention as you read to accurately identify the *actual* question so that you can eliminate irrelevant and insignificant information.

Formula-Based Questions

The formula-based questions are more thought-provoking. You must know both the formula and how to perform the calculation in order to reach the correct answer.

Knowledge-Based Questions

The knowledge-based questions will require you to know your facts. These questions test your knowledge of different HR laws. Sometimes you will be asked to identify an example chart or graph, so pay attention to the figures that are included in the chapters.

Interpretational Questions

The interpretational questions will test your ability to deduce a situation or condition and to select the most appropriate answer. All answers may actually be correct, yet selecting the *best* answer could apply.

Specific Technique Questions

With the specific technique questions, you will be tested on how to apply a tool or technique.

NOTE The questions included at the end of the chapters and on the CD-ROM practice exams will provide you with good examples of these different question types.

Preparing for the Exam

Preparing for any type of certification exam is not about memorizing information. The PHR and SPHR exams require that established HR professionals with the requisite years of experience be able to demonstrate that they can apply their experience and knowledge in a host of different situations.

NOTE You have already invested in an education for your career; investing in serious study time and preparation will pay off so that you can pass your exam.

For those with a more limited or the minimal experience qualifications, let us suggest you begin preparation and study six months prior to your exam date. For those with significantly more experience and time on-the-job as an HR professional, three months should be your yardstick. If you want to "*shoot from the hip*" and not study the material outlined in this book, your chances of passing one of these professional exams will likely by low—even if you have been in an HR exempt position for years. We aren't saying that it can't be done, but your chances of passing the exams are much better if you study the information in this book and the questions on the accompanying CD-ROM as well as use the companion practice exam book, *PHR/SPHR Professional in Human Resources Certification Practice Exams*, to prepare for the time when you will sit in that room with a hundred other candidates to spend three hours selecting the correct answers. Guessing strategies are not foolproof and not a good substitute for solid study habits in preparation for an exam. The best preparation strategy is one that is focused on committed preparation with study time spent in a productive manner.

Exam Tips

The following exam tips are exactly what they sound like, tips to assist you in your preparation for the exam. From Dory's years of experience coaching people to achieve goals and achievements, she has compiled a list of tips from exam takers of all disciplines. First let's start with studying:

- Before studying, go for a brief walk to take in some fresh air and clear your mind in preparation for the focused time and new concentration. Put all the other thoughts and projects of the day on a back burner and allow your mind to be a clean slate, setting the intention that this specific amount of time is for the exclusive intention of HRCI studying.

- Make sure your "do not disturb" sign is on your door if you are at home or in the office, so others clearly know that nothing is to disturb you during your hour long study time. Speaking of an hour, that's plenty of time to devote to studying on a regular set schedule. Most people find that four or five hours a week is sufficient for this type of material.

- Clear your study area. It should be free of anything else that might distract you from studying. Keep your focus on the studying at hand, and to add a little incentive, create a bit of visual incentive for yourself—the desired end result of a letter stating you have successfully passed your exam. Spoof a letter from HRCI, print it, and put it in a nice picture frame and place it in front of your every time you begin your study time. What the mind can conceive you can achieve!

- Select a time of day that is optimum for you to study. Are you best in the wee hours of the early morning with a cup of coffee prior to work, or perhaps it's the noon hour. Maybe your rhythm is one of a person who kicks in just after dinner. Find that sweet hour and make the appointment on your calendar, listing it as VIP-HRCI. *You* are the very important person and this appointment will cause you to think twice before allowing another activity to slip in on your time slot.

- The old adage "practice makes perfect" is not quite right. *Perfect practice makes perfect* is a better way to state the intention. As you make your study time perfect and practice saying "no thank you" to others and other things that would interrupt your study time, you are practicing the perfect combination that will allow you to stay focused and produce the results you are after.

- Beginning two days before the exam, be sure to get a full night's sleep each night, which is typically 7–9 hours for most people. Studies prove that a REM state of sleeping is extremely helpful for brain function.

- Hydrate, hydrate, hydrate the day before and the day of the exam. Try to avoid massive amounts of caffeine (it will keep you awake and rob you of precious hydration). Water is good for the body, but even better for the brain, bringing oxygen which helps your brain functions improve.

A couple of other helpful tips about the HRCI exams in particular:

- Nothing that has occurred in the last two years will be covered on your exam. It takes HRCI almost two years to process questions and add them to an exam. So don't worry about current events or a new law that just passed.

- Trust your gut, your first impression. First impressions of the correct answer are many times the best choice. This should not be confused with "guessing along." This refers to topics you know that you know.

- Be careful not to base your answer solely on what your current organization's policy is. Keep focused on generally accepted HR practices.

- There will be no patterns, so don't even try to look for them. The psychometric exam process used for the HRCI exams prevents questions from falling into patterns.

- Only *federal* laws apply—don't mix up federal laws with your state laws.

- The most common weakness of HR test takers is over-analyzing the options. Be thorough but be reasonable in your analysis and selection of the options.

- When stumped, try to eliminate the obvious answers and then just focus on what remains.

- *Do read* all four answer choices—it may be that you need to select the *best* answer choice and yet all answer choices are correct.

- Resist the urge to change your answers—this goes hand in hand with tip 1. If you are absolutely, positively sure that you have an incorrect answer, go ahead. But for the most part, resist the urge to change answers.

- Don't rush. Manage your time. You will have a little over a minute for each question. A clock is visible on your monitor screen counting down what amount of time is left. Keep an eye on it.

Final Thoughts

This book has been designed to not only assist you, the HRCI exam candidate, in studying for the PHR and SPHR exams, but also to serve as a reliable reference book to be placed on the shelf in your office as a resource. There is a lot for a human resources professional to remember. It is our hope that this book becomes a convenient resource that guides you when something pops up that you need a refresher on. At a minimum, we hope it gives you direction in your effort to improve your HR circumstance.

And finally, thank you for selecting this book. We sincerely hope your PHR or SPHR exam goes well, and wish you the absolute best on exam day!

Human Resources Certifications

The skills and abilities that an HR professional uses to produce desired results requires a mastery of sorts. Mastery of any profession will involve a continuous career-long commitment to learning, and that is a foundational truth within the Human Resources profession. HR has been, and continues to be, an evolving component of an organization because its basic focus is on people. The constant changes and outside influences on an organization's workforce increase the demands on HR professionals. HR professionals today walk a tight line and must master the art of staying two steps ahead while having one foot firmly planted in the present.

The HR Certification Institute (HRCI, http://www.hrci.org) was established in 1976 as an internationally recognized certifying organization for the human resource profession. Its mission has been to develop and deliver the highest quality certification programs that validate mastery in the field of human resource management and contribute to the continued improvement of individual and organizational performance. More than 130,000 HR professionals in more than 100 countries have been certified.

Professional Certification

Credentialing as an HR professional demonstrates to your colleagues and your organization that you are committed to a higher standard and ethic, and dedicated to the HR profession. When you achieve your HR credential, it signals your mastery of core practices and principles in HR management, raising the confidence of an employer and your peers in your abilities.

A professional certification is not to be confused with a certificate program. Professional certifications are based on work experience and education along with recertification requirements. Certificate programs do not require work experience or an educational component, nor do they require recertification. Figure 1-1 shows the HRCI April 2014 certification study.

Figure 1-1
HRCI
certification
study 2014

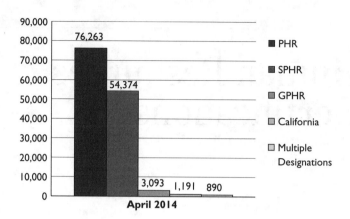

The Benefits of Certification

Earning a credential as a PHR (Professional in Human Resources), or SPHR (Senior Professional in Human Resources), adds a level of recognition as an expert in the HR profession. This certification is a distinction that sets you apart in the profession, indicating you have a high level of knowledge and skills. It adds to your career value and to the organization you work in. Your HR Certification could mean the difference between you and your competition. In fact, 96 percent of employers say that an HR-certified candidate applying for a job would have an advantage over a non-certified candidate. And HR professionals who hold the PHR or SPHR tend to make more money than their peers who do not.[1] According to PayScale Human Capital, this pattern is true for all industries and metropolitan areas in the United States. HR certification is becoming an important means for employers to recognize HR expertise and for HR professionals to increase their value and worth.

According to a 2012 HRCI exit survey,[2] earning a PHR or SPHR credential can help you:

- Boost your confidence with recognition as an HR expert
- Master the knowledge most important to expert HR professionals as defined by the current HRCI body of knowledge
- Expand your outlook on the HR field and bring new ideas to your workplace
- Keep up with HR developments including the latest legislative changes
- Protect your organization from risk by ensuring regulatory compliance
- Stand out from other HR candidates in a job search
- Demonstrate your long-term commitment to the HR profession

The HR Certification Institute Certifications

The Professional in Human Resources (PHR) and Senior Professional in Human Resources (SPHR) exams are created using HRCIs competencies defined as the HR Body of Knowledge, which outlines the responsibilities of and knowledge needed by today's HR professional. The HR Body of Knowledge (BOK) is created by HR subject matter experts through a rigorous practice analysis study and validated by HR professionals working in the field through an extensive survey instrument. It is updated every five years to ensure it is consistent with current practices in the HR field.

This book focuses on the PHR and SPHR exams and the knowledge required to pass those exams. The main difference between the PHR and SPHR exams is with the weighting of the questions (see the section, "The Exam's Design" later in this chapter).

NOTE Table 1-1 lists all of the other various HR certifications administered by HRCI for your information.

HRCI has compiled a list of criteria for the ideal PHR and SPHR candidates.[3] Compare this list in Table 1-1 to your experience and abilities to determine which exam you are best qualified and suited for.

PHR	SPHR
Primary focus is on carrying out established HR programs rather than their design and development.	Primary focus is on the design, planning, and implementation of HR policies and programs as compared to implementing HR programs.
Main responsibility is for transactional operational HR matters.	Recognized as the primary source of HR authority in the organization.
Typically reports to another HR professional within the organization.	Typically reports to top-level organizational management.
Has at least one to four years of professional-level HR experience, depending on education, handling a number of general HR responsibilities.	Has at least four to seven years of wide-ranging and complex HR generalist experience handling organizational issues.
Responsibilities focus on one or more HR functions rather than organization-wide HR services.	Responsibilities include addressing and resolving complicated organizational issues that require extensive HR knowledge and experience.
Follows established HR policies and guidelines for decision-making.	Understands the business beyond HR and has influence applicable to the overall organization.
Establishes credibility through the consistent application of HR knowledge and experience.	Contributes to the organization's public reputation and position in the marketplace through the application of extensive HR knowledge, skills, and abilities.

Table 1-1   HRCI PHR/SPHR Eligibility Requirements

PHR

The Professional in Human Resources (PHR) certification demonstrates mastery of the technical and operational aspects of HR practices and U.S. laws and regulations. This credential is for the HR professional who focuses on program implementation, has a tactical/logistical orientation, is accountable to another HR professional within the organization, and has responsibilities that focus on the HR department rather than the whole organization. The body of knowledge breakdown for the HRCI PHR exam is as follows:[4]

- Business Management and Strategy (11%)
- Workforce Planning and Employment (24%)
- Human Resource Development (18%)
- Compensation and Benefits (19%)
- Employee and Labor Relations (20%)
- Risk Management (8%)

Eligibility Requirements   To take The PHR exam, you must meet *one* of the following requirements:

- A minimum of one year of experience in an exempt-level HR position with a master's degree or higher, or
- A minimum of two years of experience in an exempt-level HR position with a bachelor's degree, or
- A minimum of four years of experience in an exempt-level HR position with a high school diploma

SPHR

The Senior Professional in Human Resources (SPHR) certification is recognized as a professionally relevant credential for those who have mastered the strategic and policy-making aspects of HR management in the United States. It is designed for the HR professional who plans, rather than implements, HR policy, focuses on the "big picture," has ultimate accountability in the HR department, has breadth and depth of knowledge in all HR disciplines, understands the business beyond the HR function, and influences the overall organization. The body of knowledge breakdown for the HRCI SPHR exam is as follows:

- The Business Management and Strategy (30%)
- Workforce Planning and Employment (17%)
- Human Resource Development (19%)
- Compensation and Benefits (13%)
- Employee and Labor Relations (14%)
- Risk Management (7%)

Eligibility Requirements   Eligible candidates for the SPHR exam have:

- A minimum of four years of experience in an exempt-level HR position with a master's degree or higher, or
- A minimum of five years of experience in an exempt-level HR position with a bachelor's degree, or
- A minimum of seven years of experience in an exempt-level HR position with a high school diploma

 NOTE   If you are not a good "test taker," you might want to start out with the PHR exam before jumping into the SPHR exam.

GPHR

HRCI offers a separate certification called Global Professional in Human Resources (GPHR). It focuses on international employment issues associated with widely varying legal requirements and cultural differences. This book is not intended to prepare you for the GPHR exam. This HRCI credential demonstrates the mastery of cross-border HR responsibilities to include strategies of globalization, development of HR policies and initiatives that support organizational global growth and employer retention, and creation of organizational programs, processes, and tools that achieve worldwide business goals. HRCI breaks down its competency and body of knowledge areas on global issues and certification expectations for the GPHR exam as follows:[5]

- Strategic HR Management (25%)
- Global Talent Acquisition and Mobility (21%)
- Global Compensation and Benefits (17%)
- Talent and Organizational Development (22%)
- Workforce Relations and Risk Management (15%)

Eligibility Requirements   Eligible candidates for the GPHR exam have:

- A minimum of two years of global experience in an exempt-level HR position with a master's degree or higher, or
- A minimum of three years of experience (with two of the three being global HR experience) in an exempt-level HR position with a bachelor's degree, or
- A minimum of four years of experience (with two of the four being global HR experience) in an exempt-level HR position with less than a bachelor's degree

PHR-CA/SPHR-CA

Both the PHR-CA and the SPHR-CA augment the PHR and SPHR certification exams with a focus on California HR-related laws and practices. HR professionals who earn a PHR-CA or SPHR-CA have proven that they are experts in the laws, rules, regulations, and legal mandates specific to the state of California. These exams do not test knowledge already covered on the PHR or SPHR exam. Candidates must hold a current PHR or SPHR certification to be eligible to sit for the California certification exam. The exam content areas of body of knowledge are the same for both the PHR-CA and the SPHR-CA as follows:[6]

- Compensation/Wage and Hour (22%)
- Employment and Employee Relations (46%)
- Benefits and Leaves of Absence (20%)
- Health, Safety and Workers' Compensation (12%)

Eligibility Requirements   You must hold a current PHR or SPHR designation to sit for the California exam.

HRBP

The Human Resource Business Professional (HRBP) is a competency-based credential that is designed to validate professional-level core HR knowledge and skills. The credential demonstrates mastery of generally accepted technical and operational HR principles, independent of geographic region, from professionals practicing HR outside of the United States. HRCI's body of knowledge breaks down for the HRBP as follows:[7]

- HR Administration (22%)
- Recruitment and Selection (22%)
- Employee Relations and Communication (20%)
- Training and Development (15%)
- Compensation and Benefits (14%)
- Health, Safety and Security (7%)

Eligibility Requirements   The HRBP is eligible to candidates outside of the United States with:

- A minimum of one year of professional-level experience in an HR position with a master's degree or global equivalent, or
- A minimum of two years of professional-level experience in an HR position with a bachelor's degree or global equivalent, or
- A minimum of four years of professional-level experience in an HR position with a high school diploma or global equivalent

HRMP

The Human Resource Management Professional (HRMP) demonstrates mastery of generally accepted HR principles in strategy, policy development, and service delivery. The credential is developed to validate the following core HR knowledge and skills, and demonstrated mastery of generally accepted principles, independent of geographic region, from professionals practicing human resources outside of the United States. The HRMP exam content areas are:[8]

- HR as a Business Leader (32%)
- People Development and Talent Management (29%)
- HR Service Delivery (32%)
- Measurement (16%)

Eligibility Requirements

- A minimum of four years of professional-level experience in an HR position with a master's degree or global equivalent, or
- A minimum of five years of professional-level experience in an HR position with a bachelor's degree or global equivalent, or
- A minimum of seven years of professional-level experience in an HR position with a high school diploma or global equivalent

Additionally, applicants for the HRMP must demonstrate knowledge of their local HR laws. This requirement may be demonstrated in a variety of ways, including the following:

- Having a national or local certification (such as PHR, SPHR, GPHR) that includes knowledge of employment laws, or
- Having a bachelor's degree (or global equivalent) or higher in Human Resources, or
- Completing a university- or college-level course in employment law, or
- Completing a formal training class or certificate program in employment law sponsored by a university/college, HR association, or other approved training provider

Recertification

After you are certified, you have to recertify every three years on or before your certification expiration date to keep your designation current. If you do not recertify within the three years, your certification will expire. All certifications are valid for three years. Recertification can be accomplished through demonstrated professional HR activities (which HRCI prefers), by earning 60 recertification credit hours, or retaking the exam.

The simplest way is to complete and track a minimum of 60 credit hours of HR-related continuing education activities within the three year period. The "hard" way is to retake the exam, which needs to occur before your current certification expires.

There are several on-the-job activities that earn credit in addition to attending seminars and classes. You can earn recertification credit for a first-time on-the-job project if it has added to your overall HR knowledge. A maximum of 20 credit hours applies. These projects are commonly overlooked and may include examples such as:

- Implementation of a new benefit plan or compensation rollout
- Research, design and implementation of a wellness program
- Research and design of a performance-management system
- Implementation of an HR Information System (HRIS) system
- Participating in labor negotiations
- Creation of an employee handbook

Additionally, teaching HR-related skills or knowledge via training, coaching, and instruction, along with research/publishing in the HR field, will provide recertification credits. Even volunteer activities using HR skills qualifies, as does active professional membership in an HR-related organization such as the Society of Human Resource Management (SHRM) and its many chapters.

NOTE The GPHR requires 15 of the 60 recertification credit hours to be in International HR. The SPHR and HRMP require 15 credit hours of the 60 to be in Business Management and Strategy. The PHR-CA and SPHR-CA require 15 of the 60 recertification credit hours to be specific to California.

HR Certification Institute's Role

The HR Certification Institute (HRCI) exists to enhance the professionalism of HR professionals with the various certification processes. The institute is a non-profit separate entity from the Society of Human Resource Professionals (SHRM). HRCI is responsible for:

- Conducting the practice analysis that results in the HR Body of Knowledge
- Developing test questions and maintaining the test bank versions
- Determining candidates' eligibility to take the exams
- Managing the details of test registration and the testing process
- Approving recertification activities by which certified HR professionals retain their designations

HRCI was accredited by the national Commission for Certifying Agencies (NCCA) in 2008. It partners with Prometric (www.prometric.com) for computerized exam delivery.

The Significance of the Body of Knowledge

The HRCI body of knowledge (BOK) is the description of the complete set of concepts, tasks, responsibilities, and the knowledge required to successfully understand and perform generalist HR-related duties associated with each of its credentials. The BOK is periodically updated, typically every five years, to ensure it is consistent with and reflects current practices in the HR field. All exam test questions are specifically linked to a BOK item.

The Test Development Process

HRCI follows certification-industry best practices to create and keep their exams updated. The institute's question writing and question review processes are designed to reflect the best practices for exam question writing and review in the certification industry. The institute also ensures that questions are developed by actual HR practitioners for the HR practitioner. The following are the steps used in developing its exams:

- **Step 1** The process begins with a practice analysis study that defines the HR body of knowledge (BOK) from which exam questions are created. The BOK is a source document that identifies the basic principles, concepts, and knowledge requirements for HR generalists to successfully carry out their duties and responsibilities for each level and type of certification offered by HRCI. A 10-member practice analysis task force is organized that is responsible for conducting critical incident interviews and focus panels to identify and collect current information and practice patterns for HR generalists. This information is sorted into process and content-based approaches to functional areas of responsibility. The final results are submitted to the HRCI Board of Directors for approval. The approved result is the "HR body of knowledge," also called "exam content." Practice analysis studies are typically conducted every five years. The next PHR/SPHR practice analysis study will occur in 2018.

- **Step 2** Exam item development begins with two U.S. 15-member item writing panels consisting of certified HR professionals who received special training and are tasked to write 35 new test items (questions) each year. Separate 15-member writing panels write test items for the GPHR and the California certification exams.

- **Step 3** Questions prepared by the item writing panels are reviewed by item review panels consisting of veteran-writers. These item review panels look to ensure the test questions are reflective of the applicable BOK, are relevant to the HR field, and are adequately supported by the evidence and subject matter expert literature—literature reviewed by a panel that checks for accuracy and proper coding to the HRCI functional area. Items that pass this review screen are collected into an "item bank" to be selected as appropriate for upcoming exams.

- **Step 4** All questions must pass validity and reliability testing requirements. This happens when a new test item is initially used on an exam. The new test item is part of 25 unscored items randomly distributed on the exam. Their initial appearance is to develop a statistical profile that will determine whether the item meets validity and reliability requirements based on exam results, thus usable as a scored item on future exams.

- **Step 5** Exams consist of 175 questions, 25 of which are unscored, and multiple versions of the exam are created and reviewed by another panel.

- **Step 6** A passing score is determined for each of the seven different exam versions.

- **Step 7** Each question on the exam version is pre-equated to determine the difficulty level of that version. Item Response Theory (IRT) is used to pre-equate. Because all versions of the exam are pre-equated, the number of questions answered correctly to earn a passing score varies depending on the exam form version. The minimum passing score is a scaled score of 500. This is a floating score based on the degree of difficulty of the exam; that is, a more difficult exam will have a lower floating score while a less difficult exam will have a high floating score.

Figure 1-2 provides a flowchart of the exam test development.

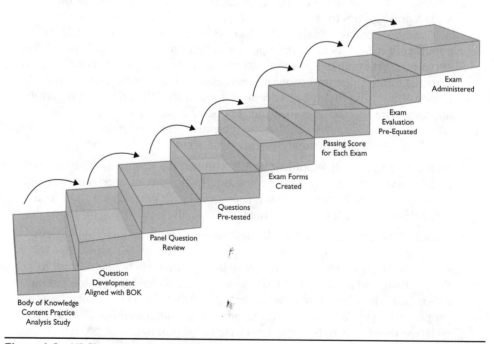

Figure 1-2 HRCI exam development process

All questions appearing on the PHR and SPHR exams are linked to HRCI's body of knowledge and responsibilities statements, which are located in Chapter 3 and at the front of each functional area in Chapters 4 through 9.

The Exam Experience

All exams are delivered by computer-based testing (CBT). Computer-based testing is the standard for many other test delivery programs. CBT is testing done in person, on a computer, at an approved testing center. CBT offers a more consistent test delivery, faster scoring and reporting, and enhanced test security. Exam takers receive their preliminary pass/fail results before walking out of the testing center. Official pass/fail notices come in the mail a few weeks after the exam.

The PHR, SPHR, and GPHR exams are three hours in length for testing. Both the PHR and SPHR have the same number of multiple-choice questions, 175, of which 150 are scored questions and 25 are pre-test (unscored). The GPHR's make-up of questions is 165 multiple-choice (140 scored questions and 25 pre-test). The HRBP is lengthier with 170 questions (145 of those are scored, 26 are pre-test), allowing 3 hours and 25 minutes for the exam. The HRMP allows 2 hours and 30 minutes for the exam consisting of 130 questions (105 scored questions and 25 pre-test questions). Both the PHR-CA and the SPHR-CA are allotted 2 hours and 15 minutes and have 125 multiple-choice questions.

Seventy-five percent of the PHR exam and 85 percent of the SPHR exam are heavily experiential—that is, application- or situation-based. The exams test a knowledge or cognitive comprehension level of 25 percent for the PHR and 15 percent for the SPHR. The PHR and the SPHR exams have test questions that require the following:

- Knowledge and comprehension (recall of factual material, translation, or interpretation of a concept)

- Application and problem solving (solving new, real-life problems through application of familiar principles or generalizations)

- Synthesis and evaluation (combining distantly related elements into a whole involving critical judgments in terms of accuracy or consistency of logic)[9]

Strict rules are enforced at the testing centers to ensure a secure, consistent, and fair test experience for all exam takers. Reviewing the "What to Expect" located at www .prometric.com/en-us/for-test-takers/Prepare-for-Test-Day/Pages/what-to-expect.aspx is advisable for preparation. For example, you will be asked to empty your pockets and turn your pockets inside-out, and a purse must be stored in a locker during the test.

Registering for the Exam

Exams are given twice a year (May/June and December/January) depending on the geographical area of the testing center. An easy-to-follow online step-by-step process to register is located at www.hrci.org/apply/application-process/phr-sphr-gphr-ca-application-process. Because of the time it takes to review documentation supporting the application process, there are deadlines associated with registration. We suggest you register early. There are also fees associated with registering, depending on the exam you will be taking. When your application has been deemed eligible, you will receive an Authorization to Test (ATT) letter, which details how you will schedule your exam appointment.

The Exam's Design

The PHR and SPHR exams will consist of 175 multiple-choice questions. The PHR exam is more heavily weighted in the functional area of Workforce Planning and Employment (24%), whereas the SPHR exam is weighted heavily in the functional area of Business Management and Strategy (30%). Table 1-2 illustrates the differences in the weightings for each exam and indicates the number of questions you can expect in the specific functional areas.

HRCI produces multiple versions of the exam for each testing level (PHR and SPHR). Prometric operates computerized-based testing centers across the United States and its system is programmed so that any one of the multiple versions may be used for a testing candidate, which means that the person sitting next to you very well may be taking a different exam. Some test versions have a number of questions where knowledge of the related legislation or the name of a court case will be needed (see Chapter 2 and Appendix B); other versions may not dive into that, or only indirectly. The other variable is whether there are any math questions on the exam; some exams have them, some don't. As a result, preparing for the exam should address all of this.

According to SHRM, the Spring 2013 national pass rates were as follows:

- PHR: 60%
- SPHR: 58%
- GPHR: 48%

NOTE If you already hold a PHR certification and you do not pass the SPHR exam, you will still retain your PHR certification.

HRCI Functional Area	PHR		SPHR	
	Weighting	Questions	Weighting	Questions
Risk Management	8%	14	7%	12
Workforce Planning and Employment	24%	42	17%	30
Business Management and Strategy	11%	19	30%	52
Employee and Labor Relations	20%	35	14%	25
Human Resource Development	18%	32	19%	33
Compensation and Benefits	19%	33	13%	23

Table 1-2 PHR/SPHR Exam Weighting

Chapter Review

Professional HR certification serves as an acknowledg[e] demonstrated mastery of core HR skills, principles, and to the best practice in Human Resources. This book pro edge and principles needed to pass your PHR or SPHR ex rience can provide you with the hands-on experience ar that are an additional essential part to earning the PHR

HR certification consists of four key components:

- Eligibility through a combination of past work exp[erience]
- Commitment and demonstration to a high profess[ional]
- Demonstrated applied knowledge and skills throu[gh]
- Ongoing professional development for career lifelong learning through recertification requirements

Having a thorough and complete understanding of the HRCI Body of Knowledge, which is located in Chapter 3 of this book, and the front matter of each functional area in Chapters 4–9, is absolutely vital for identifying a correct answer for both the PHR and SPHR exams. You need to know the objective of those laws and regulations inside-out.

Remember that the PHR and SPHR exams are based on federal laws and cases and not local state laws and ordinances (only the PHR-CA and SPHR-CA have a basis in state law and that would be California).

Last, the HRCI website (www.HRCI.org) goes into far greater detail about exam eligibility, registration, recertification, and what the exam questions may look like. Prepare yourself for scenario types of questions and be sure to take the sample test questions at the end of each chapter in this book. Guessing as a test tactic is not a good substitute for studying in test preparation. Correct answers come from sufficient studying and test practice.

Endnotes

1. PayScale Human Capital research report, "The Market Value of PHR and SPHR Certifications", http://resources.payscale.com/rs/payscale/images/report_SPHR_PHR.pdf

2. "The Value of HR Certification Around the World", exit study 2012, http://www.hrci.org/docs/default-source/web-files/2014-certification-handbook-pdf.pdf?sfvrsn=8

3. *HRCI Certification Policies and Procedures Handbook*, http://staging.hrci.org/uploadedfiles/Content/Resource_Library/Certification_Handbooks_and_Other_Publications/2010%20Certification%20Handbook.pdf

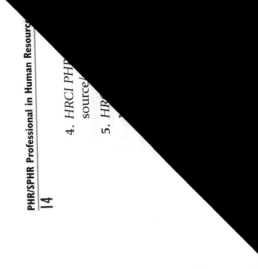

/SPHR *Body of Knowledge Handbook*, www.hrci.org/docs/default-
web-files/phr_sphr-body-of-knowledge-pdf.pdf?sfvrsn=14

CI GPHR *Body of Knowledge Handbook*, www.hrci.org/docs/default-source/
web-files/gphr-bok-pdf?sfvrsn=0

6. HRCI PHR-CA/SPHR-CA *Body of Knowledge Handbook*, www.hrci.org/docs/
default-source/web-files/2013-california-body-of-knowledge.pdf?sfvrsn=4

7. HRCI HRBP *Body of Knowledge Handbook*, www.hrci.org/docs/default-source/
web-files/hrbpbok-pdf.pdf?sfvrsn=0

8. HRCI HRMP *Body of Knowledge Handbook*, www.hrci.org/docs/default-source/
web-files/hrmpbok-pdf.pdf?sfvrsn=0

9. HRCI *Certification Policies and Procedures Handbook*, http://staging.hrci.org/
uploadedfiles/Content/Resource_Library/Certification_Handbooks_and_
Other_Publications/2010%20Certification%20Handbook.pdf

U.S. Laws and Regulations

In this chapter we introduce the federal laws and legislation that the human resource professional must be knowledgeable of. After studying this chapter and completing the test questions, you should have an understanding of the relevance of these laws to the employment relationship. HR professionals in both small and large companies play an important role in dealing with day-to-day employment issues relating to recruiting, hiring, managing, and training of employees. Ensuring that an employer's policies and actions follow the law, and keeping employers out of legal jeopardy, are essential function valued by employers.

What You Need to Know
Concerning Employee Management

We have structured this chapter so that it not only covers the necessary knowledge needed for the HRCI exams, but can also be used as a reference tool in your day-to-day needs working in human resources. The laws are summarized and listed in groupings according to the number of employees an organization employs, from 1 to 100+. Included is a reference URL that points to the law's full description. Legal regulation constantly evolves, so when using this guide as a reference book, be sure to reference the URL provided and specific state laws that govern your work locations.

- If you have from 1 to 14 employees there are 53 federal laws you must abide by.
- If you have from 15 to 19 employees, there are an additional 10 federal laws for your attention.
- If you have from 20 to 49 employees, add another 4 laws to the list.
- If you have from 50 to 99 employees, add another 6 laws to the list.
- If you have 100 or more employees, there are a total of 74 federal laws you must know and be in compliance with.
- If you are in a federal agency, you must comply with 6 laws specifically focused on your employee management issues.

In Part II of this guide, the body of knowledge areas within each chapter will direct you back to this chapter's specific law for reference. We suggest that you thoroughly explore this chapter's information before moving into Part II, for greater ease with the HRCI exam's body of knowledge. Then gauge your understanding of the laws by taking the pretest at the end of this chapter.

1. When You Have One or More Employees

Employers sometimes forget that the moment they hire their first employee they become subject to a host of legal requirements. Below are 53 laws that will impact an employer with one or more employees on the payroll.

1.1 The Clayton Act (1914)

This legislation modified the Sherman Anti-Trust Act by prohibiting mergers and acquisitions that would lessen competition. It also prohibited a single person from being a Director of two or more competing corporations. The act also restricts the use of injunctions against labor and legalized peaceful strikes, picketing, and boycotts.

For more information, see 15 U.S.C. Sec.12, www.law.cornell.edu/uscode/text/15/12.

1.2 The Consumer Credit Protection Act (1968)

Congress expressed limits to the amount of wages that can be garnished or withheld in any one week by an employer to satisfy creditors. This law also prohibits employee dismissal because of garnishment for any one indebtedness.

For more information, see www.dol.gov/compliance/laws/comp-ccpa.htm.

1.3 The Copeland "Anti-Kickback" Act (1934)

This act precludes a federal contractor or subcontractor from inducing an employee to give up any part of his or her wages to the employer for the benefit of having a job.

For more information, see www.dol.gov/whd/regs/statutes/copeland.htm.

1.4 The Copyright Act (1976)

The Copyright Act offers protection of "original works" for authors so others may not print, duplicate, distribute, or sell their work. In 1998, the Copyright Term Extension Act further extended copyright protection to the duration of the author's life plus 70 years for general copyrights and to 95 years for works made for hire and works copyrighted before 1978. If anyone in the organization writes technical instructions, policies and procedures, manuals, or even e-mail responses to customer inquiries, it would be a good idea to speak with your attorney and arrange some copyright agreements to clarify whether the employer or the employee who authored those documents will be designated the copyright owner. Written agreements can be helpful in clearing any possible misunderstandings.

For more information, see www.copyright.gov/title17/92appa.pdf.

1.5 The Davis-Bacon Act (1931)

This law requires contractors and subcontractors on certain federally funded or assisted construction projects over $2,000 in the United States to pay wages and fringe benefits at least equal to those prevailing in the local area where the work is performed. This law applies only to laborers and mechanics. It also allows trainees and apprentices to be paid less than the predetermined rates under certain circumstances.

For more information, see www.dol.gov/whd/regs/statutes/dbra.htm.

1.6 The Dodd-Frank Wall Street Reform and Consumer Protection Act (2010)

This law offers a very wide range of mandates affecting all federal financial regulatory agencies and almost every part of the nation's financial services industry. It includes a non-binding vote for shareholders on executive compensation, golden parachutes, and return of executive compensation based on inaccurate financial statements. Also included are requirements to report CEO pay compared to the average employee compensation and provision of financial rewards for whistleblowers.

For more information, see www.sec.gov/about/laws/wallstreetreform-cpa.pdf.

1.7 The Economic Growth and Tax Relief Reconciliation Act (EGTRRA) (2001)

Here are modifications to the Internal Revenue Code that adjust pension vesting schedules, increasing retirement plan limits, permitting pre-tax catch-up contributions by participants over the age of 50 in certain plans (which are not tested for discrimination when made available to the entire workforce) and modification of distribution and rollover rules.

For more information, see www.irs.gov/pub/irs-tege/epchd104.pdf.

1.8 The Electronic Communications Privacy Act (ECPA) (1986)

This is actually and uniquely a law composed of two pieces of legislation, the Wiretap Act and the Stored Communications Act. Combined, they provide rules for access, use, disclosure, interpretation, and privacy protections of electronic communications, and provide the possibility of both civil and criminal penalties for violations. They prohibit interception of e-mails in transmission and access to e-mails in storage. The implications for HR have to do with recording employee conversations. Warnings such as "This call may be monitored or recorded for quality purposes" are intended to provide the notice required by this legislation. Having cameras in the workplace to record employee or visitor activities is also covered and notices must be given to anyone subject to observation or recording. Recording without such a notice can be a violation of this act. If employers make observations of employee activities and/or record telephone and other conversations between employees and others, and proper notice is given to employees, employees will have no expectation of privacy during the time they are in the workplace.

For more information, see www.justice.gov/jmd/ls/legislative_histories/pl99-508/pl99-508.html.

1.9 The Employee Polygraph Protection Act (1988)

Before 1988, it was common for employers to use "lie detectors" as tools in investigations of inappropriate employee behavior. That changed when this act prohibited the use of lie detector tests for job applicants and employees of companies engaged in interstate commerce. Exceptions are made for certain conditions, including law enforcement and national security. There is a federal poster requirement.

 NOTE Many state laws also prohibit the use of lie detector tests.

For more information, see www.dol.gov/compliance/laws/comp-eppa.htm.

1.10 The Employee Retirement Income Security Act (ERISA) (1974)

This law doesn't require employers to establish pension plans, but governs how those plans are managed once they are established. It establishes uniform minimum standards to ensure that employee benefit plans are established and maintained in a fair and financially sound manner; protects employees covered by a pension plan from losses in benefits due to job changes, plant closings, bankruptcies, or mismanagement; and protects plan beneficiaries. It covers most employers engaged in interstate commerce. Public-sector employees and many churches are not subject to ERISA. Employers who offer retirement plans must also conform with IRS code in order to receive tax advantages.

For more information, see www.dol.gov/compliance/laws/comp-erisa.htm.

1.11 The Equal Pay Act (EPA) (Amendment to the FLSA) (1963)

Equal pay requirements apply to all employers. The act is an amendment to the FLSA and is enforced by the EEOC. It prohibits employers from discriminating on the basis of sex by paying wages to employees at a rate less than the rate paid to employees of the opposite sex for equal work on jobs requiring equal skill, effort, and responsibility, and which are performed under similar working conditions. It does not address the concept of comparable worth.

For more information, see www.eeoc.gov/laws/statutes/epa.cfm.

1.12 The FAA Modernization and Reform Act (2012)

Congress took these actions in 2012 to amend the Railway Labor Act to change union certification election processes in the railroad and airline industries and impose greater oversight of the regulatory activities of the National Mediation Board. This law requires the Government Accountability Office (GAO) initially to evaluate the NMB's certification procedures and then audit the NMB's operations every two years.

For more information, see www.faa.gov/regulations_policies/reauthorization/media/PLAW-112publ95[1].pdf.

1.13 The Fair and Accurate Credit Transactions Act (FACT) (2003)

The financial privacy of employees and job applicants was enhanced in 2003 with these amendments to the Fair Credit Reporting Act, providing for certain requirements in third-party investigations of employee misconduct charges. Employers are released from obligations to disclose requirements and obtain employee consent if the investigation involves suspected misconduct, a violation of the law or regulations, or a violation of pre-existing written employer policies. A written plan to prevent identity theft is required.

For more information, see www.gpo.gov/fdsys/pkg/PLAW-108publ159/pdf/PLAW-108publ159.pdf.

1.14 The Fair Credit Reporting Act (FCRA) (1970)

This was the first major legislation to regulate the collection, dissemination, and use of consumer information, including consumer credit information. It requires employers to notify any individual in writing if a credit report may be used in making an employment decision. Employers must also get a written authorization from the subject individual before asking a credit bureau for a credit report. The FCRA also protects the privacy of background investigation information and provides methods for insuring that information is accurate. Employers who take adverse action against a job applicant or current employee based on information contained in the prospective or current employee's consumer report will have additional disclosures to make to that individual.

For more information, see www.ftc.gov/os/statutes/031224fcra.pdf.

1.15 The Fair Labor Standards Act (FLSA) (1938)

The FLSA is one of a handful of federal laws that establish the foundation for employee treatment. It is a major influence in how people are paid, in employment of young people, and in how records are to be kept on employment issues such as hours of work. The law introduced a maximum 44-hour 7-day workweek, established a national minimum wage, guaranteed "time-and-a-half" for overtime in certain jobs, and prohibited most employment of minors in "oppressive child labor," a term that is defined in the statute. It applies to employees engaged in interstate commerce or employed by an enterprise engaged in commerce or in the production of goods for commerce, unless the employer can claim an exemption from coverage. It is interesting to note that the FLSA, rather than the Civil Rights Act of 1964, is the first federal law to require employers to maintain records on employee race and sex identification.

Provisions and Protections

Employers covered under the "enterprise" provisions of this law include: public agencies; private employers whose annual gross sales exceed $500,000 or those operating a hospital or a school for mentally or physically disabled or gifted children; a preschool, an elementary or secondary school, or an institution of higher education (profit or non-profit). Individuals can still be covered, even if they don't fit into one of the enterprises listed. If the employees' work regularly involves them in commerce between the states they would be covered. These include employees who: work in communications or transportation; regularly use the mail, telephone, or telegraph for interstate communication, or keep records of interstate transactions; handle shipping and receiving goods moving in interstate commerce; regularly cross state lines in the course of employment; or work for independent employers who contract to do clerical, custodial, maintenance, or other work for firms engaged in interstate commerce or in the production of goods for interstate commerce. The FLSA establishes a federal minimum wage that has been raised from time to time since the law was originally passed. The FLSA prohibits shipment of goods in interstate commerce that were produced in violation of the minimum wage, overtime pay, child labor, or special minimum wage provisions of the law.

Recordkeeping

The FLSA proscribes methods for determining if a job is exempt or non-exempt from overtime pay requirements of the act. If a job is exempt from those requirements, incumbents can work as many hours of overtime as the job requires without being paid for their overtime. Exempt vs. Non-Exempt status attaches to the job, not the incumbent. So, someone with an advanced degree who is working in a clerical job, may be non-exempt because of the job requirements, not their personal qualifications. Employers are permitted to have a policy that calls for paying exempt employees when they work overtime. That is a voluntary provision of a benefit in excess of federal requirements. State laws may have additional requirements. People who work in non-exempt jobs must be paid overtime according to the rate computation methods provided for in the act. Usually, this is a requirement for overtime after 40 hours of regular time worked during a single workweek. The act also describes how a workweek is to be determined.

Each employer covered by the FLSA must keep records for each covered, nonexempt worker. Those records must include:

- Employee's full name and Social Security number.
- Address, including zip code.
- Birth date, if younger than 19.
- Sex.

- Occupation.
- Time and day of week when employee's workweek begins.
- Hours worked each day and total hours worked each workweek. (This includes a record of the time work began at the start of the day, when the employee left for a meal break, the time the employee returned to work from the meal break, and the time work ended for the day.)
- Basis on which employee's wages are paid (hourly, weekly, piecework).
- Regular hourly pay rate.
- Total daily or weekly straight-time earnings.
- Total overtime earnings for the workweek.
- All additions or deductions from the employee's wages.
- Total wages paid each pay period.
- Date of payment and the pay period covered by the payment.

There is no limit in the FLSA to the number of hours employees age 16 and older may work in any workweek. There is a provision for employers to retain all payroll records, collective bargaining agreements, sales, and purchase records for at least three years. Any time card, piecework record, wage rate tables, and work and time schedules should be retained for at least two years. A workplace poster is required to notify employees of the federal minimum wage.

The federal child labor provisions of the FLSA, also known as the child labor laws, were enacted to ensure that when young people work, the work is safe and does not jeopardize their health, well-being, or educational opportunities. These provisions also provide limited exemptions. Workers under 14 years of age are restricted to jobs such as newspaper delivery to local customers; baby-sitting on a casual basis; acting in movies, TV, radio, or theatre; working as a home worker gathering evergreens and making evergreen wreaths. Under no circumstances, even if the business is family owned, may a person this young work in any of the 17 most hazardous jobs. See Figure 1-1 for a list of the 17 most hazardous jobs.

For workers aged 14 and 15, all work must be performed outside school hours and these workers may not work

- More than 3 hours on a school day, including Friday
- More than 18 hours per week when school is in session
- More than 8 hours per day when school is not in session
- More than 40 hours per week when school is not in session
- Before 7 a.m. or after 7 p.m. on any day, except from June 1 through Labor Day, when nighttime work hours are extended to 9 p.m.

- Manufacturing or storing of explosives
- Driving a motor vehicle or working as an outside helper on motor vehicles
- Coal mining
- Forest fire fighting and forest fire prevention, timber tract, forestry service, and occupations in logging and sawmilling
- Using power-driven woodworking machines
- Exposure to radioactive substances and ionizing radiation
- Using power-driven hoisting apparatus
- Using power-driven metal-forming, punching, and shearing machines
- Mining, other than coal

- Using power-driven meat-processing machines, slaughtering, meat and poultry packing, processing, or rendering
- Using power-driven bakery machines
- Using balers, compactors, and power-driven paper-products machines
- Manufacturing brick, tile, and related products
- Using power-driven circular saws, band saws, guillotine shears, chain saws, reciprocating saws, wood chippers, and abrasive cutting discs
- Working in wrecking, demolition, and ship-breaking operations
- Roofing and work performed on or about a roof
- Trenching or excavating

Source: "U.S. Department of Labor, eLaws Fair Labor Standards Act Advisor" on July 9, 2013, www.dol.gov/elaws/esa/flsa/docs/haznonag.asp

Figure 1-1   17 Most Dangerous Jobs That May Not Be Performed by Workers Under 18 Years of Age

Until employees reach the age of 18, it is necessary for them to obtain a work permit from their school district. For workers aged 16 through 17, there is no restriction on the number of hours worked per week. There continues to be a ban on working any job among the 17 most hazardous industries. All of these conditions must be met or the employer will be subject to penalties from the U.S. Department of Labor.

Overtime Computation

Overtime is required at a rate of 1.5 times the normal pay rate for all hours worked over 40 in a single workweek. An employer may designate that their workweek begins at a given day and hour and continues until that same day and hour seven days later. Once selected, that same workweek definition must be maintained consistently until there is a legitimate business reason for making a change. That change must be clearly communicated in advance to all employees who will be affected by the change. No pay may be forfeit because the employer changes its workweek definition. Compensating time off is permitted under the FLSA if it is given at the same rates required for overtime pay.

Enforcement

Provisions of the FLSA are enforced by the U.S. Department of Labor's Wage and Hour Division. With offices around the country, this agency is able to interact with employees on complaints and follow up with employers by making an on-site visit if necessary. If violations are found during an investigation, the agency has the authority to make recommendations for changes that would bring the employer into compliance. Retaliation against any employee for filing a complaint under the FLSA or in any other way availing himself or herself of the legal rights it offers, is subject to additional penalties. Willful violations may bring criminal prosecution and fines up to $10,000. Employers who are convicted a second time for willfully violating the FLSA can find themselves in prison.

The Wage and Hour Division may, if it finds products produced during violations of the act, prevent an employer from shipping any of those goods. It may also "freeze" shipments of any product manufactured while overtime payment requirements were violated. A two-year limit applies to recovery of back-pay unless there was a willful violation, which triggers a three-year liability.

For more information, see www.dol.gov/whd/regs/statutes/FairLaborStandAct.pdf.

1.16 The Foreign Corrupt Practices Act (FCPA) (1997)

The FCPA prohibits American companies from making bribery payments to foreign officials for the purpose of obtaining or keeping business. Training for employees who are involved with international negotiations should include a warning to avoid anything even looking like bribery payment to a foreign company or its employees.

For more information, see www.justice.gov/criminal/fraud/fcpa/.

1.17 The Health Information Technology for Economic and Clinical Health Act (HITECH) (2009)

The HITECH requires that anyone with custody of personal health records send notification to affected individuals if their personal health records have been disclosed, or the employer believes they have been disclosed, to any unauthorized person. Enacted as part of the American Recovery and Reinvestment Act (ARRA), this law made several changes to HIPAA, including the establishment of a federal standard for security breach notifications that requires covered entities, in the event of a breach of any personal health records (PHI) information, to notify each individual whose PHI has been disclosed without authorization.

For more information, see www.hhs.gov/ocr/privacy/hipaa/administrative/enforcementrule/hitechenforcementifr.html.

1.18 The Health Insurance Portability and Accountability Act (HIPAA) (1996)

This law ensures that individuals who leave or lose their jobs can obtain health coverage even if they or someone in their family has a serious illness or injury, or is pregnant. It also provides privacy requirements related to medical records for individuals as young as 12 years old. It also limits exclusions for pre-existing conditions, and guarantees renewability of health coverage to employers and employees, allowing people to change jobs without the worry of loss of coverage. It also restricts the ability of employers to impose actively-at-work requirements as preconditions for health plan eligibility, as well as a number of other benefits.

For more information, see www.hhs.gov/ocr/privacy.

1.19 The Immigration and Nationality Act (INA) (1952)

The INA is the first law that pulled together all of the issues associated with immigration and is considered the foundation on which all following immigration laws have been built. It addresses employment eligibility and employment verification. It defines the conditions for the temporary and permanent employment of aliens in the United States.[1]

The INA defines an "alien" as any person lacking citizenship or status as a national of the United States. The INA differentiates aliens as:

- Resident or nonresident
- Immigrant or nonimmigrant
- Documented and undocumented

The need to curtail illegal immigration led to the enactment of the Immigration Reform and Control Act (IRCA).

For more information, see www.dol.gov/compliance/laws/comp-ina.htm.

1.20 The Immigration Reform and Control Act (IRCA) (1986)

This is the first law to require new employees to prove both their identity and right to work in this country. Regulations implementing this law created the Form I-9i, which must be completed by each new employee and the employer. Form I-9 has changed many times since 1986. Please be sure you keep track of the changes as they are issued by the government and that you are using the most current version of the form. There are document retention requirements. The law prohibits discrimination against job applicants on the basis of national origin or citizenship. It establishes penalties for employers who hire illegal aliens.

For more information, see www.eeoc.gov/eeoc/history/35th/thelaw/irca.html.

1.21 The IRS Intermediate Sanctions (2002)

Here we find guidelines for determining reasonable compensation for executives of nonprofit organizations. These were enacted by the IRS and applied to non-profit organizations who engage in the transactions that inure to the benefit of a disqualified person within the organization. These rules allow the IRS to impose penalties when it determines that top officials have received excessive compensation from their organizations. Intermediate sanctions may be imposed either in addition to or instead of revocation of the exempt state of the organization.

For more information, see www.irs.gov/pub/irs-tege/eotopice03.pdf.

1.22 The Labor-Management Relations Act (LMRA) (1947)

Also called the Taft-Hartley Act, this is the first national legislation that placed controls on unions. It prohibits unfair labor practices by unions and outlaws closed shops, where union membership is required in order to get and keep a job. Employers may not form closed shop agreements with unions. It requires both parties to bargain in good faith and covers non-management employees in private industry who are not covered by the Railway Labor Act.

For more information, see 29 U.S.C. Sec.141, www.casefilemethod.com/Statuters/LMRA.pdf.

1.23 The Labor-Management Reporting and Disclosure Act (1959)

Also called the Landrum-Griffin Act, this law outlines procedures for redressing internal union problems, protects the rights of union members from corrupt or discriminatory labor unions, and applies to all labor organizations. Specific requirements include:

- Unions must conduct secret elections, the results of which can be reviewed by the U.S. Department of Labor.

- A Bill of Rights guarantees union members certain rights, including free speech.

- Convicted felons and members of the Communist Party cannot hold office in unions.

- Annual financial reporting from unions to the Department of Labor is required.

- All union officials have a fiduciary responsibility in managing union assets and conducting the business of the union.

- Union power to place subordinate organizations in trusteeship is limited.

- Minimum standards for union disciplinary action against its members is provided.

For more information, see www.dol.gov/compliance/laws/comp-lmrda.htm.

1.24 The Mine Safety and Health Act (1977)

Following a series of deadly mining disasters, the American people demanded that Congress take action to prevent similar events in the future. This law converted the existing Mine Enforcement Safety Administration (MESA) to the Mine Safety and Health Administration (MSHA). For the first time, it brought all coal, metal, and nonmetal mining operations under the same Department of Labor jurisdiction. Regulations and safety procedures for the coal mining industry were not altered, just carried into the new agency for oversight.

For more information, see www.dol.gov/compliance/laws/comp-fmsha.htm.

Provisions and Protections

This law requires the Secretaries of Labor and Health, Education, and Welfare to create regulations governing the country's mines. All mines are covered if they are involved in commerce, which any active mining operation would be. Regulations that implement this law specify that employees must be provided with certain protective equipment while working in a mine. These devices relate to respiration and fire prevention, among other protections. Protecting against "Black Lung Disease" is a key concern, even today, in the coal mining industry.

Recordkeeping Requirements

Employers engaged in mining operations must inspect their worksites and document the results, reflecting hazards and actions taken to reduce or eliminate the hazards. Employees are to be given access to information related to accident prevention, fatal accident statistics for the year, and instructions on specific hazards they will face while working in the mine. Requirements detail the content of written emergency response plans, emergency mapping, and rescue procedures. Individual employee exposure records must be maintained. Each mine operator is required to conduct surveys of mine exposures and hazards, a plan to deal with those problems, and a record of the results. This information must be made available to MSHA inspectors if they request it.

MSHA Standards

The agency enforces mine safety standards that involve ventilation, chemical exposure, noise, forklifts and other mining equipment, mine shoring, and more. Material Safety Data Sheets (MSDS) must be available to employees in mining as they are in other industries overseen by the OSHA agency.

MSHA Enforcement

MSHA has a team of federal inspectors that conduct on-site audits of mining operations. MSHA has the authority to cite mine operators for violations of its regulations, and citations can carry a $1,000 per day penalty in some circumstances.[2]

1.25 The National Industrial Recovery Act (1933)

This was an attempt to help the country get out from the Great Depression. It proposed the creation of "Codes of Fair Competition" for each of several different industries. Essentially, every business would have to identify with and belong to a trade association. The association would then be required to create a Code of Fair Competition for the industry. Antitrust laws would be suspended in favor of the code. Of course, the code would have to be approved by the President of the United States and the administration would issue federal licenses to every business in the country. If a business refused to participate in the code, its license could be suspended and that would be the signal for that business to end all operations. There were financial penalties as well. This law didn't fair very well. It was declared unconstitutional by the United States Supreme Court in 1935 and was replaced by the National Labor Relations Act later that same year.

For more information, see www.ourdocuments.gov/doc.php?flash=true&doc=66.

1.26 The National Labor Relations Act (NLRA) (1935)

This is the "granddaddy" of all labor relations laws in the United States. It initially provided that employees have a right to form unions and negotiate wage and hour issues with employers on behalf of the union membership. Specifically, the NLRA grants employees rights to organize, join unions, and engage in collective bargaining and other "concerted activities." It also protects against unfair labor practices by employers. It established the National Labor Relations Board (NLRB), which hears charges of violation and makes rulings as a court would.

Following on the heels of the National Industrial Recovery Act's failures, this law stepped into the void and addressed both union and employer obligations in labor relations issues. It established the National Labor Relations Board (NLRB), which would help define fair labor practices in the following decades. The NLRB has the power to accept and investigate complaints of unfair labor practices by either management or labor unions. It plays a judicial role within an administrative setting. This law is sometimes called the Wagner Act. Some key provisions include:

- The right of workers to organize into unions for collective bargaining
- The requirement of employers to bargain in good faith when employees have voted in favor of a union to represent them
- The requirement that unions represent all members equally.
- Covers non-management employees in private industry who are not already covered by the Railway Labor Act.

For more information, see www.nlrb.gov/national-labor-relations-act.

1.27 The Needlestick Safety and Prevention Act (2000)

This law modifies the Occupational Safety and Health Act by introducing a new group of requirements in the medical community. Sharps, as they are called, are needles, puncture devices, knives, scalpels, and other tools that can harm either the person using them or someone else. The law and its regulations provides rules related to handling these devices, disposing of them, and encouraging invention of new devices that will reduce or eliminate the risk associated with injury due to sharps. Sharps injuries are to be recorded on the OSHA 300 log with "privacy case" listed and not the employee's name. Blood-borne pathogens and transmission of human blood-borne illnesses such as AIDS/HIV and hepatitis are key targets of this law. Reducing the amount of injury and subsequent illness due to puncture, stab, or cut wounds is a primary objective. There are communication requirements including employment poster content requirements.

For more information, see www.gpo.gov/fdsys/pkg/PLAW-106publ430/html/PLAW-106publ430.htm.

1.28 The Norris-LaGuardia Act (1932)

Remember that this was still three years before the NLRA came to pass. When unions tried to use strikes and boycotts, employers would trot into court and ask for an injunction to prevent such activity. More often than not, they were successful and judges provided the injunctions. Congress had been pressured by organized labor to restore their primary tools that could force employers to bargain issues unions saw as important. Key provisions of this law include:

- It prohibited "yellow-dog" contracts. Those were agreements in which employees promised employers that they would not join unions. This new law declared such contracts to be unenforceable in any federal court.

- It prohibited federal courts from issuing injunctions of any kind against peaceful strikes, boycotts, or picketing when used by a union in connection with a labor dispute.

- It defined labor dispute to include any disagreement about working conditions.

For more information, see 29 U.S.C., Chapter 6, http://uscode.house.gov/download/pls/29C6.txt.

1.29 The Occupational Safety and Health Act (OSHA) (1970)

Signed into law by President Richard M. Nixon on December 29, 1970, the Occupational Safety and Health Act created an administrative agency within the U.S. Department of Labor called the Occupational Safety and Health Administration (OSHA). It also created the National Institute of Occupational Safety and Health (NIOSH), which resides inside the Centers for Disease Control (CDC).

Provisions and Protections

Regulations implementing this legislation have grown over time. They are complex and detailed. It is important that HR professionals understand the basics and how to obtain additional detailed information that applies to their particular employer circumstance. There are many standards that specify what employers must do to comply with their legal obligations. Overall, however, the law holds employers accountable for providing a safe and healthy working environment. The "General Duty Clause" in OSHA's regulations says employers shall furnish each employee with a place of employment free from recognized hazards that are likely to cause death or serious injury. It also holds employees responsible for abiding by all safety rules and regulations in the workplace. Some provisions require notices be posted in the workplace covering some of the OSHA requirements. Posters are available for download from the OSHA website without charge. The law applies to *all* employers regardless of the employee population size.

Recordkeeping Requirements

OSHA regulations require that records be kept for many purposes. It is necessary to conduct and document inspections of the workplace, looking for safety and health hazards. It is necessary to document and make available to employees records about hazardous materials and how they must be properly handled. Employers with ten or more people on the payroll must summarize all injury and illness instances and post that summary in a conspicuous place within the workplace. That report must remain posted from February 1 to April 30 each year. Certain employers are exempt from some OSHA recordkeeping requirements. They generally are classified by industry SIC Code (Standard Industrial Classification). A list is available on OSHA's website at www. OSHA.gov. Any time there is a serious or fatal accident, a full incident report must be prepared by the employer and maintained in the safety file. These records must be maintained for a minimum of 5 years from the date of the incident. Known as a log of occupational injury or illness, it must include a record of each incident resulting in medical treatment (other than first aid), loss of consciousness, restriction of work or motion, or transfer or termination of employment. If you are in the medical industry, construction industry, or manufacturing industry, or you use nuclear materials of any kind, there are other requirements you must meet. Key to compliance with OSHA rules is communication with employees. Training is often provided by employers to meet this hazard communication requirement. In summary, then, OSHA recordkeeping involves:

- Periodic safety inspections of the workplace
- Injury or Illness Incident Reports
- Annual summary of incidents during the previous calendar year
- Injury and Illness Prevention Program (if required by rules governing your industry)
- Employee training on safety procedures and expectations
- Records of training participation
- Material Safety Data Sheets (MSDS) for each chemical used in the workplace (made available to all employees in a well-marked file or binder that can be accessed at any time during work hours)

Occupational Safety and Health Act Enforcement

OSHA inspections may include:

- **On-site visits that are conducted without advance notice** Inspectors can just walk into a place of employment and request that you permit an inspection. You don't have to agree unless the inspector has a search warrant. In the absence of the warrant, you can delay the inspection until your attorney is present.

- **On-site inspections, or phone/fax investigations**   Depending on urgency of the hazard and agreement of the person filing the complaint, inspectors may telephone or fax inquiries to employers. The employer has five working days to respond with a detailed description of inspection findings, corrective action taken, and additional action planned.

- **Highly trained compliance officers**   OSHA Training Institute provides training for OSHA's compliance officers, state compliance officers, state consultants, other federal agency personnel, and the private sector.

Inspection priorities include:

- **Imminent danger**   Situations where death or serious injury are highly likely. Compliance Officers will ask employers to correct the conditions immediately or remove employees from danger.

- **Fatalities and catastrophes**   Incidents that involve a death or the hospitalization of three or more employees. Employers must report these incidents to OSHA within 8 hours.

- **Worker complaints**   Allegations of workplace hazards or OSHA violations. Employees may request anonymity when they file complaints with OSHA.

- **Referrals**   Other federal, state, or local agencies, individuals, organizations, or the media can make referrals to OSHA so the agency may consider making an inspection.

- **Follow-ups**   Checks for abatement of violations cited during previous inspections are also conducted by OSHA personnel in certain circumstances.

- **Planned or programmed investigations**   Inspections aimed at specific high-hazard industries or individual workplaces that have experienced high rates of injuries and illnesses. These are sometimes called "targeted investigations."

Two Types of Standards

The law provides for two types of safety and health standards. The agency has therefore developed its regulations and standards in those two categories.

Normal Standards   If OSHA determines that a specific standard is needed, any of several advisory committees may be called upon to develop specific recommendations. There are two standing committees, and ad hoc committees may be appointed to examine special areas of concern to OSHA. All advisory committees, standing or ad hoc, must have members representing management, labor, and state agencies, as well as one or more designees of the Secretary of Health and Human Services (HHS). The occupational safety and health professions and the general public also may be represented.[3]

Emergency Temporary Standards "Under certain limited conditions, OSHA is authorized to set emergency temporary standards that take effect immediately. First, OSHA must determine that workers are in grave danger due to exposure to toxic substances or agents determined to be toxic or physically harmful or to new hazards and that an emergency standard is needed to protect them. Then, OSHA publishes the emergency temporary standard in the *Federal Register*, where it also serves as a proposed permanent standard. It is then subject to the usual procedure for adopting a permanent standard except that a final ruling must be made within six months. The validity of an emergency temporary standard may be challenged in an appropriate U.S. Court of Appeals."[4]

For more information, see www.dol.gov/compliance/guide/osha.htm.

1.30 The Omnibus Budget Reconciliation Act (OBRA) (1993)

Signed into law by President Bill Clinton on August 10, 1993, this legislation reduces compensation limits in qualified retirement programs and triggers increased activity in nonqualified retirement programs. It also calls for termination of some plans.

For more information, see www.gpo.gov/fdsys/pkg/BILLS-103hr2264enr/pdf/BILLS-103hr2264enr.pdf.

1.31 The Pension Protection Act (PPA) (2006)

Focused solely on pensions, this law requires employers that have under-funded pension plans to pay a higher premium to the Pension Benefit Guarantee Corporation (PBGC). It also requires employers that terminate pension plans to provide additional funding to those plans. This legislation impacted nearly all aspects of retirement planning, including changes to rules about Individual Retirement Accounts (IRAs).

For more information, see www.dol.gov/ebsa/pensionreform.html.

1.32 The Personal Responsibility and Work Opportunity Reconciliation Act (1996)

This law requires all states to establish and maintain a New Hire Reporting System designed to enhance enforcement of child support payments. It requires welfare recipients to begin working after two years of receiving benefits. States may exempt parents with children under age one from the work requirements. Parents with children under the age of one may use this exemption only once; they cannot use it again for subsequent children. These parents also are still subject to the five-year time limit for cash assistance. HR professionals will need to establish and maintain reporting systems to meet these tracking requirements.

For more information, see www.acf.hhs.gov/programs/css/resource/the-personal-responsibility-and-work-opportunity-reconcilliation-act.

1.33 The Portal-to-Portal Act (1947)

By amending the Fair Labor Standards Act (FLSA), this law defines "hours worked" and establishes rules about payment of wages to employees who travel before and/or after their scheduled work shift. The act provides that minimum wages and overtime are not required for "traveling to and from the actual place of performance of the principal activity or activities which such employee is to perform" or for "activities which are preliminary to or postliminary to said principal activity or activities," unless there is a custom or contract to the contrary.

For more information, see 29 U.S.C., Chapter 9, http://uscode.house.gov/download/pls/29C9.txt.

1.34 The Railway Labor Act (1926)

Originally, this law was created to allow railway employees to organize into labor unions. Over the years, it has been expanded in coverage to include airline employees. Covered employers are encouraged to use the Board of Mediation, which has since morphed into the National Mediation Board (NMB), a permanent independent agency.

For more information, see www.nmb.gov/documents/rla.html.

1.35 The Rehabilitation Act (1973)

This replaced the Vocational Rehabilitation Act and created support for states to establish vocational rehabilitation programs. The term originally used in this legislation was "handicapped." The law was later modified to replace that term with "disabled."

Table 2-1 notes some of the most important sections of the Rehabilitation Act.

1.36 The Retirement Equity Act (REA) (1984)

Signed into law by President Ronald Reagan on August 23, 1984, the REA provides certain legal protections for spousal beneficiaries of qualified retirement programs. It prohibits changes to retirement plan elections, spousal beneficiary designations, or in-service withdrawals without the consent of a spouse. Changing withdrawal options does not require spousal consent. It permits plan administrators to presume spousal

Section	Requirement
Section 501	Requires nondiscrimination and affirmative action in hiring disabled workers by federal agencies within the executive branch.
Section 503	Requires nondiscrimination and affirmative action by federal contractors and subcontractors with contracts valued at $10,000 or more.
Section 504	Requires employers subject to the law to provide reasonable accommodation for disabled individuals who can perform the major job duties with or without accommodation.

Table 2-1 Key Employment Provisions of the Rehabilitation Act of 1973

survivors annuity and reduce primary pension amounts accordingly. Specific written waivers are required to avoid spousal annuity.

For more information, see www.law.cornell.edu/uscode/text/29/1055.

1.37 The Revenue Act (1978)

This law added two important sections to the Internal Revenue Tax Code relevant to employee benefits: Section 125, Cafeteria Benefit Plans, and Section 401(k), originally a pre-tax savings program for private sector employees known as Individual Retirement Accounts (IRAs), subsequently expanded to a second plan opportunity known as "Roth IRA" that permitted funding with after-tax savings.

For more information, see www.irs.gov/pub/irs-utl/irpac-br_530_relief_-_appendix_natrm_paper_09032009.pdf.

1.38 The Sarbanes-Oxley Act (SOX) (2002)

In response to many corrupt practices in the financial industry, and the economic disasters they created, Congress passed the Sarbanes-Oxley Act to address the need for oversight and disclosure of information by publicly traded companies.

Provisions and Protections

This law brought some strict oversight to corporate governance and financial reporting for publicly held companies. It holds corporate officers accountable for proper recordkeeping and reporting of financial information, including internal control systems to assure those systems are working properly. There are also requirements for reporting any unexpected changes in financial condition, including potential new liabilities such as lawsuits. Those lawsuits can involve things such as employee complaints of illegal employment discrimination.

It requires administrators of defined contribution plans to provide notice of covered blackout periods and provides whistleblower protection for employees.

This law protects anyone who reports wrongdoing to a supervisor, appointed company officials who handle these matters, a federal regulatory or law enforcement agency, or a member or committee of Congress. It even extends to claims that prove to be false as long as the employee reasonably believed the conduct is a violation of SEC rules or a federal law involving fraud against shareholders.

On March 4, 2014, the United States Supreme Court issued its opinion in the case of *Lawson v. FMR LLC.* (No. 12–3).[5] The 6-3 decision held that all contractors and subcontractors of publicly held companies are subject to the Sarbanes-Oxley Act, even if they are not publicly held. The takeaway from this ruling is that nearly everyone is now subject to the whistleblower provisions of the Sarbanes-Oxley Act. As Justice Sotomayor suggested in her dissenting opinion:

> For example, public companies often hire "independent contractors," of whom there are more than 10 million, and contract workers, of whom there are more than 11 million. And, they employ outside lawyers, accountants, and auditors

as well. While not every person who works for a public company in these nonemployee capacities may be positioned to threaten or harass employees of the public company, many are.

Under [the majority opinion] a babysitter can bring a ... retaliation suit against his employer if his employer is a checkout clerk for the local PetSmart (a public company) but not if she is a checkout clerk for the local Petco (a private company). Likewise the day laborer who works for a construction business can avail himself of [this ruling] if her company has been hired to remodel the local Dick's Sporting Goods store (a public company), but not if it is remodeling a nearby Sports Authority (a private company).

Recordkeeping Requirements

Internal control systems are required to assure that public disclosure of financial information is done as required. The registered accounting firm responsible for reviewing the company's financial reports must attest to the proper implementation of internal control systems and procedures for financial reporting.

SOX Enforcement

Enforcement of the law is done by private-firm audits overseen by the Public Company Accounting Oversight Board (PCAOB). The PCAOB is a nonprofit corporation created by the act to oversee accounting professionals who provide independent audit reports for publicly traded companies. It essentially audits the auditors.

Companies and corporate officers in violation of the act can find themselves subject to fines and/or up to 20 years imprisonment for altering, destroying, mutilating, concealing, or falsifying records, documents, or tangible objects with the intent to obstruct, impede, or influence a legal investigation.

For more information, see http://taft.law.uc.edu/CCL/SOact/soact.pdf.

1.39 The Securities and Exchange Act (1934)

When companies "go public" by issuing common stock for trade, it is done on the "primary market." This law provides for governance in the "secondary market," which is all trading after the initial public offering. It also created the Securities and Exchange Commission (SEC), which has oversight authority for the trading of stocks in this country. It extends the "disclosure" doctrine of investor protection to securities listed and registered for public trading on any of the U.S. exchanges.

For more information, see www.law.cornell.edu/wex/securities_exchange_act_of_1934.

1.40 The Service Contract Act (SCA) (1965)

Applying to federal contractors (and subcontractors) offering goods and services to the government, this law calls for payment of prevailing wages and benefit requirements to all employees providing service under the agreement. All contractors and subcontractors, other than construction services, with contract value in excess of $2,500 are covered. Safety and health standards also apply to such contracts.

The compensation requirements of this law are enforced by the Wage and Hour Division in the U.S. Department of Labor (DOL). The SCA safety and health requirements are enforced by the Occupational Safety and Health Administration (OSHA), also an agency within DOL.

For more information, see 41 U.S.C. 351, www.dol.gov/oasam/regs/statutes/351.htm.

1.41 The Sherman Anti-Trust Act (1890)

If you allow yourself to travel back to the latter part of the nineteenth century, you will find that big business dominated the landscape. There was Standard Oil, Morgan Bank, U.S. Steel, and a handful of railroads. They were huge by comparison with other similar enterprises at the time. And people were concerned that they were monopolizing the marketplace and holding prices high just because they could. John Sherman, a Republican Senator from Ohio, was chairman of the Senate Finance Committee. He suggested that the country needed some protections against monopolies and cartels. Thus, the law was created and subsequently used by federal prosecutors to break up the Standard Oil Company into smaller units. Over the years, case law has developed that concludes that attempting to restrict competition, or fix prices, can be seen as a violation of this law. Restraint of trade is also prohibited.

For more information, see 15 U.S.C. Secs. 1–7, www.law.cornell.edu/uscode/text/15/1.

1.42 The Small Business Job Protection Act (1996) (SBJPA)

This law increased federal minimum wage levels and provided some tax incentives to small business owners to protect jobs and increase take-home pay. It also amended the Portal-to-Portal Act for employees who use employer-owned vehicles. It created the SIMPLE 401(k) retirement plan to make pension plans easier for small businesses. Other tax incentives created by this law include:

- Employee education incentive—allowed small business owners to exclude up to $5,250 from an employee's taxable income for educational assistance provided by the employer

- Increased the maximum amount of capital expense allowed for a small business to $7,000 per year

- Replaced the Targeted Jobs Tax Credit with the Work Opportunity Tax Credit

- Provided a tax credit to individuals who adopted a child (up to $5,000 per child) and a tax credit of up to $6,000 for adoption of a child with special needs

For more information, see www.ssa.gov/legislation/legis_bulletin_082096.html.

1.43 The Social Security Act (1935)

The Social Security program began in 1935 in the heart of the Great Depression. It was initially designed to help senior citizens when that group was suffering a poverty rate of 50 percent. It currently includes social welfare and social insurance programs that can help support disabled workers who are no longer able to earn their wages.

The Social Security program is supported through payroll taxes with contributions from both the employee and the employer. Those payroll tax rates are set by the Federal Insurance Contributions Act (FICA) and have been adjusted many times over the years. There are many programs currently under the control of the Social Security Act and its amendments. These include:

- Federal old-age benefits (retirement)
- Survivors benefits (spouse benefits, dependent children and widow/widower benefits)
- Disability insurance for workers no longer able to work
- Temporary Assistance for Needy Families
- Medicare Health Insurance for Aged and Disabled
- Medicaid Grants to States for Medical Assistance Programs
- Supplemental Security Income (SSI)
- State Children's Health Insurance Program (SCHIP)
- Patient Protection and Affordable Care Act

There is currently a separate payroll deduction for Medicare Health Insurance, which is also funded by both the employee and employer. And the Patient Protection and Affordable Care Act is rolling out over the next few years and offers the opportunity to provide medical insurance coverage to a greater number of people.

A personal Social Security number is used as a tax identification number for federal income tax, including bank records, and to prove work authorization in this country. Social Security numbers can be used in completing Form I-9, which must be completed for every new employee on the payroll. Also required for the I-9 is proof of identity.

For more information, see www.ssa.gov/history/35act.html.

1.44 The Tax Reform Act (1986)

This law made extensive changes to the Internal Revenue Service (IRS) tax code, including a reduction in tax brackets and all tax rates for individuals. Payroll withholdings were affected, many passive losses and tax shelters were eliminated, and changes were made to the alternative minimum tax computation. This is the law that required all dependent children to have Social Security numbers. That provision reduced the number of fraudulent dependent children claimed on income tax returns by seven million in its first year. For HR professionals, answers to employee questions about the number of exemptions to claim on their Form W-4 is greatly influenced by this requirement for dependent Social Security numbers.

For more information, see http://archive.org/stream/summaryofhr3838t1486unit/summaryofhr3838t1486unit_djvu.txt.

1.45 The Taxpayer Relief Act (1997)

Congress wanted to give taxpayers a couple of ways to lower their tax payments during retirement, so the Taxpayer Relief Act was passed to create new savings programs called Roth IRAs and Education IRAs. Many individuals were able to achieve a better tax position through these tools.

For more information, see www.gpo.gov/fdsys/pkg/BILLS-105hr2014enr/pdf/BILLS-105hr2014enr.pdf.

1.46 The Trademark Act (1946)

This is the legislation that created federal protections for trademarks and service marks. Officially it was called the Lanham (Trademark) Act and it set forth the requirements for registering a trademark or service mark to obtain those legal protections. HR people may well have a role to play in training employees in how to properly handle organizational trademarks and the policies that govern those uses.

For more information, see www.uspto.gov/trademarks/law/tmlaw.pdf.

1.47 The Unemployment Compensation Amendments Act (UCA) (1992)

This law established 20 percent (20%) as the amount to be withheld from payment of employee savings accounts when leaving an employer and not placing the funds (rolling over) into another tax-approved IRA or 401(k).

For more information, see www.socialsecurity.gov/policy/docs/ssb/v56n1/v56n1p87.pdf.

1.48 The Uniformed Services Employment and Reemployment Rights Act (USERRA) (1994)

USERRA provides instructions for handling employees who are in the reserves and receive orders to report for active duty. The law protects the employment, reemployment, and retention rights of anyone who voluntarily or involuntarily serves or has served in the uniformed services. It requires that employers continue paying for the employee's benefits to the extent they paid for those benefits before the callup. It also requires that employers continue giving credit for length of service as though the military service was equivalent to company service. There are specific detailed parameters for how long an employee has to engage the employer in return-to-work conversations after being released from active military duty.

This law and its provisions cover all eight U.S. military services and other uniformed services. They are:

- Army
- Navy
- Air Force
- Marines
- Public Health Service Commissioned Corps
- National Oceanic and Atmospheric Administration Commissioned Corps
- Coast Guard
- National Guard groups that have been called into active duty

For more information, see www.dol.gov/compliance/laws/comp-userra.htm.

1.49 The Vietnam Era Veterans Readjustment Assistance Act (VEVRAA) (1974) [as amended by the Jobs for Veterans Act (JVA) (2008)]

Current covered veterans include:

- Disabled veterans
- Veterans who served on active duty in the United States military during a war or campaign or expedition for which a campaign badge was awarded
- Veterans who, while serving on active duty in the Armed Forces, participated in a United States military operation for which an Armed Forces service medal was awarded pursuant to Executive Order 12985
- Recently separated veterans (veterans within 36 months from discharge or release from active duty)

These requirements apply to all federal contractors with a contract valued at $25,000 or more, regardless of the number of total employees.

This veteran support legislation requires all employers subject to the law to post their job openings with their local state employment service. There are three exceptions to that requirement:

- Jobs that will last three days or less
- Jobs that will be filled by an internal candidate
- Jobs that are senior executive positions

Affirmative action outreach and recruiting of veterans is required for federal contractors meeting the contract value threshold. For more information, see www.dol.gov/compliance/laws/comp-vevraa.htm.

1.50 The Wagner-Peyser Act (1933)
[as amended by the Workforce Investment Act of 1998]

The Wagner-Peyser Act created a nationwide system of employment offices known as Employment Service Offices. They were run by the U.S. Department of Labor's Employment and Training Administration (ETA). These offices provided job seekers with assistance in their job search, assistance in searching jobs for Unemployment Insurance recipients, and recruitment services for employers.

The Workforce Investment Act created the "One Stop" centers within Employment Service Offices. The federal government contracts with states to run the Employment Service Offices and One Stop centers. Funds are allocated to states based on a complicated formula.

For more information, see www.doleta.gov/programs/w-pact_amended98.cfm.

1.51 The Walsh-Healey Act (Public Contracts Act) (1936)

President Franklin Roosevelt signed this into law during the Great Depression. It was designed to assure the government paid a fair wage to manufacturers and supplies of goods for federal government contracts in excess of $10,000 each. The provisions of the law included:

- Overtime pay requirements for work done over 8 hours in a day or 40 hours in a week

- A minimum wage equal to the prevailing wage

- Prohibition on employing anyone under 16 years of age or a current convict

The Defense Authorization Act (1968) later excluded federal contractors from overtime payments in excess of 8 hours in a day.

For more information, see www.dol.gov/compliance/laws/comp-pca.htm.

1.52 The Work Opportunity Tax Credit (WOTC) (1996)

This law provides federal income tax credits to employers who hire from certain targeted groups of job seekers who face employment barriers. The amount of tax credit is adjusted from time to time and currently stands at $9,600 per employee.

Targeted groups include:

- Qualified recipients of Temporary Assistance to Needy Families (TANF).

- Qualified veterans receiving SNAP (Supplemental Nutrition Assistance Program) or qualified veterans with a service connected disability who:

- Have a hiring date that is not more than one year after having been discharged or released from active duty, or

- Have aggregate periods of unemployment during the one-year period ending on the hiring date that equals or exceeds six months

- WOTC also includes family members of a veteran who received SNAP for at least a 3-month period during the 15-month period ending on the hiring date or a disabled veteran entitled to compensation for a service-related disability hired within one year of discharge or unemployed for a period totaling at least 6 months of the year ending on the hiring date. .

- Ex-felons hired no later than one year after conviction or release from prison.

- Designated Community Resident—an individual who is between the ages 18 and 40 on the hiring date and who resides in an Empowerment Zone, Renewal Community, or Rural Renewal County.

- Vocational rehabilitation referrals, including Ticket Holders with an individual work plan developed and implemented by an Employment Network.

- Qualified summer youth ages 16 through 17 who reside in an Empowerment Zone, Enterprise Community, or Renewal Community.

- Qualified SNAP recipients between the ages of 18 and 40 on the hiring date.

- Qualified recipients of Supplemental Security Income (SSI).

- Long-term family assistance recipients.

These categories change from time to time as well.

In addition to these specific federal laws, there are laws dealing with payroll that HR professionals need to understand. While it is true that Accounting people normally handle the payroll function in an employer's organization, occasionally HR professionals get involved and have to work with Accounting people to explain deductions and provide input about open enrollment for healthcare benefit programs, among other things. Those things can include garnishments, wage liens, savings programs, benefit premium contributions, and income tax, FICA, and Medicare withholdings.

For more information, see www.gao.gov/new.items/d01329.pdf.

1.53 Whistleblowing

Finally, it is important to highlight the issue of whistleblowing. We do not have a separate section for whistleblowing because protections against retaliation are embedded in various laws we cover in this chapter. Laws with those provisions and protections include the Civil Rights Acts, OSHA, MSHA, the Sarbanes-Oxley Act, ADA, and more.

Whistleblower laws usually apply to public sector employees and employees of organizations contracting with the federal government or state governments. They are designed to protect individuals who publicly disclose information about corrupt practices or illegal activities within their employer's organization. Often, such events occur when someone is mishandling money, contracts, or other assets. Construction projects not being built to specifications can result in whistleblowing by governmental employees. Employees of financial services companies (banks, credit unions, stock brokerages, and investment firms) have been in the headlines during recent years. They uncovered and disclosed misbehavior among people in their companies and were protected under whistleblower provisions of various laws. Whistleblowers are protected from disciplinary action, termination, or other penalty.

For more information, see www.osc.gov/documents/pubs/post_wb.htm.

2. When You Have 15 or More Employees

Once employers have added 15 of more employees to their payroll it becomes necessary to comply with an additional 10 major federal laws.

2.1 Americans with Disabilities Act (ADA) (1990)

Prior to this legislation, the only employees who were protected against employment discrimination were the ones working for the federal, state, or local government and federal government contractors. They were captured by the Rehabilitation Act. As a matter of fact, it was the Rehabilitation Act that was used as a model for developing the ADA. Five years after the Rehabilitation Act, the Developmental Disabilities Act of 1978 spoke specifically to people with developmental disabilities. It provided for federally funded state programs to assist people in that category of the population. The ADA had been first proposed in 1988 and it was backed by thousands of individuals around the country who had been fighting for rights of their family members, friends, and coworkers. They thought it was only appropriate for those people to have equal access to community services, jobs, training, and promotions. It was signed into law by President George H. W. Bush on July 26, 1990. It became fully effective for all employers with 15 or more workers on July 26, 1992.

Provisions and Protections

Title I—Employment—applies to employers with 15 or more workers on the payroll. Those employers may not discriminate against a physically or mentally disabled individual in recruitment, hiring, promotions, training, pay, social activities, and other privileges of employment. Qualified individuals with a disability are to be treated as other job applicants and employees are treated. If a job accommodation is required for a qualified individual to perform the assigned job, employers are required to provide that accommodation or recommend an alternative that would be equally effective. The interactive process between employers and employees should result in an accommodation or explanation about why making the accommodation would provide an undue hardship on the employer. Title I is enforced by the Equal Employment Opportunity Commission (EEOC). Part of the interactive discussion about accommodation requests involves the employer investigating other accommodations that may be equally effective, yet lower in cost or other resource requirements. Employers are not obligated to accept the employee's request without alteration.

U.S. Supreme Court Interpretation of the ADA

There were several U.S. Supreme Court cases that interpreted the ADA very narrowly. They limited the number of people who could qualify as disabled under the Court's interpretation of Congress's initial intent. Reacting to those cases, Congress enacted the ADA Amendments Act in September 2008. It became effective on January 1, 2009.

ADA Amendments Act of 2008

Following the U.S. Supreme Court decisions in *Sutton v. United Airlines*[6] and *Toyota Motor Manufacturing, Kentucky, Inc. v. William*,[7] Congress felt that the Court had been too restrictive in its explanation of who is disabled. It was the intent of Congress to be more broad in that definition. Consequently, Congress passed the ADA Amendments Act to capture a wider range of people in the disabled classification. A disability is now defined as "an impairment that substantially limits one or more major life activities, having a record of such an impairment, or being regarded as having such an impairment." Although the words remain the same as the original definition, the Amendments Act went farther. It said, when determining whether or not someone is disabled, *there may be no consideration of mitigating circumstances*. In the past, we used to treat people who had a disability under control as not disabled. An employee with a prosthetic limb did everything a whole-bodied person could do. An employee with migraines that disappeared with medication wasn't considered disabled. Under the old law, epilepsy and diabetes were not considered disabilities if they were controlled with medication. Now, because the law prohibits a consideration of either medication or prosthesis, they are considered disabilities. You can see that a great many more people will be defined as disabled under these more recent changes. The only specifically excluded condition is the one involving eyeglasses and contact lenses. Congress specifically said having a corrected eye problem through the use of glasses is not considered a disability.

An individual can be officially disabled, but quite able to do his or her job without an accommodation of any sort. Having more people defined as disabled doesn't necessarily mean there will be more people asking for job accommodations.

For more information, see www.eeoc.gov/laws/statutes/adaaa.cfm.

"Substantially Limits"

Employers are required to consider as disabled anyone with a condition that "substantially limits," but does not "significantly restrict," a major life activity. Even though the limitation might be reduced or eliminated with medication or other alleviation, the treatment may not be considered when determining the limitations. So, people who use shoe inserts to correct a back problem or who take prescription sleeping pills may now be classified as disabled. The same might be said of people who are allergic to peanuts or bee stings. Yet there may be no need for any of them to request a job accommodation.

"Major Life Activities"

Caring for oneself, seeing, hearing, touching, eating, sleeping, walking, standing, sitting, reaching, lifting, bending, speaking, breathing, learning, reading, concentrating, thinking, communicating, interacting with others, and working...all are considered "major life activities." Also included are major bodily functions such as normal cell growth, reproduction, immune system, blood circulation, and the like. Some conditions are specifically designated as disabilities by the EEOC. They include: diabetes, cancer, HIV/AIDS (Human Immunodeficiency Virus and Acquired Immunodeficiency Syndrome), MS (Multiple Sclerosis), CP (Cerebral Palsy), and CF (Cystic Fibrosis) because they interfere with one or more of our major life activities.

"Essential Job Function"

An essential job function is defined as "A portion of a job assignment that cannot be removed from the job without significantly changing the nature of the job." An essential function is highly specialized, and the incumbent has been hired because he or she has special qualifications, skills, or abilities to perform that function among others.

"Job Accommodation"

Someone with a disability doesn't necessarily need a job accommodation. Remember that we select people and place them in jobs if they are qualified for the performance of the essential functions, with or without a job accommodation. Someone with diabetes may have the disease under control with medication and proper diet. No accommodation would be required. However, if it were essential that the employee had food intake at certain times of the day, there could be a legitimate request for accommodation of that need. The employer might be asked to consistently permit the employee to have meal breaks at specific times each day.

Job accommodations are situationally dependent. First, there must be a disability and an ability to do the essential functions of the job. Next, there must be a request for accommodation from the employee. If there is no request for accommodation, no action is required by the employer. It is perfectly acceptable for an employer to request supporting documentation from medical experts identifying the disability. There might even be recommendations for specific accommodations, including those requested by the employee.

Once an accommodation is requested, the employer is obliged to enter into an interactive discussion with the employee. For example, an employee might ask for something specific, perhaps a new piece of equipment (a special ergonomic chair) that will eliminate the impact of disability on their job performance. The employer must consider that specific request. Employers are obligated to search for alternatives that could satisfy the accommodation request only when the specific request cannot be reasonably accommodated. This is the point where the Job Accommodation Network (JAN)[8] can become a resource. They can usually provide help for even unusual situations.

Once specific alternatives have been explored, a specific accommodation should be determined. The employer must consider if making that accommodation would be an "undue hardship" considering all it would involve. You should note that most job accommodations carry a very low cost. Often they cost nothing. The larger an employer's payroll headcount, the more difficult it is to fully justify using "undue hardship" as a reason for not agreeing to provide an accommodation. Very large corporations or governments have vast resources and the cost of one job accommodation, even if it does cost some large dollar amount, won't likely cause an undue hardship on that employer.

Recordkeeping Requirements

There is nothing in the Americans with Disabilities Act of 1990, or its amendments, that requires employers to create job descriptions. However, smart employers are doing that in order to identify physical and mental requirements of each job. Job descriptions also make it easy to identify essential job functions that any qualified individual would have to perform, with or without job accommodation. It is easier to administer job accommodation request procedures and to defend against false claims of discrimination when an employer has job descriptions that clearly list all of the job's requirements. It also makes screening job applicants easier because it shows them in writing what the job will entail; then an employer's recruiters may ask, "Is there anything in this list of essential job functions that you can't do with or without a job accommodation?"

If a job requires an incumbent to drive a delivery truck, driving would be an essential function of that job. A disability that prevented the incumbent from driving the delivery truck would likely block that employee from working—unless an accommodation could be found that would permit the incumbent to drive in spite of the disability.

People are sometimes confused about temporary suspension of duty being a permanent job accommodation. If that temporary suspension means the incumbent no longer is responsible for performing an essential job function, the job could not be performed as it was designed by the employer. It is not necessary for an employer to redesign job content to make a job accommodation. It is possible for such voluntary efforts to be made on behalf of an employee the organization wishes to retain. Those situations are not job accommodations, however. They are job reassignments.

EEOC procedures prohibit employers from inviting job applicants to identify their disability status prior to receiving a job offer.

Annual review of job description content is required under the EEOC guidelines. It is important to maintain accurate listings of essential job functions and physical and mental job requirements. Annual review will help assure that you always have current information in your job descriptions.

ADA Enforcement

The EEOC enforces Title I of the ADA. The agency will accept complaints of illegal discrimination based on mental or physical disability. Once an employee has established that they are disabled and claim that they have been prohibited some employment benefit because of their disability (hiring, promotion, access to training, or inappropriate termination) there is a *prima facie* case (meaning it is true *on its surface*). Then the agency notifies the employer of the complaint and asks for the employer's response. This process can work back and forth from employer response to employee response for several cycles. Ultimately, the agency will determine that the case has cause (was a valid claim of discrimination), had no cause (the claim could not be substantiated), or the case was closed for administrative purposes (the employee asked for the case to be closed). Each of those three outcomes is followed by a "Right to Sue" letter, allowing the employee to get an attorney and file a lawsuit in federal court seeking remedies under the law.[9]

Once a complaint (called a "charge of illegal discrimination") is filed with the EEOC, employers are instructed to cease talking about the issue directly with their employee. All conversation about the complaint must be directed through the EEOC. Unfortunately, that complicates the communication process, and it provides a very strong incentive for employers to resolve complaints internally before they reach the formal external complaint stage. Working directly with an employee on the subject of accommodation, or any other personnel issue, is preferable to working through an agent such as the EEOC.

For more information, see www.ada.gov/.

2.2 The Civil Rights Act (Title VII) (1964)

Although this was not the first federal civil rights act in the country,[10] it came to us through a great deal of controversy. It was signed into law by President Lyndon Johnson on July 2, 1964. Following the assassination of President John F. Kennedy the previous November, President Johnson took it upon himself to carry the civil rights banner and urge Congress to pass the law.

For more information, see www.eeoc.gov/laws/statutes/titlevii.cfm.

Employment Protections

Title VII of the act speaks to employment discrimination and cites five protected classes of people. Before the final days when Congress was discussing the issues, there were only four protected classes listed: Race, Color, Religion, and National Origin. There was a great deal of opposition in the Senate from Southern states. They decided that they would strategically add another protected category to the list. They thought that if "sex" was added to the list, the bill would surely fail because no one would vote for having women protected in the workplace. Well, it passed…with all five protected categories in place. From that time forward, when making employment decisions, it has been illegal to take into account any employee's membership in any of the protected classifications.

Penalties for Violations

Penalties can be assessed by a federal court. Protocol requires a complaint be filed with the Equal Employment Opportunity Commission (EEOC), the administrative agency tasked with the duty to investigate claims of illegal employment discrimination. Regardless of the outcome of that administrative review, a "Right to Sue" letter is given to the complaining employee so the case can move forward to federal court if that is what the employee wishes to do next.

Penalties that can be assessed if an employer is found to have illegally discriminated against an employee include:

- **Actual damages**   Costs for medical bills, travel to medical appointments, equipment loss reimbursement, lost wages (back pay), lost promotional increase, and lost future earnings (front pay). The limitation is usually two years into the past and unlimited number of years into the future.

- **Compensatory damages**   Dollars to reimburse the victim for "pain and suffering" caused by this illegal discrimination.

- **Punitive damages**   Dollars assessed by the court to "punish" the employer for treatment of the employee that was egregious in its nature. This is usually thought of as "making an example" of one case so as to send a message to other employers that doing such things to an employee or job applicant will be severely punished.

2.3 The Civil Rights Act (1991)

This act modified the 1964 Civil Rights Act in several ways:

- It provided for employees to receive a jury trial if they wished. Up to this point, judges always heard cases and decided them from the bench.

- It established requirements for any employer defense.

- It placed a limitation on punitive damage awards by using a sliding scale depending on the size of the employer organization (payroll headcount):

  - For employers with 15 to 100 employees, damages are capped at $50,000.

  - For employers with 100 to 200 employees, damages are capped at $100,000.

  - For employers with 201 to 500 employees, damages are capped at $200,000.

  - For employers with more than 500 employees, damages are capped at $300,000.

For more information, see www.eeoc.gov/eeoc/history/35th/1990s/civilrights.html.

2.4 The Drug-Free Workplace Act (1988)

This legislation requires some employers to maintain a drug-free workplace. Employee compliance must be assured by subject employers.

Provisions and Protections

This law applies to federal contractors and all organizations receiving grants from the federal government. If you are covered, you are required to assure that all the employees working on the contract or grant are in compliance with its drug-free requirements. Covered employers are required to have a drug-free policy that applies to its employees.

In order to determine that an employer is in compliance with the requirements, drug testing is usually performed on employees and applicants who have received a job offer. Random drug testing is also used in some organizations to assure employees subject to the law or policy are continuing to comply with the requirements. Any federal contractor under the jurisdiction of the Office of Federal Contract Compliance Programs (OFCCP) in the Department of Labor must comply with this legislation.

Employee notification about the policy must include information about the consequences of failing a drug test. Whenever an employee has been convicted of a criminal drug violation in the workplace, the employer must notify the contracting or granting agency within 10 days.

Recordkeeping Requirements

Covered employers are required to publish a written policy statement that clearly covers all employees or just those employees who are associated with the federal contract or grant. Each covered employee must be given a copy of the policy statement, and it is a good idea, although it is not required, to have employees sign for receipt of that policy statement. The statement must contain a list of prohibited substances. At a minimum it must cite controlled substances.[11]

Some employers choose to include in the policy prohibition of alcohol and prescription drug misuse, although that is not a requirement. Subject employers must also establish a drug-free awareness training program to make employees aware of (a) the dangers of drug abuse in the workplace; (b) the policy of maintaining a drug-free workplace; (c) any available drug counseling, rehabilitation, and employee assistance programs; and (d) the penalties that may be imposed on employees for drug abuse violations. Records should be maintained showing each employee who received the training and the date it occurred.

Drug-Free Workplace Act Enforcement

Federal contractors under the jurisdiction of the OFCCP will find that the agency requires proof of compliance when it conducts a general compliance evaluation of affirmative action plans. Any employee who fails a drug test must be referred to a treatment program or given appropriate disciplinary action. Care should be given to treating similar cases in the same way. It is fairly easy to be challenged under Title VII for unequal treatment based on one of the Title VII protected groups.

Each federal agency responsible for contracting or providing grants is also responsible for enforcing the Drug-Free Workplace Act requirements. These responsibilities are spelled out in the Federal Acquisition Regulation (FAR). Failing to maintain a drug-free workplace can result in the following:[12]

- Suspension of payments for contract or grant activities
- Suspension or cancellation of grant or contract
- Up to five-years prohibition for any further contracts or grants

For more information, see www.dol.gov/elaws/asp/drugfree/require.htm.

2.5 The Equal Employment Opportunity Act (EEOA) (1972)

Amended the Civil Rights Act of 1964 by redefining some terms. It also required a new employment poster for all subject work locations explaining that "EEO is the Law."

For more information, see www.eeoc.gov/eeoc/history/35th/thelaw/eeo_1972.html.

2.6 The Genetic Information Nondiscrimination Act (GINA) (2008)

In general terms, GINA prohibits employers from using genetic information to make employment decisions. This legislation was brought about by insurance companies using genetic information to determine who would likely have expensive diseases in the future. That information allowed decisions to exclude them from hiring or enrollment in medical insurance programs. With the implementation of this law, those considerations are no longer legal.

For more information see www.eeoc.gov/laws/statutes/gina.cfm.

2.7 Guidelines on Discrimination Because of Sex (1980)

The Equal Employment Opportunity Commission (EEOC) published these guidelines to help employers understand what constituted unwanted behavior and harassment. They were issued long before the U.S. Supreme Court considered the leading cases on sexual harassment. This is about the only thing at the time that employers were able to turn to for help in managing the problem of sexual harassment in the workplace.

For more information, see www.ecfr.gov/cgi-bin/text-idx?SID=948f17132a22640b2 59f8e238d0dd410&node=29:4.1.4.1.5.0.21.11&rgn=div8.

2.8 The Lilly Ledbetter Fair Pay Act (2009)

This was the first piece of legislation signed by President Barack Obama after he was inaugurated the 44th President of the United States. It was passed in reaction to the U.S. Supreme Court decision in *Ledbetter v. Goodyear Tire & Rubber Co., Inc.*, 550 U.S. 618 (2007).

This law amends the Civil Rights Act of 1964 and states that the clock will begin running anew each time an illegal act of discrimination is experienced by an employee. In Lilly Ledbetter's situation, her pay was less than that for men doing the same job. The old law didn't permit her to succeed in her complaint of discrimination because she failed to file 20 years earlier on the first occasion of her receiving a paycheck for less than her male counterparts. Under the new law, the 180-day statute of limitations for filing an equal-pay lawsuit regarding pay discrimination resets with each new paycheck affected by that discriminatory action.

For more information, see www.eeoc.gov/laws/statutes/epa_ledbetter.cfm.

2.9 The Pregnancy Discrimination Act (1978)

This law modified (amended) the Civil Rights Act of 1964. It defined pregnancy as protected within the definition of "sex" for the purpose of coverage under the Civil Rights Act. It also specifically said that no employer shall illegally discriminate against an employee due to pregnancy. It defines pregnancy as a temporary disability and requires accommodation on the job if it is necessary. It guarantees the employee rights to return to work to the same or similar job with the same pay following her pregnancy disability.

For more information, see www.eeoc.gov/laws/types/pregnancy.cfm.

2.10 Uniform Guidelines on Employee Selection Procedures (1976)

This set of regulations is often overlooked by employers and HR professionals alike. Details can be found in 41 C.F.R. 60-3. For covered employers with 15 or more people on the payroll, this set of requirements is essential in preventing claims of discrimination.

There are two types of illegal employment discrimination: Adverse Treatment and Adverse or Disparate Impact. The latter almost always results from seemingly neutral policies having a statistically adverse impact on a specific group of people. To avoid illegal discrimination, the guidelines require that all steps in a hiring decision be validated for application to the job being filled. Validity of a selection device can be determined through a validity study or by applying a job analysis to demonstrate the specific relationship between the selection device and the job requirements. Selection devices include things like a written test, an oral test, an interview, a requirement to write something for consideration, and a physical ability test.

Employers can get into trouble when they use selection tools that have not been validated for their specific applications. For example, buying a clerical test battery of written tests and using it to make selection decisions for administrative assistants as well as general office clerks may not be supportable. Only a validity analysis will tell for sure. What specific validation studies have been done for the test battery by the publisher? Any publisher should be able to provide you with a copy of the validation study showing how the test is supposed to be used and the specific skills, knowledge, or abilities that are analyzed when using it. If you can't prove the test measures things required by your job content, don't use the test. According to the Uniform Guidelines, "While publishers of selection procedures have a professional obligation to provide evidence of validity which meets generally accepted professional standards, users are cautioned that they are responsible for compliance with these guidelines."[13] That means the employer, not the test publisher, is liable for the results.

For more information, see www.eeoc.gov/policy/docs/factemployment_procedures.html.

3. When You Have 20 or More Employees

The next threshold for employers occurs when they reach a headcount of 20 employees. At that point another four major federal laws begin their influence on the organization.

3.1 The Age Discrimination in Employment Act (ADEA) (1967)

When this law was first passed, it specified the protected age range of 40 to 70. Anyone under 40 or over 70 was not covered for age discrimination in the workplace. Amendments were made a few years later that removed the upper limit. Today, the law bans employment discrimination based on age if the employee is 40 years old or older. Remedies under this law are the same as under the Civil Rights Act. They include reinstatement, back pay, front pay, and payment for benefits in arrears. Some exceptions to the "unlimited" upper age exist. One example is the rule that airline pilots may not fly commercial airplanes after the age of 65.[14]

For more information, see www.eeoc.gov/laws/statutes/adea.cfm.

3.2 The American Recovery and Reinvestment Act (ARRA) (2009)

The thrust of this legislation was to create government infrastructure projects such as highways, buildings, dams, and such. It was an attempt to find ways to re-employ many of the workers who had become unemployed since the great recession began in 2007. There was a provision that provided partial payment of COBRA premiums for people who still had not found permanent job placement. It applied to individuals who experienced involuntary terminations prior to May 31, 2010.

ARRA also modified HIPAA privacy rules. It applies HIPAA's security and privacy requirements to business associates. Business associates are defined under ARRA as individuals or organizations that transmit protected medical data, store that data, process that data, or in any other way have contact with that private medical information. All parties are responsible for proper handling and compliance with the HIPAA rules.

For more information, see www.irs.gov/uac/The-American-Recovery-and-Reinvestment-Act-of-2009:-Information-Center.

3.3 The Consolidated Omnibus Budget Reconciliation Act (COBRA) (1986)

The law requires employers with group health insurance programs to offer terminating employees the opportunity to continue their health plan coverage after they are no longer on the payroll or no longer qualify for benefits coverage due to a change in employment status, i.e., reduction in hours. The cost must be at group rates and the employer can add a small administrative service charge. It turns out that many employers turn these programs over to vendors who administer the COBRA benefits for former employees. They send out billing statements and provide collection services. Two percent (2%) is the maximum administrative overhead fee that can be added.

The total cost of COBRA premiums and administrative fees is paid by employees participating in COBRA. The duration of coverage is dependent on some variables, so it may be different from one person to another.

For more information, see www.dol.gov/dol/topic/health-plans/cobra.htm.

3.4 The Older Workers Benefit Protection Act (OWBPA) (1990)

In the 1980s, it was common for employers, particularly large employers, to implement staff reduction programs as a means of addressing expenses. Often those programs were targeted at more senior workers because, generally speaking, their compensation was greater than that of new employees. Reducing one senior worker could save more money than the reduction of a more recently hired worker. Congress took action to prevent such treatment based on age when it passed this law.

The key purposes of the Older Workers Benefit Protection Act (OWBPA) are to prohibit an employer from:

- Using an employee's age as the basis for discrimination in benefits

- Targeting older workers during staff reductions or downsizing

- Requiring older workers to waive their rights without the opportunity for review with their legal advisor

For more information, see www.eeoc.gov/eeoc/history/35th/thelaw/owbpa.html.

4. When You Have 50 to 100 Employees

Once the employee headcount reaches these higher levels, additional legal obligations become effective for employers. Some of them only apply if the employer is subject to affirmation action requirements as a federal contractor.

4.1 Executive Order 11246—Affirmative Action (1965)

This is the presidential order that created what we now know as employment-based affirmative action. In 1965, President Johnson was past the days when he approved the Civil Rights Act, and he was in the process of examining how it was being implemented around the country by employers. He concluded that the law was pretty much being ignored. He needed something to stimulate implementation of the employment provisions in the Civil Rights Act, Title VII. His staff suggested they require affirmative action programs from federal contractors. A new program was born. President Johnson said that if a company wanted to receive revenue by contracting with the federal government, it would have to implement equal employment opportunity and establish outreach programs for minorities and women. At the time, minorities and women were being excluded from candidate selection pools. If they couldn't get into the selection pools, there was no way for them to be selected.

So, affirmative action programs were created. Outreach and recruiting was the name of the game in these programs. Analysis of the incumbent workforce, the available pool of qualified job candidates, and the training of managers involved in the employment selection process all contributed to a slow movement toward full equality for minorities and women.

The OFCCP (Office of Federal Contract Compliance Programs) is the law enforcement agency that currently has responsibility for enforcing the Executive Order along with other laws. Federal contractors must meet several conditions in return for the contracting privilege. One is the requirement to abide by a set of rules known as the FAR, Federal Acquisition Regulations. And, then, there is affirmative action for the disabled and veterans. Any business that doesn't want to abide by these requirements can make the business decision to abandon federal revenues and contracts. If you want the contracts, you also have to agree to the affirmative action requirements.[15]

For more information, see www.dol.gov/ofccp/regs/statutes/eo11246.htm.

4.2 The Family and Medical Leave Act (FMLA) (1993)

In general, the Family and Medical Leave Act (FMLA) sets in place new benefits for some employees in the country. If their employer has 50 or more people on the payroll, then they are required to permit FMLA leave of absence for their workers. FMLA provides for leaves lasting up to 12 weeks in a 12-month period, and it is unpaid unless the employer has a policy to pay for the leave time. The 12-month period begins on the first day of leave. A new leave availability will occur 12 months from the date the first leave began. During the leave, it is an obligation of the employer to continue paying any benefit plan premiums that the employer would have paid if the employee had remained on the job. If there is a portion of the premium for health insurance that is normally paid by the employee, that obligation for co-payment continues during the employee's leave time. The 12 weeks of leave may be taken in increments of one day or less.

To qualify, employees must have more than one year of service. The leave is authorized to cover childbirth or adoption; to care for a seriously ill child, spouse, or parent; or in case of the employee's own serious illness. The employee is guaranteed return to work on the same job, at the same pay, under the same conditions as prior to the leave of absence.

There are provisions for "Military Caregiver Leave" lasting up to 26 weeks of unpaid leave of absence for employees with family members needing care due to a military duty–related injury or illness. The 26-week limit renews every 12 months. The law provides for "National Guard and Military Reserve Family Leave." Employees who are family members of National Guard or Military Reservists who are called to active duty may take FMLA leave to assist with preparing financial and legal arrangements, and other family issues associated with rapid deployment or post-deployment activities. An employer may agree to any non-listed condition as a qualifier for FMLA leave as well.

FMLA provides for "Light Duty Assignments." It clarifies that "light duty" work does not count against an employee's FMLA leave entitlement. It also provides that an employee's right to job restoration is held in abeyance during the light duty period. An employee voluntarily doing light duty work is not on FMLA leave.

There is an employment poster requirement. The notice must be posted at each work location where employees can see it without trouble. A "Medical Certification Process" is part of the new provisions. DOL regulations have specified who may contact the employee's medical advisor for information, written or otherwise, and specifically prohibits the employee's supervisor from making contact with the employee's medical advisor.

Specific prohibitions are made against illegal discrimination for an employee taking advantage of the benefits offered under this law. These provisions are enforced by the EEOC.

For more information, see www.dol.gov/whd/fmla/.

4.3 The Mental Health Parity Act (MHPA) (1996)

This legislation requires health insurance issuers and group health plans to adopt the same annual and lifetime dollar limits for mental health benefits as for other medical benefits.

For more information, see www.dol.gov/ebsa/mentalhealthparity/.

4.4 The Mental Health Parity and Addiction Equity Act (MHPAEA) (2008)

This is an amendment of the Mental Health Parity Act of 1996. It requires that plans that offer both medical/surgical benefits and mental health and/or substance abuse treatment benefits provide parity between both types of benefits. All financial requirements (for example, deductibles, copayments, coinsurance, out-of-pocket expenses, and annual limits) and treatment requirements (for example, frequency of treatment, number of visits, days of coverage) must be the same for treatment of both mental and physical medical problems.

For more information, see www.dol.gov/ebsa/newsroom/fsmhpaea.html.

4.5 The National Defense Authorization Act (2008)

This is the origin of benefit provisions under FMLA for leaves of absence due to military reasons. Qualifying events include notice of deployment, return from deployment, and treatment for an injury sustained while on deployment. The provision is for up to 26 weeks, which can be taken in increments of a day or less if, for example, treatment is required for a service-related injury.

For more information, see www.dol.gov/whd/fmla/NDAA_fmla.htm.

4.6 The Patient Protection and Affordable Care Act (PPACA) (2010)

Signed into law by President Barack Obama on March 23, 2010, this law is commonly referred to as the Affordable Care Act. It has created health insurance trading centers in each state where employees and those who are unemployed can shop for health insurance coverage. These trading centers are the American Health Benefit Exchanges and Small Business Health Options Program (SHOP). Individuals and business owners of organizations with less than 100 workers can purchase insurance through these exchanges.

It applies to all employers with 50 or more full-time workers on the payroll. Employers with fewer than 50 full-time workers are exempt from coverage under the law. Effective January 1, 2014, covered employers must either provide minimum health insurance coverage to their full-time employees or face a fine of $2,000 per employee, excluding the first 30 from the assessment. Employers with fewer than 25 employees will receive a tax credit if they provide health insurance to their workers. In 2014, that credit will amount to 50 percent (50%) of the employer's contribution to the employee's healthcare program, if the employer pays at least that amount for insurance costs. A full credit is available for employers with fewer than 10 workers earning an average annual wage of less than $25,000. The credit will last for two years.

For more information, see www.dol.gov/ebsa/healthreform/.

5. When You Have 100 or More Employees

The final major threshold for employers is reached when the payroll reaches 100 employees. At that time employers become subject to the WARN Act and are required to submit annual reports to the federal government summarizing their race and sex demographics.

5.1 The Worker Adjustment and Retraining Notification Act (WARN) (1988)

This was the first attempt by Congress to involve local communities early in the private sector's downsizing process. It also prevented employers from just shutting the door and walking away without any worker benefits. It applies to all employers with 100 or more full-time workers at a single facility. The law specifies a qualifying employer to be one that has 100 or more employees who in the aggregate work at least 4,000 hours per week (exclusive of hours of overtime).

Definitions

The term "plant closing" refers to the permanent or temporary shutdown of a single site of employment, or one or more facilities or operating units within a single site of employment, if the shutdown results in an employment loss at the single site of employment during any 30-day period for 50 or more employees excluding any part-time employees.

The term "mass layoff" refers to a reduction in force that is not the result of a plant closing and results in an employment loss at the single site of employment during any 30-day period for (1) at least 500 full-time employees or (2) 33 percent of the total number of full-time employees for employers with 50 to 499 employees.

Required Actions

The law requires 60 days advance notice to employees of plant closing or mass layoffs. Any employment loss of 50 or more people, excluding part-time workers, is considered a trigger event to activate the requirements. Notification of public officials in the surrounding community in addition to notification of employees is a requirement. The local community leaders must be informed and invited to participate in the process of finding new jobs for laid-off workers. There is a provision that says an employer can pay 60 days separation allowance if it gives no notice to workers who will be terminated.

Exemptions to Notice Requirement

Notice is not required, regardless of the size of layoff, if the layoff, downsizing, or terminations result from the completion of a contract or project that employees understood would constitute their term of employment. It is not uncommon for workers to be hired in a "term" classification that designates them as employees for the life of a project. If they understand that from the beginning of their employment, their termination would not trigger the WARN Act.

WARN is not triggered

- In the event of strikes or lockouts that are not intended to evade the requirements of this law.

- In the event the layoff will be for less than 6 months.

- If state and local governments are downsizing. They are exempt from the notice requirement.

- In the event that less than 50 people will be laid off or terminated from a single site.

- If 50 to 499 workers lose their jobs and that number is less than 33 percent of the active workforce at the single site.

For more information, see www.dol.gov/compliance/laws/comp-warn.htm.

6. For Federal Government Employees

The federal government is subject to some of the same laws as the private sector employers. Yet, there are additional obligations the government employers have. Some of those obligations stem from the United States Constitution. Others come from the following laws.

6.1 The Civil Service Reform Act (1978)

This legislation eliminated the U.S. Civil Service Commission and created three new agencies to take its place:

- **The Office of Personnel Management (OPM)** This is the executive branch's human resources department. It handles all HR issues for agencies reporting to the President.

- **The Merit Systems Protection Board (MSPB)**   This part of the law prohibits consideration of marital status, political activity, or political affiliation in dealing with federal civilian employees. It also created the Office of Special Counsel, which accepts employee complaints and investigates and resolves them.

- **The Federal Labor Relations Authority (FLRA)**   This is the agency that enforces federal civilian employee rights to form unions and bargain with their agencies. It establishes standards of behavior for union officers and these standards are enforced by the Office of Labor-Management Standards in the U.S. Department of Labor.

For more information, see www.eeoc.gov/eeoc/history/35th/thelaw/civil_service_reform-1978.html.

6.2 The Congressional Accountability Act (1995)

Until this law was implemented, the legislative branch of the government was exempt from nearly all employment-related requirements that applied to other federal agencies and private employers. This law requires Congress and its affiliated agencies to abide by 12 specific laws that already applied to other employers, in and out of government.

- Americans with Disabilities Act of 1990
- Age Discrimination in Employment Act of 1967
- Employee Polygraph Protection Act of 1988
- Federal Service Labor-Management Relations Statute
- Rehabilitation Act of 1973
- Civil Rights Act of 1964 (Title VII)
- Fair Labor Standards Act of 1938
- Family and Medical Leave Act of 1993
- Occupational Safety and Health Act of 1970
- Veterans Employment Opportunities Act of 1998
- Worker Adjustment and Retraining Notification Act of 1989
- Occupational Safety and Health Act of 1970

For more information, see www.compliance.gov/publications/caa-overview/.

6.3 The False Claims Act (1863)

During the Civil War, people were selling defective food and arms to the Union military. This law, sometimes referred to as the Lincoln Law, prohibits such dishonest transactions. It prohibits making and using false records to get those claims paid. It also prohibits selling the government goods that are known to be defective. For HR professionals today, it is wise to train all employees about the need to avoid creating records that are inaccurate or, even worse, fictitious. Doing things that are illegal, just because the boss says you should, will still be illegal. Employees need to understand that concept.

For more information, see www.justice.gov/civil/docs_forms/C-FRAUDS_FCA_Primer.pdf.

6.4 The Homeland Security Act (2002)

This Cabinet-level organization (Department of Homeland Security) was created by Congress and President George W. Bush to consolidate security efforts related to protecting U.S. geography. Immigration and Customs Enforcement (ICE) is a part of this department. The E-Verify system resides here. Used by federal contractors as part of their affirmative action obligations, and other private employers on a voluntary basis, the system is intended to assist in rapid verification of Social Security numbers (SSNs) and confirm that the individual attached to the SSN has a valid right to work in this country.

For more information, see https://www.dhs.gov/homeland-security-act-2002.

6.5 The Privacy Act (1974)

This law provides that governmental agencies must make known to the public their data collection and storage activities, and must provide copies of pertinent records to the individual citizen when requested—with some specific exemptions. Those exemptions include law enforcement, Congressional investigations, Census use, "archival purposes," and other administrative purposes. In all, there are 12 statutory exemptions from disclosure requirements. If employees are concerned about employers using their Social Security numbers in records sent to the government, this act ensures privacy. Although such private information is required by the government, they are prohibited from releasing it to third parties without proper authorization or court order.

For more information, see www.justice.gov/opcl/privstat.htm.

6.6 The USA Patriot Act (2001)

The Patriot Act was passed immediately following the September 11, 2001 terrorist attacks in New York City and at the Pentagon in Virginia. It gives the government authority to intercept wire, oral, and electronic communications relating to terrorism, computer fraud, and abuse offenses. It also provides the authorization for collecting agencies to share the information they collect in the interest of law enforcement. This law can have an impact on private sector employers in the communications industry. It can also have an impact on any employer when the government asks for support to identify and track "lone wolves" suspected of terrorism without being affiliated with known terrorist organizations. HR professionals may find themselves involved in handling the collection and release of personal, confidential information about one or more employees. When legal documents such as subpoenas and court orders are involved, it is always a good idea to have the organization's attorney review them before taking any other action.

For more information, see www.justice.gov/archive/ll/highlights.htm.

Employment Visas for Foreign Nationals

Under some circumstances, it is possible for people from other countries to come work in the United States. There are several classifications of workers that can be used depending on the type of work to be done and the level of responsibilities.

E Nonimmigrant Visas

There are two types of E Nonimmigrant Visas: E-1 Treaty Traders and E-2 Treaty Investors. For more information on E Nonimmigrant Visas, see www.uscis.gov/portal/site/uscis.

E-1 Treaty Traders

The individual must be a citizen of the treaty country; there must be substantial trade; the trade must be principally with the treaty country; the individual must have executive, supervisory or essential skills; and the individual must intend to depart the United States when the trading is completed.

E-2 Treaty Investors

The individual must be a citizen of the treaty country and be invested personally in the enterprise. The business must be a *bona fide* enterprise and not marginal, and the investment must be substantial. E-2 employees must have executive, supervisory, or essential skills, and E-2 investors must direct and develop the enterprise. The E-2 investor must depart the United States when the investment is concluded.

H Visas

There are five types of H visas that are specific for temporary workers. For more information about H visas, see www.uscis.gov/portal/site/uscis.

HI-B Special Occupations and Fashion Models

These visas require a bachelor's or higher degree or its equivalent. The job must be so complex that it can only be performed by a person with the degree. The employer normally requires a degree or its equivalent for this job. Fashion models also fall into this category.

HI-C Registered Nurse Working in a Health Professional Shortage Area

Requires a full and unrestricted nursing license in the country where your nursing education was obtained. Or, you must have received your nursing education and license in the United States. It also requires that you have appropriate authorization from the U.S. State Board of Nursing to practice within the United States. H1-C requires that you have passed the examination given by the Commission on Graduates for Foreign Nursing Schools (CGFNS) or have a full and unrestricted license to practice as a Registered Nurse in the state where you will work.

H-2A Temporary Agricultural Workers
The employer must be able to demonstrate that there are not sufficient U.S. workers who are able, willing, qualified, and available to do the temporary seasonal work. The employer must also show that the employment of H-2A workers will not adversely affect the wages and working conditions of similarly employed U.S. workers.

H-2B Temporary Non-Agricultural Workers
The employer must show that there are not enough U.S. workers who are able, willing, qualified, and available to do the temporary work, and that the employment of H-2B workers will not adversely affect the wages and working conditions of similarly employed U.S. workers. The employer must also show that the need for the prospective worker's services is temporary, regardless of whether the underlying job can be described as temporary.

H-3 Nonimmigrant Trainee
To qualify, employees must be trainees receiving training in any field of endeavor, other than graduate medical education, that is not available in their home country. Or, they must be a Special Education Exchange Visitor who will participate in a special education training program focused on the education of children with physical, mental, or emotional disabilities.

L-1 Intra-Company Transferee
This allows a qualifying organization to move an employee from another qualifying country into the United States for a temporary assignment that is either managerial in nature or that requires specialized knowledge.

L1-A Managers and Executives
These are intra-company transferees coming to the United States to work in a managerial or executive capacity. The maximum stay in the United States allowed under this visa is seven years.

Specialized Knowledge
This is someone with specialized knowledge of the employer's product, service, research, equipment, techniques, management, or other interests and its application in international markets, or an advanced level of knowledge or expertise in the organization's processes and procedures. An L1-B visa holder may only stay in the United States for five years.

O-1 Alien of Extraordinary Ability in Arts, Science, Education, Business, Athletics

These people have a level of expertise indicating that they are among the small percentage who have risen to the very top of their field of endeavor. Alternatively, they represent extraordinary achievement in motion picture and television productions, or they have extraordinary ability and distinction in the arts.

P Visa Categories

There are seven variations of athletics-based or art-based occupations visas:

- P1-A: Individual Athletes or Athletic Teams
- P1-B: Entertainment Groups
- P1-S: Essential Support needed for P1-A or P1-B
- P2: Artist or Entertainer Under a Reciprocal Exchange Program
- P2-S: Essential Support for P2
- P3: Artist or Entertainer Under a Culturally Unique Program
- P3-S: Essential Support for P3

EB Employment-Based Visas

There are five levels of employment-based visas. They are prioritized so that once the first-level immigrant applicants are processed, the next level of priority will be considered. That will continue until the maximum allotment of visas is reached. In recent years, about 140,000 employment-based visas were permitted each year.

EB-1: Alien of Extraordinary Ability

The employer must demonstrate that the alien has extraordinary ability in the sciences, arts, education, business, or athletics, which has been demonstrated by sustained national or international acclaim and whose achievements have been recognized in the field through extensive documentation. It must also be shown that the work to be done in the United States will continue in the individual's area of extraordinary ability. It shall also be shown how the alien's entry into this country will benefit the United States. 28.6% of the total employment-based visas are allocated to this category.

EB-2: Alien of Extraordinary Ability

This is a classification that applies to any job that requires advanced degrees and persons of exceptional ability. 28.6% of the employment-based visas are allocated to this category.

EB-32: Skilled Workers

This category requires professionals and even unskilled workers who are sponsored by employers in the United States. 28.6% of the employment-based visas are allocated to this category.

EB-4: Certain Special Immigrants

Included here are some broadcasters, ministers of religion, and employees or former employees of the United States government, as well as Iraqi or Afghan interpreters and translators and other similar workers. 7.1% of the employment-based visas are allocated to this category.

EB-5: Immigrant Investors

These are people who will create new commercial enterprises in the United States that will provide job creation. 7.1% of the employment-based visas are allocated to this category.

Chapter Review

While this summary list is not meant to be a comprehensive statement of each law, studying and learning these laws will help you understand the basics as you perform your human resource management responsibilities. As you read through the chapters in Part II of this book, it's important to remember that one or more of these laws is the underlying basis in the HRCI's Body of Knowledge subject matter. Additionally, using this list as a reference guide in your day-to-day application as a Human Resource professional, please also consult the statutes and regulations themselves via the URLs we have provided. A thorough understanding of the various laws and regulations that impact the employment relationship will enhance your ability to protect your organization in matters involving employment and employee relations.

Questions

The following are all questions about U.S. laws and regulations concerning employee management.

1. John, a new employee has just arrived at the orientation program where everyone completes their payroll forms and signs up for healthcare benefits. He brings his W-4 form up to you and says he isn't subject to payroll withholding because he pays his taxes directly each quarter. What is your response?

   A. That's okay. We won't process a W-4 form for you. We will give you a Form 1099.

   B. I'll check with the accounting department to find out if you can do that.

   C. Unfortunately, all employees are subject to payroll tax withholding.

   D. If you can show me a W-10 form you have submitted to the IRS, we can block your paycheck withholding.

2. The Wagner-Peyser Act protects employees who are:

   A. Unemployed

   B. Injured on the job

    C. Unable to work because of pregnancy

    D. Have two or more jobs

3. Mary has had a very bad encounter with her supervisor, Henry. That evening after getting home from work, she pulls out her computer and sends a blistering blog post to her Facebook page. She names her company and her supervisor. She calls him unfair, pigheaded, and without principles. What can the company do about her posting?

    A. The company can demand that she remove the offensive post. If she doesn't, the company can file legal action against her.

    B. The company can demand that Facebook remove the offensive post. If it doesn't, the company can file legal action against Facebook.

    C. The company is protected against such employee comments by the Fair and Decent Treatment Act and can take disciplinary action against Mary.

    D. The company is prohibited from any action against Mary because she is engaging in protected concerted activity.

4. Pete is very sensitive about security of his personal identity information since his credit card has been stolen twice in the past year. He is trying to clear up his credit rating because of the problems with the stolen cards. Now, he has approached the HR Manager at his organization and requested that his Social Security number be removed from all of the company records. He thinks that a mistake could cause him more grief if the Social Security number were to be obtained by thieves. As the HR Manager, what should you do?

    A. The company can and should delete the Social Security number from its records to protect Pete.

    B. There is a need for the company to keep the Social Security number for tax reporting.

    C. There is a need for the company to keep the Social Security number for Census reporting.

    D. The company has no need for the Social Security number, but should keep it regardless.

5. Pat is talking with her colleagues about illegal discrimination at work. Someone mentions that the company is going to be sending out a request for updated race and sex information. Pat says that isn't legal. The company isn't supposed to track any of that information.

    A. Pat has not understood the FLSA requirements that employers keep race and sex data on employees.

    B. The EEOC has issued guidelines that agree with Pat's belief that it is illegal to maintain that information in company records.

C. Only federal contractors are required to maintain the race and sex identification for employees.

D. It is only the public sector employees who are exempt from providing their race and sex identification to employers.

6. The Tractor and Belt Company (TBC) handles conveyor belt installations for many small firms. Each of the customer projects begins on a day that is most convenient for the customer. Sometimes, that's Monday; sometimes it's Thursday or some other day. The HR Manager says that the company will adjust its workweek to begin when the customer's project starts. That way, each installation team has a separate workweek and those workweeks can shift several times a month. It's better for the payroll system that way and the company can usually avoid paying overtime. What would you advise the HR Manager to do if you disagree with the policy of changing workweeks?

A. The HR Manager is taking advantage of the FLSA's provisions for flexible workweeks that support small business.

B. Once the workweek has been designated to begin on a certain day of the week it should not be changed by the HR Manager.

C. It depends on state laws and regulations whether the workweek begins on any specific day of the week.

D. The FLSA says a workweek should always begin on Sunday.

7. Sandy is 15 years old and a sophomore at Central High School. She gets a job at the local hamburger drive-in. Her boss says he needs her to work the following schedule during the Spring Break week: 4 hours at lunch time every day, 9 hours on Saturday and 6 hours on Sunday. Is that schedule acceptable for Sandy given that she has a work permit from the school?

A. Because it is a school vacation week, there are no restrictions on the hours that Sandy can work.

B. Only state laws impact what hours Sandy can work because it happens during a vacation week.

C. Federal law says Sandy cannot work over 8 hours a day when it is a vacation week.

D. Because Sandy won't be working more than 40 hours for the week, there is no problem.

8. Gary is a junior at Southpark High School. He is 17 years old. The school needs some help in its warehouse during the summer and Gary needs a job so he can save money for college. His boss is the Manager of Facilities. Gary is assigned to work 9 hours every day during the week because one of the other employees is on disability leave. And, because the other employee was the forklift driver, Gary

has been given training in how to drive that equipment around the warehouse and loading dock. He likes that duty because he has been driving a car for only a few months. The forklift is cool. Is there any difficulty with the Facilities Manager's requirements of Gary?

A. Everything the Facilities Manager has required Gary to do is permissible under federal laws.

B. Since there is no restriction to the number of hours Gary can work, everything should be okay.

C. Whatever the Facilities Manager wants Gary to do is okay because it's only a summer job.

D. Even though Gary can work unlimited hours, he cannot be assigned to drive the forklift.

9. Hank puts in the following hours at work: Sunday, 0; Monday, 8; Tuesday, 8; Wednesday, 9; Thursday, 8; Friday, 8; Saturday, 7. His boss says he will give Hank compensating time off for every hour of overtime Hank works. How many compensating hours off should Hank receive for this work time?

A. One day of compensating time off.

B. 1.5 days of compensating time off.

C. 7 hours of compensating time off.

D. Compensating time off is not permitted under the FLSA.

10. The Tractor and Belt Company (TBC) doesn't have an HR Manager. HR is handled by the payroll clerk. When a new employee is assigned to the Production Department as an assembler, the payroll clerk raises a question. Should the new person be paid the same as all the other employees, all women, in the department or is it okay to pay her more because she made more at her former job?

A. There are no restrictions on the amount a new employee can be paid. It is market driven.

B. The Fair and Decent Treatment Act requires all people doing the same work to be paid the same amount.

C. There is no restriction on the amount paid because all the incumbents are women.

D. Once a valid market survey has been done, it can be used to determine starting pay for new people.

11. Finding a life insurance company to provide benefits to its workforce has been difficult for Joan, the HR Manager. She decides to recommend that they offer a self-insured plan. What controls might Joan have to consider in her planning?

A. There are no federal restrictions on a company providing its own life insurance plan to employees.

    B. The Employee Retirement Income Security Act regulates welfare benefit plans, including life insurance.

    C. The Life Insurance Benefit Plans Act has control over what Joan is able to do with her idea.

    D. Only state laws will have an influence on Joan's development of a self-insured benefit plan.

12. Simone has just been hired and is asked to complete a Form I-9. She offers her driver's license as proof of her identity. What else is required for her to complete the document?

    A. She may offer any document authorized on the Form I-9 instructions as proof of her authorization to work in this country.

    B. She must have a Social Security number to submit on the form.

    C. Simone has a U.S. passport but is told that she can't use it for her Form I-9.

    D. As long as Simone offers to get a Social Security number in the next 30 days, she can submit her Form I-9.

13. Steve is the HR Director for a crane operations company. He just got a phone call from one of his field supervisors with tragic news. One of their units has collapsed and their operator is in the hospital with serious injuries. What should Steve do with that information?

    A. Steve should immediately call the hospital to be sure all the insurance information is on file for their employee.

    B. He should notify the Occupational Safety and Health Administration about the accident and the injuries.

    C. He should notify the Crane Safety Institute of America to be sure they are able to add this accident to their database.

    D. Steve should call the crane operator's spouse to let her know about the tragedy.

14. Every year Donna has to attend training on the use of the company vehicles she drives. She thinks this is a silly waste of time. Donna knows how to drive and she knows the company vehicles. Why should she attend training every year?

    A. There is no federal requirement for Donna to take yearly training.

    B. OSHA only requires training be done once for vehicle operation.

    C. Only state safety provisions govern how frequently training must be done in Donna's situation.

    D. Safety programs must be developed that provide for refresher training on all equipment operating procedures.

15. Jerry just arrived at work and found a sinkhole in the parking lot. He is early enough that other people have not yet begun arriving for work. Because the hole is about 10 feet across at the moment, what should Jerry be doing about the problem?

   A. If Jerry is a management employee he should take charge of the situation and begin the process of alerting others to the danger posed by the sinkhole.

   B. If Jerry is a non-management employee he should give his boss a call and leave a voicemail message, if necessary, about the sinkhole.

   C. If the sink hole poses an immediate danger of death or serious injury Jerry should call 911 and report it. He should barricade the perimeter of the sinkhole with tape or something else to prevent people from falling in.

   D. Jerry should first test the edges of the sinkhole to see if it could grow in size. Then he should barricade the perimeter so no one else will fall in.

16. Theresa attended a seminar recently that pointed out the need to post a yearly summary of injury and illness cases. Her boss doesn't want to do that, saying he doesn't want to publicize the problems the organization has had. Theresa should tell him:

   A. Posting requirements call for display of the report in a prominent location if there are 10 or more people on the payroll.

   B. Posting requirements can be met by putting a report on the back of the closet door in the employee lounge.

   C. Posting requirements can be met by making the report available in a binder in the HR Manager's office.

   D. Posting requirements are optional, but good employers are using the report as a "best practice" in safety programs.

17. An employer routinely works with hazardous chemicals trucking them for delivery to various customer locations. After each load, the truck must be cleaned before being loaded with a different chemical. Cleaning has to be done by someone inside the tanker using special absorbent materials. What else should be considered?

   A. Personal protective equipment should be provided by the employer, including breathing apparatus and hazmat suits.

   B. Standard coveralls and boot covers should be provided for employees to use if they wish.

   C. Workers should never be sent into a tanker truck for any reason.

   D. Breathing equipment is absolutely a requirement if someone will be in the tanker truck for longer than 30 minutes.

18. Shelly has worked for the same dentist for over ten years. In all that time, there has been no mention of any special requirements for handling syringes. She arranges the doctor's equipment trays every day and cleans them up after they have been used. She just tosses the used equipment into the autoclave or into the trash if it won't be used again. If you were advising Shelly about the practices used in her dental office, what would you say?

   A. Needles should be broken off before they are thrown into the trash can.

   B. Sharps should be triple wrapped in a stiff paper to protect from sticking someone handling the trash.

   C. Any possible harm can be prevented if used syringes are placed into an approved sharps container.

   D. Putting used syringes into any solid container that is wrapped in red paper is sufficient to meet requirements.

19. The price of gold is climbing and folks at the Golden Nugget Mine are planning to reopen their operation. They know that safety is an important consideration. But what about federal regulations for gold mines? Are there such things?

   A. There are only OSHA regulations in general. All of those rules still apply.

   B. There are MSHA regulations to be considered, but because they are not in the coal mining business, the Golden Nugget Mine won't have to worry about them.

   C. MSHA rules apply to all mining operations in the United States. The Golden Nugget Mine will have to study those rules and get ready for inspections by the government.

   D. MSHA can tell the mine what to do, but it has no authority to conduct inspections because the Golden Nugget is not a coal mine.

20. Olivia suspects her payroll clerk of embezzlement. She has inspected the records for the past three months and the pattern is clear. But to be sure it is the payroll clerk and not the accounts payable clerk, Olivia wants to confront her and demand she take a lie detector test.

   A. Good going, Olivia. You caught her. Sure enough, demanding that she take a lie detector test is a good way to confirm your suspicions.

   B. While lie detector tests can be used for some employees, accounting employees are exempt. You can't test her.

   C. Lie detector tests are not permitted for any use by any employer. You can't test her.

   D. Lie detector tests can be required only in limited circumstances and this isn't one of them. You can't test her.

21. For the past 6 years, Sam's company has been a federal contractor working on equipment for the Department of Defense. They have additional contract opportunities coming up and Sam isn't sure if there will be an extra burden related to disabled workers because they are subject to both the Americans with Disabilities Act and the Rehabilitation Act.

    A. Sam should rest easy. The ADA and the Rehabilitation Act are identical in their content and requirements.

    B. Sam's company has already met its recruiting obligations and now only has to worry about meeting ADA requirements.

    C. Handling job accommodation requests is a requirement of the ADA but not the Rehabilitation Act. Things should be easier.

    D. Whatever Sam thinks, the ADA and Rehabilitation Act requirements have applied to his company for 6 years already. Adding more contracts won't change his current obligations.

22. Arthur has applied for a job with the AB Transit Company. He is told he must take and pass a urine drug test. If he fails the test, and any subsequent random drug test after he is hired, he will be dismissed from the company. Arthur reacts loudly and says, "That's an invasion of my privacy! I won't do it." What happens now?

    A. Arthur can call his lawyer and have the drug test waived since he doesn't wish to take it.

    B. Arthur can discontinue his participation in the AB Transit Company's employment process.

    C. Arthur can take the test now and still refuse to participate in random tests later on.

    D. Arthur can have his friend take the test for him.

23. Cynthia works for a large multi-state manufacturing company and approaches her boss one morning and tells him that her husband has just received orders from the Coast Guard to report for deployment to the Middle East. They have a week to get everything ready for his departure. She wants to know if she can have excused time off during the coming week. If you were her boss what would you tell her?

    A. She can have the time off, but it will be logged as unpaid and charged as FMLA leave.

    B. She can take the time off, but it will be unexcused because she didn't give more than a week's notice.

    C. If she wants the time off, she will have to use her paid vacation time for the week.

    D. Jennifer has already requested the week off for vacation and only one person can be off at any one time or the unit won't be able to function. Cynthia's request is denied with regrets.

24. Robert works for a Congressional representative and suffers a disabling injury in an automobile accident. Robert cannot work more than three hours per day according to his doctor. Weeks later, when he returns to work, he asks for a job accommodation and is told that it can't be done. When he presses the point, his supervisor says the reason is:

    A. Congressional staff people aren't covered by the ADA so they don't have to even discuss his request.

    B. The request he has made would exempt him from several of his job's key responsibilities.

    C. The request he has made would set a precedent that other Representatives' offices would have to follow.

    D. Because Congressional staff members have to meet the public every day, they can't have people seeing disabled workers in the office. It doesn't look good.

25. Jimmy has heard that he will be getting healthcare coverage from his company because of the new Obamacare law. His company employs only 10 people, but Jimmy is excited that he will finally get some insurance. He hasn't been feeling very good lately.

    A. Jimmy might have to wait until he can arrange for insurance through one of the exchanges.

    B. Jimmy should get an enrollment form from his boss because all employees will be covered by the new requirements that employers must provide health insurance for workers.

    C. Jimmy is out of luck. The new law only covers employers with 50 or more people and there is no way Jimmy will be getting health insurance under the new law.

    D. Jimmy's boss just ran out of forms, but he will get some more from HR and then have Jimmy sign up for his coverage.

Is Safety the Most Important Policy?—A Case Study

A company manufactured batteries for automobiles. The battery manufacturing process used lead as a main ingredient. It is generally known that exposure to lead can cause serious health problems. Even though the company provided personal protective equipment (PPE) to its workers, there was still a chance that some exposure could happen to the folks out on the manufacturing line. One of the dangers was related to harm that could be done during pregnancy to both the mother and the baby.

Because of the sensitivity the company had to the safety and health of its employees, its policy was to prohibit any pregnant worker from being on the production line. It didn't want to be responsible for harming any of its employees or their children.

One pregnant employee objected to that policy and her union sued the company. The company stood by its policy claiming safety trumps all other concerns.
Did the company have a valid policy? Why?

Answers

1. **C.** If the new worker is classified as an employee, on the payroll, the IRS demands that income tax, Social Security tax, and Medicare tax be withheld. People are not allowed to opt out because they wish to file their own tax payments each quarter.

2. **A.** The Wagner-Peyser Act of 1933 provides for federal unemployment insurance and sets guidelines for state unemployment insurance programs.

3. **D.** Mary is protected by the National Labor Relations Act (NLRA) of 1935. The National Labor Relations Board has taken the position that almost all postings on the Internet, whether complaining about supervisors or employers or making charges that employees are treated unfairly, are protected concerted activities under the act.

4. **B.** Both the FLSA and the IRS regulations require employers to obtain and report Social Security numbers from all employees. A Social Security number is required for completion of the Form I-9 to prove authorization to work in this country. The company may not remove it from its records, regardless of how concerned Pete may be.

5. **A.** Race and sex data is specifically required by the FLSA. For employers with 15 or more people on the payroll, who are engaged in interstate commerce, EEOC regulations also require maintenance of those data records.

6. **B.** The FLSA requires employers to designate a day as the beginning of the workweek. To change that designation, there should be a significant business reason. Moving the workweek to begin based on projects is not acceptable. The FLSA requires consistency because of the need to pay overtime for hours in excess of 40 in a workweek. Constantly moving a workweek could deprive employees of earned overtime.

7. **C.** The FLSA prohibits people aged 14 and 15 from working over 8 hours in a day even when school is not in session.

8. **D.** Driving a "power driven hoisting apparatus" is one of the 17 most dangerous jobs that may not be performed by workers under the age of 18. At Gary's age, the FLSA has no restriction on the hours he may work in a week.

9. **B.** The FLSA requires all hours of work in excess of 40 in a week be paid overtime at the rate of 1.5 times the normal hourly pay rate. Compensating time off, in lieu of overtime pay, must be given at the rate of 1.5 hours for every overtime hour. So, a day of overtime (8 hours) should be compensated for with one and a half days of compensating time off.

10. **C.** The Equal Pay Act requires men and women doing the same work to be paid the same rate. If there are no men in the job, only women, there is no Equal Pay Act issue. If all the incumbents are women, there is no employment discrimination based on sex because there is only one sex represented. So, with those conditions, there is no barrier to paying the new employee more based on her previous job's compensation.

11. **B.** ERISA specifically regulates welfare benefit plans such as health insurance and life insurance. That is in addition to regulation of pension and retirement plans offered by employers. It makes no difference who underwrites the life insurance—the employer or a vendor. ERISA will still provide requirements.

12. **A.** The deadline for completing a Form I-9 is three days after hire. Any documents listed on the form are acceptable. The employer may not designate certain documents as requirements. A Social Security number is one way to demonstrate authorization to work in this country. A valid U.S. passport is also a way to demonstrate *both* identity and work authorization.

13. **B.** The company has 8 hours after the accident to file its report of serious injury with OSHA. We don't know how long ago the accident happened, but it was long enough that the operator is now in the hospital. Steve should gather all the information needed for the report and get it called in to the OSHA office.

14. **D.** Injury and Illness Prevention Programs are required by OSHA. Part of the identification and remediation of workplace hazards is employee training. Even if employees have been trained on equipment operation, periodic refresher programs can help overcome bad habits that might have developed. Refresher programs conducted on a yearly basis represent a reasonable interval for Donna's situation.

15. **C.** It doesn't matter if Jerry is a manager or not. All employees should be trained to react to imminent dangers by taking immediate action to prevent anyone from serious injury. And walking up to the edge to see if it is going to collapse is just nuts.

16. **A.** If she must, Theresa should show her boss the requirement in OSHA regulations. A prominent display location excludes places such as the back of a closet door or inside a binder somewhere in the manager's office.

17. **A.** Working inside an enclosed space with dangerous fumes calls for hazmat equipment and adequate breathing equipment. OSHA regulations specify the personal protective equipment (PPE) necessary in this and other working conditions.

18. **C.** The Needlestick Safety and Prevention Act requires all sharps be disposed of in approved sharps containers. It also requires posting of warnings and information about blood-borne pathogens.

19. **C.** The Mine Safety and Health Administration has jurisdiction over all mining operations, not just coal mines. It handles safety complaints and conducts inspections of both above-ground and underground mining operations. All mine operators are required to conduct their internal safety inspections and maintain records of those inspections.

20. **D.** Except for law enforcement, security officers, and people who handle controlled substances, lie detectors are no longer permitted in the workplace. They were commonly used prior to 1988's Employee Polygraph Protection Act.

21. **D.** Sam's company will not incur any additional obligations for disabled workers if they seek additional government contracts. They have been obligated under both laws for six years.

22. **B.** Arthur has to decide if he wishes to continue seeking employment with the AB Transit Company. If so, he must participate in their drug testing program. If he wishes to avoid testing, he must drop out of the job application process and seek employment elsewhere.

23. **A.** Under the FMLA, Cynthia is entitled to an unpaid leave of absence as a spouse of a covered medical service worker. It will be logged as unpaid time off, unless she wishes to use some of her accrued paid time off. It will also be logged in her record as FMLA leave.

24. **B.** Even the Congressional offices are subject to the ADA's requirement to consider and discuss requests for job accommodation. Job accommodations must be made to make it easier for an employee to perform one of the job's essential functions. If he can't do that, even with an accommodation, he is not eligible for assignment to that job. If there is no other job available, the employer can't return him to work until his status changes.

25. **A.** Employers are required to provide health insurance coverage, or pay a penalty in lieu of that insurance, only if they have 50 or more full-time workers. With only 10 employees, Jimmy's employer is not obligated to provide health insurance coverage. Jimmy may purchase it for himself through one of the exchanges set up for that purpose.

Case Study Outcome

The case was *Automobile Workers v. Johnson Controls, Inc.* 499 U.S. 197 (1991). The decision of the Court was that the company policy on fetal protection was a violation of Title VII of the Civil Rights Act of 1964 as amended by the Pregnancy Discrimination Act (PDA). It impacted only women and, as such, was illegally discriminating against women based on sex.

Justice Harry A. Blackmun wrote, "danger to a woman herself does not justify discrimination." The Court concluded that it is the woman's decision to make about her safety and that of her fetus. Blackmun then said, these decisions "Must be left to the parents…rather than the employers. It is no more appropriate for the courts than it is for individual employers to decide whether a woman's reproductive role is more important to herself and her family than her economic role." Thus, in this instance, Title VII trumps safety concerns for the employer. (For a copy of the complete Supreme Court Opinion, go to http://supreme.justia.com/cases/federal/us/499/187/case.html.)

Endnotes

1. "Instructions for Employment Eligibility Verification," U.S. Department of Homeland Security, U.S. Citizenship and Immigration Services, accessed July 9, 2013, www.uscis.gov/files/form/i-9.pdf.

2. "Federal Mine Safety & Health Act of 1977, Public Law 91-173, as amended by Public Law 95-164," U.S. Department of Labor, Mine Safety and Health Administration, accessed July 9, 2013, www.msha.gov/regs/act/acttc.htm.

3. "OSH Act, OSHA Standards, Inspections, Citations and Penalties," U.S. Department of Labor, Occupational Safety and Health Administration, accessed July 9, 2013, www.osha.gov/doc/outreachtraining/htmlfiles/introsha.html.

4. Ibid.

5. *Lawson v. FMR LLC*, U.S. No. 12-3, retrieved from www.supremecourt.gov/opinions/13pdf/12-3_4f57.pdf on 3/7/2014.

6. *Sutton v. United Air Lines, Inc.*, 527 U.S. 471 (1999).

7. *Toyota Motor Manufacturing, Kentucky, Inc. v. Williams*, 534 U.S. 184 (2002).

8. The Job Accommodation Network (http://askjan.org or 800-526-7234) is a free resource for employers. It is a service provided by the U.S. Department of Labor's Office of Disability Employment Policy (ODEP). Jan has been providing services for over 25 years.

9. "Disability Discrimination," U.S. Equal Employment Opportunity Commission, accessed July 10, 2013, http://eeoc.gov/laws/types/disability.cfm.

10. The first was the Civil Rights Act of 1866, which protected the right to enter into contracts regardless of race.

11. A list of controlled substances can be found in Schedules I through V of Section 202 of the Controlled Substances Act (21 U.S.C. 812) and as further defined in Regulation 21 CFR 1308.11–1308.15.

12. "eLaws—Drug-Free Workplace Advisor," U.S. Department of Labor, accessed July 10, 2013, www.dol.gov/elaws/asp/drugfree/screenr.htm.

13. 41 C.F.R. 60-3.7.

14. Fair Treatment of Experienced Pilots Act (December 13, 2007) Public Law 110-135.

15. 41 CFR 60.

Core Knowledge

The Human Resource Certification Institute (HRCI) has identified 23 knowledge items that it considers "core knowledge" applying to the HR profession overall. Consider these prerequisites or foundations. HRCI believes that certification candidates should have a good grasp of these 23 knowledge areas.

In this chapter, we discuss each of the 23 knowledge items individually and show how they link to the other knowledge mastery requirements in the certification process.

23 Core Knowledge Requirements

Some of these core knowledge requirements apply to a few functional areas. Nearly all of them apply to more than one. That's why they are considered core requirements. Just because one area of knowledge might be designated as applying to a single function doesn't mean there are not other applications as well. In this analysis, we are identifying major applications and linkages. The related functional areas are listed in the gray boxes under each core knowledge requirement.

Needs Assessment and Analysis

- Workforce Planning and Employment
  - Organizational Staffing Requirements
- Human Resource Development
  - Training and Development
- Risk Management
  - Organizational Risk

Needs assessment is a structured process of measuring the difference between current status and the desired level or quantity of any given organizational condition. A needs assessment can become input to strategic planning or training program development. It can also be done in support of individual developmental planning for career enhancement.

The following are the most common steps in needs assessment analysis:

1. Describe the objective.

2. Define the current condition.

3. Conduct a gap analysis.

4. Prioritize a list of what must occur.

5. Determine options.

6. Evaluate best options with cost/budget associations.

7. Recommend a solution and action plan.

Third-Party or Vendor Selection, Contract Negotiation, and Management, Including Development of Requests for Proposals (RFPs)

- Business and Strategy
  - HR Business Management Skills
- Risk Management
  - Organizational Risk
- Human Resource Development
  - Training and Development

Requests for Proposals are a common tool used in selection of vendors for fulfillment of projects that usually carry a significant cost. They are a structured method for outlining the desired organizational outcome while allowing competing vendors to demonstrate how they will reach that outcome and how much the project will cost. RFPs allow organizations to compare "bid" responses from multiple vendors using the same format. Negotiation of final details can be facilitated through the RFP content.

With the increasing number of HR functions being outsourced, the need for HR professionals to effectively manage third-party contractors becomes vitally important. For a successful contractor relationship, it is critical that a clear understanding of the deliverable be established in the RFP and final contract.

Generally, an RFP will follow a format such as this:

1. Brief overview

2. Qualifications of vendor

3. How the service/product will be supplied by the vendor

4. Project team from both vendor and client organization—with responsibilities and accountabilities described

5. Delivery timeline

6. Billing and pricing schedule

7. Deadline for final submission of RFPs

Once the RFPs have been submitted, an evaluation of the proposals occurs. There are various factors to consider that will be specific to the needs request, including the reputation of the vendor. Once a vendor is selected and the contract drafted, negotiated, and entered into, it is important to have an ongoing evaluation of the project/service to ensure the deliverable is meeting the expectations as outlined in the contract.

Communication Skills and Strategies (For Example: Presentation, Collaboration, Sensitivity)

- Human Resource Development
  - Developing Leaders
- Business Management and Strategy
  - Role of Human Resources and Organizations

Presentation skills are applicable in all functional areas for HR professionals. Having the ability to make presentations to small groups as well as large gatherings is critical when addressing policy makers in the boardroom and employee assemblies to present or discuss policy or program changes. Understanding how to select the proper communication tool contributes to strategic plans for policy implementation.

HR professionals will find themselves presenting a variety of timely messages to a vast array of audiences. The skills needed for effective communications include written and verbal skills that involve persuasion, collaboration, influencing, sensitivity, tact, and diplomacy.

Organizational Documentation Requirements to Meet Federal and State Guidelines

- Workforce Planning and Employment
  - Key Legislation Affecting Employee Rights
  - Key Legislation Affecting Privacy and Consumer Protection
  - Equal Employment Opportunity/Affirmative Action, Recruitment
  - Employee Records Management
- Human Resource Development
  - Performance Management
- Compensation and Benefits
  - Key Compensation Legislation
- Compensation Systems
  - Introduction to Benefit Programs and Key Benefits Legislation
- Risk Management
  - Safety Programs, Security Programs, Return to Work Programs

Documentation is the lifeblood of human resource managers. Attorneys are careful to point out, "If it isn't documented...it didn't happen." When legal challenges pit employees against their employers, jury sympathy tends to swing to the "little guy" (the employee) rather than to the employer organization. Employers are expected to spend the energy necessary to make a record of events that take place during employee management. Supervisors must be trained in effective documentation techniques for employment actions and performance issues, and it is the responsibility of HR professionals to be sure supervisors are fulfilling that duty.

Adult Learning Processes

- Human Resource Development
  - Human Resource Development and the Organization
  - Adult Learning and Motivation
  - Training and Development
- Compensation and Benefits
  - Introduction to Benefit Programs and Key Benefits Legislation

Recent decades have brought us a continuing flow of behavioral science about how adult learning is different from children's learning. While the working of brain synapses may be similar, there are huge differences in what it takes to motivate students to learn. Adults must be shown "what's in it for them." What benefit will they derive from their efforts to learn new materials? HR professionals are often thrust into the role of instructor and must understand the adult learning process so they are able to properly facilitate the training experience for their employees.

Malcolm Knowles identified the following characteristics of adult learning:

- **Self-concept**   Moving from dependency on others to autonomy and self-directed learning.

- **Experiential learning**   Drawing on past experience for future learning

- **Readiness to learn**   Needs-specific to the current condition

- **Orientation to learning**   Applying information in current situations to solve immediate issues

- **Motivation**   Coming from a source of personal inspiration and desire vs. outside conditions

Knowles also identified three different types of learners. They are:

- **Auditory learners**   A process of learning that suits those who have a preference to "hear" information

- **Visual learners**   A process of learning that suits those who have a preference to see information to commit it to memory

- **Tactile/kinesthetic learners**   A process that suits those who have a preference to be physical, involving a sense of touch and hands-on learning

Motivation Concepts and Applications

- Human Resource Development
  - Adult Learning and Motivation
  - Training and Development
  - Developing Leaders

Contemporary motivation of human beings in a work environment is based on the early scientific studies conducted by Herzberg, Skinner, and Maslow among others. HR professionals must understand the differences between hygiene factors and motivational factors, between social needs and self-actualization. McGregor's X-Y Theory of motivation impacts decisions about which tools to use and which approaches to take based on the personal beliefs and orientation of the employee in question. Motivation is a complex subject that impacts HR professionals every day, often with challenges that have not yet been experienced. Each of the HRCI functional areas is affected by employee motivation or demotivation at work. Understanding the basic motivational theories, and keeping up-to-date with newly developed theories, is a lifelong learning objective of the HR professional.

Training Techniques
(For Example: Virtual, Classroom, On-the-Job)

- Human Resource Development
  - Training and Development

With current technology, remote instruction is possible, including both virtual classroom and self-paced computer education. Employees can participate in computer-based learning programs from terminals at kiosks in the workplace or from remote locations. In sophisticated organizations, job assignments often have identified prerequisites, and developmental training programs are made available for those who wish to participate in them. Classroom instruction, either in-person or virtually, is still an appropriate technique for some programs that require group discussions, sub-group activities, or physical involvement among participants. Selection of the best technique is the role of HR professionals and training professionals. Training techniques are discussed more fully in Chapter 8.

Leadership Concepts and Applications

- Human Resource Development
  - Developing Leaders

HR professionals must understand the concepts of leadership—how to recognize it in others, and how to develop leadership skills in themselves and in others. Key support in that effort exists in the Michigan Bell Management Progress Studies, conducted by psychologists at the American Telephone and Telegraph Company (AT&T). Out of those studies came the modern industrial assessment centers that can be used to observe, rate, and develop management skills, including leadership skills. HR professionals know that leadership is more than someone making suggestions. It involves getting others to follow those suggestions willingly.

Leadership styles have been identified to fall into the following labels. Many leaders will adopt a blend of several different styles. Identification and development of leadership styles should be ideally suited and aligned with the organization's desired culture and values.

- Directive
- Democratic
- Coaching
- Laissez-faire
- Transformational
- Transactional

Project Management Concepts and Applications

- Business and Strategy
  - HR Business Management Skills

The area of project management represents skills involving planning, executing, controlling, accountability, and lessons learned. Project management involves working with Project Evaluation and Review Techniques (PERT) charts, Critical Path Method (CPM) planning processes, and other similar techniques to guide a project through to completion while controlling resources, manpower, and deliverables. For HR professionals, managing projects is a necessary skill and factor for success. Projects can occur in just about every area of the HRCI listed functional areas.

Diversity Concepts and Applications
(For Example: Generational,
Cultural Competency, Learning Styles)

- Workforce Planning and Employment
  - Equal Employment Opportunity/Affirmative Action
- Human Resource Development
  - Diversity Initiatives

Diversity issues impact every aspect of employment these days. Types of diversity include employee representation (demographics), educational background, and cultural experience. Taking advantage of viewpoints molded by those differing experiences can result in more effective decisions.

It can also take longer to resolve questions simply because you need to discuss differing viewpoints. A key consideration involves people from different generations having different values, beliefs, and expectations that can lead to difficulties and conflict.

Making decisions in a group of people with similar backgrounds and experiences can be faster, but may not include considerations of cultural issues outside that experience. And so even though groups with a multitude of backgrounds and experiences will discuss issues for a longer period, the decisions they make will typically be more sound and apply to a broader target population.

This same variety of perspectives from a diverse workforce can also create a cultural competence to add strength to an organization. Military Veterans will have had different experiences and will have developed the ability to problem solve in different ways than those without such background. Disabled people are able to bring viewpoints that those without disabilities cannot readily see. The amalgam of all these differences can bring together organizational policies and outcomes. The results can be much stronger and more effective than are seen in organizations without such diversity.

Human Relations Concepts and Applications (For Example: Emotional Intelligence, Organizational Behavior)

- Human Resource Development
  - Human Resource Development and the Organization
  - Organizational Development Initiatives
  - Developing Leaders

Human relations focuses on the relationship between supervisors and subordinates in an employment organization. Organizational behavior is what results from the impact individuals, systems, and groups have on the overall organizational effectiveness. Emotional intelligence refers to the ability to perceive, control, and evaluate emotions. Emotionally intelligent individuals are able to motivate themselves, have awareness of others' emotions, are able to manage relationships, and can control their reactions to emotions. Applying these concepts can provide a valuable benefit to any employment organization. The more supervisors understand these concepts, the better they will be able to influence subordinate behavior and organizational results.

Ethical and Professional Standards

- Business and Strategy
  - Ethical Issues Affecting Organizations
- Human Resource Development
  - Human Resource Development and the Organization

Ethics is a field of intense interest among many organizations these days. For HR professionals, ethics is tied to the proper and fair methods used to manage employees in an employment environment. It also involves HR professionals participating with senior management to define ethics standards for their organizational behavior and employee expectations. SHRM and HRCI have standards for professional behavior for the HR profession. The SHRM Code of Ethical and Professional Standards in Human Resource Management may be viewed in its entirety at www.shrm.org/about/pages/code-of-ethics.aspx. Ethical standards follow six core principles:

- Professional Responsibility
- Professional Development
- Ethical Leadership
- Fairness and Justice
- Conflicts of Interest
- Use of Information

HRCI's Model of Professional Excellence sets standards for honesty, reliability, fairness, and cooperation.

Technology to Support HR Activities
(For Example: HR Information Systems, Employee
Self-Service, e-Learning, Applicant Tracking Systems)

- Business and Strategy
  - HR Business Management Skills
- Workforce Planning and Employment
  - Employee Records Management
- Human Resource Development
  - Training and Development
- Compensation and Benefits
  - Compensation Systems
  - Evaluating the Compensation and Benefits System and Communicating It to Employees

Technology can accomplish many things. It can reduce the number of employees necessary in performing repetitive and menial duties. It can assist employees with records management, updating information as it changes through time. Technology can assist with employee training, processing job applicants, and employee information. Exactly which technology to use in any given situation is the decision to be made by HR professionals and their colleagues. There are four mainstays of technology in Human Resources:

- **HRIS (Human Resource Information System)**   A repository of information for storing employment files

- **Applicant Tracking & Hiring Systems**   Automated methods for keeping track of applicants and the hiring process

- **Employee Self-Service Systems**   Allows employees access to their own employment and benefit records on the company intranet 24/7

- **Learning Management Systems**   Track, enroll and organize employee training requirements, needs, and progression

Qualitative and Quantitative Methods and Tools for Analysis, Interpretation, and Decision-Making Purposes (For Example: Metrics and Measurements, Cost/Benefit Analysis, Financial Statement Analysis)

- Business and Strategy
  - Measuring Strategic Outcomes
- Workforce Planning and Employment
  - Organizational Staffing Requirements
  - Recruitment, Human Resource Development
  - Training and Development
- Compensation and Benefits
  - Compensation Structure
- Human Resource Development
  - Training and Development

As HR professionals gain access to the executive suites of senior management, knowledge of business strategies and measurements is critical. It is not just a question of how many employees it takes to produce a given product, or the cost of health care plans per employee. Now it is a question of the dollar benefits produced by a diversity program and the increased production per employee realized by providing an in-house childcare center. All of those are fair game for measurements (metrics) that demonstrate they add value to the employer's organization and its ultimate mission. Knowing which method to utilize for research, data collection, and analysis is essential for the information presented.

Change Management Theory, Methods, and Application

> • Business and Strategy
>   ○ HR Business Management Skills

In 1962, Everett Rogers wrote a book called *Diffusion of Innovations* that described how people adapt to new ideas and technologies. Many scientists have followed with their own versions of studies examining how organizations can identify an end result and then plan to manage the change process in order to achieve that result. Particularly in large businesses, change management has become an identifiable function on the organization chart. In others, it is a function that is either part time or hired in through consulting firms. The notion that large organizational changes can be properly managed is important in the fast-paced world of mergers, acquisitions, and other upheavals such as restructuring and downsizing. Only 10 percent of the population is known as a "change agent"—people simply resist change.[1] HR professionals must be masters of understanding, orchestrating, and getting others to accept change. As the saying goes, "Change is good—you go first!"

Job Analysis and Job Description Methods

> • Workforce Planning and Employment
>   ○ Job Analysis and Documentation
> • Compensation and Benefits
>   ○ Job Evaluation

There are many different ways to put a job description on paper (or into electronic format), but most will contain these segments of information:

- **Summary** A statement about the overall job responsibilities
- **List of duties and responsibilities** A detailed list of duties assigned to this position with corresponding allocation of time spent on each—by percentage—so the weight of activities can be determined by looking over the list
- **List of qualifications** Including educational requirements, experience required, and other specific prerequisites for successful job candidates
- **List of physical job requirements** Description of the environment in which the incumbent works—noise level, heat/cold exposure, standing/sitting/walking/running, arm and hand movement, sight/hearing requirements
- **List of mental job requirements** Language, math, science
- **Expression of time requirements** Full-time, part-time, overtime

The main purpose of a job description is to help communicate the standards and expectations of each position in an organization. It is the basis for performance management, determination of pay levels, and outreach for applicants, and serves as a guideline for requests of reasonable accommodation.

Employee Records Management
(For Example: Electronic/Paper, Retention, Disposal)

- Workforce Planning and Employment
  - Recruitment, Employee Records Management
  - Compensation and Benefits

Knowing what records to keep is critical. So is knowing what records to destroy. Records management is an area of responsibility that can be a part-time assignment in a small organization or a full staff responsibility in a large organization. Employee records include an employee's personnel file, medical records, investigation records, training records, and security clearances. Depending on the organization, there can be other categories of records retained for employees—for example, safety records. Some records are required for government compliance, such as the W-4, I-9, W-2, work time records, hazardous exposure records, workers' compensation reports, and more. Other records are maintained for the convenience and use of the employer—for example, commendation and disciplinary records, training records, and performance appraisals. Some records are required by law and must be retained for designated periods of time. Other records have no retention requirements. Generally speaking, any record other than one made by an attorney can be discovered through legal process and are often sought in lawsuits against employers, including informal electronic communications. Retaining records beyond their required period can be detrimental to employers so create and follow a purging schedule, especially of electronic records.

Techniques for Forecasting, Planning, and Predicting
the Impact of HR Activities and Programs
Across Functional Areas

- Workforce Planning and Employment
  - Organizational Staffing Requirements
  - Recruitment

HR activities embrace many different organizational functions, including employment, payroll, benefits programs, policy development and implementation, governmental reporting, and labor relations. It is important that HR professionals be constantly looking into the future to determine what will be using resources. Union contract negotiations, government tax requirements, medical benefit cost increases, and issuance of a new employee handbook are examples of activities or issues that will require some amount of organizational resources. Identifying strategies for maximizing the benefit of each and minimizing the cost is a key role of the HR professional. Developing proper forecasting and planning techniques for organizational requirements is a key contribution of the HR department.

Types of Organizational Structures (For Example: Matrix, Hierarchy)

- Business and Strategy
  - Assessing the Internal Environment

HR professionals can make a significant contribution to the organization when designing its structure. There are three key types of structures employers usually implement: functional, divisional, and matrix. Other structures less used are product-based and geographic. Functional structures are those that group organizational segments according to their purpose—for example, production, accounting, and shipping. Divisional structures group organizational segments according to product type or market segments—for example, large screen TV division, computer monitor division, audio equipment division, Pacific states division, and Midwest division. Matrix organizations rely on relationships to determine the structure. For example, a reorganization task force can pull members from traditional accounting, HR, manufacturing, marketing, and other functional areas. Matrix organizations can often create situations where individuals report to more than one supervisor.

Environmental Scanning Concepts and Applications (For Example: Strengths, Weaknesses, Opportunities, and Threats [SWOT], and Political, Economic, Social, and Technological [PEST])

- Business and Strategy
  - Scanning the External Environment
  - The Strategic Management Process

Environmental scanning is the process of monitoring for and detecting events or conditions that will have an impact on the employer's organization. Over time, the process has been structured by some scientists to produce methods that can be applied by lay people in HR management and other functional areas. SWOT and PEST are two examples of methods for environmental scanning. The degree to which the internal environment of an organization matches its external environment is expressed as its *strategic fit*. Strengths and weaknesses are considered by the method as internal elements, while opportunities and threats are considered external elements. PEST analysis has been expanded since its inception as a strategic management tool and can be represented by the acronym STEEPLED: Social, Technological, Environmental, Economic, Political, Legal, Ethics, and Demographics. Through quantification and anecdotal examples, this method allows for unmasking issues to be considered in strategically preparing for the organization's future.

Methods for Assessing Employee Attitudes, Opinions, and Satisfaction (For Example: Surveys, Focus Groups/Panels)

- Human Resource Development
  - Training and Development
- Employee and Labor Relations
  - Measuring Employee Attitudes

It is wise for any organization large enough to have one or more HR professionals on staff to engage in activities to gather feedback from employees about their experience on the job. Even smaller organizations can avail themselves of consulting support to do the same thing. Providing employees with an opportunity to be heard and express their opinions assists management and HR in many areas, including building good employee relationships and avoiding third-party interventions. Structured investigations through the use of focus groups, surveys, or panel discussions can yield a wealth of information about employee reactions, attitudes, and expectations. That information is important as a component of strategic planning and in design of HR systems and programs. The process of gathering employee input should be repeated periodically because attitudes, expectations, and reactions change over time as the environment changes.

Budgeting, Accounting, and Financial Concepts

- Business and Strategy
  - HR Business Management and Acumen

Business competence is a requirement of HR professionals just as it is of any other member of senior management. It is necessary for HR professionals to be able to create and manage within a financial budget, understand accounting reports, and be able to discuss financing issues. Chief Executive Officers (CEOs) expect HR professionals to have a grasp of business concerns and be able to express in financial terms how HR programs are contributing to the "bottom line." HR programs often must be justified in business terms so senior executives can understand the impact they will have on organizational financial results. There are several different types of budget development processes. The most used are Zero-Based Budgeting and Historical Information Budgeting.

Risk-Management Techniques

- Risk Management
  - Organizational Risk, Safety, Health, Security, and Privacy

Nearly every aspect of HR management impacts the function of risk management in one way or another. Employee satisfaction can be captured through monitoring of complaints. Safety can be expressed in terms of workers' compensation experience. The cost of employee health benefits is impacted by employer programs that support smoking cessation, exercise, and good diet. Computer security programs can block unauthorized access to confidential employee and business records. Privacy of records can be expressed in financial terms. All of these issues are potential impacts on the profit or loss of an employer's organization. Even non-profits and governmental agencies have budgets they are expected to live within. Huge, unexpected expenses related to risks can cause instant budget failure. HR professionals can have a great impact on the organizational finances by preventing large losses through proper risk management programs.

Chapter Review

This chapter has provided you with an overview and basic understanding of the concepts and applications. As you read the specific topic information in Part II, notice how these core knowledge statements have implications in several functional areas. There are volumes of books, courses of study, and journals that address the many subject topics presented here. An understanding of the concepts is what will be required for the HRCI exams.

Questions

1. HRCI has identified ____ knowledge items that it considers "core knowledge," which every HR professional should master.

   A. 45

   B. 23

   C. 15

   D. 17

2. Needs Assessment and Analysis is an area of required knowledge that applies to these functional areas:

   A. Workforce Planning and Employment, Human Resource Development, Risk Management

   B. Risk Management, Business Management and Strategy, Employee and Labor Relations.

   C. Employee and Labor Relations, Compensation and Benefits, Human Resource Development

   D. Business Management and Strategy, Human Resource Development, Employee and Labor Relations

3. Needs assessment can be applied to any of these processes:

   A. Benefits planning, vacation assessments, attendance programs, and employee training needs

   B. Strategic planning, public relations, and emergency awareness

   C. Any given organizational condition, training programs, and strategic planning

   D. Staffing forecasts, training planning, and budgeting

4. Vendor selection can involve each of the following activities:

   A. Reference checking, financial assessment, comparison with similar projects

   B. Interviewing, background checking, financial stability assessment

   C. Appointment of contract manager, review of financial statements, review of similar projects

   D. Development of RFPs, evaluation of match to project requirements for each vendor, background checking, and financial stability

5. Organizational documentation requirements can impact these functional areas of professional HR management:

   A. Parking policy, payroll compliance, orientation

   B. EEO/AA, employee records management, performance management

   C. Magazine subscriptions, amusement park discount programs, forms management

   D. Vacation selection system, cafeteria menu planning, parking lot space assignments

6. HR professionals must be concerned about adult learning processes because they impact these areas of the organization:

   A. Human Resource development, training and development, compensation and benefits

   B. Payroll, employee orientation programs, training and development

    C. Job description development, vacation planning, government compliance

    D. Safety compliance, compensation and benefits, employee training

7. Employee motivation is influenced by HR management and so HR professionals must understand these scientists and their studies:

    A. McDonald, McGregor, McJohnson

    B. Herzberg, Underwood, McDonald

    C. Byonberg, Skinner, Maslow

    D. Herzberg, Maslow, McGregor

8. Employee training is a function that falls within Human Resources Development. The following are generally accepted training techniques:

    A. Texting, lecturing, small group discussions

    B. Reading, group discussions, email

    C. Lecturing, self-paced online, sub-group exercises

    D. On-the-job, classroom, recess

9. Diversity management falls within an HR professional's responsibility because:

    A. It is the most recent academic HR subject studied and recommended.

    B. It is considered to have both a representation component and an inclusion component, both of which are HR responsibilities.

    C. Racial demographics are a critical component of successful organizations.

    D. All of the Fortune 100 organizations have mastered diversity programs and demand that other organizations do the same.

10. Ethics management is important to HR professionals because:

    A. No one should have to do anything unethical at work.

    B. Ethics is tied to the proper and fair methods used to manage employees in an employment environment.

    C. Ethics management programs are a requirement for government compliance.

    D. Ethics management programs are required by most state laws.

Answers

1. **B.** There are 23 knowledge items HRCI considers prerequisites (or foundation requirements) for every HR professional.

2. **A.** The three major areas of involvement for this knowledge area are Workforce Planning and Employment, Human Resource Development, and Risk Management.

3. **C.** Needs assessment can be a component of any organizational condition, including benefits. It is also a key component of employee training programs and strategic planning processes.

4. **D.** RFPs should be the foundation of vendor-assigned projects. Vendor selection should be based on the match of vendor capabilities to RFP requirements, background investigation, and financial stability.

5. **B.** In fact all of these things are going to require documentation. The most correct answer is B because it has the widest impact across the employer's organization.

6. **A.** Like the previous question, this is the correct answer because it has the widest impact on an employer's organization.

7. **D.** Herzberg, Maslow, and McGregor were behavioral scientists who made real contributions to the field of employee management. The other names were made up.

8. **C.** Texting, email, and recess are not commonly accepted training techniques.

9. **B.** Diversity and inclusion are key components of successful diversity management programs. Representation extends beyond race and gender to cultural background, sexual orientation, disability, veteran status, and any other identifiable characteristic.

10. **B.** While some federal legislation requires ethical management programs, not every employer must comply with those requirements. Ethics is an important part of HR management because it is based on meeting employee expectations for fairness and proper decision making.

Endnote

1. Barker, Brenda, "Energizing Organizational Readiness," Queen's University (2007). http://irc.queensu.ca/articles/energizing-organizational-readiness.

Risk Management

Risk management covers many functional areas in the employment world. Some of them are: compliance with federal employment laws, identification of workplace hazards and developing safety plans to protect employees and the public, and preparation of job descriptions to be used both as a communication tool and also as a means to address physical and mental requirements of each job. Risk management explores how technology can help manage the liability that comes with operating an employment organization. And, finally, risk management addresses the rapidly evolving field of social media, Internet, technology, and e-mail use. Eight percent of the PHR exam and 7 percent of the SPHR exam will focus on this area of knowledge.

Risk management addresses issues related to employees, customers, clients, the public, and vendors/suppliers. Risk management is the process of managing liabilities related to these populations in ways that will protect the employer organization and not be so heavy-handed that the organization can't function well in performing its mission. HR professionals are the key to striking a balance in that delicate effort—developing, implementing/administering, and evaluating programs, procedures, and policies in order to provide a safe, secure working environment and to protect the organization from potential liability. Lots of exciting things to think about.

The official HRCI Risk Management functional area responsibilities and knowledge statements are as follows:

Responsibilities

- Ensure that workplace health, safety, security, and privacy activities are compliant with applicable federal laws and regulations.

- Conduct a needs analysis to identify the organization's safety requirements.

- Develop/select and implement/administer occupational injury and illness prevention programs (i.e., OSHA, workers' compensation).

 • Establish and administer a return-to-work process after illness or injury to ensure a safe workplace (for example: modified duty assignment, reasonable accommodations, independent medical exam).

- Develop/select, implement, and evaluate plans and policies to protect employees and other individuals, and to minimize the organization's loss and liability (for example: emergency response, workplace violence, substance abuse).
- Communicate and train the workforce on security plans and policies.
- Develop, monitor, and test business continuity and disaster recovery plans.
- Communicate and train the workforce on the business continuity and disaster recovery plans.
- Develop policies and procedures to direct the appropriate use of electronic media and hardware (for example: e-mail, social media, and appropriate website access).
- Develop and administer internal and external privacy policies (for example: identity theft, data protection, and workplace monitoring).

Knowledge of

- Applicable federal laws and regulations related to workplace health, safety, security, and privacy (for example: OSHA, Drug-Free Workplace Act, ADA, HIPAA, Sarbanes-Oxley Act)
- Occupational injury and illness prevention (safety) and compensation programs
- Investigation procedures of workplace safety, health, and security enforcement agencies
- Return to work procedures (for example: interactive dialog, job modification, accommodations)
- Workplace safety risks (for example: trip hazards, blood-borne pathogens)
- Workplace security risks (for example: theft, corporate espionage, sabotage)
- Potential violent behavior and workplace violence conditions
- General health and safety practices (for example: evacuation, hazard communication, ergonomic evaluations)
- Organizational incident and emergency response plans
- Internal investigation, monitoring, and surveillance techniques
- Employer/employee rights related to substance abuse
- Business continuity and disaster recovery plans (for example: data sharing, password usage, social engineering)
- Data integrity techniques and technology (for example: data sharing, password usage, social engineering)
- Technology and applications (for example: social media, monitoring software, biometrics)
- Financial management practices (for example: procurement policies, credit card policies and guidelines, expense policies)

Core Knowledge of

- Needs assessment and analysis
- Third-party or vendor selection, contract negotiation, and management, including development of requests for proposals (RFPs)
- Communication skills and strategies
- Organizational documentation requirements to meet federal and state guidelines
- Adult learning processes
- Motivation concepts and applications
- Training techniques
- Leadership concepts and applications
- Project management concepts and applications
- Diversity concepts and applications
- Human relations concepts and applications
- Ethical and professional standards
- Technology to support HR activities
- Qualitative and quantitative methods and tools for analysis, interpretation, and decision-making purposes
- Change management theory, methods, and application
- Job analysis and job description methods
- Employee records management
- Techniques for forecasting, planning, and predicting the impact of HR activities and programs across the functional areas
- Types of organizational structures
- Environmental scanning concepts and applications
- Methods for assessing employee attitudes, opinions, and satisfaction
- Budgeting, accounting, and financial
- Risk-management techniques

Key Legislation Governing Risk Management

Now that you've reviewed the Risk Management HRCI responsibilities and knowledge statements, we recommend that you review the federal laws that apply to Risk Management as outlined in Figure 4-1. It would be helpful to refer back to Chapter 2 on these specific laws prior to reading any further in this chapter. A great many of them impact organizational liability, requiring HR professionals to make plans to address how those liabilities will be managed properly.

- National Labor Relations Act
- Equal Pay Act
- Occupational Safety and Health Act
- Uniformed Services Employment and Re-Employment Rights Act
- Fair Credit Reporting Act
- Whistleblower Provisions of Several Laws
- Health Insurance Portability and Accountability Act
- Davis-Bacon Act
- Service Contract Act
- Drug-Free Workplace Act
- Age Discrimination in Employment Act
- Workers Adjustment and Retraining Notification Act

- Fair Labor Standards Act
- Immigration Reform and Control Act
- Needlestick Safety and Prevention Act
- Consumer Credit Protection Act
- Fair and Accurate Credit Transaction Act
- Civil Rights Act
- Sarbanes-Oxley Act
- Walsh-Healey Public Contracts Act
- Pregnancy Discrimination Act
- Americans with Disabilities Act
- Family and Medical Leave Act
- Patient Protection and Affordable Care Act

Figure 4-1   Key federal laws impacting employer liability

NOTE   If you are a federal contractor or subcontractor you will want to be very familiar with the Executive Order and legislation that govern how employers must comply when they are receiving certain amounts of federal revenues through goods and service contracts.

Cross-Reference to Other Legislation Requirements and Enforcement Agencies That Impact Risk Management

As you reference each of these pieces of legislation listed in Figure 4-1, you will understand how they individually bring liability for noncompliance to the workplace. There are some additional federal laws that aren't highlighted in the figure. That is because they are special condition laws that don't apply to all employers. If your organization is a federal contractor or subcontractor, for example, you most likely have to comply with Executive Order 11246, the Rehabilitation Act, and the Vietnam Era Veterans' Readjustment Assistance Act in your affirmative action efforts. But those requirements don't apply to every employer, or even most employers.[1]

Applicable Legal Cases Involving Risk Management

We suggest that you understand the nature of case law prior to reading the chapter to correlate the topics with the legalities involved. There is only one recent case that is related to risk management, the 1991 case involving Johnson Controls. For more information on this case, see Appendix D.

A very common type of employer liability is employee complaints of discrimination. Typically, these complaints arise because an employee feels mistreated by a decision made about his or her employment conditions. They include complaints of race, sex, religious, or age discrimination. Also common are complaints of national origin discrimination and pregnancy discrimination. But the most frequent of all complaints is that "my employer retaliated against me because I filed a complaint." The retaliation charge is one that most judges don't like to hear and have little patience for. If an employer doesn't understand that things must change when settling an initial complaint, and then does something to retaliate against the complaining employee, it is likely to raise the ire of any judge you find yourself before.

Hazard (Risk) Identification and Communication

The process of protecting an organization from financial harm by identifying, analyzing, financing, and controlling risk is a shared responsibility among several areas in an organization. Risk is the threat of an event or action that will adversely affect an organization. Risk arises from missed opportunities as well as possible threats. HR is relied upon to be the keeper of accountability and the developer of policies and procedures in risk management.[2] Effective risk management is a progression of actions that are taken with the purpose of minimizing losses or injuries within the organization. HR's responsibilities fall within the following areas:

- Occupational safety and health
- Legal compliance
- Privacy
- Security
- Disaster recovery for business continuity

The identification of current and potential risks is an essential role for the Human Resource professional. Weighing in on the probability and acceptability of the risk is valuable to integrate with business decisions that are made with other business units. It is a goal for the HR professional to be consulted as a business partner within the organization. Focus should be on *proactive* and *management*.

Needs Analysis (Audits)

Conducting a comprehensive risk management needs analysis is an important activity. A comprehensive risk management assessment is a useful tool to uncover and identify risks. When you conduct a risk management needs assessment, you must start with identifying a number of areas and goals and use an appropriate method for audit.

Qualitative and quantitative methods and tools for analysis, interpretation, and decision-making purposes—such as metrics and measurements, costs-benefit analysis, and financial statement analysis—are frequently used in risk management.

There are numerous risks possible in the modern workplace. For HR, the focus is usually on things related to the employee's body and its day-to-day exposures. Some HR risks include:

- Employee complaints of illegal discrimination (EEO issues)
- Employee complaints of illegal financial processes (Sarbanes-Oxley and SEC issues)
- Employee injuries on the job (workers' compensation issues)
- Safety practices and procedures (OSHA/MSHA issues)
- Emergency plans for use in the event of fire, earthquake, tornado, flood, hurricane (OSHA/MSHA issues)
- Imbalance of compensation programs (equal pay issues)
- Loss of federal contract revenues by noncompliance with affirmative action requirements
- Responses to crisis conditions (embezzlement, production interruption, natural disaster, key person disappearance)

Recordkeeping Requirements

There is a saying among HR professionals: "If it isn't documented, it didn't happen." Actually, many management attorneys agree with that sentiment. When employer meets employee in a courtroom, juries have a tendency to root for the little guy (the employee) and have little sympathy for the big guy (the employer). That means the employer must be ready to "prove" everything they claim during the course of defending themselves against claims such as wrongful termination, illegal discrimination, failure to (fill in the blank).

Documentation is so important that almost every management attorney will offer instructions to their clients about how to prepare documentation of actions involving employee treatment. The problem is that people are inherently lazy. It takes time and effort to prepare documentation. If there is a choice between spending a half hour writing up the conversation a supervisor just had about an employee performance problem or getting out of work early, the documentation will slide. Eventually, it will be forgotten. And, there will be nothing in the file to prove a supervisor had that conversation with that employee about that performance problem. Whatever the supervisor claims to recall will be suspect without the written document to demonstrate that the recollection is accurate.

 NOTE One of the highest impact activities an HR professional can have on any organization is to teach managers and supervisors the proper way to prepare documentation.

Once prepared, it is usually dependent upon state laws and company policy whether or not the employee is given a copy. In some states, that is a requirement, while it is not in other states. Federal law doesn't specify one way or the other. It is not necessary for an employee to sign documentation about a disciplinary conversation with the supervisor, but if you get an employee signature, it is a good practice to provide a copy of the document to that employee. Why isn't it necessary to get an employee signature? Supervisor notes are made by the employer and don't require employee agreement. Unless it is a contract with the employee, the supervisor is merely writing what happened from his/her perspective.

Generally speaking, documentation should include the following:

- The date of the event and when the documentation was prepared. (They should be the same in most situations. Supervisors should always prepare their notes for file soon after the event took place.)

- A description of what was said. It is not necessary to quote verbatim. It is important to capture the key thoughts, who agreed to what, and the details about any deficiencies or issues the supervisor pointed out. The level of detail depends on the topic and how important details were to the conversation.

- How the conversation ended. What action plan was agreed to by both people?

- Will there be a follow-up meeting?

These same guidelines should apply to HR professionals in their documentation of conversations they have with employees, supervisors, and managers. It may be necessary at a future date to show someone your notes about what was said on a particular occasion.

The thing about documentation is that you don't know if it will be important until you reach the future when someone requests it. By the time you discover it is important, it's too late to create it.

Here is a quick word about creating documentation after the fact. While it is always best to be able to say that your notes were made right after the event or conversation, it is also possible to create your notes in the days following that event. When you write notes after the fact, always put the date on them representing when you wrote them. If you had a conversation on January 2 with an employee but didn't get around to writing your notes until three days later, mark your notes with the January 5 date. That way, there will be no question about the fact that you prepared them after the event. It could be beneficial if you stuck in a note saying what caused the delay in preparing the documentation.

Investigating Complaints

There are several ways in which HR professionals can manage the employee complaint process, and there are several reasons why you could be faced with the need for an investigation. It may become necessary because of a discrimination complaint, employee

In the Trenches

Investigating a Sexual Harassment Complaint

It was a Friday morning when the phone rang and a young man on the other end of the line said he wanted to file a complaint about his supervisor. He said he was calling from an airport 2,500 miles away from his work location and some of his coworkers helped him escape from his boss. He claimed that his life was at risk because his boss threatened him when he was confronted.

That began a complaint investigation that lasted for six months, involved travel halfway across the country for the investigators, consumed six investigators for the entire six months, and cost an enormous amount of money...just for the investigation. This young man claimed his supervisor (another male) had physically assaulted him and made sexual advances in the process.

Because he was a new hire and would be relocating from another state, the boss invited him to live at his house temporarily. The boss said it would save money and give them time out of work hours to get to know one another. The boss was single, having divorced several years before.

The assault, as it was told, took place in the boss's home while the two men were working out together. When the sexual advances were rebuffed by the young man, he said his boss got angry and started to punch him. The boss threatened to kill the new employee if he ever told anyone about the incident.

Over the next three weeks, while still living at the boss's home, the young man identified two people in his workgroup that he felt he could trust. He enlisted them in a plan so he could escape the constant oversight of the boss. The boss wanted to know where the young man was at every moment of the day. He wasn't permitted to leave the work site, nor was he permitted to make any trips without supervision away from the home. It was claimed that everything the boss did was intended to isolate this employee from the rest of the workgroup. Still, he managed to get two coworkers to help him get away.

There was no way the employee could take his clothing or personal effects from the house so he abandoned them. The coworkers arranged an off-site meeting as an excuse for being away from the office. The employee claimed he was going to use the restroom, but instead, he left the building and climbed into the trunk of his coworker's car. The coworker drove directly to the airport where the employee got out of the trunk and bought a ticket with borrowed money. The plane was headed 2,500 miles away. And, that's where he made the call to the company HR Manager.

That investigation yielded a "He said...He said" situation. Interviews with the accused manager and with the employee produced credible stories from

(Continued)

each one. Sometime after the investigation began, documentation revealed that the boss had been found to have done something similar in years past. That history of behavior tipped the balance. Deeper digging revealed some of the young man's coworkers had also experienced some form of sexual advance from the accused manager.

The case was closed after the manager was fired. Criminal assault charges were never brought.

bad behavior (code of conduct violation, embezzlement), safety issue (serious employee injury or death), disagreement with the employee's supervisor, and so on.

When you recognize the need for an investigation, you can take one of several approaches to getting that done:

- *Investigate the complaint yourself.* As an HR professional, investigations are often just another of the many responsibilities that come with the job.

- *Hire an outside expert to conduct the complaint investigation.* This might be a consultant specializing in the investigation of complaints of the type you face. It might also be an attorney who specializes in investigating complaints for clients. It is generally possible to protect files created by an outside legal counsel as attorney work product. The files are part of the legal advice provided to the client organization. You should be aware of any state or local requirements that investigators be licensed before performing such work. Using unlicensed investigators when a license is required could expose the organization to additional risks.

- *Have your internal legal expert conduct the complaint investigation.* It may or may not be possible to protect investigation materials from disclosure under attorney client privilege when you use your internal attorney. An argument is sometimes made that a lawyer who provides legal advice and is also a participant (investigator) in the same situation invalidates the claim to attorney-client privilege. You'll have to talk with your own legal counsel to determine the best course of action for your organization.

The following steps should be taken in an investigation:

- *Plan the investigation.* Identify the key people involved (complainant, supervisor, witnesses, experts). Identify what is needed from each of them. What questions should be asked based about the complaint. Who saw what? Who did what? Is there any documentation available? Are there any videos or photos available?

- *Interview the employee who filed the complaint.* Determine the details. Be sure the complaint is in writing, naming names and being specific about what happened. Document the encounter.

- *Interview the witnesses.* Determine if they can corroborate the claims of the complaining employee. Find out if they have any documentation or other evidence to support their observations. That might include videos or photographs. Document each interview.

- *Interview the accused.* Explain the charges. Explain the documentation and witness testimony about what happened. Ask for comments from the accused in reaction to each of those pieces of input. Document the responses.

- *Follow up on any questions remaining.* Re-interview individuals if necessary.

- *Make a determination and provide feedback to both the accused and the complaining employee.*

Documentation of each step in the process is very important. Note that it will be difficult to protect the documents you create from disclosure requests in the event of a lawsuit at some point in the future. That means you should "write for the jury" by explaining everything in detail, especially the reasons you had for making the decisions you made as you progressed through the investigation. Make sure your written documentation can stand on its own if you are not available to testify about what you did in that investigation.

Communication Skills and Strategies

Not much happens properly within a modern workplace unless adequate communication systems are in place to help workers understand what work needs to be done, how safety enters into the process, when to stop a given procedure, and hundreds of other applications you can think of each day.

Successful communication depends on completing the Communication Cycle, which is shown in Figure 4-2.

When someone sends a message, it is generally received by the other person. However, the sender doesn't really know that what was said has been understood unless there is some sort of feedback to indicate understanding.

Think about driving a car. When you step on the brakes, your brake light turns on to alert the driver behind you. When that message is received, the car behind begins to slow, giving you feedback that the message was received. If the car doesn't slow, well… bad things happen.

Similar disasters can happen when communication between people goes awry. If your boss tells you not to send the announcement until later, and you understand the message to be, "Send the announcement, it will get there later," the outcome won't be what the boss wants and he may send you another message. When your doctor tells you take three pills twice a day and you hear, "Take three pills every two days," things won't go as planned in your recovery. Communication clarity matters.

One of the claims that invariably emerges from every complaint of sexual harassment is, "That isn't what I meant at all." Confusion in communication is reduced substantially when people insist upon getting feedback about what they have just said.

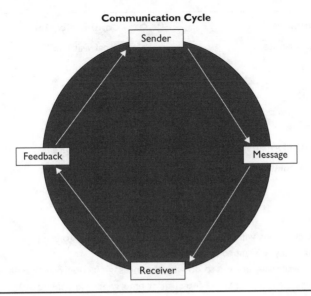

Figure 4-2   Communication cycle

One tactic for making sure that the communication cycle is working as you want is to ask for feedback after you have given an important set of instructions. "Tell me what you are going to do…" Or, "What do you understand I just said?" Any number of other tests will solicit the feedback you want so that there is assurance your message got across as you wanted.

A second important part of communication is the realization that the sender controls intent, but the received controls the impact. Remember what accused parties usually say when confronted with a complaint that they sexually harassed someone? "That isn't what I meant at all." Well, it is often true. That isn't what they intended the message to be. The receiver in our example heard something other than what the sender of the message intended. Incomplete or inaccurate communication can create very large liabilities for both individuals and organizations.

In the employment world, communication is critical to proper and successful running of the organization. Supervisors must successfully communicate to subordinates their task assignments, deadlines, expectations, methods, guidelines, and more.

Communication Methods

With today's technology and real-time accessibility, a conscientious approach and clarity of message is vital. HR becomes a bridge communicating to various sectors within the organization and also outside the organization. Determining the most effective method to communicate can be just as important as what is communicated. Figure 4-3 illustrates the various communication methods for HR.

Written Communication

- Personal letter or note
- E-mail message
- Website message
- Webinar
- Newsletter article
- Form filled with information
- PowerPoint presentation
- Texting

Oral Communication

- Personal visit/talk
- Group meeting
- Conference call
- Personal telephone call
- Voicemail message
- Speech or lecture
- Artistic performance

Strategic Communication Planning

Answering these questions will help you determine what strategy to use in your communication.

1. What message do you want to send?
2. What do you want the receiver to do with the message (action, planning, etc.)?
3. How fast must the message arrive (no rush or emergency/life dependent)?
4. Should the message go to a group or only an individual (one worker or whole staff)?
5. Do you want to be known as the sender (author or agent for author/boss)?
6. Is the message confidential or public information (medical condition or Congressional testimony)?
7. Must the message meet some legal requirements for content (Security and Exchange Commission filing or vendor contract)?
8. Is a form required to convey the message (performance appraisal or job application)?
9. What professional conventions must be met (patient treatment record, investigation interview documentation, training learning points)?
10. Who should convey the message (you or someone else)?

Figure 4-3 Communication methods

Strategy involves selecting the best tool for the job. In terms of communication strategy, how a message is to be communicated is often as important as what the message contains. Timing of a message can also be critical. Getting an e-mail message saying all performance appraisals were due last Thursday isn't much help if you don't get it on time to meet the deadline. When you are asked to provide some content to a bid proposal, delay can mean you lose business and the revenues associated with it. Picking the proper communication channel or media is often quite important.

Strategic Communication Planning

You can control the message in many different ways. What strategy you elect to use in conveying your message is dependent upon your answers to the key questions: Who, What, When, Where, Why? It's not silly. And it's not inane. These are important questions for anyone who doesn't want to go through their professional career "winging it." That cavalier approach won't work for long in the role of an HR professional.

Ask yourself who should receive the message. What is the purpose of the message? When should your message arrive? Where will it be going? And, finally, why should the message be sent? If you can answer those questions you can select the best strategic communication process/media for your message.

Obviously, this analytical approach isn't necessary for all messages. We send many messages every day as a matter of routine. Some, however, will require more thought. If you are involved in a merger or acquisition, a corporate downsizing, or introduction of a new vendor for your healthcare programs, some amount of thought should be put into what your message will be and how you will communicate it properly. Your employees will depend on your message being clear and easy to understand. Your executive team will be depending on you to accomplish the objective you have targeted. Success of your communication will depend a great deal on the strategy you select for its delivery.

Human Relations Concepts and Applications

Helping structure an organization's policies and culture to make people feel welcome is a critical HR responsibility. If done properly, morale will remain high and risks can be controlled.

Job Analysis and Job Description Methods

As noted in Part I under Laws Affecting HR Management, the Americans with Disabilities Act (ADA) does not require employers to prepare job descriptions, but it does require that those who do shall review them for accuracy at least once each year. Federal contractors, subject to affirmative action obligations, must review their job descriptions every year. Therefore, most federal contractors are required to prepare and maintain proper job descriptions. If that requirement doesn't apply to you, your organization may choose to have them or not have them. More information on job analysis appears in Chapter 9, "Compensation and Benefits."

Preparing and Reviewing Job Descriptions

So, why should you write job descriptions for your organization? Job descriptions can:

- Identify key duties and responsibilities
- Communicate to incumbents their job content
- Communicate to job applicants the job content
- Communicate to job supervisors/managers what an incumbent should be doing
- Aid in organizational structuring to identify which jobs will perform which duties
- Provide input for evaluation of job value in compensation system
- Assist in determining how much incumbents should be paid
- Provide objective reference for preparation of work performance reviews or evaluations
- Assist in succession planning
- Provide reference for disability accommodation requests

Usually, job descriptions contain some typical subjects. They might be described as:

- List of duties and responsibilities
- Identification of the amount of time spent (by percentage) on each duty and/or responsibility
- List of knowledge categories required to perform the job
- List of skill categories required to perform the job
- List of ability categories required to perform the job
- List of physical requirements of the job
- List of mental requirements of the job
- Identification of qualifications not mentioned elsewhere in the job description (such as educational requirements, amount of specific experience required to be successful on the job)

Figure 4-4 is an example of a standard job description.

Organizational Name
Job Description*

Job Title: Administrative Support Specialist
Department: Marketing
Reports to: J. C. Jones, Marketing Manager
FLSA Status: Non-Exempt
Prepared by: J. C. Jones, Marketing Manager
Prepared Date: 3/5/2019
Approved by: T. L. Smith, Vice President
Approved Date: 3/10/2019

<u>Summary</u>: Schedules appointments, gives information to callers, processes inventory orders, and otherwise relieves Marketing Manager of clerical work and minor administrative and business detail by performing the following duties.

<u>Essential Duties and Responsibilities:</u>
Include the following. Other duties may be assigned.

20%	Writes, types, or enters information into computer to prepare correspondence, bills, statements, receipts, checks, or other documents, copying information from one record to another.
5%	Proofreads records or forms. Counts, weighs, or measures material. Sorts and files records.
15%	Processes orders for catalog merchandise from customers. Shrink-wraps products as orders and inventory demand. Receives money from customers and deposits money in bank. Processes credit card payments using credit card processing agent to secure authorization on each purchase.
5%	Composes and types routine correspondence.
5%	Organizes and maintains file system, and files correspondence and other records.

Figure 4-4 Job description example

5%	Answers and screens telephone calls, conveys messages, and runs errands. Answers basic questions on products or product order processing.
5%	Arranges and coordinates travel schedules and reservations.
10%	Conducts research, and compiles and types statistical reports.
5%	Coordinates and arranges meetings, prepares agendas, reserves and prepares facilities.
10%	Makes copies of correspondence and other printed materials.
10%	Prepares outgoing male and correspondence, including e-mail and faxes. Processes outgoing bulk mailings as required.
5%	Orders and maintains supplies, and arranges for equipment maintenance.
100%	Total Time Allocation

Supervisory Responsibilities: This job has no supervisory responsibilities.

Qualifications: To perform this job successfully, an individual must be able to meet each of the essential duties satisfactorily. The requirements listed below are representative of the knowledge, skill, and/or ability required. Reasonable accommodations may be made to enable individuals with disabilities to perform the essential functions.

Education and/or Experience: High school diploma or general education degree (GED); or one to three months related experience and/or training; or equivalent combination of education and experience.

Language Skills: Ability to read and interpret documents such as safety rules, operating and maintenance instructions, and procedure manuals prepared in the English language. Spanish language skills would be an advantage, but are not a requirement.

Mathematical Skills: Requires an ability to add, subtract, multiply, and divide in all units of measure, using whole numbers, common fractions, and decimals. Also requires an ability to compare rate, ratio, and percent and to draw and interpret bar graphs.

Reasoning Ability: The job requires ability to apply commonsense understanding to carry out instructions furnished in written, oral, or diagram form. This job requires an ability to deal with problems involving several concrete variables in standardized situations.

Certificates, Licenses or Registrations Required: None

Physical Demands: While performing the duties of this job, the employee is regularly required to sit. The employee frequently is required to use hands to finger, handle, or feel; reach with hands and arms; and talk or hear. The employee is occasionally required to stand and walk. Stooping and bending are required when accessing filing cabinet contents and supplies in the storage room. The employee must occasionally lift and/or move up to 50 pounds. Specific vision abilities required by this job include close vision. Keyboard typing skills are required and used up to 50% of any work day. Hands and fingers are involved with repetitive movements on standard keyboard.

Work Environment: While performing the duties of this job, the employee is occasionally exposed to moving mechanical parts (computer printers), toxic or caustic chemicals (copy machine toner, correction fluid, etc.), risk of electrical shock (computers and related equipment), and risk of radiation (computer monitors). The noise level in the work environment is usually quiet.

[* Prepared with the help of *DescriptionsNow* software, Insperity, Kingwood, Texas]

Figure 4-4 Job description example

NOTE Reviewing your job descriptions at least once each year is essential if you are to keep them representative of the actual job content and incumbent requirements. If you are a federal contractor, you must be prepared to attest that you have periodically reviewed your job descriptions to be sure they are accurate.

Job Analysis

When trying to determine the content of a job so a job description can be written, there are several approaches to the task:

- **Observation**   A job analyst prepares lists of all activities and behaviors performed by an incumbent or group of incumbents, and then consolidates those lists of duties and responsibilities. Observation can involve time and motion studies. For accuracy of results, job analysts should be properly trained in the process rather than using untrained observers.

- **Questionnaire**   A written questionnaire can be used to gather input from incumbents, supervisors, and managers about job content and incumbent requirements.

- **Interview**   A job analyst interviews incumbent(s) to determine the job content, qualifications for successful incumbents, and the physical and mental requirements required of the job.

After a draft of the job description has been prepared, it should be shared with the incumbents, supervisors, and managers so they can have an opportunity to comment on the content. After considering the feedback received from the subject matter experts, a final description should be prepared and submitted for approval.

Each year, or at some more frequent schedule if the job is undergoing rapid changes, the incumbent and supervisor should be asked to submit their comments about changes needed in the written job description. Those changes should be worked into the description and resubmitted for approval.

There is more information about job descriptions and essential functions in Chapter 5, "Workforce Planning and Employment," and Chapter 9, "Compensation and Benefits."

Review of Job Descriptions

While job descriptions are not required, affirmative action compliance requires employers to review physical and mental job qualification standards annually. This review must be in writing and made available to Compliance Officers from the Office of Federal Contract Compliance Programs if requested during an audit of Affirmative Action Plans for the Disabled.[3]

Communication to Employees

Organizations live and die by communication. It is when people stop talking with one another that their organizations get into trouble and flounder. To prevent such a disastrous result, HR professionals should be alert to healthy communications within the organization and do all they can to foster those conversations.

Keys to Healthy Organizational Communication

Each of the following types of communication should be encouraged within any employment organization. It is incumbent upon the HR professional to be sure each type thrives and is reinforced and encouraged.

- *Keep employees up to date on what is happening in the organization.* Senior executives (and HR professionals) sometimes overlook how important it is to the average worker to understand what's going on with the organization. If employees can be made to feel that they are given information about situations as developments occur, it will be easier for them to believe they really are contributing to the organizational success.

- *Reinforce with employees why their jobs are important.* When employees understand the "big picture" about where the organization is headed (and why), they will be more willing to keep their performance levels high. If they think they are being excluded from the "big picture," their enthusiasm for the job will diminish.

- *Deal effectively and immediately with rumors.* Organizational effectiveness can be severely impacted by rumors working their way through the workforce. Rumors often start when people "suspect" something will happen, but don't have confirmation that it is really true. Sometimes rumors are intentionally started in an effort to derail what is thought to be something bad for workers. It could be something to do with the organization, or something to do with individuals in the workgroup. Whenever untrue rumors take hold, managers should react quickly to address them openly and correct misunderstandings where they exist. If rumors deal with confidential issues, they should still be dealt with quickly and with as much openness as possible. You can always say, "We don't have information about that yet, but as soon as we do, we'll let you know." Or, "These things are personal and hurtful to those involved. Consider how you would feel hearing something like this about yourself. Even though we can't discuss them because of their personal nature, we hope you will not discuss things like this that can't be confirmed as accurate."

- *Ask for feedback.* Many employees would be willing to contribute ideas or suggestions if they thought there was a chance someone would actually listen. If we believe no one will listen, or worse, have actually been told to keep our ideas to ourselves, we are not very likely to be open with ideas in the future. HR managers should protect upward communication by requesting input from employees when it is appropriate. That may mean training managers and supervisors in how to request and accept employee feedback. You might have to prepare organizational leaders in how to behave when employee suggestions surface. Some of those ideas will be good ones. It is not necessary to have formal "Employee Suggestion Programs" for there to be requests for employee feedback. Feedback can be handled formally or informally, but if it is not handled at all, workers will become discouraged at not being able to contribute. Frustration will lead to dissatisfaction and lower production. Give folks the chance to contribute their ideas.

- *Give feedback.* Let your workers know how they are doing. If they are meeting your expectations, give them that acknowledgment. You don't need a formal job performance appraisal system in order to provide that input to your employees. When something happens that you like, or there is a remarkable achievement, let employees know that you appreciate what they did. Likewise, when things go wrong that could have been handled differently, make suggestions for doing it differently next time. People have a need to understand where they fit into an organization and what their supervisors think of the contributions they are making.

HR Technology Activities

Besides the government, the HR function was notorious for being an intensive paper user. It was one of the first organizational functions to jump into the paperless movement via the development of technology, specifically human resource information systems and, soon after, applicant tracking systems. The cost savings of going digital and paperless were astounding. HR technology continues to develop and basically serves two purposes: as a repository of necessary information and as an aid to good decision making. Let's review the various technology that exists today for HR.

Employee Records Management

These days, records management invokes thinking about not only the method of recordkeeping, but the safety of those records as well. For employers larger than 10 to 20 employees, keeping records manually is very difficult. That is particularly true with the reporting requirements that exist for federal contractors and subcontractors. A great deal of attention is given to record security, yet there are not many pieces of legislation that speak to employer obligations in that regard. Most of them on the books deal with medical information. (See Chapter 2, 1.14—The *Fair Credit Reporting Act* [CRA]; 1.18— The *Health Insurance Portability and Accountability Act* [HIPAA]; 2.1—*Americans with Disabilities Act* [ADA].) Today, hardly a week goes by that there isn't news of another illegitimate access and release of private information from some database somewhere. From a risk management perspective, there are many commonsense protections that can be put in place to prevent the embarrassment of such disclosures and the expense of following up with people whose records have been jeopardized. It can be very costly to notify hundreds or thousands of employees that their records have been subject to theft. It erodes employee relations along with HR trust and credibility.

HR Information Systems (HRIS)

Employee records involve fields of data including those shown in Figure 4-5. This is not an exhaustive list. Many other records are maintained by some employers.

Birthdate	Department	Home phone	Original job title
Building code	Educational degree	Home state	Original pay rate
Cell phone	Employee ID number	Home zip	Past job title
Certifications	Exempt/non-exempt	Job group/EEO code	Race/ethnicity
Current job title	Healthcare plan	Last employer	Sex
Current pay rate	Home address	Licenses	Social Security number
Dental plan	Home city	Name	Vision plan

Figure 4-5 Types of data included in employee records

HRIS programs range from those serving employee groups up to 100 people to systems that can handle unlimited data fields and unlimited numbers of employees. Obviously, the prices of such software systems vary according to the capabilities they offer. PII (Personal Identity Information) is a crucial concern with HRIS and other systems in protecting employee data.

Employee Self-Service

There are many ways to offer employee self-service related to personal employee records. Some large employers use kiosks in central locations equipped with computer terminals that offer individual employees the opportunity to make changes to their employee records. Those changes might include marital status, health plan selections during open enrollment, addition of licenses or certifications, and more.

Employers often offer employee self-service through remote access and internal intranets so they can connect from the convenience of home during off-duty hours. It is obvious that such systems require security to assure that only authorized employees can gain access and that employees can only access their own personal record and not others. It's not a good thing to have one employee searching through other employee records. In some cases, employers have even offered telephone access to employee data with the ability to make updates from the touch tone keypad. The latest hardware, offering touch screen technology, makes reviewing and updating employee records quick and easy.

It used to be that employers would default to using Social Security numbers as employee numbers in their HRIS, or even file folders. That is no longer such a good idea with identity theft on the rise. In some states, it is no longer permissible to print the entire Social Security number on paychecks for that same reason. Instead, consider using sequential numbers, 1 representing the first employee hired, and so on. Or you could use compound numbers such as 2013-1 to reflect the year and the hiring priority within the year. Another approach is to use the employee's phone number as the employee number. Because Social Security numbers are used for so many sensitive purposes such as bank account reporting to the Internal Revenue Service, income tax filings, and payroll withholding reports, protecting them by not using them as employee ID numbers is a reasonable protection to take.

e-Learning

Only a few years ago, e-learning was not an option in the workplace. Learning was accomplished by attending a classroom session lasting from a few hours to several days, weeks, or months. Today, employees are able to log on to a computer access point and participate in training programs at their own pace, on their own schedule. These e-learning systems provide materials, review, and testing to assure the employee has accomplished specific learning objectives before moving to the next training step. They also offer an audit trail to report on who has participated in each program. That is handy when you have to be sure everyone has gone through specific training programs. There is no need for an instructor. Each individual works with the materials presented, and perhaps some reference materials, to meet the training objectives.

One of the more popular e-learning systems involves classroom-type groups with an instructor and a group of students, all participating remotely from anywhere in the world. There is no longer a need when using these systems for the group to collect into one physical setting. The savings on travel time alone has been significant for organizations using these types of learning programs. This approach is used by almost all of the major universities and colleges around the country.

Applicant Tracking Systems

For most small employers, an applicant tracking system consists of a file folder filled with job application forms. Larger employers are not able to operate with manual records any longer. During the great recession, with unemployment running up to double digits, an employer could count on receiving hundreds or thousands of job applications for every job opening announcement. Processing them manually was not feasible.

More and more, applicant tracking is accomplished on employer websites. People interested in a given job opening can submit their application information online and in some cases can even submit resume files and cover letters for consideration. These mechanized programs allow employers to sort through the massive amounts of data to find the few candidates who might be a good fit for the job opening.

Federal contractors with 50 or more employees and $50,000 or more in contracts are required to maintain applicant flow logs so they can perform analysis compared to new hire data.[4] The objective, of course, is to determine if there are significant disparities among various groups for race and gender. Don't forget that "race" includes all races. All people have a race, and all races are protected…not just minorities.

See more about applicant tracking systems in Chapter 5.

Techniques for Forecasting, Planning, and Predicting Impact of HR Activities

One of the largest challenges facing HR professionals is having the right people resources available for the organizational needs precisely when they will be needed. Forecasting can be accomplished in many ways but often relies on the professional experience of people with institutional knowledge about organizational history.

Mathematically Based Forecasting Techniques

In some situations it is possible to bring objective analysis to the forecasting effort. Using mathematical techniques can help create confidence in the forecast.

- **Staffing ratios**   Compare the number of support personnel needed for each 10 production workers. This method can be used to estimate any support group requirements from accounting to HR to legal.

- **Sales ratios**   Compare the number of employees required to support each different level of sales activity.

- **Regression analysis**   Can be used much like the other ratio approaches to use various pieces of information to determine the likely workload and employee requirements based on sales, production levels, economic indicators, and so on. This method can get very complicated very quickly, but is aided somewhat by the availability of software aids within programs such as Microsoft Excel.

Judgment-Based Forecasting Techniques

Judgment requires experience and knowledge to be effective in forecasting. Some manners of judgment-based forecasting techniques are:

- **Simple estimates**   Based on what input may be available to the HR manager, this is simply an approximate valuation for the number of people required based on what is known subjectively and objectively about the future.

- **The Delphi Technique**   Using input from a group of individuals who are experts in the area of HR forecasting. Input is gathered through the use of questionnaires; it is compiled/aggregated and then the anonymous responses are recirculated to the experts for another set of opinions. It is a type of orchestrated survey system that seeks to reach a "correct" response through consensus.

- **Focus group or panel estimates**   Using people gathered into a conference room setting, the group is asked to voice their opinions based on a set of facts given to them.

- **Historically based estimates**   Using historical records, best judgments are made extrapolating history into the future.

In the Trenches

Historical Telephone Company Operator Scheduling

In the 1920s through the 1970s, the telephone company used to schedule its operator work schedules based on 15-minute increments of workload projection. Many years of data were retained and used by the "Force Manager" to determine how work schedules would be allocated. Notes were kept on such things as special events for the day (Super Bowl, Mother's Day, political inaugurations, or elections) and local events or celebrations (parades, sports contests with local rival organizations, special TV programming). People used the telephone at TV commercial time, just like they used the bathroom at those program breaks. Of course, there are times when historical events cannot reliably project into the future for workforce planning. Examples include the assassination of President Kennedy, explosion of the space shuttle Challenger, 9/11, the 2013 Boston Marathon bombing, and other disasters. Success in using this approach to forecasting relies a great deal on personal experience and professional judgment. Today, the retail industry lives and dies by these kinds of staffing forecasts.

Risk Management Techniques

There are four techniques for managing risk:

- **Risk avoidance**   Eliminate the risk at any cost. For example: Terminate an employee who had a car accident in a company vehicle to avoid claims of negligent retention. Or do not permit public tours of the facilities because of the possibility for liability if a visitor gets hurt.

- **Loss control**   Reduce the number of occasions that loss occurs. For example: At least once a month, an employee gets injured by slipping and falling when the bathroom floors are being washed. Control could be obtained by washing the floors at a time when employees would not be using the facilities.

- **Risk retention**   For larger employers, this is common when they self-insure such things as workers' compensation or other loss risks. This approach requires that a reserve fund be established to pay for any loss since the employer is self-insured under this model.

- **Risk transfer**   Insuring against a particular loss will move the liability from the employer to an insurance carrier. For a fee, nearly everything is insurable. Employers are more frequently turning to insurance to prevent large financial losses due to things such as sexual harassment or supervisor misbehavior. Those types of policies carry very large deductibles (paid by the employer) before the insurance begins paying for additional loss.

Occupational Injury and Illness Prevention Programs

On January 26, 1989, OSHA published in the Federal Register[5] a notice with general guidelines for voluntary adoption by employers. That set of guidelines was identified as standards 1910; 1910.1200; 1915; 1917; 1918; and 1926.

OSHA refers to these Injury and Illness Prevention Programs as Voluntary Protection Programs (VPP) because employers are not required to adopt them, but encouraged instead. The VPP is broken down into four sections, as noted in the following outline, and although not a requirement, it would benefit organizations to create and maintain policies and programs that correlate with the VPP outline.

Injury and Illness Prevention Programs

- Section 1: Management Leadership and Employee Involvement
  - Written safety and health management system
  - Management commitment and leadership
  - Planning
  - Authority and line accountability
  - Contract employees
  - Employee involvement
  - Safety and health management system evaluation
- Section 2: Worksite Analysis
  - Baseline hazard analysis
  - Hazard analysis and significant changes
  - Hazard analysis and routine activities
  - Routine inspections
  - Hazard reporting
  - Hazard tracking
  - Accident/incident investigations
  - Trend analysis
- Section 3: Hazard Prevention and Control
  - Disciplinary system
  - Emergency procedures
  - Preventative/predictive maintenance
  - Personal Protective Equipment (PPE)
  - Process safety management
  - Occupational healthcare program
  - Recordkeeping

- Section 4: Safety and Health Training
  - Requirements for managers and employees
  - Delivery systems
  - Results measurement

A key component of any safety program, as listed in Section 3, is the provision of Personal Protective Equipment (PPE). This can be as simple as safety glasses and earplugs to hard hats, breathing apparatus, and hazmat suits. PPE is provided by the employer based on the job conditions and hazards faced in doing that work. Employers who are cavalier about these protection requirements are liable to find themselves in jail or paying a big fine if one of their workers is injured because of a bad decision on their part.

What are some of the consequences of failure to keep workers safe and free of injury?

- Employee injuries or death.
- Workers' compensation costs increase due to experience modifications.
- Executives and management risk criminal prosecution for negligence or intentional acts.
- Company assessed financial penalties for workplace injuries.
- Company existence threatened because of marketplace reactions to accidents.

Safety programs should be part of a business's strategic plan. Because of that level of importance, this topic is considered critical for SPHR certification.

General Health Practices

Policies will vary from employer to employer primarily because the health risks associated with employers vary widely. An accounting firm employee will face health risks that are quite different from those faced by Level 4 Containment Lab workers at the Centers for Disease Control, or even people in a local physician's office. And, in all work locations, the objective is the same…protect workers from health risks whenever possible.

Personal Protective Equipment (PPE)

In high risk environments, Personal Protective Equipment (PPE) plays a key role in health protection. In some environments, full hazmat suits are a requirement. In other environments, a gauze mask may be appropriate because of the number of people coughing and sneezing. In a normal office environment, there may be no PPE requirements. Other examples of PPE include:

- Rubber/latex/nitrile gloves
- Protective aprons or overcoats
- Goggles or safety glasses

Workplace Environment Management

Developing a checklist for auditing the environment is something every HR professional should be able to do. There should be an identification of health hazards caused by the workplace, and those brought into the workplace by employees and visitors. On that list should be considerations such as those in an environmental hazard checklist of considerations and inspections. Here are some items you may find on such a checklist:

- **Dust, debris, hazards (construction environment)** Are these in the primary work site or are they intruding from outside the site. What mitigation options exist?

- **Electrical and gas hazards** Are there exposed electrical terminals? Are there devices used in the workplace that pose an electrical hazard? Is natural gas, propane gas, gasoline, or other fuel used in the workplace posing a hazard? What potential for leaking gas exists in the workplace? What mitigation options exist?

- **Respiratory hazards** Is there a risk of exhaust from gasoline engines entering the workplace? Is there a risk of carbon monoxide poisoning from gas heaters or other appliances? Could other substances such as refrigerant gasses like ammonia or Freon escape into the workplace? Is it possible for chlorine gas to find a way into the workplace and cause problems for workers? What mitigation options exist?

- **Noise** Are there machine noises in the workplace? Are other sources of noise generating potentially damaging noise? What mitigation options exist?

- **Moisture** Are there sources of water that could potentially cause flooding in the workplace? Are there misting sources in the workplace that could cause respiratory issues for workers? Might they cause slip and fall hazards? Could moisture cause skin reactions for workers? What mitigation options exist?

- **Temperature** Does the workplace experience extreme high or low temperatures. Is work done outside in direct sun without shade? Is work done in a refrigerated environment? What mitigation options exist?

- **Ergonomic** Does the work require constant movement in repetitive motion? Are there physical response requirements that demand fast reaction, or extreme extensions of limbs? Are long periods of sitting, standing, or walking required? What mitigation options exist?

ISO 14001 is known as a generic environmental management system standard, meaning that it is relevant to any organization seeking to improve and manage its environment more effectively.[6] The International Standards Organization (ISO) develops and publishes organizational and product standards for the world stage. This includes:

- Single site to large multinational companies
- High-risk companies to low-risk service organizations

- Manufacturing and the service industries, including local governments
- All industry sectors including public and private sectors
- Original equipment manufacturers and their suppliers

 NOTE The key for any employer is to perform an analysis of the workplace to determine what type of health hazards exist and then develop plans for dealing with those hazards.

General Safety Practices

Because all employers are accountable under federal law for maintaining a safe and healthy work environment (General Duty Clause), and in many industries, are required to have written safety programs called Injury and Illness Prevention Programs (IIPP), it is necessary to understand what key components exist within those programs.[7]

Evacuation Plans

A basic component of every safety plan is evacuation. Fire is a threat in nearly every workplace. And, although fire is likely the primary reason, it is not the only reason for having an evacuation plan for your work space.

Employer work spaces vary from single office facilities to multiple floors in high-rise buildings to entire campus installations composed of many buildings. In each case, employees should be provided with instructions about how to evacuate their work site and what to do following evacuation. Re-assembly areas should be designated in the evacuation plan and someone should be designated as the authority to verify that everyone successfully got out of the quarters. Figure 4-6 provides a sample evaluation plan.

Once the plan has been properly drawn up, employees should be trained in how it should be implemented and the signals that will alert them to the need to evacuate.

Ergonomic Evaluations

These days, finding employees who have no need for ergonomic work stations is only a dream. Fortunately, these days, more and more resources are available to assist employers in prevention of injury due to ergonomic problems. Some of the areas for concern are:

- Repetitive motion injuries (wrists, hands, arms, legs, backs)
- Sitting (desk chairs, table height "standing" desks)
- Keyboard use, including use of the mouse (carpal tunnel syndrome, arm and shoulder ailments) (split keyboards, separate portions for each hand, wrist support pads for mouse and keyboard)

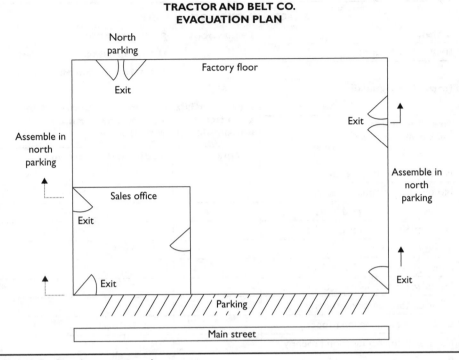

**TRACTOR AND BELT CO.
EVACUATION PLAN**

Figure 4-6   Sample evacuation plan

- Lifting, bending (cranes, exo-skeletons, robot substitute)
- Telephone use (neck pain, shoulder pain) (headset with microphone to avoid having to hold handset between ear and neck)

Safety Audit and Communication Plans

A good safety program will always have periodic inspections built into the program. As a function, "safety" can often be included in the Human Resources department. In some organizations, it is found in a department all its own (the Safety Department). Or, it can be located in another part of the organization such as Operations or Facilities Management.

It is a good idea to have each manager and supervisor perform monthly inspections of their individual and crew work areas. If there is a safety officer for the organization, that person should inspect every part of the physical facility at least once per quarter. Each inspection should be documented and notations made about the need for follow-up and problem correction. Part of every supervisor's personal safety responsibility is to inspect the audit reports made by his or her subordinates. If nobody checks to be sure safety inspections were actually done, they will sometimes get "missed" because of other important things that demand a supervisor's attention.

SAFETY INSPECTION REPORT		
Date:	**Evaluations:**	**S = Satisfactory**
Inspector Name:		**U = Unsatisfactory**
		NA = Not Applicable to Area
Inspector Signature:		
Area Inspected: Desks, Work Stations, Chairs	**If an unsatisfactory rating is provided for a particular item, company Form 4 must be completed for that item.**	
	Rating	**Additional Comments**
Pencils stored, points away		
No overhanging objects on desks		
Cords not a trip hazard		
Storage: Knives, letter openers		
Storage: Scissors		
Ashtrays: Not near flammables		
Plants/water not near electric outlets		
Chair castors function properly		
Chair armrests function properly		
Chair adjustments function properly		
Broken furniture is not being used		
This sheet is Page _____ of _____ pages		

Figure 4-7   Safety Inspection Report

See Figure 4-7 for a sample Safety Inspection Report. It is necessary to create one inspection form for every type of work area and hazard present. Figure 4-8 illustrates a sample Safety Action Report.

Inspector/Manager Name:		Telephone Extension:		
Inspector/Manager Signature:		Date Report Completed:		
Description and Location of Unsafe Condition and Date			Completion Date	
Discovered by Management	Action to be Taken		Planned	Actual
Concrete cracked and chipped at front entrance.	Work with facilities management to repair.			
Carpet at the entrance to the warehouse is frayed and a trip hazard.	Ask facilities management to repair the damage.			
Binders are stacked on top of filing cabinets creating a hazard if they should fall on someone.	Relocate binders to proper storage site.			
File drawers left open and unattended.	Train staff to close file drawers when not in use.			

IMPORTANT: Hazards which pose a risk of serious or substantial injury to employees must be corrected immediately. Other hazards should be corrected as soon as reasonably possible but in no case later than __ days from the date of discovery by management. Any deviation from these time requirements must be reported to the Program Administrator immediately.

This is page _____ of _____ pages

Figure 4-8 Safety Action Report

Return to Work Policies

When choosing a policy, employers have a wide range of choices. On the one hand is a policy that says no one may return to work until they are 100 percent (100%) recovered and able to perform the full range of work duties their job requires. On the other hand is a policy that says, just as soon as an employee is able to perform some of the job functions, he or she should return to work, and the balance of their duties can be handled by others until they regain full recovery.

Modified Duty Assignments

Somewhere in the middle of that spectrum is a policy that says that once an employee is able to return to work, we will modify her job responsibilities on a temporary basis so we can get her back to work as early as possible. Some medical people suggest that returning to work early can aid in recovery. Because what we do in our job is so often integral to the person we see ourselves as being, assurances that the job will still be available to the employee can be psychologically beneficial.

In a Modified Duty Assignment, some tasks or duties will be forgiven or handed off to other employees for a period of time. If the employee has just returned from back surgery, waiving the need to lift objects that would be normal work tasks could be an example of modified duty.

Reasonable Accommodation

Reasonable accommodations can present an opportunity to get the employee back on the job with some alterations to the job that don't relieve the employee of any duties or responsibilities. The same employee who had back surgery may find it necessary to alternate standing and sitting. Providing the opportunity for that to take place is an example of job accommodation. If frequent rest breaks are needed to help someone return to work, the employer could agree to allow the employee to take several additional breaks throughout the day. In many cases these accommodations are temporary and will go away in time. In other cases, the job accommodation may be a permanent thing. When an employee returns to work after having been diagnosed with diabetes, it may be that you are faced with an accommodation request to provide a firm schedule of meal and rest breaks so there are opportunities to take insulin injections and eat food at precise intervals throughout the day.

Independent Medical Exam

Of course, any injury or illness that requires medical attention will be followed closely by the employee's own medical team. But, when the employee calls and say he is ready to return to work, what do you do?

First, if the absence has required medical attention, you should ask for a return to work release from the employee's physician.

Second, you should make an appointment for the employee to visit a physician who is hired by the employer to evaluate the individual's abilities to perform the specific job requirements. That means a physician who is an expert in occupational medicine. You should provide to that physician a copy of the employee's job description, including a listing of the physical and mental requirements of the job.

If there is a difference of opinion between the two physicians, you can send the employee for a third evaluation, or you can simply elect to use the guidance from your employer's medical expert. HR professionals should be cautioned that it is unwise to make conclusions of a medical nature if you are not a qualified physician yourself. Allow protocol and procedure to obtain the required expert input, and then rely on it for your decision making about the situation.

Plans to Protect Employees and Minimize Organization Liability

HR professionals are responsible for the workforce in many ways, including recruiting and counseling on employee management issues, record management, and the management of organizational liabilities related to employees. There are many disasters that can befall an employer. Airlines experience airplane crashes. Investment institutions experience embezzlement. Manufacturers experience product contamination or other defects. There may just be an accident that causes fire in the building. Who knows what will happen when they get up in the morning?

Emergency Response Plans

A primary safety axiom is that proper planning can save lives and property. It is a good idea to have a written plan specifying what actions will be taken in any of many various scenarios. There are some basic alternatives for dealing with a disaster, large or small.

This consideration goes beyond the Emergency Evacuation Plans discussed earlier in this chapter. Here we are talking about the entire universe of emergency planning. Evacuation is just one type of response to an emergency.

The first step toward having an emergency response plan is to conduct a risk assessment for your work location. Look at the physical facilities, emergency exits, fire suppression systems, electrical and gas shut-off access, hazardous materials used in the workplace, protective equipment needed for operations, employee training for special equipment, use of proper lock-out tag-out procedures when working on electrical equipment, and proper handling of carcinogenic substances such as copy machine toner. Answer hypothetical questions such as: "What would we do if someone with a gun walked through our front door?"

Engage key personnel in the development process. Ask people on the production line and in the office what they would do in some circumstances. Get input from experts and non-experts alike. Then list the responses that should happen for each emergency you listed.

Finally, once the plan is developed, be sure everyone in the workplace knows about it and what to do if an emergency happens.

Business Continuation

If there is a flood or fire and your workplace is destroyed, the computers, hard drives, on-site backup systems, and filing cabinets may no longer be available. How will you open your business tomorrow morning?

Employers must have a plan for how they will continue operating their organization. What about customer records, accounting records, client data, and payroll information?

This is an area of responsibility where HR professionals should work with others in the organization such as professionals in Information Technology (IT) and Accounting. It should be common practice for backups to be made of all technology systems, especially an HRIS system. And, those backups, or at least duplicates of them, should be stored off-site at some secure location. It is necessary for the survival of your organization that it be able to continue operations as quickly as possible with all the records it requires for that to happen.

What will your plan dictate regarding where employees should report to work after such a disaster? Do you plan to use e-mail, text messages, or a telephone tree to contact everyone and pass along instructions? How will you keep supervisors and managers informed? Who will handle media inquiries about the disaster and your plans for the future?

Password Usage

Some common mistakes are made by employees in handling passwords for computer program access. If you look around your workplace, you will likely find examples of these:

Password Problems

Here are some common problems found when analyzing password usage:

- **Sticky pad note passwords** Passwords written on sticky pad types of notes. This is for the convenience of the employee who can't seem to remember his password. No effort is made to conceal the password. Sometimes this note is pressed to the computer monitor to make it even more available.

- **Desk drawer passwords** You will find some employees who make a list of their passwords and stick that list into their top desk drawer, or workbench drawer. Again, this is for convenience, but it is easily discoverable by anyone with dishonorable intentions.

- **Personal information passwords** Employees will often create passwords by using their birthday, their home street address, their child's name, or their wedding anniversary. Any of these can be fairly easily discovered by looking elsewhere in the workstation. A family photo with a special date stamp, a diary with the password notations in the front or back, or some other personal notations will be available to anyone wishing to access the employee's work information.

- **Password binders** What could be more handy for a thief than to have sitting in plain sight a binder labeled "Passwords"? With all the access points we must have in the HR world these days, it is common for people to keep binders and address books filled with passwords for each of those programs. But keeping the binder in plain sight shows a very low level of concern for security. Perhaps it could be locked up in a cabinet or desk drawer?

Password Examples

Passwords should be made of random or nonsensical characters. They should not be recognizable words.

Bad passwords might look something like this: Easter2015; Hellen1234; 1776July4th; InkPen; RadioKQRT; Mary7789; Phone593.

Strong passwords might look something like this: HyRtP73N; 84XcMH59; Ak9BrzE45. Some software today requires the use of symbols in passwords to add further complexity (for example, * & % $ # @ + = !). Use both upper- and lowercase letters interspersed with numerical characters.

Why Passwords Matter

HR professionals have many pieces of information entrusted to them. You know from Chapter 2 that you have a legal obligation to protect the privacy of employee data and medical information. If you take that responsibility seriously, you will treat passwords with the respect they deserve. The last thing you want to have to tell someone is, "I'm afraid someone has accessed your data file and taken a copy."

Social Engineering

Social engineering refers to using electronic communications and the Internet to manipulate someone into compromising their organization's cyber security by revealing critical information. With the role of Human Resources, personal identification information (referred to as PII) is the target. It is a term that describes a kind of intrusion that often involves tricking other people to break normal security procedures.

A social engineer runs what used to be called a "con game." Social engineers often rely on the natural helpfulness of people as well as on their weaknesses. Virus writers use social engineering tactics to persuade people to run malware-laden e-mail attachments, phishers use social engineering to convince people to divulge sensitive information, and scareware vendors use social engineering to frighten people into running software that is useless at best and dangerous at worst. They might, for example, call the authorized employee with some kind of urgent problem that requires immediate network access. Appeals to vanity, appeals to authority, appeals to greed, and old-fashioned eavesdropping are other typical social engineering techniques. Social engineers may even be internal within an organization, searching wastebaskets for valuable information, or gaining access codes by looking over someone's shoulder (shoulder surfing).

Security experts propose that as our culture becomes more dependent on information, social engineering will remain the greatest threat to any records and data system. Organizations need to raise the level of awareness of all their people about the dangers of social engineering, and keep it at a high level at all times. Con and scamming games are as old as civilization itself. The methods never really change because human nature never changes. Only the technology does.

Disaster Recovery

There are many resources for disaster recovery on the Internet. Here are some of those you may find useful:

- **Federal Small Business Administration** www.sba.gov/content/disaster-recovery-plan

- **Federal Emergency Management Agency** www.fema.gov/disaster-recovery-centers

- **Federal Disaster Assistance Web Service** www.disasterassistance.gov

Needless to say, every employer organization should have a disaster recovery plan. It should identify the types of disasters that might hit the organization (for example, earthquake, fire, flood, workplace violence), how each of those situations would be handled, who would be assigned to speak for the organization (to the employees and to the press), what should employees do following a disaster, how the organization could regain an ability to resume operations, and how employee injuries or fatalities should be handled. What alternate work site has been chosen to accommodate resumption of operations? Who will manage the business if the existing leaders are not available for some reason?

If you want a model of crisis management planning, look to the airline industry. They have worked through almost every possible scenario that could impact their business, and have developed plans for how each would be handled. They know it is possible for a disaster to happen in their business and they have prepared themselves for managing those possibilities.

If you would like to have a desk reference on the subject of disaster recovery, we suggest *Manager's Guide to Crisis Management*, also published by McGraw-Hill, at www.mhprofessional.com/product.php?isbn=0071776133.

Workplace Violence

Like the other areas of risk management, the area of workplace violence demands planning. HR professionals will be required to have written workplace violence prevention programs in some states. Under the "General Duty Clause" of OSHA requirements, employers are responsible for providing a safe work environment. Preventing workplace violence would fall within that requirement.

Preventing workplace violence begins with identifying the types of violence that might occur in your workplace. Sources can come from inside or outside the organization. Retail establishments might consider robbery as a possible risk. The same could be said for banks or credit unions. Disgruntled customers or former employees can pose a risk.

Once identified, each risk should be addressed with an action plan detailing how the organization will respond if the violence actually happens. What will the business leaders do? What will the HR manager do? What are employees expected to do? Where should employees go in a violent event? How should they protect themselves if violence happens? Who will address the media? Who will coordinate with law enforcement?

Perhaps the most important consideration is employee communication. Keeping people informed as events unfold is a big part of keeping them safe and reassured. But making sure employees know where to go and what to do in advance depends on careful planning and training. HR professionals must allocate resources to those things or a disaster can result.

Budgeting, Accounting, and Financial

There is always a risk of employee theft. Embezzlement can happen in the smartest of organizations. If someone wants to game the system, it is only a matter of time before that happens. It is an area for more planning. The senior financial executive in the organization (Chief Financial Officer—CFO) should be involved with that planning effort.

There are commonsense things to consider when planning for financial security of the organization. For example, never allow a single person to have access to money or other resources without a second person involved in the transaction. When two or more people are required to access accounts, the likelihood of theft is reduced. Having a record of each financial transaction and who did it will serve as an audit trail so it will be possible to identify who is accessing funds for any purpose.

But oversight is going to remain a primary requirement. Frequent review by managers is important. When employees know they will be observed and their work reviewed, there is less chance they will try to take what they shouldn't.

These types of financial risks can be significant depending on the employer. Planning should include identification of the type of risk that could occur, what action plans will be activated in each instance, and how the organization will recover from the problem after the fact.

In some situations, it will be necessary to inform federal agencies of the problem. This is often required when the employer is a publicly held entity. The Securities and Exchange Commission (SEC) and other federal agencies may have requirements that specifically address your type of organization. You should plan accordingly.

Substance Abuse

Substance abuse is a risk not only because it can harm employee health and personal life, but also because it can lead to problems such as embezzlement, workplace violence, and workplace injuries.

In some organizations, it is necessary to assure that you are maintaining a drug-free workplace. (See information about the Drug-Free Workplace Act in Chapter 2.) That can involve drug testing on either a regular or random basis. It can also require drug testing following accidents when an employee has been operating equipment or motor vehicles. Federal laws require drug testing for some truck drivers, train engineers, and airline pilots if they are involved in an accident.

If employees must be able to drive on their job, they must do so without impairment by drugs or alcohol, whether the drugs are prescription or illegal. It is up to the HR professional to establish systems necessary to assure that happens and can be verified.

Employers risk the torts of Negligent Hiring and Negligent Retention if they knowingly hire or keep on the payroll someone who is a drug or alcohol abuser who does harm to someone else while on the job. If the employee is involved in an automobile accident while under the influence on the job, the employer can be held accountable in some situations.

Policies must be developed that specify what will happen to employees if they fail to pass one or more drug tests. Sometimes, policies will provide for employees to use a leave of absence to address drug or alcohol dependence. Chapter 9, "Compensation and Benefits," will explain more about the types of leaves of absence that can be used for this purpose and whether they provide for paid or unpaid time off. Will the employer sponsor employee participation in a rehabilitation program? Is there a state or local program that will help pay for the type of program? What will happen if the employee has another incident of involvement with drugs? How will someone who appears to be under the influence of drugs or alcohol be handled if they report to work while impaired?

Don't forget to develop action plans for how you will handle the situation when one of your employees does become involved in an on-the-job incident because of drugs or alcohol.

Theft

There are lots of ways theft can happen in the workplace. Here are some examples:

- Embezzlement of funds
- Taking company equipment (for example, computers, printers, scanners, calculators)
- Taking company supplies (for example, paper, toner/ink, staplers, tape, batteries)
- Taking time (for example, long breaks for coffee and meals, wandering through the workplace chatting with other workers, playing games on the computer, texting and social media)
- Falsifying records (for example, time cards/payroll input, untrue overtime claim, extended time off for union activities, untrue sickness reports)
- Unauthorized credit card charges—claiming personal expense as company expense
- Copying employer software for personal use in violation of copyright law

HR professionals need to work with the accounting professionals to develop appropriate policies that explain how these things are unacceptable under the organization's Code of Conduct. Policy should be clear about what will happen if an employee is discovered to have participated in these types of activities. And management should follow through with discipline according to that policy. Consistency in treatment is critical. Inconsistency can bring charges of illegal discrimination based on any number of classifications.

Sabotage

The term "sabotage" is believed to have originated in the fifteenth century.

Today, workplace sabotage includes such things as:

- Throwing items into machinery to destroy or disrupt production
- Removing parts of equipment to cause a shutdown

- Tampering with software or passwords for access to programs
- Attacking computer systems by hacking
- Destroying computer records
- Creating a false workload by filing inaccurate or false claims

Without a doubt, sabotage is a difficult problem to handle. HR professionals should approach such issues with basic investigative techniques. Conduct a proper investigation, and it is possible that some witnesses will surface, or the code of silence will be broken, and the truth will come out. When sabotage reaches the criminal vandalism level, always involve law enforcement with proper reports so they can conduct their own inquiries.

Social Media, Internet, and E-mail Use Policies

Social media is here to stay. There is no going back. According to one source, in February 2014 the membership and usage of some principal social media websites was very impressive[8]:

- **eBay**   120 million active users
- **Facebook**   1.23 billion users
- **Instagram**   150 million users
- **LinkedIn**   259 million users
- **Pinterest**   70 million users
- **Skype**   300 million users
- **Twitter**   240 million users
- **YouTube**   1 billion users (4 billion views per day)

This is just a sampling of websites involved in e-commerce and personal communication. Needless to say, with these membership and usage numbers growing each month, how employees use social media and e-commerce sites is an issue that employers must address in their policies and workplace practices. (Please note: These usage figures change daily. If you need exact usage figures, please conduct a current investigation to be sure you have the accurate data you need.)

Social Media

Social media embraces Internet sites that permit person-to-person communications or posting of general comments on almost any subject. Messages can be directed to a single individual or to the world at large. Also included are services such as YouTube. com that permit people to upload video files that can then be accessed by anyone with an interest. Consider a policy that explains to employees that they should have no

In the Trenches

Social Media's Impact on the Workplace Community

Jane E. Henderson, Ed.D., timner@comcast.net

The iconic potluck dinner and ice cream social have long been traditions across America. These events brought communities together to share stories and pictures, make new friends, welcome new neighbors, and build bonds that often lasted a lifetime, all while enjoying delicious food and sweet treats. Originally, foods such as ice cream were considered delicacies that were enjoyed only by royalty, but eventually American Presidents served it to their guests who attended gatherings. However, these community gatherings quickly became universally adopted as centerpieces of social life in the early communities. Today, social networks such as Facebook, Flickr, Twitter, LinkedIn, live chat, blogs, and MySpace, offer a virtual environment in which people replicate these types of community activities but with an added benefit. Now, more than 400 social media and social networking sites allow millions of people to connect both in general socializing and more specifically for the purpose of sharing common interests, such as education, cooking, music, and movies.

Traditional "networking" in the workplace and through professional organizations required physical appearances either on company grounds or travel to conference sites. The technologically savvy employee today will have an advantage by being comfortable in the new world of online networking and community building. This advantage will not only enhance the employee's potential within the organization, but will also contribute to career development goals. Also, as companies expand globally, online social media provide employees opportunities to build relationships and to nurture them over time without sharing the same physical space.

It is in the connection to such virtual social networks that the concepts of the "potluck dinner or ice cream social" can be applied in order to provide an environment in which employees have the opportunity to build stronger team bonds, especially if they are working on projects with peers in remote locations. It further supports the notion that the skills and behaviors practiced in the online environment enhance workplace skills and career development.

Despite concerns, social media will expand its influence in the workplace if in no other way than through use by tech savvy employees who are accustomed to multitasking and integrating such tools throughout their workday.

expectation of privacy while in the workplace. Of course, careful review of all policies should involve your attorney before any announcements are made to employees.

Internet Access

When it is necessary for employees to have access to the Internet to conduct their business, there should be a written policy describing how that access is to be accomplished, and what websites are unacceptable. The policy should also provide for disciplinary activity for someone who engages in accessing Internet sites that are unacceptable. Unacceptable websites can include personal use of pornographic sites, political sites, gaming sites, shopping sites, or others. Use of company equipment and company time to access such sites could be cause for discipline as a misuse of work time and employer equipment.

E-mail Use

E-mail has grown to include texting as a means of written communication from one person to another. It is so common now that we've seen distracted people get into car accidents, walk into automobile traffic, and stumble into water fountains while concentrating on text messaging. Here, once again, employers should consider policy content that controls the use of organizational equipment and the limitation of personal use. But also consider the issue of employees using personal smart phones for texting and e-mail. If this happens during work time, it can be as big a problem as other non-work diversions. Policies should explain that work equipment is intended only for work applications.

Diversity Concepts and Applications

Diversity and inclusion practices embrace internal and external groups. Social media can be effectively used to reach out to groups you have found are underrepresented in your workforce, your vendor and supplier groups, or your customer and client groups. One example is found in how popular LinkedIn.com has become in the recruiting arena. It has been said that over half of white-collar workers are being placed through that website each year. Why not use those avenues of communication to increase diversity of the employee population?

Of course, the risk of liability for failing to treat people equally is that complaints about disparate treatment will be filed. When cases go directly to external enforcement agencies, the employer loses the ability to provide an early remedy, or explain to employees why the actions were not discriminatory.

Ethical and Professional Standards

The Society of Human Resource Management (SHRM) has compiled and published a Code of Ethics.[9] It calls for HR professionals to set an example for others in their organization: "HR professionals are expected to exhibit individual leadership as a role model for maintaining the highest standards of ethical conduct."

Privacy Issues

The United States Supreme Court has weighed in on the question of employee privacy when using employer-owned equipment intended for use as a business tool and not a private communication device. The Court has said, regarding public employees, they should have no expectation of privacy when the equipment is owned by the employer and they are directed to use it for work-related business only.[10]

Social media has become such a powerful influence in the lives of American citizens that private employers in some locations began asking job applicants for their Facebook passwords so a review of their Facebook content could be included in the background check. In 2012 Congress failed to pass the Password Protection Act, but that didn't stop six states from passing their own legislation preventing employers from demanding such information.[11]

Another privacy issue for employers is embedded in the National Labor Relations Board ruling on employee freedom to engage in "concerted activities." Late in 2012, the Board ruled that employees have a right to discuss employer policies and their personal treatment in a forum such as Facebook.[12]

Internal Privacy Issues

Privacy issues within an organization surround employee expectations and the type of business the organization conducts. Here are some reasons why you might want to explain to employees that they should have no expectation of privacy while at work:

- Security cameras monitor work areas as well as the grounds outside.
- Telephone calls are monitored and recorded for training and quality purposes.
- Computer use is monitored and reviewed for quality purposes.
- E-mails are subject to review at any time.
- Lockers and desks are employer property and subject to search at any time without notice.
- Personal bags and briefcases are subject to search when entering or leaving the building.

External Privacy Issues

When communicating with people and locations outside the employer's organization, it is necessary to consider the possibility that those communications could be intercepted and read by unauthorized people. Today, there is a growing problem of "bad guys" stealing e-mail messages to mine personal data such as credit cards and Social Security numbers. One way to contain the problem is to use encryption for e-mail messages. That scrambles the message so it is not readable by anyone other than someone with the encryption tool needed to decode the message.

Electronic access to bank accounts, tax records, credit card merchant accounts, or other sensitive data are all at risk. Such data transfer processes should only be done with a secure link on the Internet. Credit card information should only be transmitted across secure connections. It is time to recognize that there are people sitting and watching electronic traffic. If they have an opportunity to steal such information for personal gain they will do so. It is incumbent upon the HR professional to assist the organization in constructing systems to prevent that from happening.

Protection of Data

Risks abound in the subject of data protection. Consider the types of data employers generally handle:

- Personal and private employee information (name, Social Security number, bank account number for payroll deposit, drivers license number, passport number, medical records, disability identification)
- Financial records belonging to customers (credit card number, credit card expiration date, credit card security code, bank account number for wire transfers)
- Financial records belonging to the employer's organization (tax records, bank account numbers, accounting records including customer contact information)

The question becomes one of how to protect such information from unauthorized disclosure. Here are some considerations:

- Provide an audit trail in software so financial records can be checked.
- Require two people for authorization of transactions above a given dollar amount.
- Secure employee records with physical locks and sufficient password policy.
- Restrict access to customer records through sufficient password policy.
- If it is warranted, require a supervisor to input authorization on each occasion before an employee can gain access to sensitive record systems.

Ensuring that such policies and procedures are not only implemented but properly maintained by all people in the organization is something HR professionals can help with. The alternative is the unauthorized disclosure of employee personal information or customer financial information and the expense it will require to "clean up" after the fact. And that doesn't include the loss of trust people will have in the organization having once experienced exposure that should not have happened. Typically, organizations that have had a breach of security and loss of personal or financial data will offer six to twelve months of credit report monitoring through one of the three major credit bureaus. Even with the expense that represents for thousands of people whose records may have been disclosed, often the basic security for the data systems doesn't get changed and the same risk carries forward. Through proper attention to such matters, HR professionals can help their organizations avoid such catastrophes.

Password Protections, Monitoring Software, and Biometrics

Passwords are problematic because people generally treat them in a very cavalier manner. They are posted on notes under plastic desktop protectors or taped to the computer monitor in plain sight. Sometimes, a modicum of effort is made to hide them by putting the note inside the desk drawer or under a blotter.

Employers and HR professionals should have well-considered policies about passwords. The best systems have passwords controlled by a single coordinator who changes passwords on a regular basis or require users to create new passwords on a regular basis. Storing passwords is an issue that should be discussed with all departments. Proper handling can easily be the subject of a brief employee training program.

Monitoring software is available that will permit employers to track the type of usage on company PCs. Some of the types of tracking that can be done include:

- Websites visited
- Searches conducted
- Keystroke logging
- E-mail sent and received
- Document tracking
- Website blocking
- Application blocking
- Keyword blocking

All of these types of tracking can be performed remotely by supervisors or other authorized surveillance personnel. There are many such programs available for less than $100.

NOTE It is necessary to inform employees that such monitoring systems are being used and that they have no privacy when working on company equipment.

Biometrics is the use of personal biological characteristics to identify authorized personnel for system access. Biometrics can include retina scans, fingerprint scans, or palm print scans. The level of sophistication in this technology is increasing rapidly. A quick Internet search will unveil hundreds of websites that offer information or products related to biometric security systems. The federal government even has a website dedicated to the subject at www.biometrics.gov/.

Identity Theft

This is the result we wish to avoid. Identity theft is the generic term used to describe the situation when someone co-opts personal information such as credit card numbers and Social Security numbers to steal money from the person those things belong to. Often that happens without anyone being aware of it until the arrival of the next credit card statement. It should be noted, however, that banks and other credit card issuing organizations are becoming much more sophisticated about their monitoring of credit card purchases. They look for purchases that don't belong in the individual's buying pattern, or for charges made outside the country.

When someone has had their identity stolen, and their credit rating demolished, they will need to invest a significant amount of effort to set things right again. That can take months or years and some amount of money in correspondence and notary fees.

If employee information is jeopardized, a policy should be in place that specifies how the organization will respond to the problem. It should lay out the communication that will take place and any support that will be provided to employees who experience identity theft–type events as a result of the data loss.

Workplace Monitoring

Aside from the computer monitoring we have already discussed, there are some organizations that find it beneficial to monitor their workplace by using video equipment. Examples include gas stations, convenience stores, check cashing businesses, and banks. Monitoring is done for the benefit of employees as much as for the organization's protection.

Of course, retail establishments are concerned about theft of products as well as robbery. "Shrinkage," as product theft is called, costs retailers $119 billion in 2011 according to the *RFID Journal*. Radio Frequency Identification (RFID) is being used more and more to protect expensive products from pilferage. As the cost of those small devices decreases, they are finding their way into less expensive products. A transponder chip inserted into the packaging will trigger an alarm when exiting the store if it is not disarmed at the cash register first.

Policies should be in writing and clearly communicated to employees so they understand any monitoring that is conducted in the workplace.

Methods for Assessing Employee Attitudes, Opinions, and Satisfaction

Some risks can be reduced if employers are aware of them in advance. If employee attitudes are sliding from positive to negative, the employer would want to know that and have a chance to correct whatever problems exist before they become irreversible.

Small employer organizations can make use of PC-based software products that can perform surveys and survey reporting with some limitations. Larger organizations will likely want to use more sophisticated software or the help of external survey experts. Often these are members of the American Psychological Association (APA).

Most organizational success experts stress the importance of monitoring employee attitudes and opinions on a regular basis. Almost every large organization spends a great deal of energy and resources on monitoring customer satisfaction. But that's only half of the equation. It takes satisfied customers to support an organization's march into the future. However, it also takes satisfied employees as the other part of the equation. HR professionals can help their organizations understand the benefits and importance of budgeting for this important effort.

Use of Third Parties or Vendors

There will come a time in the professional life of every HR manager when there won't be sufficient internal resources available to do the tasks required. It could be the need to do open benefits enrollment, affirmative action plan development, employee attitude surveys, or HR Information Systems (HRIS) implementation. It could be any number of other things.

When vendors are needed to perform a function or task, selecting them should be a serious undertaking. It is a multi-step process.

Developing Requests for Proposals (RFPs)

A Request for Proposals (RFP) is different from Requests for Information (RFI) or Requests for Quotation (RFQ).

RFI is a formal request for information about products or services available on the market that might fit the buyer's needs. Think of them as "off the shelf" or "ready to wear." There is little or no customization involved with an RFI. Examples are software packages that will track job applicants or an HRIS database for employee information.

An RFQ seeks pricing for a product or service that the buyer already understands. There is no need for the buyer to engage a vendor in discussions about how the request will be fulfilled. The basic information needed is a price for the deliverable. This can be useful when shopping for salary survey reports, or safety kits to be posted throughout the workplace.

The RFP is generally used for more complex products and services. When you need to have a vendor provide healthcare benefits programs or payroll services, you will want to publish an RFP and distribute it to vendors you believe would be able to respond adequately.

Contents of an RFP should include:

- **Organization and project background**   This is a statement about the organizational history that brought about the need for this program or project. What generated the need?

- **Work to be done**   A statement about what the project will entail. This is where a description of the product or service will be found. It can be brief or extensive depending on the complexity of the deliverable involved.

- **Timelines and deadlines**   Clear expectations about milestones to be met during the project. Attach dates to each step or review point. Vendor responses should be based on these deadlines and expectations. If payments are to be made to the vendor at interim points along the way, that should be explained here.

- **Vendor bid**   This is the statement of expense the vendor will provide. If necessary, the buyer may request more than a "bottom line number" for the cost statement. It might be that there are identifiable subdivisions of work that can be priced for budgeting purposes.

- **Payment conditions**   Explain the number of days it will take to generate a check after a vendor invoice is received. Of course, this is something that should involve the Accounting department and any policy on the subject. Will there be monthly invoice requirements, one invoice at the end of the project, or only one invoice for delivery of the product being purchased?

- **RFP evaluation criteria**   This is the statement about how the buyer will evaluate the RFP responses. Will there be interviews? Will there be follow-up questions requiring vendor response? Will a committee be making the decision or is that to be done by an individual? What will be taken into account for evaluating the RFPs? Cost will be one, but other factors could include the ability to meet the milestone dates, background and experience of the vendor and its staff, responses from references provided by the vendor, and the location of the vendor's work site in relation to the buyer's facilities. Almost any business criteria could be applied to evaluating vendor responses. But whatever they are should be included in the RFP document.

Contract Negotiation

If you are going to select a vendor or supplier without going through the RFP process, it will be necessary to reach agreement on the details of delivery and payment. These things are usually covered in an RFP.

When negotiating, first identify the legal requirements for the situation. Are there local or state laws that govern building permits, or zoning that will impact your project? Are there sales tax requirements that will be involved with the purchase? Your organization's legal advisor or financial officer can be very helpful in identifying these requirements.

Next, prepare for your negotiating session(s):

- *Prepare a list of topics you want to address.* Identify the facts and figures associated with each topic. Know the details before you go into the meeting.

- *Identify the facts that you think both parties might be able to agree on.* List those that you think will be controversial.

- *Highlight the items you believe are absolute requirements and those you would be willing to compromise on.* Attach some cost estimates to each of the items so you will be ready to discuss the expenses if you do compromise.

- *Meet the other side with respect.* Treat the vendor, or others, as you want to be treated.

Contract Management

Once a contract has been negotiated and approved, someone should be designated as the contract manager. This should be a single person who will be responsible for following up to assure the contract requirements are met. These include verifying that the timeline is working as planned and that all deadlines or milestones are met. If contract changes are needed, work with the attorney to prepare an amendment and then implement the changes. Your organizational attorney will be of help in identifying how to oversee the contract's implementation.

Chapter Review

In this chapter, we have identified how HR professionals can help their organization manage risks. There are risks to people and risks to budget. Some risks can be shifted away from the organization through insurance policies. Others must be managed and minimized. When HR professionals ask to be included in executive-level discussions, explaining how risks have been controlled is one way to gain that inclusion. Real contributions to business goals and financial bottom line will gain attention every time.

Questions

1. A hazard identification survey should be performed:
   A. If there is an obvious problem or someone has filed a complaint
   B. Every month in manufacturing organizations and every quarter for all other types of organizations
   C. On a regular planned schedule that involves most management people
   D. Only when the designated Safety Officer says it should be done

2. Hugo has just had a conversation with one of his subordinates about his performance. Now that it is over, Hugo should prepare documentation:
   A. That must be approved by in-house counsel and the HR Manager
   B. That is filed in the employee's personnel folder
   C. That is signed by the employee and sent to legal
   D. That is at least four or five pages long with quotations from both supervisor and employee

3. Alexia has just received a complaint of discrimination from Marshall, one of her employees. She should now:
   A. Determine if there is a *prime facie* case and investigate if there is
   B. Determine if the complaint sounds reasonable and immediately call the employee's supervisor to discuss things

    C. Determine if the employee has a history of complaints and treat this one accordingly

    D. Determine if the employee's supervisor is going to be receptive to the complaint and an investigation before moving forward

4. Andre has just given instructions to his employee concerning a new sales order. This is not a routine order and there are a couple of unusual requirements. What should Andre do to be sure things will go the way he has instructed?

    A. Tell the employee to check in after the order is completed to be sure it has been done properly.

    B. Tell the employee that this customer is very important and if this order is done properly, there will be more orders to come in the future.

    C. Give the employee a chance to explain his understanding of the instructions that have just been given. Because they are complicated, Andre should follow up with written instructions or checklist.

    D. Andre should carefully supervise exactly how the employee works on the order, staying close and giving input all along the way.

5. Sylvia has just been asked to make a presentation to senior management about the new healthcare benefit program. To be sure it goes well Sylvia should:

    A. Practice her presentation in front of a mirror and be sure she wears her best business suit on that day.

    B. Prepare a brief summary sheet with key points about the new healthcare benefits that the managers can take back to their employee groups for discussion.

    C. Make sure she has included the answers to the questions Who, What, When, Where, and Why in her presentation.

    D. Ask the senior managers if any of them have already learned about the new program.

6. John is told he has been assigned the task of preparing written job descriptions for each job in the organization. He questions the idea that physical and mental requirements should be in writing. It sounds to John like the employer is more likely to be sued if those things are committed to paper. What would you tell John if you were his boss?

    A. If physical and mental requirements have any possibility for excluding disabled people, John's right. They shouldn't be included in the description of job content.

    B. Physical and mental job requirements should only be discussed if a disabled job candidate applies for the position. Otherwise, they should be left out of the description.

    C. Actually, there should be two versions of every job description. One should have the mental and physical requirements and the other should not. The one without that content is what should be published announcing the opening.

    D. Each job should have both physical and mental job requirements identified. Those requirements should be discussed with job candidates to determine if each candidate feels they can meet those requirements, or if they will need an accommodation of some sort.

7. Hilario has just been asked to prepare a written job description for a newly created position. Because this job has never existed before, can Hilario just make things up and correct them later?

    A. Of course. The description can be updated after someone has been assigned to do it and discovers what responsibilities actually exist.

    B. A job description should be prepared in advance, with help from the supervisor. It is up to the employer to determine job content. Listing those responsibilities is important because they can help in selecting a new employee for the new job.

    C. In the beginning, it's not too important to be accurate about the job content. It will develop over time and the description can be updated later.

    D. When the supervisor isn't sure what responsibilities will be assigned to the job, Hilario should reschedule development of the job description until the supervisor is more confident about the job content.

8. Lynell just got a call from a manager in Production asking if the rumor is true about a new policy on pension plans. As the HR Manager, what should Susan do about that phone call?

    A. She should explain to senior management that the rumor is working its way through the organization. If it is true, she should encourage senior managers to move forward with announcements so the truth about new pension changes can be heard directly from the employer. If it is not true, Lynell should work with managers to communicate with employees that there is no foundation for the rumor.

    B. Lynell should do nothing. It's just one person who has raised the question. It will go away on its own without causing upset among the employees.

    C. She should announce to all employees that the pension plan is being changed, or that the rumor is false.

    D. Lynell should tell the production manager not to say anything about the pension issue until senior management is ready to unveil the changes.

9. Tobias has just been appointed the first HR Manager for his company. He wants to organize employee records as one of his first projects. He isn't sure how to separate records into various categories of information. How would you advise Tobias?

   A. All records for each employee should be consolidated into one file per person. That file should be kept in the HR office and secured in locked file cabinets.

   B. Separate files should be created for each employee's personnel records, medical records, and investigation files if necessary. All files should be secured in locked file cabinets.

   C. The HR staff should only be concerned with personnel files. Medical records and investigation records should be handled by someone outside the HR organization.

   D. According to the Employee Records Stability Act, employee files should contain personnel records and medical records but never investigation information. Securing them is a requirement.

10. Gary is converting paper records to a computerized Human Resource Information System (HRIS). He wants to make it easy for employees to update their personal records in the new system. What approach would you recommend he use?

    A. It is a good idea to give a hard copy of their personal information to each employee so they can verify the accuracy of the data. Ask for feedback with corrections or additions.

    B. Call each employee and review each personal data element to be sure they are all accurate. Take corrections over the telephone.

    C. Send an e-mail to each employee with the employee's personal information asking for corrections and additions.

    D. Send out a notice to all employees that the new system is being created and ask anyone with questions to contact Gary.

11. Jerrod works for a federal contractor with 145 employees. He knows he should keep a log of job applicants, but his boss doesn't want to give him the clerical support he needs to keep the log current. If you were Jerrod, what would you do?

    A. Because the employer has fewer than 150 employees, it's not an issue. He can ignore the log until he hires five more people.

    B. The CEO should understand that federal regulations permit the Department of Labor to presume illegal discrimination if they don't track applicants.

    C. The CEO should understand that an applicant log is something that can be created at the end of the year and that's when critical clerical support will be needed.

    D. Because the employer hasn't kept an applicant log up to now, Jerrod should wait until next year to start fresh with the new year.

12. Valerie has just begun work as HR Manager for a new non-profit organization. She has been tasked with developing many policies, including one on workplace safety. Valerie isn't sure that she needs to be concerned about Injury and Illness Prevention Plans (IIPP). What would your advice to her be?

    A. She is right. Non-profits don't have to be concerned about meeting requirements for written IIPPs.

    B. She should start creating her IIPP right away. Liability is present from day one of the employer's operations.

    C. She should develop a policy about safety, but there is no need for her to go to the trouble of creating an IIPP. That is just for government and for-profit companies.

    D. She should take advantage of the 120-day grace period offered by OSHA rules and put creation of a safety program on her "To Do" list for later in the year.

13. If you are responsible for developing the safety plan for your organization, how would you be able to determine if everyone got out of your building in an emergency?

    A. Always have the employee roster on your iPad and take that with you when you evacuate.

    B. Have the Safety Officer check the number of people who made it to the gathering location away from the building.

    C. Ask everyone who made it out if they know that the people they were talking to earlier were all present at the emergency gathering location.

    D. Gather all evacuees in a predetermined location outside the building and have supervisors report on their group headcount.

14. Bill is going to return to work after a skiing accident had him recovering from a broken leg for six weeks. His doctor has written return to work instructions prohibiting Bill from standing for more than 30 minutes at a time. Because his job requires constant standing at the customer service counter, you have to determine whether to have him return to work or not.

    A. You should have a frank discussion with Bill about what he can do and what he can't do. From that conversation, you should determine if some accommodation can be made for the restrictions and how long that will need to last. Perhaps he can be reassigned to another job temporarily, or it might be that he can't return until he can take on all of his responsibilities.

    B. Sure, let Bill return to work and give him a stool to sit on while talking with customers. If he has to get something from the parts inventory, you can hire a temp to do the running for him.

C. You should have a frank discussion with Bill's coworkers and tell them they will have to do more running to help Bill when parts are needed. They can object but you can require them to help out.

D. There is no way that Bill can return to work until he is able to perform all of the essential functions of his job, including walking to get parts when necessary.

15. Lanny supervises the accounting operations. He has several of the passwords he needs for software he uses on his job taped to his computer monitor. He knows that he shouldn't do that but says he can't remember them and doesn't want to go digging for them every time he needs to do some work on the computer. What are you going to say to him?

A. Tell Lanny that he should put the note under the glass desktop protector. That way it won't be obvious to anyone who looks at his computer monitor.

B. Tell Lanny that he can put the password list on the bottom of his keyboard. No one will think of looking there.

C. If he can't remember the passwords, he should keep a list of them in a locked desk drawer.

D. Lanny should never write down his passwords. He should prove that he has them memorized before being allowed back into the software programs.

16. Monika works hard and parties hard. On Monday morning, she comes in to work and seems to be slurring her words and not really focusing on the things she looks at. The supervisor calls you to see what you recommend as the HR Manager. What will you tell the supervisor?

A. Tell the supervisor to take Monika home. She isn't fit for duty and the organization doesn't want the liability of having her at work.

B. Tell the supervisor that he should keep an eye on her to be sure she doesn't get hurt. It should be just fine. Monika can handle this type of thing.

C. Tell the supervisor that we can't get too personal with Monika by asking how she got stoned, so just send her to the break room for a half-hour to see how she feels after that.

D. Tell the supervisor we should get Monika to the company doctor for drug and alcohol screening. Be sure he takes her and doesn't let her drive herself.

17. The accounting manager comes to you with a stack of printouts showing a long list of embezzlements by one of the employees. Best practices would suggest the following treatment.

A. Confirm that the data is accurate and shows employee theft. Notify senior management if necessary and obtain authorization to call in police for an arrest. Send the employee a letter confirming their employment termination.

B. Once the data has been confirmed, it should be used to confront the employee and demand repayment.

    C. With the proof in hand, call the employee and the employee's supervisor into a conference and terminate the employee on the spot. Send a letter confirming the termination.

    D. Confront the employee and offer the opportunity to resign if the employee promises to repay the stolen funds.

18. Almost everyone in the Tiger Tooth Dental Office has and uses social media on their personal cell phones. Doctor Tiger has asked that employees only use their cell phones during breaks, lunch, or in emergencies. Sherlene can't seem to restrain herself and the cell phone hardly ever leaves her hands. What would you advise Doctor Tiger to do?

    A. Confiscate Sherlene's cell phone. Tell her she can get it back at the end of the day.

    B. Have Sherlene store her cell phone in the doctor's private office and allow her to have it back at lunch and after work.

    C. Make the Office Manager responsible for enforcing the policy and tell her that Sherlene will not be able to bring her cell phone to work if she doesn't start abiding by the policy.

    D. Explain to Sherlene that one more incident of her using her cell phone during work time will result in disciplinary action. Include the Office Manager in those discussions.

19. Alden has always considered himself a benevolent employer, trying to make decisions about employee issues in favor of the employees whenever he could. Yet in all the years he has been in business, he has never had a worker like Mickey. Mickey has been on the payroll for a little over two years and all of a sudden has started missing work two days a week. He has no more accrued sick time and has blown through all of his accrued vacation time. How should Alden handle the problem?

    A. Talk with Mickey and try to determine what has suddenly changed in his life. If he is ill or has a family problem, it may be possible to offer a leave of absence so he can deal with whatever has happened.

    B. Talk with Mickey and explain how important attendance is to personal performance. He can't do his job if he isn't here every day. Get a commitment from Mickey that he will not miss any more work days.

    C. Talk with Mickey and tell him that he will be disciplined if he doesn't end his attendance problem. Any more unauthorized time off and he might have all of his days free.

    D. Talk with Mickey and explain that you are thinking of getting a replacement for him. As a matter of fact, you have already posted the job opening on Craig's List. Tell him perfect attendance from now on is the only thing that can save his job.

20. Ivory wants to hire a benefits consultant to help assess the organization's healthcare benefit options. Her boss tells her to draft an RFP to be used in obtaining input from other benefit consultants. Ivory has never prepared an RFP before. As her boss you should tell her:

    A. Getting a list of qualifications and the bid amount are the two most important components of the RFP process.

    B. Having responses include a list of deadlines that will be met for the project is something Ivory should not overlook.

    C. It is important to begin by developing a list of criteria for evaluating each response from consultants.

    D. If you have someone in mind for the work, write the RFP so only that person will qualify and be selected.

21. Doyle is wrestling with the idea of creating job descriptions for his organization. As the HR Manager, he is wondering how he can convince the line managers to invest the time it will require. How can job descriptions speak to risk management?

    A. Used properly, they can help in employee selection (reduce turnover), assist in discussions about job accommodation requests (workers' compensation), and help in performance management.

    B. Used properly, job descriptions will give supervisors something to prove why they can't accept a job accommodation request. There are too many actual requirements to be able to allow some of them to slide without getting done.

    C. Used properly, supervisors will be able to talk with job candidates about the kinds of educational requirements needed in the job. A job description enables you to weed out unqualified people without wasting interview time.

    D. Used properly, job descriptions will include a statement that says, "...and all other duties as may be assigned." Supervisors should be pleased by that.

22. The AB Trucking company has never had a safety program until now. The CEO has said HR will develop one and make sure it is implemented the right way. What should the HR Manager include in the project outline for the safety program to succeed?

    A. Supervisors should be required to spend a minimal amount of time or they won't support the project.

    B. The written program should include MSDS and an annual walkthrough by the CEO to reinforce the importance of safety.

    C. The HR Manager should include all of the OSHA-specified content in the written IIPP. That will mean supervisors will have to spend time on safety issues.

    D. Only the CEO can make safety a reality. It is up to the policy statements to carry the weight and produce the results.

23. Damion has just called saying he wants to file a complaint that he's being discriminated against by his supervisor. What should you do if you are the HR Manager?

   A. Give Damion the phone number for the EEOC. They are the experts in handling discrimination complaints. You couldn't do as good a job if you handled it.

   B. Ask Damion to explain what happened. Get him to describe the supervisor's decision that caused him harm, and how that was linked to his membership in a protected group. Ask him how other people have been treated in similar circumstances.

   C. Make some notes and explain to Damion that his accusations are very serious and you will get back to him after you talk with his supervisor. In the meantime, he should consider taking some time off.

   D. It doesn't matter how other people are treated, Damion has had such a difficult time. He should get some special recognition and a reward for turning in his supervisor.

24. For quality control purposes, you sit in on random interviews your recruiters conduct with finalists in the employment selection process. Your recruiter Samantha has just been asked, "I'm interested in a permanent job that will last for the rest of my career. Is this the job that will do that for me?" What would you like to hear Samantha say in a response?

   A. Not a problem. We treat our people like members of a family. You won't have anything to worry about.

   B. The company's not going anywhere and you can expect to be here for life.

   C. We can't guarantee lifetime employment.

   D. We can't give you promises, but you can expect that this job is going to last for a very long time.

25. Augustine filed a discrimination complaint saying her supervisor made sexual advances toward her. Now, her supervisor tells her she is being moved to a job at a different work location. She doesn't like that much because it means a longer commute. Does she have any recourse?

   A. Actually, she does. Making an employee move work locations against her wishes can be considered retaliation for having filed the complaint. The supervisor should have been moved instead. She should file a retaliation complaint.

   B. Separating Augustine from her supervisor's control is the best way to handle this situation. If it means she has to move, then at least she will be protected from him. She has no recourse.

C. Augustine's supervisor is hopping mad to begin with. There is no way he will keep her in his group, so she is going to move one way or another. Augustine is just going to have to accept the move as a consequence of her complaint.

D. If there had been any openings for supervisors at other work locations, her supervisor would have been moved. She'll just have to tough it out with the longer commute. Maybe later she can get a job at the original work location when something opens up.

Answers

1. **C.** Safety should be a concern and responsibility of every management person in the organization. There should be a plan or schedule for regular safety inspections and action plans should be developed for hazards discovered.

2. **B.** Unless state law or union agreement requires a copy be given to the employee, supervisor documentation is considered to be an employer-owned record of the conversation. It should be filed in the employee's personnel file along with other performance-related documents such as appraisals and commendations. In some jurisdictions, a copy must be given to the employee if the employee signs the document.

3. **A.** If the complaint claims an employment penalty caused by membership in a protected group, and that people not in that group were given better treatment, the complaint seems valid on its surface (at first glance). It should be investigated to see if the facts support the employee's charges.

4. **C.** Asking for feedback about the instructions is necessary to be sure Andre's message has been received as it was intended. If Andre puts his instructions on paper as a follow-up, he can help the employee recall each unusual requirement for the order. Hovering over the employee as the order is processed would probably not be a good idea. Waiting until the order is completed means any problems would require that someone do the work all over again.

5. **C.** Both B and C are good answers, but for assurance that all the key information is conveyed successfully, each of the basic five questions should be addressed in her presentation. A simple fact sheet could be used if it contained the answers to all five of these questions.

6. **D.** Any employer subject to the Americans with Disabilities Act (ADA) would be well served to include physical and mental job requirements in each job description. When asked for a job accommodation, the job description can be helpful in determining how an accommodation will assist in accomplishing job responsibilities. While including them is not a federal requirement (nor is it required that job descriptions be created), stating the job requirements can be a good management tool.

7. **B.** If the supervisor doesn't know what the new employee will be expected to do, how can someone be hired to do the job? The supervisor should decide what responsibilities will be assigned to the new position and help Hilario describe that in a written document. That will be an aid in selecting someone to fill the position.

8. **A.** Pension plans are important to employees. Any changes in those plans will be seen as having important personal impact by all affected workers. It is likely that the HR Manager will need to work with senior management to coordinate the announcement of any pension plan changes. Because the rumor exists, she should encourage a swift response with facts so workers will have accurate information.

9. **B.** There is no requirement for records to be locked up, but best practice says that it is a good idea. Medical records, including disability information, should be kept separate from personnel files. Investigation records should be created when necessary and kept separate from other employee records. Electronic files should be treated in the same way.

10. **A.** This is confidential information and it should probably not be transmitted by e-mail. Calling each employee will take a great deal of time and verbal corrections are subject to errors. By far, the best practice would be to send a confidential copy of the employee's record for review with an invitation to submit corrections or additions.

11. **B.** Federal regulations (41 CFR 60-1.12(e)) provide, "Where the contractor has destroyed or failed to preserve records as required by this section, there may be a presumption that the information destroyed or not preserved would have been unfavorable to the contractor." The CEO should be made aware that illegal discrimination can be expensive to remedy.

12. **B.** Liability exists from day one of operations. Non-profits are not exempt from OSHA rules, and there is no grace period offered by federal regulations.

13. **D.** The most reliable method is to have supervisors identify who among their group is present in the emergency evacuation location. Supervisors know who is working and who is off for vacation, illness, and so on. They should be able to accurately identify anyone missing from the muster point. If people are identified as missing, first responders should be notified.

14. **A.** It is important to engage Bill in a conversation about his medical restrictions and ask him how he thinks he can do the job within those restrictions. Seeking an honest outcome is the goal. Determining what to do with him before such a conversation will likely risk undesirable outcomes.

15. **C.** Passwords are sensitive enough that they deserve to be locked up all the time. Leaving them on the desk or monitor invites security problems.

16. **D.** Anyone who appears impaired physically or mentally should be taken to the employer's physician for a drug and alcohol screen. They should not be permitted to remain at work until that has been accomplished. Depending on

the outcome of the testing, the employer may decide on discipline or some other treatment. Under no circumstances should someone who is impaired be allowed to drive home or to the doctor. If the supervisor can't take them, call a taxi.

17. **A.** It's always a good idea to confirm the evidence is accurate before taking action. Embezzlement is a criminal problem and should be turned over to the local police. Arrange a meeting with the employee and have the police present. Explain the evidence and ask for the employee's admission to the embezzlement. Ask the police to arrest the employee. If you have insurance covering such issues, you can file a claim for the missing funds.

18. **D.** When a policy is broken by employees, there should be proper progressive disciplinary procedures used to correct the situation. It is difficult to prevent people from bringing their cell phones to work. However, controlling how they are used during work time is a different matter.

19. **A.** Determining what is causing the attendance problem will help in determining how to manage it. Sick spouses, children, or even aging parents can suddenly create care-giving circumstances that hadn't been anticipated. Attendance policies are important, but so are an employee's personal needs. If it is possible, Alden should identify the root of the problem before taking action.

20. **C.** Listing evaluation criteria will include identifying milestones and costs as evaluation items. Determining how responses will be evaluated will make the sorting and selection of a benefit consultant easier and more accurate. Writing an RFP in such a way that only one consultant will qualify may be okay for this project, but the organization will soon get a reputation among vendors and service providers that will limit participation in future RFPs.

21. **A.** A properly developed job description is a good communication tool that helps with hiring and with firing. It helps defend the employer when essential duties may not be ignored during job accommodation discussions. It also helps physicians understand physical and mental job requirements when evaluating workers' compensation issues or return to work.

22. **C.** A valid safety program will include all of the OSHA-specified content and involve supervisors directly in the process. Injuries and illnesses can make the supervisors' job more difficult because of employee absences. Controlling workplace injury and illness is beneficial to everyone, employees and supervisors alike.

23. **B.** A *prima facie* case requires a statement of employment penalty, a statement of membership in a protected group, and a statement that people outside that group are treated differently in similar circumstances. Do everything possible to keep the complaint internal and not in a government enforcement agency such as the EEOC. Because the complaint is about Damion's supervisor, talking with the supervisor initially is not a good idea.

24. **C.** Liability for oral contracts made by recruiters or other selecting managers can cost an employer a great deal of money. It is best to say, simply, we have no guarantees of long-term (or lifetime) employment.

25. **A.** Forcing an employee to endure additional penalties (moving to a job farther away) can be considered retaliation for the original complaint. If anyone moves, it should be the supervisor. Of course any action should depend upon the results of a thorough investigation, but imposing additional negative treatment on the employee is not a good idea.

Endnotes

1. Roughly 600,000 employers are federal contractors or subcontractors, subject to affirmative action requirements. According to the Bureau of the Census, there are more than 6,000,000 employers in the United States (organizations with payroll). Overall, there are nearly 28,000,000 non-employers in the United States. These are business firms with no payroll—nearly always, single entrepreneurs.

2. 29 CFR 1910.1200

3. 60-741.44(c)

4. 41 CFR 60–2.17(b)(2)

5. 54:3904–3916

6. "International Standards Organization" website as of July 11, 2013, www.iso .org/iso/home/standards/management-standards/iso14000.htm.

7. "How Many People Use the Top Social Media, Apps & Services," July 14, 2013, Craig Smith, Digital Marketing Ramblings blog. Retrieved on February 8, 2014 from http://expandedramblings.com/index.php/ resource-how-many-people-use-the-top-social-media/.

8. "SHRM Code of Ethics," November 16, 2007, www.shrm.org/about/pages/ code-of-ethics.aspx.

9. Public Employee Privacy Expectations, *City of Ontario, California vs. Quon*, No. 08–1332, June 17, 2010, www.supremecourt.gov/opinions/09pdf/08-1332.pdf.

10. States with laws barring employers from demanding social media account passwords from employees or job applicants as of January 2013 include: California, Delaware, Illinois, Maryland, Michigan, and New Jersey. *Wired Magazine*, www.wired.com/threatlevel/2013/01/password-protected-states/.

11. NLRB Case Ruling, *Hispanics United of Buffalo, Inc. and Carlos Ortiz*. Case 03–CA–027872.

12. December 14, 2012, www.employmentmattersblog.com/Board%20 Decision%20%282%29.pdf.

Workforce Planning and Employment

A wealth of information is available in case law to guide HR professionals in their compliance with federal legislation and regulations. Common sense can help as well. Workforce planning and employment is important to both PHR and SPHR candidates. Twenty-four percent of the PHR exam and 17 percent of the SPHR exam will focus on this area of knowledge.

Workforce planning and employment is where you will find all the information about staffing, recruiting, interviewing, equal employment opportunity, affirmative action, new employee orientation, retention, terminations, and employee records management. These are core functions for HR management in any organization. Master these and you will have a strong foundation for HR performance in your employment group.

The official HRCI Workforce Planning and Employment functional area responsibilities and knowledge statements are as follows:

Responsibilities

- Ensure that workforce planning and employment activities are compliant with applicable federal laws and regulations.
- Identify workforce requirements to achieve the organization's short- and long-term goals and objectives (for example: corporate restructuring, workforce expansion or reduction).
- Conduct job analyses to create and/or update job descriptions and identify job competencies.
- Identify, review, document, and update essential job functions for positions.
- Influence and establish criteria for hiring, retaining, and promoting based on job descriptions and required competencies.
- Analyze labor market for trends that impact the ability to meet workforce requirements (for example: federal/state data reports).

- Assess skill sets of internal workforce and external labor market to determine the availability of qualified candidates, utilizing third-party vendors or agencies as appropriate.

- Identify internal and external recruitment sources (for example: employee referrals, diversity groups, social media) and implement selected recruitment methods.

- Establish metrics for workforce planning (for example: recruitment and turnover statistics, costs).

- Brand and market the organization to potential qualified applicants.

- Develop and implement selection procedures (for example: applicant tracking, interviewing, reference and background checking).

- Develop and extend employment offers and conduct negotiations as necessary.

- Administer post-offer employment activities (for example: execute employment agreements, complete I-9/eVerify process, coordinate relocations, and immigration).

- Develop, implement, and evaluate orientation and on-boarding processes for new hires, rehires, and transfers.

- Develop, implement, and evaluate employee retention strategies and practices.

SPHR • Develop, implement, and evaluate the succession planning process.

- Develop and implement the organizational exit/off-boarding process for both voluntary and involuntary terminations, including planning for reductions in force (RIF).

- Develop, implement, and evaluate an affirmative action plan (AAP) as required.

- Develop and implement a record retention process for handling documents and employee files (for example: pre-employment files, medical files, and benefits files).

Knowledge of

- Applicable federal laws and regulations related to workforce planning and employment activities (for example: Title VII, ADA, EEOC Uniform Guidelines on Employee Selection Procedures, Immigration Reform and Control Act)

- Methods to assess past and future staffing effectiveness (for example: costs per hire, selection ratios, adverse impact)

- Recruitment sources (for example: employee referral, social networking/social media) for targeting passive, semi-active, and active candidates

- Recruitment strategies

- Staffing alternatives (for example: outsourcing, job sharing, phased retirement)

- Planning techniques (for example: succession planning, forecasting)

- Reliability and validity of selection tests/tools/methods

- Use and interpretation of selection tests (for example: psychological/personality, cognitive, motor/physical assessments, performance, assessment center)

- Interviewing techniques (for example: behavioral, situational, panel)

- Impact of compensation and benefits on recruitment and retention

- International HR and implications of global workforce for workforce planning and employment

- Voluntary and involuntary terminations, downsizing, restructuring, and outplacement strategies and practices

- Internal workforce assessment techniques (for example: skills testing, skills inventory, workforce demographic analysis)

- Employment policies, practices, and procedures (for example: orientation, on-boarding, and retention)

- Employer marketing and branding techniques

- Negotiation skills and techniques

Core Knowledge of

- Needs assessment and analysis

- Organizational documentation requirements to meet federal and state guidelines

- Diversity concepts and applications

- Technology to support HJR activities

- Qualitative and quantitative methods and tools for analysis, interpretation, and decision-making purposes

- Employee records management

- Techniques for forecasting, planning and predicting the impact of HR activities and programs across functional areas

Key Legislation Governing Workforce Planning and Employment

Now that you've reviewed the Workforce Planning and Employment responsibilities and knowledge statements, we recommend that you review the federal laws that apply to Workforce Planning and Employment (see Figure 5-1). It would benefit you, the reader, to refer back to Chapter 2 on these specific laws prior to reading any further in this chapter.

While legislation is important, of equal value is the case law that comes from court interpretations. Over the decades since the civil rights laws began to impact the country in earnest, the U.S. Supreme Court has heard and provided its clarification to many questions. See Figure 5-2 for the vitally important cases dealing with Workforce Planning and Employment.

For more information on each of these cases, see Appendix B.

- The Civil Rights Act of 1964
- The Civil Rights Act of 1991
- Pregnancy Discrimination Act of 1978
- Age Discrimination in Employment Act of 1967
- Americans with Disabilities Act of 1990
- Americans with Disabilities Act Amendments Act of 2012
- Genetic Information Nondiscrimination Act of 2008
- The Fair Credit Reporting Act of 1970
- The Immigration and Nationality Act of 1952
- The Portal to Portal Act of 1947
- Drug-Free Workplace Act of 1988

- Federal Contractors & Subcontractors: Executive Order 11246 (41 CFR 60-1, 60-2 & 60-4)
- Federal Contractors & Subcontractors: Rehabilitation Act of 1973
- Federal Contractors & Subcontractors: Vietnam Era Veterans' Readjustment Assistance Act of 1974
- Federal Contractors & Subcontractors: Jobs for Veterans Act of 1974
- The Uniformed Services Employment and Reemployment Rights Act of 1994
- The Employee Polygraph Protection Act of 1988
- The Equal Pay Act of 1963
- The Fair Labor Standards Act of 1938
- The Immigration Reform and Control Act of 1986
- The Work Opportunity Tax Credit of 1996
- The Lilly Ledbetter Fair Pay Act of 2009

Figure 5-1   Key legislation governing workforce planning and employment

Case Citations

- *Griggs v. Duke Power Co.* (401 U.S. 424)
- *Phillips v. Martin Marietta Corp.* (400 U.S. 542)
- *McDonnell Douglas Corp. v. Green* (411 U.S. 792)
- *Espinoza v. Farah Manufacturing Co.* (414 U.S. 86)
- *Corning Glass Works v. Brennan* (417 U.S. 188)

- *St. Mary's Honor Center v. Hicks* (509 U.S. 502)
- *Taxman v. Board of Education of Piscataway* (91 F.3d 1547, 3rd Circuit)
- *McKennon v. Nashville Banner Publishing Co.* (513 U.S. 352)
- *Robinson v. Shell Oil* (519 U.S. 337)
- *Faragher v. City of Boca Raton* (524 U.S. 775)

Figure 5-2   Case law that applies to workforce planning and employment

Case Citations

- *Albermarle Paper v. Moody* (422 U.S. 405)

- *Washington v. Davis* (426 U.S. 229)

- *McDonald v. Santa Fe Transportation Co.* (427 U.S. 273)

- *Hazelwood School District v. U.S.* (433 U.S. 299)

- *Trans World Airlines, Inc. v. Hardison* (432 U.S. 63)

- *Regents of University of California v. Bakke* (438 U.S. 265)

- *United Steelworkers v. Weber* (443 U.S. 193)

- *Connecticut v. Teal* (457 U.S. 440)

- *EEOC v. Shell Oil Co.* (466 U.S. 54)

- *Meritor Savings Bank v. Vinson* (477 U.S. 57)

- *Johnson v. Santa Clara County Transportation Agency* (480 U.S. 616)

- *School Board of Nassau v. Arline* (480 U.S. 273)

- *Watson v. Fort Worth Bank & Trust* (487 U.S. 977)

- *City of Richmond v. J.A. Croson Company* (488 U.S. 469)

- *Price Waterhouse v. Hopkins* (490 U.S. 288)

- *Wards Cove Packing Co. v. Antonio* (490 U.S. 642)

- *Harris v. Forklift Systems Inc.* (510 U.S. 17)

- *O'Connor v. Consolidated Coin Caterers Corp.* (517 U.S. 308)

- *Oncale v. Sundowner Offshore Service, Inc.* (523 U.S. 75)

- *Bragdon v. Abbott* (524 U.S. 624)

- *Kolstad v. American Dental Association* (527 U.S. 526)

- *Gibson v. West* (527 U.S. 212)

- *Grutter v. Bollinger* (539 U.S. 306)

- *Gratz v. Bollinger* (539 U.S. 244)

- *General Dynamics Land Systems, Inc. v. Cline* (540 U.S. 581)

- *Pennsylvania State Police v. Suders* (542 U.S. 129)

- *Smith v. Jackson, Mississippi* (544 U.S. 228)

- *Leonel v. American Airlines* (400 F.3d 702, 9th Circuit)

- *Ledbetter v. Goodyear Tire & Rubber Co.* (550 U.S. 618)

- *Ricci v. DeStefano* (No. 07-1428)

- *Vance v. Ball State Univ.* (No. 11-556)

- *University of Texas Sw. Med. Ctr. v. Nassar* (No 12-484)

- *St. Mary's Honor Center v. Hicks* (509 U.S. 502)

- *Taxman v. Board of Education of Piscataway* (91 F.3d 1547, 3rd Circuit)

- *O'Connor v. Consolidated Coin Caterers Corp.* (517 U.S. 308)

- *Ellerth v. Burlington Northern Industries* (524 U.S. 742)

Figure 5-2   Case law that applies to workforce planning and employment

Equal Employment Opportunity and Affirmative Action

While it is true that the Civil Rights Act of 1964 was the first civil rights law in the United States that embraced employment issues, it was not the first civil rights law in the country. That would have been the Civil Rights Act of 1866, which said that anyone born in the United States is a citizen and any citizen, regardless of race, has the right to enter into contracts, sue and be sued.

Before the assassination of President John Kennedy in November 1963, Congress had argued for many months about extending protections from discrimination based on race, religion, national origin, and color. The Senate just couldn't make any progress. Then some Senators from Southern states devised a strategy to end the arguments and defeat the bill once and for all. They proposed an amendment that would add "sex" as a protected category. They reasoned that nobody would vote in favor of protecting women against discrimination in the workplace. Well, the idea didn't work out so well for them. It backfired and the bill passed with five protected categories, including sex. President Johnson signed the bill into law in 1964.

In 1965, President Johnson looked around the country and noticed that the Civil Rights Act he had signed the previous year was pretty much being ignored by employers of all sizes. He asked his staff to evaluate the problem and come up with some recommendations about how he should address it. They devised a program called "Affirmative Action" that would force certain federal contractors to implement the Civil Rights Act. President Johnson issued Executive Order 11246 requiring contractors to take affirmative action for minorities and women in their hiring and promotion programs. That didn't have much impact, however. It wasn't until President Nixon's administration implemented some regulations and created an oversight agency that employers began to pay attention.

Equal Employment Opportunity Commission (EEOC)

In 1964, President Johnson signed the Civil Rights Act, which had been working its way through Congress since the time of Presidents Eisenhower and Kennedy. Title VII of that law deals with employment-related equal opportunity provisions. Sometimes these terms are used interchangeably, although they should not be. The Civil Rights Act of 1964 has other titles dealing with public housing, education, and more. (A title in a law is like a chapter in a book.)

The Civil Rights Act of 1964 created a five-member commission that stands alone with allegiance to no government department. Its Commissioners are appointed to five-year staggered terms. A Council General, the Commission's head lawyer, is also appointed by the President. All appointments must be confirmed by the U.S. Senate. There is a Chair, Vice Chair, and three Commissioners. By design, three of the positions are appointed from the sitting President's political party and the other two are selected from the political party not in power. Even though the President appoints the Commissioners, the EEOC does not report to the White House. It is independent.

Commissioners can file charges against employers, but more often the EEOC staff receives complaints of employment discrimination from employees and job applicants.

Because the Civil Rights Act of 1964 applies only to employers with 15 or more employees, whose business is engaged in interstate commerce, smaller employers are not subject to its oversight. The EEOC also has jurisdiction over federal government agencies that are considered part of the Executive Branch, reporting to the President, and state and local governmental units as well. Size of payroll does not matter for governmental employers. That limitation applies to private employers only. EEOC has divided its staff into two specialty groups, one handling the public sector and the other handling the private sector.

The EEOC has enforcement authority for:

- Civil Rights Act of 1964
- Age Discrimination in Employment Act of 1967
- Pregnancy Discrimination Act of 1978
- Americans with Disabilities Act of 1990
- Equal Pay Act of 1963
- Genetic Information Nondiscrimination Act of 2008

When the EEOC investigates a complaint and determines that there is justification for that complaint, it says the case has "cause." When a case has "cause" the EEOC will attempt to find a "make-whole" remedy that can include any of the following reimbursements:

- Back pay (for up to two years)
- Reimbursement for out-of-pocket expenses (for example, job search, doctor visits)
- Front pay—unlimited (based on how long it might take to get another job)
- Compensatory damages (for example, pain and suffering, emotional distress)
- Punitive damages (for example, punishment of the employer with dollar limits based on payroll headcount as specified by the Civil Rights Act of 1991, shown in the following table)

Table 5-1 notes the limits on punitive damages relative to the number of employees within an organization.

Table 5-2 notes the number and nature of EEOC charges filed in fiscal year 2012.

Table 5-1 Cap on Punitive Damages for Title VII Cases[1]	Employer Headcount	Limit on Punitive Damages
	15 to 100 employees	$50,000
	101 to 200 employees	$100,000
	201 to 300 employees	$200,000
	Over 300 employees	$300,000

Table 5-2	Basis for Charge	FY 2012 Count	FY 2012 Percentage
Quantity of EEOC Charges in Fiscal Year 2012[2]	Total	99,412	100
	Race	33,512	33.7
	Sex	30,356	30.5
	National Origin	10,883	10.9
	Religion	3,811	3.8
	Color	2,662	2.7
	Retaliation—All Statutes	37,836	38.1
	Retaliation—Title VII Only	31,208	31.4
	Age	22,857	23.0
	Disability	26,379	26.5
	Equal Pay	1,082	1.1
	GINA	280	.3

EEOC Complaint Investigation Procedures

Complaints must be filed with the EEOC within 180 days from the date on which the action was taken that caused the charge of illegal discrimination. In states that have a reciprocity agreement between the state's Fair Employment Practices agency and the EEOC, the filing period is 300 days.

The charge must be made in writing. It must contain:

- The employee's name, address, and telephone number
- The name, address, and telephone number of the employer (or employment agency or union) the employee wants to file this charge against
- The number of employees employed there (if known)
- A short description of the events the employee believes were discriminatory (for example, the employee was fired, demoted, harassed)
- When the events took place
- Why the employee believes (s)he was discriminated against (for example, because of race, color, religion, sex [including pregnancy], national origin, age [40 or older], disability or genetic information)
- The employee's signature

It is common for the Compliance Officer to ask the employee what remedy (s)he would like in the situation. That can become important during a conciliation conference if the charge is found to have merit.

Once the complaint has been received by the Commission, a letter will be sent to the employer within 10 days explaining the charge and asking for the employer's response.

The employer should conduct an internal investigation using the steps outlined in Chapter 4 if that has not already been done. Unfortunately, once a charge has been filed with either the EEOC or a state enforcement agency, the employer is banned from speaking about it with the employee. There may be no direct contact between the employee and employer on that issue. Of course, normal day-to-day interactions are permitted, but nothing related to the charge of illegal discrimination. If an internal investigation has not been conducted before the EEOC's notice of filing, it will be handicapped by the ban on interaction with the employee.

At the completion of the internal investigation, the employer will prepare a written response to the Commission explaining what it has found in its investigation. This is the employer's opportunity to explain its side of the story. Based on that input, the EEOC's Compliance Officer (CO) will either suggest mediation or open an investigation so it can gather more information. There may be requests for more written information from the employer. There may be an on-site visit so interviews can be conducted with people involved in the issue, and witnesses to what happened. How long that will take is an open question. It could be a relatively short period of time (2 or 3 months), or it could go on for a couple of years. Typically, cases are resolved within 12 to 18 months. The EEOC's case backlog continues to hover around 100,000.

At the conclusion of the EEOC's investigation, it will always issue a Right to Sue or a Notice of Rights, which explains to the employee their right to file a lawsuit in federal court. Each investigation concludes with one of the following types of findings:

- **No Reasonable Cause**   The charge of illegal discrimination could not be substantiated.

- **Reasonable Cause**   The charge of illegal discrimination is substantiated by the evidence and a Letter of Determination is sent to the employer and employee inviting the parties to join the agency in seeking to resolve the charge through conciliation. If conciliation fails, the EEOC will issue a Right to Sue letter to the employee who is then free to locate an attorney and proceed to federal court. The Commission may also decide to pursue legal action itself. It can sue the employer on behalf of the employee.

- **Administrative Closure**   If the employee requests the case be closed without an investigation or during an investigation, the Commission will cease its activities on the case and issue the employee a notice that (s)he has the right to proceed to federal court.

Remedies for cases found to have merit can range from back pay (up to 2 years), retroactive promotion, retroactive benefits, reimbursement of medical expenses, and other out-of-pocket costs along with other "make whole" compensation. Those are called actual damages. If the employee wants to pursue reimbursement for compensatory damages (emotional and psychological damages) and punitive damages (punishment to the employer) it is necessary to pursue the complaint in federal court.

EEOC Guidelines

Since 1979, the EEOC has issued over 40 policy statements, policy guidance, enforcement guidance, and revised guidelines. Some of them have been rescinded. Among the most important are:

- Consideration of Arrest and Conviction Records in Employment Decisions under Title VII (April 2012)

- Employment Tests and Selection Procedures (December 2007)

- Unlawful Disparate Treatment of Workers with Caregiving Responsibilities (May 2007)

- Reasonable Accommodation and Undue Hardship Under the Americans with Disabilities Act (October 2002)

- Disability-Related Inquiries and Medical Examinations of Employees Under the Americans with Disabilities Act (July 2000)

- Application of EEO Laws to Contingent Workers Placed by Temporary Employment Agencies and Other Staffing Firms (December 1997)

- Americans with Disabilities Act and Psychiatric Disabilities (March 1997)

- Workers' Compensation and the ADA (September 1996)

- Current Issues of Sexual Harassment (March 1990)

- Veterans' Preference Under Title VII (August 1990)

- Indian Preference Under Title VII (May 1988)

- Guidelines on Sexual Harassment (1980)

 NOTE You can find a complete listing on the Commission's website at www.eeoc.gov.

One particular highlight in the Commission's publications are the *Guidelines on Sexual Harassment from 1980*. These were issued to aid employers in traversing the legal minefield of evolving employment requirements *before* the U.S. Supreme Court began issuing its opinions on the subject in the 1990s. They are still relevant today.

Uniform Guidelines on Employee Selection Procedures (1978)

The Uniform Guidelines, as they are generally known, are among the least understood regulations in equal employment law. They are actually ensconced in the Code of Federal Regulations at 41 CFR 60-3.

Refer to Chapter 7 for more information about the application of the Uniform Guidelines on Employee and Labor Relations. Chapter 9 has additional information—about how the Uniform Guidelines apply to compensation and benefits.

NOTE If you don't wish to purchase a copy of the regulations from the U.S. Printing Office, you can search the Internet for "41 CFR 60-3." Any professionally certified Human Resource Manager should possess a copy of this regulation.

Any employer with 15 or more workers on the payroll is subject to the Uniform Guidelines. (Any employer subject to the Civil Rights Act of 1964 is also subject to the Uniform Guidelines.) They require validation of all employment selection steps and tools. As an example, let's assume that our employment selection process involves the following steps. We are required to determine that each step is free from illegal discrimination (disparate impact) and that it has validity for selecting someone to fill the specific job in question.

Our employment selection steps are as follows:

- Job application form completed (or resume submitted)
- Written test (specific skills such as typing or accounting and specific knowledge such as building codes or engineering practices)
- Interview with job's supervisor
- Interview with coworkers
- Background check

One of the greatest liabilities employers accept comes through purchasing an "off the shelf" employment test. If said test has not been validated as a nondiscriminatory selection tool for your specific job content, you probably shouldn't use it. You can find paper-and-pencil written tests for clerks and accountants in some stationery stores and large office supply warehouses. They often have no validation information that would indicate what type of job knowledge or skills they are designed to test. Employers should avoid these products if they don't plan to conduct validation studies themselves.

The Uniform Guidelines requirements exist so that disparate impact can be controlled. Disparate impact, also known as *adverse impact,* means one or more groups suffer a numerical disadvantage compared to other group(s). This usually occurs when a seemingly neutral policy or employment selection device (or process) results in discrimination against a Title VII protected class. Numerical and statistical analysis are tools used to detect disparate impact. HR professionals should be acquainted with the "80% test" which is sometimes called the "4/5ths rule." Simply said, if any protected group is selected at a rate (percentage) that is less than 80 percent the selection rate of the most favorably treated group, there is possibly a problem. An example is shown in Chapter 7. Courts have acknowledged that it is necessary to use statistical analysis techniques to eliminate the possibility of chance in the selection results. So, often we see statistical significance testing methods such as standard deviations and probability analysis being used. Ultimately, the only method available to "prove" disparate impact is linear regression analysis. Statisticians love that because they are usually the only ones who understand it. Regulations say, "Users are cautioned that they are responsible for compliance with these guidelines." It is not the publishers of the test that are liable; it is the employer who uses the test that carries the liability.

 NOTE HR professionals will be very cautious about what employment selection tools are used in their organizations. While it may be difficult to corral managers and executives who feel it is okay to use any technique or tool they wish, it is necessary to have them understand that they can single-handedly cost the organization a lot of money if they are cavalier about these requirements.

Validation of Each Selection Step Is Required by the Uniform Guidelines

The Uniform Guidelines say, "If the information [required] shows that the total selection process for a job has an adverse impact, the individual components of the selection process should be evaluated for adverse impact." For our purposes, the terms Adverse Impact and Disparate Impact will have the same meaning. So, test the overall results and if a problem pops up in that test, drill down to the individual steps in the selection process and test each of those.

You may find the following information about validation on the exam.

Jumping back into the selection process, recall that we have discussed the Uniform Guidelines on Employee Selection Procedures (Chapter 2 and earlier in this chapter). If you have 15 or more employees and are involved in interstate commerce, or are a government entity at the state or local level, you must comply with these requirements for validation of your employment selection steps.

Content Validity

If you use testing that is specifically related to what is done on the job and how it is done on the job, then you will have met the Uniform Guidelines requirements. This is called *content validity*. Don't fudge. You must test for the knowledge, skills, and abilities that are specifically required on the job. And you must test them in the same way they are used on the job.

For example, a township fire department asked each firefighter candidate to take a physical test that was conducted out in back of the firehouse. There was a starting line, a ladder, and a hose connected to a water source. The candidate was required to pick up the ladder and run it over to the firehouse, lift it into position against the firehouse, return for the hose, carry it up the ladder, and squirt the roof of the building. Some people objected to that test and the judge hearing the case asked if that was exactly what was done on the job. The fire chief said, "Yes, it is, except for one thing." The judge asked was that one thing was. The chief replied, "The job requires all of those things to be done, but we normally assign people to work in pairs." So the department was testing for what was done on the job, but not the way it was done on the job.

Criterion-Related Validity

Demonstrating this type of validity involves empirical studies producing data that show the selection procedure(s) are predictive or significantly related with important elements of job performance. This is a scientific study of the test used with a sufficient number of successful incumbents to determine there is a statistically significant correlation with the job content. These studies are, by their very nature, long and expensive. They should be performed by the test publisher. Or, by the test user...employer. Remember that the Guidelines tell us that it is the test user (employer) who is responsible for any disparate impact caused by use of the test. It isn't the publisher who is liable.

You can use your own written test without a criterion-related validity study *if* you make the test specifically related to the work done on the job. Otherwise, if you purchase a written clerical test "off the shelf," for example, you must be able to demonstrate that it is predictive of success on the clerical job for which you will use it.

One employer purchased a general clerical test battery that tested basic arithmetic skills, typing skills, and spelling skills. That test battery was administered to *all* job applicants in the organization. So anyone applying for a clerical job would have to take the tests, but so would anyone applying for a laboratory cleaning job, a delivery driver job, or a food service job. Clearly, the test battery didn't apply to many of the jobs for which it was being used. The employer was wrong in how it applied the tests.

Construct Validity

Construct validity is another data-based way of determining that an employment test has validity for the job in question. It should show the "procedure measures the degree to which candidates have identifiable characteristics which have been determined to be important in successful performance in the job..."[3] Those measurements are done through detailed study of the test results and success of incumbents on the job. Such validation can be extremely expensive to demonstrate.

Federal Contracting and Affirmative Action Requirements

In 1965, President Johnson recognized that employers were not implementing Equal Employment Opportunity provided for in the Civil Rights Act of 1964, so his administration created affirmative action requirements to force the portion of the employer community engaged in federal contracting to implement the new law. Affirmative action requirements demand the inclusion of all qualified individuals in consideration for job openings.

It was common practice in 1965 to fill jobs without any announcement. Decisions were made in private (secret) and, in particular, minorities and women had no knowledge that a job opening even existed. Affirmative action rules changed that for federal contractors. They said contractors had to assess their workforce and determine where there was a need for more minorities and women. Then the regulations required contractors to implement "outreach and recruiting programs" to invite qualified minority and female candidates to participate in the selection process.

Federal Regulations

Congress passes laws that direct the Executive Branch of our government to do certain things. It is up to the Administration to write the regulations that will cause those Congressional mandates to happen. Regulations have the force and effect of law. Regulations are sometimes referred to as "rules." On the other hand, "guidelines" issued by agencies such as the EEOC do not have the same weight as regulations. Employers may not be forced to abide by guidelines, while they are compelled to abide by regulations.

When an employer decides it wishes to get revenue from the federal government, it subjects itself to these rules governing that process. Just as it is necessary for any organization earning money in this country to pay income taxes according to the IRS regulations, it is necessary to abide by U.S. federal government contracting rules if you wish to have the revenue from selling goods or services to the government.

 NOTE Construction contractors who wish to get revenues from building roads, dams, or office buildings for the government are also subject to affirmative action requirements, although rules for construction contractors are different from those for goods and service contractors.

Goods and Services Contractors

If the employer has 50 or more employees (full time, part time, casual, term) on the payroll *and* it has contracts valued at $50,000 or more, there are affirmative action obligations that must be met. There are also other obligations under the Federal Acquisition Regulation (FAR)—FAR obligations are usually managed by the accounting department and affirmative action obligations are usually managed by the human resource department.

Under the employment affirmative action obligations there are three types of affirmative action plans required. One covers minorities and women. Another covers disabled people. And, the third covers certain veterans of the U.S. uniformed services. Written plans are required for each type of affirmative action effort. As we said earlier, affirmative action requirements are the government's way of ensuring that equal employment opportunity laws were properly implemented. They got a bad reputation because people used them in ways that they should not have. Today, the U.S. Supreme Court has clarified that affirmative action programs are not quota systems. Nor are they set-aside or preferential treatment systems.

Executive Order 11246 sets the basic requirements upon which these regulations were established. 41 CFR 60-1 and 60-2 set out what is required for minorities and

Affirmative Action Plans (AAP)

Affirmative Action Plans (AAP) are documents containing information and commitments to take action that will improve the representation of minorities, women, disabled and veterans in the workforce. Specifically, there are affirmative action plans required for: (1) Minorities and Women; (2) Disabled; and (3) Veterans. There are narrative requirements, action plan requirements, and data analysis requirements. All together these are referred to as affirmative action. Employment affirmative action has nothing to do with affirmative action for educational admissions or affirmative action for minority- or female-owned supplier enterprise programs.

Sometimes, "affirmative action program" is used to describe the "affirmative action plan." "Affirmative action requirements" is a term referring to the federal regulation requirements. Plans and programs are the synonymous documents and action plans needed to meet those regulations. An "action plan" is a step-by-step list of actions to be taken to accomplish a specific goal. AAP documents must contain action plans for reaching the AAP goals in each AAP Establishment. "AAP Establishment" can be either (1) a street address (or campus) where 50 or more of the contractor's employees work, or (2) a functional segment of the workforce such as Marketing or Engineering at all work locations in the country. AAP regulations apply only to U.S.-based employee locations.[4]

women. Affirmative action for disabled is regulated by 41 CFR 60-741. Finally, affirmative action programs for covered veterans is governed by 41 CFR 60-250 and 60-300.

Affirmative action programs involve outreach and recruiting. Equal employment opportunity means equal access. So, if you are building a pool of candidates for a given job opening, anyone who is qualified for the position should have access to the pool (equal opportunity) and you should reach out to qualified groups of minorities and women to invite them to participate in the selection process (affirmative action). Once the pool has been established with qualified candidates, the nondiscriminatory selection process should be applied to ultimately make a job offer to the best qualified person. The notion of affirmative action is that if someone isn't in the candidate pool, they can't possibly be selected. So, we must be sure that minorities and women are represented in the candidate pools.

Construction Contractors

Unlike the obligations for goods and service contractors, those who engage in construction projects have a different set of requirements. Known as the 16-point program, the regulations are found at 41 CFR 60-4 and apply to any contractor or subcontractor with a federal or federally assisted construction contract in excess of $10,000. The construction affirmative action plan requirements focus on craft and laborer jobs with specific numerical targets for total minorities based on the job location. A table of locations and goals for minorities can be found in 46 F.R. 7533. If you haven't looked at this table recently don't worry; the table has not been changed since 1980. There is one uniform goal for representation of women in construction jobs and that is 6.9 percent. No management or professional jobs are included in these requirements.

 NOTE An employer who must meet the construction contractor requirements may not need to meet the requirements of goods and services contractors. An exception to that rule might be a design and build engineering and construction company that has both a service contract for engineering and a construction contract for building the project.

A separate set of AAP documents must be created for each work location (or campus facility) where 50 or more people are assigned to work. Work locations with fewer than 50 people should have those jobs and incumbents "rolled up" into the plan where their boss works. If there are no remote work locations with 50 or more people, all company employees should be reported in the corporate headquarters plan.

Compliance Evaluations by OFCCP

Enforcement of affirmative action regulations is accomplished by an agency in the United States Department of Labor called the Office of Federal Contract Compliance Programs (OFCCP).

There are approximately 160,000 federal contractors and subcontractors in the United States that are large enough to warrant preparation of affirmative action plans. Of that number, around 4,000 goods and service providers are selected each year for compliance evaluations as a test of their compliance with all the federal regulatory requirements. That equates to roughly a 2.5 percent chance that any one of them will be selected for audit. An additional 450 construction contractors are selected each year to undergo audits of their 16-step Construction AAPs. There are three primary types of compliance evaluation that the OFCCP conducts.

- **Normal Compliance Evaluation**   Audit of physical establishment identified by a street address or campus location. This can be for either a goods and services contractor or a construction contractor. The requirements are different, but the off-site and on-site activities are much the same.

  - **Opening Conference**   The Compliance Officer will visit the contractor and interview the senior executive, discussing the employer's EEO/AA policy and its implementation.

  - **Desk Audit**   A Scheduling Letter is sent by the OFCCP to the contractor requesting a response with specific documentation in the employer's response. These documents will be examined by the OFCCP Compliance Officer (CO) in the OFCCP office. There may be additional documentation demands and those will be examined in the OFCCP office as well. If all compliance requirements have been met, the evaluation can be closed with a Letter of No Violation.

- **On-Site Visit**   The Compliance Officer may find it necessary to visit the contractor's work location to interview management or non-management personnel. The CO also may find a need to inspect the physical facilities to determine that there are proper and equal restrooms or changing rooms for both men and women. Poster inspection is another task undertaken during the on-site visit. The OFCCP has said it will make an on-site visit in every fiftieth audit even if there is no "indication" of a problem at the desk audit stage.

- **Closing Conference**   A meeting when the CO provides feedback to the contractor about violations found and expectations for corrective action.

- **Closure of the Evaluation**   The OFCCP will close the audit once it has finished its evaluation of all regulatory requirements.

  - **Notice of No Violation**   Given to contractors that meet all the requirements.

  - **Notice of Violation**   Given to contractors that have one or more deficiencies in meeting the requirements. This usually results in a Conciliation Agreement, which can permit the OFCCP to monitor the contractor for up to two years going forward. A Conciliation Agreement is a formal contract with the government that specifies specific corrective actions the contractor must take. It can also specify a remedy for a discriminatory practice with back pay awards and other such financial settlements.

- **Functional AAP Compliance Evaluation**   When a contractor has gained approval of the OFCCP for its functional establishment, it becomes subject to selection of a compliance evaluation of that functional establishment. A functional establishment is composed of everyone in the contractor's enterprise working in a functional area such as sales and marketing or administrative support.

- **Corporate Management Compliance Evaluation**   Sometimes called a "Glass Ceiling Audit," this audit looks at the corporate headquarters organization and analyzes issues surrounding executive compensation, succession planning, mentoring programs, and developmental programs. This type of compliance evaluation was created by the OFCCP to identify illegal discrimination at senior corporate levels. *Glass ceiling* is the term that refers to an invisible barrier beyond which women may not progress in the organization. Since the term was first used, its meaning has expanded to encompass minorities as well as women.

It is the current policy of the OFCCP to avoid another compliance evaluation in the same AAP establishment for a period of two years following the successful closure of an audit.

Affirmative Action Reporting Requirements

In addition to the Affirmation Action requirements for contracting, there are also annual reporting requirements for federal contractors. EEOC rules require all employers with 100 or more employees to submit a report showing sex and race/ethnicity headcount by job category, and that report is also required of federal contractors subject to affirmative action requirements. That means federal contractors with 50 or more workers must submit the required reports even before they have grown to a 100-person payroll.

One report set is known as Standard Form 100. Today, it includes the EEO-1, EEO-3, EEO-4, and EEO-5. Reports labeled EEO-2, EEO-2E, and EEO-6 have all been discontinued.

- EEO-1 applies to private sector employers and is required annually by September 30.

- EEO-3 applies to local unions with 100 or more members. Filing is required biennially in even numbered years.

- EEO-4 applies to state and local governments with 100 or more employees. Filing is required biennially in odd numbered years.

- EEO-5 is formerly known as the Elementary-Secondary Staff Information Report, and is a joint requirement of the EEOC and the Office for Civil Rights (OCR) and the National Center for Education Statistics (NCES) of the U.S. Department of Education. It is conducted biennially, in the even numbered years, and covers all public elementary and secondary school districts with 100 or more employees in the United States.

Another report that is required of all federal contractors by September 30 each year is the VETS-4212, previously the VETS 100A. Effective 2015 the VETS-100A report is being renamed to VETS-4212. This form was changed to collect information about the currently defined categories of covered veterans. Any federal contract dated after December 2003 requires submission of the VETS-4212 report.

The Vietnam Era Veterans' Readjustment Act (VEVRA) requires federal contractors and subcontractors with contracts worth $25,000 or more to annually collect and report certain data on the covered veterans in their workforce on the Federal Contractor Veterans' Employment Report VETS-100 report form. The Jobs for Veterans Act of 2002 (JVA) amended VEVRA's reporting requirements and tasked the DOL with the responsibility for these amendments. In 2008, the DOL issued regulations that created new requirements for the VETS-4212 report form starting September 30, 2009, for all contracts entered into or modified after December 1, 2003, of $100,000 or more.

The following are the covered veteran categories for the VETS-4212 form:

- Disabled veterans

- Active duty or wartime campaign badge veterans

- Recently separated veterans (within the past three years)

- Armed Forces Service Medal veterans

NOTE Completion of each report, the Standard Form 100 and the VETS-4212, requires an employer identification number that can be obtained online. Once the employer identification number has been issued for each report, it will be reused in each subsequent filing period.

Contrary to what some people believe, it is not necessary to "file" your affirmative action plans with the government each year. Only when you get a notice of audit called a Scheduling Letter is it necessary to send copies of your AAP documents to the Office of Federal Contract Compliance Programs (OFCCP). That is the U.S. Department of Labor agency that has been given authority and responsibility to enforce the federal regulations requiring affirmative action on the part of federal contractors. AAP documents are created by the contractor for use by the contractor in the implementation of action plans contained in the AAPs.

It wasn't long ago that the EEOC changed the race/ethnic and job categories in the EEO-1 Report. Those changes were not made in the EEO-4 or any other Standard Form 100. Tables 5-3 and 5-4 show how race/ethnicity and occupational categories are now defined.

Race	Definition
Hispanic or Latino (Can be combined with any race, but is reported as Hispanic.)	A person of Cuban, Mexican, Puerto Rican, South or Central American, or other Spanish culture or origin regardless of race.
White (not Hispanic or Latino) race	A person having origins in any of the original peoples of Europe, the Middle East, or North Africa.
Black or African American (not Hispanic or Latino) race	A person having origins in any of the black racial groups of Africa.
Native Hawaiian or other Pacific Islander (not Hispanic or Latino) race	A person having origins in any of the peoples of Hawaii, Guam, Samoa, or other Pacific Islands.
Asian (not Hispanic or Latino) race	A person having origins in any of the original peoples of the Far East, Southeast Asia, or the Indian Subcontinent, including, for example, Cambodia, China, India, Japan, Korea, Malaysia, Pakistan, the Philippine Islands, Thailand, and Vietnam.
American Indian or Alaska Native (not Hispanic or Latino) race	A person having origins in any of the original peoples of North and South America (including Central America), and who maintain tribal affiliation or community attachment.
Two or more races (not Hispanic or Latino)	All persons who identify with more than one of the above five races.

Table 5-3 New EEO-1 Report Race/Ethnicity Categories

Occupational Category	Definition
Executive/Senior Level Officials and Managers Category 1.1	Individuals who plan, direct, and formulate policies; set strategy; and provide the overall direction of enterprises/organizations for the development and delivery of products or services within the parameters approved by boards of directors or other governing bodies. Examples are: chief executive officers, chief operating officers, chief financial officers, line of business heads, presidents or executive vice presidents of functional areas or operating groups, chief information officers, chief human resources officers, chief marketing officers, chief legal officers, management directors, and managing partners.
First/Mid Level Officials and Managers Category 1.2	Individuals who serve as managers, other than those who are in the more senior Category 1.1 jobs, including those who oversee and direct the delivery of products, services, or functions at group, regional, or divisional levels of organizations. These managers receive direction from more senior managers. They implement policies, programs, and directives of senior executives through subordinate managers and within the parameters set by senior executives. Examples of these jobs are: vice presidents and directors; group, regional, or divisional controllers; treasurers; human resources, information systems, marketing, and operations managers. Also included are first-line managers and supervisors, team managers, unit managers, and branch managers.
Professionals Category 2	Most jobs in this category require bachelor and graduate degrees, and/or professional licensing or certification. Examples of these jobs are: accountants, auditors, airplane pilots and flight engineers, architects, artists, chemists, computer programmers, designers, dieticians, editors, engineers, lawyers, librarians, scientists, physicians and surgeons, teachers, and surveyors.
Technicians Category 3	Jobs in this category include activities requiring applied scientific skills, usually obtained by post-secondary education of varying lengths. Examples of these jobs are: drafters, emergency medical technicians, chemical technicians, and broadcast and sound engineering technicians.
Sales Workers Category 4	These jobs include non-managerial activities that wholly and primarily involve direct sales. Examples of these jobs are: advertising sales agents, insurance sales agents, real estate brokers and sales agents, wholesale sales representatives, securities or other financial services sales agents, telemarketers, demonstrators, retail salespersons, counter and rental clerks and cashiers.
Administrative Support Workers Category 5	These jobs involve non-managerial tasks providing administrative and support assistance, primarily in office settings. Examples of these jobs are: bookkeeping, accounting and auditing clerks, cargo and freight agents, dispatchers, couriers, data entry operators, administrative assistants, typists, proofreaders, and general office clerks.
Craft Workers Category 6	Most jobs in this category include higher skilled occupations in construction and natural resource extraction. Examples of these jobs are: boilermakers, brick and stone masons, carpenters, electricians, painters, glaziers, pipe layers, plumbers, pipe and steam fitters, plasterers, roofers, elevator installers, and derrick operators.

Table 5-4 New EEO-1 Occupational Categories

Occupational Category	Definition
Operatives Category 7	Most jobs in this category include intermediate skilled occupations and include workers who operate machines or factory-related processing equipment. Jobs in this category include: textile machine workers, laundry and dry cleaning workers, photographic process workers, weaving machine operators, electrical and electronic equipment assemblers, semiconductor processors, and testers, graders, and sorters.
Laborers and Helpers Category 8	Jobs in this category require only brief training to perform tasks that require little or no independent judgment. Examples include: production and construction worker helpers, vehicle and equipment cleaners, laborers, freight or material movers, service station attendants, septic tank servicers, and refuse materials collectors.
Service Workers Category 9	Jobs in this category include food service, cleaning service, and protective service activities. In this category are medical assistance, hairdressers, janitors, porters, transit and railroad police, and fire fighters, guards, private detectives, and investigators.

Table 5-4 New EEO-1 Occupational Categories

Placement-Rate Goals and Good Faith Efforts

As part of affirmative action, each year qualifying federal contractors also have to re-compute the gap between their incumbency race and sex mix and the availability of qualified workforce within a reasonable recruiting area. This must be done for every job group separately. A job group is a collection of similar job titles with similar responsibilities and compensation with similar developmental or promotional opportunities. The gap can be large enough to require a placement-rate goal. That means for the coming year, special outreach and recruiting efforts will be made for the job group to ensure representation of each candidate pool created for that job group will contain at least the percentage of minorities and women that availability analysis tells us exist.

 NOTE Even the government recognizes that it is difficult to hire less than one whole person. Therefore, goals need only be set when the gap exceeds one whole person.

Federal regulations require the contractor to make "Good Faith Efforts" to address the placement-rate goal. These efforts will likely involve special outreach and recruiting actions, such as contacting associations of minority or women professionals and asking for qualified candidates for job openings, or reaching out to universities and technical clubs specifically for minorities and women. Remember that it is necessary to document all of the good faith efforts so they can be discussed during any possible audit from the OFCCP.

In the Trenches

Control Your Applicant Flow—Beware the Law of Big Numbers

John C. Fox, Partner, Fox, Wang & Morgan P.C., San Jose, California
jfox@foxwangmorgan.com

This is *the* most important lesson of the FedEx settlement (OFCCP conciliation agreement with FedEx Ground Package System Inc. and FedEx SmartPost Inc., March 2012). This was not a case of unlawful discrimination. This was a series of what I call "the law of big numbers" cases defense lawyers see weekly. FedEx's greatest crime was that it allowed its applicant flow to swell to too large a size. *Any* employer—*any* employer—that allows an Applicant Flow of greater than approximately 1,000 to occur for even a large number of jobs will trip a statistical violation meter known as 2 Standard Deviations...unless the employer hires literally "by the numbers"...meaning that the employer hires very close to the exact percentage of protected groups represented in their Applicant Flow. And the more applicants the establishment in question has, the larger the statistical confidence level (the more standard deviations) will be. This is because the "law of big numbers" will cause a *prima facie* finding of unlawful discrimination *almost always* when you have thousands of applicants. The U.S. Supreme Court was not thinking about this complex law of statistics when it sanctioned the "pattern and practice" disparate treatment class-type theory of unlawful discrimination in the *Hazelwood* and *Teamsters* case decisions on May 31, 1977. Had an attack on the statistics been in one of those cases, I doubt we would today have the pattern and practice (P&P) theory. It is time for the courts to revisit the P&P theory with the advance in statistical education the last 30 years of class litigation has brought us.

Office of Federal Contract Compliance Programs (OFCCP)

When affirmative action programs were first created, there were several enforcement agencies, nearly one in each federal department. It wasn't until 1978 that President Jimmy Carter consolidated all of the enforcement groups into one agency that would eventually be called the Office of Federal Contract Compliance Programs (OFCCP). Organizationally, it came to rest in the U.S. Department of Labor (DOL).

The OFCCP has responsibility for enforcing the following:

- Executive Order 11246 (Affirmative Action Plan requirements for minorities and women)

- Section 503 of the Rehabilitation Act (affirmative action requirements for disabled)

- Vietnam Era Veterans' Readjustment Assistance Act (affirmative action requirements for veterans)

- Americans with Disabilities Act (job accommodation requirements for disabled)

- Americans with Disabilities Act Amendments Act

The OFCCP has developed regulations for contractors to follow during their implementation of these laws and Executive Orders. Those regulations have the weight of law and specify what federal contractors are expected to do and how they will be audited by the OFCCP when they are randomly selected from the contractor pool. In that regard, the OFCCP is a law enforcement agency. The EEOC is also a law enforcement agency. They are just enforcing administrative laws rather than criminal laws. These regulations are in the Code of Federal Regulations at 41 CFR 60. Chapter 60 has many different components that give the OFCCP its administrative power over contractor affirmative action programs.

Affirmative Action Plans for minorities and women must contain:

- Commitment to Equal Employment Opportunity

- Responsibility for implementation

- Internal review and reporting systems

- Problem identification

- Development and execution of action-oriented programs

- Statistical analysis reports (including: Workforce Analysis [or Organizational Structure Report], Job Group Analysis, Availability Analysis, Analysis of Incumbents Compared to Availability, Placement Rate Goals & Goals Progress Report)

Affirmative Action Plans for disabled and veterans categories do not currently have any statistical analysis requirements, although the OFCCP has proposed some regulatory changes that would establish those requirements. If your organization is a federal contractor, it is a good idea to remain current on these requirements as they evolve. At the time of this writing, only narrative sections are required in AAPs for disabled and veterans.[5]

Outreach and Recruiting Requirements for Affirmative Action

The purpose of affirmative action programs is the establishment of outreach and recruiting efforts. To better understand this, it is helpful to look at a comparison of EEO and affirmative action.

Equal Employment Opportunity (EEO) is the foundation of affirmative action. EEO means anyone who is qualified for a job opening should have access to that job opening. Before the Civil Rights Act of 1964 it was common practice for employers to fill some job openings with "hand selected" incumbents. Sometimes the position was never even announced until it had been filled. The Civil Rights Act of 1964 said that type of employment practice was not acceptable. Today, openings should be announced and candidate pools established. Anyone who is qualified for a job should be given access to the candidate pool. Then, sorting, and selection should be done based on nondiscriminatory procedures. (Remember the discussion of the Uniform Guidelines on Employee Selection Procedures earlier in this chapter?) The objective of EEO selection procedures should be to include everyone who is qualified and then select the best qualified from among all candidates.

As EEO is supposed to provide equal access, affirmative action is supposed to provide outreach and recruiting efforts where there are gaps between incumbent representation and computed availability. If you compute availability of women among professional civil engineers to be 40 percent in your recruiting geography and your incumbents have a 20 percent representation of women, you will likely be required to establish a placement rate goal of 40 percent for your professional civil engineer job group. That means you should have at least 40 percent women in your candidate pool for that job group. Each time you have a job opening in that job group, at least 40 percent of the candidates will be women. And, because there are more trained and experienced women in that type of work these days, you will undoubtedly be finding some to be best qualified in your selection process. Gradually, your female representation will grow. It may take a few years of effort, but you will see the demographics shift so that your incumbency more closely mirrors availability. The same type of comparisons need to be done for each of the minority race and ethnic categories.

In summary, employers must abide by many administrative laws. EEO and affirmative action requirements are only two of them. EEO is equal employment opportunity. It requires all individuals to be given access to job opportunities for which they are qualified. Affirmative action is a program requiring employers who are federal contractors to engage in outreach and recruiting to entice qualified minorities, women, disabled individuals, and veterans into the job applicant process.

Recordkeeping Requirements

One regulation the OFCCP has put in place is a definition for *Internet Applicant* that governs much of how federal contractors collect and retain data on job applicants. This definition applies to applications submitted through the Internet, by fax, or by any other electronic process. It does not apply to applications taken in person or through the U.S. mail unless the contractor wishes to apply the same definition to those sources.

An Internet applicant is someone who

- Submits an application, resume, or other expression of interest in employment
- Has been considered for a specific job opening
- Possesses all the basic job qualifications for the open job
- Did not self-eliminate from considerations by taking another job elsewhere, stating she/he is no longer interested, or failing to respond to employer communications

In addition to the job applicant records, contractors are required (under 41 CFR 60-1.12) to keep and maintain

- Any record created by the employer pertaining to hiring, assignment, promotion, demotion, transfer, layoff or termination, rates of pay or other terms of compensation and selection for training or apprenticeship.

- Other records having to do with request for reasonable accommodation, and results of any physical examination

- Job advertisements or postings

- Applications

- Resumes

- Any and all expressions of interest through the Internet or related electronic data technologies...such as online resumes or internal resume databases

- Records identifying job seekers contacted regarding their interest in a particular position

- A record of each resume added to its internal resume databases, and a record of the date each resume was added to the database

- A record of each position for which a search of an internal database was made and, corresponding to each search, the substantive search criteria used and the date of the search

- A record of the position for which each search of an external database was made, and corresponding to each search, the substantive search criteria used, the date of the search, and the resumes of job seekers who met the basic qualifications for the particular position who are considered by the contractor

- Tests for employment screening or selection

- Interview notes

Gender Discrimination and Harassment in the Workplace

As much as we would like to think that discrimination against employees based on sex or gender has been eradicated from the workplace, there is still a thriving complaint-handling business in both the private and public sectors. To help combat that problem, the federal government has provided general guidelines.

Gender-Neutral Job Advertisements

Returning to the discussion of EEOC guidelines, the EEOC has issued guidance on how employment ads should be constructed. Back in 1964, most employment advertisements were seen in local newspaper classified sections. Prior to the Civil Rights Act, it was common practice for newspapers to have separate categories for "Jobs for Men" and "Jobs for Women."

The EEOC guidelines say such designations are illegal under the law. There are some exceptions where jobs require either men or women, but those are few and they must be justified based on a Bona Fide Occupational Qualification (BFOQ). Examples of jobs that might be gender or sex-specific would include restroom attendant, wet nurse, actor, or actress. Today most gender-specific job titles have been changed to gender-neutral titles. For example, mailman has been changed to mail carrier; waitress and waiter have been changed to server; and, stewardess has been changed to flight attendant.

The EEOC guidelines also require a "tag line" in all job advertisements. At a minimum employers should show "EEO Employer" or "Equal Opportunity Employer" at the bottom of each of their job advertisements. Additional wording may be added if the employer wishes. Some have used sentences such as, "Minorities, women, disabled, and veterans encouraged to apply."

Types of Harassment

In addition to providing protection for gender discrimination, the Civil Rights Act has provided for protection against harassment as well. Before the Civil Rights Act and the case law that has come out of its application, harassment on the job was a fact of life for some individuals and these folks were faced with the option of putting up with the harassment or quitting their job and going to work somewhere else, hoping that harassment wouldn't be a problem at the new location.

Sexual Harassment

Sexual harassment has been defined by the courts over the last several decades (see Figure 5-2: *Meritor Savings Bank v. Vinson; Harris v. Forklift Systems Inc.; Faragher v. City of Boca Raton; Ellerth v. Burlington Northern Industries; Oncale v. Sundowner Offshore Service, Inc.*). If you go back to the Civil Rights Act of 1964, you will not find the term "sexual harassment" in the law. It has been created from these court cases. And, as it turns out, there are two types of sexual harassment: quid pro quo and hostile environment.

Quid pro quo means "this for that." It is usually an issue when a supervisor makes sexual demands of a subordinate. It represents abuse of power. It can literally mean, "If you give me sexual favors, I'll let you keep your job."

Hostile environment harassment can happen to employees by other employees (peers), or even people who are not employees—for example, by vendor representatives just visiting the employee's workplace to deliver drinking water or office supplies. Hostile environment sexual harassment exists when behavior is repeatedly unwelcome and of a sexual nature. It can be verbal, physical, or visual, involving any of these types of behavior:

- Verbal conduct such as epithets, derogatory jokes or comments, slurs or unwanted sexual advances, invitations or comments

- Visual conduct such as derogatory and/or sexually oriented posters, photography, cartoons, drawings, or gestures

- Physical conduct such as assault, unwanted touching, blocking normal movement, or interfering with work because of sex, race, or any other protected basis

- Threats and demands to submit to sexual requests as a condition of continued employment, or to avoid some other loss, and offers of employment benefits in return for sexual favors

- Retaliation for having reported or threatened to report harassment

It should be noted that an employee is not required to give notice to the employer that the behavior is unwelcome. Sometimes, fear for one's job or simple social discomfort will prevent people from speaking up to say they don't like what is going on. It might only come out in a complaint to the EEOC at some later time. "She laughed along with the rest of us" is not a valid defense to charges of sexual harassment if the behavior was something that should have not been permitted in the workplace to begin with. The only acceptable form of touching in the American workplace these days is the handshake.

What is the standard for employers who learn of a problem with sexual harassment in their organization? The federal requirement is that employers address the problem rapidly and thoroughly. Some state laws require employers to go as far as to guarantee that the problem does not occur again, which is beyond federal requirements.

Harassment of Other Types

It isn't only sexual harassment that is illegal in the American workplace. Harassment based on race, age, religion, national origin, color, disability, or pregnancy is also illegal. In fact, harassment on the basis of any protected class is illegal.

NOTE Remember that jokes at the expense of others are usually not a good idea. And if you are a supervisor or manager engaging in such behavior, you can plan on some serious consequences if you end up in court.

Employment liability for workplace injuries is usually handled with liability insurance. These days, insurance is available to address employment decisions but it is very expensive and it comes with a very high deductible. That insurance is called Employment Practices Liability Insurance (EPLI). It does offer employers some amount of coverage to protect against judgments against the employer and the punitive compensation awards that might accompany those judgments. EPLI covers employers for harassment or other illegal discrimination complaint charges and violation of laws about working conditions, among similar alleged bad acts. They usually have a very large deductible requirement and carry expensive premiums.

These injuries are not Workers' Compensation injuries. They are psychological and financial impacts felt by employees subjected to illegal employment discrimination. Peace of mind and the financial security of employment can be taken away in these situations. Courts assign dollar damage awards to compensate for such injuries.

For individual supervisors and managers who engage in employee harassment, no insurance protection is available, and the employer is not obligated to defend the supervisor against legal challenges. Ordinarily a supervisor would be indemnified by the employer because, although the supervisor was making individual decisions, it was done within the scope of their job as an agent of the employer. It is when the supervisor steps outside the boundaries of the normal job requirements that things get sticky. Employers depend on managers and supervisors to make decisions every day. However, harassment is not a duty assigned by the employer to any manager or supervisor. It is behavior that is illegal, and in most cases runs counter to employer policy. No insurance policy will pay for such illegal behavior unless it is a specific covered hazard in the policy. Additionally, supervisors who engage in harassing behavior with their employees will find that their homeowner's liability coverage won't protect them either. It will decline coverage saying that it was an intentional act, not an accident. Think of someone who gets behind the wheel of their car and intentionally runs over the neighbor's garden. Their automobile policy won't cover them because it was an intentional act. Thus, any court assessments or fines will have to come from the supervisor's personal financial resources. Some have lost their houses because of that insurance provision.

Employer Prevention Obligations

Under federal provisions, employers subject to the Civil Rights Act of 1964 are responsible for having a policy that clearly states what behaviors are considered unacceptable in the workplace. Additionally, they are responsible for enforcing that policy with disciplinary actions when necessary. That may include dismissal in some instances.

As with any other discipline, it should be consistently applied. Similar situations should produce similar outcomes. Treating people differently because of their race, sex, or other basis could generate its own set of discrimination complaints.

Organizational Staffing Requirements

Staffing is the lifeblood of an organization as people are required to make any organization run. Getting the right ones into the right jobs is the function known as *staffing*.

Forecasting Placement Opportunities

Forecasting results can be converted into employee headcount and budget impact, and the consequences can demand other staffing needs. Adding production workers can cause an increase in payroll support work levels, for example.

Identifying job openings before they exist is the activity known as *forecasting*. It is best performed with the aid of operations managers who will be supervising the new positions. Given what is anticipated for growth (or force reduction) a manager is able to convert workload into staff requirements. Determining the portion of jobs that will be part time versus those that will be full time is another contribution of the forecasting process.

Forecasting staffing needs is usually done in terms of the number of full time equivalent people. That unit value is also favored for budgeting activities. Full Time Equivalent People (FTE) Required = Total Functional Work Load / Work Load Handled by One Person

Compliance with WARN Act

In contrast to forecasting for growth, when you have 100 or more employees and undergo a large downsizing of your staff, as you read in Chapter 2, you may be subject to the WARN (Worker Adjustment and Retraining Notification) Act.

Should it be necessary to reduce your employee headcount by 50 or more full-time workers, you must comply with the WARN Act requirements. At least 60 days before the layoff is to occur, or the plant is to be closed, notice should be sent to the State Rapid Response Dislocated Worker Unit as well as the chief elected official of the local government where the layoff or closure will occur. Notice must also be given to each union or other employee representative at the facility that will experience the force reduction. In companies without union representation, each affected worker must receive this notice. Specific content is required of these notices, including the following:

- The name and address where the mass layoff or plant closing is to occur, along with the name and telephone number of a company contact person who can provide additional information

- A statement as to whether the planned action is expected to be permanent or temporary and, if the entire plant is to be closed, a statement to that effect

- The expected date of the first separation and the anticipated schedule for making separations

- The job titles of positions to be affected and the name of affected employees in each job classification

The WARN Act Employers Guide states, "An employer who violates WARN is liable to each affected employee for an amount equal to back pay and benefits for the period of violation, up to 60 days. This liability may be reduced by any wages the employer pays over the notice period. WARN liability may also be reduced by any voluntary and unconditional payment not required by a legal obligation."[6]

Workforce Planning, Forecasting, and Predicting Metrics

The Society for Human Resource Management (SHRM) represents over 250,000 members around the world. It has partnered with the American National Standards Institute (ANSI) to develop standards for the business of human resource management. Just as there are standards for sizes of nails, nuts, and bolts, there will soon be a variety of standards dealing with employee management issues, including diversity management, staffing, and retention. To learn more about the most recent developments, check in with SHRM for announcements of new standards.

Basic Workforce Planning and Forecasting includes these action steps or tasks:

- Establish list of assumptions about the future period in months or years (revenue growth rate, facility plans—new locations, acquisition plans involving other organizations, downsizing projections).

- Compute FTE requirements for each organizational grouping (department, division, group, and so on).

- Establish comparison of FTE forecast with incumbency to determine new opportunities or downsizing amounts.

- Identify internal sources for qualified job candidates (review inventory of job skills for each employee).

- Identify external sources for qualified job candidates (include sources that may not yet have been utilized for diversity or new skill requirements).

- Develop a plan for recruiting from external sources that identifies specific actions to be taken. (Internet sources should be identified as well as any other media that targets groups that should be represented in candidate pools when jobs open up.) Social media has shot to the top of the recruiting sources list. Even smaller organizations are finding that websites such as Facebook.com and LinkedIn.com can produce job candidates quickly and inexpensively.

Workforce Analysis Techniques

Often, managers will have a need to assess their workforce and what things are influencing it. Questions arise such as, "Why is turnover so high?" "Why are new hires only lasting for six months before leaving?" Some of the following analysis techniques can help determine the answers.

- **Supply analysis techniques**   A strategic evaluation of supply chain options such as sourcing alternatives, plant locations, and warehouse locations.

- **Trend and ratio analysis**   Ratio analysis compares current results or historic results, but always at a point in time. Trend analysis compares historical results with current results and identifies what may happen in the future based on the trend of data in the past.

- **Turnover analysis**   There are many possible reasons for employees leaving the payroll, including resignation, dismissal, death, long-term disability, and transfer to another subordinate company within the same parent company. Identifying the reasons that employees are leaving provides the data needed to analyze trends and identify potential problems within the organization. If supervisors are causing high resignation rates, it may be appropriate to train the supervisors, or take some other action to reduce the rate at which their subordinates are leaving.

- **Flow analysis**   This can involve analysis of data, analysis of production line movement, or analysis of order processing, among other possibilities. How processes operate and how flows of products, data, or other items go through those processes is the objective of this type of monitoring.

- **Demand analysis techniques**   It is interesting to look forward to determine what customers, clients, or patrons will want in the future.

- **Judgmental forecasts**   These are projections based on subjective inputs. This method is often used when there is a very short time for drawing a conclusion, or data is outdated or unavailable.

- **Managerial estimates**   An individual or a group of management people use their experience and knowledge to identify the most likely future characteristics without any additional data analysis.

- **Delphi technique**   This is a method of determining the future outcome and then manipulating a group to reach that conclusion or goal statement. A group of people is forced into polarized positions; then the facilitator suggests a resolution and guides people to support that idea. Ultimately, the group will endorse the facilitator's suggestion because the group has accepted the facilitator as one of its own. It is unethical and used more frequently than might be suspected.

- **Nominal group technique**   A variation on the brainstorming process for group creativity, the nominal group technique alters that process a bit. As a forecasting process, the facilitator can ask a question such as, "What will be our best selling product next year?" The large group is then divided into small groups of five or six members. Then each person spends several minutes silently brainstorming on their own, seeking all the possible ideas they can come up with. Next, each group collects its members' ideas by sharing them around the table, and each is written on a flipchart. No criticism is allowed, but clarification in response to questions is encouraged. Each person then evaluates the ideas and individually and anonymously votes for the best ones using some form of grading system (for example, a score of 5 for the best idea, 4 for the next best, and so on). The group then collects and tabulates the points awarded to each idea and the one with the highest score is the winner.

- **Statistical forecasts**   These approaches to analysis use mathematical formulas to identify patterns and trends. Once identified, the trends are analyzed again for mathematical reasonableness.

- **Regression analysis**   Linear regression is a tool often used in forecasting and financial analysis. It compares relationships among several variables. A variable is something for which the value changes over time. In hiring, one variable is the number of job openings to be filled. Another variable is the number of job applicants received for each job opening. How these things can be related and used in predicting the number of people who will meet the job requirements can be determined through linear regression analysis.

Multiple regression analysis allows us to ask the question, "What is the best predictor of...?" If we want new employees to remain on the job successfully for at least one year after hiring them, we can use multiple regression analysis to determine how factors such as educational degree, educational institution, general experience, specific job experience, multiple language skills, or community involvement can contribute to that longevity requirement.

- **Simulations**   We can simulate a process or condition in order to predict an outcome. For example, we can build a simulation of a management problem in order to measure how non-management people handle the problem. That allows us in turn to predict whether or not each participant would be successful if promoted to a management position. This is commonly done in industrial assessment centers.

- **Gap analysis techniques**   Measuring the distance (or difference) between where you are and where you wish to be is known as gap analysis. If you have to train all employees in certain safety procedures, you can use gap analysis to determine what portion of the population has yet to receive the training, or any portion of the training.

- **Solution analysis techniques**   Another approach is to define the problem, identify a variety of solutions, and then assess each solution through use of statistical comparisons. It involves asking the question, "What is the likelihood of success for this solution?" It can employ the mathematical process of regression analysis to assess the variables influencing each solution's implementation. For example, it might be possible to solve the problem of turnover by creating a management skills training program. It also might be possible to solve the turnover problem by providing different employee benefits, more appealing to the workers. It could also be that offering continuing education to employees would have an impact on turnover. Each of those solutions could work. You can determine how well each works by using regression analysis to calculate the contribution each could make to the problem of turnover control. This analysis considers that there is some value to be contributed by each different solution. If you can't choose all of them, where will you get the greatest impact for your investment of time and money?

Staffing Effectiveness Assessment and Metrics

When considering staffing metrics specifically, there are actually two types of staffing to consider measuring: staffing of the overall employer organization and staffing for the HR organization within the larger employer group.

Effectiveness of staffing in HR is usually measured by the ratio of HR workers to the total organizational headcount. It used to be that executives expected one HR person for every 100 employees. Today, those ratios are influenced by more sophisticated considerations having to do with strategic planning (succession planning, training, and development) and implementation of special programs (mergers and acquisitions with large cultural differences). "Cheap" isn't always the most effective route to success.

Overall staffing success can be measured through consideration of turnover rates (before and after mergers and acquisitions), the level of professional staff remaining after a raid by a respected research university, or the quantity of employees who remain on their job for at least 12 months after being hired.

Each organization must devise its own measures for staffing effectiveness. Identify the factors that affect staffing and retention. Isolate those factors that are unique to the organization because of special conditions. Create measurements for normal conditions and a separate set of measurements for the unique conditions. Complete the statement for each condition, "I know our staffing programs have been successfully effective because they _____."

Strategic Workforce Planning

SPHR Strategic workforce planning involves all of the basic processes with the addition of key components such as succession planning. Succession planning is a sensitive subject because it identifies top candidates for each executive position and the developmental steps necessary for each of them to become qualified for the higher level job when an opening occurs.

To begin, a succession plan should contain an assessment of each employee, detailing whether that person is "Ready now for promotion," "Ready in the future for promotion," "Best to remain in current position," and "On performance improvement program."

- *Ready now for promotion* means the employee could move into a specific higher position and be successful without further developmental activities. The employee currently has all of the knowledge, skills, and abilities required of the higher job.

- *Ready in the future for promotion* means that there are some specific knowledge, skills, or abilities the employee must attain before being ready for the higher level job. There may be specific plans to send the individual to training programs, or to move them into other specific jobs for experience needed before being ready for the promotion. Other developmental activities might include assignment to specific task force groups or additional education in certain university programs. If an advanced degree is needed, that should be identified (for example, Master of Business Administration).

- *Best to remain in current position* means the employee has a satisfactory or better job performance rating in the current position. Performance appraisals indicate that there is not a high chance of success if promoted. It might be that the individual participated in a formal assessment program and was judged unlikely to succeed if promoted. In any event, remaining in the current job is the best for both the employee and the organization.

- *On performance improvement program* means anyone who is less than satisfactory in their current job should be provided with a specific plan for development of the deficiencies so he or she can be successful. If the improvement program does not help generate successful knowledge, skills, or abilities, the employee should be moved into a job where existing skills would be adequate, or the individual should be terminated.

Once the inventory of employees has been completed, identification of likely internal candidates for each executive position can begin. Usually, three people are identified as potential successors for each executive job. When doing so, first identify those who are "ready now" and then those who still need some developmental work.

When you are done, a chart of positions and likely successors can be created and published. Distribution of such plans is normally tightly controlled. There are many reasons for exercising restraint in distribution of succession plans. They include:

- If incumbents know they are identified as the possible successor to an executive, contractual expectations could be created that would raise legal liability problems.
- People who are identified as successors might conclude that they no longer need to produce at exceptional levels in the current job.
- People who are not identified as successors can experience a drop in morale resulting in production issues.

Those not identified as successors may leave the organization and the resulting turnover could reach unacceptable levels. In summary, succession plans are important when disaster strikes an employer's organization or when large numbers are expected to retire, causing a gap in skills and knowledge, which is what has been predicted with the baby boomer exodus. Succession plans typically involve plans for filling vacancies at the most senior levels of management. However, it is possible to expand the coverage to any level of management. They can ensure trained, experienced people ready to take over a more senior job once the job becomes vacant. A successful succession plan will prevent uncertainty and costly delays in searching for qualified job candidates.

Job Analysis and Documentation

There are still many organizational leaders who think it is problematic to have job descriptions. Even with the passage of the Americans with Disabilities Act, job descriptions did not become a legal requirement. Yet, consider this question: If job responsibilities and duties are not clearly identified, how can an incumbent be held accountable for performance? Absent a written job description, communication issues can be serious and organizational efficiency easily suffers. Table 5-5 identifies the key content in a job description as recommended by SHRM.

Please also refer to Chapters 4 and 9 for more information about job descriptions, job evaluation, and essential functions.

Job Description Element	What the Element Contains
Date	When the job description was written
Position title	The name of the position
Job status	Exempt or non-exempt under FLSA regulations; full time or part time
Objective of the position	What the position is supposed to accomplish; how it affects other positions and the organization
Supervision received	The reporting structure for this position—to whom does the position report
Supervisory responsibilities	The number of direct reports, if any, and the level of supervision it provides
Job summary	An outline of job responsibilities
Essential functions	Detailed tasks, duties, and responsibilities that must be performed
Competency or position requirements	The knowledge, skills, and abilities to perform the job
Quality and quantity standards	The minimum levels required to meet the job requirements and performance expectations
Education and experience	The required minimum levels required by the job content
Physical factors	The type of environment associated with the job: indoor/outdoor, including movement requirements (sitting, standing, walking), lighting conditions, hearing, speaking, grasping, carrying, lifting, finger or hand movement, arm and leg movement, entire body involvement, temperature ranges, and so forth
Working conditions	Shift hours and overtime requirements
Unplanned activities	Examples of other duties that could be assigned
Review and approval	The name and title of senior person reviewing and approving the job description

Table 5-5 Job Description Key Content

Identifying Key Job Responsibilities and Essential Functions

When beginning the process of creating a job description, a job analyst, if your organization has one, should work with the manager of the position to develop a list of key job responsibilities and essential duties. (If there is no job analyst, managers are sometimes left to do the description development themselves.) A job description may be assigned to a single incumbent or represent a job that has many incumbents. Either way, it should identify the key functions to be performed by those incumbents.

Essential job functions are those things done by the incumbent that cannot be changed without altering the job so much that it becomes a different job. A complaint investigator receives complaints from employees and investigates them. Alter or remove that function and the job won't be the same. It will become a different job.

To begin, one would ask what responsibilities are assigned to this particular job (for example, accuracy of all correspondence, bills, statements, receipts, checks, and other documents generated in the vice president's office; or, developing protocol for use by laboratory assistants in generating research data). Responsibilities are things for which someone is accountable. One can be responsible for production on a given work shift, or for delivery of newspapers to a specific neighborhood.

Next, what duties are going to be assigned to the job (for example, coordinate and arrange meetings for the vice president and immediate staff members; or, develop the budget for laboratory operations and maintain control over budget expenses)? Duties are assigned tasks. One can be assigned to prepare all outgoing mail with proper postage, or to conduct training for laboratory personnel in proper safety procedures.

Third, what are the essential job functions (for example, all order processing, inventory management, and production of printed products; or, management of laboratory employees so that research objectives are met each quarter)? Each job may have many essential job functions or duties. While production of budget reports might be essential for an administrative assistant, maintaining a list of employee birthdays may be incidental to the job. Remember that it is only essential functions that are important when considering job accommodation requests.

Identifying Job Qualifications

Having identified the responsibilities and duties, it is a good idea to next make a list of job qualifications.

 NOTE Remember that you must be able to prove that each qualification is valid under requirements of the Uniform Guidelines on Employee Selection Procedures.

First begin with qualification categories. Basic job qualifications can include education, specific experience, specific duration at certain responsibility levels (general management or senior operations management, for example), designated minimum test scores, or other such requirement. For each qualification category, there should be a list of standards and examples that can be used for all job descriptions. Selection from the list under each qualification category can result in a carefully thought out set of criteria to be used in preparing the job opening announcement and in the evaluation of job applicants during the selection process.

Some job requirements will specify mental and physical demands or there may be legal requirements such as certification and licensing. Some jobs may not be staffed by anyone without proper licenses—for example, attorneys, physicians, librarians, pharmacists, and in many locations around the country, a construction contractor. In some jurisdictions, it is permissible for someone to work on a job while in the process of being certified or licensed. Failure to achieve the proper level of certification by a given deadline can result in removal from the job.

Identifying Physical and Mental Job Requirements

As we mentioned, some job requirements will specify mental and physical demands. Physical demands of a job involve physical activity and work environment. If the job requires working in a warehouse freezer, temperature will be a factor. If the job involves roofing during the summer when temperatures reach 100 degrees or more, temperature will be a factor. If the job requires bending, stretching, lifting, carrying, sitting, fingering, grasping, reaching, standing, or walking, the incumbent will need to be able to do those things, or achieve an understanding with the employer for a reasonable job accommodation.

Mental demands of a job can involve things such as reasoning ability and mathematical and language skills. When setting mental job requirements ask questions about the job such as these:

- What education or experience is required for success on the job? Is a high school diploma needed? If so, why? What responsibility or duty in the job could not be fulfilled without a high school diploma? Is it possible that some level of experience could be a substitute for formal education?

- What language skills are needed on the job? Is it necessary to read and write English to perform this job? Why? What part of the job requires those skills? Perhaps the job requires response to verbal or written safety instructions. Perhaps it requires preparation of reports or delivery of briefings to senior management. Describe not only the verbal and written skills required but also what duties they will be used to perform.

- Are mathematical skills required by the job? If so, at what level? Is it necessary to be able to add and subtract so that proper change can be made at a cash register? Maybe it is necessary to use math skills to measure and cut proper lengths of lumber for a construction job. Or it might be necessary to have advanced calculus skills to understand movement of space vehicles in relation to the planets.

- What reasoning ability is needed on the job? Is it necessary to follow specific and detailed instructions? Or does the job require a level of thinking associated with problem solving and consideration of alternatives?

Job Competencies

Job competency is the ability to properly perform a job.[7] According to Washington State Human Resources, there are four types of job competency: knowledge, skill, ability, and behavioral competency. It seems logical that knowledge of the job content is an essential part of performance success. It also appears realistic that employers could expect someone to have the skills and abilities to competently perform their jobs. We don't always think of behavioral competencies, however. These are patterns of action or conduct that people exhibit that lead to job performance success.

Point Systems for Job Evaluation

Point systems for job evaluation are often found in use at very large organizations. They are also sometimes used by consulting firms such as the Hay Group (*Hay System* of job evaluation). Sometimes they are used by internal groups dedicated to evaluating job content to be sure the jobs are properly graded for compensation purposes.

The point-factor method, as described by SHRM, is one of four different evaluation methods. The four methods include job ranking, job classification, factor comparison, and the point-factor method. The four methods are further divided into two categories: non-quantitative and quantitative.

The discussion of job evaluation and each of the four methods is addressed in more detail in Chapter 9, "Compensation and Benefits."

Point factors are designed to evaluate each job's content based on a series of scales. For example, a job evaluation program might consider these rating factors:

- **Mental development**   The degree of knowledge required to understand and think about the duties. (A scale might go from "1" requiring incumbents to follow orders to "10," where professional competence equivalent to a doctorate level is required.)

- **Experience**   The time required to accumulate practical knowledge needed for the job. (A scale could be built on the number of months in a career path.)

- **Difficulty**   The degree of difficulty in making decisions required by the job. (A scale might go from "1," requiring a choice between two solutions, to a "10," where causes of problems and potential solutions are very difficult to establish.)

- **Functional variety**   The number of functions performed on the job. (A scale could be based on the number of distinct functions performed by the job.)

- **Inventiveness**   The amount of innovation or creativity demanded by the job. (A scale might go from "1," no requirement for inventiveness, to "10," where devising original concepts and techniques is a dominant component of the job.)

- **Freedom**   The amount of freedom from rigid supervision and prescribed practices. (A scale could go from "1," where there is no freedom to deviate from instructions, to "10," where freedom exists to produce and results are judged on their overall impact on the organization.)

- **Magnitude**   The amount of impact the job has on the overall organization. (A scale could go from "1," with only slight impact on its local organization, to "10," where there is a major impact on goals of the overall organization.)

- **Supervision**   The number of subordinates reporting to this job. (A scale could be developed based on the size of subordinate groupings.)

When using a point system, after each factor has been evaluated, the points are added up and the total points will determine the organizational level and/or the compensation grade for the job. The employer specifies a scale of point totals that is segmented into job levels or compensation amounts and can also be interpreted by organizational responsibility level.

NOTE A system designed to measure management jobs may not be appropriate for non-management positions. There may be a need for two different rating systems.

In order for any system of job rating to have value, the team of people that make up the rating board should establish a standard or benchmark that represents each level of rating possible. All other jobs should be rated in comparison to those benchmarks.

Annual Review of Job Contents

Although it is a "best practice," an annual review of job descriptions is only a requirement for federal contractors, subject to affirmative action requirements for disabled individuals. Under affirmative action, while written job descriptions are not required, an annual review of job content is. In practical terms, it is difficult to review job content without a written job description.

Recruitment and the Application Process

New employees either replace or expand incumbency in any employer organization. Even a stable, healthy organization will need to replace employee losses due to resignation, death, disability, and other causes. These are some recruiting issues that must be faced in the process.

Internal and External Recruitment Sources

Often, employers search both inside and outside their organizations for someone who can fill a job opening.

Internal Sources

Some organizations overlook their own workforce as a legitimate source of qualified candidates when job openings occur. Internal recruiting can be handled either formally or informally. In union-represented organizations, a procedure for internal job postings is usually specified in the Memorandum of Understanding (MOU) or union contract (Collective Bargaining Agreement—CBA). Details within union contracts (CBAs) might specify what information should be included in job postings and how long job openings will remain posted. Sometimes internal recruiting must happen for a specified number of days prior to any external recruiting efforts being made. In the absence of unions, the employer will have the opportunity to develop its own policies and procedures in this staffing area.

Often there are internal resources that might fill the needs of the job opening in question. Current employees are constantly changing, through education or temporary job assignments. They may be working on certifications that would better qualify them for a different job. It is important to consider these resources because they represent less expensive candidate pools than those built with external candidates. And it begs the question of whether it is necessary to have a database that tracks current employee skills and certifications. Training accomplishments, new educational achievements, and demonstrated skill performance should all be identified periodically (annually or more often) and the data entered into these types of databases.

Succession planning is a process of organizing the internal staffing process. It depends on identifying when job openings may occur, who is currently qualified to perform that job, and alternatively, who could be qualified through more training and/or development. Properly done, succession planning will enable you to identify two or three key candidates for each senior executive position in the organization. It will also enable you to identify the developmental process that will be implemented to prepare each of those candidates for the ultimate placement in the higher position. Developmental activities can include temporary task force assignments, temporary job assignments, rotational job assignments, or job swapping where two people change positions for mutual benefit. Succession plans are usually closely guarded because they contain very special and sensitive information. Sometimes HR professionals below the senior executive in HR are not even privy to succession plan content. Implementing a quality succession plan can take a year or more.

One tool that can assist the internal recruiting process is an employee skills database. Information tracked in this database will be confidential to a large extent. Yet it can help you identify qualified candidates for internal placement when the need arises. Your list of data content will likely be different from that created by other HR professionals in different types of organizations. Some of the basics could include:

- Typing (rate and accuracy)
- Specific software application skills (Microsoft Office, accounting programs)
- Driving (automobiles, trucks, forklifts)
- Licenses (attorney, physician, pharmacist, private investigation, nursing)
- Certifications (CPA, PHR, SPHR, surveyor, architect)
- Computer programming (languages)
- CPR/First Aid
- Credentials (teaching specialty)
- Craft specialty (welding, plumbing, electrician, carpentry)
- Advanced degree (MBA, functional specialty)
- Executive training
- Task force leadership
- Languages (specific language fluency)

Internal recruiting can contribute substantially to your overall placement needs. And, generally speaking, internal candidates are less expensive to obtain than external candidates.

Employers often find it is less expensive to recruit job candidates from internal sources. When people are already on the payroll, transferring them to a new job assignment reduces the costs associated with recruiting, hiring, and even sometimes Social Security and Medicare tax.

Here are some internal sources that can be considered before publishing a job opening in external sources.

- **Promotions and transfers** Internal sources include promotions and transfers. People can transfer within the same department, to other departments, or to other associated subsidiary companies. A promotion can be defined as an increase in job level, an increase in compensation, or an increase in responsibilities. Usually, morale is positively affected when workers see the employer making opportunities available to the existing workforce before searching outside for job candidates. Upgrades and, strangely, downgrades or demotions can also be considered internal sources for job placements.

- **Diversity groups** Diversity groups are sometimes called Employee Affinity Groups. They typically are organized along race, gender, disability, or veteran status (for example, African American Employees Association, Women Engineers Club, or AB Trucking Veterans Association). Sometimes they are sponsored by employers; sometimes they are not. Often, employers provide meeting space and refreshments in exchange for conversations with the groups on topics of diversity management, employee relations, employee development, and so on. Such groups can be a valuable resource for employer human resource management. Diversity groups should be included in external recruiting efforts, encouraging further referrals of job candidates from minority, women, disabled, and veteran populations.

- **Retired employees** A resource that is already trained, has organizational knowledge, and is experienced in job requirements should not be overlooked. It may be cheaper in the short run to bring back a retired worker to "fill in" temporarily than to hire another type of temporary worker.

External Sources

In contrast to internal recruiting is external recruiting, which is just as it sounds. External recruiting sources include the following:

- **State employment services** Free posting for job openings of all kinds.

- **Industrial associations** If the employer is a member of an industrial association, there are frequently job posting services offered by such associations, and they are usually free.

- **Local educational Institutions** High schools, community colleges, and universities will usually be glad to post job opening information so their graduating students can find employment in their chosen field of work.

- **Veterans organizations** Sometimes state employment agencies have linkages to veterans organizations and often have Veteran Coordinators on their staff to maintain those relationships. Get to know these people and how they can help with your recruiting efforts.

- **Organizations for disabled** Many qualified job seekers are classified as "disabled" for one reason or another. In many cases, the disability will have no impact on that person's ability to perform the essential job functions. Don't overlook a valuable resource.

- **Advertising or posting on paid web services**   It has been said that, today, more than half of all white collar jobs are being filled through LinkedIn. LinkedIn.com is a paid resource for employers. Posting job openings requires payment of a fee. Other similar posting-for-a-fee web services include Monster.com, Amazon.com, ZipRecruiter.com, and others. Craigslist.com, as of this writing, is still a free service for employers.

- **Traditional advertising**   Newspaper and magazine print advertising can take the form of classified ads or display ads. These days, magazines and newspapers have companion editions online. Buying advertising in one format can also provide the same advertising in the other format. There are also free job search newspapers that can be found in dispensing racks at local supermarkets, on street corners, and at newsstands. These list only job openings within a given geography. They are sustained by paid advertising related to job opportunities and placement, like those related to training institutions and universities, for example.

In the Trenches

Req-less Recruiting

Grant D. Bassett, VP of Talent, Workday, Inc.

As the advantages of creating connections through social media grow, online professional networks continue to make finding talent easier and easier. I believe we're at the cusp of a hard left turn in the recruiting profession where the real value of a recruiting function will clearly be talent engagement and conversion.

Imagine a company with 10,000 employees, all of whom actively manage their social networks as well as cultivate their professional networks. It is reasonable to believe that through the connections of those 10,000 employees, every person that company might want to hire is known to someone within that network. So finding them isn't the issue any more. It's curating and distributing content in a way that attracts, engages, and ultimately converts those individuals into people who will be interested in talking about a career move.

All of this points away from a job requisition being the order that is placed to kick off recruiting efforts, and towards a model where key talent profiles are built and communicated across a company, communities are created that will feed those profiles, and compelling, engaging content is developed that can be used by all employees to share with their networks.

Every employee becomes a recruiter and the ultimate goal is 100% employee referral, or stated another way, 100% of hires come from our networks. The requisition goes away, the success profile becomes key, and the role of the talent acquisition function becomes a true COE focused on successful profile creation, talent community creation, content creation and distribution, and other key programs aimed at enabling all employees to engage and convert talent that feeds the needs of the company.

State Employment Services

Each state maintains an agency that serves the function of job placement assistant.[8] Usually it is the same agency that manages the unemployment insurance distribution system. Federal contractors are required to post their job openings with the state employment service for the state in which the job will be located. Other employers are encouraged to post their job openings at these agencies, but they are not required to do so. There is no fee for employer use of these agencies. Anyone using the sites should retain a copy of the filings they post so there is no confusion in the future about what job content was described.

Recruitment Strategies

While for some posting job openings at state employment agencies is a requirement, it is nonetheless a recruitment strategy. Generally speaking, there are four key components of recruiting strategies that every organization should employ:

- **Identifying your brand**   If you are the leading company in a specific arena, let people know that.

- **Targeting specific candidate sources**   Identify the most likely sources for the type of candidates you seek. If you want professional engineers, look in engineering associations and college institutions. If you want electricians, look at the union organizations in the locations where your need exists. Target the specific sources you know will give you the qualified candidates you need.

- **Working with your key sources**   When you find organizations that have job candidates that will fill your needs, cultivate relationships with the people in those organizations. Give them tours of your facilities and stress how it is possible for you to work together to reach mutually dependent goals. Federal contractors have obligations to foster these types of relationships with sources of veterans and disabled job candidates in addition to those serving the female and minority job seekers.

- **Prepare your sales pitch**   Be prepared to sell your best job candidate on the benefits of working for your organization. Explain the environment, the working conditions, the side benefits, and the culture in a way that entices the job candidate to want to accept your job offer.

Branding and Marketing the Organization

Branding is a key recruiting strategy but branding differs from marketing. Branding is a strategic exercise, whereas marketing is a tactical process. Branding is also a method of conveying the key organization values while marketing is a process of encouraging people to purchase the organization product or service. They are often confused simply because they are so closely related.

HR professionals can help the organization advance its brand when discussing the organization with job candidates and employees. "Here are the things we value as an employer." "Here is the way we do things around here." "Here we have a culture that values _____." All of these are statements about the organization's brand.

When we hear things like, "We can provide that solution for you with our product/ service," we know we are hearing a marketing statement. It says "buy me." It is more direct and pointed than a branding statement. HR professionals can assist with marketing when they support submission of responses to Requests for Proposals or Sales Proposals.

Applicant Tracking

SPHR ── With recruiting underway, it is a matter of good management that some form of applicant tracking be used in any organization hiring employees. In federal contractor organizations and employers with 100 or more workers, there are additional obligations that require maintaining records of job applicants. Table 5-6 provides basic information that an applicant tracking records system should track.

Information Element	Element Content
Applicant name	Applicant name
Address	Applicant's current mailing address
Telephone number	Applicant's current telephone number (home, cell, work)
Email or other method of contact	Applicant's email address
Self-identification of race and sex	This information should not be passed on to the selecting manager(s).
Self-identification of protected veteran and disabled status	This information should not be passed on to the selecting manager(s).
Source	How did this person get information about your job opening?
Position applied for	Always insist on applicants identifying the specific job opening they are interested in. This might be a job requisition number or a job title.
Job location	If more than one location is available, ask for a preference.
Qualifications for the job	This could be satisfied by a resume or CV. Or you can require every applicant to complete your specific job application form.
Availability	How soon will the candidate be available to start work?
Compensation desired	While many people won't answer this question, it is good to ask it anyway. If someone replies with a number significantly above your budget range, you do not need to waste any more time on their candidacy.
References	Be sure to track references provided by the job applicant, including educational institutions (and degrees), former employers (with job titles and compensation amounts), and personal references.

Table 5-6 Applicant Tracking Data

Resumes vs. Job Applications

So far, no state or federal law or regulation requires employers to use job applications or resume forms in their employment process. That means employers are left to their own devices about how to process job applicants. Evaluating differences among job applicants is the primary task. Carefully crafted job application forms can help HR professionals in that evaluation process.

What is required by state and federal law is that employers meet the requirements of equal employment opportunity laws and be able to demonstrate that they made their employment decisions without regard to any of the protected categories. Some organizations prefer to use resumes rather than job applications, and in some companies neither is a requirement.

If a job application is used, it can be designed by the employer to contain requests for information the employer deems to be necessary in making the employment decision. Obviously, information categories should not include things such as birth date, race, sex, marital status, or other reference to protected categories.

Race and gender/sex are required data points for employees. Employers must either capture that information through employee self-identification or by observation best guess. Affirmative action employers (federal goods and service contractors) must invite job applicants to self-identify their race and gender/sex when they submit their application. That information is supposed to be diverted from view of the hiring manager or recruiter. Normally, it is routed to the HR professional responsible for accumulating and analyzing the database it will be entered into.

There are countless ways to write a resume, and not all of them will contain the same data elements. Further, resumes almost never provide written authorization for employers to gather information from previous employers. Job application forms can be designed with those authorizations and liability release statements to facilitate background checking.

Online vs. Hard Copy

There are many folks today who prefer to dispense with paper copies of documents and there are legitimate environmental reasons for moving to electronic copies. There are advantages to each approach.

Hard-Copy Records Job applications and resumes can provide an insight into the candidate's organization and language skills. Sloppiness and misspellings can be readily detected on paper records, particularly on resumes. Asking applicants to fill out a form can offer some insights into their reading skill, penmanship, written articulation, and inner work standards. When such records are converted to electronic format, the same types of information may not be as obvious.

Online Records The most obvious advantage of electronic records is that they can be shared by multiple people at the same time. In the case of group interviews, this can be particularly nice. Many years ago there were problems with the legality of electronic signatures on e-documents. The Uniform Electronic Transactions Act of 1999[9] remedied that problem for the most part.

Advantages of Job Application Forms

While there is no requirement for employers to use job application forms, they can be enormously helpful. As an employer, you might expect to gain some or all of these benefits:

- Consistently gather the same data in the same format from each prospective employee. With an employment application, employers gain standardization of information requested.

- Gather information about the applicant's credentials that candidates would not usually include in a resume or cover letter. Examples include reasons why the applicant left the employ of a prior employer, felony or misdemeanor crime convictions, and names and contact information for immediate supervisors.

- Obtain the applicant's signature attesting that all statements on the employment application are true.

- Obtain the applicant's signature enabling a potential employer to check the veracity of all data provided on the employment application, including employment history, education history, degrees earned, and so forth. Fraudulent claims and information on application materials, including fake degrees, exaggerated claims about former job responsibilities or compensation, fake dates of employment, and other falsehoods are a significant problem.

- Get the applicant's signature to attest that he or she has read and understands certain employer policies and procedures that are spelled out on the employment application. These typically include the fact that the employer is an at will employer, that the employer is an equal opportunity, nondiscriminating employer, and any other facts that the employer wants the applicant to read and understand on the employment application. When applicable, this may include the requirement that the applicant must pass a drug test prior to hire.

- Obtain the applicant's signature agreeing to a background check, including criminal history, creditworthiness (for certain jobs), driving record (for certain jobs), and anything else required by the job.

- Obtain voluntary self-identification data about race, sex, disability, and veteran status to enable proper reporting to government organizations as required and analysis of employment data by the employer.

These days, it is more a function of employer policy and organizational preference as to which type of record format will be used.

Invitations to Self-Identify as Part of the Application Process

We know from the Fair Labor Standards Act (see Chapter 2) and the EEOC requirement for annual filing of the EEO-1 Report that many employers are required to establish and maintain records of employee demographics. This information should be treated as confidential just as all other HR data is considered confidential.

Race and Gender/Sex

All employers with 100 or more employees and all federal contractors with 50 or more employees and contracts of $50,000 or more (or a construction contract valued at $10,000 or more) must maintain sex and ethnic identification of each employee.

There are seven race/ethnic categories on the EEO-1 form. So an invitation to self-identify given to employees and job applicants should contain all seven categories. They are:

- White (Not Hispanic)
- Black or African American (Not Hispanic)
- Hispanic
- Asian (Not Hispanic)
- Native Hawaiian or Other Pacific Islander (Not Hispanic)
- American Indian, Native American, Alaska Native (Not Hispanic)
- Two or More Races (Not Hispanic)

In the public sector, the EEO-4 Report has not expanded its list of five race/ethnic categories. They remain:

- White (Not Hispanic)
- Black or African American (Not Hispanic)
- Hispanic
- Asian (Not Hispanic) (Including Hawaiian and Other Pacific Islander)
- American Indian, Native American, Alaska Native (Not Hispanic)

 NOTE Any form requesting job applicants or employees to identify their race should conform the choices to the type of EEO report you will have to file.

When an employee fails to self-identify, the employer is responsible for making an observation and best guess as to the race category in which the employee should be reported. If the employee later decides to report their race/ethnicity, that information should be accepted and recorded by the employer.

The government has decided that for tracking and reporting purposes, the Hispanic ethnicity trumps all race categories. That is to say, someone who says they are Hispanic and some other race in addition should be recorded as Hispanic. Race categories are only used for Non-Hispanic individuals.

The invitation to self-identify should also ask for identification of gender/sex either Male or Female. Again, if the individual refuses to self-identify, the employer is obligated to make a selection based on observation.

Veteran and Disabled Status

Federal contractors with $25,000 or more in contract value must abide by regulations related to affirmative action requirements for disabled and veterans. As of 2014, all federal contractors are required to invite self-identification as disabled and veteran from both applicants and employees. When talking about veterans, we mean U.S. veterans. Someone who has served in the armed forces of a foreign country is not included in the government's definition.

The EEOC has determined that it is acceptable to request identification of disability prior to an employment offer being extended as long as the invitation form is the one specified by the Office of Federal Contract Compliance Programs (OFCCP) and it is in an effort to comply with affirmative action obligations. Of course, any request for accommodation during the application process should be handled as required by the Americans with Disabilities Act.

 NOTE There is a new requirement as of March 24, 2014 for federal contractors to invite job applicants to self-identify their disability and veteran status. Then the invitation will be repeated for any new hires.

Each of the four categories of veteran should be clearly identified on the self-ID request form. The applicant or employee should be able to choose from that list. And a brief explanation of each category should be given so the form user can understand what they mean.

The disability identification should be available as a selection, along with an opportunity to request any job accommodation or applicant accommodation that might be desired.

Analysis of Labor Market Data

Labor market data can be used in a couple of important ways within the recruitment process. First, it offers demographics on race and sex that can be used in affirmative action plan preparation. Occupational categories are available in the U.S. Census American Community Survey and each occupational category has a count of sex and race/ethnic representation. There are 488 occupational codes in the 2010 Census. These data are used to create affirmative action benchmarks in computing availability of qualified workers. A visit to the Census Bureau's website can yield a wealth of information.[10]

The second type of labor market data application is in the function of compensation management. Market studies by geography can be very helpful in determining how much money people in designated job titles are earning. That can support both calculation of internal compensation ranges and new hire salary offers.

Diversity Management

Diversity and Inclusion (D&I) are no longer just topics of interest; they are essential components of any large organization's strategic planning process. SHRM has been working with ANSI to develop standards of measurement for Diversity and Inclusion. Those are expected to be released sometime in 2014 or early 2015. They will provide guidance to HR professionals and executives alike. The standards will recognize there are differences among organizations of various size when it comes to resources that can be allocated to diversity and inclusion management. In organizations of any size, however, D&I need to be addressed.

If the foundation of employee management is equal employment opportunity (EEO), and a tool for ensuring organizations meet those EEO obligations is affirmative action, then diversity and inclusion are the next step in ensuring that human contributions come from all sectors of the employee population. D&I is based on the premise that all employees have contributions to offer based on their experiences and that different experience histories can make a collective group of employees more effective in addressing organizational problems, including production and revenue generation.

At the most basic level of D&I program measurement are the demographic comparisons between incumbents and computed availability. Ensuring diversity in employee recruiting programs is another first stage effort. Advanced D&I management will include executive-level diversity (including board of directors membership) and an active focus on D&I in advertising programs and customer appreciation programs. Focus groups, climate surveys, and employee opinion monitoring will all play a role in advanced diversity management. Management training will be essential for the success of serious D&I programs. Managing people from extremely different cultural backgrounds and with different generational representation will be a challenge into the future. In several states currently, there is no racial majority group. All racial groups are in the minority. That means, any employer organization will be required to hire, train, and tap into the various talents and cultural assets of a human pool with multiple levels of sophistication. While it may be human nature to feel most comfortable with people like ourselves, it is going to be more and more necessary to push that comfort boundary and include people unlike ourselves if we are to be successful as an organization.

Measurements and Metrics of Recruitment

Overall there are many measurements that can be applied to human resource management. In fact, many books have been written about the subject. One of particular value is *How to Measure Human Resources Management* by Jac Fitz-enz and Barbara Davison.[11]

Measuring recruiting is valuable because it can tell you the cost of each step in the process as well as the overall cost of a new hire, and knowing costs associated with recruiting can help with budgeting for future staffing requirements. In February 2012, SHRM and ANSI published a formal standard on cost per hire.[12] In its most basic form, this standard is computed by adding the sum of costs for internal hires to the sum of costs for external hires and dividing the result by the number of hires. This can be done for the total organization or for subdivisions of the organization, such as a department. Cost per hire includes the cost of advertising a position, processing responses, interviewing, background checks, necessary medical exams, and processing a new employee onto the payroll and into benefit programs.

Some Ways to Measure Hiring

Other valuable recruitment measurements that can be undertaken include:

- **Response time to obtain a new hire**   How long it takes from the authorization to hire until someone is actually on the payroll. This can be monitored separately for various candidate sources (newspapers, social media, employer website, or other source).

- **Recruiting efficiency**   The amount of time it takes to collect a viable number of qualified candidates, process candidates through interviews, and get people on the payroll. Each can be measured individually and the total can be measured.

- **Quality of hire**   Considerations include the job performance rating of new hires, the percentage of new hires promoted within a year, the percentage of new hires retained after a year, and any number of other possibilities.

- **Employee retention**   Grasps the percentage of new hires that are retained for a year (or any other designated period of time). Retention can be computed in budget terms because the cost per hire can be computed and allow identification of retention costs.

- **Turnover cost**   The opposite of retention, turnover measures the rate of employee loss. It can include unemployment insurance expense, workers' compensation expense, the cost of training a replacement, the cost of recruiting and hiring a new employee, and other factors.

There are a host of possible measurements associated with compensation programs as well (payroll taxes, revenue per employee, employee cost including benefits, net income per employee, average pay per grade, percentage of employees paid over grade maximum, and so forth). There are also measurements for employee training, production tooling, engineering expense, percentage of project cost associated with permits, inspections, and reworking. Almost anything you can observe in a workplace can be measured. Chapter 9 offers an expansion on this topic.

American National Standards Institute (ANSI) Standards for Hiring Metrics

The Society for Human Resource Management (SHRM) has partnered with ANSI to develop and publish many types of measurements for HR management. One set of those standards relating to hiring has been published. It offers methods for measuring cost per hire and a Recruiting Cost Ratio.[13]

Cost Per Hire   This measurement uses external costs and internal costs to determine overall cost per person hired during any given time period. This formula looks at the number of hires and the costs to obtain them. It enables us to derive expenses for each new hire stated as an average.

$$\text{Cost Per Hire} = \left(\frac{\text{(S(External Costs)} + \text{S(Internal Costs))}}{\text{(Total Number of Hires in a Time Period)}} \right)$$

External costs are those expenses such as external agency fees, advertising costs, job fair costs, travel costs, and other similar expenses for the time period being analyzed.

Internal costs are expenses that can include fully loaded salary and benefits of the recruiting team and fixed costs such as physical infrastructure.

$$\text{Cost Per Hire} = \left(\frac{\text{(External Costs} = 100{,}000 + \text{Internal Costs} = \$100{,}000)}{\text{(Total Number of Hires in a Time Period} = 50)} \right)$$

$$\text{Cost Per Hire} = \$4{,}000$$

Recruiting Cost Ratio   This measurement looks at the cost per hire based on compensation rather than headcount.

$$\text{Recruiting Cost Ratio} = \left(\frac{\text{(S(External Costs)} + \text{S(Internal Costs))}}{\text{(Total First-Year Compensation of Hires in a Time Period)}} \times 100 \right)$$

The RCR tells us how much we spent recruiting for every dollar of first-year compensation paid to the new hires.

$$\text{Recruiting Cost Ratio} = \left(\frac{\text{(External Costs} = \$100{,}000 + \text{Internal Costs} = \$100{,}000)}{\text{(Total First-Year Compensation of Hires in a Time Period} = \$2{,}000{,}000)} \times 100 \right)$$

$$\text{RCR} = 10\%$$

Obviously, the lower the percentage, the better (more efficient).

Recruitment Yield Ratio Another measure of recruiting efficiency and effectiveness is the Recruitment Yield Ratio. It can be calculated at each step of the recruiting and hiring process to determine how successful you are at each stage of the process.

- How many people were minimally qualified compared to total responses?
- How many people were sent to the hiring manager compared to minimally qualified?
- How many people were interviewed compared to those sent to the hiring manager?
- How many people were hired compared to those interviewed?
- At each stage, you can compute a ratio or percentage. The greater the percentage, the better.

$$\text{RYR} = \frac{\text{Number of Hires}}{\text{Number of Interviews}}$$

$$\text{RYR} = 3 / 15 = 20\%$$

Achieving a higher ratio (percentage) means your yield is greater for whatever comparative group you are using.

Here is an example:

We have hired 25 new computer programmers. It took an average of four interviews for each new hire. So our Recruitment Yield Ratio is 25 / 4 = 6.25. If we only required an average of three interviews per new hire the RYR would be 25 / 3 = 8.33. The higher our RYR the better. It allows us to recognize that many interviews in the hiring process add to the cost of hiring. Lowering the average number of interviews per new hire will raise our ratio.

The Impact of Compensation and Benefits on Recruitment and Retention

Compensation and benefits are, among other things, tools for recruiting and retaining quality employees. An employer can't hope to recruit top talent unless it is willing to pay a wage or salary that is competitive in the marketplace. Benefits take on a similar role and help with recruiting and retention.

Recall that there are no legal requirements that demand employers provide paid vacation time to employees. Vacation is an invention that comes through either union agreements/contracts or from the need to be competitive in the employment market. Imagine a company trying to hire people today if it did not offer some competitive number of paid vacation days. Not many people would like to work at that place if vacation weren't a part of the employment package. So, by policy, employers offer paid time off to their workers. Other benefit programs that add to the employment enticement package include retirement programs, savings plans, medical benefits, employee cafeterias, employee spas, rest and recovery centers, and pizza Fridays.

All of the benefits can be quantified and their contribution to employment and retention efforts can be computed. There is no doubt that both compensation and benefits are major factors in every employer's efforts to attract and retain talent on its payroll. We discuss compensation and benefits in detail in Chapter 9.

Flexible Staffing

Traditionally, full-time employment was thought of as one of the three 8-hour periods in a workday: 8:00 AM to 5:00 PM, 4:00 PM to 1:00 AM, or 12:00 AM to 9:00 AM. (Each is nine hours long because of a planned meal period of one hour.) These days, we don't have quite the lock-step approach to staffing that used to exist and there are many alternatives to full-time employees.

Temporary Employees

One change to full-time employment is the use of temporary employees. It is not necessary to hire people by putting them on the payroll. Employers can expand their workforce quickly and easily by contracting with temporary talent agencies to satisfy their need for additional people. Temporary workers can be used on production lines, in accounting departments, or any other portion of an organization experiencing a workload that cannot be handled by the permanent staff. Agencies pay their employees, take care of payroll withholding and tax reporting, add a profit margin, and then pass the final rate to the employer contracting for that help.

Job Sharing

Job sharing is an employment technique that you hear about more and more these days. It offers two or more workers the opportunity to collectively constitute one full-time equivalent employee. One person works the job in the morning, and another works the same job in the afternoon. Considerations involve briefing the "job sharing partner" on the current issues to be dealt with during the next portion of work time. There are some financial considerations, too. Each employee will require the employer's full contribution toward Social Security and Medicare. That may cost the employee more than if one person were to occupy the position.

 NOTE Job sharing can increase morale and provide staffing in situations that otherwise might be difficult.

In the Trenches

Mother Nature, the Sherpa of Job Sharing/Telecommuting

In 1989 a catastrophic earthquake, Loma Prieta, hit the San Francisco Bay Area, causing freeways to collapse, modes of public transportation to hiccup, and buildings to be red-tagged as uninhabitable. With all of that disruption, the launch of the era of telecommuting was officially born. Companies were scrambling to figure out how to get business done when key employees were unable to physically make it into the workplace due to lengthy road and bridge closures. The terms telecommuting and job sharing were tossed into the ring as viable options for keeping business moving. It was helpful that San Francisco was in close proximity to the technology capital of the world, Silicon Valley, whose professional and technical types of employees had already been successfully working within the parameters of telecommuting.

Yet this was a time when most other industry organizations were still struggling to get their executive and senior management staff to learn how to dial into bridge/conference lines, let alone use a PC. Many HR professionals turned to the California Telecommuting Pilot Project, which was initially planned in 1985 and began with its pilot in mid-1987 as a resource for help. Though this pilot program had a controlled group of mostly supervisory personnel and individual contributors such as technical staff, nevertheless, it was helpful to review the "how to" on implementing telecommuting. Organizations didn't have the luxury of time to create a well-thought-out project plan, and most were just plain shell-shocked by the events, so the local media was brought into the loop to help spread the option. IT staff were taking laptops to key employee's homes, setting them up with modems, and dialing in to intranet email systems, providing personal one-on-one instructions on the use of keyboard function keys (those were the days prior to a "mouse").

And the story expands from there, because folks were having issues with their own personal matters from the earthquake's aftermath and having to juggle family/home issues while still attending to their careers. That's when the concept of job sharing expanded. In that era, job sharing was mostly for new parents in the workplace whose job capacity was identical to others, such as accounting. With Mother Nature as a catalyst, it caused many more occupations and employees to design the job share to help overcome both the needs of the business and take care of the personal crisis. And eventually, there was no turning back once business as usual resumed and the transportation infrastructure was fixed. Telecommuting and new roles for job sharing were here to stay as the effectiveness and productivity became widespread. HR was quickly developing aligned policies and IT groups geared up for the technology training and hookups.

(Continued)

Today, telecommuting and job sharing have affected almost every aspect of contemporary life, from fundamental job patterns like having to reserve office space (i.e., hoteling) when going into the office, to the physical structure of communities, such as solo home offices and the additions of cable/fiber optics to the suburbs. Interesting how a kick from Mother Nature can cause an idea to explode into reality and the everyday way of now doing work.

Part-Time vs. Full-Time

In addition to contributions toward Social Security and Medicare, there are many financial considerations related to full-time versus part-time workers. Where local employment taxes are based on headcount, part-time workers can cost more than a full-time staff.

Under the Affordable Care Act, employers can escape paying for benefit coverage of some workers if they maintain a part-time status. By policy, other benefit programs may or may not be available to part-time workers. It is not uncommon to have access to IRA or other retirement programs based on the number of hours worked each week. The amount of supervision available can also impact the ratio of full-time to part-time workers.

Project Hires/Contract Labor

Using project hires and contract labor is another alternative to full-time employment. Project hires are people who are recruited and placed on the payroll with the understanding that their employment will be terminated once the project is completed. It is common in organizations that seek out projects from client organizations. A staff is hired for the project and then let go when the project comes to an end.

"Contract labor" refers to people who are hired for a specific period of time. An organization may believe that the workload will last until this time next year. So it contracts with people to handle that workload for the year. At the end of the contract, those folks will come off the payroll, whether or not the project has concluded. They could be "extended" (payroll status maintained) for a designated period of time if the workload has not diminished.

Phased Retirement

As opposed to instant full-time retirement, phased retirement is another alternative to full-time employment, which allows an individual to take partial retirement while continuing to work a reduced schedule. It can take the form of job sharing, part-time, seasonal, temporary, or project work.

NOTE A major advantage of phased retirement is that it allows employees to get used to working less and having more time to themselves. It prevents the sudden shock of not having a work routine that comes with traditional retirement.

Retiree Annuitants

Retiree annuitants are folks who have retired from the organization but are called back to work because of emergencies, unexpected workload, or other unforeseen need. They are defined by the Internal Revenue Service (IRS)[14] as people who are entitled to be drawing benefits from their retirement program while earning compensation from their employer for continuing employment whether or not they are continuing to pay into the retirement program.

Payrolling

When a job needs to be done and the organization does not wish to hire someone onto its own payroll to do that job, an alternative is to contract with a vendor who will hire someone to do the job at the client organization. Contractor payrolling is used when you need to adjust to seasonal fluctuations, fill a vacancy while searching for a permanent replacement, bridge the gap in personnel when there is unexpected growth, or use interns for a set period of time. It has many applications and the greatest benefit is in protecting against charges that the person hired is not an independent contractor but an employee, a problem that cost the company Microsoft just under a hundred million dollars in payroll taxes, penalties, fines, and legal fees. This is usually a process used for less than an entire workforce. When single employees or small groups of employees are needed, payrolling services can solve the need.

Employee Leasing and Professional Employer Organizations (PEOs)

Similar to payrolling, employee leasing is a process of moving employees to another company's payroll as a service for a client organization. Typically, Professional Employer Organizations (PEOs) will take over the entire workforce in a client company. PEOs provide payroll services, tax tracking and depositing, retirement program management, healthcare benefit program management, and even employee counseling and support services. In essence, employee leasing is the outsourcing of the Human Resources department and the payroll function together. Employees usually become employees of both organizations, the client where they perform their work, and the vendor (PEO) that handles the payroll and HR functions for the client. It means both employers are liable for legal compliance.

Outsourcing and Managed Service Providers (MSPs)

Another alternative is outsourcing. Outsourcing is shifting a workload out of the organization through a contract with another employer organization, either here in this country or somewhere else in the world. Managed Service Providers (MSPs) offer to manage functions as part of a strategic decision to move operations or support functions out of an employment organization to a vendor which can perform them less expensively. Such a decision is designed to allow the client company to focus on key activities within its core business while a vendor handles support activities for the client.

Temp-to-Lease Programs

When a need exists for employees on a seasonal basis or for jobs that will last longer than a few days or weeks, it is possible for employers to lease their workers from a vendor organization. The vendor provides the underlying employment relationship with the worker. When temporary needs stretch into longer-term needs, it still may not be wise to increase payroll in the client organization. That's when contracting for temporary agency workers can be converted into long-term employee leases. These workers often have no benefits provided to them. The client organization pays an employment agency a fee in addition to the pay received by the worker assigned to the client. All payroll operations are maintained by the temporary service agency.

Rehires and Transfers

When workloads rise unexpectedly it is sometimes difficult to bring in new hires quickly enough to respond to that increased demand. Rehiring laid-off workers and bringing in transfers from other portions of the organization can sometimes be good solutions. Rehired workers are already trained and can be productive immediately. Transfers from other portions of the organization have the advantage of already knowing the culture, and if coming from similar or identical types of work, can also be productive rather quickly.

Relocation

Moving workers from one location to another outside the normal commute radius requires finding them new living quarters. This can be done on a temporary or permanent basis. If relocation is used to respond to union strikes or increased workload, it will likely be a temporary condition. Employers sometimes rent blocks of rooms in long-term hotel facilities so workers can have cooking and laundry facilities along with living quarters.

Permanent relocation can involve workers selling and buying homes, and packing household belongings and shipping them long distances, sometimes across the country or internationally. There are many variables in such action on the part of the employer. Enticing employees to accept relocation can be a high hurdle to overcome. Forcing the change for a spouse's employment, moving children from one school to another, and accepting a higher cost of living at the new location can require employers to provide financial incentives. Those incentives can include such things as:

- **Home purchase/lease escape fees** Guaranteed purchase of the employee's old home following an appraisal of value. The employee can accept or reject the company's offer if it might be possible to achieve a higher selling price some other way. When there is a fee involved for canceling property leases, employers can pay that fee for employees.

- **Real estate processing fees**   Escrow fees for selling and buying real property can amount to many dollars. Paying these expenses for a relocating employee can lift that burden and remove another objection to relocating.

- **Mortgage subsidy**   In an inflationary economy, mortgage rates rise. It can sometimes be necessary for employers to pay a portion or all of the increased mortgage rate to get an employee to accept relocation.

- **Packing/shipping/unpacking**   Paying the bill for a moving company to pack, ship, and unpack at the destination is another way to relieve employees of financial burden.

- **Funds for taxes on increased taxable income**   When there are income tax consequences for employees as a result of a relocation, employers sometimes compute a "tax obligation roll-up" and pay that to the employee in a lump sum as withholdings.

Selection

"Pick me. Pick me!" Employment selection is a competition of talent identification. It is rare for someone to walk into a business and ask for a job and then to be hired on the spot. Although it might still happen in small employer organizations, more typically, selection is a multiple-step process. It can involve, as we discussed earlier in this chapter, an initial application and/or resume, telephone interview, written testing, in-person interview (perhaps several), a team interview (panel interview), background check, job offer, and post-offer physical exam. Then, there is usually a probationary period that is now more often called a *training period* or *initial job experience*.

Selection Systems

There is a host of possible selection systems. Pick every sixth person on the list, presuming all on the list meet the basic qualifications of the job. Pick the tenth person, without any further consideration or screening. Pick the first person to respond. These are all valid selection processes, and they are nondiscriminatory. They don't, however, offer much in the way of screening or filtering for nuances of skills and abilities.

Quantitative Selection Systems

How often have you heard operations managers say, "I want to pick my own people." Usually, what they are saying is, "I want to be sure the chemistry is right and that I can work with the person who is selected."

Quantitative selection systems are those that use numerical performance levels and allow for specific numerical cut-offs as qualification thresholds. Written paper and pencil tests are the easiest example. Giving a test involving true-false or multiple choice answers permits scoring the test by the number of correct responses. The raw number of right answers can be used, or it can be converted into a rate or percentage. The percentage of 76 correct out of 134 questions is 57 percent. If the "pass" level was initially set at 66 percent, this person would not have passed the written test.

NOTE The PHR/SPHR exam is another example of a quantitative selection system. Only those with a passing score will be awarded the certification.

Subjective Selection Systems

How often have you heard someone say, "I'll know it when I see it, but it can't be measured…it's too subjective." Of course, that's nonsense. Anything can be measured. Things such as behaviors and accomplishments can be measured in relation to other things, similar or not. Behaviors are what we say and do. Behaviors can be measured along a scale that is created just to measure those behaviors or their characteristics. Think of measuring the amount of leadership someone demonstrates. Or measuring the amount of communication skill they can display. Behaviors can be measured against a standard or norm and a person can be determined to have less or more of that behavior than the norm. Consider a measurement of inner work standards. A furniture painter with exceptionally high inner work standards compared to a typical furniture painter is a person who paints the top of the top shelf and the bottom of the bottom shelf, even if no one will ever see those surfaces.

Teachers and instructors are perfect examples of people who perform jobs that some folks think would be difficult to measure. It's not so. Giving it a little thought, you will discover that the behaviors of good teachers can be thought of as the norm or standard you would like all teachers to "measure up to." Then it is only necessary to identify the specific behaviors you would like to measure in teachers. Here are some examples:[15]

- **Skills**   Verbal, interpersonal, leadership, reading, organizing and planning, platform skills, decision making, analytical, problem solving, feedback, questioning, writing, management of diverse groups

- **Knowledge**   Subject matter, organization, adult learning needs, trainee group

- **Qualifications**   Educational degree, license, certification, train-the-trainer course

- **Experience**   Technical, training, supervisory, management, operations or staff

- **Characteristics**   Energy, enthusiasm, commitment, integrity, self-objectivity

Pick any of those on the list and you will be able to create a measurement for it. For example, let's choose "leadership." First we must define what the term means related to the job at hand. So, we will say, "Leadership is the ability to get other people to willingly follow suggestions." Now, we can create a scale on which we can measure the amount of "leadership" each instructor demonstrates. It might look like Figure 5-3.

"N" is the amount of leadership seen in the person being referenced as the norm. "X" is the amount of leadership being seen in the person being evaluated against the norm.

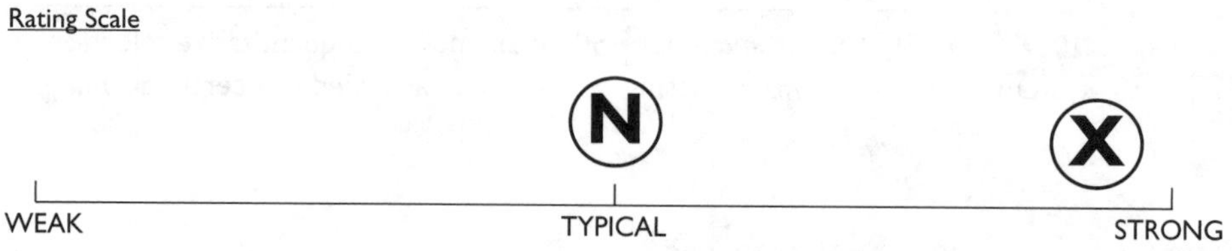

Rating Scale

WEAK   TYPICAL   STRONG

Shows all possible amounts of leadership skills from weak to strong. The N is the norm. It represents the amount of leadership skills observed in the person or group of successful individuals who are at the same job level as the incumbent being rated. X represents the incumbent's amount of leadership skills observed.

Figure 5-3 The amount of leadership observed

Measuring performance in HR functions can be done in the same way. Consider the "norm" for each behavior, characteristic, skill, or knowledge to be "What you would expect to see in someone performing the job successfully." Not the best ever. Not what just gets by. But what you expect to see in a successful performer.

Criteria for Selection

Before beginning the actual selection process, criteria for selection should be determined. This criteria should measure the degree to which a candidate possesses the job qualifications listed in the job description. Lack of a college degree may be a problem, or it may be compensated for by demonstration of specific experience on identified duties and responsibilities. Criteria might specify the degree of physical involvement required by citing how heavy the materials are that must be lifted and carried a specified number of times during a work shift. Mental criteria could include certain mathematical abilities, literacy achievements, or speaking ability. Demonstrated leadership skills could also constitute a job selection criterion.

Whatever is listed as a basic requirement must be demonstrated by any person selected for the position. Selecting someone who does not have a required qualification invalidates the job requirements and could entirely invalidate the employer's selection process. Care should be taken to be sure the basic qualifications are actually required and that no one is selected who does not have all of them.

Employment Testing

Proper testing is conducted by using validated selection tools. That was explained earlier in this chapter. Be sure to understand the various types of validation studies that can be used under the Uniform Guidelines on Employee Selection Procedures.

In addition to testing, interviewing is an important part of the selection process. A large portion of the workforce is hired only after one or more interviews with the prospective employer. There are several primary types of interviews employers can select from.

Structured

An interviewer asks every applicant the same questions along with follow-up probes that may be different depending on the initial response. Structured interviews make it possible to gather similar information from all candidates.

Patterned

In the patterned interview, sometimes called a targeted interview, an interviewer asks each applicant questions that are from the same knowledge, skill, or ability (KSA) area; however, the questions are not necessarily the same. They differ depending on the candidate's background. For example, questions asked of a recent college graduate may differ from those asked of a candidate with years of related experience.

Stress

In this type of interview, an interviewer creates an aggressive posture—in other words, deliberately creating some type of stress to see how the candidate reacts to stressful situations. For example, using a room where the candidate has to face an open window with the sun in his or her eyes can put the candidate under stress. This type of interview is used more often in law enforcement, air traffic control, and similar high-stress occupations. The stress interview was more common in the '70s and '80s. Today, it is not recommended due to the likelihood that it will be interpreted as personal bias.

Directive

In this type of interview, an interviewer poses specific questions to the candidate, maintaining tight control; it is a highly structured interview. Every candidate is asked exactly the same questions.

Nondirective

In this type of interview, the interviewer asks open-ended questions and provides only general direction; the interviewer allows the candidate to guide the process. A response to one question dictates what the next question will be.

Behavioral

In a behavioral interview, an interviewer focuses on how the applicant previously handled actual situations (real, not hypothetical). The interviewer probes very specific situations looking for past behaviors and how the applicant handled those experiences. The questions probe the knowledge, skills, abilities, and other personal characteristics identified as essential to success on the job. The interviewer looks for three things; a description of an actual situation or task, the action taken, and the result or outcome. The principle behind behavioral interviewing is that past performance is the best predictor of future performance.

Situational

In a situational interview, the interviewer elicits stories and examples that illustrate the applicant's skills and qualifications for the job. Situational interviewing is similar to behavioral interviewing; the only difference is that in a behavioral interview, the interviewer is probing for actual past experiences, whereas in a situational interview, the interviewer develops hypothetical situations and asks the applicant how he or she would handle them.

Group

Group interviews happen when multiple job candidates are interviewed by one or more interviewers at the same time. Group interviews are used in specific situations where a number of candidates are being considered for the same job in which the duties are limited and clearly defined, such as a merry-go-round operator. A *fishbowl interview* brings multiple candidates together to work with each other in an actual group activity or exercise. It is similar to an in-basket exercise except it involves a group of candidates. A *team interview* typically involves a group of interviewers with a perspective of the actual interactions associated with the job. This might include supervisors, subordinates, peers, customers, and so on. It is like a 360° exercise. Finally, in a *panel interview*, questions are distributed among a group of interviewers, typically, those most qualified in a particular area. At the conclusion of the panel interview, the panel caucuses with the purpose of coming to a group consensus regarding the result.

NOTE Panels can be structured or unstructured. In the public sector, consistency is often a key factor in selection decisions, so structured interviews are conducted by panels.

Panel members will sometimes ask the same question of each candidate, and sometimes the panel members will alternate their selection of questions to be asked. Panel size also varies from two to something more. It is common to see panels composed of three to four individuals. Because this is an expensive approach to interviewing (it requires multiple people to spend their time) it is usually reserved for professional and managerial job selections.

Job Accommodation Requests

An accommodation request can come to an employer from either a job applicant or an employee. An applicant may find it necessary for someone to read test questions to him or her to accommodate a vision limitation. An employee may find it helpful to have a standing desk because of sitting restrictions.

There is a specific protocol for handling a request for job or applicant accommodation. This protocol has been developed by the Equal Employment Opportunity Commission (EEOC) and is available online at the EEOC website.[16] It is labeled "Enforcement Guidance" and should be followed.

Request

A request for job accommodation can be either written or oral. It can come from either a job applicant or employee. A legitimate request for accommodation could also come from a family member, friend, or medical professional.

Documentation of Disability Requiring Accommodation

Employers are permitted to request medical documentation that explains the individual disability and how a job accommodation could make it possible for the individual to continue performing the job's essential functions. That might include asking the employee or applicant to go to an appropriate medical professional, selected by the employer, so that an evaluation of the disability can be made.

Interactive Discussion About Request

The employer is required to enter into an interactive discussion with the applicant or employee about the specific request. This is the time for an employer to present any alternative accommodations it has determined would work as well but cost less or interfere with work performance less. When a job accommodation request would cause a violation of work rules under a union contract (Memorandum of Understanding), in most cases, the labor agreement will prevail and the requested accommodation will not work out—for example, an accommodation that requests day shift assignment only, when the union agreement specifies rotation of shift assignments based on seniority.

Decision About Accommodation and Implementation

It is sometimes difficult to explain a job accommodation to the rest of the workforce. Disability information is confidential under HIPAA and the ADA (see Chapter 2). Therefore, details of the disability and reasons for the accommodation should not be discussed with other workers. Managers and supervisors, with counsel from their HR staff, should let coworkers know that a job accommodation has been made in response to a request from the employee. That's about as far as you can go without getting into trouble with the privacy requirements.

The process of job accommodation involves an interactive process of discussion between the employer and the employee making the accommodation request. The content of those discussions should be documented to act as evidence that the employer met its obligations to participate in the interactive process. Whatever decision is made should also be documented with reasons for that decision.

Documentation of Selection Decisions

Once you've gone through testing and interviewing, you have a decision to make. All employment decisions should be documented, none more so than those that involve hiring and termination. All notes made about the reasons for selecting one candidate over another are subject to the retention requirements for holding documentation up to two years beyond the decision.

Documentation about interviews and hiring decisions should:

- Be factual
- Contain job-related information only
- Not contain opinions or personal biases

Marginal notes on resumes should not contain comments about age, disability, race, or other protected category. As surprising as it seems, there are still interviewing supervisors who write things such as "This one is too fat!" "She's way too old for the job," "Customers will never accept an Asian." It is OK for marginal comments to contain notes about how resume content relates to job requirements.

The Selection Approval Process

Each organization has its own structure of approving authorities. That is usually controlled by the Accounting Department. Those structures tell what management level is authorized to approve expenditures of given amounts, approve the hiring of people at given job levels, and so forth. Policies are established based on those structures. Authority to hire is closely related to authority to spend money. Sometimes there are multiple steps in the authorization process. First, the budget must contain authorization for the Full Time Equivalent (FTE) position. Then, there must be authorization to fill the position. And, finally, there must be authorization to hire a specific individual to fill that job. Small organizations have fewer steps, larger organizations can have more steps in the process. Before making a job offer, be sure you have the approval of your "hiring authority" to do so.

Employment Policies, Practices, and Procedures

Employment policies, practices, and procedures all impact selection efforts. An employer with a policy requiring all hiring decisions to be approved by executives at a certain authority level in the organization wants definite budget control over the hiring process. A staffing practice that says a job opening may not be advertised outside the organization until internal postings have lasted for at least three days gives existing employees "first chance" at any new opportunities. A procedure requiring at least two in-person interviews will have an impact on budget because it involves two or more interviewers and it may cost money to bring a candidate in from out of town. All of these organizational preferences have consequences. Those consequences can be financial, production impacts, government compliance issues, or morale-related. It is up to the HR professionals to analyze them all and make senior management aware of those consequences so they may consider them before approving any changes.

Negotiation Skills and Techniques

When you are ready to make an offer, first identify the outcomes you want to achieve from the process. It might be as simple as "hiring the best candidate for an amount of money that doesn't break the budget." Before a written offer is made, then, the amount of compensation should be discussed and agreed on by both you and the candidate. You explain what amount is offered, and the candidate accepts or explains that more is wanted. If you have more to give without violating some equal pay circumstance, then make the enhanced offer. Other points of negotiation can include: hours of work, frequency of shift changes, work location assignment(s), travel requirements, bonus provisions, criteria for performance, and stock awards.

> **NOTE** The best negotiators are those who make it seem like a common conversation rather than a championship boxing match.

Employment Offers

Once the candidate has accepted all the job conditions that you have explained, it is time to put the offer in writing. The offer letter will detail the compensation, start date, job title, organization, and immediate supervisor. You should have a signature block at the bottom of the letter for the candidate to sign as acceptance of the terms. One copy should be returned to you with the signature.

> **NOTE** It is wise to attach a copy of the job description to the offer letter.

Employment Reference Checks, Background Checks, and Credit Reports

Job offers are often conditioned upon successful completion of background checks, reference checks, and sometimes even credit checks. In some instances, a job offer could be conditioned on passing a medical evaluation or a drug screen.

Before conducting background checks or credit checks, review the current legal limitations on their use. The EEOC has issued guidelines on consideration of conviction records because the population of convicted felons is so heavily skewed with Blacks and Hispanics. Considering conviction records has a disparate impact on those two racial groups.[17] Thus, only if the conviction has a direct relationship to the job content will considering it in the hiring decision be permitted by the EEOC.[18]

New Employee Orientation

It is a common belief that the first 90 days of a worker's experience on a new job will determine how the relationship goes for the balance of her/his employment. One way to get off on the right foot is to provide a quality orientation program (also referred to as onboarding) to every new employee.

A strong orientation program will include such things as:

- **Welcome by the CEO/senior executive**   Providing evidence that senior management cares about employees can begin during orientation. Senior executives who believe it isn't worth their time convey a strong message also.

- **Discussion about culture**   An opportunity to discuss "the way we do things around here." What does the employer value? What gets rewarded in the organization? What type of image does the employer want to project to the world? What are expectations of ethics?

- **Enrollment in benefit programs**   An opportunity to complete payroll tax forms, benefit enrollment forms, and self-identification forms for race, sex, disability, and veteran status.

- **Tour of employee common areas**   This can include the cafeteria or break room, the location for labor law compliance posters, and restrooms.

- **Safety equipment and emergency exits**   This is often overlooked when it should be on the orientation agenda. If there are emergency breathing apparatus, eye wash stations, emergency shutdown switches, first aid stations, or other important safety points of interest, this is the time to show each new worker where they are. Safety training in how to use emergency equipment will come later.

- **Introduction to coworkers and supervisors**   Guide the employees to their new work locations and introduce them to their new coworkers and supervisors, even if they may have met some of them during the interviewing process. Have someone designated to explain where to get office supplies, how to access computer terminals, and whom to ask when questions come up. These things are just common employment courtesy.

Retention

Once you've hired a new employee, you want to keep them. Retention is the collection of programs and techniques that result in good employees staying on the job. Retaining employees means the employer does not have to undertake the expenses involved with recruiting, hiring, and training new workers.

Management Training

Few things can irritate employees more quickly than poor supervision and management. Employers must allocate budget to management skills training so their supervisors and managers are competent and capable in their jobs. These skills include:

- **Interpersonal skills**   Including social and situational perception, questioning techniques, and empathy skills

- **Leadership skills**   The ability to get people to follow willingly and produce desired results

- **Decision-making skills**   Both the willingness to make decisions and the quality of those decisions (will they work?)

- **Communication skills**   Both oral and written communication skills

The higher a manager or supervisor scores on these skill scales, the stronger will be their performance effectiveness on the job. Management and supervisory training is a constant ongoing learning throughout a management person's career. Measurement of skill effectiveness should include feedback instruments such as 360-degree evaluations that superiors, peers, and subordinates complete. They are designed to assist with identifying where skill development efforts should be focused.

Rewards

Human beings do things for rewards. Those rewards may be monetary, altruistic, or physiological. If we hunt for food and bring home a game animal or fish, bagging what we hunt is reward for the effort that went into hunting. If we hold the door open for someone and get a "Thank you" for our kindness, we have been rewarded. Absence of a "Thank you" can also be said to be a reward (negative), just not the kind we would prefer.

Monetary Rewards

Money is one way to reward people. In an employment context it is a common reward. A paycheck is reward for having spent hours working during the pay period. Bonus checks are rewards for extra contributions or participation in a winning team effort. According to studies done by industrial psychologists such as Herzberg and McGregor, money is a motivator for employees but it does not have a very long life as a motivator. As soon as we get used to our new earnings level, we begin the cycle again and want more.

Non-monetary Rewards

There are countless ways to reward employees that don't involve cash. Some of them are:

- **Gift certificates**   For shopping, a dinner out, or a movie and popcorn

- **Recognition**   Employee of the Week (Month or Year), plaques, certificates, use of special parking spaces, or use of a private elevator

- **Awards**   Jackets with the company logo, clocks, watches, or a week in Hawaii

- **Time off**   An extra vacation day, floating holiday, or the first Friday of every month in the next calendar quarter

What is important with the intended recognition of non-monetary rewards is that they are selected with the recipient in mind in terms of what he or she would value.

Metrics and Measurements for Retention

There are many measurements used in monitoring human resources effectiveness. Production organizations measure units per hour and accidents per quarter. Human resources professionals measure things such as retention rates, recruiting costs, BIS (butts in seats), and termination rates. HR professionals are also interested in demographic targets in measuring affirmative action plan effectiveness and average recruiting days required for placement. Any activity can be measured and, once measured, targets set for achievement.

Organizational Exit

Everyone will eventually leave an employer. The question isn't "If?" but "How?" Some departures are voluntary; some are involuntary. Some are performance related and some are for retirement. Sadly, people also become disabled and die. HR is involved with all of them in one way or another.

Involuntary Separations

People sometimes have their employment status terminated despite not wanting to lose their job. Individual separations can happen because of performance deficiencies. They can happen because of an employee's inability to maintain a satisfactory attendance record.

When work goes away, however, both individuals and groups of people can be affected at once. If no work is available for which they are qualified, employees are usually laid off. The absence of work in the Engineering department can result in the loss of one Full Time Equivalent (FTE) position. At the same time, the loss of a customer contract can result in a need for many fewer delivery drivers. The term "reduction in force" (RIF) is used to describe both circumstances. It represents a cutback in employee headcount. See the following section, "Reductions in Force (RIF)."

Sometimes those layoffs happen with a "separation allowance" based on length of service or the boss's largesse. Sometimes there is no financial benefit provided to laid-off employees.

Involuntary separations are governed by union contracts where they exist. Nearly always, when unions are involved, separations are determined based on inverse seniority for people in the affected work groups. Seniority lists are sometimes used even when there are no unions representing workers. Determinations can be made based on performance evaluation ratings, area of specialty or expertise, or the length of time employees have been in the workgroup.

Reductions in Force (RIF)

When workloads fall, sales take a tumble, or contracts are canceled, staffing needs suddenly shift. It is sometimes necessary to reduce force by large amounts which will involve layoffs.

A RIF can happen to one person or to a group of people. Outsourcing functions performed by our jobs can reduce the need for employees. When the job goes away and there is no more work to be done in that function, the individual is removed from the payroll as a reduction in force.

If the entire painting function is subcontracted out to a vendor who can do it cheaper, the group of painters who used to do that work in-house will be surplus employees and subject to a reduction in force.

HR professionals should be particularly careful to avoid removing individuals from the payroll claiming a RIF when the real reason for payroll separation is performance deficiency. That type of action can cause complaints of illegal discrimination. When the RIF is pretext for discrimination, nobody wins.

You already know that state and federal laws come into play when groups of people are going to be separated from the payroll at a single location. Chapter 2 has information about the *WARN Act* (Worker Adjustment and Retraining Notification Act), which governs layoffs for employers with 100 or more workers.

Needless to say, the determination of who gets a separation notice should not be based on any protected category membership. It is even advisable to forecast who will be separated and conduct some disparity analyses to determine if any protected group (people over 40 years old, women, disabled, and so on) will be experiencing higher than acceptable rates of separation.

COBRA qualifying events are the triggers for making COBRA benefits available to employees. The type of qualifying event will dictate the maximum number of months the employee may retain coverage of health insurance using COBRA. Table 5-7 provides an easy reference about COBRA availability periods; this information has a high probability of showing up on the PHR/SPHR exams.

COBRA coverage gives employees the right to continue health insurance coverage by paying 100 percent of the premiums required for the coverage. How much of the premium was paid by the employer prior to the qualifying event is irrelevant in computing

Qualifying Event	Minimum Required Duration of COBRA Availability to Employee
Termination of employment (voluntary or involuntary)	18 months for coverage of employee, spouse, and dependent child
Reduction in work hours	18 months for coverage of employee, spouse, and dependent child
Employee's Medicare entitlement begins	36 months for coverage of spouse and dependent child
Divorce or separation (of employee and spouse)	36 months for coverage of spouse and dependent child
Death of employee	36 months for coverage of spouse and dependent child
Loss of dependent child status	36 months for former dependent child
Qualified disabled beneficiaries (those disabled within the first 60 days of COBRA coverage become eligible for an additional 11 months of coverage in addition to the basic 18 months)	29 months total for disabled person

Table 5-7 COBRA Coverage Provisions

the amount of COBRA cost to the employee. Unless the employer offers to voluntarily pay for a portion of COBRA premiums, the employee is obliged to assume all of the cost of continued health plan coverage. COBRA just means the coverage may not be taken away during the entitlement period if the employee wishes to pay for continuation.

Voluntary Separations

Under some circumstances, people willingly leave the payroll. This can happen if an employee receives a better job offer, the employee's spouse gets a job out of town, the employee must relocate because of their child's health, or the employee has finally made it to retirement. Sometimes voluntary resignations can be predicted. Sometimes they cannot. It is up to HR to react appropriately to the staffing need left by a resignation.

Another consideration is the Older Workers Benefit Protection Act (OWBPA), which is an amendment to the Age Discrimination in Employment Act (ADEA). Please refer to Chapter 2 for more detailed information about each of these laws.

During large workforce reductions it is common for "separation packages" to be offered to certain qualifying groups of employees as an enticement that can prevent involuntary reductions. These enticement packages can include cash incentives based on length of service, additional retirement benefits, continuing health benefits, and about anything else you can imagine. If enough employees accept the offered separation packages, then involuntary layoffs can be cut back. Ideally, the headcount reduction goal can be met by voluntary means and no layoffs will be required. Separation packages are normally accompanied by a waiver that asks employees to waive their rights to sue the company or file discrimination complaints in exchange for the separation payment.

The OWBPA requires that voluntary waivers of rights or claims under the ADEA are valid only when they are "knowingly and voluntarily" made. OWBPA requires:

- The waivers must be in writing and signed.
- The employee must receive severance payment(s) or something else of value they would not otherwise receive.
- The employee must be advised in writing to consult an attorney before signing the waiver.
- The employee must be given 21 days to consider the terms (45 days if more than one employee) and be able to revoke the agreement for up to 7 days after.
- Employees must be given (when more than one employee) certain disclosure information designed to allow the employee or his/her attorney to determine if the terminations will have an adverse impact on older workers.

Exit Interviews

An exit interviews is a tool used to seek feedback from employees who are leaving the payroll. There are times when employees resign unexpectedly and the employer would like to know why that happened. Exit interviews are the tool to help discover those things.

Often, exit interviews seek information and opinions from the departing employee about supervision or management. How did they feel they were treated? What would they like to have had their supervisor or manager do differently? How were the working conditions? What did they think about their coworkers? Did they feel appreciated on the job for their work? Almost anything is "fair game" for probing and discovery.

Unfortunately, not every departing employee will be willing to participate in an exit interview. It is up to HR to try to convince an employee that it will help the organization get better.

Employee Records Management

Records are critical for any organization with employees. With the advent of privacy legislation, and many mandatory records retention requirements, employers are today faced with an array of compliance requirements. It is important to know what records must be made, and equally important to understand when to destroy those records.

Employment Authorization (Form I-9)

The Immigration Reform and Control Act of 1986 (see Chapter 2) introduced the requirement for all employees in the United States to provide proof of identity and proof that they have the legal right to work in this country. That law brought us the Form I-9. Every person hired after November 30, 1986, must furnish information on a Form I-9, and the employer must complete the document citing the specific identification presented by the new worker. The employer must also cite the document used to prove the new employee has authorization to work in this country. This form changes from time to time, so employers should visit www.uscis.gov/files/form/i-9.pdf to be sure they are using the most current version of the form.

- **Proof of identity** Also required for employment is a photo identification of some variety, issued by a governmental agency that contains the individual's name as well as a current or recent image. This can be a U.S. passport (Passport Book or Passport Card), or in most cases, a driver's license issued by the state in which the person lives. All states will issue a non-driver identification card if requested to do so. A list of acceptable documents is included on the instructions for Form I-9.

- **Proof of work authorization** A Social Security Card number is the usual form of authorization offered by new employees. It does not provide proof of identity because it does not have a photo of the card owner, but it does offer proof that the owner is authorized to work in this country. Documents accepted for work authorization include visas of various types, and any other form specified on the instructions for Form I-9. Refer to Chapter 2 for a detailed outline of Visa types related to employment.

Employers have three workdays from the time of hire to complete the Form I-9 and have it ready for inspection by any authorized federal investigator. If, at the end of three days, the employee has not provided the required documentation, the employer is instructed to remove the worker from the payroll. Retaining someone who is not properly documented will represent a violation of the federal law. There are fines of up to $1,000 per error on Form I-9 and court-imposed fines for retaining illegal aliens on the payroll.

E-Verify System

E-Verify began life as a voluntary program offered by the government as a way for employers to get online verification of new employee's Social Security numbers. It has evolved into a combination voluntary/involuntary program as federal and state governments mandate portions of the employer community to participate. The program was intended to reduce the number of false positives received when the Social Security Administration was checking new hire reports for invalid Social Security number matches.

The Department of Labor now requires federal contractors who are subject to the affirmative action regulations to participate in E-Verify. And, as time has passed, the accuracy of the Social Security number database has improved.

As of August 2013, nine states require all employers to participate in the E-Verify program. There is pending legislation in eleven additional states that would require some or all employers to participate in the program. In addition to that, there are many states that require state agencies to participate in the program, and some local jurisdictions that have their own requirements. The message here is that HR professionals should check their local and state requirements frequently so they remain in compliance.

Employee Files

There are three reasons why proper record keeping is a requirement for employers. First, it simply makes good business sense to have accurate information handy and organized when you want to use it. Second, most business owners and managers will eventually encounter the need to produce documentation about employee performance and work history. Having the proper records to retrieve is vital when the need presents itself. Third, some employee records are required by federal or state governments and must be kept somewhere. Organizing them by employee name makes access easy.

There are some important cautions to be given about the subject of identifiable employee information. Generally, state laws permit employees the right to examine their personal employment records. This simply allows individuals the opportunity to confirm information in the file and identify any specific information that is believed to be incorrect. Employees are not universally guaranteed the right to copies of all file contents, however. As the employer, you usually have the right to control the time and location of these examinations as long as you are reasonable in doing so. The objective, of course, is to ensure accuracy of information about each person. In most states, ownership of the personnel file and its contents rests with the employer who maintains it.

Access to information about employees should be strictly limited to those people in your business with a need to use the information in their jobs. Many states are aggressive protectors of employee privacy and random or unauthorized access to personnel files can bring on severe penalties. Make sure that you store personnel files in a secure location and that they are not left unattended even during the business day. When asked by people outside the company to provide "verification" of certain employment information about your employees, make it a practice to confirm only the information your employees have authorized you to release. Employment verifications are usually required to support such things as mortgage applications, credit applications, and the like. Employee authorization should be in writing and specify the information they wish you to reveal. Tell your employee the policy is designed for his/her protection.

Job applicants may not have decisions about their applications made based on protected categories such as race, color, sex, religion, national origin, and so on. Therefore, having any information on the application that identifies these categories is inappropriate and may be considered illegal. It is permissible, and for some employers required, to request demographic data from job applicants. This information is directed to a location separate from the hiring manager, however, to avoid even the suspicion of discrimination.

For employees (someone you have put on your payroll), it is necessary to have information in the personnel file that would be considered illegal to gather prior to the job offer being made. For example, you need a birth date to enroll your employee in health insurance and life insurance programs. As long as such information is used for legitimate purposes, employers will have no problem (see Chapter 2).

Personnel File

A "personnel file" is often a collection of record files maintained by various people in various locations. The central file is usually maintained by the HR department. However, additional employee records could be located in the training department, the labor relations department, and in the desk of the immediate supervisor. Each of these files contains different information, yet they all comprise personnel records. Taken together, they represent the "personnel file."

The following should be in a personnel file when circumstances require them:

Employment

- Request for application
- Employee's original employment application
- Prescreening application notes
- College recruiting interview report form
- Employment interview report form
- Education verification
- Employment verification
- Other background verification
- Rejection letter
- Employment offer letter

- Employment agency agreement if hired through an agency
- Employee Handbook acknowledgment form showing receipt of Handbook
- Checklist from new employee orientation showing subjects covered
- Veterans/Disabled self-identification form
- Transfer requests
- Relocation offer records
- Relocation report
- Security clearance status

Payroll

- W-4 form
- Weekly time sheets
- Individual attendance record
- Pay advance request record

- Garnishment orders and records
- Authorization for release of private information
- Authorization for all other payroll actions

Performance Appraisals

- New employee progress reports
- Performance appraisal forms

- Performance improvement program records

Training and Development

- Training history records
- Training program applications/requests
- Skills inventory questionnaire

- Training evaluation forms
- In-house training notification letters
- Training expense reimbursement records

Employee Separations

- Exit interview form
- Final employee performance appraisal

- Exit interviewer's comment form
- Record of documents given with final paycheck

Benefits

- Emergency Contact form
- Medical/Dental/Vision coverage waiver/drop form
- Vacation accrual/taken form
- Request for non-medical leave of absence
- Retirement application
- Payroll deduction authorizations
- COBRA notification/election

- Hazardous substance notification and or reports
- Tuition reimbursement application and or payment records
- Employer concession and or discount authorization
- Annual benefits statement acknowledgment
- Safety training/meeting attendance/summary forms

Wage/Salary Administration

- Job description form
- Job analysis questionnaire
- Payroll authorization form
- Fair Labor Standards Act exemption test

- Compensation history record
- Compensation recommendations
- Notification of wage and/or salary increase/decrease

Employee Relations

- Report of coaching/counseling session
- Employee Assistance Program consent form
- Commendations
- Employee written warning notice
- Completed employee suggestion forms
- Suggestion status reports

The following should *not* be in a personnel file:

Medical Records

- Physician records of examination
- Diagnostic records
- Laboratory test records
- Drug screening records
- Any of the records listed previously in the discussion on HIPAA
- Any other medical records with personally identifiable information about individual employees

Investigation Records

- Discrimination complaint investigation information
- Legal case data
- Accusations of policy/legal violations

Security Clearance Investigation Records

- Background investigation information
- Personal credit history
- Personal criminal conviction history
- Arrest records

The following should *never* be in a personnel file:

Insupportable Opinions

- Marginal notes on any document indicating management bias or discrimination (for example: comments about an applicant's race, sex, age, disability, national origin, or other protected class membership)

Medical File

The federal Health Insurance Portability and Accountability Act of 1996, (HIPAA) requires employers and health care providers to protect medical records as confidential, separate, and apart from other business records. That means you may no longer retain medical information in a personnel file. Here are some examples of information you should extract from your personnel files and place in separately protected files as medical information:

- Health insurance application form
- Life insurance application form

- Request for medical leave of absence regardless of reason
- Personal accident reports
- Workers' compensation report of injury or illness
- OSHA injury and illness reports
- Any other form or document that contains private medical information for a specific employee

Questions about employee access to review their personnel file come up frequently. Each employer should have a policy addressing such questions that complies with state requirements. Federal law does not address the question. Government employees and private sector employers are usually controlled by state laws. So, multi-state employers must comply with requirements in all of the states in which they operate.

Investigation File

Any time a complaint is lodged or law enforcement agencies get involved with individual employees, it may be necessary to conduct an investigation of facts. Each time that happens, a written record should be created that documents what investigative steps were taken and what resulted from them. Complaints of illegal employment discrimination are a good example.

These files will have specific employee-identifiable information that may be of a very sensitive personal nature. Facts may involve criminal activity or behavior that could result in civil action. For the sake of privacy, each investigation file should be held under the same security provisions as are medical records. Only those people having a need to access the content of the files should be allowed access. Records should be secured at all times so passersby cannot pull open a file drawer and remove documents.

Documentation Techniques and Guidelines

There are many reasons for creating documentation. Often, conversations with employees are held to provide feedback on job performance, or about behavioral problems that have led to disciplinary decisions. Other types of documentation relate to projects, proposals, or other employment issues. Whatever the reason for creating documentation, it should contain answers to these questions:

- Who
- What
- When
- Where
- Why (if employee discussions provide this information)

Documentation should not include guesses, suppositions, assumptions, or other nonfactual information. Opinions only belong in documentation if they are labeled as opinions. They should never be unlabeled and presented as facts. Documentation should contain a date identifying when it was created, and a name to indicate who created it. If a document is created some time after the event it describes, it should be dated on the day it was created, not pre-dated to the time of the event.

Documentation of employee conversations does not ordinarily need to be signed by the employee. Exceptions to that include requirements of union agreements or employer policy to the contrary. Remember to follow the basic rule that any time an employee signs a document of any type, a copy of that signed document should be given to the employee. It is a requirement in some states that those copies be provided. Otherwise, depending again on your legal jurisdiction, documents about employee conversations can be considered the property of the employer.

Retention Requirements

As with many HR issues, retention requirements do change from time to time. Be sure you confirm the requirements for your situation before destroying any records. Because these requirements are fluid in nature, we suggest you confirm your specific needs through discussion with your management attorney or by checking on the Internet for guidance. Be careful about relying on the Internet without knowing your source, however. You still have the responsibility and the liability for proper records retention even if you get bad advice from an Internet source.

Some possible sources include:

- www.management-advantage.com/products/retainrecords.htm
- https://www.shrm.org/templatestools/samples/documents/federal%20 record%20retention%20chart%20-%20revision%20by%20regan%208-12.doc
- www.shrm.org/LegalIssues/StateandLocalResources/StateandLocalStatutesand Regulations/Documents/Recordkeeping-access%20to%20files.pdf
- http://nctc.fws.gov/courses/references/job-aids/supervisors/suprefdocs/ documents/FederalRecordRetentionGuidelines.pdf
- www.nationalscanning.com/document-retention-guidelines.html

Records Destruction

Once a record has reached its expiration date (been retained for the period required by law), it should be destroyed. Destruction is something that should be done by shredding so that records cannot be reconstructed by someone rifling through the trash bin.

There are commercial records storage and destruction companies almost everywhere in the United States. For a fee, they will come to your work site, collect the records you wish to have destroyed, and either shred them in their truck while at your location, or take them back to a central location where the documents will be shredded. Some specialize in certain industries such as medical record shredding services.

Employee Skill Sets Database

Another set of records that is important to employee management is a database of employee skill sets. Such a database will reflect the employee skills you can draw upon when searching for promotable workers and in planning your succession for executive positions. Consider making a survey of your workforce, asking each person to identify the skills they have that apply to your organization's needs. This type of database will contain private information that must be protected from unauthorized access. It also contains information that will change over time so the database must be properly maintained.

Employers who are subject to affirmative action regulations related to disabled and veterans are required to maintain an inventory of employee skills.

Workforce Assessment Techniques

As part of the employee skill database, fields of data are often gathered through assessment of individual employees. At the same time, a different database of records can be maintained containing organizational assessment information. There are different reasons for performing an assessment of an organization and its employees. First, the organization may need to be assessed for effectiveness. Second, employees may need assessment as a way of determining developmental needs as well as current strengths.

Organizational Assessment

If you believe that you need more information about the health of your organization, these assessment tools can be of help.

- **360-degree evaluations** Designed to assist individual managers and management teams in knowing where developmental effort should be focused
- **Workforce involvement** Identification of the degree of engagement felt by the people on your payroll

Individual Assessment

Once you are sure about the health of your organization, it may be helpful to add more information about individual employees. These techniques can do that.

- **Job assessment** Identifies the best fit for individual interests and skill sets
- **Talent profile** Identifies specific current skills
- **Readiness for promotion** Likelihood of success if promoted now

Many of these assessments are done by professional psychologists or through the use of tests developed by psychologists. Any HR professional considering such programs would be best served by consulting with someone qualified in the field to determine the best approach for the current need.

⬛SPHR⬛ International Workforce Management

More organizations each day are finding that they have needs related to multinational employment. And, it's not just the private sector that is experiencing these added workforce management issues. Many governmental organizations are finding that they have overlapping responsibilities that embrace international issues.

International Workforce Planning

Labor laws are significantly different in other countries. Not only is it necessary for international organizations to understand and abide by those rules, but it is essential that they understand the customs and expectations of people in any new remote location in which they wish to establish new operations.

Types of International Workers

It is necessary to understand the types of worker classifications that appear on the international stage. There are people who originate in the home country, people who originate in the remote country, and people who come from some other country altogether.

Parent-Country Nationals (PCNs)

These people are expatriates or parent-country nationals. They come from the country where the employer is based at the corporate level. Royal Dutch Shell is based in The Netherlands. Nestle is based in Switzerland. General Motors is based in the United States. Each of them is an international enterprise. Anyone sent from the country where headquarters is located to another country is known as a PCN.

Third-Country Nationals (TCNs)

It is common for an international organization to have PCNs assigned to remote countries. When the organization wishes to open operations in a new location in some other country, it can move TCN staff from the first remote location to the new remote location. These people become third-country nationals (TCNs). When Shell wants to build a refinery in Chile, it might move key management people from its refinery in the United States to work on establishing the new facility in Chile. They become TCNs. They do not originate from the country where headquarters is located (The Netherlands), and they do not originate from the host country (Chile). They have been moved from a third country (the United States).

Host-Country Nationals (HCNs)

Also called local nationals, host-country nationals (HCNs) originate in the country where the remote location is being established. When General Motors wishes to build a new manufacturing facility in Mexico, for example, it can hire Mexican nationals to run that facility. They are HCNs.

Expatriates

Sometimes these people are referred to as "expats," probably because we love to shorten words by removing syllables. Expatriates are people who are working in a country other than the one of their origin. They are expatriates of the country in which they originated. International relocation expenses can be extremely high so it is usual to only see professionals and managerial people moved internationally. It is often less expensive to obtain lower skilled workers who are already in the host country.

Inpatriates

These are people who are working at corporate headquarters who originated in another country. Transferring management people to headquarters on a rotational assignment is commonly used for career development. Later, inpatriates can return to their home country or be assigned to another position elsewhere.

Repatriates

When employees return to their home country from a foreign assignment, they are repatriates. They are said to have been repatriated.

Organizational and Staffing Approaches to International Business

Not only are there different laws and customs to be considered, but there are definite differences in the possible approaches to staffing a remote international organization. Here are the primary strategies for international staffing strategies. Immigration policies of the countries involved in international staffing methods will have a profound impact on the level of success that can be achieved with any of the following policy types.

Ethnocentric

This policy provides for all key management positions to be filled by expatriates. If all management personnel are from the headquarters organization, they know what is expected by the corporate office. Communications can be expedited because there are no language or idiom barriers to overcome when every manager in the remote location is from the home office.

Polycentric

When corporate headquarters positions are staffed with inpatriates (people from other countries) and remote locations are staffed with expatriates (people from the headquarters country) they are engaging in a multiple-centered staffing practice known as polycentricism. This policy can reduce corporate and cultural myopia because it "mixes things up" and forces integration of cultures.

Regiocentric

Staffing and planning organizational issues around regionalization is what we find with regiocentric organizations. We think of examples such as "European," "Asian," or "South American." They become extensive, multinational organizations that are adapted to the cultural, economic, and sometimes language commonalities of a given region.

Geocentric

This type of staffing policy seeks to place the best qualified individuals into job openings regardless of their country of origin.

Types of International Assignments

Many different types of assignments are possible when international staffing is involved. Table 5-8 outlines typical international assignments.

Type of Assignment—Global Mobility	Definition
Short-term assignees	Relocation from one country to another for the duration of the assignment, lasting from six months to one year.
Long-term assignees	Relocation from one country to another for the duration of the assignment, lasting more than one year.
Sequential/rotational employees	Workers who move laterally within an employer organization to a different job title or department with the objective of building new skills or enhancing professional development.
International commuting employees	Employee works in one country of assignment and commutes frequently to the home country.
Frequent flyers/extended business travelers	Employee does not relocate, but travels regularly to the assignment location.
Stealth expats/stealth pats/stealth assignees	Employees who are working in other countries outside the employer's formal global mobility program without the knowledge of human resources.
Local hires	People who are hired within the vicinity of the work location.
Localized transfer	Cross-border move in which employee is ultimately moved to permanent local status.
Permanent assignees	Employees who are assigned to a work location on a permanent basis.
Interns/trainees	People who are in a training status that may or may not lead to a regular job assignment.
Returnees	People who are enticed to return to their home country to work for the same or a different employer.
Virtual employees	Workers who are not physically present at the workplace.
Retirees	Workers who have left employment on a formal or informal program of retirement.
Part-time employees	Workers who work less than a designated number of hours per week or per month, as established by the employer. Typically less than 40 hours per week, which is usually considered to be full-time status.
Temporary employees	Employees who have been hired for a designated task that is expected to last for a short period of time, usually less than six months.
Temp-to-hire employees	Workers who are engaged through a temporary service agency for a specific assignment and converted from non-employee to regular employee status. These are usually non-competitive new hires.
Outsourced employees	People who work for another employer who are assigned tasks otherwise performed by employees at the outsourcing organization. Work is performed by the vendor organization under contract, so the vendor's employees are not on the outsourcing organization's payroll. Employment taxes, employee benefits, and other employment issues are managed by the vendor.

Table 5-8 Types of International Assignments

Chapter Review

Workforce Planning and Employment covers a wide swath of knowledge and responsibility. There are many laws that impact this area of expertise and a great deal of experience-based talent to be developed. It takes some time for HR professionals to acquire the skills needed to implement what they may know about this portion of the PHR and SPHR requirements.

From sexual harassment to job descriptions, from illegal employment discrimination to leaves of absence and hiring practices, HR professionals have extensive responsibilities and knowledge requirements.

Don't forget that this functional area makes up from 17 to 24 percent of the exam depending on the test you will be taking. More emphasis is placed on this area in the PHR exam than in the SPHR exam.

Questions

1. Stewart was working late when his boss approached him and asked if he would like to go get a drink. His boss then put his hand on Stewart's backside and gave it a little squeeze. What is going on here?

   A. Nothing. It is simply his boss showing a little affection for Stewart. No problem.

   B. Whether or not it is a problem depends on Stewart's reaction. If it is unwelcome, there might be a problem.

   C. If Stewart agrees, they can have a drink without anyone being the wiser.

   D. It is only a problem if one of Stewart's coworkers saw what happened.

2. Charlene is the HR Manager for her company. She opens her mail one day and finds a letter from the Equal Employment Opportunity Commission (EEOC) saying one of the company's employees has filed a charge of illegal discrimination. How seriously should Charlene take this letter?

   A. This is a very serious issue. Charlene should investigate the charge without talking to the complaining employee. Then, she should write a response to the EEOC.

   B. This is a very serious issue. Charlene has 90 days in which to get her response together.

   C. This is not very serious. These things happen all the time. Charlene can talk it over with the complaining employee and try to get it resolved.

   D. This is not very serious. There isn't much the EEOC can do even if the complaint has some merit. Charlene can set it aside and deal with it later when she gets time.

3. Lebron serves his employer as the HR Director. It is a startup company and his bosses want him to hire people fast so they have given him some tests to use in the screening process. He was told to hire the applicants with the best scores. Are these tests something Lebron should use?

   A. It is okay to use tests if they are job-specific in their measurement.

   B. No way. He should not use any tests that he hasn't bought from a legitimate test publisher.

   C. Tests are just fine. He should be sure the passing scores are set so they can get the best people.

   D. If the boss says to use the tests, he has little choice. He just has to be sure to score them properly.

4. Pat has just discovered that her organization has signed a contract with the federal government to provide computer products and installation services. The contract value is $600,000. The organization just hired its 61st employee. Does Pat's organization now need to prepare an affirmative action plan?

   A. No. When they get to 100 employees, they will need to develop an AAP.

   B. Because the contract value is less than $1,000,000 they are exempt from the AAP requirement.

   C. Yes. An AAP is needed for Minorities and Women, Disabled and Veterans.

   D. Yes. Only an AAP for Minorities and Women is necessary.

5. Elton heads a company that contracts to build office buildings for the federal government. He isn't sure if he has any affirmative action obligations because of his work. What would you tell him if you were his HR advisor?

   A. Don't worry. Construction firms are not classified as providers of goods and services. There is no affirmative action plan obligation for Elton's company.

   B. Elton may have to prepare a 16-point affirmative action plan that is required of all federal construction contractors if the contract value exceeds $10,000.

   C. Elton has to meet the same requirements as all other federal contractors who sell anything to the government.

   D. Elton should revisit the question once his contracts exceed $1,000,000.

6. Julia has been asked to identify her race and sex for her employer. She is uncomfortable doing that, thinking that she might be the target of some discrimination if she tells them. If you were Julia's HR Manager, what would you tell her?

   A. It's okay. We can put down whatever we want to identify your race and sex.

   B. Don't be concerned, Julia. Discrimination is something we don't tolerate and it is also illegal. We are required by the government to keep the race and sex data.

C. If you don't tell us what you want recorded, we will just have to leave your information blank in the database.

D. Julia should be sent to the HR department so they can tell her she has no choice. She must identify her race and sex for the company records.

7. Irene has a limp that she says is the result of a war wound. She was in the Canadian Army during the Gulf War and got hit in the leg by shrapnel. She is a decorated veteran of that war. She asks what category of veteran she should select on her self-identification form. What will you tell her?

A. Irene can't identify as a veteran because it applies only to veterans of the Vietnam War.

B. She has been out of the military for more than 6 months, so she would not qualify as a recently separated veteran.

C. When she was discharged, she should have been given a document that told her what category of veteran she should identify with.

D. Irene is not able to claim veteran status on her self-identification form because her service was not in the U.S. military. She can identify herself as disabled, however, if the wound interferes with one of her major life activities.

8. Solomon is from an island off the coast of India and has always been told he is classified as Asian. Now Andrew, his HR Manager, is telling him something else. How should Solomon be classified?

A. Always default to White when there is a question.

B. Solomon should identify himself as being two or more races.

C. Because he comes from an island off the coast of India, he really should be classified as a Pacific Islander.

D. People who originate in the Indian subcontinent should be classified as Asian.

9. Affirmative action plans have a great deal to do with altering the demographics of an employer's organization. They do this by:

A. Creating "set asides" for job openings that are underrepresented in certain race categories.

B. Providing preferential selection for the underrepresented race category.

C. Creating placement rate goals and letting a nondiscriminatory selection process select the best qualified people.

D. Moving applicants with a certain race up to the top of the selection list.

10. Gerardo manages the HR function along with the accounting department. He is involved in an OFCCP audit of his affirmative action plans. The agency wants him to sign a conciliation agreement saying he will hire a certain number of

women into one job title and give back pay to a group of Hispanics who weren't hired. What would you advise Gerardo to do with the conciliation agreement?

A. Review it with his legal counsel and senior executives. Determine if the OFCCP claims are accurate and negotiate something else as a consequence if they are not.

B. Go ahead and sign the conciliation agreement. It's just a promise and doesn't really matter.

C. Whenever there is a document like this coming from the federal government, there should be a set of instructions that comes along with it telling the contractor what to do. Gerardo should look for that list.

D. Gerardo should read it and make sure there isn't anything that talks about illegal discrimination. He should scratch out any references to discrimination and send it back to the OFCCP with his signature.

11. Guillermo supervises a group of six women in the accounting department. They are responsible for all payments and receipts. On Friday, Eleanor invites Guillermo to her apartment for a home-cooked dinner. He accepts. Under the various U.S. Supreme Court opinions on the subject, is this classified as sexual harassment?

A. Very likely. Anytime a supervisor has a relationship with a subordinate it is classified as sexual harassment.

B. Probably not. The subordinate initiated the relationship, if indeed there actually is one. It is hard for a subordinate to harass a supervisor because in the end the supervisor is the one with the organizational power.

C. It all depends on what happens after dinner. Guillermo is the one with the supervisory power. If he initiates anything, he can be in trouble.

D. If they are having an affair, there is likely sexual harassment involved.

12. Every month, Ali has to provide a report to the executives that details what employee complaints have been received. This month's report shows complaints of harassment from two people. One was based on race and the other was based on religion. The executives are challenging those classifications, saying harassment can only be based on sexual conditions. What would you tell the executives if you were Ali?

A. It shouldn't have been classified as harassment rather just plain discrimination. There really can't be any harassment other than sexual harassment.

B. We should really get our attorney to set the classifications for us. We're not sure if there can be harassment based on anything other than sex.

C. Of course there can be harassment based on race, religion, age, national origin, or a number of other categories.

D. Executives should be encouraged to avoid getting into such details. It isn't really important. In the end, we just have two complaints of discrimination.

13. Times are still hard for the AB Trucking Company. They are going to have to close one of their work locations. That will take 146 full-time people off the payroll who will have to look for other work with other employers. What should the company consider in their layoff planning?

    A. WARN kicks in and they must notify the local government as well as employees who will be affected at least 60 days before the layoff date.

    B. WARN kicks in but they don't have to notify anybody until a week before the layoff date.

    C. Because they are in the transportation industry, the WARN Act doesn't apply. They have *carte blanche* in how they handle the layoff.

    D. WARN kicks in and they have to notify employees 60 days in advance, but notifying the local government is a voluntary decision.

14. Lawana has just been given the job of preparing an EEO-1 for her employer group. She finds some gaps in the employee race and gender data she will need to use in reporting. How should she handle that problem?

    A. Ignore the missing data and just report what data she has. She should not guess about any of the race or gender identifications.

    B. Talk with each employee and ask if they have been invited to self-identify. If they choose not to self-identify, speak with the supervisor and get a determination based on observation.

    C. Take the best guess possible and fill in the blanks.

    D. Where data is missing, it is usually a good idea to default to White as a race and Male as a gender. Statistically, those are the most common entries.

15. Harriet has just taken over for the HR Manager in her group and her boss is asking for an update on the succession plan. He wants to see the employee skill inventory as soon as possible. Harriet didn't even know there was a succession plan. What should Harriet be looking for in her files?

    A. A confidential record that lists each employee's skills and abilities

    B. A list of only the top-rated people in the group who have computer skills

    C. A list of everyone in the group identifying each person's skills and whether or not they are currently ready for promotion

    D. A list of people showing what individuals are capable of doing now, without regard for any future assignment

16. Pearl will be writing a lot of job descriptions over the coming months. Her CEO has just given her the task because the organization doesn't currently have job descriptions. What should Pearl be sure to include in the job descriptions?

    A. She should be sure that all general duties are included and that "Other duties as assigned" is the last one.

    B. She should include duties and responsibilities in every job description based on what she knows about the job content.

    C. She should find a way to use generic descriptions from her job description library. It is important to be consistent with what has already been published in case she needs to defend those documents later on.

    D. She should plan to interview incumbents and their supervisors to identify the job duties and responsibilities.

17. When Pearl gets around to actually writing the job descriptions, should she include the physical and mental requirements of the job?

    A. Those are things that should be written into a separate document. They should not be in the job description because that would violate the Americans with Disabilities Act.

    B. Yes, Pearl should include a list of physical and mental requirements for each job as part of the job description.

    C. No, Pearl would be exposing her employer to unnecessary risks of lawsuits if she put those things into the job descriptions.

    D. Perhaps. If there are some unusual physical or mental requirements in a certain job, she should put those things into the job descriptions. Otherwise, it isn't necessary.

18. Lydia finds that her job descriptions are all written and current. Now, she wants to use them to be sure each job is properly assigned to a compensation level. She doesn't want to get caught in an OFCCP audit with the government telling her she needs to make large adjustments all at once. How should Lydia's organization be evaluating their jobs for compensation levels?

    A. Lydia should call one of the job evaluation consulting firms to have them review all the jobs in her organization.

    B. She can create her own point system and arbitrarily set compensation levels wherever she wants.

    C. A point system is not necessary for determining what similarities exist between job content descriptions. She can assign compensation groups based on her assessment of those similarities and differences in the level of job responsibilities.

    D. Lydia should avoid any type of job evaluation program if it hasn't been statistically proven to be 100 percent accurate.

19. AB Trucking has had a policy that nobody will be hired unless they complete the company's job application. Now, all of their job applications are being processed online, and some applicants want to submit their resumes instead of a job application form. What can AB Trucking do about the resume-versus-application controversy?

    A. It is entirely up to the company how it wants to handle the policy. Application forms are not a legal requirement, but using them is generally considered a best practice in the employment arena. Job candidates can be forced to go through the company's process of completing an application form, online or offline.

B. The government has set up regulations that say employers have to accept resumes if they are submitted in a job search. The company doesn't really have any choice but to accept them.

C. Job applications are old school. Almost no employer uses them these days. The company should change its policy and use only resumes in the future.

D. Resumes don't have all of the information that can be gathered on a job application and people lie on resumes anyway. That alone is reason for the company to continue using its job application forms.

20. An employee in Cortez's organization came to him and suggested that she and her coworker could consolidate their duties into one job and each work part-time, sharing the 40 hours each week so the work got done as always. What would you say if you were Cortez?

A. Unfortunately, the Fair Labor Standards Act and the Unified Job Consolidation Act say that sharing jobs is not permitted because it would violate union agreements.

B. There is no reason that it couldn't work if Cortez believes the two people are capable and want to make it work.

C. Having more than one person and one Social Security number on one job assignment won't work. It makes tax reporting impossible.

D. It's not a good idea because it doubles the liability for workers' compensation and unemployment insurance.

21. The local county's workforce has been decimated in recent months because the pension plan is changing and folks wanted to get their higher level calculation before the changes cut that formula. The result, however, has been that a great deal of organizational intelligence walked out the door. The senior staff are suggesting you hire back some of the key personnel as temporary workers until you are able to get replacements trained. Is that a good idea?

A. Hardly ever. It gives the newly retired people a way to "double dip" and make more money than they would have if they had stayed on the job without retiring.

B. Sometimes. If the temporary period is truly used to train a replacement, it could get the organization across the institutional knowledge gap, passing along that information to someone new.

C. Always. There is no downside to bringing back retirees as temporary workers. So what if they make a bit more? The work gets done without interruption.

D. Maybe. If there is a limit of 6 months on the temporary assignment in compliance with the Fair Labor Standards Act.

22. Abel has been having trouble selecting quality accounting people. Everyone claims to be able to use Excel spreadsheets but few actually can once they get on the job. In the end, he has had to terminate people because of poor performance. He is thinking he will use a test he saw at the local office supply warehouse. If you were the HR Manager in Abel's organization, what advice would you give him about his plans for testing?

   A. It sounds like a good idea. It certainly could control the cost of turnover. We should try it.

   B. It sounds like a good idea. Will he be able to show that the test actually predicts success on the jobs he wishes to use it for? If not, he should find a different screening tool.

   C. It doesn't sound like a good idea. With everyone talking about the liability of written tests these days, we can't take that risk for any job.

   D. It doesn't sound like a good idea. It is going to create more paperwork for HR and we can't stand any workload increase.

23. Jo is trying to standardize the selection system for instructors in her training group. Having one procedure to screen candidates should yield both consistency and accuracy. What she hasn't decided is whether she should use an objective or subjective system. What would you tell her?

   A. Only objective systems are able to "slice and dice" candidates effectively. Jo should use numeric devices only.

   B. It is so hard to pin down clear delineations of skill using a numeric system. Jo should rely on a subjective process that gives her greater flexibility in grading candidates.

   C. There is no way to quantify everything about an instructor's job. Therefore, it is impossible to use a quantitative system for that job set. Go with the subjective.

   D. Both subjective and objective approaches can be used on instructor jobs as long as they both have been validated according to the Uniform Guidelines.

24. When Ophelia had her weekend automobile accident, everyone in the office rushed to show her support. Now that she is confined to a wheelchair, she is asking her employer to support her by giving her a job accommodation so she can still do her job as the scheduling clerk. What should her employer do?

   A. They should listen politely and take her written request. There isn't anything they really have to do about an accommodation because it doesn't involve a workplace injury.

   B. They should listen politely and take her written request. They should investigate other possible accommodations and give her some suggestions if those might be better than what she requested.

    C. They should listen politely and take her written request. It is just a matter of time before they will have to approve the request because of the ADA requirements.

    D. Because Ophelia is a member of the union that represents office workers, the contract will contain a specification explaining whether anyone in the workplace will be given a job accommodation and under what conditions.

25. When Gretta approached her supervisor and asked to review the contents of her personnel file, the supervisor told her she would check with HR about the request. As the HR Manager, what will you tell the supervisor?

    A. Sure. No problem. Now we have to gather up the files from the supervisor, HR, and training so Gretta can see all of them because, under company policy and state laws, the personnel file comprises all of these files.

    B. Sure. But only the official file maintained by HR should be provided for Gretta's review even though we have no policy on the issue.

    C. Sure. We'll get around to it at some point in the next few months. There are a lot of other more important priorities at the moment.

    D. Gretta is out of luck. We don't allow that under any circumstance regardless of what anyone thinks.

Answers

1. **B.** If the behavior of his boss is unwelcome, this could be an incident of *quid pro quo* sexual harassment. We need more information to know for sure. If Stewart's coworkers saw what happened, they might also object should Stewart go along with the boss's sexual advance. Coworkers could be negatively affected because of favoritism or perceived favoritism toward Stewart on the part of his boss, and there could be other problems as well.

2. **A.** The EEOC is a law enforcement agency so it is a serious matter. Charlene has 30 days to get her written response to the Commission, and she is barred from discussing the complaint with the employee who filed it.

3. **A.** Remember that it is the user of a test that holds the liability, not the publisher of the test. If a test has been validated to properly predict success in specific jobs with specific knowledge and skill requirements, it can be used for those jobs. Using it for *all* jobs is not a good idea. If the boss insists, he needs to be told what the consequences can be.

4. **C.** The contract exceeds $50,000, and there are more than 50 employees, so an AAP is required for minorities and women. A plan for disabled and another for veterans are required as well because the contract is over $10,000 for disabled AAP requirements and $100,000 for veteran AAP requirements.

5. **B.** If his contract exceeds $10,000, Elton will need an affirmative action plan that satisfies regulatory requirements for construction contractors. The 16-point plan they must develop is not the same as the plans required of goods and services contractors.

6. **B.** Identifying race and sex is voluntary. The employer is required to keep records of every employee's race and sex identification, however. When someone doesn't volunteer the information, the employer must make a determination by observation and keep a record of the race and sex of the individual.

7. **D.** Only veterans of the United States military are able to claim veteran status. Veterans of military organizations in other countries are not to be counted. Veterans are people who served in an area for which a medal or award was made. Definitions are contained in the regulations.

8. **D.** According to the EEO-1 instructions, the category of Asian includes all people from the Indian subcontinent. The fact that he lived on an island off the coast is irrelevant.

9. **C.** Preferences and set-asides are illegal under case law. Outreach and recruiting so a candidate pool reflects a mix of race and sex can allow a nondiscriminatory selection system to pick the best qualified person. In some cases, that will be a woman or racial minority.

10. **A.** A conciliation agreement is a legal contract. When it comes from OFCCP, it means they will come back every six months or so to be sure you are doing what it promises you will do. If not, they can take you through the enforcement process to force you to comply. Always get your management attorney involved before signing such a contract.

11. **B.** It's probably not *quid pro quo* harassment because the invitation came from a subordinate. It's likely not hostile environment harassment because the person being harassed has to suffer unwanted advances of a sexual nature. She is actually the one initiating the invitation.

12. **C.** Harassment has been recognized by the courts when it is based on sex but also when it is based on race, ethnicity, religion, and other protected categories. Executives need to understand that these are all liabilities for the organization.

13. **A.** WARN applies because the layoff will involve more than 100 full-time people at a single location. It requires 60 days advance notification to both the employees and the local government officials.

14. **B.** Employees should always be invited to self-identify. If they refuse, and since employers are obligated to maintain the data, the next best way to get it is to ask the supervisor to make a personal observation and record it in the data fields.

15. **C.** The list should show what skills each person has now and whether or not they are ready for promotion now or need further experience or training before being ready for promotion.

16. **D.** The only way to determine what a job actually does is to interview the incumbent(s) and the supervisor. Job descriptions should be specific to each job.

17. **B.** Every job description should have in it a list of the physical and mental requirements for that job. That helps in selecting employees and in working on job accommodations for workers' compensation and disabilities.

18. **C.** It isn't necessary to use a point system to evaluate job content for compensation purposes. Making comparisons of responsibility levels can be done and compensation levels determined based on those comparisons. Lydia should attempt to be consistent in how she makes those comparisons so the compensation decisions will be consistent.

19. **A.** The company is not constrained by the government on how it designs its job application process. If it wishes to have a certain form completed, it can establish that policy. A decision should be made about what documents it will accept from job applicants. Consistency in how the process is applied is critical in avoiding complaints of bias.

20. **B.** Sometimes, using part-time workers to accomplish one job is a good solution. A great deal depends on the reliability of incumbents.

21. **B.** One reason these arrangements sometimes fail is that they go on and on and on. There is no real replacement training going on. The retired employee is doing the same work as before they retired, and nobody is being transferred, promoted, or hired into that job as a replacement.

22. **B.** The test should measure Excel skills because those are the predictors of success for Abel's accounting positions.

23. **D.** There is no reason that both objective and subjective selection systems cannot be used together in sorting candidates for instructor jobs.

24. **B.** The interactive process requires employers to determine if there might be other ways to accommodate the needs of their employee. Discussing those other possibilities will come next in the process.

25. **A.** State law will determine requirements. Policy can go beyond state law if desired by the employer. Presuming both state law and policy require providing an opportunity for employee review of the file, it should be scheduled as soon as reasonably possible.

Endnotes

1. Civil Rights Act of 1991 (see Chapter 2).

2. EEOC Charge Statistics, EEOC website, http://eeoc.gov/eeoc/statistics/enforcement/charges.cfm (as of 7/30/2013).

3. 41 CFR 60-3.5B.

4. Truesdell, William H. SPHR, *Secrets of Affirmative Action Compliance*, The Management Advantage, Inc., Walnut Creek, CA 2014.

5. U.S. Department of Labor, WARN Act Employer Guide, www.doleta.gov/layoff/pdf/EmployerWARN09_2003.pdf (as of 8/5/2013).

6. U.S. Department of Labor, WARN Act Employer Guide, www.doleta.gov/layoff/pdf/EmployerWARN09_2003.pdf (as of 8/5/2013).

7. Washington State HR website, retrieved on 5/18/2014, www.hr.wa.gov/WorkforceDataAndPlanning/WorkforcePlanning/Competencies/Pages/default.aspx.

8. "State Employment Sites," retrieved on 2/8/2014, www.statelocalgov.net/50states-jobs.cfm.

9. "The Uniform Electronic Transaction Act," retrieved from the Uniform Law Commission on 2/8/2014 from www.uniformlaws.org/ActSummary.aspx?title=Electronic%20Transactions%20Act.

10. U.S. Bureau of the Census, www.census.gov (as of 8/6/2013).

11. Fitz-enz, Jac, and Barbara Davison, *How to Measure Human Resources Management*, 3rd edition, McGraw-Hill, 2002.

12. SHRM-ANSI Standard on Cost Per Hire, free copy available from SHRM by sending email to HRSTDS@SHRM.org.

13. Cost per hire standard developed by SHRM, referenced on 5/20/2014, www.shrm.org/hrstandards/publishedstandards/documents/cost-per-hire%20american%20national%20standard.pdf.

14. Internal Revenue Service, "Retiree Annuitants," retrieved on 2/8/2014 from www.irs.gov/Government-Entities/Federal,-State-&-Local-Governments/Rehired-Annuitants.

15. Powers, Bob, and William J. Rothwell, *Instructor Excellence: Mastering the Delivery of Training*, 2nd edition, Pfeiffer (John Wiley and Sons), San Francisco, CA 2007.

16. EEOC Guidelines on Job Accommodation Requests, www.eeoc.gov/policy/docs/accommodation.html (as of 8/11/2013).

17. Equal Employment Opportunity Commission, "Consideration of Arrest and Conviction Records in Employment Decisions under Title VII of the Civil Rights Act of 1964," www.eeoc.gov/laws/guidance/arrest_conviction.cfm, published 4/25/12

18. U.S. Department of Justice, Bureau of Justice Statistics, "Prisoners in 2012—Advance Counts," www.bjs.gov/content/pub/pdf/p12ac.pdf, published July 2013.

CHAPTER 6

Business Management and Strategy

Business Management and Strategy is probably the most important functional area for PHR, and especially SPHR, candidates, because it assists them in developing into the role of an essential internal business consultant for their organizations. Twelve percent of the PHR exam and a hefty 29 percent of the SPHR exam will focus on Business Management and Strategy.

Business Management and Strategy is where you will glean all the essential information about the skills and responsibilities of HR as a business partner, strategist, and protector of organizational assets. HR professionals not only need to understand the organization's business, but they must also understand the external environments in which it operates, its competition, and trends that influence it. These continue to be expanding and evolving functions for HR in our current business environment with the emphasis on helping the organization compete in new global markets and respond to rapidly changing conditions. Embrace these skills and you will surely become a key internal consultant for your organization's management team.

The official HRCI Business Management and Strategy functional area responsibilities and knowledge statements are as follows:

Responsibilities

- Interpret and apply information related to the organization's operations from internal sources, including finance, accounting, business development, marketing, sales, operations, and information technology, in order to contribute to the development of the organization's strategic plan.

- Interpret information from external sources related to the general business environment, industry practices and developments, technological advances, economic environment, labor force, and the legal and regulatory environment, in order to contribute to the development of the organization's strategic plan.

- **SPHR** Participate as a contributing partner in the organization's strategic planning process (for example: provide and lead workforce planning discussion with management, develop and present long-term forecast of human capital needs at the organizational level).

- Establish strategic relationships with key individuals in the organization to influence organizational decision-making.

- Establish relationships/alliances with key individuals and outside organizations to assist in achieving the organization's strategic goals and objectives (for example: corporate social responsibility and community partnership).

SPHR • Develop and utilize business metrics to measure the achievement of the organization's strategic goals and objectives (for example: key performance indicators, balanced scorecard).

- Develop, influence, and execute strategies for managing organizational change that balance the expectations and needs of the organization, its employees, and other stakeholders.

SPHR • Develop and align the human resource strategic plan with the organization's strategic plan.

- Facilitate the development and communication of the organization's core values, vision, mission, and ethical behaviors.

- Reinforce the organization's core values and behavioral expectations through modeling, communication, and coaching.

- Provide data such as human capital projections and costs that support the organization's overall budget.

SPHR • Develop and execute business plans (for example: annual goals and objectives) that correlate with the organization's strategic plan's performance expectations to include growth targets, new programs/services, and net income expectations.

SPHR • Perform cost/benefit analyses on proposed projects.

SPHR • Develop and manage an HR budget that supports the organization's strategic goals, objectives, and values.

- Monitor the legislative and regulatory environment for proposed changes and their potential impact to the organization, taking appropriate proactive steps to support, modify, or oppose the proposed changes.

SPHR • Develop policies and procedures to support corporate governance initiatives (for example: whistleblower protection, code of ethics).

- Participate in enterprise risk management by ensuring that policies contribute to protecting the organization from potential risks.

SPHR • Identify and evaluate alternatives and recommend strategies for vendor selection and/or outsourcing.

SPHR • Oversee or lead the transition and/or implementation of new systems, service centers, and outsourcing.

SPHR • Participate in strategic decision-making and due diligence activities related to organizational structure and design (for example: corporate restructuring, mergers and acquisitions [M&A], divestitures).

SPHR • Determine strategic application of integrated technical tools and systems (for example: new enterprise software, performance management tools, self-service technologies).

Knowledge of

- The organization's mission, vision, values, business goals, objectives, plans, and processes

- Legislative and regulatory processes

- Strategic planning process, design, implementation, and evaluation

- Management functions, including planning, organizing, directing, and controlling

- Corporate governance procedures and compliance (for example: Sarbanes-Oxley Act)

- **SPHR** Due diligence processes (for example: M&A, divestitures)

- **SPHR** Transition techniques for corporate restructuring, M&A, offshoring, and divestitures

- Elements of a cost-benefit analysis during the life cycle of the business (such as scenarios for growth, including expected, economic stressed, and worst case conditions) and the impact to net worth/earnings for short-, mid-, and long-term horizons

- Business concepts (for example: competitive advantage, organizational branding, business case development, corporate responsibility)

Core Knowledge of

- Third-party or vendor selection, contract negotiation, and management, including development of requests for proposals (RFPs)

- Project management concepts and applications

- Ethical and professional standards

- Technology to support HR activities

- Qualitative and quantitative methods and tools for analysis, interpretation, and decision-making purposes

- Change management theory, methods, and application

- Types of organizational structures

- Environmental scanning concepts and applications

- Budgeting, accounting, and financial concepts

Key Legislation Governing Business Management and Strategy

Now that you've reviewed the Business Management and Strategy responsibilities and knowledge statements, we recommend that you review the federal laws that apply to Business Management and Strategy as outlined in Figure 6-1. It would be helpful to refer back to Chapter 2 on these specific laws prior to reading any further in this chapter.

Electronic Communications Privacy Act (ECPA) of 1986	Foreign Corrupt Practices Act (FCPA) 1977
False Claims Act of 1863	Sarbanes-Oxley Act of 2002
The Dodd-Frank Wall Street Reform and Consumer Protection Act (2010)	The IRS Intermediate Sanctions (2002)
The Securities and Exchange Act (1934)	The Tax Reform Act (1986)

Figure 6-1   Federal laws that apply to business management and strategy

Role of Human Resources in Organizations

The role of Human Resource Management (HRM) has evolved over the years, probably more so than any other department function in an organization. In the early twentieth century, HR as a specialized function began with a narrow focus of hiring and keeping records of employees, an operational and administrative function. Changes in HR have been stimulated by external changes, as illustrated below in Table 6-1.

HR's staff typically provided three types of support: advice, service, and control.

- **Advice**   Advising line management on workforce matters, including policies and laws, providing solutions and procedural steps, offering assistance and guidance on employee issues, diagnosing problems or gathering facts, and providing resources.

- **Service**   Maintaining records, hiring, training, answering, and clarifying information within a broad customer base, including management, employees, legal and regulatory agencies, applicants, retirees, families of employees, and vendors.

- **Control**   An authoritative role involved in consistency of policy application, evaluation of employee performance, corrective action, and designing or implementation of employee programs.

While the focus continues to have a foundational basis in the day-to-day operational role (acquisition, development, resolving issues, and communications), along with administrative transactional activities (maintaining a Human Resource Information System, or HRIS), the significance of HR's contributions has become more apparent as a business strategist with a forward-thinking, long-term global focus that includes protecting the organization from potential risks. HR professionals have earned a seat at the executive round table, contributing to the organization's direction with strategic solutions for talent management, creating organizational culture, formulating and developing strategies, and balancing the external or internal environments to help the organization achieve its goals. The title of Chief Human Resource Officer (CHRO) is common in today's large organizations—a recognition that indicates HR has come a long way up the perceived value added scale. In today's global competitive business climate the HR role must contribute in quantifiable business terms, outlining a return on investment (ROI) that ensures the effective and efficient use of its human capital.

Era	HR's Identity	Business Era	Issues for HR
Pre-1900	HR did not exist	Gilded Age—most small businesses and a few large corporations called "trusts"	Responsibilities mostly associated with payroll/hiring done by owners or accounting personnel
1900–19	Referred to as *Labor Relations*	Industrial Revolution	People could be replaced with machinery
1920–39	Referred to as *Employee and Industrial Relations*	World War I and civil service	Formalized processes brought in; worker's rights issues
1940–59	Referred to as *Personnel Administration*	World War II and scientific research	Efficiency productivity experts, benefits administration, women in the workforce
1960–79	Referred to as *Personnel Management*	Civil Rights and government compliance	Legal compliance reporting and policing, policy application consistency
1980–99	Referred to as *Human Resources Management*	Knowledge and service economy; hostile takeovers; M&A; technology	HR theories for employee motivation, training and development, RIFs, immigration hiring
2000–09	Referred to as *People or Talent Management*	9/11 attack on U.S. and homeland security; global competitiveness	Cultural diversity, outsourcing, technology, cultural blending, talent acquisition, offshoring
2010–Present	Evolving: *HR Business Consultants within the Human Asset Department* is trending.	Global Economy; Mobile Technology Age; Great Recession	Talent retention, organizational restructuring, employee engagement, cost containment

Table 6-1   Evolution of Human Resources

Table 6-1 provides a brief historical perspective of the evolution of the Human Resources function.

Strategic Alliances

As a strategic business partner, the role of an HR professional requires partnering with others in an alliance of collaboration that aims for a synergy where each partner's benefits will be greater than those from individual efforts. Cooperation on planning, organizational design, and other broader HR activities are major emphases for these strategic relationships with an organization's management. Strategic relationships are between individuals, defined as stakeholders, who could be employees, the management hierarchy, the shareholder, or the community and industry.

Building partnerships across the organization requires an understanding of the differing perspectives, views, and needs of the stakeholders, and how all areas are interrelated and affect one another. Having a broader perspective outside of the organization within its industry or its communities is necessary, too, for a big picture view.

HR's Internal Business Partners

Every organization, regardless of size, has basic key business functions: sales and marketing, operations, information technology, finance and accounting. Larger organizations will have even more: Customer Service and Relations, Research and Development, Quality Assurance. They each have a connection and collaboration associated with the Human Resources function. HR professionals need to form partnerships within their organization's key business functions to fully understand the key functional areas in an effort to become a true strategic business partner.

Sales and Marketing   The sales function in an organization is normally the revenue generator. It is responsible for selling the organization's service or product. The marketing function has responsibilities for promoting, pricing, and locating/identifying the customer base.

Operations   Operations is considered the heartbeat of the organization. Operations will create the goods or services, acquire the resources, and ensure the customer receives those goods or services. Five concepts drive operations: capacity, scheduling, inventory, standards, and control.

Information Technology   Information Technology is the brain of today's organizations. The systems, tools, and information required for all other key functions to do what they do are dependent on the responsibilities of IT.

Finance and Accounting   Similar to sales and marketing functions, the finance and accounting functions go hand-in-hand, yet are distinctively different. Finance has its focus on funding sources, such as bank loans and stock sales, along with budgeting for income generation and expenses. Accounting, on the other hand, is associated with the movement of the monies going in and out, such as payables and receivables processing, payroll, and taxes.

Influencing Decision Making

HR experts have experience and knowledge about how to build human capital in an organization, and there's nothing more vital to a company's success than its people. They deserve to have the CEO's ear. Yet even today in the twenty-first century, there are many HR professionals who are not included in executive meetings where critical business is discussed and budgetary allocations are made. It's a disservice if HR does not have a voice at the upper echelons in an organization to advocate for the funding of projects that will boost workforce morale, efficiency, retention, and engagement.

HR is viewed by some executives in an organization as the soft side of the business, mostly handling transactions such as hiring, onboarding, and training. Executives may need help in understanding that HR fits into discussions about the financial and operational issues facing the company. The following tips will help you make that shift:

- *Become fluent in the language of economics.* HR focuses primarily on human capital, yet there are four other kinds of capital—structural, financial, social, and intellectual—that require equal consideration in decisions. Understand how HR intersects with each area.

- *Present concrete analysis.* Be prepared with concrete analysis of how HR impacts the business function and aligns with the organization's larger goals. Explain the cost versus value from an HR perspective, how a decision might impact human capital in areas such as hiring, training, and morale. This is how executives think. They are constantly using analytical techniques to make decisions and judgments that will move the organization forward. Those HR leaders who can master number-crunching, who not only explain the reasoning for something but show it via research and analytical evidence, will have a valued opinion in decision making.

- *Become known as a problem solver and collaborator.* Pulling together various options for emerging problems, collaborating with management, and having a focus on holistic solutions (the greater of the whole) will definitely earn respect. Keep in mind the desired end result and what's in the best interest for all stakeholders. Create scenarios with probability analysis to help decision makers make their decisions.

In the Trenches

Be an Influencer: Five Key Competencies of the Most Influential HR Practitioners
Joel Garfinkle, Executive Coach, Garfinkle Executive Coaching, San Francisco, California

Being an influential leader is a necessity in organizations today. Especially for Human Resource professionals who need to rely on the power of their influence to drive change, improve situations, and produce game-changing results. As an Executive Coach, I've observed five specific traits that influential people have developed to a significantly higher degree than others. Developing these competencies will help you increase HR's impact in top-level decisions and gain an influential seat at the round table:

- *Build a solid reputation.* Reputations take time to build. As you build, your accomplishments will begin proving your worth to the company. As a result of your consistently helpful and effective behavior, others will start to view you as reliable and come to both know and respect

(Continued)

you. They will find your character trustworthy and know that your actions will be consistent. They will value you and depend on you to get the job done.

- *Enhance your skill set.* Having an enhanced skill set is all about knowing how to do your job exceedingly well. People throughout the company recognize and know you as someone who is extremely competent. You do quality work and perform at the highest level.

- *Project executive presence.* Executive presence is about having a powerful and confident persona. You don't hesitate. You are decisive and confident with your choices and in your speaking. People trust in your leadership, and feed off of your assured sense of self.

- *Be likeable.* Likeability means you have a solid internal comfort level interacting with others, whether they are your own team members or someone from top management. You share information about yourself and ask open-ended questions that help others open up about themselves. You make eye contact and focus totally on what the other person is saying.

- *Utilize your power of persuasion.* When you're persuasive, you sway others to your side and win them over. They follow your direction and adopt your aspirations. Being able to persuade others requires that you compel them to believe in you and your information, and to feel as though you have their best interests at heart. They trust the integrity you bring to a given situation and recognize sound reasoning in your ideas.

You will be perceived as a leader by your C-level executives and others in the company when you learn to consistently lead with influence. Hone these traits and consider where you can begin applying these today in your work. It may be speaking more authoritatively in meetings, or volunteering to take on a high profile project that highlights your skills. Be sure to take stock annually at how well you increased your influence, where you can shift into a new influencing gear, and with whom. Your future as a leader is in your hands.

SPHR **Business Case** A major responsibility falling on the shoulders of HR professionals these days is development and presentation of a business case for the organizational programs that will solve specific problems. For example, a business case is needed when recommending certain medical insurance programs, particularly if the employer has not provided such benefits in the past.

A business case is a written or oral presentation that identifies a problem, analyzes the various possible solutions, and makes a recommendation for implementing one of them. It will almost always have an analysis of financial impact, personnel impact, and customer impact. It is designed and presented using business terminology. For example, a recommendation for medical insurance would include the current cost plus a forecast of future costs both in total dollars and in dollars per employee. It will have specific information about the way in which the recommendation will solve the problem that has been identified. (For example, retention of employees is significantly improved if the employer offers medical insurance to workers. Higher retention means less turnover and lower recruiting and training costs.) All of the benefits will have dollar values assigned to them in a business case presentation.

"Making a business case" means assembling business reasons for taking some action. The case will be ultimately presented to the decision maker, be it an executive or the Board of Directors. Business case content includes the following:

- **Executive summary** Short statement that summarizes the problem and recommendation with key reasons for choosing the recommended solution.

- **Definition of the problem** Identifying the issue that is being addressed in the business case. It could be changes in employee benefits, alterations in payroll, policy changes, or other HR-related issues. The definition should include a statement of how the organization is impacted by the problem.

- **Objectives** Statements of key results expected in solving the stated problem.

- **Possible solutions** List of key solutions possible for the stated problem.

- **Recommended solution** Identification of the solution that is being recommended and why. The list of reasons for making the choice should include statements of impact on the organization, its workforce, its customers/clients, and its other stakeholders. Those impacts should be quantified if possible.

- **Implementation plan** The steps needed to implement the solution and solve the problem. It could be a short list of steps or something quite complicated. An action plan should always include an action to be taken, who is responsible for that action, and the target date for completion of that action.

- **Support documents** All documents related to the selection decision. They might include financial analysis, statements of impact on profit and loss or balance sheet, analysis of HR impacts (for example, turnover, diversity, morale), organizational branding impacts, influences on competitive advantage, corporate responsibility changes, and staffing required for implementation.

Business Partner Consultant Over the last decade or so, a lot of excitement and focus has been around HR professionals evolving into business partners and no longer being pegged to just a support function role—thus the evolution of the title HR Generalist to HR Business Partner, which acts as an internal consultant to management, chiming in on human capital management. To be effective as a business partner consultant, HR professionals need to position themselves as a consultant does: providing advice, solutions, options, and not being the decision maker. They should provide proposals and factual data to back up recommendations, which gain credibility with the value of data and information.

With more HR professionals jumping on the bandwagon to partner with their business leaders, employees perceived that the pendulum might have swung too far, which left employees feeling left out of the equation; thus evolved the title of HR Employee Partner to provide a counterbalance.

Community Partnership

Community partnership, here referred to as corporate responsibility (CR), involves keeping a watchful eye within the organization's communities—local, national, and even international. CR strives to enhance the organization's reputation. Strategic relationships and behaviors include CR activities such as Chamber of Commerce membership or sponsoring a local non-profit fundraiser, creating a *Corporate Citizenship*. Multiple departments may have corporate responsibility in creating community relationships, yet HR is typically the department primarily at the core, absent an organization's official CR or public relations department.

Corporate philanthropy has been around for decades and was typically under the control and influence of senior management within a corporation. Although corporate philanthropic activities such as monetary donations, percentage of sale, and cooperative programs are still widely in existence, the tide has shifted to a more strategic focus on donations, one that affiliates with the organization's relevant business or branding. A good example of this is the cosmetic company Avon, which is widely known as a corporate sponsor for breast cancer research. The company's customer base is relevant to the majority of affected individuals with breast cancer, women.

Sustainability and the associated accountability efforts within sustainability (behavior that is cognizant of depleting resources that the organization is intertwined with) have also become front and center for CR. Time, labor, and finances are where HR is involved with the design or implementation of programs. An example of a program would be re-entry into the workforce by former stay-at-home parents. "Green initiatives" along with "environmental footprints" are now a prime attention grabber within CR. Green initiatives might include an HR department reducing its paper printing needs by converting to online, paperless employment and benefit forms, employee handbooks, and newsletters. A paid time-off volunteerism policy for employees is another popular initiative in CR.

The external forces that typically drive goals and objectives in CR can be better understood by looking at Figure 6-2.

When identifying the goals and objectives for CR, it is ideal to use the same analysis tools as used with strategic planning (see the section "Environmental Scanning" later in this chapter) to identify the long-term investment and involvement for the organization.

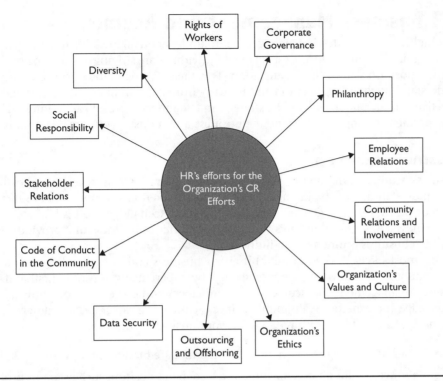

Figure 6-2 Corporate responsibility

Facilitation and Communication

One important role that HR plays is facilitator of communications to the workforce at large. That includes serving as a bridge to link the workforce with new and/or existing strategic plans. The organization's vision, mission, values, and ethics are foundational and should be linked by HR with its recruitment, onboarding, enrollment, development, and performance review materials and activities, just to name a few. There is also the role of communicator of change management, as discussed in this chapter.

Given the accessibility to information that is now in the hands of all levels of employees, and the manner in which employees access and share information, the role HR plays as Chief Communicator is a daunting one. The lines of transparency become blurred, and both accurate and inaccurate information can spread like wildfire. HR professionals are required to hone their writing skills, and visual presentation skills (such as those used for weekly intranet videos), in order to manage the accelerated flow of communications. Chapter 7 explores the various tactics and methods of communication for the HR professional.

HR Business Management and Acumen

It is highly important for HR management to understand all business functions within the organization and industry, especially if individuals are striving towards the business partner position within the organization. This means recognizing business issues and understanding their organization and industry from both an internal and external perspective. Simply put, in order to be strategic in HR and to be trusted as an internal business partner, you must understand the business and industry your organization is in.

Business Acumen

Business acumen is defined in SHRM's Business Literacy Glossary as "the knowledge and understanding of the financial, accounting, marketing and operational functions of an organization." It is generally considered to be a keen judge about all things related to business. Figure 6-3 illustrates the many categories of business that provide a well-rounded business acumen for an individual.

You most likely learned quite a bit about business concepts in college courses. A good amount of knowledge is also gained by experiencing business firsthand. HR business management and acumen as a competency come about as you apply all that knowledge and experience. Building business acumen is a career tactic that never ends. Activities you can do to continue to build your business acumen are:

- Voracious reading of journals and media that are broader in topic than just HR
- Volunteering for an organization in a leadership position such as a non-profit credit union in a board of director's position
- Studying your organization's financials and regulatory compliances
- Knowledge of your organization's competitive unique propositions and market share

Figure 6-3
Business Acumen

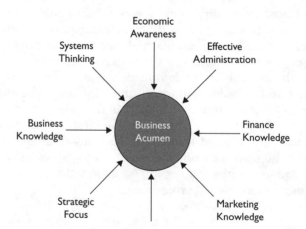

- Staying tuned in to your organization's industry threats and opportunities

- Researching your competitors and staying abreast of their developments

- Asking questions of other managers within the organization to learn about the issues and opportunities affecting their departments

- Enrolling a mentor or hiring an outside Executive Coach that will broaden your perspective and paradigms

- Taking classes or executive education programs on a continual basis

Budgeting and Financial Analysis

SPHR — Budgeting is the process of estimating the amount of income and expenses that will occur within a given period of time. It is usually done on an annual basis, although budgets can be created for multiple years and for shorter periods of time such as months and quarters. Accuracy of budgeting can be improved when there is some historical data on which to rely. And, generally speaking, budgets in the short term can be easier to construct and are usually more accurate than long-range budgets. The reason, simply, is that many unforeseen influences can enter the long-range picture. Fewer unpredictable influences tend to occur in shorter periods of time. Figure 6-4 illustrates the basis of budgeting.

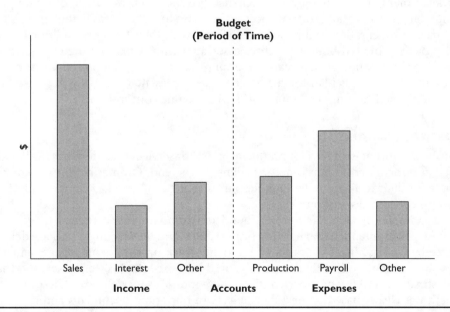

Figure 6-4 Budget chart

Whether in a for-profit enterprise or a governmental agency, a non-profit or a volunteer service organization, there is need for money management. Budgeting and financial analysis are critical to any organization large enough to have employees. Understanding how to plan for earnings and expenses, and then manage the process and ultimately conduct analyses of what happened after the fact, is key to any individual's success in a management role.

There are two key financial reports that any organization should be preparing and studying. One measures the income and expenses over a defined period of time. That can be a year, a calendar/fiscal quarter, or a month. It is usually called the Profit and Loss Statement, or "P & L." The second is a balance sheet that shows the assets (furniture, buildings, vehicles, cash, and accounts receivable) compared to the liabilities outstanding (accounts payable, taxes payable, credit card balances, and payroll payables). A balance sheet also shows the amount of equity owned by investors in the organization. "Equity" is the difference between income and liabilities in a for-profit organization. In a non-profit organization, it is called "net assets."

 NOTE This basic formula will help you understand balance sheets: Assets = Liabilities + Equity.

HR professionals at management levels will generally participate in the creation of the HR department's budget to outline anticipated specific expenses, such as office supplies, equipment purchases, and software licenses, but also for other areas in the organization that have compensation and benefits associated with their budgets. Additionally, HR will provide projected budget expenses associated with plans that the organization's strategic plan may pursue that year—for example, a strategic plan objective that creates a new incentive bonus plan for customer service representatives. HR will project how those additional earnings will impact 401(k) matching contributions.

Business Concepts

A business concept is an idea for producing goods or services that identifies the benefits that can be achieved for customers or clients in the end. Ordinarily, concepts rely on people for their realization. Human Resources thus becomes a key component of any business concept description.

For example, in 1971, Fred Smith founded a company called Federal Express. His business plan contended that it would be possible to provide overnight package delivery service by having a fleet of trucks and airplanes pick up shipments from originating cities around the country, fly them to a central hub in Memphis, Tennessee, sort them by destination, and fly them back to the remote locations for delivery the next day. The benefit was clearly based on next-day delivery of important documents and materials. The process involved using assets including trucks and airplanes and a sorting facility at a central airport. The sorting, driving, and flying had to be done by people. He had to design a system for human resource management that would permit him to successfully implement the concept.

In 2001, Dean Kamen unveiled his invention called the Segway Human Transporter. He had a business concept that he could create and sell a product that would solve some problems people had with transportation. His product is now used in factories, warehouses, and law enforcement. Segways are also rented as a means of transportation for city tours in numerous cities.

An employer's enterprise or agency begins with a business concept. Someone has an idea for solving a problem he or she has noticed in the world. Fleshing out a statement about the assets and human resources that will be required to implement the concept is the process of preparing a business concept statement.

Management Skills

Management skills were first measured scientifically in the American Telephone and Telegraph "Management Progress Study,"[1] which began in 1956 and lasted for over 30 years. It followed the careers of managers within the Bell System, first in Michigan Bell, then nationally. That study led to the first industrial assessment centers, measuring the amount of management skills exhibited by participants in the assessment process.

Skills measured in the program included:

- Oral and written communication skill
- Human relations skill (later called "leadership skill")
- Personal impact (forcefulness and likeability)
- Perception (environmental and perception of people)
- Creativity
- Self-objectivity
- Social objectivity
- Behavior flexibility
- Goal flexibility
- Organization and planning
- Decision making (willingness to make decisions and effectiveness of decisions)

In addition, non-skills were observed and measured. These included things such as:

- Tolerance of uncertainty
- Resistance to stress
- Energy
- Range of interests
- Primacy of work

- Inner work standards
- Need for approval of supervisors
- Need for approval of peers
- Need for advancement

There are other functions involved in managing. These typically involve four identified management functions that the early management theorist Henri Fayol identified and are the basis of most of today's management theories.

Planning

Forecasting, setting goals and objects, determining actions and courses of direction—these activities are key to keeping HR activities in a proactive position rather than a reactive one. The HR department needs to perform strategic planning for its function to ensure that its programs and activities are aligned with the organization's needs. Having a big picture view of how HR activities intertwine with the organization's objectives is necessary.

Organizing

Organizing is the process of creating order out of chaos. It involves collecting process steps and information about the desired goal, and then structuring the methods to achieve the goal. Ordering and sequencing are things done while organizing.

HR professionals have huge organizational responsibilities. There are employee data systems to construct, benefit programs to identify, open enrollment to conduct, the interview selection process to design, and payroll processing to handle. HR professionals must create structures that effectively align the people of an organization with the organization's goals and administration.

Directing

These days, directing work in an organization is thought of as leadership. It involves getting people to willingly do what is wanted or needed. Even in military organizations, it is rare for managers/officers to issue blunt orders. In most situations, it is appropriate to lead a group of people to the desired end without dictating. (That doesn't necessarily apply to combat.)

Once a goal has been determined and a path chosen, the task of directing requires a manager to encourage people to willingly do what is necessary by engaging people in activities that contribute to the desired business's outcomes.

Controlling

The function of controlling involves a monitoring activity to ensure that everything is carried out according to a plan. Managers monitor their organizations' activities and results, determine the difference between what was planned and what actually happened, and then take corrective action to redirect the organization to the goal(s).

HR Management Skill Development

HRCI identified four critical skill development areas that prepare HR professionals for the career challenges they will face:

- Project management
- Managing change
- Managing third-party contractors
- Managing technology

Project Management

Projects come and go in the life of HR professionals. There are projects for implementation of new benefit programs, assessment of new recruiting sources, and all the projects associated with new paths of business that the organization is embarking on. Being able to juggle all those things at the same time while ensuring that each gets the proper amount of attention and actually moves toward a conclusion is the mark of a good project manager.

A project consists of a series of activities and tasks that have been identified that need to be performed to accomplish an outcome. Dates are identified, people assigned to the tasks, and resources such as budget and people allocated. Overseeing a project is project management.

A standard tool used in project management is the Gantt chart, also known as an activity log or milestone chart and is widely available as a template or dedicated software programs. A Gantt chart normally identifies in chronological order the simultaneous tasks that have to occur (see Figure 6-5). The benefit of a Gantt chart is the visual

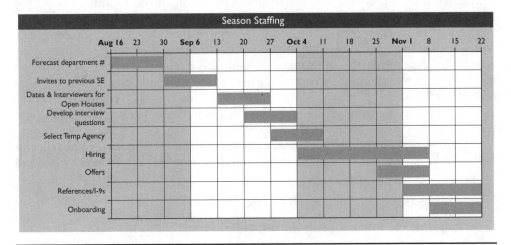

Figure 6-5 Sample Gantt chart

monitoring and communication of who is on first base and doing what task, what needs to occur before progression to second base, and where the results have to be before a run is counted at home plate.

PERT Program evaluation and review technique (PERT) is a project management tool used to organize, schedule, and manage tasks of a project. The U.S. Navy developed the methodology in the 1950s. The Critical Path Math (CPM) methodology is similar to PERT and you will frequently see CPM/PERT associated with one another—they both use visual charts. Large projects that employ cross-functional tasks for several interrelated departments will use the PERT/CPM process tool. Milestones are identified to keep the project on path progression and in a manner that illustrates what must happen before what. The input for a PERT/CPM chart is different from a Gantt chart (a Gantt chart shows the relationship of a task to time); the PERT/CPM is not fueled by time, but by the sequence of events that must occur first. With a PERT/CPM, only two inputs are required: the specific events with associated duration, and the sequence of the events. Advantages of using the PERT/CPM technique include the identification of tasks that can be delayed due to other resource priorities (money, labor). This, however, slows down the progression of the project.

Managing Change

Also referred to as change management; Chapter 8 elaborates more extensively on this skill development. Suffice it to say that managing change is the largest driving force behind employee relations. Change is a process that people and organizations undergo as a response; it is a transformation toward flexibility. HR is involved in the managing of the people issues resulting from change, either planned changed or a reactive change, such as something occurring from an external source (for example, an employment-related law that regulates behavior in the workplace).

Helping both employees and management in an organized process through the rollercoaster ride of change, as identified by Elisabeth Kubler-Ross in her book *On Death and Dying*,[2] is an emotional intelligent (EQ) competency skill for HR professionals and leaders. First, shock and denial about the change is awakened within people. Anger is the next response. Depression eventually sets in about the "loss" of status quo resulting from the change. Then movement toward bargaining and dialogue occurs related to the change. Finally, the rollercoaster ride ends as employees reach a level of acceptance about the change. The key knowledge is in understanding the change and the management of the anticipated reactions.

Donald Kirkpatrick's *How to Manage Change Effectively*[3] discusses a model with the seven basic steps in the change management process to be followed by HR and organizations:

- Determining the need or desire for change
- Preparing the tentative plans for change
- Discussing alternative and probable reactions to the change

- Making a final decision about the change
- Establishing a project plan and associated timetable
- Communicating the change
- Implementing the change and evaluation

Managing Third-Party Contractors

SPHR *Outsourcing* is now a regular everyday word impacting the HR function. It refers to third-party or outside contractors/companies that are able to more cost effectively and efficiently handle functions associated with HR activities. Staffing, benefit and compensation administration, relocation transfers of employees, and training and coaching are just a few of the services easily outsourced today. The value with internal HR personnel is not necessarily the administrative functions they may provide; the value lies with the strategic business management and development activities they offer.

More detailed information about the process of selecting a third-party contractor, requesting proposals, negotiating contracts, and management of contracts can be found in Chapter 4.

Managing Technology

SPHR New technology has increased the efficiency and cost effectiveness of HR greatly over the past two decades. The capability to respond to hundreds of applicants with timeliness and personalization, or for employees to have real-time access to their organization's policies and procedures—these are examples of ways that technology has transformed HR. Electronic signatures, online recordkeeping, enrollment and ordering systems, and ASPs (application service providers) and the technology applications keep HR professionals on their toes. They must be keenly aware of the trends, security, and privacy issues, and the improvement capabilities that HR technology offers. HR professionals must assess and evaluate not only the positive effects of a new technology for HR, but also the negative uninvited effects, such as missing out on a wonderful applicant because her resume was not coded correctly for screening into the applicant tracking system.

As with all technological innovations, a live person needs to sit at the helm of control monitoring and ensure that what goes in comes out correctly, and to monitor hacking and security breaches. This is not just the function of the IT department; it is the function of the owner or the system—in the case of HR, the HR department.

Organizational Structures

Aligning the way the parts of an organization relate to one another is considered the organizational structure. HR professionals need to be familiar with organizational structures so they may act as a guide for management in the selection and determination as to which structure would be best to gain the best performance.

Business Structures and Functions

There are six types of organizational structures:

- Departmental
- Chain of command
- Span of control
- Work specialization
- Formalized
- Centralized or decentralized
- Matrix

Departmental

For this structure, tasks are divided into separate duties, grouping people and jobs together. The purpose is so that work can be coordinated. It can be functional in nature, divisional, or matrix.

Chain of Command

It is a structure where an employee typically reports to one manager in an up-down format, a clear line of decisions and authority. Chain of command is becoming less recognized in organizations today because, more and more often, organizations are pushing decision-making down matrix lines, which causes the line of authority to look more lateral.

Span of Control

This organizational structure refers to the number of individuals who report to a single supervisor. It's hierarchical in nature through a chain of command: executives at the top, managers, then supervisors, and then direct reports—much like a pyramid. In organizations where many workers are skilled and require little supervision, employees may report to one supervisor. This would be considered a "flat organization."

Work Specialization

Work specialization was first associated with the assembly line. It is where tasks are divided into specific jobs and workers are considered skilled labor. It may offer a more efficient manner of productivity, but it can lead to worker boredom. Today's organizations using this organizational structure will typically rotate job functions on a regular basis, training the workers in skills that add variety to their tasks.

Centralized or Decentralized

To centralize or decentralize, that seems to be the question and the cycle of several long-standing organizations. Centralizing pulls decision-making authority to a central level of management, such as headquarters. Decentralizing is pushing the authority level and decisions out to units, such as regional divisions.

The centralizing and decentralizing continuum is also applicable to HR departments. With decentralized structures, corporate headquarters will create policy and develop programs—rollout and application are then carried out by the HR staff in the regional divisions. When it is centralized, HR headquarters would make the policy *and* coordinate the rollout activities or administrative functions.

Matrix

Matrix structures create a dual, rather than a single chain of command. A function, such as HR, would report to the local division executive at a facility, along with a direct reporting function to the head of HR in the headquarters office, which is typically located in another geographical area. As a result, the HR manager at the division location would have two managers, neither manager having a superior role over the other in this reporting relationship. A huge disadvantage of this type of reporting relationship is the conflicting priorities of the division and the headquarters. The employee with two direct superiors is attempting to follow the direction of one, and the other is competing for their priority. It can be a bit of a tug-of-war.

Corporate Culture

Corporate culture is deliberately created by management to achieve specific strategic end results. It is achieved through identifying the specific values, norms, working language, systems, ethics, beliefs, and habits that are aligned and connected with achieving the organization's vision and mission. An organization determines its own corporate culture based on how it wants to be perceived. It is also the pattern of such collective behaviors that are taught to new employees as a way of perceiving, acting, thinking, and even feeling. Ideally, corporate culture is clearly defined and communicated by HR in the onboarding of new hires and in the alignment of HR policies and practices, and it is reinforced within the leadership/employee training functions. Management has the responsibility to "walk the talk" of the desired corporate culture, along with setting expectations and evaluating employee performance against corporate culture expectations. Culture affects the manner and way employees interact with one another, with customers, and with all stakeholders.

Life Cycles of Organizations

Just like the life cycle of people, organizations have life cycles, too. Life cycles are predictable and lead to levels of growth or decline. There are phases in the organizational life cycle: startup, growth, maturity, decline, rebirth, and death. Figure 6-6 is an adaptation of the original Five Stage Organizational Life Cycle Model by Lester, as it includes the newer phases of death and rebirth stages.[4]

After the formation and sometimes turbulent, yet exciting, start-up phase, the lucrative growth phase sets in, which is when the organization begins to settle and reaches its maturity stage. In the maturity stage, the organization establishes its market share and niche loyal customer base. The brand identity and image of the organization

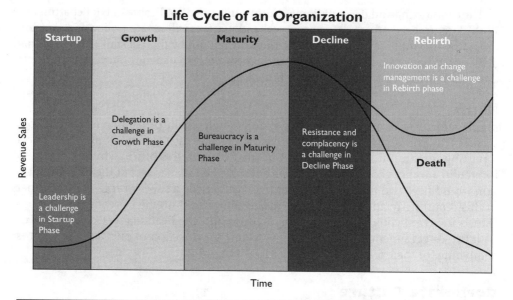

Figure 6-6   Life cycle of an organization

is well established in its market at this point. During this phase, cash flows stabilize and organizational functions are operational and optimized.

The maturity phase can be the most profitable stage of the life cycle if the primary area of business has gained control of a sizable market share that yields profits. Sales and revenue in the maturity phase are no longer exponential; rather, they are normally consistent and regular. Profit margins are stable as revenue/sales have reached a considerable volume and require fewer resources from the creation of a new service/ product stage to the new item promotion stage.

The maturity stage is the key phase in the organizational life cycle as it will determine if the organization survives in the long term. This phase is characterized by a slowdown and a false sense of security. A watchful eye needs to be kept on external factors that could affect the organization's business, such as competition, or substitutions that obliterate the need for the product or service the organization provides, which then leads to the death phase. A recent example of an entire industry being affected by substitutions is the direct marketing product fundraising industry. Within the last decade and a half, what has evolved in fundraising for schools and nonprofit organizations has been the invention of *scrip*, which is a percentage of sales at businesses (such as grocery stores and restaurants) given to schools and nonprofit organizations, thus no longer requiring the need for fundraising through products (magazines, gift wrap, and candy sales).

When organizations fail to implement growth measures to improve sales/revenue, they will eventually enter the final phase of decline, becoming inefficient and top-heavy with bureaucracy. To remain viable, restructuring may be a course of action by reducing the workforce and divesting certain lines of the business. The rebirth phase is characterized by a need for reinvigoration in order to survive, which means a retooling of the business with new vision, focus, and strategies. Rebirth requires the strategic planning process; outside facilitation assistance can be helpful in stretching the organization's leaders to think outside the box.

SPHR Corporate Restructuring

The act of recognizing the structures of an organization for the purpose of making it more profitable, or better organized, is known as corporate restructuring. Additional changes can necessitate restructuring such as a change of ownership or a bankruptcy filing. Restructuring can include selling off portions, or divesting, to reduce debt or operations. The 1980s experienced a heyday of restructuring due to the rampant under-valuation of publicly traded organizations that attracted hostile takeover attempts. If the targeted organization was lucky enough to find a major investor to ward off the hostile takeover attempt (known as a White Knight), the aftermath usually involved a tremendous amount of debt and then restructuring and divesting to pay off the White Knight and debt.

During the recent great recession, corporate restructuring occurred as a result of economic decline to reduce financial losses from the lack of revenue. The basic nature of restructuring is a zero-sum game. It can quickly reduce financial losses and simultaneously reduce the tensions between major stakeholders (shareholders) and the overriding condition prompting the distressed situation.

Divestiture

Organizations divest to refocus, rethink, and restructure their core business capabilities with an ultimate goal in mind to be leaner and more cost effective. Going from big to smaller, or refocusing on the core product/service that the organization offers by selling off a separate line of business arms, can present a variety of challenges for HR. To minimize disruption of operations and employees during divestiture, HR may need to redefine some of the organizational structure that is currently in place. Reviewing re-employment policies, severance packages, and employee classifications and job descriptions for either increased or decreased responsibilities are just a few considerations.

Mergers and Acquisitions

Mergers and acquisitions (M&A) are intended to enhance an organization by accessing market share or increasing assets. It is best to involve HR right from the get-go to plan for the effects that mergers and acquisitions have on an organization, such as culture blending, job function redundancy, and comparison of benefits/compensation/job titles, along with effects on HR information systems, policies/procedures/ethics, and, if there is a union, collective bargaining.

The M&A process has four basic phases, which are covered in the following sections.

Preparation

You must first ascertain if the HR staff has the necessary knowledge, strategic planning, and project management skills, for managing the transition of an M&A.

Due Diligence

The due diligence stage is next, which includes scrutinizing not just the financials, but many of the other risks associated with HR. The organization's workforce-related risks are just the tip of the iceberg. Factoring in people matters are more difficult to quantify, and yet absolutely crucial.

Research and investigation are needed on the proposed M&A organization to determine the technology differences and needs, structural and talent risks, and cultural issues that will arise. The sheer recognition that two cultures must be brought together and blended to create a collaborative, high-performance new organization is daunting. Compliance, corporate governance, and legal claims/lawsuit information—those in process and those that appear on the horizon as a potential threat—would additionally be reviewed and understood at this phase. It is important to understand that oversimplifying these risks can lead to misguided integration planning, unexpected costs, and loss of critical talent.

Integration Planning

Here's where a good strategic planning process resulting in goals and objectives is necessary, along with project management implementation. A change management plan associated with a culture blending process, communication strategies, and consolidation activities occurs during this phase.

Implementation, Measurement, and Monitoring Results

The process is not complete when the organizations are finished with the M&A. HR plays a vital role in monitoring the pulse and mood, assisting with workforces that have blended successfully, and helping to troubleshoot new issues that may have occurred during integration. Employees, after all, will be the implementers of the changes to enable an organization to realize the goals of the merger. Creating metrics and milestones that measure the intended results the organization set out to achieve, with respect to the people related value of the deal, is the last phase for HR.

Transition Tactics

During a major transition, management often expects leadership transitions to happen without major changes in the acquired business. When clarity and trust are most needed, it's possible that leadership may appear more focused on itself (individuals impacted personally by the transition) than on taking care of its anxious people. Employees can't help noticing the disconnection between leadership's actions and words, with potentially damaging effects of costly turnover of valued employees and serious morale and productivity problems. Poor people management and communication drain financial value from many changeovers.

Having a clear vision and consistent frequent communication about organizational transition is vital. Creating a strategic blueprint should revolve around communication, not just to the workforce, but also to other stakeholders such as the customers and communities served by the organization (plural in the case of M&A). The best transition tactics revolve around trust and communication. Leadership groups must move forward together, fully aligned, and "owning" the strategic blueprint of the newly created vision in sharing its messages. If the messages and themes that are expressed to all parties are not consistent, then confusion, fear, and a lack of faith in the transition process will likely occur. Those signals could send tremors of uncertainty throughout the organization. The workforce can surely be counted on to fill a vacuum of information with worst-case scenario rumors, in terms of who will be retained, who will be let go, and how the everyday rules of the game will change.

Outsourcing and Offshoring

Sometimes the terms "outsourcing" and "offshoring" are used interchangeably; however, they do have distinctly different meanings. Offshoring is moving a function, such as a manufacturing plant or customer call center, to another country away from the "home" of the organization. The plant or call center is still part of the organization, and the workforce are employees of the organization.

With outsourcing, a function is moved to a third-party entity, a business separate from the organization. Order fulfillment and benefit and payroll administration are functions that might be outsourced. The third-party company that the function has been outsourced to may or may not be within the organization's country.

There are nine identifiable steps in the outsourcing process:

1. Define the needs and goals for outsourcing.
2. Establish the budget.
3. Create the RFP (Request for Proposal).
4. Select third-party contractors to send the RFP to.
5. Evaluate the return proposals.
6. Select the third-party contractor.
7. Negotiate the contract.
8. Create the project plan schedule and implementation of the function move to the third-party contractor.
9. Evaluate the project's implementation and continued measurement of intended results.

Chapter 4 contains detailed information about RFPs and negotiating third-party contracts. With both outsourcing and offshoring, there is generally a cost savings strategy at play, typically involving labor costs.

Strategic Planning

Strategic planning is an important process in the life cycle and health of an organization. The process produces a blueprint for the organization's growth intentions, typically from three to five years. It helps define the foundational premises for growth: Where is the organization now, where does the organization intend to go (vision), and how will it get there (strategies, goals, and objectives), and lastly, what will be the milestones and measurements of success?

All major organizational functions are involved in the strategic planning process: finance, marketing, sales, operations, IT, customer service, public relations, and human resources. Many types of organizations are required to do strategic planning as part of their legal governance requirements. The benefits of strategic planning include maintaining a competitive position within the organization's market and industry, and internally, the goal of strategic planning is to communicate to the workforce a big picture view of what lies ahead, keeping everyone singing from the same hymnbook page.

In previous decades, the strategic planning process was initiated generally by the sales or revenue producing functions. The focus was narrow with financial objectives and sales/revenue initiatives. HR's involvement has come about through the recognition of the human capital component in planning and its impact on business strategy, and the recognition that HR as a whole has moved away from just a transactional role to a more strategic role within organizations.

Developing Goals and Objectives

After a strategy has been created and identified in the strategic planning process, goals and objectives are then created to set a course of action for how to achieve the stated strategy. There may be more than one goal associated with a single strategy. Strategies might look like this: increasing market share to 24 percent; opening a fulfillment center in the Midwest to decrease transit time to client; launching a new line of gluten-free products with a private label brand name.

Goals might be problem solving in nature, correcting something that is not right yet. Or they might be development goals that foster a growth initiative. A third type of goal is an ongoing goal, one that keeps routine events occurring. The following are examples of goals: year-end decrease in the number of customer complaint calls by 20 percent; partner with the Main Street Merchants Association as a sponsor for the community's Fourth of July parade; maintain social media presence with weekly guest expert blog posts.

Objectives fall under goals, and include the basics steps for accomplishing the goal. They are specific, clearly stated, and relate to a time frame. Typically, a single goal will include several objectives. In an organization, different functions will have objectives related to an organizational goal—finance will have one that relates to the finance function, IT and HR will have theirs, and so on. The following are examples of objectives related to the first goal example, to decrease the number of customer complaint calls by 20 percent:

- Evaluate 2013's customer complaint categories by March 1.

- QA to retool IT's inspection process of the ABC widget by Quarter 2.

- Sales and marketing staff initiates round-robin scheduling for listening in on 500 customer service calls during Quarter 1, identifying the typical FAQ and associated responses.

- IT streamlines the automated response generator on the website with FAQs by end of Quarter 2.

There is a memorable acronym for the creation of goals and objectives, SMART.

> S = Specific
> M = Measurable
> A = Attainable
> R = Relevant and realistic
> T = Time bound

Environmental Scanning

When developing a strategic plan, leaders need to understand and know what is going on in their organization's industry, the market it serves, and within the organization itself. They need to be acutely aware of risks such as technological advances and how that may impact the organization or its business. The framework to collecting, analyzing, and interpreting relevant information of threats and opportunities is known as *environmental scanning*. It's not always easy to define what is going on outside an organization, yet it is vitally important for the outcome of strategic planning.

The following factors will shape an organization's external environment and need to be considered when doing environmental scanning:

- Demographic factors, such as age, gender, ethnicity, generations, shifts in population, education trends, and labor force.

- Economic factors, which can be a host of things such as the current day recession, rising health and retirement costs, and emerging global economies—just to name a few. The Gross Domestic Product (GDP), Consumer Price Index (CPI), interest rates, and inflation all can have an immediate and direct effect on financial planning, which includes wage increases, benefit costs, and retirement notices.

- Political factors must weigh in because one thing that U.S.-based organizations can count on is an ever fluid regulatory and legislative government arm continually being enacted at the federal, state, and local levels.

- Employment factors are looked at in environmental scanning. Retention, turnover, skilled labor competition, unions, immigration, and even attitude and generational trends and realities are determined.

- International factors are interwoven into the environmental scanning due to the nature of our growing global connections as a world. Trade agreements, offshoring, and international labor laws may impact the organization or its industry.

- Social factors have a place in the scanning review and research. For example, the prominence of single parents in the workforce and a generation that is working past normal Social Security retirement age will necessitate planning and consideration.

- Forever increasing in their speed of change are technological factors. The advances we have seen in just the past five years are astounding when it comes to information access and the speed of that access. The awareness of technological skills and the training to keep workforces up-to-speed on ever-changing software programs and equipment is required. A digital divide has been created, in much the same manner as the divide created during the first years of automobile ownership in the early 1900s. The haves and have-nots are apparent again in terms of broadband access.

SWOT Analysis

SWOT stands for strengths, weaknesses, opportunities, and threats. Strengths and weaknesses are looked at as internal factors within the organization that can be managed. Opportunities and threats are controlled by external forces. It is a long-standing simple process used in strategic planning for collecting information about an organization's current state. Four foundational questions are posed:

- **S:** What are the organization's strengths?

- **W:** What are the organization's weaknesses?

- **O:** What external opportunities might help the organization to progress toward its vision?

- **T:** What external threats could foil the organization's plans and business?

Assessments are helpful in SWOT analysis, including customer focus groups or surveys, current employee attitude surveys, and exiting employee interviews. It's important to ask these groups open-ended questions such as:

- What's going well and right with the organization?

- What would be more ideal with the organization?

- What needs improvement or is not working so well?

PEST Analysis PEST analysis is also referred to as STEP analysis—they are the same tool used within the SWOT process. The acronym stands for political, economic, social, and technological factors. The PEST process is focused on the external scanning and gathering of information. Today, software has been developed to use the PEST process, which is widely helpful in reducing the amount of time for research, in particular with opportunities and threats. An additional way to obtain information from the organization's marketplace is through a third-party consulting firm. Those firms have collected vast amounts of data and information, including data about trends and other predictions of information.

Porter's Five Forces

This is another analytical tool created by a Harvard Business School professor, Michael E. Porter. Porter asserts in his book *Competitive Strategy: Techniques for Analyzing Industries and Competitors*[5] that there are five forces found in all industries—competitors, suppliers, buyers, alternative products for consumers, and the type/level of competition in the industry. Porter's model of analysis targets the specific issues of the industry in which the organization operates, keeping an eye on the horizon and futuristic events. Five questions are posed:

- What new competition might enter the organization's market?
- What level of reliance does the organization have with its suppliers?
- What is the diversity of the organization's customer base?
- What substitutions as a more reasonable cost to the customer might pop up?
- What is the level of competition in the current marketplace?

Internal Environment Scanning

As mentioned previously, in SWOT analysis, the internal environment of the organization also plays a role in the gathering and analysis of information prior to the strategic planning process. It's essential to be able to read the strengths and weaknesses of the organization's internal environment and assess whether the structure of the organization is helping or hampering its effectiveness. This can include functional reporting relationships and also policies that are conflicting in nature, such as a customer service policy that clamps down on customer service authority and is in direct violation of the organization's expressed value of employee empowerment.

Gathering information in the form of facilitating employee discussion groups, assessments, and surveys is helpful with the internal environmental scanning process. Employee surveys, interviews, focus groups, suggestion systems, confidential hotlines, and steering committees are just a few of the ways this scanning can occur.

Strategic Planning Contributions

SPHR When HR earns a seat in the strategic planning team process, it is expected to contribute as a consultant, not as a decision maker. You can leverage your authority and credibility by providing the environmental scanning data and backing up opinions with objective data to support your recommendations. To contribute effectively as a consultant, you must know all the internal functions in the organization and have a broader perspective, and again, you should have that big picture view of what is in the best interest of the greater whole. You must not just be the voice and advocate for the human capital in an organization, or just perform the HR function, but you must also represent the entire constituency of an organization. SHRM cites in its 2008 report *HR's Evolving Role in Organizations and Its Impact on Business Strategy* that the top-three HR critical functional areas that contributed to organizations' business strategies were: [6]

- Staffing, employment, and recruitment
- Training and development
- Employee benefits

Employee relations and strategic planning followed this list with close percentages.

Forecasting Human Capital

SPHR — Predicting human capital aligned with the organization's objectives is known as forecasting. And in order to forecast, the information gathered from the internal and external scanning is needed. Like forecasting the weather, information from the past, current, and future is used to identify an expected condition. The methods used to forecast can either be judgmental or mathematical. More detailed information about the methods for forecasting is located in Chapter 5.

Aligning HR Initiatives or Organizational Objectives

SPHR — The purpose of aligning HR's initiatives and objectives with the organization's objectives is to ensure that the functions and responsibilities HR is accountable for are in alignment with the organization's plans and are helping move the organization toward its vision. This is the "big picture" view that we've been referring to in this book and is expressed in the "In the Trenches" sections. Having the right number of people, with the right capabilities, at the right times, and in the right places, engaged and motivated to do the right things is HR's primary support role for the organization. Basically, HR is charged with aligning the human capital with the organization's strategy plans. For example recruitment initiatives must correlate with plans for opening a new facility. Retention incentives such as compensation and benefits would fit into the organization's plans for holding on to key employee groups. Or culture-creating initiatives to heighten the engagement of the workforce could involve HR policies and procedures. It is the human capital in an organization that actually produces the desired results from a strategic plan, and HR is a gatekeeper of the human capital.

In the Trenches

Adding Value: Proactive vs. Reactive

The human capital in a company can account for up to 80% of the costs of doing business. How HR hires, retains, and manages that human capital directly impacts the company's bottom line. When employees have such a big stake in the success of a company, the value of HR's role is easy to see. At one time, HR professionals were known as firefighters, putting out fires left and right that involved employees in the workplace. Preventing those fires in the first place—now that's where HR has progressed, wearing a proactive hat.

What does it take to be proactive? It takes a plan that views the entire organization and its goals—a 'big picture view." Without a proactive plan, it's easy to find yourself in that firefighting, reactive role, wherein you are not in control of one of the largest expenses of doing business.

Let me use the example of a janitorial company to illustrate how this can be detrimental to a business. If the janitorial company supplies staff for bank buildings and retail malls, there will be different security requirements for each type of facility. The staff being sent to the retail mall may only need to complete a two-hour security clearance process, whereas the staff utilized at bank buildings are required to go through a three-day process to obtain a different level of security clearance.

Since the janitorial industry is a high turnover one, the company is constantly having to hire and replace staff. The three-day security clearance time will cause a delay in the hiring process and will create a staff shortage for the cleaning of bank buildings. This is where wearing your proactive HR hat and having a proactive plan comes into play.

In this circumstance, the janitorial company should be using a proactive talent pipeline. HR would select and schedule employees who have been working satisfactorily in the retail mall cleaning position, for the three-day bank security training programs, to create a pipeline of ready staff to be moved in a moment's notice. Simultaneously, HR could collaborate with the local Welfare Recipients Back to Work Program in their county by sponsoring the security training required for a retail mall to be included in the county's retraining program. This then creates a talent pipeline whereby easier-to-fill positions act as a "talent bank" for the janitorial company.

(Continued)

> Without proactive recruitment practices, the janitorial company will experience service interruptions, and incur unwanted liability that may lead to a loss of revenue and contracts for the company.
>
> Acting proactively instead of reactively is something we'd all like to do as professionals because it's easier to manage our time and plan out our activities. But fires will happen and working from a proactive plan offers the *gold* time management principle, which provides for less disruption when an unplanned event happens requiring urgency and reactiveness. As an HR professional you can hold the proactive keys by reviewing your company's goals and making sure HR's activities are aligned to support those goals. Look for what is causing pain in the company and treat that as a symptom, peeling back what is at the root cause of the pain. Therein lays the real problem to be working on and figuring out how to head it off at the pass.

Measuring Strategic Results

Quarterly, if not more frequently, the results being achieved from strategic planning initiatives, goals, and objectives should be reviewed to determine whether plans and projects are "on track" or "off course," requiring corrective action. Too many organizations skip this important stage of strategic planning and, instead, dust off the planning binders from the previous year just prior to the new year's planning session to evaluate how well they executed the year's goals and objectives. Change is inevitable during the year and something could occur that causes a shift in priority and allocation of resources.

It's helpful to have milestones set for each objective and goal on a quarterly basis. Those milestones set the short-term placards of what should have been achieved and by what function. Quarterly review meetings should be held to review the progress against objectives and to keep an eye on the plan. A scorecard of sorts is necessary to account for the expense, resources, and results that are being (or not being) achieved. The HR professional is likely to facilitate these types of quarterly reviews, or minimally, to be present as a contributor.

Methods and Tools Used in Decision Making

The process of decision making is complex. When coupled with building a business case for the recommended solution to a specific problem, there is need for supporting documentation that provides legitimate rationale for the recommendation.

Decision-Making Methods

In the book *Crucial Conversations: Tools for Talking When Stakes Are High*,[7] Kerry Patterson and his coauthors outline four specific methods for making decisions: command, consult, vote, and consensus:

- **Command decisions**   Made by the decision maker with no involvement from other people.

- **Consult decisions**   Decisions made following invitations from decision maker to others requesting their input.

- **Voting decisions**   Following discussion of the problem and alternative solutions, the group takes a vote on the solution it wishes to support. Majority rules.

- **Consensus decisions**   Discussion continues until everyone in the group agrees on a decisions.

Analysis of Research

Decisions are often based on research that comes either from primary or secondary sources.

- **Primary source**   An original work such as a study, eyewitness account, or literary paper

- **Secondary source**   A document written about a primary source

If a primary source is a study about costs of medical insurance, a secondary source could be a white paper that refers to the study and evaluates how it describes medical insurance costs.

Then, there are quantitative and qualitative approaches to analysis:

- **Qualitative analysis**   Based on stories and pictures without numerical support. Often based on interviews, the depth of information gathered about each individual is usually more extensive than with numerical analysis techniques. Fewer samples are included than with a quantitative approach.

- **Quantitative analysis**   Based on statistics from a large sample or population. Results can be used to predict what an entire population looks like or will do.

Informational Formats

Presenting the information gathered as part of the decision-making process is ultimately what the process is all about. It is necessary to communicate the gathered information to a decision maker or group of decision makers. Here are some ways that this can be accomplished:

- **Descriptive statistics**   These techniques involve preparation of charts or graphs to allow visual descriptions of the results from research and analysis.

- **Measuring central tendency**   There are three basic measurements that are commonly used for central tendency. They are "mean," "median," and "mode." Mean is the arithmetic average of all data points. Median is the data point in the middle of the sequence. Mode is the most frequently appearing data point. For example, the following data set will result in the results indicated.

Length of Employee Service with Employer in Years
17 employees
1,1,1,2,3,4,4,5,5,6,6,6,6,7,7,8,9
Mean = 1+1+1+2+3+4+4+5+5+6+6+6+6+7+7+8+9 = 81/17 = 4.76 years
Median = 5
Mode = 6

Statistical Analysis

Statistical measurements can be used to infer conclusions. For example, they can be used to show that certain things could not have happened by chance. Disparate impact is one such measurement. When applied with enough data points, regression and correlation analysis can demonstrate beyond the shadow of a doubt that a conclusion is accurate.

Correlation analysis measures the relationship of two or more variables. It can be used to track how one variable reacts in response to the other variables. Perhaps the amount of vacation an employee receives is positively correlated with the length of that employee's service with the employer. Employees with five years of service are entitled to three weeks of vacation while employees with under five years of service are entitled to only two weeks of vacation. A negative correlation exists when one variable goes up and the other goes down, or vice versa. Volume discounts offer a good representation of this type of statistical analysis. The unit price of a widget is set at $5.00. But if a customer orders 100 widgets at once, the unit price is only $4.50. There is a negative correlation between the number of units ordered and the unit price.

Regression analysis can show how one variable is responsible for a specific result regardless of the influence from other variables. One application is the determination that there is disparate impact discrimination in compensation against women regardless of their length of service, age, educational levels, job history, and perhaps other variables. If a statistical significance can be shown at levels beyond two standard deviations or 5 percent probability, a conclusion can be drawn that there could have been discrimination. Proof requires analysis of many more variables and the entire employee workforce. Courts accept regression analysis as evidence of illegal discrimination so the process holds value for HR professionals.

Variation analysis is a mathematical process that allows the comparison of how much two or more things vary from one another. Perhaps those variations fluctuate over time. In HR terms, it could measure the turnover rate with the employee survey satisfaction rate and the cost per employee for company-provided benefits.

All of these methods give us mathematical tools to draw conclusions (inferences) about the likelihood of what will happen in the future. We may be able to predict the lowering of turnover rates if we improve our employee satisfaction survey results.

Develop Metrics to Measure Milestones/Results

SPHR Creating and reporting on metrics and milestone results are good ways for HR to express its value and achievements. There are several ways that expand on measurement reporting such as six sigma, total quality management, management by objectives, and the balanced scorecard (Figure 6-7).

Figure 6-7
Balanced
scorecard

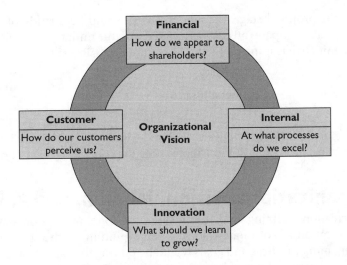

The balanced scorecard is a tool developed by Robert Kaplan and David Norton[8] to help organizations expand the level of measurements from solely financial results to include other key elements that impact an organization's success. A balanced scorecard tracks information in four key areas:

- Financial results
- Customer results
- Key internal processes organization excels with
- Innovation

Examples and instructions on the concept and use can be located at The Balanced Scorecard Institute, www.balancedscorecard.org/basics/bscl.html.

Chapters 5 and 8 have more information on the specifics of metrics used with hiring and training activities.

Performance Cost and Benefit (ROI) Analyses

SPHR The most commonly used metric for measuring results in an organization is a return on investment (ROI) metric. It is one of the most effective manners for HR to communicate and evaluate its impact on strategic initiatives. ROI is calculated by dividing the benefits realized from an initiative, such as hiring or training, by the total related costs (direct or indirect). ROI occurs after-the-fact and not as a tool for projecting. The formula is:

$$\frac{\text{Value of benefit received}}{\text{Costs to produce benefit}}$$

In the proposal stage, the analysis used would be a study of cost benefit analysis (CBA). CBA compares all costs associated with the initiative or project that are forecasted if the initiative is implemented. The formula for CBA is:

$$\text{Cost benefit ratio} = \frac{\text{Value of projected benefits}}{\text{Cost}}$$

The main difference between ROI and CBA is that CBA includes projected soft costs in its calculation, and ROI calculates only the concrete costs that occurred.

Organizational Vision, Mission, and Values

The creation, defining, and composing of vision and mission statements, along with identification of corporate values, is the beginning of the strategic planning process. Diving into objectives and goals would be putting the cart before the horse. Facilitating the development along with communicating the vision, mission, core values, and ethical standards of an organization typically lies within the HR function, beginning with the onboarding orientation process of new hires.

A vision statement speaks of what the organization intends to "be" in its future—the direction it is headed in. The mission statement is the organization's clear definition of what business it intends to be in and for whom, which is the method of how it will achieve its vision. And the corporate core values provide the compass of behaviors on its journey toward achieving the vision. Standards of ethics address the attitude and actions.

Vision Statement

A corporate vision statement is the guiding and compelling image of a desired future for an organization, a big picture view of what company leadership is developing the organization into. It is what convinces people to hire on with an organization, to contribute their work to that organization, and align their own values, morals, and goals with the result the organization desires to achieve. A vision statement provides clear direction like a pinpoint on a map. Following are two examples of a vision statement:

> To be the preferred choice of hotels for business travels in the nine western states.
> To be the largest provider of durable widgets to the U.S. defense industry contractors.

Mission Statement

The mission statement describes what an organization does and for whom. It specifies a general outline of how its vision will be achieved. Mission statements are helpful for keeping employees directed toward the same common goal, defining the purpose of the organization and who its intended customers are. They have been excellent points of reference for decisions by management and policy creation, along with charting the course for new ventures. Mission statements also act as an organization's promise to its customer as to what they can expect from the organization and its employees. The following is an example of a well-conceived mission statement:

> The mission of ABC Corporation is to manufacture and distribute to U.S. defense industry contractors, the highest quality of widgets that are safe, reliable, durable, and low cost, on a just-in-time order basis, and in an environmentally Green manner.

Values

Corporate values are the behaviors that an organization has that dictate to employees how they will act, interact, and what will drive their decisions and behaviors for business performance. They are guiding principles that help define not only how the employees will behave and act, but also how the organization as a whole will act, and the building blocks to corporate culture. Some values are written and purposefully identified by management in order to set an expectation of desired employee behavior (right from wrong) with customers and with representatives of the organization. The values can align with branding of the organization to help set those expectations of what customers and employees can anticipate from the organization. Many core corporate values are also expressed in the organization's mission statement. Others might be the unwritten values, positive or negative, that have an undercurrent that drives behavior, actions, and decisions—they are important as a core to the organization and thus referred to as *core values*. A core value, however, is only a true core value if it influences employees' actions the majority of the time. A few examples are listed in Table 6-2.

Corporate Ethics

Corporate ethics define the moral principles and values that establish an organization's expectations of conduct from its leadership and employees. Where corporate values define desired behaviors, corporate ethics are the code for attitude and norms. Identifying

Positive Core Values	Negative Core Values
Treating everyone, regardless of position, with respect.	Managers expected to answer text messages or phone calls during vacations.
Innovation, thinking outside paradigms.	Creative tension, challenging everything.
Acting in an environmentally friendly way.	Management personnel arrive prior to non-exempt employees in the morning.
The customer is always right.	Providing preference to parent employees over single employees for vacation requests during school recess.
Quality and safety first.	Eating and working at desk during lunch break.

Table 6-2   Driving Core Organizational Values

and establishing an organization's ethics go hand-in-hand with creating its vision, mission, and values, helping clearly identify what an ethical workplace is for new hires and existing employees.

Organizations have a responsibility and even a legal requirement thanks to the Sarbanes-Oxley Act (SOX, see Chapter 2) to interact with its employees, stakeholders, and communities in an ethical and trustworthy manner. Responsibilities are wide and vary ranging from decisions involving local community environmental hazard notifications, to the treatment of customers or employees with truth and integrity. HR's role in organizational ethics is an important one because ethical issues raised are generally about honesty, truthfulness, fairness, social responsibility, and legal governance, typically coming from within the workforce.

SOX made many of the practices of organizations come under added scrutiny, providing penalties and even jail time for executives for violations. The following are scrutinized under SOX:

- Insider trading, which is illegal and monitored by the Securities and Exchange Commission, occurs when investors receive information that could only be known by internal organizational sources, and this information impacts buy-sell shares of that company. For example: Your benefits manager in HR discloses a planned merger (that has not been made public yet and would likely increase the value of shares) to your third-party employee benefit firm's account executive. If that account executive were to increase his shares and/or share that information with friends who invested, this would be considered insider trading.

- Conflicts of interests where either an individual or the organization is involved in a situation of multiple interests, one of which could possibly influence or corrupt motivation. For example: An executive in an organization has a spouse with a separate business that provides products or services to the organization, and that executive has a say in awarding the contract.

- Kickbacks, bribes, and payoffs are common terms used for payoffs of some nature for doing something such as awarding a contract. For example, buyers in the procurement department of an organization can get caught in this unethical behavior if they accept tickets to the Super Bowl from a vendor in exchange for awarding the procurement contract to that vendor. Acceptance of gifts by an employee and the amount of the gift needs to be clearly defined in policy.

 NOTE   Not all unethical behavior may be breaking the law.

Whistleblower Retaliation Protection

Employees who report to government agencies real or perceived illegal activity committed by their organizations are called whistleblowers. Encouragement to inform on organizations that are acting illegally arose from the False Claims Act of 1863 (see Chapter 2), where persons could report government contractors to the federal government.

Over the last couple of decades, whistleblowing incidents have occurred that have made it to lawsuits and headlines in the news. Enron, AOL, WorldCom are just a few. The most noteworthy and largest payout occurred when a former employee at Warner-Lambert reported (and brought a lawsuit) that the pharmaceutical firm used illegal means to market a drug. Some states have specific statutes protecting whistleblowers, but even if there is no specific statute, protection is provided under the "public policy" exception in the employer-at-will doctrine. HR professionals need to be familiar with their local laws in the states where their organization is located.

The degree to which employees report wrongdoings outside of the organization is a direct reflection on the culture of the organization. HR needs to create reporting avenues that maintain a strong level of confidentiality, and be aware of signs, such as when a performance review rating discloses that an employee is insubordinate and not following procedures.

Retaliation against whistleblowers is clearly not allowed according to numerous court decisions (see Chapter 2, Sarbanes-Oxley Act).

Corporate Governance Compliance

SPHR The manner in which an organization is managed (shareholders, management, and board of directors) is known as corporate governance. Its system of structures, obligations, rights, and duties by which the organization is directed and controlled influences the decisions that are made by those in charge (be it top management or a board of directors). They all have a fiduciary responsibility, aligned with the values and ethics of the organization, to act in the best interests of the shareholders.

An owner, board of directors, and/or top management committed to standards of corporate governance, business integrity, and standards of conduct in all activities are the cornerstone of fiduciary responsibility. They are ultimately accountable to the shareholders and must show that the organization is appropriately governed; follows compliance rules, regulations, and standards; and delivers on its strategy and mission statement.

Assessment of Policies/Procedures

SPHR Each year, human resource professionals should conduct a review of the organization's policies and procedures. It is necessary because federal or state laws may have changed, causing new requirements for monitoring and oversight. It is also appropriate to re-evaluate policies in light of financial obligations. For example, health insurance benefit programs are experiencing a rise in expense from year to year. To manage that expense, it may be necessary to reconfigure health insurance benefits, offering less expensive options to employees. It might also be necessary to make major changes by instituting different benefits for new hires who begin after a certain date in order to lower the organization's financial obligations. Pension programs are obviously another example of policies that need review from time to time.

When legal requirements change, employers must adapt to the new rules. One example might be the addition of genetic information as a protected category in equal employment law. Policy statements may need to be rewritten to include the new protections.

Keeping policies current will contribute to proper employee communication and can help reduce financial liabilities should a lawsuit challenge employer treatment.

In the Trenches

Shaping Culture Through Policy Development

Christina Nishiyama, MBA, PHR, Human Resources Director, Las Vegas, Nevada

The policy development process is your opportunity to shape the work environment. Gone are the days of the dreaded personnel encyclopedia; make it a map of the culture!

Although this policy mantra is clear to me now, it was not so clear upon my initiation into policy development. On my first day at a new job, in a new industry, I vividly remember walking away from a brief meeting with a thousand-page collection of reference materials and a daunting number of employment law acronyms scribbled on a notepad.

I began the policy development process with a laser focus on legal compliance and a vast amount of research. Although important, the hours I put in lurched over a computer, assuring that every word was carefully phrased and thoughtfully evaluated, are not what made my experience with policy creation successful. In taking a step back and thinking about how critical a policy manual was, I learned how to draft it not merely as a document that should be read once and strewn aside, but as an opportunity to shape the organization's culture.

No two organizations are alike, and whether from a written or administrative perspective, neither are the policies that shape them. For a small organization with mostly exempt staff, an attendance policy may be much less critical than it is for the eight-hundred-employee casino across the street. Furthermore, a dress code may not be quite so "standard" across an organization with a technical operation in one state and a retail operation in another.

When granted the opportunity to create policies, it is important to begin the process by evaluating the culture of the organization—what are the mission, vision, and core values? How do staff and department heads view the organization in its current state, and where do they want it to be? Policies serve as a reference for decision-making across the organization. The verbiage you place to a seemingly simple corrective action procedure may change how the entire organization views the training, coaching, and performance management processes.

(Continued)

As you ascertain that each policy is compatible with legal requirements, conduct thoughtful research of policies at comparable organizations, and confirm that all relevant topics are covered in the manual, take your assignment a step further and think about actually implementing each policy in the workplace. Do staff members thrive on immediate recognition? If so, maybe the standard employee-of-the-quarter program is not right for the group. Do staff members struggle with communicating grievances through the right avenues? Think about a way to communicate the grievance procedure in a manner that is relatable to staff and tie it back to your founding principles. Taking the time to thoughtfully research innovative communication practices targeted to the workplace demographic may entirely change the way the policy manual is viewed. Finally, keeping language simple, clear, and easy to follow will make policies a useful resource for both supervisory management and employees to adhere to.

Ethics Investigations

SHRM's *Business Literacy Glossary of Terms* defines "business ethics" as, "A philosophy principle concerned with opinions about appropriate and inappropriate business conduct or behavior by individuals or groups of individuals." Some organizations are subject to legal expectations about ethical behavior. (See Chapter 2 and the *Sarbanes-Oxley Act of 2002*.)

It is fairly common these days for employers to have telephone hotlines for employees to report instances of unethical behavior. Once reported, the employer can investigate and resolve any problems that may exist.

Behavior is influenced by rewards so it is critical that HR professionals be sure to think through how behavior is rewarded. For example, are sales representatives told that they should reach their sales quotas "at all costs"? If that is the case, there may be some incentive for people to cut corners and do things that aren't exactly proper. Some people may find it reasonable to do things that aren't even legal in order to reach their quotas. That disconnect between rewards and behavioral expectations is something to guard against.

Monitoring Legislative and Regulatory Issues

Some industry associations have legislative monitors or lobbyists to keep track of state and federal legislatures. It is only the larger employers who would find it beneficial to employ their own representatives to the legislative process. Collective funding for common interests is often quite effective and it is done by most industries, including the pharmaceutical, automobile, high technology, and the lumber and paper industries. Many more can be added to that list.

When legislation is proposed that will have an impact on the employers within an industry, these representatives work with legislators and their staffs to understand the impact proposals will have on the work done by people in those groups. It is common for these discussions to take place and for lobbyists to try to convince legislative representatives that their industry's interests should be taken into account when considering legislative action.

Individual employers may find it advantageous to perform their own monitoring of state and federal legislatures so they can participate by testifying at hearings or submitting comments regarding their suggestions for new laws.

Federal regulations are published in the Federal Register and thus are available for review by the general public. When new regulations are developed, opportunities are available for employers to offer comments on the impact those regulations will have on them. It is frequently in the best interest of employers to participate in that process, yet few actually do. All employers should be alert to what is going on in Washington, D.C., and state capitals.

The Legislative Process

While each state legislature follows much the same process, the following are the steps for a federal law:

1. The bill is introduced in either the House of Representatives or the Senate.

2. One of the House or Senate committees is assigned to consider the bill.

3. Either a sub-committee or the full committee considers the bill, marks it up, and votes on whether or not to pass it along to the full House or Senate. Sub-committees must "report out" on the bill to the full committee by a majority vote. The committee must report out on the bill to the full House or Senate. The report out includes a recommendation for passage.

4. The bill goes to the full House or Senate for a vote by all members. Amendments can be made by representatives or senators. If an amendment passes, it becomes part of the bill. A vote of the entire body will result in passage by simple majority or defeat if a majority is not achieved.

5. The bill is sent to the other body for consideration. The same process is followed. Committees and sub-committees are involved and may hold hearings to listen to experts talk about the proposed law. Once passed by the committee, the bill goes to the full body for consideration.

6. If the Senate version and the House version of the bill are different, it goes to a joint committee of both bodies to resolve those differences. It is now called a "conference bill." When a final joint agreement is reached, the bill goes back to each body for another vote.

7. Once passed by both Congressional bodies, the bill goes to the president for his signature. If he signs the bill, it becomes law in the time specified in the law. If

the president opposes the bill, he can veto it. It then goes back to Congress for a veto override consideration. If the president takes no action after Congress has adjourned its second session, it is a pocket veto and the legislation dies.

8. Congress can override the president's veto by a two-thirds roll call vote of the members who are present (meeting sufficient numbers for a quorum) in each house.

Chapter Review

If you were beginning your HR career today, you would most likely notice a significant difference than if you had entered the field just a decade ago. While the HR role traditionally was one of a transactional administrative nature, it has now grown and shifted into an area of responsibility and focus as a strategic element to an organization's competitive advantage. The role of HR now encompasses: strategic business planning, change facilitation, and employee advocacy.

The greatest way of showing that the HR function is strategic is through the partnering with organizational management as an internal business consultant. A true business consultant presents all the factual data and necessary information, along with recommendations from their broader perspective in an effort to help their client reach a decision. For the HR professional, that includes presenting credible data, understanding all functions of the organization, aligning HR initiatives with the organization's strategy, and knowing how to monitor and measure the results. The Business Management and Strategy area of the HRCI exam is heavily emphasized on the SPHR exam with 29 percent of the test questions focused in this functional competency area.

Questions

1. A statement that describes what the organization does and its customer base is a:

   A. Vision statement

   B. Statement of position

   C. Lofty statement

   D. Mission statement

2. A strategy that focuses on launching a new line of business would most likely occur at which stage in the organization's life cycle?

   A. Maturity

   B. Startup

   C. Growth

   D. Rebirth

3. Which of the following is not part of a SMART goal?

   A. Relevant

   B. Strength

   C. Time bound

   D. Measurable

4. Mikayel is the shipping and receiving manager at your Russian parts plant. He has experienced problems with getting shipments through Customs for timely delivery to the United States. His contact at Customs informs him that he can expedite the shipments if Mikayel would pay him a gratuity for his service in cash. Your organization's ethics clearly state that bribes are considered unethical behavior; however, this "gratuity" seems to be in the best interest of the organization. What is your *best* course of action?

   A. Authorize Mikayel to make the payments out of petty cash.

   B. Report the bribe incident to the local Russian Customs head officer.

   C. Ask executive management for "special outside-of-policy" authorization.

   D. Adhere to the organization's no-bribe ethics policy and seek other solutions for the shipment delay issue.

5. Taylor is the Quality Assurance director at her organization and reports to both the Division VP at her facility and the VP of Quality Assurance located at the headquarters office. This is an example of what type of organizational structure?

   A. Span of control

   B. Formalized

   C. Matrix

   D. Chain of command

6. Elton has hired a consultancy firm to perform an environmental scanning on his organization. The report comes back indicating that a global competitor is moving into a state where Elton's company has existed for decades. Elton should present this information to executive management as a(n):

   A. Opportunity

   B. Weakness

   C. Strength

   D. Threat

7. Which of the following HR functions is not appropriate for outsourcing?

   A. Benefit administration

   B. Development of HR goals aligned with the organization's strategy plan

    C. New employee orientation/onboarding

    D. Open enrollment

8. Which is the *most* important foundational issue of organizational effectiveness?

    A. Ethics

    B. Governance

    C. Policies

    D. Rewards

9. Which of the following actions taken by HR Manager Chris is the *most* ethical?

    A. Working exclusively with a technical contracting agency for the IT group to qualify for a random prize drawing for customers

    B. Not standing up and voicing displeasure about a discriminatory decision made by a superior

    C. Referring a qualified friend for a vacant position at the company

    D. Deleting low-paying companies from salary survey results of HR positions

10. The matrix type of organizational structure is uniquely suited to managing a group of activities that are:

    A. Narrow and interrelated

    B. Narrow in focus and unrelated

    C. Diverse and unrelated

    D. Diverse and interrelated

11. The process of analyzing and identifying the need for availability of human resources so that the organization can meet its objectives is known as:

    A. Strategic planning

    B. PEST analysis

    C. Human resource planning

    D. Organization planning

12. In an organizational structure, what is centralized?

    A. The degree to which decision-making authority is restricted to senior management.

    B. The degree to which decision-making authority is given to lower levels in an organization's hierarchy.

    C. The hierarchical division of labor that distributes formal authority and establishes how critical decisions will be made.

    D. The degree to which decisions are made by committees.

13. A balance sheet shows:

    A. Historical budgeting

    B. Amount of equity owned by investors

    C. Taxes paid last year

    D. The income and expenses over a defined period of time

14. Colin is the HR manager at a tax preparation firm. During the tax season, Colin contracts with a temporary agency for seasonal help. The seasonal workers receive payroll checks from the temporary agency and not Colin's organization. What type of contract will Colin sign with the temporary agency for the seasonal workers?

    A. Temporary contract

    B. Seasonal contract

    C. Third-party contract

    D. Direct contract

15. Yoko's organization is acquiring another smaller company. What is the first step for her HR department to be involved with?

    A. Survey the existing workforce of both companies.

    B. Eliminate the redundant positions.

    C. Review the collective bargaining agreements that exist.

    D. Assurance of OSHA compliance.

16. Which of the following is a legal consequence of the Sarbanes-Oxley Act?

    A. Organizations are allowed to conduct their own stock appraisal.

    B. Shareholders are prevented from suing the company.

    C. CEOs may be punished, including jail time, for fraudulent financial reports.

    D. Audit firms must alternate every two years.

17. Antonio has been assigned as the HR project manager for the implementation of the new HRIS. The IT staff, Training and Development group, Risk Management department, and the Compensation and Benefits group will be involved in the implementation. What project management tool will be best for Antonio to use for scheduling and managing the tasks with all groups?

    A. Gantt chart

    B. PERT chart

    C. Implementation schedule

    D. Balanced scorecard

18. The role of human resource management has changed over the last few decades because more focus is now placed on

    A. Finding people with qualifications in high technology that can meet today's challenges

    B. Strategic management of the organization and less focus on labor relations

    C. Recruiting and less focus on paperwork

    D. Supporting the executive suite and the programs that the officers want implemented

19. Financial contributions from the HR department are important because

    A. Training and staffing are the easiest areas to cut and gain back budget.

    B. Executives expect the HR department to be the most flexible in budget terms.

    C. There is little impact from reducing the HR department's budget.

    D. Every strategic decision must contribute to the financial performance of the organization.

20. Management skills have been identified over a long period of time through the work of

    A. Various universities around the country and their studies of manufacturing plants

    B. Various consulting firms across the country and their studies of university environments

    C. Studies such as the Management Progress Study conducted by American Telephone and Telegraph beginning in 1956 and continuing over the next 30 years

    D. IBM's study of management individuals that lasted for 35 years

21. Complex project management is made easier through the use of

    A. PARK/ITEM planning charts

    B. Gaunt PERK planning charts

    C. PACK/CWA planning charts

    D. PERT/CPM planning charts

22. The AB Trucking Co. is expanding its routes and hiring more people. Those changes will mean that employees will have to take on different work assignments. How should the HR manager handle those changes with the workforce?

    A. Explain the coming changes to all employees and solicit their help in deciding how to assign the new routes. Prepare a project plan and make sure everyone has a chance to see it before the implementation date.

  B. Explain the coming changes and tell the truckers that assignments will be made based on seniority. The new people will be assigned last.

  C. Explain the coming changes and let the senior executives handle the questions about how new job assignments will be made.

  D. Explain the coming changes and let the employees discuss among themselves how they want to assign routes to the workforce.

23. When the AB Trucking Co. makes its organizational changes, it plans to alter its reporting relationships. If it elects to have each supervisor report to an operations manager and also to a financial manager, what type of organizational structure will AB Trucking Co. be using?

  A. Formalized. A firm structure that can be charted, regardless of how many reporting lines exist from one job to another.

  B. Matrix. A perfect example when multiple reporting relationships exist for certain jobs.

  C. Span of control. The span of control will be exceedingly easier to manage with multiple reporting relationships.

  D. Work specialization. Because there are multiple reporting relationships, the specialization of each will increase.

24. Mergers and acquisitions (M&A) provide HR managers with special problems of cultural differences. In order to make sure that the cultures don't clash after the merger, the HR manager should

  A. Assign a subordinate to monitor the complaint levels and report on problems that are being addressed.

  B. Conduct meetings with key players from each organization to outline the cultural values of each organization and determine how best to protect them in the blended employer unit.

  C. Send memos to department heads that specify the new cultural characteristics and express the expectation that the department heads will "make it happen."

  D. Provide written complaint forms to all employees and express a willingness to listen to any comments the employees have to make about the merger.

25. The AB Trucking Co. is considering outsourcing its HR, accounting, and safety functions to vendors. What considerations should be given to issues impacting that decision.

  A. How the decision will fit into the organization's strategic plan and whether it will be cost effective

  B. How the employees will react

C. How much money can be saved and what workload can be eliminated from the company executives

D. How all the compliance work can be done by someone else

Answers

1. **D.** A mission statement contains a description of both organizational products/services and the customer base for which it exists.

2. **D.** When organizations move past maturity and enter the rebirth phase of existence, they begin actively assessing their structure and lines of business.

3. **B.** SMART goals and objectives are Specific, Measurable, Attainable, Relevant/Realistic, and Time Bound. Strength is not included in the list.

4. **D.** A bribery demand is not only a violation of the company's policy but also a violation of the Foreign Corrupt Practices Act of 1997 (see Chapter 2). To pay such a bribe could be a criminal act under federal law.

5. **C.** When the organization calls for reporting to two or more supervisors, the organization is known as a matrix organization.

6. **D.** Competition constitutes a threat to the company. During strategic planning and SWOT analysis, all perceived threats should be considered seriously.

7. **B.** The employer should always retain control of its goal determination function so it can be assured the goals will support the organization's strategic plan.

8. **A.** Ethics determine how we behave with employees, vendors, customers, clients, and other stakeholders. They govern "how we do things around here." They are constant references for employee decision making and behavior.

9. **C.** Suggesting a friend apply for a job opening at the employer's organization is perfectly ethical. It even demonstrates a willingness to support the employer as a good place to work.

10. **D.** Matrix organizations allow for great flexibility and quick reaction to outside changes.

11. **C.** Human resource planning involves all facets of people management issues. Forecasting the need for more or fewer people, budget considerations, and recruiting sources comes into play. How HR can be used to support the organization's strategic plans is critical.

12. **A.** The greater grasp senior management retains on decision making, the more centralized the organization.

13. **B.** Balance sheets show assets, liabilities, and owner's equity.

14. **C.** Because Colin doesn't contract directly with the employees, he instead contracts with a third party for the services of the employees.

15. **A.** Part of the due diligence is surveying the workforce to determine not only how many employees are in the organization but what they are doing and their certifications/licenses/skills.

16. **C.** SOX brought criminal liability to the most senior manager in the organization. There is some personal incentive for the CEO to insist that employees behave and follow the rules.

17. **B.** Program Evaluation and Review Technique is the project management tool that will allow multiple groups and many tasks to be tracked at once.

18. **B.** Designing strategic support programs for human resource management is critical in today's fast-paced employment world. Competition is more stringent and legal requirements are constantly expanding. While supporting executive wishes has always been part of the HR job, the design of strategic programs is relatively new.

19. **D.** It is not just a matter of budget dollars, but the contribution they make toward the organizational "bottom line."

20. **C.** It was the psychologists at AT&T that gathered data about management skills over a 30+ year period of time. They identified characteristics of successful managers in the process.

21. **D.** Program Evaluation and Review Technique charts handle multiple project requirements and can be enhanced by the Critical Path Method in visual charts.

22. **A.** Whenever possible, involving employees in designing the plan for accommodating organizational changes will be the best for employee morale.

23. **B.** Matrix structures involve multiple reporting relationships.

24. **B.** Involving key managers from each organization can provide a foundation for whatever cultural values the new organization could like to build.

25. **A.** Key factors are the organizational strategic plan and the budget. If outsourcing will fit nicely into those two considerations, it may be a good alternative. But there are also other factors to be considered such as employee morale, responsiveness of the vendor, and more.

Endnotes

1. Douglas W. Bray, Richard J. Campbell, and Donald L. Grant, *Formative Years in Business: A Long-Term AT&T Study of Management Lives* (John Wiley & Sons, Inc., 1974).

2. Elisabeth Kubler-Ross, *On Death and Dying* (Scribner; Reprint Edition June 1997).

3. Dr. Donald L. Kirkpatrick, *How to Manage Change Effectively* (Jossey-Bass, October 1985).

4. Donald L. Lester, John A. Parnell, and Shawn Carraher, "Organizational Life Cycle: A Five-Stage Empirical Scale,"*International Journal of Organizational Analysis* 11, no. 4(2003), 339–54.

5. Michael E. Porter, *Competitive Strategy: Techniques for Analyzing Industries and Competitors* (Free Press, 1980).

6. SHRM Research Department, *HR's Evolving Role in Organizations and Its Impact on Business Strategy*, Project leader Amanda Benedict, M.A. (2008) http://www.shrm.org/research.

7. Kerry Patterson, Joseph Grenny, Ron McMillan, Al Switzler, and Stephen R. Covey, *Crucial Conversations: Tools for Talking When Stakes Are High* (New York: McGraw-Hill, 2002).

8. Robert Kaplan and David Norton, *The Balanced Scorecard: Translating Strategy into Action* (Harvard Business Review Press, September 1, 1996).

Employee and Labor Relations

Early in the existence of employee-employer relationships, there was little a worker could do but say "yes" to every employer instruction or demand. There was no recourse for employees. If the employee didn't like the employer or the way he or she was being treated, the only option in many cases was to resign the position and look for another. Unfortunately, good references were often required by new, would-be employers so they would know the worker was responsive and responsible. Without those written references, obtaining work elsewhere was difficult at best.

In the nineteenth century, a fledgling union movement from the previous century began to gain traction and employee recruitment to union organizations swelled. It seems employees don't like being powerless in the employment relationship. And, who can blame them?

In this chapter, we examine the nuances of employee and labor relations. You will learn how the early union protections regarding work rules, terminations, and other actions have been recently migrating into law. Today, even non-union-represented employees have many protections that once were afforded only to union members.

The official HRCI Workforce Planning and Employment functional area responsibilities and knowledge statements are as follows:

Responsibilities

- Ensure that employee and labor relations activities are compliant with applicable federal laws and regulations.

- Assess organizational climate by obtaining employee input (for example: focus groups, employee surveys, staff meetings).

- Develop and implement employee relations programs (for example: recognition, special events, diversity programs) that promote a positive organizational culture.

- Evaluate effectiveness of employee relations programs through the use of metrics (for example: exit interviews, employee surveys, turnover rates).

- Establish, update, and communicate workplace policies and procedures (for example: employee handbook, reference guides, or standard operating procedures) and monitor their application and enforcement to ensure consistency.

- Develop and implement a discipline policy based on organizational code of conduct/ ethics, ensuring that no disparate impact or other legal issues arise.

- Create and administer a termination process (for example: reductions in force [RIF], policy violations, poor performance), ensuring that no disparate impact or other legal issues arise.

- Develop, administer, and evaluate grievance/dispute resolution and performance improvement policies and procedures.

- Investigate and resolve employee complaints filed with federal agencies involving employment practices or working conditions, utilizing professional resources as necessary (for example: legal counsel, mediation/arbitration specialists, investigators).

 - Develop and direct proactive employee relations strategies for remaining union-free in non-organized locations.

- Direct and/or participate in collective bargaining activities, including contract negotiation, costing, and administration.

Knowledge of

- Applicable federal laws affecting employment in union and non-union environments, such as laws regarding antidiscrimination policies, sexual harassment, labor relations, and privacy (for example: WARN Act, Title VII, NLRA)

- Techniques and tools for facilitating positive employee relations (for example: employee surveys, dispute/conflict resolution, labor/management cooperative strategies)

- Employee involvement strategies (for example: employee management committees, self-directed work teams, staff meetings)

- Individual employment rights issues and practices (for example: employment at will, negligent hiring, defamation)

- Workplace behavior issues/practices (for example: absenteeism and performance improvement)

- Unfair labor practices

- The collective bargaining process, strategies, and concepts (for example: contract negotiation, costing, and administration)

- Legal disciplinary procedures

- Positive employee relations strategies and non-monetary rewards

- Techniques for conducting unbiased investigations

- Legal termination procedures

Core Knowledge of

- Methods for assessing employee attitudes, opinions, and satisfaction

Federal Laws That Apply to This Body of Knowledge

Now that you've reviewed the Employee and Labor Relations responsibilities and knowledge statements, we recommend that you review the federal laws that apply to employee and labor Relations, as listed in Figure 7-1. It would benefit you, the reader, to refer back to Chapter 2 on these specific laws prior to reading any further in this chapter.

While legislation is important, of equal value is the case law that comes from court interpretations. Over the past five decades, the U.S. Supreme Court has heard and provided its clarification to many challenges involving employment and labor laws. Figure 7-2 lists the vitally important cases applying to Employee and Labor Relations.

For more information on each of these cases, see Appendix B.

- Davis-Bacon Act of 1931

- Employee Polygraph Protection Act of 1988

- Fair and Accurate Credit Transactions Act of 2003

- Fair Labor Standards Act of 1938

- Immigration Reform and Control Act of 1986

- Labor-Management Reporting and Disclosure Act of 1959 (Landrum-Griffin Act)

- Norris-LaGuardia Act of 1932

- Railway Labor Act of 1926

- Federal Insurance Contributions Act of 1935 (Social Security Act)

- Vietnam Era Veterans Readjustment Assistance Act of 1974

- Walsh-Healey Act of 1936 (Public Contracts Act)

- Civil Rights Act of 1991

- Genetic Information Nondiscrimination Act of 2008

- Pregnancy Discrimination Act of 1978

- Age Discrimination in Employment Act of 1967

- Electronic Communications Privacy Act of 1986

- Equal Pay Act of 1963

- Fair Credit Reporting Act of 1970

- Immigration and Nationality Act of 1952

- Labor-Management Relations Act of 1947 (Taft-Hartley Act)

- National Labor Relations Act of 1935

- Portal-to-Portal Act of 1947

- Service Contract Act of 1965

- Uniformed Services Employment and Reemployment Rights Act of 1994

- Wagner-Peyser Act of 1933 (Amended by Workforce Investment Act of 1998)

- Civil Rights Act of 1964 (Title VII)

- Drug-Free Workplace Act of 1988

- Lilly Ledbetter Fair Pay Act of 2009

- Uniform Guidelines on Employee Selection Procedures of 1976

- Worker Adjustment and Retraining Notification Act of 1988

Figure 7-1   Key federal laws impacting employee and labor relations

---

Case Citations

- *DeBartolo Corp. v. Gulf Coast Trades Council* (485 U.S. 568)

- *E. I. DuPont & Company v. NLRB* (311 NLRB 893)

- *PepsiCo. Inc. v. Redmond* (No. 94-3942 7th Cir)

- *NLRB v. Weingarten, Inc.* (420 U.S. 251, 254)

- *Ronald Lesh v. Crown Cork and Seal Company* (334 NLRB 699)

- *Phoenix Transit System v. NLRB* (337 NLRB 510)

- *Oil Capitol Sheet Metal, Inc., v. NLRB* (349 NLRB 1348)

- *Syracuse University v. NLRB* (350 NLRB 755)

- *Staub v. Proctor* (131 U.S. 1186)

- *Kepas v. Ebay* (131 S.Ct. 2160)

- *UGL-UNICCO Service Company v. NLRB* (01-RC-022447)

- *Harris v. Quinn* (S.Ct. No. 11-681)

- *Electromation, Inc., v. NLRB* (Nos. 92-4129, 93-1169 7th Cir)

- *NLRB v. Town & Country Electric* (516 U.S. 85)

- *Circuit City Stores v. Adams* (532 U.S. 105)

- *IBM Corp. v. NLRB* (341 NLRB 148)

- *EEOC v. Waffle House* (534 U.S. 279)

- *Toering Electric Company v. NLRB* (351 NLRB 225)

- *Dana Corporation/Metaldyne Corporation v. NLRB* (351 NLRB 434)

- *KenMor Electric Co., Inc. v. NLRB* (355 NLRB 173)

- *AT&T Mobility v. Concepcion* (S.Ct. No. 09-893)

- *Specialty Healthcare and Rehabilitation Center of Mobile v. NLRB* (15-RC-008773)

- *D. R. Horton, Inc. v. NLRB* (12-CA-25764)

- *Wright v. Universal Maritime Service Corp.* (525 U.S. 70)

Figure 7-2 Case law that applies to employee and labor relations

Common Law and the Napoleonic Code

There are two separate legal heritages we draw from in the United States. One is from England and the other is from France. They are quite different.

Napoleonic Code

This type of law comes from old Roman law, which predominated in Europe. Germanic law influenced how the Napoleonic Code developed and it all came together in France. Napoleon I between 1800 and 1804 established a written set of laws called the Napoleonic Code. It drew upon the private laws of France that governed transactions and relationships between individuals. It was intended that these laws could be available to all citizens. The Napoleonic Code specifically forbade judges from altering laws through establishment of precedence in their rulings. Our modern civil codes come from this type of legal system. The Provence of Quebec and the State of Louisiana use a legal system based on the Napoleonic Code.

Common Law

The system called Common Law comes to us from medieval English law. Judges were expected to create precedence through their interpretations of the King's laws. Other judges were then bound by those precedent decisions and the result was known as Common Law. In the United States, it is the state courts that are primarily responsible for creating and using common law.

Labor Laws Currently

Over the years, many things have changed in the area of labor law. There are differences between public sector and private sector provisions for labor laws. Many legal protections exist for employees and are the same in each of the two major employment sectors, for instance equal employment opportunity protections against employment discrimination and wage and hour requirements requiring payroll actions. Benefit and pension programs, on the other hand, are governed by different laws but generally offer similar protections to employees. It is in the area of privacy expectations that the two sectors diverge:

- **Private sector**   Generally, private employers are able to apply an employment at will relationship with their employees as long as they don't violate public policy when terminating someone. Warrants are not required for employers to access lockers, desks, computer files, or e-mail accounts. Even social media is subject to content review if the employer wishes to do so.

- **Public sector**   Constitutional protections against unreasonable search and seizure in the Fourth Amendment protect employees of the federal government and, in some cases, those in state and local governments as well. These conditions have an impact on an employee's right to privacy in the workplace. Government employers can find themselves in a position where they either need the employee's permission or a court warrant to access lockers, desks, computer files, e-mail accounts, and the like.

Employment Types

Employment types are usually defined under applicable employment laws. They have evolved over the years from early European legal foundations.

Employment at Will

"During the late 19th and early 20th centuries a new set of legal rules emerged in the United States governing the relationship between employer and employee. These rules were called 'employment-at-will' and provided that, absent express agreement to the contrary, employment was for an indefinite time and could be terminated by either party, for any reason, or for no reason at all. This doctrine is a unique product of American common law, created by state and federal judges, and continues, substantially unchanged, until today."[1]

Currently, employment at will exists in most states, and it is state law that usually governs these employee relationships. In other countries, using different legal systems, employment may be terminated only for cause. That means employers must justify their decisions to end the employment relationship with someone. Behavior of the individual is usually the justification.

Employment at will only exists in the absence of a contract that details the employment agreement between employer and employee. Those contracts can be related to a group, as union memorandums of understanding, or to individuals, such as Chief Executive Officers. Since roughly the 1930s, American courts have been instrumental in identifying conditions under which employers may not arbitrarily discharge people, even though they are at-will employees. Some of those restrictions include:

- Civil service rules
- Constitutional protections
- Protections against employment discrimination (based on race, color, national origin, religion, sex, age, genetic information, physical disability, mental disability, pregnancy, veteran status, use of Family and Medical Leave)
- Whistleblowing protections

Written Employment Agreements and Oral Contracts

When it is in the best interest of both parties, an employment agreement can be developed. For senior executives (usually CEOs and other positions particularly sensitive to the employer organization, for example a Chief Information Technology Officer in a high-tech company) employment contracts are particularly desirable. They protect the individual in compensation issues and in the term of the agreement. They also protect the employer by citing the performance requirements that must be met for compensation thresholds. They also protect the company by requiring the individual to remain in the position for a specified period of time, saving the organization the recruiting expense of an early departure, or limiting the ability to immediately work with a competitor.

Written Employment Contracts

Written Employment Contracts will typically contain several sections, such as:

- **Job description**   Lists duties and responsibilities.
- **Statement of authority**   Details expenditure limits, hiring authority, and what conditions require approval of the Board of Directors or other authority.
- **Agreement length**   Identifies the beginning and ending dates of the contract.
- **Performance requirements**   Documents performance requirements for compensation increases or bonuses. These can include revenue targets, sales targets, or other measurable performance standard.

- **Compensation and benefits**   Details the base rate of pay, pay calculation (hourly, salaried, commissioned), how increases will be achieved, how bonuses will be achieved, how compensation will be paid (cash, stock, bonds, future payments), pension program (company and employee contribution scheme), health care benefits programs (medical, dental, vision, individual or family), perquisites (company car, airplane, driver, concierge, entertainment tickets for concerts and sporting events), and any other compensation condition upon which the relationship will be based.

- **Other important issues**   Can include agreements about who owns copyright and patent rights to things produced by the employee during the contract period, non-disclosure agreements for employer intellectual property protection, and non-compete provisions.

- **Termination provisions**   Can include personal behavior and ethics requirements, and other reasons or "causes" for separating the employee from the organization. In many contracts these reasons are specified in great detail. If there is to be a "buy out" for time remaining on the agreement, that should be specified here. "Golden Parachutes" are often large sums representing the "buy out" for early separation such as in a merger.

Oral Employment Contracts

Oral Employment Contracts can be expressly made, or made by mistake, and still be valid and enforceable, much to the dismay of employers who fall into those traps.

Oral contracts can be created in some unusual circumstances. Supervisors and managers can inadvertently enter into oral contracts and should receive training to help them avoid such pitfalls.

Some examples of oral contracts include:

- An in-house recruiter tells a job applicant that this is a great organization and anyone who keeps their record clean "can expect to have a lifelong career here." Within a year, the new employee's division was closed and all employees laid off.

- A manager tells a subordinate that "nothing short of stealing from the company" will be cause for termination. Within a year the employee was terminated for inadequate performance.

- A manager tells a new employee, sure "you can bet that you'll be here at least five years so go ahead and sell your house in another state and move your family here." The employee was part of a downsizing six months later.

- A supervisor says to an employee, "Don't worry about your performance rating. Nobody pays any attention to them here anyway." Within a few months the employee is terminated due to poor performance.

Collective Bargaining Agreements

When workers have chosen to be represented by a union, the employer and the union discuss and agree on a written contract through the process of collective bargaining. The contract specifies the working conditions in their workplace and the duties of each of the parties. Normally, a collective bargaining agreement will contain specifications for these and other topics:

- Shift assignments and scheduling (for example, hours of work, overtime)
- Seniority provisions
- Time off (for example, vacation, sick time, leave of absence, holidays)
- Termination procedures
- Other benefits (for example, health insurance, disability insurance)
- Rights of management
- Rights of the union
- Grievance procedure (complaint procedure)
- Compensation schedule (for example, by title, by location, by level, by seniority)
- Labor-Management Committee
- Health and safety
- Length of contract agreement (start date, end date)

Union contracts are sometimes referred to as Memoranda of Agreement (MOU). Contracts are negotiated following an election brought about by a qualifying event such as a show of interest among employees that is sufficient to generate the National Labor Relations Board (NLRB) sanctioning the election. There is usually a period between qualifying and the election that allows both union and management to present their positions to employees. Once the vote is taken and it authorizes the union to represent workers, the process of negotiating begins.

When the negotiations are completed and the contract has been submitted to the general employee body for approval, implementation begins. Periodically, union contracts must be renegotiated. They usually last from two to five years. Some are shorter. Some are longer.

Some unions are national in scope. Others are local. It is not uncommon for a local branch of a national union to be the point of contact for a particular employer. One example is the local union office of the International Brotherhood of Teamsters. Other examples are the Communication Workers of America, the Service Employees International, United Food and Commercial Workers International Union, American Federation of Teachers, National Association of Letter Carriers, Longshore and Warehouse Union, and the International Brotherhood of Electrical Workers. There are dozens of others. When an employer works with one of these large union organizations, it is almost always through a local that has its own cadre of officers and workplace stewards. The stewards are the first point of contact between the union and employees. It is often the stewards who are appointed to represent employees in a grievance handling process, in an attempt to settle any workplace disagreements.

Right to Work States

There are 24 states that have passed Right to Work laws. A Right to Work law guarantees that no person can be compelled, as a condition of employment, to join a labor union. They also prohibit unions from collecting mandatory dues from every employee. That means a Closed Shop (employers may hire only dues-paying union members) is not a legal form of unionization in those states. A Union Shop is one in which employers agree to hire only union members or those non-members it hires must join the union within a designated time. Union dues are required. An Agency Shop does not require employees to join the representing union, but they are required to pay a fee to the union for its representation if they don't join as members. Open Shops are workplaces where the employees do not have to pay dues to or join the representing union.

Limitations to Agency Shop

On June 30, 2014, the U.S. Supreme Court issued its ruling in the case of *Harris v. Quinn* (S.Ct. No 11-681). The Court said, "The First Amendment prohibits the collection of an agency fee from [employees] who do not want to join or support the union."[2]

Exceptions to Employment at Will

The idea that employers can hire and fire at will, with or without a valid reason, left open the possibility that there would be improper treatment of employees through management by whim of the boss.

Public Policy

Over the years, legislative bodies have created laws limiting employers' at-will rights and courts have reached conclusions that public policy takes precedence over individual employer interests, thus also limiting employment at will. An example is the body of non-discrimination law that exists at both state and federal levels. Public policy says we may not dismiss employees based on race, color, national origin, religion, sex, genetic information, and other characteristics (depending on jurisdiction). So, employers are not free to take employment action against any employee if that action would violate public policy.

Implied Contract

Employers can sometimes create an implied contract for employment by doing things that seem to be okay on the surface, but actually make promises that the employer must then keep. For example, a supervisor makes a job offer to a job applicant and says, "You're going to love it here. Nobody gets laid off here." That is a promise that can be interpreted as an implied contract. The employer implies a contract for lifetime employment. That invalidates the claim of employment at will.

Covenant of Good Faith and Fair Dealing

There is a general assumption in the law of contracts that says people will treat each other with respect and honesty, that they will fulfill their promises to one another. It is known as the Covenant of Good Faith and Fair Dealing. In employment terms, it means the employer must not do things in an underhanded way when dealing with employees. Employment may not be ended based on a trumped-up charge without any basis in fact. If a new worker was promised access to certain benefits and left their former job based on that promise, the employer is obligated to fulfill the promise. To do otherwise would break the Covenant of Good Faith and Fair Dealing.

Invasion of Privacy

The electronic age has brought with it faster communication, communication that can sometimes contain information that is illegal or inappropriate in the workplace. Sexual and racial jokes are two examples. Employers want to prevent these things from happening in their workplaces. To do that, they often resort to monitoring telephone and e-mail message content. There are legal limitations to that monitoring, however. Wiretapping laws require that participants in the telephone communication be notified that the conversation is being recorded or monitored: thus, the announcement you are familiar with at the beginning of every call to a help desk that says something like, "Your call may be monitored or recorded for training and security purposes." That puts you, the caller, on notice that you will be monitored and the practice is acceptable. If you continue the call, you are presumed to have agreed with the condition.

Claims of Invasion of Privacy are hard to support when the parties have been placed on notice that they will be subject to inspection of one sort or another. That is the reason employee policy manuals and handbooks have privacy policies that state something like, "While at work, you should have no expectation of privacy. Anything placed in your company-owned desk or conversations held over company-owned equipment are subject to review by the employer if conditions should indicate that it is necessary. Lockers assigned to employees, company vehicles assigned to employees, desks assigned to employees, and computers and computer systems owned by the company are all examples of tools that the company has the right to inspect if it chooses to do so. It is usually a good idea to place employees on notice that they should have no expectation of privacy and all company equipment, systems, and facilities are subject to search at any time without notice.

Privacy issues are wrapped up in other topics such as personal financial information, criminal background checks, polygraph tests, and credit reports. You will find more information about those topics elsewhere in this book.

Public sector employees have different rights of privacy because public sector employers are constrained by the Constitution's Fourth Amendment. That Amendment prohibits unreasonable search and seizure by government entities. Federal and sometimes state employers are prohibited from inspecting personal work spaces in some instances without getting either the employee's permission or a warrant from a judge.

Common Law Tort Claims

A tort is harm done to someone in legal terms. Negligent hiring and negligent retention are examples of legal torts.

Defamation (Slander/Libel)

Defamation is the act of damaging someone's reputation. Slander is verbal defamation and libel is written defamation. It someone says or writes something about another person and it is true, there is no defamation. The truth is an absolute defense against a claim of defamation. However, if someone says or writes something about another person that is false, made up, or unfounded, it can be defamation if it harms that person's reputation. Employees can cause themselves problems on the Internet by posting comments about others (including supervisors) that are not true. Employers (including supervisors) who respond with untrue comments can also find themselves in hot water.

Fraudulent Misrepresentation

When someone represents something to be true, knowing it is false, or represents something as fact, recklessly without knowing it is true, there can be the possibility of fraudulent misrepresentation. Some other things have to come into the equation before we can say for sure. Such misrepresentations must be made with the intention that another person rely on them. Finally, the other person must have suffered damages as a result. For example, an employer makes a statement such as, "If you join our company, you can plan on getting at least a 20 percent bonus payment every year." Should a job applicant leave an existing job and come to work for the employer promising a bonus, the harm comes when the bonus isn't paid and overall compensation falls below what would have been earned at the previous job.

Other Factors Involved in the Employment Relationship

The employment relationship depends on other factors beyond employment at will and the Covenant of Good Faith and Fair Dealing.

Employer Expectation of Employee Loyalty

From common law comes this concept of the duty owed to employers by employees. Some states have added it to their laws. In California, it is part of the Labor Code. Section 2860 says, "Everything which an employee acquires by virtue of his employment, except the compensation which is due to him from his employer, belongs to the employer, whether acquired lawfully or unlawfully, or during or after the expiration of the term of his employment." The Duty of Loyalty requires that employees will not compete with the employer by running a similar business, or take from the employer private and confidential information such as customer lists.

Unfair Competition and Non-Compete Clauses

Employers depend on their workers to keep confidential all the information that might benefit competitive organizations. Disclosure of proprietary and confidential information can harm the employer whose information is lost in the process. Employees have an obligation to avoid helping anyone outside their employer's organization if that could bring harm to their employer. Giving aid to a competitor can foster unfair advantage to the other company. That is described as Unfair Competition.

Employers have sometimes tried to protect themselves by having employees sign Non-Compete Agreements. In some cases, when challenged, state courts have determined that the Non-Compete Agreement was overly broad and could not be justified. Trying to prevent an employee from ever working for some competitive company can deprive that person of the ability to make a living. If the Non-Compete Agreement simply prevented activity that directly harmed the employer it could be acceptable to court scrutiny. Insisting employees agree not to take a job with a direct competitor's organization for six months might be supportable.

Concept of Inevitable Disclosure

This legal concept holds that an employer may enjoin a former employee from working in certain jobs for competitors of the employer. It is based on the belief that if the former employee were to do so it would inevitably result in disclosure of the former employer's trade secrets to the competing employer.

Workplace Policies and Procedures

Organizations need a set of guidelines that explain how the workplace will be managed, what will happen when there are disagreements, and what expectations employees should have for employment conditions and benefits.

Frequently, employers prepare written employee handbooks that contain their policies for employment issues. Having them written can be beneficial if they are thought out carefully. And, of course, any employee policies should be reviewed with an employment attorney before implementation.

Developing and Communicating Policies

Many states have rather strict laws about employment policies and their communication to workers. Case law helps clarify what expectations employees should have about policies and their implementation. Generally, it is not acceptable to make policies effective retroactively. Plan to circulate any policy changes or additions to your employees with sufficient time for them to digest and adjust to the requirements before the implementation date.

 NOTE Some attorneys recommend having employees sign a document acknowledging receipt of the policy changes. It doesn't mean they agree, but that they have received a personal copy. This is particularly important when there are changes having to do with privacy and other similarly sensitive issues.

Policy development is a process that can take a short time or considerable time. Some organizations use teams of people in policy development; other organizations have one person generate policies. In all cases, it is a good idea to have the proposed policy circulated among executives and select employees to get feedback about their content and the changes that they will bring. If the organization has unions, it may be necessary to negotiate policy changes through the collective bargaining process.

Employee Handbooks

Employee handbooks are the documents that represent the employer's policies concerning employee management. They outline the following types of topics:

- Equal employment opportunity
- Sexual and other types of harassment
- Selection and placement of employees
- Employment at will employment relationship
- Personnel records and personal employee information
- Employee conduct
  - Weapons
  - Violence
  - Insubordination
  - Sabotage and negligence
  - Theft
  - Confidential information
  - Ethics
  - Attendance and punctuality
  - Use of employer equipment
  - Use of personal telephone or computer
  - Use of employer vehicles
  - Dress code
  - Records maintenance and worktime cards/reporting
- Performance evaluations
- Progressive discipline
- Employment termination
- Payday and paychecks or direct deposit
- Holidays and vacation time off (paid and unpaid)
- Leaves of absence
- Drug-free workplace and drug testing

- Employee healthcare benefits
- Employee assistance program benefit
- Employee expectations of privacy

There are often other subjects included as well. Some are the personal preferences of the organizations that explain "the way we do things around here." Some are cultural issues reduced to writing. There was a time when male employees of IBM all wore white dress shirts and ties. Colored shirts were not acceptable. The dress code was very clear and in writing.

Whenever someone joins the organization as a new hire, a copy of the employee handbook should be provided to him or her in the new-employee orientation session. At that time, other actions should be taken to complete payroll forms (for example, W-4 and I-9), and benefit election forms for insurances, and so forth. It is at that time all policies should be reviewed with the new hire. Everyone should have the advantage of knowing what the rules are before they begin their employment.

Discipline and Termination

In small organizations, discipline and termination are handled without many written procedures. The "boss" simply tells one of the employees that they are being disciplined because of a specific infraction. In larger organizations, the procedures for disciplinary action are written down in a step-by-step format and followed by managers.

Usually, discipline and termination are a multi-step process. It doesn't have to be a formal process, but it can be. Here are the typical steps in that process:

1. **Oral warning** Observing the employee violating a policy, procedure, or instruction. In a personal discussion with the employee, the boss explains the problem and issues a verbal warning that the problem should not happen again.

2. **Written warning** Observing the employee doing the same behavior for which he/she received the oral warning. This is an "escalation" of discipline to the next step. A warning in writing should explain the infraction and why it is unacceptable. It should also explain the consequence of the same thing happening again.

3. **Suspension** Although this step is not always included in the process, it is available for use to emphasize to the employee how serious the behavioral problem is. In most cases, a suspension will be unpaid time off. It can last from a day to several weeks. The length of time should be dependent upon the seriousness of the behavioral problem and the employee's length of service.

4. **Termination** The final stage of the disciplinary process is removing the employee from employment. Use of this step acknowledges that the employee cannot be salvaged.

NOTE Whatever disciplinary procedures you elect to use in your organization, they should be applied consistently in similar situations. It is not a good idea to treat people differently when their situations are similar. That will surely land you in court or present you with a union grievance.

Employers can avoid locking themselves into strict disciplinary procedures if they provide a policy for discretionary disciplinary decisions based on the circumstances of a situation. Hard rules about steps to be used in the process can prevent flexibility and discretion.

In the Trenches

From Employee to Ex-Employee in Five Minutes

Gerald was upset about the merit rating he received from his supervisor. When his boss's boss came to the office, Gerald was ready with his list of grievances and was going to let the executive have it right between the eyes.

Gerald got the attention of his senior manager and began with his statement explaining how upset he was about the situation. He was threatening in his tone. Muriel, the executive, said to him, "Gerald, please lower your voice and change your tone. We can't have a discussion until you are more reasonable in your approach." Gerald continued with his rant.

Muriel said, "Gerald, I'm warning you that you must change your tone or there will be consequences." Gerald continued.

Muriel said, "Gerald, I'm giving you an oral warning that you will be suspended for two days if you don't stop threatening me." That didn't even slow him down.

Muriel said, "Gerald, you are now suspended for two days without pay. You should go home and give some thought to how people need to communicate in the workplace."

Did Gerald stop? It only made him more angry. His rant continued.

Muriel said, "Gerald, you have already been suspended for two days without pay. If you don't stop right this minute, you will be risking your job. I will terminate your employment if you continue your behavior."

Gerald was so worked up that he could only see that he was not getting his message across. So, he raised his voice and volume for the next few sentences.

Muriel said, "Gerald, it is with sadness that I tell you that you are being terminated. I will have your final paycheck ready for you in 30 minutes. Please gather your personal things and prepare to leave the building."

Progressive discipline in action. From caution to dismissal in five minutes.

Background Investigations

For decades, legal advisors have been telling their employer clients to conduct background checks on every new employee. These investigations have helped detect inaccuracies on application forms and resumes.

Typically, background investigations involve verification of employment history and educational achievements. Occasionally they will also delve into personal references and professional references. These are often less than helpful, however, because a job candidate will only list references that are known to provide good comments if asked.

In 2012, the Equal Employment Opportunity Commission (EEOC) published its guidelines on use of arrest and conviction records in employment decisions.[3] These guidelines are not legal requirements but will be considered if complaints of illegal discrimination are filed against an employer. Basically, the guidelines say that disparate impact against Hispanics and Blacks results from consideration of criminal records because there is a higher percentage of those races/ethnicities represented in the prison and ex-convict population. There have been many voices raised against this position, yet the guidelines remain. There are exceptions allowed by the guidelines for a direct link between job requirements and the reason for conviction. The guidelines prohibit use of any conviction or arrest record if it is not specifically job related.

Credit Checks

Credit checks are another area of controversy in the employment world. It has been common for employers to use credit checks in their employment decision making based on the premise that someone with bad credit would constitute a bad risk on the job. Without specifics, however, the relationship between job requirements and credit history wasn't generally made.

The Fair Credit Reporting Act (FCRA) (see Chapter 2) requires employers to obtain a job applicant's permission to seek a credit report from one of the major credit reporting agencies. It also requires the information obtained be maintained as private and confidential. If a negative decision is made based on the credit report information, the candidate (or employee) must be given a copy of the credit report that was used in making the employment decision.

Work Rules/Codes of Conduct

Almost all legal advisors recommend that employers have a written code of conduct or a set of work rules that lay out expectations for employee behavior. Table 7-1 lists the topics a written code of conduct should cover.

Non-Monetary Rewards

Non-monetary rewards are often given because they are effective and do not impact the budget. Monetary rewards are such things as merit pay increase, bonus payment, or other cash payment. Non-monetary rewards can include such things as a day off,

Topic	Subjects Often Included
Personal appearance	Sometimes called a "dress code," this can specify the expectations of an employer and reduce confusion about employee clothing and other adornments. This category can include clothing, uniforms, headwear, jewelry, hair styles, tattoos, piercings, and other appearance considerations.
Use of company communication/ computer equipment	If an employer allows workers to use company equipment for personal use, this is where those permissions will reside. If an employer wishes to ban personal use of organization-owned equipment, this is the place where those rules can be outlined. Included in this category, you usually find telephone equipment (including cell phones, smart phones, tablets, pagers, and walkie-talkies), office computer equipment, private television circuits, and company accounts for Internet services such as Skype and My Meeting.
Moonlighting	Some employers object to workers having more than one job. Moonlighting is the practice of holding more than one job at a time. Objections include employee fatigue, loss of concentration, and safety concerns. Other employers don't mind as long as the employee is able to perform the work as assigned and be prompt for each day's schedule.
Gifts and tipping	Allowing employees to receive gifts or tips from vendors or customers can be sensitive in some work groups. If the employee has a relationship with the vendor or supplier, for example, gifts or tips could be perceived as bribes for purchasing more product or service from the vendor. If that is objectionable, then this is the place to specify its prohibition.
Smoking	Smoking is receiving a great deal of attention in many parts of the country. There are many public facilities (airports, hospitals, restaurants, and sporting venues for example) where smoking has been banned altogether. Some states have prohibited smoking in the workplace. Others leave the decision up to the employers. Here is where the policy on smoking can appear to communicate those expectations to the employee body.
Conflict of interest	Akin to gifts and tipping, conflict of interest can embrace any condition that might suggest the possibility of undue influence over the decisions an employee is required to make in the course of his or her employment. That could apply to purchasing agents, but also to janitors who have authority to recommend certain products. If there is a personal financial interest or potential financial gain from activities performed in the course of doing a job, the employer has a right to prohibit an employee from participating in those activities.
Political contributions	In some jurisdictions, it is not permissible for employers to make political contributions. If it is, the employer has a right to control how its name and resources are used in any political context. If there are rules, they should be included in the Code of Conduct.
Work time and time records	Payroll depends upon accurate work time recordkeeping. If an employee is permitted to make or change work time records for herself/himself or a coworker, that should be explained in the code of conduct. Likewise, if making changes is not permitted, that should also be explained. Of course, it is a good idea to specify that falsifying time records is cause for disciplinary action.

Table 7-1   Common Topics in a Code of Conduct

Topic	Subjects Often Included
Personal behavior	Unacceptable personal behavior includes arguing, fighting, threatening, and harassing. Acceptable behavior includes working a full day with appropriate effort to accomplish the job assigned. It includes getting along with coworkers and others with whom the employee interacts routinely.
Safeguarding organizational property and funds	Every employee has responsibility for safeguarding organization property. Even if the employee is a copy clerk, the reproduction equipment is expensive and should not be abused. Managers and supervisors have responsibility for properly using employee resources by scheduling work appropriately and not allowing resources to be used for things other than organizational business. Personal expense accounts, office cash funds, checking account transactions, receivables, and other financial instruments are obvious targets of policy protection. Employer property, including note pads, pencils, and batteries, should never be taken for personal use.
Integrity and ethics	Working up to the best possible performance should be everyone's responsibility. Ethics means employees should not solicit or accept any payment, gift, commission, service, or favor in the transactions performed on behalf of the employer. It also means personal issues should not interfere with responsibilities to the employer for honest performance of the job. Honesty should prevail in all activities.

Table 7-1   Common Topics in a Code of Conduct (*Continued*)

picnics, recognition of birthdays, free lunches, restaurant gift certificates, plaques, designated parking space, or company jackets reserved for special performers. Chapter 9 has more information on non-monetary compensation.

Still, the most effective and least expensive form of non-monetary reward is a sincere "Thank you" from the boss. Done publicly, with detailed explanation of the employee's accomplishments, it can be even more effective.

Employee Relations Programs and Organizational Culture

Organizational culture is often defined, at least in part, by the type of employee relations programs that exist. We are talking about structured programs that are designed to help employees feel a part of the organization in positive ways. Creating a positive culture is not a simple matter and is an essential influential factor for recruiting and retaining talent. HR devotes much effort and time to champion a positive culture with effective employee relations programs. The Human Resources Department also serves as an employee advocate. Culture is defined by the way an organization treats its employees, customers, and others. It is also influenced by the way power is distributed within the organization, and the amount of power employees sense they have. What follows is an overview of different types of employee relationship programs.

Recognition

The larger an organization grows, the greater the likelihood that its recognition programs will be structured. In small organizations, recognition can be given in many forms, often as events unfold and accomplishments are achieved.

Employee recognition can include service anniversary awards (watches, clocks, plaques, certificates, pins), employee-of-the-month awards (designated parking space, plaque or bulletin board posting, special benefit like a dinner gift certificate), cost savings suggestions, sales achievement awards, team achievement awards, or individual achievement awards. Obviously, that is not an exhaustive list. You can add others and apply them as your organization finds a fit between the recognition and the accomplishment.

Special Events

Taken in context as employee relations programs, special events can include free pizza Fridays, after-hours beer parties, company day at the county fair, or political rallies with presidential candidates. It can also involve the organization and its employees in news coverage of its products or services being used in historical situations like the moon landings. Special events can embrace new product introductions and unveiling of innovative service offerings. Events involving employees in activities that contribute to a sense of pride in the organization and for being a member of the employment family would qualify in this category of employee relations programs.

Diversity Programs

Aside from the outreach and recruiting of minorities, women, disabled, and veterans, diversity programs can include additional employee activities. Common among them are employee affinity groups (Black engineers, Hispanic professional women, Veteran employees). These groups are endorsed by employers in many cases and are sometimes provided with facilities in which to conduct meetings or informal gatherings. When employees have an opportunity to meet with people like themselves and discuss issues associated with succeeding in the workplace, they can adjust more readily and feel better about their employer and themselves.

Some employers schedule special events or celebrations based on specific cultural groupings, such as International Food Day, unique cultural celebrations exhibits, or Gay Pride Day. Almost anything that recognizes and supports differences between people and cultures can expand individual employee tolerance and add value to decision-making processes.

In the Trenches

Tapping the Riches of Global Diversity

Susan Farwell, President, The Executive Communicator, LLC, New York City
sf@executivecommunicator.com

Although today's workplaces often consist of bland looking cubicles and rows of uniform offices, if we take an aerial view, we will see a rich tapestry of color, culture, custom, and belief in the employees working in those spaces. Organizations equipped to tap into the vibrancy of this diversity will draw from a larger pool of ideas and experiences and will increase their ability to stay competitive well into the future.

There is greater opportunity for cross-cultural interaction in business today than in just about any other place in the world. In cities, neighborhoods and villages around the globe people still often gravitate into culturally-familiar groupings. This is no longer an option in the business world. Employees in today's global business environment are collaborating and negotiating with others whose ancestry, religious beliefs, leadership and communication practices are often quite dissimilar to theirs.

I worked with a senior team that consisted of division leaders from Britain, Thailand, Egypt and the U.S. The team was encountering considerable difficulty communicating and resolving conflict and yet they had not considered their cultural differences as having any impact on this dysfunction. When I broached the subject of culture with the team, the executive in charge dismissed it saying, "All of us have had many years of international work experience, so I don't see how we can still be influenced by the country we grew up in."

We learn our culture's values and communication practices very early on: consciously through adults who praise, criticize, and give instructions nonverbally and verbally and unconsciously by observing adults who are acting in consistent ways. Because communication practices are adopted from birth they are held in the subconscious and they just seem right; common sense.

So, for the Brit on this team it felt right to employ clever quips and to practice understatement; while for the Egyptian, it was right to speak passionately and to defend his team's "honor." The Americans were expected to say what they mean and not beat around the bush while for the Thai member of the team it was common sense to "save face of others" by being selective and implicit in communication style.

Each of these approaches is valid in the individual's country-of-origin, but on this team the behaviors collided. Of course, we can't assume that all communication choices the team members were making were culturally derived; however, once the topic of culture was discussed, the dynamics on the team

(Continued)

changed and respect grew. Team members were able to then agree on a set of communication ground-rules that they practiced going forward. In my experience facilitating diversity dialogues, leading intercultural workshops and coaching global leaders and teams, I have had the opportunity to see firsthand how openly discussing diversity enriches interaction and creativity.

Globalization and the seismic shift in workforce demographics are two mega-trends that drive the confluence of diverse peoples, values, beliefs and practices. Success in today's business world dictates the need for increased cultural awareness and agility, an essential role that the HR professional holds.

Self-Directed Work Teams

In organizations that do not have labor unions (and in a few that do), self-directed work teams are used to tackle projects or problems when multiple disciplines are needed for the effort. This is a very common approach in the high-technology industry. It is even found in some old-line manufacturing companies when adapting and implementing new technologies on the production line. The automobile industry is a prime example of a long-established, union-represented industry that uses work teams to tackle quality problems.

When an issue is systemic in its nature, gathering representatives from all the affected functional disciplines can bring the appropriate talent to bear on finding a solution to the problem. Such teams can work without designated leaders or can appoint their own leaders when necessary. They work independent of management oversight except for their accountability for the end result of their efforts. Once the problem has been solved, the team disbands and people return to their normal job assignments.

Employee-Management Committees

The National Labor Relations Board (NLRB) has issued decisions in several cases over the past two decades that have both criticized and endorsed different forms of employee-management committees.

The Board has held illegal committees that were charged with suggesting policies or courses of action to management that would subsequently decide whether or not to accept the committee recommendations. The Board said that such a committee was engaged in issues of working conditions.[4]

Later, the NLRB decided that committees that were assigned management authority to oversee certain aspects of the business with limited power were not negotiating groups, but management agencies. In that format, such committees are legal, said the Board.[5]

NOTE Employee-Management Committees are becoming increasingly popular as a method of involving workers in the management of an enterprise. Given the rocky experiences in front of the NLRB on this issue, it would be wise to seek the advice of your labor attorney before implementing any program of this nature. The same is true of employee brainstorming committees and suggestion box offerings.

Labor Leadership Concepts and Applications

In both the public and private sectors, the movement toward a more cooperative and collaborative labor-management practice is in force. Efforts are characterized by:

- Increased willingness to share power
- Candid sharing of more information
- Joint decision making on issues of common concern
- Win-Win-Win bargaining techniques (organization/union/customer)
- Shared accountability of results and responsibilities

Employee Complaints and Grievances

Several conditions impact how employee complaints and grievances are handled within an employer's organization. One large determining factor is whether or not the employer has labor unions involved in the workplace. Labor agreements/contracts (or Memorandum of Understanding) will usually contain a structured method for dealing with employee grievances. Those designate steps for handling complaints about working conditions or other provisions of the labor union contract. Complaints about issues outside working conditions are not usually addressed within the confines of a labor union contract. Those are handled by other employer policies.

Using Employee Input to Prevent Complaints

There are many methods for gathering employee input regarding organizational changes and how they would react to those changes. Some techniques are: formal employee focus groups (facilitated discussions describing certain programs or conditions and gathering employee reactions to those ideas), employee surveys (written or computer-based gathering of employee responses to multiple-choice or narrative alternatives in designated situations), or individual interviews (one-on-one sessions to ask for specific feedback about specific proposals).

Taking employee thoughts into consideration before implementing changes is one way to help prevent complaints later on. Organizational changes that can evoke strong employee reactions include: organizational structure modifications (new divisions, departments, or hierarchy), employee benefit programs (changes to existing benefit programs, proposed new benefit programs, or elimination of benefit programs), or alterations to employee development programs (training opportunities, temporary assignment opportunities, or advanced education sponsorship programs).

NOTE When employees have the opportunity to review and comment on proposals for change, they will have a higher level of acceptance for whatever decisions are made about those proposals. Presenting decisions as a *fait accompli* can result in bruised feelings, resentment, and sometimes passive sabotage.

Conflict Resolution

Some amount of conflict will always be present in the workplace. The fact that it exists is not necessarily an unhealthy thing. When it is resolved quickly and effectively, it can lead to personal and professional growth. In many cases, effective conflict resolution can make the difference between positive and negative outcomes. The Leader's 5-Step Guide to Conflict Resolution[6] recommends five steps in the conflict resolution process:

1. **Affirm the relationship**   I am here because I value your friendship more than I value the discomfort of confronting my hurt feelings.

2. **Seek to understand**   Stephen Covey's thoughts on listening are worth their weight in gold, teaching one to seek the other person's feelings, thoughts, and perspectives first.

3. **Seek to be understood**   After understanding, share one's feelings, thoughts, and perspectives, not in an attacking mode, but in an effort for the other party to see one's views.

4. **Own responsibility by apologizing**   Seek to see where any, if not all, of the conflict is one's responsibility, learning to respond differently in the future. A genuine apology not only affirms the relationship but can do wonders in releasing hurt feelings.

5. **Seek agreement**   After both parties have apologized, accepting responsibility for their parts in the conflict, seeking agreement means reuniting on the common vision that drew both sides together in the first place, agreeing that the cause is bigger than the conflict is for both parties.

Complaint/Grievance Handling

Employee grievances can relate to any subject but always indicate a feeling of upset or discontent about something going on in the workplace . . . the way they are being treated, organizational policies, and the big category of "fairness."

In union-represented organizations, the union contract (Memorandum of Understanding) will usually explain what steps exist in the grievance procedure. They are designed to permit union members the opportunity to formally protest application of any contract provision. Most will deal with working conditions such as hours of work, how shifts are assigned, or seniority practices.

In non-union organizations, employee handbooks will often detail the steps for submitting and processing an employee complaint.

 NOTE Rarely will such complaints be called "grievances" in non-union groups. That is usually a term reserved for union contracts.

Here are the typical grievance handling steps you will find in most organizations:

1. **Submit a written complaint** The employee describes in writing what is causing the upset or discontent.

2. **Supervisor-level discussion** The employee's supervisor (or another group's supervisor) will discuss the complaint with the employee, reviewing facts and reasons for the decision that resulted in the complaint. If the explanation is sufficient, the grievance ends here. If the employee presents information that causes the decision to be changed, the grievance can also end here.

3. **Management- or HR-level discussion** If the supervisor and employee can't agree, the next discussion is with a management person and/or the human resource department. If an agreement is reached, the matter is settled. If not, it can go to a final step with senior management.

4. **Senior management** The final step is usually with a senior management official. Sometimes that is the Chief Executive Officer, but it can be with any other designated official who has authority to make any adjustments or decisions deemed appropriate in settling the grievance. If no agreement is reached at this step, the employee will have to either drop the complaint or seek legal advice in a potential civil suit.

Conducting Unbiased Investigations

Investigations are appropriate in several circumstances within an employer's organization. They can be helpful in a grievance handling effort and are essential in determining the validity of discrimination complaints. Whenever there is a need to determine facts surrounding a complaint, an investigation should be conducted.

Internal HR professionals are almost always given authority in state and federal law to conduct an investigation on behalf of the employer. If the organization wishes to have an external investigator handle the fact finding, there are some limitations imposed by certain state laws. In California, for example, external investigators who are not licensed attorneys must be licensed private investigators. Other states have different requirements.

Legal advisors suggest that internal attorneys are not the best people to conduct investigations because they could be placed in the position of having to testify to their investigative activities while still providing legal advice to their employer.

Whoever is designated as the investigator should normally follow these steps:

1. **Obtain a written complaint**   The employee should write out a complaint that states she was treated differently from others in similar situations based on a legally protected category and that category should be identified. If she can do this, she will have provided a *prima facie* case, which means it sounds good on its face.

2. **Interviews**   Next it is necessary to interview the complaining employee, the supervisor or management person who is named as the offending decision maker, and any witnesses the employee says were there at the time. Sometimes, it is a peer who has been the offending party. When that is the case, at least one interview of the offending party should be scheduled. The investigation should follow whatever leads are uncovered until the investigator is satisfied that all the facts have been uncovered that can be uncovered. Each step of the process should be documented in writing and maintained in a complaint investigation file.

3. **Determination**   Once the facts have been determined as best as possible, a determination should be made about the validity of the complaint. If the complaint is valid, a remedy should be sought based on both legal and reasonable requirements. If the complaint is determined not to have valid grounds, that will be the determination. The decision should be documented in writing and included in the investigation folder.

4. **Feedback**   The employee who filed the complaint should be given feedback about the investigation results and any decisions made as a result. It may or may not be advisable to provide specific information about disciplinary action taken against an employee. Your legal advisor can give you guidance about that in your specific circumstances.

Internal vs. External Complaints

Internal complaints can run the gamut from "it isn't fair" to "I was discriminated against illegally." Especially in non-union organizations, it is important to let employees know that their complaints are taken seriously. Each one should be handled in a way that conveys that message. If necessary, the four steps of an investigation should be followed as just outlined.

Internal complaints give an employer the opportunity to resolve issues with employees before they fester further and generate formal external agency complaints. Wise HR professionals will make every effort to encourage employees to file complaints internally so they will have the opportunity to investigate and resolve them. Dealing with issues internally is always preferable to having them registered with third-party law enforcement agencies.

External complaints are those filed with state or federal fair employment practices agencies (for example, Equal Employment Opportunity Commission), wage and hour enforcement agencies (for example, U.S. Department of Labor, Wage and Hour Division), or safety enforcement agencies (for example, Organizational Safety and Health Administration or Mine Safety and Health Administration). When a formal complaint is filed with an external agency, it is often a signal that the employer may no longer speak with their own employee about that issue. All discussions with the employee after a complaint is filed must be handled through the enforcement agency. As a practical matter, that means the employer will face some limitations.

Before a response can be prepared explaining what happened and why, the employer will need to conduct an investigation to determine if the complaint has merit. Based on that result, and with the help from legal counsel, a formal response can be prepared explaining the employer's position.

Remember that these are law enforcement agencies with authority to require employers to take certain actions to remedy complaints if that is warranted. Your legal advisor is always your best ally when working with external agencies. There are usually complaint filing deadlines, designated response deadlines, and deadlines for implementing remedies. Those will vary depending on the agency involved and provisions of the relevant laws.

Mediation and Arbitration (Alternative Dispute Resolution—ADR)

Mediation and arbitration are alternative methods for dispute resolution. Some employers require one or the other in lieu of lawsuits to resolve employment problems with workers. Each requires certification by a national or state board and also requires compliance with strict ethical standards.

Mediation is the less formal of the two problem-solving methods. Since 1995, the American Arbitration Association (www.adr.org) has used a Due Process Protocol that requires fair hearing of an issue. Mediation is usually not binding on the parties involved. That means employers and employees can go through the process, arrive at a conclusion, and still not accept it, though why that would happen seems odd.

Arbitration is a stricter alternative. It is usually binding on the parties because they accept that condition before the process begins. Arbitration is nearly always conducted by an arbitrator who is a neutral party and a member of the American Arbitration Association. Binding arbitration is sometimes used as an alternative to lawsuits because the expense is considerably less than court and attorney costs, and it can be quicker.

Cost of mediation or arbitration is often split equally by the parties, although it is possible for the employer to agree to accept responsibility for paying all costs involved. In union contracts there is frequently a provision that costs will be split between the union and the employer. The method for selecting an arbitrator is usually specified in a union contract when that step is included in the grievance handling process.

Using External Experts

There are many different types of external experts who can be resources when appropriate. They include lawyers, consultants, investigators, and educators or trainers. The key to using external experts is to determine there is a benefit to be gained over performing the required tasks using internal personnel. The benefit might be a cost reduction or simply relief of the workload being carried by internal people. Sometimes it doesn't make sense to have a special talent or resource on the payroll because the frequency at which it is used seems so low. When the "growing your own" internal resource isn't practical, calling upon external resources is the next best thing. They can be used for the project and then the expense can be ended.

Expert witnesses are sometimes hired by employers and their legal representatives to support their position in lawsuits. When that happens, the people hired as experts offer knowledge and experience that fits the issues being disputed.

HR's Role in the Litigation Process

Employee and vendor lawsuits are quite common—much more than employers would like. The question here is, "What is the role of HR management in that litigation process?" The answer is, "Several roles come to mind."

- **Preserving documentation**   Once a lawsuit has been filed, your employment attorney will notify you and instruct everyone in the organization to preserve all records related to that suit. Because the HR department has custody of most employment-related records, a bulk of the responsibility for record preservation rests with the HR professionals. Preservation means records may not be destroyed or altered. Records may be in hard copy or on computer files, or stored in archive form somehow. It is necessary that they all be flagged in some way to indicate that they may not be destroyed until a release is provided by the organization's attorney.

- **Witness information**   With help from the organization's attorney, HR professionals should identify appropriate witnesses in the lawsuit. Those people should be contacted to be sure they are aware that they may be called to testify. Any records they have about the issue at hand must be preserved until the matter is settled.

- **Identifying others involved**   The complaining employee's supervisor, the decision maker, even coworkers who were present at the time, and other employees who are in similar situations as the complaining employee.

- **Communication with involved employees**   Notify all employees involved in the lawsuit that they may not discuss it with the complaining employee or with that employee's legal counsel. They should report to HR or Legal any attempt by the complaining employee or her/his lawyer to contact them to discuss the case.

Collective Bargaining

Collective bargaining is a process of negotiation that is required by the National Labor Relations Act (NLRA) (see Chapter 2). Once an election has resulted in a union being certified as the representative of a work group, the next step is to develop a written contract that will lay out all the working conditions appropriate to the relationship and the work group requirements. That process of contract development is called *collective bargaining*.

Governance of the Union-Employer Relationship

The National Labor Relations Act (NLRA) was passed by Congress in 1935 to encourage employers and employees to work together through collective bargaining. It protects rights of employees and provides procedures for establishing and eliminating bargaining units from the employment relationship. Union representation is always conducted under written contract with employers. Because represented employees have a written contract for their employment, they are no longer considered employment at will employees.

Contract Negotiation

Negotiating a contract requires identifying the subjects to be addressed by the agreement. Then, each party prepares its preferred position on each subject. Then the process of comparing those positions begins. Often, dollars are attached to contract subjects. For example, the length of work shift, the amount of overtime to be paid, and the cost of healthcare benefits all can be represented by dollar values. If the union wants greater benefits for its members, a dollar value can be assigned to that increase. Employers argue budget restraint and use dollar values to justify their reasoning.

According to the Negotiation Board, there are eight steps in the negotiation process.[7] Here is a list of the process step flow in contract negotiations:

- **Step 1: Prepare**   Do your research ahead of time so that you know your opponent and you know what you want from the negotiation.

- **Step 2: Open**   Let the other side know what you want and let them tell you what they want.

- **Step 3: Argue**   Back up your case with evidence and uncover defects in your opponent's argument.

- **Step 4: Explore**   Search for common ground and agreeable outcomes.

- **Step 5: Signal**   Show that you are ready to reach an agreement.

- **Step 6: Package**   Put together different acceptable options for both parties.

- **Step 7: Close**   Come to an agreement and finalize the negotiation.

- **Step 8: Sustain**   Ensure that their side, and yours, follows through with the negotiated agreement.

Establishing Contract Costs

Each component of a contract agreement can be assigned a cost in dollars. Adding all of those component costs can produce the total contract value. For example, health benefits will cost several hundreds of dollars each month to cover an employee and family members. The employer can agree to cover a percentage of that cost, with the balance being paid by the employee. A union will ask for more employer contribution to that formula. And, should the employer agree, the increased contribution can be assigned an incremental cost increase value. Adding that to other cost increases, such as increased pay schedules and overtime rates, will produce a total increase of contract costs. Each time a new proposal is made or received, a cost analysis should be made to determine the budgetary impact. Some costs will be perpetual, such as an increase in pay rates. Other costs can be limited to one-time only such as special bonus payments. There are advantages and disadvantages to costs that will be contained to one period of time (year) versus continuing into future periods of time.

Administering Union Contracts (MoU or CBA)

The thought that only large employers have union contracts is a myth. Many small employers work with union agreements. That is often the case in the construction industry, for example. Operating Engineers, Teamsters, and Laborers, among other unions, will sometimes have agreements with governmental entities that only union-represented workers will be employed on projects funded by that entity. This is common practice for cities and counties, particularly in geographical areas where labor organizations are a strong political influence.

Memoranda of Understanding (MOU) and Collective Bargaining Agreements (CBA) are the written contracts between employer and unions. MOU is a term usually found in the public sector and CBA is a term normally used in the private sector.

Whether the employer is large or small, someone in the organization must be assigned the responsibility for coordinating work through unions and ensuring the employer abides by all requirements of the union contract. Sometimes, unions require that they process all job requisitions from their employer counterparts. Hiring through union "hiring halls" is the practice of notifying the union of a job opening and receiving a qualified union member as the new hire designee. It is a simple process that can provide staffing quickly, often with only one telephone call or e-mail with the employment requisition.

Large employers will have labor relations staff groups that are assigned responsibility for day-to-day interactions with labor unions, as well as carrying responsibility for contract negotiations. Small employers will rely on a part-time job duty assignment for the labor relations function because it doesn't require full-time attention. Small employers sometimes rely on their labor attorneys to fill the role of contract negotiator and grievance handler, while job requisitions are processed part-time by another company employee.

Unfair Labor Practices

The National Labor Relations Act (NLRA) explains that unfair labor practices can be blamed on either employers or labor unions (see Chapter 2). Common among issues evoking such claims are those revolving around the process of union elections. Unions commonly claim the employer is blocking their organizing efforts, and employers claim that the union is harassing employees and electioneering using paid-time. Another issue that generates great numbers of complaints is how management and union members behave during a work stoppage (strike).

Complaints of unfair labor practices are formally filed with the National Labor Relations Board (NLRB). The NLRB will investigate the complaints and issue a determination along with any order for corrective action or limitation on activities of the offending party.

In some instances, when an employer believes there has been a violation of civil law requirements, it will go directly to court requesting an injunction against the union to prevent the behavior which is causing the problem. That is common when striking union pickets block access to parking lots, loading docks, or employee building entrances. Municipal laws in many locations govern how public access to property must be maintained and how public sidewalks and roadways can be used appropriately.

In other instances, unions can seek court assistance when employers are being accused of inappropriate controls on picketers. Use of physical force by private security guards could be an example.

In either situation, the remedy sought through the court is an injunction preventing the offending behaviors. With an injunction in hand, it is possible to request help from law enforcement bodies such as the police department or sheriff's department to enforce the injunction.

Labor-Management Cooperative Strategies

Linking the interests of both unions and employer can be an effective way to find common ground and preserve jobs while improving productivity. Cooperation is itself a strategy.

The United States Department of Labor has some thoughts about building cooperative, service-focused relationships between unions and employers.

> "It is useful to note that labor-management cooperation that is specifically focused upon employee participation and service improvement represents a fundamentally different approach from more traditional labor-management relations. In traditional relationships employee involvement in problem-solving is limited or absent and the organization is characterized by hierarchical service delivery and decision-making systems. Workplace problems and conflicts are likely to be more difficult to identify and resolve. In a successful and stable labor-management partnership, labor and management agree to assume and allow new roles for managers, workers and their representatives in workplace decision-making. This means that employees participate on a daily basis in decisions about services in areas traditionally reserved only for supervisors and managers. In exchange, the workers and their representatives are committed to responsible improvement of . . . services."[8]

Strikes, Picketing, and Boycotts

Agreement is not always reached which negotiating the terms of a union contract. Bargaining impasses can reach the point of a deadlock that cannot be resolved. There are three arrows a union has in its quiver of actions to take against an employer. When negotiations break down, there are still some actions that can be taken. These are protected concerted activities under the NLRA.

Strikes

Work stoppages are the last resort of a failed negotiation process. When a union contract expires, and the union and management are unable to reach agreement on terms of a new contract, the union can call a strike. When that happens, all union members are directed by the union to report for duty on the picket line and not to go to their normal jobs. Should a union member fail to report for picket duty as directed by the union, he or she may be fined by the union. Some laws govern the amount of notice that must be given to management or the public before a work stoppage can be implemented. Union leadership is obligated to get a majority agreement from its members on the advisability of a strike. A strike may be unlawful if its purpose or methods are illegal such as strikes in violation of a no-strike clause in an existing agreement. Federal employees do not have the right to strike as doing so would not be in the public's interest, and can be punished with felony charges and/or dismissal.

- **Economic strike**   Based on employee desire for more compensation or benefits.
- **Unfair labor practice strike**   Some labor practices such as overtime assignment procedures are disputed and not resolved in negotiations. The union can call a strike to stop work, putting pressure on the employer in an attempt to gain the union's objectives.
- **Wildcat strike**   An illegal, unsanctioned work stoppage by the union in reaction to some dispute with the employer.
- **Jurisdictional strike**   A work stoppage precipitated by two or more unions claiming jurisdiction in representation of the work group in question.
- **Sympathy strike**   A cessation of work by a second union in support of the first union that actually called an economic or unfair labor practice strike against the employer. If negotiations break down with one union, when that union calls a strike it can seek support from other unions that it hopes will put additional pressure on the employer.

Picketing

There are two primary types of picket exercises. One is informational picketing. The other is work stoppage picketing. *Informational picketing* is a technique used by unions when they want to have the public learn about certain issues. Information pickets usually carry signs or placards containing their message. *Work stoppage* (or *primary picketing*) occurs when the union has taken a strike vote and the majority of members wish to exercise their right to strike. While employees are marching on the picket line they are not working, and therefore, not being paid. Sometimes, unions have amassed a strike fund that will provide sustenance-level support to members who need it. In most jurisdictions, strikers are not eligible for unemployment insurance while they are on strike. That is because they are without work by choice, akin to being barred from receiving unemployment insurance payments after resigning a job. Other types of picketing include:

- **Recognitional** Picketing designed to get an employer to recognize the union as the official representative of employees in that work location.

- **Organizational** Picketing designed to get workers to recognize the union as their representative.

- **Area standards** Picketing used by unions to get an employer to accept standards used in the industry within the local area.

- **Common situs** Illegal picketing of a construction site by a union because of a grievance against a single subcontractor on the worksite.

- **Consumer picketing** Picketing by a union in an effort to get consumers not to patronize a given employer organization because of a labor dispute.

- **Bannering** Use of large banners (sometimes up to 20 feet long) and passing out handbills usually on public sidewalks or streets. In those conditions, bannering is usually considered legal.

Boycotts

Primary boycotts are a form of protest that unions sometimes use to emphasize the strength of their beliefs. Boycotts are organized withholding of transactions from a target employer or group of employers. For example, in 2011, members of the Wisconsin State Employees Union, AFSCME Council 24, circulated letters to businesses in southeast Wisconsin, warning that they would face a boycott if they didn't support collective bargaining for public employee unions.[9] Boycotts are sometimes called against companies that don't sell goods produced by union-represented workers. "Buy Union Labels" is a common theme. Unions have sometimes been known to call for members to boycott certain stores because they resist union organizing attempts. Boycott International, a program of 1World Communication, called for unions around the country to boycott Walmart because the chain sold clothing made in Bangladesh where wages are low. What impact such actions have on employers is not known.

There are also secondary boycotts, which fall into the following categories:

- **Ally doctrine** A boycott against a secondary employer because it is virtually indistinguishable from the primary employer—for example, General Motors assembly plant and the General Motors painting facility next to the assembly plant. Another example is Dole fruit harvesting and Dole canning and packaging operations.

- **Single employer** A boycott against a single employer or entities that operate so closely that they are treated as a single entity.

- **Joint employer** Professional Employer Organizations (PEO) would fall into this category as joint employer with the primary employer organization against whom the union constructs a boycott.

- **Alter ego doctrine** Determines that two or more businesses are essentially the same business for the purposes of NLRA coverage. Four criteria were established by the U.S. Supreme Court to determine if only one employer exists for labor relations purposes: interrelation of operations, central control of labor relations, common management, and common ownership.[10]

- **Double-breasting** Usually used in construction where multiple corporate structures are created. One handles work performed under union agreements and another performs work where workers are not union represented. A boycott against one is a boycott against all.

- **Straight-line operations** A boycott against two separate business organizations that operate in the same industry doing the same type of work on the same or similar projects.

- **Hot cargo clauses** An illegal boycott that involves the union coercing an employer not to do business with another firm.

Lockout

Lockouts can occur when management shuts down operations to prevent union employees from working. A lockout can occur when an organization is concerned about sabotage, and can force the union to look again at its bargaining position. Employers may also have the right to transfer work to another facility, run the business with management personnel or people not associated with the bargaining unit, and to protect their property from trespass.

Employment Legal Issues

Of course, there are many legal issues faced by employers. Those resulting from the acts of hiring and firing/layoff have special meaning in many states. These issues are usually defined and governed by state laws.

Negligent Hiring

This tort (legal injury) claim is brought against an employer when a person hired by the organization caused injury to someone inside or outside the organization in a way that should have been predicted by the employer had a proper background investigation been conducted. When a new hire gets angry and physically assaults another employee, it could represent negligent hiring if the employer could have determined that the new hire was dismissed from previous jobs because of anger issues. Failure to conduct proper background checks is usually the foundation for these types of claims. If a background check was conducted and the issue of violence was investigated with prior employers, the new employer could have a defense against such claims.

Preventing negligent hiring is a matter of conducting background investigations, probing for information relevant to the specific job requirements. Behavioral issues should always be on the list of subjects investigated. Misbehavior at previous employers should be a warning signal that future problems may exist if this individual is hired. Ignoring such information is always a risk.

Negligent Retention

A cousin of negligent hiring, this tort action can be brought against an employer for keeping someone on the payroll who is known to be a danger to others inside or outside the organization. When such a person then hurts a customer, another employee, or member of the public, the employer can be liable for the damages. These types of cases usually depend on an answer to the question, "Did the employer know, or should the employer have known, that the employee could be a threat to others?" If the employer knew, or reasonably should have known, that the employee was a possible threat, then the employer should have acted to remove the employee from employment through due process.

Liability for negligent retention can be controlled if managers and supervisors are trained to take appropriate disciplinary action when behavior problems occur. If a problem of violence arises, it may be appropriate to immediately dismiss the worker. When due process calls for progressive discipline, it should be implemented diligently and fairly. Similar problems should receive similar treatment. Accepting misbehavior is a recipe leading to liability.

Defamation

When an employer publishes (writes or says) something about an employee that it knows is not true, the employee may have recourse through a charge of defamation. Damage to the employee could include loss of reputation, loss of income, loss of employability, and more. Sometimes these charges come up when an employer is asked for information about a former employee. If someone provides rumor, innuendo, or accusations that are untrue or hearsay, the employer could be "on the hook" for the damage it does to the former employee.

The way to prevent defamation charges is to train employees and management in how to handle requests for references from another employer. Directing these requests to one person can help reduce the risk that something inappropriate will be provided to the other employer.

Measuring Disparate Impact During Reduction in Force

You will recall that disparate impact is one of two types of illegal discrimination under the Civil Rights Act of 1964. It is usually proven statistically, involving groups of people rather than through comparison of individual treatment.

Proving disparate impact is a deeply mathematical process involving large linear regression tables. That measurement requires a computer, and it is a legal process. Proving illegal disparate impact requires rigorous statistical analysis.

A less time-consuming, less accurate, but simple rule of thumb has existed since 1978. The Uniform Guidelines on Employee Selection Procedures (1978)[11] say that disparate impact occurs when the selection rate for a protected group falls below 80 percent of the selection rate for the most favorably treated group involved in the selection decisions. Sometimes called the *4/5ths Rule* or the *80% Rule* or *Adverse Impact Test (Impact Ratio Analysis [IRA])*, this level of analysis falls far short of proving disparate impact according to the U.S. Supreme Court.[12]

Nonetheless, HR Managers will find it helpful to do rapid comparisons using the 80% Rule when they look at data from hiring, promotion, termination, or training decisions. Sometimes what seems to be a neutral policy can actually result in illegal discrimination. The most famous of these seemingly neutral policies involved the use of height and weight requirements for the selection of firefighters. It was ultimately determined that the height and weight requirements had a statistically provable negative impact on females, Hispanics, and Asians. In recent times, it is rare to find height and weight requirements as part of the job hiring process. The 80% Rule is our first line of defense against such problems.

 NOTE You will probably find questions about the *Adverse Impact Test* or *80% Rule* on the PHR and SPHR exams. You should know how to compute the results and what they mean. Remember that they do not prove illegal discrimination but simply act as a red flag to indicate additional analysis should be done.

Table 7-2 provides an example of how the 80% Rule can be applied.

Category	# Qualified Applicants	# Hires	Hiring Rate (Hires/Apps)	Impact Ratio
Male	141	67	67/141 = 48%	48/59 = 81% No
Female*	111	66	66/111 = 59%	Most favorably treated group
White	75	40	40/75 = 53%	53/64 = 83% No
Black/African American**	30	10	10/30 = 33%	33/64 = **52% Yes**
Hispanic**	45	20	20/45 = 44%	44/64 = **69% Yes**
Asian*	55	35	35/55 = 64%	Most favorably treated group

* This is the most favorably treated group. According to the Uniform Guidelines on Employee Selection Procedures (1978), White is not always the most favorably treated group and in this example that is the case. Asians are the most favorably treated group because they have the highest selection rate (64%). In positive employment actions such as hiring and promotion, the most favorably treated group is the one with the highest selection rate. In a negative employment action, such as layoff or downsizing, the most favorably treated group is the one with the lowest selection rate.

** There is adverse impact because the impact ratio is less than 80 percent.

Table 7-2 Hiring Analysis

The results shown in our example indicate that more analysis should be done for Black/African American and Hispanic. Even though Hispanic is an ethnicity rather than a race under Title II, it is still treated like a race in these computations.

Additional Statistical Analysis Beyond the 80% Rule or Adverse Impact Test

Employers can use probability and standard deviation analysis as the next step in their investigation of statistical anomalies. The group "Age over 40," can be added to the computations if needed to determine how a downsizing or layoff is affecting that group. It is a protected group under the Age Discrimination in Employment Act and should not suffer because of layoff decisions.

It is commonly accepted that results in excess of 2.0 standard deviations out from the center of a bell curve distribution cannot have happened by chance. Said differently, results that fall out in the tails of the bell curve could not have happened by chance. Results within the "fat" part of the curve distribution might have happened by chance. The courts have said that employers will not be held accountable for illegal discrimination (disparate impact) unless it has been demonstrated to occur with statistical certainty. The only way to prove statistical certainty is with a multiple-regression analysis. For that we turn to the statisticians.

In summary, if you wish to use a rule of thumb, the 80% Rule is a good tool. If you wish to analyze data from your employment decisions to determine if you may have a statistically significant problem, you will want to use standard deviations or probability testing as your tool.

Evaluating Program Effectiveness

Whenever an HR professional implements a new program he or she should have a plan for how results will be measured. Without measurements it is not possible to determine if the program has been successful. Establishing measurements should be a key component of any new employee program.

Turnover Rates

If the program results in employee turnover that exceeds expectations, it could be a serious problem for the employer. Turnover is expensive, and if people begin finding jobs elsewhere if you change your vacation policy, or decide to freeze wages for the coming year, the cost of recruiting and training new workers could exceed the savings from the new program or policy.

These effects can happen when implementing healthcare program changes or taking away benefits such as employee discounts, company contributions to educational expenses, or sabbatical leaves of absence. If employer contributions to employee healthcare or savings programs are reduced or eliminated, workers can get upset to the extent that they seek employment elsewhere.

One way to anticipate these types of reactions and reduce employee turnover is to conduct focus group discussions about alternatives being considered. Ask employees for their reactions to each alternative and test various explanations of the business reasons for the notion that certain employee benefits will have to be reduced or eliminated. Armed with knowledge about employee reactions, decisions can be made more intelligently by senior management and it may be possible to contain the damage represented by employee turnover.

Employee Surveys

Employee surveys are a tool that wise employers use to constantly monitor the pulse of their workplace. A strong pulse can indicate employee satisfaction and cooperation with business objectives. A weak pulse can indicate employee upset or dissatisfaction that will result in higher turnover and greater cost to the enterprise.

Some employers, particularly smaller ones, will create and use their own employee surveys. There are off-the-shelf software packages that help construct survey questions and implement the survey. Some of them even allow surveys to be conducted on company intranet web networks.

There are some do-it-yourself survey services that charge fees for online surveys that can be used by employers to test employee satisfaction as well as things such as customer satisfaction. Survey Monkey (www.surveymonkey.com) is one such service with tutorials on creating unbiased survey questions.

Then there are consultants that will prepare survey questions and implement the survey process for a fee. These are often people with doctorate-level degrees who specialize in monitoring employee attitudes and analyzing the statistics that result from their survey efforts.

For surveys to deliver benefits, they should:

- Guarantee anonymity
- Provide feedback on the results to the surveyed population
- Have a clear purpose defined and communicated

However you do it, keeping a monitoring system of some kind on the pulse of employee attitudes is a constructive human resource management effort. Surveys are one way to accomplish that and provide painful and brutally honest feedback.

SPHR Developing and Implementing Strategies to Maintain a Union-Free Environment

In the "old days," even before there were Personnel Departments, there were Labor Departments in larger employment organizations. Remember that the first half of the twentieth century was a boom time for labor unions in the United States. Employers who didn't have union-represented workers often wanted to maintain their union-free environments. The process of gaining representation in a workforce is a strict legal process. Therefore, labor-management attorneys and law firms were often involved in guiding employers through the election process and negotiating contracts with successful unions. When employers wish to prevent a union from gaining employee approval for representation, they often call on their labor attorneys for help.

NLRB Procedures for Recognizing a Union

The National Labor Relations Board has formal procedures for union recognition:

1. The NLRB receives a petition from a labor organization for specific bargaining unit certification. The union petition must demonstrate a "show of interest" from at least 30 percent of employees it wishes to organize into a collective bargaining unit. This show of interest is usually in the form of authorization cards the union asks employees to sign saying they would like that union to represent them.

2. If accepted by the NLRB, the employer may consent by voluntary agreement or request a hearing and election.

3. The NLRB conducts a hearing to determine the legitimacy of the election request. It determines the scope of the voting unit and if that is a reasonable and appropriate group for collective bargaining. A *bargaining* unit is an employee group that shares a community of interest. Factors impacting that community of interest include the following:

   - Common supervision
   - Similar wages, benefits, and working conditions
   - Similarity of skills
   - Business operations in common

   Each side (employer and union) may call or subpoena witnesses to testify during the hearing.

4. Next comes a pre-election campaign by union and employer. A period of 25 to 30 days is normally allowed after the hearing decision for each side to try to convince employees of its viewpoint. The employer must provide to the NLRB an alphabetized list of employee names and home addresses who will be eligible to vote in the election. The agency will forward that list to the union so it can contact employees if it chooses to do so. That list is called an "Excelsior List" based on the NLRB case that first required employers to offer it. Employers may actively campaign against union representation, even using company time and facilities to do so. Employers are not required to provide union representatives an opportunity to attend those sessions, nor even access to company property to refute those employer meeting presentations. All campaigning must end at least 24 hours prior to the election date as required by the NLRB 24-hour rule.

5. "Blocking Charges" can be filed by either side. Charges of unfair labor practices can be filed with the NLRB by either the union or the employer. The pre-election process will be suspended while NLRB investigates and rules on the charges. Once charges are resolved, the pre-election campaign clock can begin ticking again.

6. NLRB conducts the election. All managers and supervisors must stay away from the location where voting takes place on election day. They are not permitted to intimidate employees during the election process. People permitted at the voting location include the NLRB agent conducting the election; employee voters; one or more non-supervisory observers chosen by the employer, and the same number of observers chosen by the union. Only employees who are determined to be in jobs within the bargaining unit are eligible to vote.

7. The union is elected to represent the bargaining unit or it is not (union election requires 50 percent plus 1 vote). The NLRB counts the votes and makes its announcement about the outcome.

Employer Reactions to Union Organizing Efforts

- **Voluntary agreement** Employers may agree voluntarily to recognize a union without a formal NLRB election. The union must still show that a majority of employees wish to be represented by that union. Voluntary agreements are sometimes called neutrality agreements, where employers agree to remain neutral during the union campaign, even permitting union organizers access to employees and opportunity to address groups of workers. *Card check* is a process where a majority of employees in the bargaining unit sign a card saying they want representation from the specific union and the employer accepts that without an election.

- **Acceptance because of a requirement under the successorship doctrine** If an employer merges or acquires another employer and assumes the former union-represented workforce, it can be required to accept the union representation and its contract with the former employer.

- **Opposition to union organizing efforts** Including such actions as employee meetings, suggestion boxes, dispute resolution policies and procedures, exit interviews, open door policies, and other employee-involvement programs. Key to any employer success is proper training of managers and supervisors. There are two training objectives for supervisors: (1) instructions for prevention of unfair labor practices and (2) reinforcement of policies and procedures for employee communication of all types.

Decertification or Deauthorization of a Union

NLRB rules give new unions a full year before they are subject to decertification efforts. Once past that year, any union can be decertified if the proper procedures are followed.

What's the Difference?

Decertification of a Union: Removal of the union as the exclusive bargaining representative of the employees.

Deauthorization of a Union: Removal of "union security" (forced unionism clause) from the contract. The union remains as the exclusive bargaining representative, and the collective bargaining agreement remains in effect, but employees are not forced to be members or pay dues to the union.

Decertification begins with at least 30 percent of the employees within the bargaining unit signing cards or a petition asking that the NLRB conduct an election to remove the union. (There can be additional restrictions during the first three years of a contract existence, particularly in the healthcare industry.) A majority of votes will determine if the union stays or goes.

Common Employee Relations Strategies

Employees who feel they are well treated and included in what is happening in the workplace are not very likely to seek out union representation. Inversely, those workplaces where employees are feeling mistreated have a higher chance of seeing workers attempting to gain union representation. Unions are seen as a tool to force management to conform to certain rules of employee treatment. Preventing unions from gaining a foothold in the workplace can be accomplished by keeping the workplace happy.

The following are strategies for preventing unionization efforts in the workplace:

- **Thorough management training in management skills**   There is a mistaken belief that promoting someone to a management position will automatically result in their understanding all that is necessary for their success in the new role. Management depends on successful use of a specific skill set. Included in that group of skills are: leadership skills, communication skills, decision making skills, perception skills, team building skills, inner work standards, and more.

- **Thorough management training on organizational policies and disciplinary procedures**   Consistency of treatment is critical for employees to believe they are getting a "fair shake." Once they begin believing they are being mistreated, all is lost.

- **Training managers and supervisors to recognize the signs that employees are starting to think about pursuing union organization in your workplace**   Early detection is necessary for a successful effort at preventing the union's success.

- **Monitoring employee benefit programs** Monitor benefit programs such as vacations, medical insurance, retirement programs, and other policies to be sure that employees are receiving benefits comparable to what they would get if they worked for similar employer organizations elsewhere.

- **Monitoring employee attitudes constantly** Use focus groups, employee surveys, and management discussions to help monitor how employees are feeling about their work environment and their treatment. When problems are detected, take action to resolve them.

- **Encouraging employees to present their complaints and irritations to their managers or to human resources officials** This type of employee communication enables managers and HR officials to investigate and resolve issues. The time spent on such efforts can be returned manyfold in savings of time later on.

Prevention of employment relations problems depends on strong and open communication channels within the organization. Successful organizations encourage employees to present their complaints so they can be addressed before they reach the level of a formal complaint or legal issue. Once a complaint goes outside the organization to an enforcement agency or court, the costs to an employer will escalate exponentially. It makes good business sense, and is substantially cheaper, to handle employee complaints internally. And the sooner the better. Left to fester, employee complaints can cause thoughts of union organizing and worse.

Identifying and Addressing Union Interests in Your Workplace

When a union shows interest in organizing your workforce, they won't come to your door and announce that fact. You will have to be alert to what is going on with employees. It may be that union organizers are seeking employment so they will have access to your other workers and can "talk up" advantages of union membership and representation. You may discover that union organizers are taking up positions at your front door to talk with employees as they come and go from your facilities. It may be that the union is handing out flyers or informational packets to employees in the parking lot. Stay alert and you will be able to detect these initial signs of union organizing.

Unions will "play up" their ability to act on behalf of employees who are being treated unfairly. They can emphasize their ability to structure overtime practices and take away the pain employees are feeling because of unfairly assigned work schedules. Whether or not these things are true, the union will attempt to get workers to believe that problems (true or imagined) can be solved by getting a union to represent them. Union organizing efforts can involve unpleasant and distasteful claims by organizers. They can also test the employer's resolve to maintain order in the workplace.

If you discover that there is one key issue being pushed by union organizers, you might be able to address that issue and take away the reason for the union to succeed in your workplace. For example, if work schedules are assigned based on a first-come claim to the most desirable schedules, changing to assignment based on seniority could dull the point of union organizers' efforts.

There are law firms in the country that specialize in helping employers work their way through the process of resisting union organizing efforts. If you experience such union efforts and would rather not have a union represent your employees, contacting one of these law firms might be a good business decision.

In the Trenches

HR Prevention; More Effective and Less Expensive than Union Avoidance

Jim Foord, SPHR, jfoord@comcast.net

Anyone attending a regional or national HR conference has undoubtedly been bombarded with the ever-increasing negative sentiment toward unions. It is, therefore, no surprise that the law firms and consultants that work with organizations to assist them in staying union free have become big business. So big, in fact, that the industry now has its own designation: "union avoidance."

It is my opinion that HR's adversarial posture toward unions is not going to help it accomplish a key organizational goal: retaining a union-free workplace. In fact, I posit that organizations focused on avoiding unions are more likely to see a union form in their workplace. For it is not unions that make cultures bad, it is poor leadership that leads to bad cultures, which are a potent breeding ground for union organizing.

The basis for this argument is fairly simple. By focusing on keeping unions out, HR is probably not doing the basic HR work that, if done in a timely fashion, would naturally keep them union free. The old adage that an ounce of prevention is worth a pound of cure is spot on here. Unfortunately, many organizations wait until their workplace is in such disarray that workers are motivated to look elsewhere for remedies that should be coming from within, and it is this waiting that the union avoidance industry is poised to leverage.

We need to focus on the work of ensuring that our workplaces are keeping pace with the needs of today's workers. As a society we have fought hard to keep our economy as efficient and "free" as possible. Think, then, of the work of staying union free as a free market opportunity, an opportunity to develop and maintain a workplace where the workers have no desire to seek outside assistance. Instead of spending our valuable time and resources on a "pound of cure" type of solution provided by the union avoidance industry, let's redirect our efforts internally. These "preventive" internal efforts are bound to be in better alignment with our organization's strategic goals, and they also cost less to implement. They provide a much better value in the long run.

Recognizing Union Organizing Efforts

Unions commonly request that employers accept the result of the show of interest cards without a formal election. That can represent a showing of anything over 30 percent of employees. Called *card checks* these are short-cut recognition requests. There has been a push in Congress to require the NLRB to accept card checks as authorization for certifying unions rather than requiring full elections. So far, that has not been successful.

Another common tactic used by unions is known as *salting*.[13] It can take several forms:

- **Salting union members without identifying them as union members** After they are hired, they usually violate employer policies until they are terminated, upon which the union files unfair labor practice charges against the employer.

- **Salting using union members wearing union clothing or other identifiers** If the individuals are not hired, the union files unfair labor practice charges against the employer.

Unions will also demand to use employer facilities to address groups of workers during work time. They will try to get employer agreement to access employees while they are at work. It is simpler for them than having to contact each individual at their home. Employers have no obligation to permit union access to the organization's property, nor to provide even non-work time access to employees at work.

Strategies for Maintaining a Union-free Environment

HR professionals are a key link in the chain an organization can forge to prevent union organizations from making inroads into the employer's group. Here are some key action steps that can help prevent a successful union organizing campaign.

- **Maintain a written policy** Explain why you wish to remain union-free. Explain the advantages already provided by the company and that there are no additional advantages a union could provide.

- **Provide thorough communication** Use employee meetings, newsletters, e-mails, and webinars to provide information to employees on a regular basis. Let them know what the company is doing and where it is headed. Keep employees up to date on the latest sales successes, and spotlight key people who are good performers. Offer an equally wide spectrum of ways employees can provide the employer with feedback. Those should include employee surveys, supervisor and management access, and written feedback systems. Publish survey results and explain what actions will be taken to follow up on those results. Use skip-level interviews to reach employee groups directly, soliciting their feedback about current conditions and key issues. Again, take action on the input received, particularly if there are problems to be addressed.

- **Be honest** Always respond with honesty. If you can't comment on a particular issue, that can be acceptable to employees. If you lie to them, they will know it and your case for a union-free environment will be substantially weakened.

Chapter Review

Employee and labor relations are complex issues. They often require HR personnel to understand complex legal requirements. They depend on talented and skilled management personnel to guide employees and the organization through all requirements of day-to-day concerns. In today's employment world, HR professionals must have a great depth of legal knowledge because they will need to use that knowledge every day.

Questions

1. Alysse is setting up the human resource systems for her newly formed organization. She wants to write a policy about employment at will but isn't sure what it is. How would you explain it to her?

   A. Employment at will means either the employee or the employer can end the relationship at any time for any reason.

   B. Employment at will means the employer can terminate an employee when necessary, but the employee must give two weeks' notice.

   C. Employment at will means the employee can quit at any time, even without notice.

   D. Employment at will doesn't exist any more because of state and federal labor laws.

2. When Barack began his work with the AB Trucking Company, he established a process of sending engagement letters to all his new employees. Is he creating employment contracts by doing so?

   A. Probably. By laying out the amount of money he is going to pay them and when they will begin work, he is creating a contract agreement.

   B. Not at all. By specifying how much will be paid and the start date, there is no promise of continued work so there is no contract.

   C. Absolutely. By giving the new employee a chance to review the employee handbook and sign the engagement letter, there is a written contract for employment.

   D. Maybe not. If the letter doesn't require a signature from the new employee, there likely isn't a contract being created.

3. Caladonia was interviewing with the HR Manager of an organization she really wanted to work for. The HR Manager told her that "the employer was really good about not laying off workers." They always found another way to deal with slow periods. Can Caladonia rely on that statement as an oral contract?

   A. Perhaps. It was close to a promise that she wouldn't be laid off in the future.

   B. Absolutely. There is no question that the HR Manager made an oral contract with Caladonia.

C. Probably not. There really wasn't any promise made to not lay her off later.

D. Definitely not. The HR Manager can say anything during an interview and it can't be relied on as an oral contract.

4. Collective bargaining agreements are contracts between a union and an employer.

A. Yup. They are written expressions of a set of workplace rules and benefits the employer will provide in exchange for employee work performance.

B. Nope. They are guidelines only. The union will work out any deviations in the grievance process.

C. Hmmm. Maybe. If the agreement says it is a contract, then it is a contract. If it doesn't claim to be a contract, then it isn't.

D. Arrrggggg. Never. If the employer tells the union it isn't going to enter into a contract, then the agreement is only an informal set of working rules.

5. Seniority will always be the determining factor in a union agreement.

A. Not always. Some union contracts will use education as the determining factor over ruling seniority in the process.

B. Seniority is only used by unions that have contracts or subcontracts with federal agencies.

C. Public agencies rely on seniority and they are the only ones with those agreements.

D. Universally, unions will rely on seniority as the determining factor for all treatment under contract provisions.

6. Dabney is the HR Manager negotiating a renewal of the contract his organization has with an international union. Because the union is international, he isn't sure if the National Labor Relations Act applies to his situation. What would you tell him?

A. He's right to be concerned. It is the International Labor Relations Act (ILRA) that governs his situation with the union.

B. When the union is an international organization, it can choose between the governance of the ILRA and the NLRA.

C. The NLRA governs all union interactions regardless of the union's scope of involvement.

D. If Dabney's organization is negotiating in good faith, there is no law that will tell him what to do. Only if he isn't willing to negotiate will the NLRA take effect.

7. Is it possible for employment policies (as laid out in the employee handbook) to take precedence over union contracts.

A. If there is a conflict between the union contract and the employer's policies, the contract will always win.

B. In case a conflict arises then the policy will always prevail.

C. Whenever there are different provisions in a union contract and employer policy, the differences must be arbitrated to resolution.

D. It is up to the manager of the unit involved to determine which will be applied in a given situation.

8. Dabney is the HR Manager for his employer. He has been asked to write an employee handbook to provide all the organization's policies in writing. What will employees be able to assume about the handbook policies?

A. Handbook policies are only guidelines and they will offer general instruction about how to treat things like vacation and leaves of absence.

B. Dabney should write the handbook so policies are acceptable to most employees. There will always be some exceptions to the rules.

C. The policies are requirements. All managers and employees should use them consistently or there can be complaints of illegal discrimination.

D. With provisions for exceptions to be approved by senior management, Dabney can be confident that the handbook policies will be applied by all the managers in his organization.

9. A union contract normally details the process called "progressive discipline." How would you counsel non-union employers to deal with the process?

A. Progressive discipline is only required for union-represented organizations.

B. There is no need for non-union employers to have a progressive discipline process since they are probably "at-will" employers and can terminate employees any time.

C. Progressive discipline is a good process for any employer. It offers "due process" to workers, and it satisfies the legal covenant called "Good Faith and Fair Dealing."

D. Employers can consider using progressive discipline, but absent a union contract, there is little motivation to use the process.

10. Elaine has attended an industry meeting with other HR professionals. She came back to her office with the idea that background investigations of new hires is something she ought to implement. What would you say to Elaine about that idea?

A. The EEOC has banned background investigations in any form because they discriminate against Hispanics and Blacks.

B. The EEOC has only recommended that background checks not automatically eliminate Hispanics or Blacks because of employment history.

C. Background checks are still legal and should be conducted on applicants before a job offer is made to be sure there is no history of bad behavior that could bring liability into the new workplace.

D. Finding anyone these days with no skeleton in the closet is going to be very difficult. Background checks are not really worth the money or time they require.

11. Mary has never before had an employee who caused a physical fight with another employee. The policy in her organization calls for progressive discipline. Mary isn't sure if she should just give the employee a warning or terminate him immediately. What would you recommend?

    A. This is the reason people should learn self-defense. When someone is defending themselves, there should be no reason for employer-imposed discipline. The aggressive employee should be given a written warning, though.

    B. It is hard for someone to start a fight by themselves. Both employees should be written up, skipping the oral warning step of progressive discipline.

    C. It depends on how other aggressive behavior has been treated in the past. Even though there have not been fights per se, the employee treatment should be guided by history.

    D. Violent behavior of any kind is justification for immediate dismissal. Even if there is no policy that says violence can result in immediate termination, that is how this situation should be handled.

12. Woodrow has been awarded a paid day off because he delivered his product development project ahead of schedule. Does this mean every time someone delivers a job in advance of the deadline they should be given a paid day off?

    A. Maybe. If the situations are the same or very similar, the reward should be the same.

    B. Maybe. Assuming that the employees had the same amount of service and their projects were similar in difficulty, they should all be given a paid day off.

    C. Maybe. With an eye on illegal discrimination, the employer should err on the side of providing a day off with pay to anyone who completes work ahead of schedule.

    D. Maybe. However, if the employer can describe the reward as "special" based on the circumstances it needn't create a precedent that must be followed in each future instance.

13. Harold has heard that it is necessary to have a diversity management program under some new federal law. What would you tell Harold about that requirement?

    A. The new law won't be effective until a year after it was passed. So there is no immediate requirement for him to worry about.

    B. There is no federal law requiring diversity management programs. Sophisticated employers are moving in that direction because it is the right thing to do and production results often improve.

   C. There is no law requiring diversity management programs, and employers should not consider moving toward such programs unless they are federal contractors.

   D. The new law will require diversity management programs only for employers that have federal contracts to provide goods or services to government agencies.

14. Gianna has been asked by her boss to develop a program for use of self-directed work teams in their organization. She has limited experience with that form of organization. How would you advise her on her project?

   A. Self-directed work teams only work well in the high tech industry.

   B. Her program should have a method for determining how a leader will be appointed for each work team. There must be management control over all team efforts.

   C. Gianna should review the experience of employers in the automobile industry to determine how to design her program.

   D. She should place a sunset provision into her program so each work team is disbanded twelve months after it is formed. Everyone needs to return to their normal work group no later than that twelfth month.

15. Gwen has just been promoted to HR Manager and has no background in that area of the business. She has always been in engineering. Her boss wants her to establish an employee-management committee that he can chair. How would you advise Gwen under those circumstances?

   A. Gwen should explain to her boss that the NLRB has ruled such committees to be in violation of the law if management controls them.

   B. There is nothing wrong with an employee-management committee as long as it has representation from both management and non-management.

   C. Employee-management committees are only legal in organizations that have no union representation.

   D. When employees participate in management, they must be paid a differential to compensate for the higher-level responsibilities they are taking on.

16. Naji is wondering how he is going to describe the difference between his organization's employee grievance resolution process and the discrimination complaint handling process. What would you suggest?

   A. There isn't any difference between them. The processes for handling them is the same.

   B. Employee grievances are often regarding workplace rules and work assignment processes. Discrimination complaints have more to do with equal employment opportunity issues.

C. Grievances only happen in union-represented organizations so Naji doesn't have to worry about that. He still has to explain how discrimination complaints can be handled in his organization.

D. Handling grievances is not required by law, but handling discrimination complaints is a legal requirement under federal law.

17. When Lloyd was told that he couldn't take a personal leave of absence, he said to the HR Manager that his boss was being unfair. Lloyd wants to file a complaint of discrimination because he is being treated unfairly. As the HR Manager what would you tell Lloyd?

A. His boss has never made an unfair decision in his time with the company. It is very unlikely he would be unfair in this situation.

B. There can only be discrimination if someone else was given a leave of absence who was a different race than Lloyd.

C. You will speak with Lloyd's boss to find out why the leave of absence was denied, and you will get back to Lloyd with some feedback about the reasons why.

D. Fairness is not a protected or guaranteed outcome of every employment decision. Lloyd should just accept the decision and make other plans.

18. A discrimination complaint notice has just arrived from the EEOC. You have 30 days to respond in writing to the Commission. What should you do before submitting your response?

A. Go to the employee who filed the complaint and ask why.

B. Notify the employee's supervisor and explain that he or she cannot discuss the complaint with the employee. Conduct an investigation without talking to the complaining employee. Collect documentation that pertains to the complaint. Write the employer's rationale for the decisions and actions taken that resulted in the complaint.

C. Notify the employee that the notice of complaint was received and explain that we will be investigating to identify what happened and how to respond. Tell the employee you wish to schedule an interview to discuss what happened and what can be done to remedy the situation.

D. Tell the supervisor that you will have to explain this to the CEO and the senior legal counsel. Once they are aware of the complaint, you will get back to the supervisor with their reaction.

19. Mia has only been an HR Manager for six months. She has been told by other HR professionals that she should have a policy that requires employees to go through arbitration rather than permit lawsuits. What should she do, if anything?

A. First, Mia should speak with her legal advisors to determine if mediation or arbitration would fit into their employment culture. Not every employer is well suited to requiring all employees to use arbitration for the resolution of disputes in the workplace.

B. Mia should draft a new policy statement that can be forwarded to senior management for its approval. It should take advantage of mandatory arbitration to prevent the cost of employee lawsuits.

C. Never should a policy be drafted that doesn't already have the approval of senior management. A discussion about changing employee requirements related to dispute resolution should take place and then a new policy should be drafted and implemented.

D. Once everyone in the organization understands the concept of mandatory arbitration and what it will cost each participant, the employer can proceed with a policy requiring it as the dispute resolution method to be used.

20. When Jacob's company experienced its first union organizing effort, the union won the election and Jacob was faced with having to negotiate his first union contract. Because it was his first time, what would you recommend Jacob do?

A. He should be all right if he gets a copy of another contract to use as a model and then sticks to that language.

B. Jacob would be well advised to invite his labor relations attorney to participate in the negotiation process. He will need advice at each stage of the process to be sure he makes only wise commitments for the employer.

C. Jacob should turn the negotiations over to the labor attorney. He can do all the negotiating and Jacob doesn't even have to be involved.

D. Once the union provides its demands, the only thing Jacob needs to do is explain to the union what can be done and what can't be done.

21. Emma has never had to manage a union contract before. As the HR Manager, she is involved with the grievance handling process as the third step in the process. At her first meeting with the union steward, the steward began yelling at Emma and telling her what she had to do to satisfy the union in this situation. Emma was stunned. What should she do?

A. She has little choice but to sit there and take it. She is the employer's representative and if she gets upset it will only make matters worse.

B. Emma should call a recess and ask for a management representative to join the meeting with her so she can have some backup in a very unpleasant situation.

C. Emma should recess the meeting and tell the steward that she will not continue their conversation until the steward can conduct herself in a civil manner.

D. Once the steward has blown off all her steam, Emma should continue the discussion by explaining the employer's position.

22. Isabella is sitting at her desk in the HR Department on the first day of a union strike. Pickets have assembled at the front gate and are blocking the sidewalk and not allowing anyone to enter the employer's property. As the HR Manager, what should Isabella do?

    A. There is nothing she can do. The union has a right to picket outside the employer's gate. People will just have to wait for a break in the picket line so they can cross over and go to work.

    B. She can go out to talk with the pickets and ask them to allow people to cross over into work. She can also explain to the pickets that she will call the police if they continue to block public access to the employer's property. She should tell them she will get a restraining order if they don't open things up for people to move into the property.

    C. Without even talking with the picketers she should call the police. There is no way they should be permitted to prevent people from entering the workplace.

    D. Emma should fight fire with fire. She should organize a few management people with signs protesting the union blocking their entrance to the property and picket inside the gate. Their demonstration can counter any effect the union pickets might have.

23. Sophia makes it a practice to call each applicant's former employers to verify employment claims and determine if there were any behavioral problems in prior jobs. Her company is now being sued because a new hire had an automobile accident while on a delivery run. It turned out he had a history of reckless driving charges in his past two jobs. But she wasn't told about those when she talked with the former employers. Should Sophia be worried?

    A. Yes. Almost certainly, Sophia will be blamed for negligent hiring. She has little defense. She should have found out about the new employee's previous employment issues.

    B. No. She tried to get information from the previous employers and they wouldn't talk to her. She made a good faith effort. She is off the hook.

    C. Yes. Sophia is going to have to explain to her attorney why she hired this person when there was such a bad history of workplace behavior.

    D. Yes. In this instance, she should also have conducted a search of his driving record before hiring him into a job that required driving for deliveries. She shouldn't have relied on only former employer input.

24. Alex insists on taking all calls requesting employment verification for former employees. As the HR Manager, he refuses to give any feedback about people who were poor performers, but for those who were good performers, he

is willing to explain how well they had done. What do you think of Alex's approach to employee references?

A. It sounds good. There should be no problem since he isn't saying anything bad about anyone.

B. He should never give out any information about any former employee, good or bad.

C. His approach to references will develop a reputation for the employer, and other employers will soon be able to know if someone was a bad performer simply because Alex doesn't give them any feedback about performance. That in itself could constitute a poor reference and be cause for some upset among former employees. His approach is a risky one that could bring liability to the employer.

D. Only if a former employee signs a release of liability should Alex give out information about poor performers.

25. Olivia believes that it is a good idea to conduct an employee survey each year to get input about employee attitudes. Her Vice President thinks that employee surveys cost too much money and don't provide much value in the end. What should Olivia tell the Vice President?

A. A well-constructed employee survey can provide information about the types of employment benefits employees would find attractive, how they feel about their managers, and if they believe they are being treated fairly. All of these feedback categories can be assigned dollar values and can be compared over time as budget impacts.

B. Because the professional HR community is suggesting that employee surveys be conducted each year, it would be wise for Olivia's organization to do that also.

C. The organization Olivia worked at before did an employee survey and she thinks it would communicate to employees that the employer is willing to listen to them.

D. In the modern workplace, employee attitudes are controlling factors. Surveys will help managers regain control of the workplace.

Answers

1. **A.** Either party can end the relationship with or without notice subject to some limitations on the employer created by various laws barring illegal treatment.

2. **B.** Employment contracts require a promise to do something in return for a consideration such as work. Even if an offer is made and accepted, the letter would need to contain a promise of retention for a certain period of time to overcome the employment at will status.

3. **A.** Caladonia wasn't promised a job forever. But she was told the employer always found another way to deal with slow periods. In many jurisdictions, she can rely on that as a contract.

4. **A.** Collective bargaining agreements are contracts between the union and the employer.

5. **D.** We have yet to see a union contract that didn't use seniority as the determining factor for contract provisions.

6. **C.** The National Labor Relations Act has effect regardless of how large the union or employer may be. The key is that operations take place in the United States.

7. **A.** Contract provisions are policy. So contract provisions will prevail.

8. **D.** There will always be someone wanting an exception to a policy. Requiring senior management review and approval for each exception is key to making sure there are legitimate business reasons supporting each request. Otherwise, all managers should apply handbook policies consistently.

9. **C.** Due process is the effort made by employers who want to convey that they are treating employees fairly. It demonstrates that the employer is abiding by the Covenant of Good Faith and Fair Dealing.

10. **C.** Background checks are still legal. The EEOC simply recommends making sure they are job related and that conviction records not automatically disqualify candidates. Using background checks to help prevent claims of negligent hiring is a good idea.

11. **D.** It is hard to be absolute in any recommendation, but this situation sounds like it should result in the immediate termination of at least the aggressive employee. It may be appropriate to also discipline the other employee depending on the outcome of an investigation.

12. **D.** It is not a requirement that each person who completes their project ahead of schedule be given a paid day off. However, if we create a situation where people in similar circumstances are treated differently based on membership in a protected class, we could face a claim of illegal discrimination.

13. **B.** Diversity management programs are not a new idea, and they are not a legal requirement. More and more employers, however, are implementing them because they help with employee satisfaction and marketplace perceptions.

14. **C.** The best way to ensure success of a new employment program is to study those that have already been successful. The automobile industry has achieved a great deal of success with this method of addressing work problems. It makes sense to study their efforts and consider using some of their methods.

15. **A.** Gwen should offer her boss the insight of *NLRB v. Electromation, Inc.* It prohibits employee-management committees that are controlled by management. Committees that are given management responsibility for solving workplace issues are considered legal by the NLRB.

16. **B.** Labor relations issues are usually handled by grievance procedures whereas discrimination complaints are considered EEO issues.

17. **C.** There may be a misunderstanding between Lloyd and his boss. You should speak with the boss to determine what the business reasons were for the decision to deny Lloyd's request. Feedback to Lloyd is critical to complete the communication.

18. **B.** Once a formal complaint has been filed with the EEOC, an employer is prohibited from discussing it with the complaining employee. The employer will have to conduct its investigation without the benefit of the employee's input. That's why it is much better to handle complaints internally so everyone involved can participate in the investigation.

19. **A.** Examination of the pros and cons for mandatory arbitration should be made and it should be reviewed with legal counsel before moving forward with a policy change. Not all employers will find that mediation or arbitration are the best methods for resolving conflicts in the workplace.

20. **B.** It is always a good idea to have a labor attorney involved with the negotiation process, but Jacob needs to be involved in the details so he can assign costs to each provision of the union requests. The bottom line is that there is always a budget constraint to be considered in the negotiation process. But Jacob doesn't want to make agreements that aren't required either. Paying for the attorney to participate is a wise decision.

21. **C.** Emma does not have to sit there and take abuse from the steward. If the steward cannot behave civilly, the meeting should end. Only when the steward can control herself should Emma agree to continue. It might also be a good idea to provide some feedback to the union president about what has happened in the meeting.

22. **B.** Local and state laws will usually govern property rights and whether or not it is permissible to block entrance to private property. Law enforcement officials can be helpful to ensure access rights are not trammeled during a strike. If necessary, seeking a restraining order against the union may be necessary.

23. **D.** A background check should be tailored to the situation. For a job that requires driving, a check of DMV records and history of insurance claims should be routine. Had Sophia conducted such a check, she surely would have uncovered this history and been able to change her hiring decision.

24. **C.** Providing references only about good performers will create a reputation that no reference means a bad reference. That could bring liability. It is best to either provide references for everyone or not for anyone. Your legal advisor can provide guidance.

25. **A.** In fact, each category of employee feedback can be assigned a dollar value and those can be tracked over time as budget impacts. Benefits are only one segment of the employee experience at work. Interpersonal relations with

supervisors and managers is another big issue. Generally speaking, employees who feel well treated will be better performers, which also impacts the financial results.

Endnotes

1. Seymour Moskowitz, *Employment at Will & Code of Ethics: The Professional Dilemma*, 23 Val. U.L. Rev. 33 (1988). Available at http://scholar.valpo.edu/vulr/vol23/iss1/7. Retrieved on 8/16/2013.

2. *Harris v. Quinn* (S.Ct. No. 11-681), June 30, 2014, http://www.supremecourt.gov/opinions/13pdf/11-681_j426.pdf.

3. "Consideration of Arrest and Conviction Records in Employment Decisions Under Title VII of the Civil Rights Act of 1964," www.eeoc.gov/laws/guidance/arrest_conviction.cfm. Retrieved on 4/25/2012.

4. *National Labor Relations Board vs. Electromation, Inc.*, 309 NLRB 990 (1992), enf'd., 35 F.3d 1148 (7th Cir. 1994).

5. *National Labor Relations Board vs. Crown Cork & Seal Company*, 334 NLRB No. 92 (July 20, 2001).

6. The Center for Social Leadership, www.thesocialleader.com/2011/07/leaders-5-step-guide-conflict-resolution/. Retrieved on 10/10/2013.

7. The Negotiation Board, http://negotiationboard.com/eight-steps-to-a-successful-negotiation/, as of 10/8/2013.

8. U.S. Department of Labor, "How to Build and Sustain Cooperative, Service-Focused Workplace Relationships," www.dol.gov/dol/aboutdol/history/reich/reports/worktogether/chap4new.htm. Retrieved on 10/9/2013.

9. Milwaukee, Wisconsin *Journal Sentinal*, March 31, 2011, www.jsonline.com/news/statepolitics/118963234.html.

10. *Radio Union vs. Broadcast Services Inc.*, 380 U.S. 255 (1965).

11. 41 C.F.R 60-3.

12. *Griggs v. Duke Power Co.*, 401 U.S. 424 (1971); *Wards Cove Packing Co., Inc., et al. v. Atonio, et al.*, 490 U.S. 642 (1989).

13. NLRB Decisions: *Toering Electric Company*, September 29, 2007; *Oil Capitol Sheet Metal, Inc.*, May 31, 2007; *KenMor Electric Company, Inc.*, August 27, 2010. U.S. Supreme Court Decision: *NLRB vs. Town & Country Electric, Inc.*, 516 U.S. 85, 1995.

Human Resource Development

Human resource development (HRD) focuses on the talent, knowledge, and performance of the workforce in an organization in an effort to meet the current and future needs of the organization. Developing, implementing, and evaluating activities and programs that address employee training and development, performance appraisal, and performance management is at the core of HR responsibility. The PHR exam carries an 18 percent weight on the exam for HRD and the SPHR gives a 19 percent focus.

Responsibilities

- Ensure that human resources development activities are compliant with all applicable federal laws and regulations.

- Conduct a needs assessment to identify and establish priorities regarding human resource development activities.

- Develop/select and implement employee training programs (for example: leadership skills, harassment prevention, computer skills) to increase individual and organizational effectiveness.

SPHR ● Evaluate effectiveness of employee training programs through the use of metrics (for example: participant surveys, pre- and post-testing).

- Develop, and evaluate talent management programs that include assessing talent, developing career paths, and managing the placement of high-potential employees.

- Develop, implement, and evaluate performance appraisal processes (for example: instruments, ranking and rating scales) to increase individual and organizational effectiveness.

- Develop, implement, and evaluate performance management programs and procedures (includes training for evaluators).

SPHR ● Develop/select, implement, and evaluate programs (for example: telecommuting, diversity initiatives, repatriation) to meet the changing needs of employees and the organization.

- Provide coaching to managers and executives regarding effectively managing organizational talent.

Knowledge of

- Applicable federal laws and regulations related to human resources development activities (for example: Title VII, ADA, Title 17 [Copyright law])

- Career development and leadership development theories and applications (for example: succession planning, dual career ladders)

- Organizational development (OD) theories and applications

- Training program development techniques to create general and specialized training programs

- Facilitation techniques, instructional methods, and program delivery mechanisms

- Task/process analysis

- Performance appraisal methods (for example: instruments, ranking and rating scales)

- Performance management methods (for example: goal setting, relationship to compensation, job placements/promotions)

 - Applicable global issues (for example: international law, culture, local management approaches/practices, societal norms)

- Techniques to assess training program effectiveness, including use of applicable metrics (for example: participant surveys, pre- and post-testing)

- Mentoring and executive coaching

Core Knowledge of

- Needs assessment and analysis

- Third-party or vendor selection, contract negotiation, and management, including development or requests for proposals (RFPs)

- Adult learning processes

- Motivation concepts and applications

- Training techniques

- Leadership concepts and applications

- Human relations concepts and applications

- Ethical and professional standards

- Technology to support HR activities

- Qualitative and quantitative methods and tools for analysis, interpretation, and decision-making purposes

- Methods for assessing employee attitudes, opinions, and satisfaction

Federal Laws That Apply to This Body of Knowledge

Now that you've reviewed the Human Resources Development responsibilities and knowledge statements, we recommend that you review the federal laws that apply to HRD (see Figure 8-1). The federal laws fall into two categories:

- Laws that regulate content and intellectual property
- Laws that protect the rights of employees

It would benefit you, the reader, to refer back to Chapter 2 on these specific laws prior to reading any further in this chapter.

HR's Role in Organizational Development (OD)

First, let's define what organizational development is. The following is a longstanding definition created by Richard Beckhard in his 1969 book *Organization Development: Strategies and Models*[1]:

> Organization Development is an effort (1) planned, (2) organization-wide, and (3) managed from the top, to (4) increase organization effectiveness and health through (5) planned interventions in the organization's "processes," using behavioral-science knowledge.

The best way to describe HR's role in organizational development is as a masterful change agent because planning and managing change are the cornerstones in OD. Helping the workforce adapt to change, embrace the changes, and see the potential possibilities for the organization's benefit is the responsibility of HR professionals.

Of all the many competencies required for the HR professional, being a masterful change agent is probably the most important because HR professionals not only serve as the catalyst in communicating the change, but they will also be charged with the evaluation of the change and with design or implementation interventions for the

---

- The Copyright Act (1976)
- The Trademark Act (1946)
- Uniform Guidelines on Employee Selection Procedures (1978)
- Age Discrimination in Employment Act (1967)

- The U.S. Patent Act
- Title VII of the Civil Rights Act (1964)
- The Americans with Disabilities Act (1990)
- Uniformed Services Employment and Reemployment Rights Act (1994)

Figure 8-1   Federal laws that apply to human resources development

change. They will have their hands in diagnosing the environment to determine the readiness of the workgroup that is impacted and needing to accept the change. Then HR professionals move into developing an action plan that determines the strategies to be used to implement the plan. And lastly, they are responsible for evaluating the change to measure the planned effectiveness and behavioral results against what was intended.

Learning Organization

A learning organization is a place "where people continually expand their capacity to create the results they truly desire, where new and expansive patterns of thinking are nurtured, where collective aspiration is set free, and where people are continually learning how to learn together." It is a systems-level concept in which the organization is characterized by its capacity to adapt to changes in its environment. The organization responds quickly to situations by altering the organizational behavior. A good example is when social media became more than just staying in touch with friends and family. Businesses quickly learned how much power they had to influence customers and thus businesses began creating their own customer fan pages to communicate with customers and provide time-sensitive offers.

The importance of aligning HR initiatives and activities with the overall strategic plan of the organization will require the application of concepts of both a learning organization and organizational learning.

In a learning organization a systems-thinking approach is used, change is embraced, risk is tolerated, and failures are lessons learned. Peter Senge's *The Fifth Discipline* outlines the five disciplines that interface and support one another with this systems-thinking concept.

1. **Personal mastery** Connects personal and organizational learning, merging an individual's personal vision with their current reality. Commitments happen between the organization and the individual.

2. **Mental models** Ingrained assumptions that influence how individuals understand their reality and what actions they take.

3. **Building shared vision** Develops a projection of the future that is shared and creates a genuine commitment on all individuals involved.

4. **Team learning** Aligns the shared vision of a group and develops their capacities to produce the results the team desires.

5. **Systems thinking** A framework for seeing patterns and how things interrelate, and how to change things.

When the five disciplines are in use in an organization, learning is matched to employees' learning preferences, leaders become stewards and teachers, people take responsibility for their own development and learning, and there is an understanding on how to learn, not a sole focus on what needs to be learned. The learning is easily tied to business objectives and it creates a performance-based culture where solving problems and learning new ways not previously used are rewarded. Basically, a learning organization focuses on employees who want to learn to develop new capabilities and reacts to adapt to its environment.[2]

Organizational Learning

Organizational learning describes the particular activities or processes that occur in an organization with both individuals and teams. An example would be a new payroll cloud-based processing software that all payroll clerks are required to learn to use. In organizational learning, individual learning takes place through self-study, instruction, and observation. Group learning occurs through increasing knowledge, skills, and group instruction.

The characteristics of a culture that supports organizational learning are:

- Recognition of continuous learning in the work environment being as important as the day-to-day work itself
- Quality improvements driving organizational initiatives
- Well-defined core competencies in job descriptions
- Performance rewards based on individual and group learning achievements
- Employees having access to important information such as strategic plans
- A focus on creativity exists

The distinction between organizational learning and a learning organization is that organizational learning exists in every organization.

Change Process Theory

OD and the change process theory go hand-in-hand. Just as there is a predictable series of emotions that occur with significant emotional events, as discussed in Chapter 6, in organizational change, social psychologist Kurt Lewin[3] identified three stages of the change process in organizations, as depicted in Figure 8-2. The first stage is called "unfreezing" and involves shifting and dismantling the existing mind set or paradigms. In the second stage, labeled "moving," is the moment change occurs. It is generally a phase of confusion marked by not knowing what's next and difficulty in letting go of old ways. The final and third stage is called "freezing." This is when the new paradigm is taking shape and a tipping point of comfort with the new change is taking hold.

Like all good planning methods, with organizational changes, communication must be crystal clear on the long-term goals for the change, along with actions steps on how the change will take place.

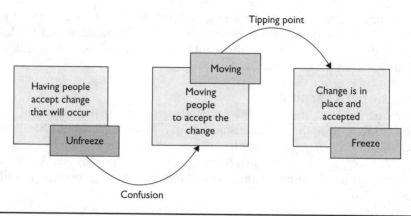

Figure 8-2   Change process theory

In the Trenches

The Five Misconceptions of What OD Really Is?
Larry Bienati, Ph.D., SPHR, CCP

   I am grateful to my HR-OD mentor Fred Jackson, who always conveyed the importance of an Organizational Development (OD) mindset in how I led the HR vision of the organization. Over the last 35 years Fred's good counsel still rings true and it has led me to lament the five misconceptions of what OD really is.

   The first misconception is thinking that it is all about "training" or anything "done to an organization." Those seeking the valued HR business partner role by their senior leadership team realize that OD is the catalyst for delivering the transformational leadership outcome in an organization. Its purest definition was captured by Wendell and French when they referred to OD as "a response to change, a complex educational strategy intended to change the beliefs, attitude values, and structure of an organization so it can better adapt to new technologies, markets and the business strategy." I have always viewed OD as a process to engage the hearts and minds of your human resources by providing a vision of the future, involving employees in that vision, enlisting their ideas, commitment, and ownership of the process to bring about a desired result.

   The second misconception is to focus strictly on the process and failing to engage the people in that process understanding. I recall many failures of process improvement strategies like TQM, reengineering and other management fads of the month. Kotter got it right in his legacy work on the 8 steps to *Leading Change*—a must read and model for any successful OD practitioner! He captured the 8 deadly sins and reminded us of the importance of creating that sense of urgency, ensuring top level commitment, sharing the vision, exhaustive communication, board-based action, removing barriers, aligning systems and celebrating success.

The third misconception is failing to clearly align the HR-OD strategy to the organizational business plan. Each year I would meet with the key functional leaders in the organization and ask how HR could support their business imperatives. This resulted in various service level agreements with each "customer" and ensuring our HR-OD program aligned in some measure to their key performance objectives. We focused two objectives per customer. We established appropriate success measures and communicated with the customer on a regular basis to show impact.

The fourth misconception is failing to demonstrate the "ROI effect in the OD process." Sadly, OD is viewed as another touchy-feely HR program by many. The Rx: Can you show in soft and hard dollars what the economic value, and cost-benefit of the OD effort will be? Will it increase revenue, decrease costs, improve productivity, or achieve some critical aspect of the business plan? Whenever possible, I always demonstrated the financial impact of our OD process—what got measured, got done.

The fifth misconception is thinking the change management process is a 90 day process of immediate success. Sure, we might see immediate returns initially if we scope the project correctly, pursue realistic objectives, and pursue small victories through deeds—actions and not words. Be prepared to stay the course, and achieve success through incremental wins realizing it may take a 36-month time frame for the full outcome effect. Good luck on your OD journey!

Training and Development

Training and development are core value functions of the HR department. The process of training provides skills and abilities, plus knowledge that is focused on a specific outcome. The intent is a short-term focus for the immediate application for on-the-job use by the trainee(s).

On the other hand, with development activities, there is a longer-term focus that prepares the intended trainee(s) for future job skill or knowledge needs, to increase their effectiveness for the organization.

In all T&D activities, it is imperative that the learning objectives and programs developed be aligned with the strategic goals and objectives of the organization, along with a strong level of support from line management.

A systematic process is used to determine the needs for training, developing the training, and evaluating the outcomes. One of the most widely used standard processes is known as the ADDIE model.

ADDIE represents:

- **Assessment**   In this first phase, data is received and collected to identify where there may be lack of productivity or gaps in desired performance. Individually or within groups, this assessment will point the way to what specific knowledge, skills, and abilities are lacking and need to be addressed for training and development objectives.

- **Design**   The initial information from the assessment phase is decided upon for course content, delivery methods, and tactics for delivery. The result is an outline of what the training design will be and the order of presentation.

- **Development**   The pencil meets the paper in this phase, and the actual training materials and coursework are created. Courses and training materials may already be available off the shelf, or a customized or modified creation may occur. For training that is highly specific and customized to the organization, a course may be developed from scratch to fit the specific objectives to reach the desired outcome, such as in a new product launch for a product that has never before existed. An example might be the new Apple watch.

- **Implementation**   In this phase, the training program is delivered to the trainees. A pilot training program might first occur to work out any kinks and revise material. Participant selection and scheduling occur during this phase and the where, when, and whom to deliver occur in this phase, too.

- **Evaluation**   Just as the label indicates, the end results and outcomes of the training require an evaluation—both from the participants trained and the learning objectives measurement. The evaluation phase will typically last some months after the training to measure the changes and performance indicators for sustained results.

Training Needs Assessment and Analysis

As the ADDIE approach suggests, the first phase in training is to conduct a needs assessment and analysis. The needs assessment is a process in which HR identifies the training needs and identifies the specific training to help the intended trainees to meet the organization's objectives. A thorough needs assessment will dive into the possible training needs on three levels: organizational, task, and individual.

When conducting a needs assessment, processes used in strategic planning are utilized (see Chapter 6 for a more in-depth discussion). Processes such as environmental scanning, and SWOT analysis (strengths, weaknesses, opportunities, threats) are helpful. A needs assessment model that follows a problem-solving structure is helpful for HR's role in strategic management. For some organizations, an outside vendor is utilized for the needs assessment phase.

Establishing Training Objectives

Determining what the training objectives are is necessary for measuring the outcome of the training. Objectives relate to the results that the participants in the training will be able to do or perform at the end of the program. They provide a focus for the design. Objectives provide a guide for training participants on what they are intended to know by the end of the training. The objectives assist in ensuring that there is the intended knowledge/skill transfer. Objectives provide a means to measure what was learned. When designing training objectives, much like the design of an individual's performance goal objects discussed in Chapter 6, employing the use of the SMART outline is helpful. (SMART stands for: specific, measurable, action-oriented and achievable, realistic/relevant, and timed.) Composing objectives with the SMART outline and the use of action verbs such as "identify," "describe," and "define," will guide the objective of the learning. An example of an objective might be something like this: "With the knowledge and techniques taught in this three-day training course on operating the new widget processor, the participant will be able to operate the widget processor at a 100 percent production capacity."

Selecting Training Programs

SPHR Once the training program has been identified and the participants targeted for training, and with the objectives set, it's now time to select the training program. The organization's size and available resources are usually the major deciding factors as to whether to develop and deliver a training program using in-house talent or to purchase a program off the shelf. Advantages for using an outside training consultant/vendor company and purchasing an off-the-shelf program include the following:

- The immediate availability for scheduling the training with an existing program.
- An off-the-shelf program is typically less expensive than developing a program in-house.
- Outside consultants can have instant credibility and respect with the participants.

On the other hand, the major disadvantages are that the training may be too "one size fits all" and not tailored to the organization 100 percent.

Developing Training Programs

SPHR When using both in-house and outside vendors for the development of training programs, it's important to avoid reinventing the wheel or covering the same subject matter that has already been done. It's important that the consistency of what has already been covered in training have a relevance and consideration in the development cycle. With the advent of newer technology, HRIS and other resource planning software systems can keep track of classifying the content of training programs. Many organizations have learning management systems (LMS) that track and manage employee training from registrations, to career development plans, to other training activities, including required legal training.

Implementing Training Programs

Implementation usually involves a number of elements that will influence the success of the training program. This is the most visible stage of the ADDIE process because success is to be measured on the learning that takes place during the delivery of the training. At this stage, the HR professional puts on a marketing hat and begins touting the benefits of the training program launch. Giving intended participants a preview of the topics and what they can expect is helpful in creating interest, preparation, and motivation. The delivery of the training success lies now with the facilitator/instructor.

█ SPHR █ Selecting a Training Facilitator

Whether an internal or external facilitator is utilized for the training delivery, effective facilitators are those who understand the various methods for delivering the content in a manner that it can be received. Deciding whether the material requires a subject matter expert or a technical expert is important for answering the questions and conducting the problem scenario exercises. The goal is to find the right mix of experience based on the program's content and the intended participants to be trained. When technical content needs delivery, the pairing of a technical training expert, perhaps with an outside vendor, with an internal training facilitator might be the best solution to meet the organization's needs.

Instructional and Delivery Methods

There is no one perfect teaching method for every situation. As a matter of fact, the method that should be used will depend upon the training circumstances and the material being covered. There are teacher-centered instructional methods and learner-centered instructional methods.[4] According to University of Tennessee's Bob Annon, instructional methods are the manner in which learning materials are presented to students.

Adult Learning Processes and Principles

Adult learning principles have a single track focus, trainability. *Trainability* is concerned with the readiness to learn and its associated motivation. *Andragogy* is the study of how adults learn, and it is based on five assumptions about learning in adults versus children. As people mature they shift to:

1. **Self-concept** Their concept of self moves toward self-direction and self-sufficiency.

2. **Experience** They accumulate more experience that they tuck away and can access in learning situations.

3. **Readiness to learn** They adjust to a readiness state for learning due to developmental requirements associated with developmental needs that correlate to the stage of life and the social roles they have (for example, parent, homeowner).

4. **Orientation to learning** They shift from subject-focused to problem-focused learning that has immediate applicability.

5. **Motivation to learn** Motivation for learning comes from an internal source within rather than external.

As training programs are being designed and delivered, these needs of adult learners should be incorporated. Real-world examples and emphasis on how the training is going to be immediately applied are helpful.

Learning Styles

All adults have a particular learning style that best suits their ability to learn. Understanding these learning styles will assist you in the creation of a learning environment within your organization, allowing you to accommodate each style with the delivery of training.

Additionally, as a presenter or trainer, knowing your own learning style will enhance your ability to adjust your preference of delivery methods, so you won't fall into the comfort of just your style, and can shift your delivery to meet the needs of all participants. Also knowing your own learning style will assist you in your career with problem solving, managing conflict, negotiations, teamwork, and career planning.

There are three learning styles: auditory, visual, and kinesthetic.

1. *Auditory learners* tend to benefit most from lecture-style. Present information by talking so they can listen. Auditory learners succeed when directions are read aloud or information is presented and requested verbally, because they interpret the underlying meanings of speech through listening to tone of voice, pitch, speed, and other nuances.

2. *Visual learners* rely upon a seeing presentation style: "Show me and I'll understand." These learners do best when seeing facial expressions and body language. It helps them understand content of what is being taught because they think in pictures, diagrams, charts, pictures, videos, computer training, and written directions. These students will value to-do lists, flip charts, and written notes. They need and want to take detailed notes to absorb the information.

3. *Kinesthetic learners* are also called tactile learners. They learn via a hands-on approach and prefer to explore the physical aspects of learning. Sitting for long periods of time is difficult for these learners for they need activity in order to learn. Kinesthetic learners are most successful when totally engaged with the learning activity such as in role playing, practicing, and with topics that can use the senses of feeling and imagining.

Learning Curves   Besides having different learning preference styles, adults also learn at different rates. This is referred to as learning curves. A learning curve is a graphical representation of the increase of learning (vertical axis) with experience (horizontal axis). The factors that determine how quickly an adult will learn are:

1. The person's motivation for learning

2. The person's prior knowledge or experience

3. The specific knowledge or task that is to be learned

4. The person's aptitude and attitude about the knowledge or skill to learn

The four most common learning curves are:

1. **Increasing returns** This is the pattern that comes into play when a person is learning something new. The start of the curve is slow while the basics are being learned. The learning increases and takes off as knowledge or skills are acquired. This curve assumes that the individual will continue to learn as time progresses. An example would be when an IT programmer needs to learn a new coding language. Learning will be slow at first until they grasp the new coding protocol, and after mastering the basics, the learning becomes easier and/or quicker as they learn more about the particular language.

2. **Decreasing returns** This pattern is when the amount of learning increases rapidly in the beginning and then the rate of learning slows down. The assumption with this learning curve is that once the learning is achieved, the learning then stops. This occurs with routine tasks learning and is the most common type of learning curve. An example is when a data entry clerk learns how to enter a sales order—the learning is complete.

3. **S-shaped** This learning curve is a blend of the increasing and decreasing returns curves. The assumption with this learning curve is that the person is learning something difficult, such as problem solving or critical thinking. Learning may be slow at the beginning until the person learning becomes familiar with the learning material, and at that point, learning takes off. The cycle continues with a slow to faster progression as new material is presented. An example of this is when a production lead is trained on new equipment, yet this equipment has not been utilized in the production of the product before. There might be a trial and error for adjustments until the new production equipment is working as expected and is adjusted to the new product. Then when another product is introduced, the equipment and process needs adjusting again until everything works smoothly.

- **Plateau curve** Just as the name suggests, learning on this curve is quick in the beginning and then flattens or plateaus. The assumption is that the plateau is not permanent and that with additional coaching, training, and support the person learning can ramp up again. With this curve, it can be frustrating to the learner if they are not getting the support and additional training needed to master the task. An example of the plateau curve is a salesperson who has met quotas in the past, and when a new line of equipment is introduced into the product line, the salesperson is provided a minimal level of training/knowledge about it, but not enough training to answer all the questions of the prospective customers. The anticipation of additional sales with the new product is not being achieved because the salesperson requires more training in order to pitch the new product and convince the customer to purchase.

The four most common learning curves are illustrated in Figure 8-3.

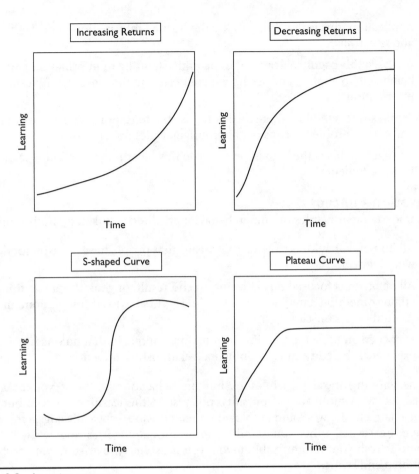

Figure 8-3   Learning curves

Learning Levels   Knowing the styles of learning and learning curves are essential, yet understanding the levels of adult learning is critical to being able to meet adult learning objectives. According to the principles of classification known as Bloom's taxonomy, training objectives are divided into three domains: cognitive, affective, and psychomotor (which is loosely described as "knowing/head," "feeling/heart," and "doing/hands"). Within the domains, there are six levels of cognitive learning[5]:

1. Knowledge: this level of cognitive learning is where the learner recalls specific facts and instruction.

2. Comprehension: this level of learning allows the learner to interpret information.

3. Application: this is the ability to use the learned information in new experiences and situations.

4. Analysis: this cognitive learning is the understanding of information and being able to apply it and see how it connects and fits together with other information.

5. Synthesis: this level is where the learner is able to respond to new experiences and dissect problems, consider appropriate tactics for solutions.

6. Evaluation: this is the highest level of cognitive learning wherein the learner will make judgments.

Motivation Concepts

Three underlying principles of human behavior are directly linked to motivation.

- All human behavior is caused. This means that people have a reason for doing what they do.

- All behavior is focused on achieving an end result, or goal. People do things to attain something, tangible or intangible. Their behavior is not random, though it could be unconscious.

- Every person has a unique fingerprint and is unique in that no one has the exact experience, heredity, or environmental/relationship influences.

Understanding these principles of human behavior will assist you as an HR professional with motivational pursuits, not just in the learning process, but in all matters related to the work and employment relationship, especially engagement.

There are several other longstanding motivational theories and we will briefly review to refresh your memory about what you most likely learned in your secondary educational endeavors.

Maslow's Hierarchy Needs   In Maslow's theory, there are five basic human needs arranged in a pyramid, necessitating that the first level (bottom of the pyramid) must be met first before moving up the pyramid. Figure 8-4 shows Maslow's hierarchy of needs. Lower-level needs on the pyramid will always have some influence on behavior. [6]

You can fulfill these needs in the workplace through the following:

- **Safety and security**   Employment security such as an employment contract, pay and benefits, working conditions

- **Belonging and love**   Teams, good leadership, participation in groups, employee associations, customer base assignments

- **Esteem**   Training, recognition, awards, special assignments

- **Self-actualization**   Job growth opportunities, project team participation, becoming a mentor

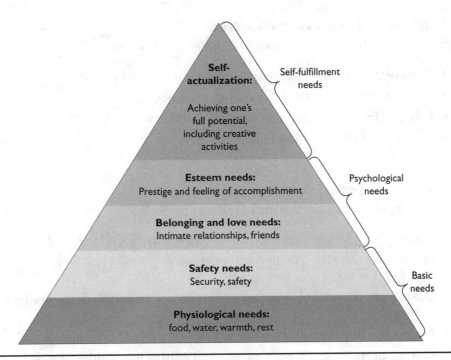

Figure 8-4 Maslow's hierarchy of needs

 NOTE It's important to recognize today that not all motivational models of Western culture, like Maslow's hierarchy of needs, are going to apply in many of the global and diverse organizations of today.

Herzberg's Motivation-Hygiene Theory This theory asserts that employees have two different categories of needs and that they are essentially independent of each other, but they affect behavior in differing ways: hygiene factors, which are considered extrinsic, and motivational factors, which are considered intrinsic. The latter is associated with recognition, achievement, and personal growth–related events in the job, whereas hygiene factors are associated with job security, pay, working conditions, supervision, and co-worker relations that can quickly lead to job dissatisfaction.

McGregor's Theory X and Theory Y McGregor's theory offers two approaches to motivating employees: Theory X, which suggests an authoritative management style because it assumes that employees inherently do not like to work and must be controlled and closely monitored; and Theory Y, which suggests a participative style of management, under the belief that employees dislike controls and inherently want to do their best. It is obvious to see that a Theory Y type of supervisor will provide better leadership and produce greater satisfaction.

Teacher-Centered Approaches

Elements of a teacher-centered approach include the following:

- **Demonstration**   Showing participants how something is done
- **Direct instruction**   Conveying concepts and skills
- **Lecture**   Passive participants reception of instruction
- **Lecture-discussions**   Questions added to lecture

Learner-Centered Approaches

The following are elements of a learner-centered approach:

- **Case studies**   Require application of knowledge to respond to a "real" problem.
- **Cooperative learning**   Small group working on solving a problem or completing a task.
- **Discussion**   Classroom or online interaction among participants and with the teacher.
- **Discovery**   Using prior knowledge and experience to discover new things.
- **Graphic organizers**   Diagrams, maps, and webs as illustrations of material.
- **Journals/blogs**   Recordings of reflections and ideas.
- **K-W-L**   Structured table showing columns with what participants know (K), what they want to know (W), and what they learned in the end (L).
- **Learning centers**   Independent or small group work aimed at completing a task.
- **Role-play**   Solving problems through action or performance.
- **Scaffolding**   Teacher modeling skills and thinking for participants, allowing participants to take over those expressions based on the initial structure provided by the teacher.
- **Problem-based learning (inquiry learning)**   Teacher provides a problem where inquiry must be utilized to reach a solution.
- **Simulations**   Situations designed to be as realistic as possible without the risk of a real-life circumstance.
- **Storytelling**   Use of multimedia technology (for example, PowerPoint) to present interactive opportunities involving any subject. .

▬ SPHR ▬ Evaluating the Effectiveness of Training

Training evaluation is dependent upon the objectives that were initially identified for the training. Specific achievement goals that training participants can demonstrate their ability to perform are essential for participants and instructors to use in determining training effectiveness. Training programs should have specific performance-related goals identified. They should answer the question, "What will participants be able to do at the end of the program that they may not have been able to do at the beginning of the program?" Objectives should be stated using verbs to describe behaviors. For example, "By the end of this program, participants will be able to list at least six management skills common to all successful managers, cite at least two sources for information related to management skills measurement, and demonstrate leadership skills in a group exercise." Each of the training objectives begins with a verb that explains exactly what the participants will be able to do, or say, or the desired behavior. Once the reason for training the target population has been identified as objectives, methods of measurement should be prepared. Sometimes, measurement can be accomplished with written tests; sometimes it requires performance or demonstration. Each measurement should be tailored to the specific objective. If participants are able to meet the training objectives, the training program can be said to be effective. Measuring instructor competencies can be undertaken as a subcategory of metrics.

SPHR **Evaluation Method**   There is one widely known model for evaluating training and HR programs, Donald Kirkpatrick's four levels. Kirkpatrick's model focuses primarily on evaluating the effectiveness of the training presented.[7] Figure 8-5 illustrates the four levels.

Figure 8-5
Kirkpatrick's
Four Levels of
Evaluating Training

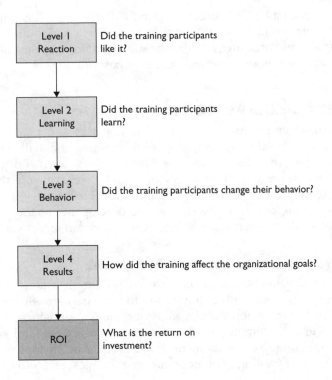

The first level measures the reaction of the participant. A survey given at the conclusion of the training is the most common method. Participants detail how they liked the training and their thoughts as to its applicability. This, however, measures the immediate reaction about the training delivery and its environment rather than their level of learning.

Level two measures how well participants in the training learned facts, concepts, theories, and behaviors. To use this measure normally requires HR professionals or consultants who are trained in statistics and studies to interpret the results. Pre- and post-training measurements are conducted, and control groups may be involved. The results will indicate the effectiveness of the training.

Level three deals with the measurement of behavior and is more difficult to measure than the previous two levels because it can be difficult to determine if behavior changed solely because of the training program; other outside influences could be involved. In level three measurement, observations, interviews, 360 feedback instruments, and simulations can be used. Critical incidents performance by the trainee's supervisor might be employed.

Level four deals with the measurement of results to determine if the planned effectiveness of the training delivered the desired results. The difficulty with this measurement is with determining if the training was the sole factor affecting the results. Typically a cost-benefit of return on investment (ROI) follows to substantiate the level four results.

When evaluating the training program's effectiveness, it is important to achieve an objective viewpoint. Solicit information from all affected sources—not just the training participants and presenter, but also the sources affected by the training, which could be other departments, management, and even customers.

Talent Management

Talent management involves all the HR strategies and processes that are involved in attracting, developing, engaging, and retaining the skills/knowledge/abilities of the workforce in order to meet the organization's needs. Talent management goals are simple: Manage the human resources initiatives that directly result in employee productivity and that address current and future business needs.

This section focuses on the strategies to develop and retain a productive workforce. Additional talent management strategies are covered in more detail in Chapters 7 and 9.

Employee Development Programs

Employee development programs are an important aspect of talent management, providing employees with opportunities to learn new knowledge and skills, preparing them for future responsibilities and job changes, and increasing their capacity to perform in their current jobs. Job rotation, enlargement, and enrichment form one avenue for employee development. Another could be an apprenticeship program that relates to skills training. (For more information, please refer to Chapter 7.)

NOTE The U.S. apprenticeship system is regulated by the Bureau of Apprenticeship and Training (BAT).

Higher education tuition reimbursement programs are also offered by many organizations as part of their employee development program. The pursuit of education is normally restricted to an employee's current occupation or an occupation that exists within the organization.

Other employee development programs that are increasingly on the rise within organizations are those associated with wellness training, stress management, and work/life balance.

Skills Training

Skills training generally encompasses specific skill sets associated with jobs as identified in job descriptions. Skill development is a constantly moving target because of the nature of changing workplace requirements. With the added complexity of technology and rules/regulations, most jobs will have changing skill set requirements throughout their existence in the organization. Categories of skills training will normally include:

- Sales training
- Technology training
- Technical skills
- Quality training
- Communication skills training
- Emotional intelligence
- Basic on-the-job training

Other skills training may be specifically targeted to supervisory-level positions such as leadership/supervisory skills training, discrimination/harassment prevention training, or diversity and ethics training.

Teams

Bringing together a group of people who can address a given set of issues or problems is the process of team creation. How effective the group will be depends on many things, such as the team leadership and the experience of each member. Teams permit the focus of talent on specific organizational goals.

Employee development strategies could include team participation, involvement on committees, and work teams to expose a group to decision making and collaborative processes. Team assignments can enrich an employee's experience and perspective, assisting with an employee's career planning initiatives.

For a team to be effective, all participants need to be clear on the goals they are working toward and what expectations they are to meet and fulfill.

Project Teams

Project teams are formed when specific projects must be completed. People with a specific talent or experience are recruited into the group to contribute their knowledge and skills to resolving the problem or accomplishing some other goal. There is often a team leader who can be an organizational superior or peer of other team members.

Self-Directed Teams

Self-directed teams are groups of people who are given general direction by assignment to resolve an issue or solve a problem. The group selects its own leadership, identifies its own direction, and holds itself accountable for accomplishments.

Task Forces

A cousin of "teams," task forces are groups of people assembled to research and address major organizational issues. They are composed of individuals with specific experience or knowledge and are expected to "fix" problems that could have significant impact on the organization. Task forces are sometimes used to address system failures (for example, computer or software) or to handle crises (for example, natural disaster or sudden inability to transport goods through a region due to a new local ordinance). Once the solution is found or issue resolved, the task force disbands.

Work Teams

When formed to facilitate production or performance, the group is sometimes referred to as a work team. These are people from the same type of work, usually of the same or similar job class who are working together to generate the production for their segment of the organization. Types of work teams include the following:

- **Functional work teams**   Groups of people from the same function working together to generate production. On an assembly line, or in the accounts receivable department, groups handle the work load as a unit rather than as individuals.

- **Cross-functional work teams**   Groups of people from different functions working together to generate production. On the assembly line, or in the engineering department, individuals with different talents work together to create a unified output. (For example, an engineer works with drafters and technicians to create work drawings for a project. The group may include electricians, construction supervisors, and other interior designers. All functions work together to create one unified result.)

- **Virtual work teams**   With virtual work teams, members are not located in the same facility and, in fact, may work in different parts of the globe. They come together via technology such as Internet facetime meetings to accomplish team assignments that could fall within the scope of work teams.

Career Development

Career development is the lifelong individual process that involves planning, managing, learning, and transitions at all ages and stages in work life. In organizations, it is an organized approach used to match employee goals with the business's current and future needs. An individual's work-related preferences and needs continuously evolve throughout life's phases. At the same time, organizations are also continuously adapting to economic, political, and societal changes.

Career Development Processes

There are two processes in career development: career planning and career management. With career planning, the focus is on the individual. Career management has a focus on the organization.

In career planning, assessing an individual's skills, talents, experiences, and potential abilities occurs to give direction to a person's career. HR professionals typically assist with these activities, but many self-assessment instruments are available online for individuals to use.

With career management, this involves implementing and monitoring employee career paths at an organizational level. The individual employee is actively involved; however, the organization is typically providing the development programs and opportunities associated with internal career progression opportunities and succession planning. The intention with career management from the organizational perspective is to assist with aligning existing workforce talent with new business objectives, create an atmosphere of positive morale, and for employee retention of needed talent.

Roles in Managing Career Development

It is not just the individual employee and HR involved in career development. The direct line of management and the organization's leaders have a role to play, too.

Individuals bear the primary responsibility for their own career. Today, individuals are required to be proactive in planning their career progression and not rely on an organization to direct their career path. Being keenly aware of current assessed traits and skills, along with needs for increased knowledge, skill, and experience associated with the individual's career ambitions, is largely the responsibility of an individual employee. Figure 8-6 illustrates the stages of an individual's career development.

The direct line of management normally serves as support in helping an individual assess his or her current effectiveness and potential, and provides a broader view of the organization's career paths. The direct supervisory management will wear many hats, including coach, appraiser, guidance counselor, and resource referral in the employee's career development planning.

The HR professionals are involved in the development of career pathing, personal development programs, and skill development training in order to enable employees to achieve their career aspirations and goals. Creating a skill inventory database along with work and educational experience of the current workforce is needed in helping the

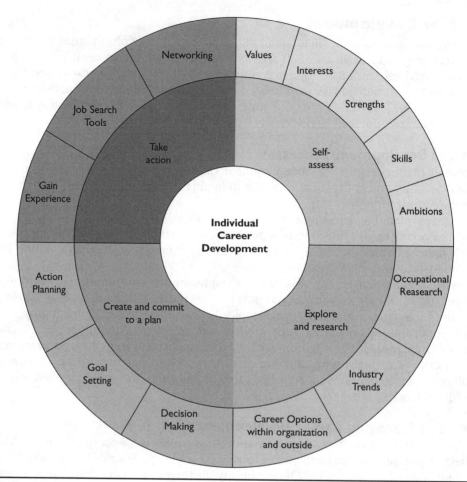

Figure 8-6 Individual career development

organization assess its current workforce talent. Additionally, HR professionals monitor training and development needs and create programs to meet those needs, along with the communication of job progression opportunities.

The organizational leader's role in career development includes the communication of the organization's mission and vision to the workforce, to link the organization's initiatives and changes with the anticipated talent needs. Fostering a culture of support and internal opportunity for career development is another important function of the organizational leader's role.

In the Trenches

Personal Branding and You

Susan Chritton, **Author** **of Personal Branding for Dummies,**
http://susanchritton.com

What do people think of when they think about you? Are you thought of as intelligent, honest, and creative or do people associate you with poor quality work and someone who doesn't finish what they start? You have a personal brand whether you know it or not.

So what exactly is a *personal brand?* Very simply it is your reputation. Your personal brand is the way others remember you through your actions, your knowledge, and the emotional connections that you make. Your personal brand becomes the promise you make about who you are and what you do that is strengthened every time people connect with you.

Personal branding is the strategic process of building a positive set of experiences for the people who need to know about you. Personal branding is about expressing your authentic self by allowing you to be the person you are meant to be. Personal branding helps you connect with your unique promise of value and employ it in the world to act as a filter that helps you make decisions that are congruent with who you are and what you stand for. It identifies what makes you unique and clearly communicates your individuality to the people who need to know about you.

Having a personal brand sounds like a great idea, but how do you get one? If you're serious about developing your personal brand, you will need a clear plan to get you there.

To begin the process, you need to spend time up front studying yourself and figuring out what you really want. Only with a strong sense of yourself can you undertake the steps to build a personal brand. You will need to define who you are and understand both your target audience and who your competitors are.

After you know your brand, your next challenge is to communicate it clearly, concisely, and consistently to the people who need to know about you. Finally, you'll want to examine your *brand ecosystem*: those things that encompass every element of your life—from your clothes to your professional colleagues—and influence how your target audience perceives you.

Personal branding supports and enhances your work. Your best success comes when you recognize your own gifts and are able to represent your personal brand in all that you do. Your personal brand helps you make the most of what you've got to offer by understanding who you are and what sets you apart from every other person. It helps you navigate the direction of your life. Your personal brand is your own success story waiting to be written.

Career Development Programs

Many large organizations create full-fledged career development programs. Some will be self-paced and opt-in by individual employees, and some are created with particular objectives in mind, such as management development programs, where high potential employees are invited to participate. A typical model for a career development program will include stages of:

- **Occupational preparation**   This stage is where occupations are assessed, an occupation is decided upon, and necessary education and skill levels are pursued.

- **Organizational entry**   This is the stage where a person obtains and decides on job offers from organizations they want to work for, or they learn of internal changes within the company they work in and they decide on if they want to go for that.

- **Early career establishment**   In this phase, an employee learns a new job, along with organizational norms and rules for fitting into the job, company, or industry. An employee gains work experience and career skills.

- **Mid career**   In this phase, an employee evaluates his or her career objectives, with an understanding of his or her current life situation, and may choose to shift career direction.

- **Late career**   In this last phase, employees focus on retirement planning, and again, choices associated with life considerations as to the hours they wish to work and the extra effort that may cause additional mental stress. Climbing career progression ladders is not normally in their career plans at this phase, yet mentoring of employees in early career phases would be.

 NOTE   By understanding the focus of each stage, HR professionals are better equipped to prepare and manage the transitions the employees in their organization will experience.

Dual-Ladder Program

Dual-ladder career development programs allow mobility for employees without requiring that they be placed into the managerial enclave. Mostly associated with technical, medical, engineering, and scientific occupations, this type of program is a way to advance employees who are not interested in pursuing a management track. These individuals exhibit one or more of the following characteristics:

- Have substantial technical or professional expertise beyond the basic levels

- Have licensure or required credentials

- Are known for innovation

- May or may not be well-suited for management or leadership roles

An objective within a dual-ladder development program is to increase complexity and value to the organization, enabling the organization to increase employee salaries to improve employee retention and satisfaction. Lateral movement may occur within a dual-ladder program such as team membership, internal consultative roles, mentorships, or larger facility rotation. Figure 8-7 shows an example of a dual-ladder career path.

Succession Planning

Succession planning systematically identifies, assesses, and develops talent as a key component for business success. It is an ongoing process that enables an organization to plan or recover when critical talent is lost. An effective succession plan includes a focus on identification, development, and preparing the placement of high-potential employees for future opportunities. It is foolish to assume that key players would

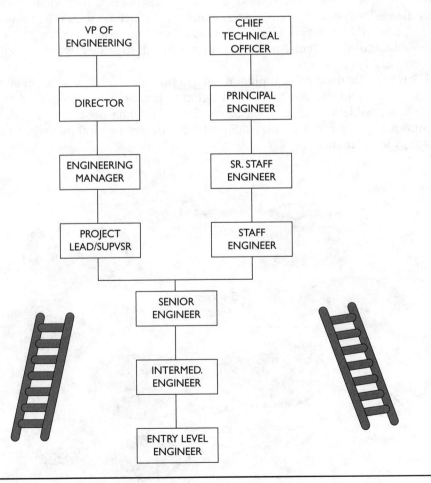

Figure 8-7   Dual-ladder career path

provide adequate notice of resignation. Succession planning is not just for the planned events such as retirements; it serves for replacement planning such as when a key player is relocating due to family, or perhaps perished in an accident. Succession should be developed to anticipate managerial staffing needs or key employee positions that would interrupt the business process if an incumbent were to vacate.

 NOTE Be careful not to exclude employees from a succession plan solely based on their age.

A succession plan contains an identification of high-risk positions along with those positions with known or potentially known vacancy dates (as with retirements). Competencies for those positions are identified and a gap analysis is performed using the current workforce reviewing potential candidates. Individuals within are identified as high-potential employees, which might include their interest/aspiration in the position. After all, not every individual may be interested in moving into a more responsible position. Tentative plans are created for shortages, which may include seeking outside candidates.

HR is typically responsible for maintaining a candidate database of skills and career development plans, along with the monitoring of development activities. Additionally, HR is responsible for the sourcing or creation of training needs for candidates and monitoring their continued interest. Figure 8-8 provides a typical progression of steps in succession planning.

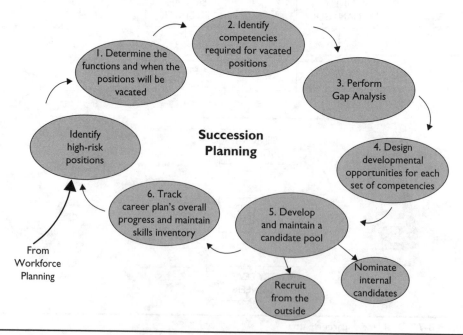

Figure 8-8 Succession planning

Knowledge Management (KM) Knowledge management is a term that relates to the retention and distribution of organizational knowledge. It is the efficient process of capturing, developing, sharing, and handling of information or resources within a business. KM efforts will generally focus on competitive advantage, innovation, the sharing of lessons from the past, integration, and the renewal cycle of continuous improvement in an organization. Its focus is on the management of internal knowledge held by incumbents as a strategic asset and the mentorship in sharing this knowledge.

In the Trenches

Keep an Eye on the Horizon: Knowledge Transfer

Rob Hyde, HR Business Partner, Kaiser Permanente

How many generations are represented throughout your workforce? Are your new employees ready to take the reins from the generation that is retiring and to continue growing the organization beyond what it is today? These are questions whose answers are self-evident. "Several" and "I really don't know" are the answers for most organizations and that likely includes yours. So now what do you do about it? The answer might lie in the success of one of our most established and what some call old-line industries.

Over the past decade or more the defense industry has been faced with a generational talent drain that's likely greater than anything you've seen in your company or your industry. You see, the baby boomers, that generation of engineers and technologists who literally won the cold war, are now retiring in droves. So how is that industry coping, retaining that basic technological know-how, passing on the whys, the errors, and the lessons learned from five decades of success that provided our nation's security? The answer is they've embarked on a program of knowledge transfer. They are replicating the passing down of knowledge that began millennia ago and has seemingly become a forgotten art. Rebuilding that art form that began at the proverbial ancient campfire and applying it to the modern office was an answer so self-evident as to be simple.

What is knowledge transfer? Mimicking those ancient councils it starts with a partnership between the elders and the new. It has to be a part of job descriptions, performance evaluations, and daily routine. In the past failing to learn resulted in a hungry family; now it equates to career stagnation and perhaps a hungry family as a result. It includes lessons on where to find the dusty data that might be the answer to tomorrow's puzzle, lists of who to call for different types of inquiries, the obscure reference material and where it can be found, and (of course) those wonderful undocumented shortcuts that have been learned the hard way. At the core of the program, however, is a system to learn specific tasks and demonstrate a capability in performing them. The list of things that need

(Continued)

to be known has to be robust and the demonstrations of capability rigorous. Managers must be engaged on reviewing these demonstrations and responsible to only open the gate to the "next step" when satisfied the knowledge and skill set that's going to depart has been replicated. Remember, things haven't changed all that much—if the student can't bring home the game then the village starves. That's still true.

Done right, a knowledge transfer regimen can be interesting, challenging, and profitable. Without one, you might be on the road to yesterday without a tomorrow to look forward to.

Coaching and Mentoring

More organizations are realizing the advantages of having coaching and mentoring programs as part of their overall career management strategy. These programs are advantageous for HR for their effectiveness in working one-on-one with individuals, allowing HR the ability to maintain an unbiased position.

Coaching involves one-on-one discussions between the employee and a "coach." The coach can be internal or external. An internal coach could be a member of the HR team or a line manager. Coaching can involve ongoing activities with a direct supervisor or HR professional that provides discussions focused on the career objectives of an employee, including perspective assessments such as poor job fit or potential growth tracks. External coaches are professionals hired at the organization's expense who typically work on the development of an employee in a particular area—for example, presentation or communication—or to hone and shift leadership skills. This type of coaching is focused solely on the employee and is confidential and private. At the level of executive coaching, which is more prevalent in organizations of all sizes, a third-party-vendor certified executive coach is utilized to allow executives the freedom to discuss aspects of career/life balance with a high level of trust and nondisclosure.

Mentoring is an action-oriented relationship between two people within the organization, usually a senior and junior colleague. It involves advising, providing opinion and perspective, role modeling, and sharing contacts and networks, along with support. The mentee receives career support and learns the ropes in the organization, and the mentor has the opportunity to share her knowledge and perhaps pass the baton of her job responsibilities on to afford the mentee a chance to move out of her current role. Mentorships can occur at all levels in an organization. They can be formally designed by HR, such as part of the onboarding orientation process, or they can be part of a succession planning program.

Employee Retention

According to the SHRM's Future of the U.S. Labor Pool Survey Report,[8] three out of ten employees in the workforce are retiring each year for the next 12 years. That creates a large knowledge gap and an emphasis on passing institutional knowledge on to employees via replacement/succession planning. Yet a plan is only going to work as designed if the identified candidates remain employed with the organization. Retention is the ability to keep talented employees. The importance of retention has moved to the top of the priority list in today's global competitive marketplace because of the following factors:

- An improved economy rebounding from the recession causing the job market to improve
- Retirement of the baby boomers and a likely shortage in skills/knowledge-based labor
- The increase of global competition
- Economic factors resulting in cost of living substantially increasing
- Technological advancements
- Generational motivation differences

Employee Suggestion Systems

Having an employee suggestion system is an employee engagement and involvement strategy that goes hand-in-hand with employee retention. When employees feel their opinion counts, or their perspective is "heard," they are more likely to turn away from third-party representation.

Employee suggestion systems, anonymous or not, can provide management with a way to "hear" the workforce for both positive ideas, and negative issues or perceptions. Many improvements are discovered through employee suggestion systems that are considered at upper management levels in an organization. Often, HR is the gatekeeper responsible for screening or compiling the employee suggestions. It's important that employee suggestions are acknowledged and given serious consideration, and that responses are provided in a timely manner.

Employee Focus Groups

When a large cross-section of employee opinions or perspectives is needed, an employee focus group from various units, functions, and facilities in an organization is used. Surveys can solicit the input from the entire employee population, and there are survey instruments that can compile this input for HR, but a focus group offers the opportunity to have two-way dialogue for clarity and probing purposes. The employees, however, must feel safe providing candid and honest feedback, which is a reason why either HR or an outside consultant will conduct employee focus groups.

When an organization is bleeding from key and high performers exiting, a focus group of existing employees might be in order to learn what the root cause of the exodus is.

Challenges in Talent Management

Organizations may not always realize why they are losing talent. There exists special challenges in talent management, even though the organization may have a plethora of training and development programs in place. Not all careers will take an upward or positive direction for every employee. In fact, some long-term employees may hit a wall and go nowhere.

Plateaued Careers

How do you maintain the productivity, loyalty, and commitment of an employee who is not considered promotable? They have been good performers in the past, and they may be years away from retirement, though suddenly their performance growth hits a mile-long plateau. The challenge is in seeking ways to expand skills, create new levels of motivation and interest, keep the employee engaged in the organization's vision, and work them into a process where their knowledge and talents due to lengthy experience can benefit the organization. Some employees see this as a pigeon-hole, and yet their high salary expense can become an issue as their cost of employment becomes inequitable to their productivity.

Glass Ceilings

Glass ceiling is another talent management issue as well as a federal legal issue. The federal government found it to be such a big issue that the Federal Glass Ceiling Commission was created in 1991 and its mandate was to identify the glass ceiling barriers that have blocked the advancement of minorities and women. The commission also studies the successful practices and policies of organizations that have led to the breaking of glass ceilings and advancing minorities and women into decision-making power positions. Organizations are recognizing that glass ceilings are not healthy for business because of shifts in labor force demographics, changes in their marketplace, and of course the globalization of their industries.

Boards of directors and senior management are creating glass-ceiling initiatives to help all employees, regardless of gender and ethnicity, reach their full employment potential. There is bottom-line value and economic advantages to the business, and then there is the practicality of keeping the EEOC from issuing a audit notice. Glass ceiling legal issues are more fully discussed in Chapter 5.

Performance Management

Performance management is a systematic process that helps improve organizational effectiveness by providing feedback to employees on their performance results and improvement needs. It is employee accomplishments and contributions that drive the business results of an organization, so a regular feedback system discussing individual performance is at the core of a good performance management system. It ensures that employees are on course for the completion of tasks and goals that are aligned with the organization's goals, and that the resources and support are provided for the employee to perform such functions.

Employee performance management systems include the following:

- Delegating and planning work
- Setting expectations for performance results

- Continually monitoring performance
- Developing a capacity to perform to new levels for personal and professional growth
- Periodically rating performance in a summary fashion
- Providing recognition and rewarding good performance

As discussed in Chapter 6, creating and communicating the organization's vision, mission, strategies, specific goals, and values form the foundation that is needed for the performance management system. Then performance standards are agreed upon by both the line management and the employee on what the job requires and what will be measured. At this stage, it is essential that employees clearly understand the standards, including expected behavior standards set forth for their jobs. Feedback is the next stage and can be both informal and formal. Formal feedback would entail a written performance appraisal.

SPHR When it comes to performance management within a global organization, there are additional considerations. Different cultural values and societal norms will affect the definition of standards and performance criteria as it relates to a global workforce. Different languages will also have to be considered for the interpretation of performance definitions and standards. Recognizing that there are differing behaviors for different cultures can be a challenge for setting behavioral standards and expectations of individuals.

Performance Standards

Employees need to know and understand what specific performance is expected of them in performing their jobs and the acceptable behavior. This communication begins with the very first discussion in a job interview and certainly with the job offer and new hire onboarding orientation. The discussion continues on a consistent basis both with the reinforcement of organizational standards that are outlined in employee handbooks and other written material, and with performance appraisal review sessions. The clearer the expectations set for employees, the greater the success in having expectations met.

 NOTE In order for employees to meet job expectations, there needs to be a direct relationship between the job description's competency requirements and the performance objectives.

Performance Appraisal Methods

Performance appraisals satisfy three purposes:

- Providing feedback and coaching
- Justifying the allocation of rewards and career opportunities
- Helping with employee career planning and development plans

For the organization, performance appraisals can foster commitment and align people to contribute to initiatives with their upcoming performance contributions. The most common performance appraisal method involves just two people: the employee and his or her direct supervisor. In some companies, others are asked to be involved in the appraisals such as peers, another level of management, and sometimes colleagues in the organization whose job function interacts with the employee. These are known as 360 degree appraisals.

Methods for rating the performance can be completely narrative, management by objectives (MBO) discussed in another section of this chapter, behaviorally anchored ratings (BARS), category rating, and comparative ratings with others in like functions.

The least complex of the methods is the category rating where the reviewer simply checks a level of rating on a form. Three types of rating formulas are typically used in category ratings:

- **Graphic scale** The most common type, where the appraiser checks a place on the scale for the categories of tasks and behaviors that are listed. A typical scale is 5 points where 1 means not meeting expectations or low, and 5 means exceeding expectations or high. These types of performance appraisals normally have a comments section that the appraiser completes that provides justification for the rating.

- **Checklist** Another common appraisal rating in which the appraiser is provided with a set list of statements/words to describe performance. The appraiser selects the one word or statement that best describes the performance—for example, "Employee consistently meets all deadlines" or "Employee consistently misses deadlines".

- **Forced choice** A variation of the checklist approach, but in the checklist method, the appraiser is required to check two of four statements. One check is for the statement that is most like the employee's performance and the other check is for the statement that is least like the employee's performance—a combination of positive and negative statements. This method can be difficult to convey to employees and understand from an employee's perspective.

With comparative methods, employee performance is compared directly with others in the same job. The appraiser will rank the employees in a group from highest to lowest in performance. This causes a forced distribution known as a bell curve. Ten percent will fall in the highest and lowest of the rating scale, another 20 percent will fall on either side, and then 40 percent will meet job standards and expectations. An obvious fault with this type of system is suggesting that a percentage of employees will fall below expectations. Figure 8-9 displays a bell curve distribution.

Narrative evaluations are time consuming for an appraiser to complete, yet they can be the most meaningful to the employee being evaluated. There are three methods that are the most common for the narrative appraisal.

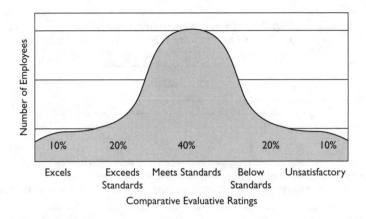

Figure 8-9 Bell curve distribution

- **Essay format** The appraiser writes an essay type of narrative describing each category of performance.

- **Critical incident** The appraiser is logging dates and details of both good and not so good performance incidents. This method requires the appraiser to be keeping good, detailed notes on a routine basis during the appraisal period and not relying solely on an employee's most recent performance.

- **Behaviorally anchored rating methods** Referred to as BARS, this appraisal method describes desirable behavior and undesirable behavior. Examples are then compared with a scale of performance level for the rating. BARS works well in circumstances in which several employees perform the same function. A BARS appraisal system requires extensive time to develop and maintain to keep the performance dimensions up-to-date as the job functions change. However, the BARS methods offer a more accurate gauge of performance measurement, provide clearer standards to employees, and have more consistency in rating.

Self-Assessment

Coupled with the direct supervisory management evaluation, many employees are asked to self-assess their performance. This approach assists with creating a truly two-way dialogue in the evaluation interview and offers an opportunity for the employee to provide his own perception of his performance. Additionally, it engages employees in a proactive means of creating goals and objectives, along with triggering a discussion about career development. Figure 8-10 provides an example of a self-assessment—both a category rating along with open-ended questions to elicit a narrative commentary.

Self-Assessment Performance Appraisal
For the appraisal period of January 1, 2014 – December 31, 2014

Employee Name: _____ EE # _____

Department: _____
Position Title: _____
Supervisor: _____
Facility: _____

Instructions:
Please complete your self-assessment evaluation and return it to your supervisor by (date)_____.
Your participation in the annual performance appraisal process helps to facilitate a comprehensive
evaluation of your performance and accomplishments against set standards, goals, and objectives.

---

1. Describe your accomplishments and contributions since last review period.
2. Describe the activities you have participated in that have produced favorable outcomes.
3. Since your last appraisal, what new skills have you acquired?
4. Describe skills that you have increased and provide an example of their effective application on the job.
5. List new training and/or development programs you have completed.
6. Describe areas you wish to improve to enhance your job performance and capabilities.
7. State three or more job objectives for this next year and how you plan to achieve them.

Please provide your self-assessment rating in the following categories using the rating scale below.

Rating Scale:

4 - Outstanding   **3** - Very Competent or High Level   **2** - Satisfactory   **1** - Inexperienced or Improvement Needed

Category	Self-Rating
a. Technical Skills (job specific)	_____
b. Job Knowledge (up-to-date on industry, articles, and best practices)	_____
c. Quality of Work Product (comprehensive, accurate, timely)	_____
d. Productivity	_____
e. Professionalism (punctuality, attendance; conduct; responsiveness and follow through)	_____
f. Collaboration & Teamwork	_____
g. Computer Skill Applications	_____
h. Time Management & Organizational Skills	_____
i. Interpersonal Skills	_____
j. Communication Skills - Verbal/Written	_____
k. Innovation or Creativity	_____

Date: _____   Employee Signature: _____

Figure 8-10   Self-assessment performance appraisal

Shortcomings of Performance Appraisals

As with any subjective system, and performance appraisals are subjective because they are based on people's perceptions and opinions, there can be shortcomings. Here are the most common errors made on the part of appraisers:

- **Halo** This occurs when the employee is doing well in one area and is therefore rated high in all areas.

- **Horn** This occurs when an employee is demonstrating a strong weakness and is thus rated low in all other areas.

- **Bias** This happens when the evaluator's bias (consciously or unconsciously) influences and distorts his or her perspective.

- **Recency** A recency error occurs when more emphasis is placed on a recent occurrence and all earlier performances during the review period are discounted.

- **Primacy** The opposite of recency. The evaluator gives more weight and emphasis to earlier performances, discounting more recent performance.

- **Strictness** An evaluator is reluctant to give high ratings, and his or her standards are higher than other evaluators.

- **Leniency** The evaluator does not provide low scores and instead gives all employees a high rating on their appraisals.

- **Central** An evaluator rates all of his or her employees in the same range and does not take into account differences of actual performance among the group rated.

- **Contrast** The evaluator is providing an employee rating based solely on a comparison to that of another employee, and not objective standards.

 NOTE These common errors can be avoided with narrative format methods.

HR Interventions

Human resource interventions can be micro level, macro level, and managerial or operational level. They can be interpersonal, technological, or even structurally related. These interventions are commonly referred to as OD interventions. At all levels, OD intervention it is about intervening to make an improvement. Deliberate processes are utilized to introduce change with the overall objective being to change a current condition.

Micro level interventions may involve behavioral or performance issues of individuals who are impacting productivity or the work environment, such as a manager who is causing undue stress and commotion due to bullying leadership tactics. It may be an employee who is causing turmoil in the work unit because he is using inappropriate language within earshot of coworkers. In such circumstances, HR is called upon to intervene if the line management efforts were not effective. The HR professional would consider which type of process or action to take to address the issue.

A macro level intervention would involve more than one individual, perhaps groups. A wellness program to address an increase in workers' compensation stress claims, teambuilding activities to bring about better relationships with sales and customer service, or a flexible telecommuting arrangement for employees affected by a natural disaster would all fall under the macro category.

An example of managerial- or operational-level interventions is sexual harassment prevention training following an increase in complaints by employees, or the development of a diversity program to combat a cultural issue caused by a global merger.

 NOTE The main goal of OD interventions is to find a suitable solution that causes the organization to successfully ride the tide of change that is required.

Conflict Resolutions

Conflict is natural and it is bound to happen in all work settings. In most conflicts, neither party is right or wrong; instead, different opinions collide to create disagreement. The process of conflict resolution involves resolving issues and maintaining effective working relationships. When a direct supervisor is unable to resolve the conflict, HR is normally brought in as an intervention. Clear and open communication is the cornerstone of successful conflict resolution, and thus HR professionals must be skilled communicators. This includes creating an open communication environment that encourages the disconnected parties to talk. Listening and probing with non-defensive inquiries will help dissipate the conflict.

Whether it is coworkers who are jockeying for the desk next to the window, or the employee who wants the room cooler and the other one who doesn't, an immediate conflict resolution is essential. Steps for conflict resolution involve:

- *Acknowledge that an opposing situation exists.* Acquaint yourself with what's happening and be open about the problem.

- *Let the individuals express their feelings.* Emotions fly and feelings of anger and/or hurt usually accompany conflicts. Before any kind of probing can take place, acknowledge the emotions and feelings.

- *Define the problem.* What is the issue? What is the negative impact on the work or relationships? Are different personality styles part of the problem? Meet with the opposing parties separately at first and gain their perspective about the situation.

- *Determine the underlying need.* There is no goal of deciding which person is right or wrong; the goal is to reach a solution that everyone can live with. Looking first for needs, rather than solutions, is a powerful tool for generating win/win options. To discover needs, you must try to find out why people want the solutions they initially propose. Once you understand the advantages their solutions have for them, you have discovered their needs.

- *Find common areas of agreement.* Agree on the problem; agree on some small change to give a feeling of compromise.
- *Find solutions to satisfy needs:*
  - Generate multiple alternatives.
  - Determine which actions will be taken.
  - Make sure involved parties buy into actions. (Total silence may be a sign of passive resistance.) Be sure you get real agreement from everyone.
- *Determine follow-up to monitor actions and sustained agreements.* Schedule a follow-up check-in to determine how the solutions are working and how those involved feel about how the solutions are working.

What if the conflict goes unresolved? If the conflict is causing a disruption in the workplace and it remains unresolved, you may need to explore other avenues. An executive from the organization or an outside consultant such as a mediator may be able to offer other insights on solving the problem. In some cases the conflict becomes a performance issue, and may become a topic for coaching sessions, performance appraisals, or disciplinary action.

Emotional Intelligence

Also referred to as EQ, emotional intelligence deals with the ability an individual has to be sensitive to and understanding of the emotions of others, and to control the expression of their own emotions. Emotional intelligence includes abilities to accurately perceive emotions and to access or generate emotions to assist thought and tap into emotional knowledge. People vary in their levels of EQ and this can affect leadership abilities. Leaders with a high level of EQ are able to influence and motivate others to accomplish goals, collaborate with others effectively, and facilitate issues.

When it comes to an HR intervention involving EQ, the goal is to improve the individual's interactions and behaviors to increase their effectiveness.

Management by Objectives

Management by Objectives, or MBO, is another HR intervention that basically helps align an employee with the organization's goals, measuring the accomplishment of goals with quality and quantity as a scorecard. It is a highly effective manner in tying results to goals, and used in HR interventions such as performance improvement programs (PIP).

The term MBO was first introduced in Peter Drucker's 1954 book *The Practice of Management.*[9] It is a management model that aims to improve performance of an organization by clearly defining objectives that are agreed to by both the individual and the line management. According to Drucker, when people have a say in goal setting and action plans, it ensures better participation and commitment on the part of the individual and alignment to organizational goals. Thus, many performance appraisal systems include MBO and incentive bonus awards are linked with an MBO list of organizational goals.

Quality Initiatives

Quality initiatives are siblings of human resources development, the latter focused on employee skills and knowledge development and the former on building excellence—all to help an organization attain the quality level of its products or services expected by its marketplace. The HR professional that links the two and sees how to increase quality in the organization via training and development programs will become the valued internal business partner to senior management. In his book *In Search of Excellence*, Tom Peters quotes IBM founder Thomas Watson: *"If you want to achieve excellence, he said, you can get there today. As of this second, quit doing less-than-excellent work."* That is where HR's binoculars should be focused, looking for the processes and situations that are producing less than excellent work.

Total Quality Management (TQM)

There are three Total Quality Management pioneers who popularized the concept and strategies for achieving total quality: W. Edwards Deming, Joseph Juran, and Phillip Crosby. Their philosophies vary somewhat.

Deming developed his 14-point program for managing productivity and quality for Japan in the 1950s. In that era, Japan was known for producing "cheap and defective" products. In the 1970s Deming's philosophy was summarized with the following "a vs. b" comparison:

> When people and organizations focus primarily on quality, defined by the following ratio, quality tends to increase and costs fall over time.

> However, when people and organizations focus primarily on *costs*, costs tend to rise and quality declines over time.

$$\text{Quality} = \frac{\text{Results of work efforts}}{\text{Total costs}}$$

Deming's message to management was that the reason for a company's poor quality of products was a direct result of management fault and no one else's. The buck stops here—accountability at the very top![10]

Juran's philosophy defines quality as "fitness to use," which focuses on the reliability of a product or service for the customer. Named The Juran Trilogy®, it incorporates quality control, quality planning, and quality improvement, a triage to identify what's first.[11]

Crosby also has a 14-point process for quality management. As the quality control manager of the Pershing missile program, Crosby was credited with a 25 percent reduction in the overall rejection rate and a 30 percent reduction in scrap costs. His process has four absolutes: a definition of quality, a prevention system, a performance standard for zero defects, and the cost of nonconformance.[12]

Quality Control Tools   There are a number of tools for management and teams to use for process improvement, but the commitment to change is first and foremost. Developing people and shifting behaviors and attitudes is the intervention of HRD, setting the foundation for quality initiatives. Once that is in place, the tools can follow. The most common QC tools are:

- A *process-flow analysis*, which is a flowchart diagram depicting the process and its results. The Delphi technique discussed in Chapter 5 is a classic example.

- A *control chart* illustrates a range of lower and upper variations to reach "normal," similar to the graphing of the weather by meteorologists when discussing normal temperatures.

- A *cause and effect diagram*, known as the fishbone diagram or Ishikawa diagram, is a visual map that lists the factors that are known to affect a problem. This tool is frequently used in process failures.

- A *scatter diagram* analyzes relationships between two variables. One variable is plotted on the horizontal axis and the other is plotted on the vertical axis. The pattern of their intersecting points graphically shows relationship patterns.

- A *histogram* is a graphical display of data using bars of different heights next to each other, also referred to as a bar graph. It represents the distribution of a measurement that answers "How many occurrences are there in each item that is being measured?"

Six Sigma   Six Sigma is a quality approach with a set of techniques and tools for process improvement. It was developed in 1986 by Motorola. General Electric CEO Jack Welch brought it fame by making Six Sigma central to his business strategy because it lends itself well to manufacturing. Basically, it is a disciplined data-driven approach and methodology for eliminating defects. Today, it is increasingly used in many sectors such as finance, health, government, and public education.

Six Sigma seeks to improve the quality of process outputs by identifying and removing the causes of defects (errors) and minimizing variability in manufacturing and business processes. The term "six sigma" originated from terminology associated with manufacturing, specifically terms associated with statistical modeling of manufacturing processes. The maturity of a manufacturing process can be described by a *sigma* rating indicating its yield or the percentage of defect-free products it creates. A six sigma process is one in which 99.99966% of the products manufactured are statistically expected to be free of defects (3.4 defective parts/million), although this defect level corresponds to only a 4.5 sigma level. A Six Sigma defect is defined as anything outside of customer specifications; a Six Sigma opportunity is the total number of chances for a defect.

Six Sigma uses two improvement processes, DMAIC and DMADV:

DMAIC stands for *define, measure, analyze, improve, control*. It is a system for existing processes falling below specifications and looking for incremental improvement.

DMADV stands for *define, measure, analyze, design, verify*. It is a system used to develop new processes or products at Six Sigma quality levels.

Both processes are carried out by employees who are experts in the methods and given titles of Black Belts, who are the project leaders, and Master Black Belts, who are quality leaders. Additional labels include Champions and Green and Yellow Belts. Each Six Sigma project carried out within an organization follows a defined sequence of steps and has quantified value targets; for example: reduce process cycle time, reduce pollution, reduce costs, increase customer satisfaction, and increase profits. Additional information on Six Sigma can be found at http://www.isixsigma.com/sixsigma/six_sigma.asp.

Leadership Development

In order to have leadership development, first an organization must have a clear understanding and definition of its effective leadership competencies, characteristics, and behaviors that are effective in its culture for producing desired results. Identifying this information is the first step so that developmental activities, measurement processes, and coaching/mentoring can be created.

Leadership is an ability to influence others toward results and goals. It entails keeping the organization's vision and mission in sight, providing the direction on how that mission and vision will be accomplished, and providing the tools and means to attain them, while motivating or encouraging people to work toward the vision.

Leaders are born and leaders are made. Early childhood experiences such as role models, hardship, mentors, education, and opportunities roll together to craft a leader. The following list consists of possible development opportunities for developing leaders:

- Mentorships from higher management and formal coaching
- Assignment to special projects such as a task force
- Participation in formal leadership development training programs
- Exposure to good leaders as role models, and also to ineffective leadership styles
- Attendance at meetings that exposure the individual to other core functions
- Fast-tracking assignments for broad exposure in their discipline

When it comes to global leadership, HR professionals should recognize that Western leadership theories may not be cohesive with other cultures in the workforce. Leaders and their development need to have a global mindset and an additional set of competencies. Executive Coach Marshall Goldsmith has identified five factors that are most important according to his book *Global Leadership*[13]:

- Thinking globally
- Appreciating cultural diversity
- Developing technological savvy
- Building partnership and alliances
- Sharing leadership

Leadership development is an ongoing lifelong process and today's leaders have the task to grow and develop leaders of tomorrow in their organizations.

Leadership Theories

In this section on leadership theories, we recognize that your formal education most likely went into great depth about each of the theories. What follows is a refresher on the basics of the leadership theories that will help you with your OD and HR initiatives.

Situational Leadership Theory

Widely referred to as the Hersey-Blanchard situational leadership theory, the fundamental underpinning of the situational leadership theory is that there is no single "best" style of leadership. Effective leadership is task-relevant, and the most successful leaders are those who adapt their leadership style to the maturity ("the capacity to set high but attainable goals, willingness and ability to take responsibility for the task, and relevant education and/or experience of an individual or a group for the task") of the individual or group they are attempting to lead or influence. Effective leadership varies, not only with the person or group that is being influenced, but also depends with the task, job, or function that needs to be accomplished. The Hersey-Blanchard Situational Leadership Model rests on two fundamental concepts: leadership style and the individual or group's maturity level. Figure 8-11 depicts the situational leadership model.

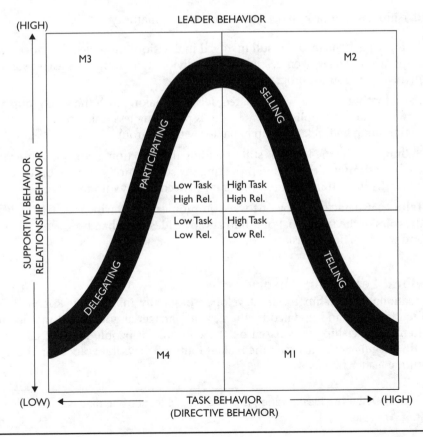

Figure 8-11 Situational leadership model

The Hersey-Blanchard Situational Leadership Theory[14] identified four levels of maturity, M1 through M4:

High	Moderate		Low
M4	M3	M2	M1
Very capable and confident	Capable but unwilling	Unable but willing	Unable and insecure

- **M1** Employees still lack the specific skills required for the job in hand and are unable and unwilling to do or to take responsibility for this job or task.

- **M2** Employees are unable to take on responsibility for the task being done; however, they are willing to work at the task. They are novice but enthusiastic.

- **M3** Employees are experienced and able to do the task but lack the confidence or the willingness to take on responsibility.

- **M4** Employees are experienced at the task, and comfortable with their own ability to do it well. They are able and willing to not only do the task, but to take responsibility for the task.

Leadership has four tasks based on an employee's maturity:

- **Delegating** The leader is still involved in decisions; however, the process and responsibility have been passed to the individual or group. The leader stays involved to monitor progress.

- **Participating** This is where shared decision-making with the workgroup about how a task is accomplished; the leader is providing less task direction while maintaining high relationship behavior with the group.

- **Selling** While the leader is still providing the direction, he or she is now using two-way communication and providing the socio-emotional support that will allow the individual or group being influenced to buy into the process.

- **Telling** Characterized by one-way communication in which the leader defines the roles of the individual or group and provides the what, how, why, when, and where to do the task.

Behavioral Leadership Theory

This situational leadership model developed originally in 1964 by Robert R. Blake and Jane Mouton,[15] and updated by them, is a managerial grid model that identifies five different leadership styles based on the concern for people and the concern for production. Figure 8-12 illustrates the Blake-Mouton Behavioral Leadership theory and the resulting leadership styles.

 NOTE The ideal position is a nine on production and nine on people.

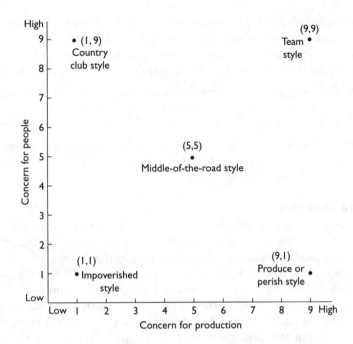

Figure 8-12
Blake-Mouton
Behavioral
Leadership Theory

- *Impoverished style (1,1): Evade and elude.* In this style, managers have low concern for both people and production. Managers use this style to preserve job and job seniority, protecting themselves by avoiding getting into trouble. The main concern for the manager is not to be held responsible for any mistakes, which results in less innovative decisions.

- *Country club style (1,9): Yield and comply.* This style has a high concern for people and a low concern for production. Managers using this style pay much attention to the security and comfort of the employees, in hopes that this will increase performance. The resulting atmosphere is usually friendly, but not necessarily very productive.

- *Produce or perish style (9,1): Control and dominate.* With a high concern for production, and a low concern for people, managers using this style find employee needs unimportant; they provide their employees with money and expect performance in return. Managers using this style also pressure their employees through rules and punishments to achieve the company goals. This style is often used in cases of crisis management.

- *Middle-of-the-road style (5,5): Balance and compromise.* Managers using this style try to balance between company goals and workers' needs. By giving some concern to both people and production, managers who use this style hope to achieve suitable performance but doing so gives away a bit of each concern so that neither production nor people needs are met.

- *Team style (9,9): Contribute and commit.* In this style, high concern is paid both to people and production. Managers choosing to use this style encourage teamwork and commitment among employees. This method relies heavily on making employees feel like they're constructive parts of the company.

- *The opportunistic style: Exploit and manipulate.* Individuals using this style, which was added to the grid theory before 1999, do not have a fixed location on the grid. They adopt whichever behavior offers the greatest personal benefit.

- *The paternalistic style: Prescribe and guide.* This style was added to the grid theory before 1999. Managers using this style praise and support, but discourage challenges to their thinking.

Trait Theories

The theory of trait leadership was developed from early leadership research, which focused primarily on finding a group of heritable attributes that differentiated leaders from non-leaders. Basically, it asserted that leaders were born and not made, and the focus was on personal characteristics and attributes that included mental and physical abilities. Although this perspective has been criticized immensely over the past century, scholars still continue to study the effects of personality traits on leader effectiveness. Past research has demonstrated that successful leaders differ from other people and possess certain core personality traits that significantly contribute to their success. It has been called the "great person" leadership theory with its assumption that leaders are different from the average person. The five traits identified are:

- Intelligence

- Dominance

- Self-confidence

- High levels of energy and vitality

- Task or technical relevance knowledge

More current research has failed to identify one set of traits that *always* differentiates a leader.

Contingency Theories

The most popular situational contingency theory was developed by Fred Fiedler.[16] The Fiedler Contingency Theory holds that group effectiveness depends on an appropriate match between a leader's style (essentially a trait measure) and the demands of the situation. Fiedler considers situational control the extent to which a leader can determine what their group is going to do to be the primary contingency factor in determining the effectiveness of leader behavior.

Fiedler's contingency model is a dynamic model where the personal characteristics and motivation of the leader are said to interact with the current situation that the group faces. Thus, the contingency model marks a shift away from the tendency to attribute leadership effectiveness to personality alone.

Fiedler asserts that there are three factors determining the favorableness of the environment for the leader:

- **Leader-member relations**   The degrees of trust, confidence, and respect that employees have in their leader
- **Task structure**   The extent to which the tasks the employees are engaged in are defined (clear or ambiguous, structured or unstructured)
- **Position power**   The degree of power and influence the leader has over their subordinates

Changing one of the three factors is a more effective route rather than trying to change the leadership's trait.

Leadership Concepts

In their book *The Leadership Challenge*,[17] authors James Kouzes and Barry Posner suggest that there are attributes that go beyond personality traits as a predisposition to lead. They assert that the following leadership practices are common to successful leaders:

- **Challenge**   Challenging the status quo and seeing a bigger need for change. Not accepting mediocrity or complacency. This practice leads to innovation.
- **Inspire**   Leaders need to be persuasive in getting others to buy in to a vision and create an engaged workgroup toward that vision, inspiring people to a common goal, a bigger vision, and especially to change when it is needed.
- **Enable**   Empowering others to do their best, providing the resources to do their best work, and forming a collaboration where everyone is aligned with the desired end result (the vision).
- **Modeling**   Demonstrating as an example the expectations they desire from others. Their values and behavior must walk-the-talk as they lead by example.
- **Encourage**   Leaders must hit the core sweet spot of those they lead—the heart and soul of people. Encourage others toward achievements, recognizing their effort and accomplishments, and celebrating milestones.

The biggest difference between managers and leaders is the way they motivate the people who work or follow them. Many management jobs require that you be both leader and manager, and thus people who are successful in such jobs display a combination of skills needed for both roles. True leaders may have management jobs, but they realize that you must influence people and lead by heart, especially if you want your employees to follow you down a difficult path. Table 8-1 provides a sense of the differences between being a leader and being a manager. This is an illustrative characterization, and there is a whole spectrum between either end of these scales.

		Leader	Manager
Table 8-1 Leaders Versus Managers	**Outcomes**	Leading people	Managing work
	Seeks	Vision	Objectives
	Approach	Sets direction	Plans detail
	Decision	Facilitates	Makes
	Power	Personal charisma	Formal authority
	Appeal to	Heart	Head
	Culture	Shapes	Enacts
	Dynamic	Proactive	Reactive
	Persuasion	Sell	Tell
	Style	Transformational	Transactional
	Wants	Achievement	Results
	Risk	Risk Taking	Risk Adverse
	Rules	Breaks	Makes
	Conflict	Uses	Avoids
	Concern	What is right	Being right

Transformational and Transactional Leadership

Leadership can be either transformational or transactional in nature. A transformational leadership approach is one that stimulates and inspires people to work together toward achieving a common goal. Transformational leaders are charismatic (which instills pride, respect, and trust in the leader's sense of mission and vision); inspirational, with the communication skills necessary to gain engagement; stimulating, where the promotion of intelligence and challenge are at play; and attentive to individual needs, giving personal attention in manners of coaching or mentoring.

Transactional leadership has characteristics associated with contingent reward, where effort is rewarded via accomplishment; management by exception, in which corrective action is taken when standards are not met or protocol is broken; and laissez faire, in which responsibility is abdicated and decision-making is delayed or avoided.

Transactional leadership has been widely used and the norm historically for decades; transformational leadership has been proven to improve productivity and morale in the long run. A blend of both transactional and transformational leadership is typically warranted and the most effective.

Fast-Track Development Programs

Fast-track development programs were originally designed for the development of future management talent. For example, in the profession of HR, a female employee who has worked for the organization and completed her college degree may be enrolled into a fast-track development program that has her fulfill roles for 18 months each in compensation, recruitment, benefits, and training in order to move her into the role of assistant director of HR within five years. In turn, this helps the organization with its plan to have more women in management. Fast-track programs today are helpful with retention of high-potential employees, such as top-of-class college recruits.

Organizational Development Initiatives

OD, as organizational development is called, is the process or function of structured analysis and planning for strategic organizational accomplishment. It involves design of organizations and strategic application of resources (for example, human resources, financial resources, supply and service resources) that result in the organizational ability to accomplish its mission through greater effectiveness and efficiency.

Theories and Applications

The University of Pennsylvania describes organizational development theory as involving three things:[18]

- **Organizational climate** The personality of the organization. It embraces attitudes and beliefs about organizational practices, employee satisfaction, stress factors, and other elements.
- **Organizational culture** Deeply seated norms, values, and behaviors, including elements of assumption, values, behavioral norms, behavioral patterns, and artifacts.
- **Organizational strategies** Design and implementation of change, including the key steps of diagnosis, action planning, intervention, and evaluation.

SPHR Diversity Initiatives

Successful organizational design generally includes consideration for diversity of its workforce. Diversity includes a variety of representation from groups based on gender, race, ethnicity, sexual orientation, cultural background, religious beliefs, economic experiences, educational background, and more. Programs that are designed to increase the diversity of an organization's workforce are often organizational development efforts, whether labeled as such or not. Diversity is built upon the foundation of equal employment opportunity and affirmative action programs. Equal employment opportunity requires that anyone who is qualified for an employment opportunity should be considered for that opportunity. Affirmative action programs represent outreach and recruiting efforts to entice people into candidate pools who may be in groups that are currently underrepresented in the organizational workforce. Diversity programs go beyond legal requirements into strategic staffing initiatives to expand the mix of people and their backgrounds that are represented in the workforce.

SPHR Programs for Organizational and Employees' Changing Needs

Developing and implementing change programs should follow the articulation of specific needs. If efficiencies can be improved through implementing new technologies (for example, use of robots on the automobile assembly line to perform routine repetitive actions), plans can be made to implement that change.

Normally, implementation plans should involve these steps:

1. Documentation of goals and specific actions required to achieve them.

2. Meetings with employees to discuss the changes and vision that require those changes.

3. Solicitation of employee support and participation in the change process.

4. Measurement of the results.

Organizational changes should always be consistent with the employer's strategic plan. Changes should represent means to achieve missions or goals. There should always be a link between the change and the organizational strategy.

SPHR Measuring Results, Establishing Metrics

Measurement is critical. Without measuring the accomplishments, there is no way to know if the stated goals have been realized. Measurements generally fall into one of two categories discussed in the following sections.

Objective Measurements

When measurements involve impartial assessment of a result, they are said to be objective. Counting items, identifying distances or temperatures, and weighing items are all examples of objective measurements. Rates (miles per hour, units per day) and ratios (error rates or failure rates) also qualify as objective measurements. These types of measurements are usually fact-based and not dependent upon the individuals doing the measuring.

Subjective Measurements

When measurements involve opinion or perceptions they are said to be subjective. Just because job performance may be difficult to evaluate doesn't mean it cannot be measured. Attorneys, teachers, HR managers, and physicians have jobs that depend on both objective and subjective measurements. Beyond the number of trials won or the number of participants passing the standardized tests, there are behaviors that should also be measured in some way. Leadership, decision making, communication, and inner work standards are all skills/behaviors that are imprecise.

Subjective measurements can be quantified by using scales representing amounts of the behavior. Usually, such efforts are best when compared with a "standard" or "benchmark" that represents the desired behavior. Watching someone who is a successful manager demonstrate leadership skills can provide a reference for comparison of leadership demonstrated by other people. It can be described in a narrative or on a scale from "Very Little" to "Excessive." Knowing where the benchmark falls on the scale is critical. Everyone else should be compared to that benchmark, not one another.

If only one person is applying subjective measurements, all of the results will likely be consistently generated from the same opinion or expectation base. When more than one person is involved in measuring using subjective means, the difference between the evaluators can become problematic. That is why using a standard or benchmark is recommended so results can be more closely controlled from one evaluator to another. Every evaluator can make adjustments based on the benchmark.

Global Issues and Considerations

There are key issues to be aware of in global organizations that apply to the topics discussed in this chapter. Things become more complex due to cultural and language barriers along with geographical and time zone differences. Managing the diverse global workplaces becomes complicated with laws, regulations, and practices differing from country to country.

Cultural Issues

There are two cultural constructs that have a great influence on communication and training/development activities: power distance and high-context/low-context culture. Dr. Geert Hofstede, well known for his pioneering research of cross-cultural groups in organizations, conducted a study of how workplace values were influenced by culture. He developed a model that identifies five primary dimensions to differentiate cultures. The five dimensions are: *power distance, individualism, uncertainty avoidance, masculinity, and long-term orientation.*

Power distance is the extent to which less-powerful members of organizations expect and accept that power is distributed unequally. In high power distance organizations, the less powerful employee accepts autocratic structures.

Individualism refers to the extent to which people are expected to stand up for themselves. With high individualism, individual's rights are most important.

Uncertainty avoidance is the extent to which members of a society cope with anxiety by minimizing uncertainty. High uncertainty avoidance cultures like structure and rules.

Masculinity also includes femininity and refers to the value placed on male or female values from a Western culture perspective. Feminine cultures place more value on relationships and harmony, wherein masculine cultures value competitiveness and assertiveness.

Long-term orientation is the degree to which the society embraces long-term devotion to traditional values. High long-term orientation has a respect for loyalty commitments and work ethic is strong. [19]

Low-context/High-context Culture

Low-context culture and the contrasting high-context culture are terms presented by Edward T. Hall in his 1976 book *Beyond Culture* that categorize the differences in communication styles.[20]

Low-context refers to cultures where people will have many connections but of shorter duration or for some specific reason. Cultural beliefs may need to be spelled out explicitly so that newcomers into the cultural environment know what is acceptable, especially with behaviors.

High-context refers to cultures where people have close connections over a long period of time. These members of the culture know what to do and what to think from years of association and interaction with each other. High-context is more common in Eastern cultures.

Training and development, talent management, developing leaders, and of course performance management may need to vary depending on whether a culture that the organization is doing business in is consider low or high context.

Chapter Review

Human Resource Development is the integrated use of training, organizational development, and career development efforts to improve individual, group, and organizational effectiveness. This HRCI functional area focuses on the behavior, skills, and competencies for employees to further the organization's goals. HRD activities need to align and support the organization's strategic goals and objectives, and it is the HR professional's responsibility to develop, evaluate, and measure the direct effectiveness to ensure that they are in alignment. By providing input in the development, and fully understanding the organization's strategic plan, they can then develop, select, and implement human resource development programs and activities that provide the organization's workforce with the necessary skills and competencies to meet the current and future organizational job demands.

HRD has a strong role to play in helping employees acquire skills and knowledge, and in assisting with the changes and outside influences through the development of training and development programs, change management, performance management, employee career planning, and job enhancement.

Questions

1. Organizations with several employees in technical and scientific careers can most effectively impact retention by providing:

    A. Dual-career ladders

    B. An employee wellness program

    C. A validated succession planning program

    D. Various telecommuting options

2. What is the name for the evaluation error to appraise most recent negative behavior or effort rather than a review of the entire appraisal period?

    A. Nonverbal bias

    B. Last function relay

    C. Recency

    D. Horn effect

3. According to Maslow's hierarchy, which needs must be met first?

   A. Social needs

   B. Security/safety needs

   C. Self-actualization needs

   D. Belonging/loving needs

4. Leslie is moved into a new supervisory position in the creative services department. She intends to set a good example for her subordinates. She recognizes that there are already strong creative partnerships within the department, so she tries to foster even more cooperation. What style of leadership is Leslie practicing?

   A. Authoritarian leadership

   B. Team style

   C. Democratic leadership

   D. Collaborative leadership

5. ADDIE is an instructional design tool. What is not a part of ADDIE?

   A. Delivery

   B. Implementation

   C. Design

   D. Development

6. What are the four styles of leadership identified by the Hersey-Blanchard theory?

   A. Telling, selling, participating, delegating

   B. Showing, growing, sowing, bestowing

   C. Managing, administrating, inspiring, following

   D. Giving, taking, making, doing

7. The Tasty Good corporation downsized due to intense global competition and modified its strategic business plan for the year. The most important task that the HR department's training and development function needs to do to support the change is to:

   A. Cost-justify training

   B. Work with employees on accepting the change

   C. Evaluate the effectiveness of all training programs

   D. Link training and development to the new strategic plan

8. Adult learners in comparison to child learners have which of the following characteristics?

   A. Resistance to change

   B. Inflexibility

   C. Focus on real-world issues

   D. Directed by others

9. One of the most important competencies of an HR professional is:

   A. Skilled project manager

   B. A masterful change agent

   C. Excellent time management skills

   D. Listening

10. When an HR intervention has a focus on emotional intelligence (EQ) the goal is to:

   A. Heighten emotions

   B. Always improve coworker relationships

   C. Cause EQ rating to align with IQ rating

   D. Improve or increase an individual's interactions and behaviors

11. Training and development manager Joey was requested by the operations director to develop a team-building program that would focus on blending the values of Gen X with the Baby Boomers. Joey does not possess the knowledge of generational issues for team building. A justification Joey can use to sell his boss on purchasing an already existing team building training program from a third-party consultant is:

   A. Outside expertise will generate higher credibility from the Gen X participants because Joey is from the Baby Boomer generation.

   B. The time required to develop a training program in-house by Joey would take too long.

   C. There are many vendors that offer this kind of specific training.

   D. A Gen X training facilitator would be better to deliver this type of training program.

12. What performance evaluation method increases employee engagement and dialogue the most?

   A. Self-assessment evaluation

   B. Behaviorally anchored rating scale method (BARS)

   C. A forced-choice method

   D. Paired comparison method

13. Brianna is the responsible HR recruiter for handling exit interviews. She has noticed that the number of accounting personnel leaving the finance division who claim not to have other jobs to go to and are too young to retire has increased in numbers over the last 18 months. To help stop the exodus and learn the root of the reason behind the increased level of resignations, Brianna should:

    A. Ask their reference checking service to determine where the former employees are working

    B. Hold a brown bag lunch with the finance employees to talk up the value of the benefits the company offers

    C. Design focus-group questions and invite select finance employees to a focus group meeting with a confidential input agreement

    D. Send out an employee survey in the finance department to ask what employees think about the recent resignations

14. Which of the following is *not* an example of a narrative evaluation method?

    A. Behaviorally anchored rating (BARS)

    B. Forced distribution

    C. Management by objectives (MBO)

    D. Essay

15. A large technology company has identified a group of key managers in various departments who were hired with employment contracts that included large equity options. The company went public two years ago and continues to see a steady increase in stock value. There is a realization that many of these managers may retire when they are eligible to exercise their stock options in three more years. What OD activity should HR be focused on related to this circumstance?

    A. Review the organization's retirement plan and begin counseling discussions

    B. Expand the vacation policy for this group of managers

    C. Design a succession plan and identify high potential employees

    D. Hire executive coaches to help this group of management with work/life balance

16. Herzberg's Motivation-Hygiene Theory is based on which two categories of needs?

    A. Psychological and basic needs

    B. Motivational and security needs

    C. Extrinsic and intrinsic needs

    D. Safety and self-esteem needs

17. What type of team involves a group that is given general direction to resolve an issue or solve a problem?

    A. Self-directed team

    B. Task force

    C. Project team

    D. Work team

18. Kiara has been working at her company for close to 18 years out of her 25 years as a programmer. What stage would probably best describe Kiara's career development:

    A. Late-career

    B. Mid-career crisis

    C. Occupational preparation

    D. Mid-career

19. Mark and Gwen are coworkers whose cubicles are located in a 12 x 10 enclosed room. Their manager is unable to resolve a conflict that they are having related to the temperature in the room and the matter has escalated to HR. Which would be the best tactic to use in resolving their conflict?

    A. Use the seniority system; the person with the most seniority gets to decide on the temperature.

    B. Provide a portable fan for the cubicle and desk of the person who is too warm.

    C. Facilitate a conversation with the two of them in the same room to try and find common agreements.

    D. Create a schedule of telecommuting so that they are not in the same office at the same time.

20. Which is *not* one of the leadership practices that Kouzes and Posner identify for effective leadership?

    A. Enable

    B. Persuade

    C. Model

    D. Encourage

21. In a low-context culture, which is true?

    A. Tasks are needed to be spelled out explicitly.

    B. Behavior are needed to be spelled out explicitly.

    C. People know how to behave.

    D. People have connections over long periods of time.

22. Which is not one of the four quality absolutes in Philip Crosby's TQM philosophy?

    A. Appraisal of quality

    B. Zero defects

    C. Cost of nonconformance

    D. Definition of quality

23. Which Quality Control tool resembles a fishbone?

    A. Scatter diagram

    B. Histogram

    C. Cause-and-effect diagram

    D. Process-flow chart

24. You have observed that your employee Matthew consistently has a notebook in hand and is taking notes in the training sessions. Which learning style is Matthew exhibiting?

    A. Visual

    B. Auditory

    C. Kinesthetic

    D. Tactile

25. Which learning curve is the most common?

    A. Increasing returns

    B. S-shaped curve

    C. Decreasing returns

    D. Plateau curve

Answers

1. **A.** Dual-career ladders provide opportunities for a parallel occupational track that recognizes and rewards different skill sets. This allows organizations to retain their technical and professional employees at a similar rate as their managerial track employees.

2. **C.** Recency is an error that occurs when an appraiser uses a recent occurrence, allowing it to discounts all other performances during the review period.

3. **B.** Safety and security needs must be met first before moving up the pyramid of hierarchal needs according to Maslow's theory.

4. **B.** Team style of leadership that encourages teamwork and commitment among employees.

5. **A.** ADDIE is an instructional design model that follows phases of assessment, design, development, implementation, and evaluation.

6. **A.** The Hersey-Blanchard Situational Leadership Model has four tasks based on an employee's maturity—delegating, participating, selling, and telling.

7. **D.** Linking training and development activities to the new strategic plan is the first step to ensure that activities and resources are aligned with the organization's new initiatives.

8. **C.** As people mature, they shift in their motivation for learning. Real-world examples and emphasis on how the training is going to be immediately applied is most helpful.

9. **B.** Although all those skills listed are important to the profession, being a masterful change agent is most important because change agents serve as a catalyst in helping others work through and accept change, along with implementing processes and programs that align with the change.

10. **D.** Emotional intelligence (EQ) interventions involve skill and coaching or mentoring to cause a person's interactions to improve by changing an ineffective behavior.

11. **B.** Sometimes it is more cost and time effective to utilize an already developed training program that is available from a third-party vendor.

12. **A.** More organizations are having their employees complete a self-assessment on their performance and submit it prior to their evaluation interview meeting. This affords an opportunity for the employee to be more engaged with setting their job goals for the next review period and focuses discussions on their career development in the organization.

13. **C.** A focus group provides an ability to have two-way dialogue for clarity and probing purposes, and Brianna needs to solicit confidential information in a trusted environment that allows the employees to express collective concerns about conditions.

14. **B.** Forced distribution is what is known as the bell curve, which assumes that a group of individuals will fall within a rating scale that includes a percentage meeting standards, a predictable group not meeting standards, and also a group exceeding standards.

15. **C.** A succession plan is a key component for business success and should be part of every organization's human resources development program to be sure that there is no gap in knowledge that cripples an organization due to the departure of key human capital.

16. **C.** Hygiene factors are considered extrinsic and associated with job security, pay, working conditions, and relationships, whereas motivational factors are

considered intrinsic, associated with recognition, achievement, and personal growth–related events in the job.

17. **A.** Self-directed teams as a group select their own leadership and identify their own direction, holding themselves accountable for the intended accomplishments.

18. **D.** Mid-career is a phase when evaluation of career objectives occurs. It is too soon for retirement but a time of life when work/life family issues are more of a factor and can shift a person's motivations about work.

19. **C.** Any and all small agreements assist with the stages of conflict resolution. Agreeing on the problem and on some small changes gives a feeling of compromise to both parties so you can begin the process of looking at all possible acceptable solutions.

20. The five leadership practices Kouzes and Posner identify in *The Leadership Challenge* are: challenge, inspire, enable, model, and encourage.

21. **B.** In low-context cultures, people need to have work behavior expectations spelled out so that they know how to behave and what is expected of them.

22. **A.** Crosby's TQM included a prevention system rather than an appraisal system of quality.

23. **C.** Cause-and-effect diagram which is used to map out all the factors that are thought to affect a problem.

24. **A.** Matthew is a visual learner. Visual learners prefer to take detailed notes in order to absorb new information.

25. **C.** Decreasing returns is the most common type of learning curve. It occurs when the amount of learning increases rapidly in the beginning and then the rate of learning slows.

Endnotes

1. Richard Beckhard, *Organization Development: Strategies and Models* (Addison-Wesley, 1969).

2. Peter Senge, *The Fifth Discipline*, Revised and Updated edition (New York: Doubleday, 2006).

3. Kurt Lewin, "Frontiers in Group Dynamics: Concept, Method and Reality in Social Science; Social Equilibria and Social Change," *Human Relations Journal* (June 1947), http://hum.sagepub.com/content/1/1/5.

4. University of Tennessee, http://edtech2.tennessee.edu/projects/bobannon/in_strategies.html, accessed on July 25, 2014.

5. Benjamin Bloom, Engelhart, M. D. Furst, E. J. Hill, W. H. Krathwohl, D. R. *Taxonomy of Educational Objectives: The Classification of Educational Goals*. Handbook I: Cognitive Domain (New York: David McKay Company, 1956).

6. Abraham Maslow, "A Theory of Human Motivation," *Psychological Review*, 50, 370–96, 1943.

7. *Don Kirkpatrick: The Father of the Four Levels* (Biographical article from *Chief Learning Officer Magazine*, November 2009).

8. SHRM, Talent Management Future of the U.S. Labor Pool Survey Report, 2013, www.shrm.org/india/hr-topics-and-strategy/strategic-hrm/talent-development-strategy.

9. Peter Drucker, *The Practice of Management* (New York: HarperBusiness, 2010).

10. W. Edwards Deming, *The New Economics for Industry, Government, and Education* (Boston: MIT Press, 1993), p. 132.

11. Joseph Juran, *Quality Control Handbook* (New York: McGraw-Hill, 1951).

12. "Philip Crosby, 75, Developer of the Zero-Defects Concept." *The New York Times*, 2001.

13. Marshall Goldsmith et al. *Global Leadership* (Upper Saddle River, NJ: FT Press, 2003).

14. Paul Hersey and Ken Blanchard, *Management of Organizational Behavior* (Upper Saddle River, NJ: Prentice Hall, 2012).

15. Robert Blake and Jane Mouton, *The Managerial Grid* (Houston, TX: Gulf Publishing, 1985).

16. Fred Fiedler, *A Theory of Leadership Effectiveness* (New York: McGraw-Hill, 1967).

17. James M. Kouzes and Barry Z. Posner, *The Leadership Challenge* (Hoboken, NJ: Jossey-Bass, 2012).

18. University of Pennsylvania, www.med.upenn.edu/hbhe4/part4-ch15-organizational-development-theory.shtml, accessed on July 25, 2014.

19. Geert Hofstede, *Culture's Consequences: Comparing Values, Behaviors, Institutions, and Organizations across Nations* (2nd ed.) (Thousand Oaks, CA: SAGE Publications, 2001).

20. *Edward T. Hall, Beyond Culture* (New York: Anchor Books, 1976).

Compensation and Benefits

Compensation and benefits are the lifeblood of the employment relationship between the worker and the employer. But this relationship reaches beyond the scope of compensation and benefits alone, including recognition programs and assorted fringe benefits; thus, "total rewards" has become a popular term that best defines this aspect of the employment relationship. Nineteen percent of the PHR exam and 13 percent of the SPHR exam will focus on this area of knowledge.

The official HRCI Compensation and Benefits functional area responsibilities and knowledge statements are as follows:

Responsibilities

- Ensure that compensation and benefits programs are compliant with applicable federal laws and regulations.

- Develop, implement, and evaluate compensation policies/programs (for example: pay structures, performance-based pay, internal and external equity).

- Manage payroll-related information (for example: new hires, adjustments, terminations).

- **SPHR** • Manage outsourced compensation and benefits components (for example: payroll vendors, COBRA administration, employee recognition vendors).

- Conduct compensation and benefits programs needs assessments (for example: benchmarking, employee surveys, trend analysis).

- Develop/select, implement/administer, update and evaluate benefit programs (for example: health and welfare, wellness, retirement, stock purchase).

- Communicate and train the workforce in the compensation and benefits programs, policies, and processes (for example: self-service technologies).

- **SPHR** • Develop/select, implement/administer, update, and evaluate an ethically sound executive compensation program (for example: stock options, bonuses, supplemental retirement plans).

- **SPHR** • Develop, implement/administer, and evaluate expatriate and foreign national compensation and benefits programs.

411

Knowledge of

- Applicable federal laws and regulations related to compensation, benefits, and tax (for example: FLSA, ERISA, FMLA, USERRA)
- Compensation and benefits strategies
- Budgeting and accounting practices related to compensation and benefits
- Job evaluation methods
- Job pricing and pay structures
- External labor markets and/or economic factors
- Pay programs (for example: variable, merit)
- **SPHR** • Executive compensation methods
- Noncash compensation methods (for example: equity programs, noncash rewards)
- Benefits programs (for example: health and welfare, retirement, Employee Assistance Programs [EAPs])
- **SPHR** • International compensation laws and practices (for example: expatriate compensation, entitlements, choice of law codes)
- Fiduciary responsibilities related to compensation and benefits

Core Knowledge of

- Organizational documentation requirements to meet federal and state guidelines
- Technology to support HR activities
- Qualitative and quantitative methods and tools for analysis, interpretation, and decision-making purposes
- Employee records management

A Total Rewards Philosophy and Strategy

People are willing to work in exchange for rewards they receive from the work they do. The objective is to provide a balance between what work is performed and the reward received for doing the work. "Total rewards" includes the financial inducements and rewards (direct pay, cash-based incentives and benefits) as well as non-financial inducements and rewards such as the value of good job content as well as a good working environment. Employers strive to offer an attractive compensation package, including a fair base pay, incentives, and benefits, in addition to a good job match and working environment to attract employees and retain them.

"Total rewards" includes compensation that is both direct and indirect. Direct compensation (e.g., "cash") applies to a variety of pay programs that are, in one way or another, cash-based, whereas indirect compensation (e.g., "benefits") applies to programs primarily designed to provide recognition and benefits and, therefore, are indirectly cash-based. Examples of these two types of compensation are listed in Table 9-1.

Direct Compensation ("Cash")	Indirect Compensation ("Benefits")
Base pay (wages and salary)	Social Security
Commissions	Unemployment insurance
Bonuses	Disability insurance
Merit pay	Pensions
Piece rate	401(k) and other similar programs
Differential pay	Health care
Cash award	Vacations
Profit sharing	Sick leave
Gainsharing	Paid time off

Table 9-1   Direct and Indirect Compensation

Some of the direct compensation programs are discretionary, i.e., cash awards, differential pay, and certain bonuses, while others are mandatory and governed by federal, state, and in some cases, local law and regulation (base pay and incentives). Some of the indirect compensation programs are also discretionary—that is, they are employed at the option of the employer. They include paid vacation, sick leave, paid time off, 401(k) and similar retirement plans, and pensions. Finally, some benefits are mandatory and governed by federal law and regulation. Social Security, workers' compensation, and unemployment insurance are examples. Even discretionary programs are subject to regulation when they are employed.

NOTE   The single difference between direct and indirect compensation is that direct compensation results in some form of a cash reward while indirect compensation results in some form of a desired benefit for the employee.

COMPENSATION

Strategic Objectives of Compensation

Direct compensation, simply referred to as "compensation," as a strategic objective, significantly impacts all of the other HR functions, including staffing, performance evaluations, training and development, and employee relations, and these HR functions likewise influence compensation. Compensation affects organizational processes, job satisfaction, productivity, and turnover. Compensation must be viewed not only on the basis of what is legal and motivating, but also on the ethical basis of what is fair and just.

Employers want to attract and retain good, qualified workers who are motivated to a degree of high productivity, but employers must make compensation decisions with competing pressures. Simply paying more or providing better company benefits may make some employees happy but will, in the long term, raise labor costs and make the company less competitive.

In the face of competitive pressures, all pay decisions should:

- **Be legal**   Must be consistent with numerous federal, state, and local laws.

- **Be adequate**   Be large enough to attract qualified employees to join the organization and stay.

- **Be motivating**   Should provide sufficient incentives to motivate employees to perform efficiently.

- **Be equitable**   Employee should feel that his or her compensation is internally equitable relative to other employees in the organization and externally equitable relative to employees doing similar work in other organizations.

- **Provide security**   Employees want to feel that their monthly income is secure and predictable. They need to feel that their pay is somewhat insulated from changes in employment, profitability, individual performance, and personal health.

- **Be cost-benefit effective**   The organization must administer the compensation system efficiently and have the financial resources to support it on a continuing basis.

Federal Laws That Impact Compensation

Federal, state, and local governments play a significant role in the management of employee compensation. The federal government sets minimum standards relative to how much and how employees are paid through the following legislation. Key federal laws that impact compensation are listed in Figure 9-1.

   NOTE   Detailed descriptions of these federal laws and regulations can be found in Chapter 2 of this book.

- Davis-Bacon Act (1931)

- Walsh Healey Act (1936)

- Portal-to-Portal Act (1947)

- Service Contract Act (1965)

- Work Opportunity Tax Credit (WOTC)

- Dodd-Frank Wall Street Reform and Consumer Protection Act (2010)

- Copeland "Anti-Kickback" Act (1934)

- Fair Labor Standards Act (FLSA) (1938)

- Equal Pay Act (EPA) (1963)

- Age Discrimination Act (ADA) (1967)

- Lilly Ledbetter Fair Pay Act (2009)

- IRS Intermediate Sanctions (1996)

Figure 9-1   Key federal laws impacting compensation

Federal Agency Non-Discrimination Enforcement

The following federal agencies have a significant legal oversight role in the rules and regulations applicable to compensation and benefits.

United States Department of Labor (DOL)

The mission of the United States Department of Labor (DOL) is to foster, promote, and develop the welfare of the wage earners, job seekers, and retirees of the United States; improve working conditions; advance opportunities for profitable employment; and assure work-related benefits and rights. The Department of Labor enforces the Fair Labor Standards Act (FLSA), which sets basic minimum wage and overtime pay standards. These standards are enforced by the Department's Wage and Hour Division.

The Department of Labor's Unemployment Insurance (UI) programs provide unemployment benefits to eligible workers who become unemployed through no fault of their own and meet certain other eligibility requirements.

Equal Employment Opportunity Commission (EEOC)

The U.S. Equal Employment Opportunity Commission (EEOC) is responsible for enforcing federal laws that make it illegal to discriminate against a job applicant or an employee because of the person's race, color, religion, sex (including pregnancy), national origin, age (40 or older), disability, or genetic information. It is also illegal to discriminate against a person because the person complained about discrimination, filed a charge of discrimination, or participated in an employment discrimination investigation or lawsuit.

Most employers with at least 15 employees are covered by EEOC laws (20 employees in age discrimination cases). Most labor unions and employment agencies are also covered.

The laws apply to all types of work situations, including hiring, firing, promotions, harassment, training, wages, and benefits.

Office of Federal Contract Compliance Programs (OFCCP)

The purpose of the Office of Federal Contract Compliance Programs (OFCCP) is to enforce, for the benefit of job seekers and wage earners, the contractual promise of affirmative action and equal employment opportunity required of those who do business with the federal government.

In carrying out its responsibilities, the OFCCP uses the following enforcement procedures:

- Offers technical assistance to federal contractors and subcontractors to help them understand the regulatory requirements and review process.

- Conducts compliance evaluations and complaint investigations of federal contractors and subcontractors' personnel policies and procedures.

- Obtains Conciliation Agreements from contractors and subcontractors who are in violation of regulatory requirements.

- Monitors, through periodic compliance reports, contractors' and subcontractors' progress in fulfilling the terms of their agreements.

- Forms linkage agreements between contractors and Labor Department job training programs to help employers identify and recruit qualified workers.

- Recommends enforcement actions to the Solicitor of Labor.

The ultimate sanction for violations is debarment—the loss of a company's federal contracts. Other forms of relief to victims of discrimination may also be available, including back pay for lost wages.

The OFCCP has close working relationships with other departmental agencies, such as the Department of Justice, the Equal Employment Opportunity Commission, and the DOL's Office of the Solicitor, which advises on ethical, legal, and enforcement issues; the Women's Bureau, which emphasizes the needs of working women; the Bureau of Apprenticeship and Training, which establishes policies to promote equal opportunities in the recruitment and selection of apprentices; and the Employment and Training Administration, which administers Labor Department job training programs for current workforce needs.

The OFCCP has a national network of six regional offices, each with district and area offices in major metropolitan centers. The OFCCP focuses its resources on finding and resolving systemic discrimination. The agency has adopted this strategy to:

- Prioritize enforcement resources by focusing on the worst offenders

- Encourage employers to engage in self-audits of their employment practices

- Achieve maximum leverage of resources to protect the greatest number of workers from discrimination

The OFCCP enforces Executive Order 11246, including the ban on compensation discrimination, consistent with Title VII's flexible, fact-specific approach to proof. This involves factual investigation and data and legal analyses that allow OFCCP to identify and remedy all forms of compensation discrimination. Compliance officers tailor the compensation investigation and analytical procedures to the facts of the case as appropriate under Title VII. This case-by-case approach to compensation discrimination includes the use of a range of investigative and analytical tools. Statistical analyses, such as multiple regression, and non-statistical analyses, such as the use of comparators or cohort analysis, are applied as feasible and appropriate given the factual questions and the available data and evidence. Compliance officers seek anecdotal evidence, but will investigate and remedy compensation discrimination regardless of whether individual workers believe they are being underpaid or whether OFCCP has any anecdotal evidence.

This case-by-case approach is designed to eliminate unnecessary barriers to OFCCP's ability to protect workers from discrimination. It ensures OFCCP fully takes into account explanations or responses from contractors and that OFCCP conducts an analysis tailored to a contractor's compensation systems and practices. These investigation procedures apply to all OFCCP reviews scheduled on or after February 28, 2013, to the extent they do not conflict with OFCCP guidance or procedures existing prior to the effective date.

Job Evaluation

The systematic determination of the relative worth of jobs in an organization is known as "job evaluation." The importance of job evaluation is that it is a critically important pay equity concept applied through a formalized process designed to prevent internal pay inequities as employers create structure within the organization's cost parameters while responding to its workforce expectations. Conducting a job evaluation is an essential first step in creating an appropriate wage structure that accommodates jobs of different worth while it preserves the core objective of internal pay equity. Market surveys are a tool that enables organizations to understand and recognize market pressures with an objective of external equity.

Job Evaluation Methods

Job evaluation methods can be non-quantitative or quantitative. The primary objective of a non-quantitative method is to establish a relative hierarchy of jobs based on the jobs' relative worth. Non-quantitative methods often are referred to as whole-job methods because they rank jobs as a whole based on their perceived worth without placing a numerical value on each job. An example of a non-quantitative method would be to rank a clerical job below a supervisory job on the basis of their relative, non-quantitative worth.

Quantitative job evaluation methods include *point-factor* and *factor comparison* methods. Quantitative methods evaluate factors on a defined measurable scale and provide a score as the result that is a measurable comparison of one job to another (see Table 9-2).

Job Ranking

The job ranking method is often called a "whole job" comparison because it is a comparison of the whole job compared to another whole job rather than a comparison based on each job's measurable factors. Job ranking using the "whole job" method is quick and easy but not very precise. It is easy to explain which is why it is popular but it leaves unanswered why one job is worth more than another as well as how much of a "gap" exists between jobs.

	Non-Quantitative Methods	**Quantitative Methods**
Job-to job comparison	Job ranking	Factor comparison
Job-to-predetermined-standard comparison	Job classification	Point-factor

Table 9-2 Job Evaluation Methods

When there are a large number of jobs to evaluate, a "paired-comparison" method of ranking can be used. This method enables each job to be compared with every other job. Jobs are methodically compared to the next job and, depending on the perceived worth, moved up or below the next job. Ultimately, the job with the highest number of upward movements is the highest ranked. Other jobs are ranked accordingly.

Job Classification

Jobs can be compared to an outside scale. This also can be done on a "whole job" basis called a "job classification" method. Job classification is the result of grouping jobs into a predetermined number of grades or classifications. Each classification has a class description. The federal government has a classification system known as the "General Schedule." The General Schedule (GS) is the predominant pay scale for federal employees, especially employees in professional, technical, administrative, or clerical positions. The system consists of 15 grades, from GS-1, the lowest level, to GS-15, the highest level. There are also 10 steps within each grade. The grade level assigned to a position determines the pay level for that job.

Classes can be further identified by using benchmark jobs that fall into each class. Benchmark jobs have the following characteristics:

- The essential functions and knowledge, skills, and abilities (KSAs) are established and stable.
- They represent the entire range of jobs in each class.
- A significant percentage of workers is employed in these jobs.
- External market rates for these jobs are an acceptable basis for setting wages.

The job classification method is a non-quantitative job evaluation method. In the job classification method, a job may be compared to a similar job or to other jobs in the General Schedule, to determine its relative ranking. This is considered a non-quantitative method called a "job-to-predetermined-standard comparison." Job classification comparisons are a good method when evaluating a large number of jobs and are understandable by employees but may not be effective when jobs overlap as they only look at whole jobs.

Point-Factor Method

The most commonly used job evaluation method is the *point-factor method*, which uses specific compensable factors as its reference points to measure relative job worth. Compensable factors are significant job characteristics that contribute to the value of the work and organization as a whole. Two well-known systems used to identify compensable factors are:

- **The Hay Plan**   Uses a standard criteria comprising three compensable factors: know-how, problem solving, and accountability.

- **The Factor Evaluation System (FES)** Determines levels of duties and responsibilities using a point rating system to evaluate selected positions. Uses weighted factors to address the major position characteristics of responsibility, education/experience, job conditions, physical requirements, supervision, training, and so on.

There are five steps involved in the point-factor method of job evaluation:

1. *Identify key jobs.* These are benchmark jobs, not necessarily the most important jobs in the organization, but jobs that are equitably paid, stable, and well-defined.

2. *Identify the compensable factors.* These are the factors that will be used to distinguish one job from another. Six to eight factors are generally sufficient. Experience, responsibility, and education are most often used. Other factors that can be considered, depending on their general applicability, include physical demands, mental requirements, skill, working conditions, and supervisory responsibilities.

3. *Weight the factors according to their overall worth.* Usually, the most heavily weighted factors are knowledge, responsibility, experience, education, degree of difficulty, and supervisory responsibilities.

4. *Divide each job factor into degrees that range from high to low.* Assign points to each degree. The number of points assigned to each degree should correspond with the weighting of the factors. As an example, if the factor for skill is weighted 40 percent, the factor of working conditions is weighted 10 percent, and both factors have five degrees, degree two for skill should have four times as many points as degree two for working conditions.

5. *The final result will be a table (see Table 9-3) that gives a complete range of points from 50 (the least number, column 1) to 200 (the most, column 5). Based on the assigned point values, the job in this example is 126 on a scale of 50 to 200 points. Points usually determine the pay grade to which the job will be assigned.*

Point-Factor Job Evaluation Method						
Compensable Factor	**Weighted Percentage**	**Degrees/Points**				
		1	2	3	4	5
Skill	(40%)	20	32	48	72	100
Responsibility	(30%)	15	24	36	54	75
Effort	(20%)	10	16	24	36	50
Working Conditions	(10%)	5	8	12	18	25

Example: Machine Operator	**Compensable Factor**	**Degree**	**Points**
	Skill	3	48
	Responsibility	2	24
	Effort	4	36
	Working Conditions	4	18
	Total points		126

Table 9-3 Point-Factor Job Evaluation Method

Factor Comparison Method

The *factor comparison method* is more complex than ranking, classification, or the point-factor methods and is rarely used. It involves ranking each job by each compensable factor and then, as an additional step, identifying dollar values for each level of each factor to develop an actual pay rate for the evaluated job.

The factor comparison method is most often used in union negotiations as part of a labor contract and in limited cases where wages are steady over a period of time and the organization uses a flat rate for each job.

Market-Based Evaluation

A market-rate system is not a true job evaluation system but, in some cases, market value can be used to price jobs—particularly when the organization is sensitive to competition. These prevailing rates are used to represent the relative worth of the jobs. In this approach, key jobs are measured and valued against market and the remaining jobs are inserted into a hierarchy based on their whole-job comparison to the benchmark jobs.

 NOTE When matching a job with the competition, it is important to compare duties, scope, and reporting relationships but not titles because they are often misleading.

Market-based evaluation can be particularly beneficial when an organization has similar jobs in various locations throughout the United States. The disadvantage of a market-based evaluation is that the data will be reliable only when gathered for a significant number of jobs in the organization. Market-based evaluation results are more vulnerable to legal challenge than job-content approaches. Another disadvantage is that market-based evaluations do not recognize internal job value and, as a result, are more likely to lead to discontent and potential from within the organization.

Pay Surveys

Many organizations rely on pay surveys as a systematic way to collect, evaluate, and classify their jobs, adjust pay structures, and provide market information to top management. Pay surveys collect data on prevailing market rates and provide information such as starting wage rates, base pay, pay ranges, overtime pay, shift differentials, and incentive pay plans.

Options to collecting pay survey data include whether the survey should be conducted internally or gathered externally. Organizations that want to maintain maximum control over their pay information often choose to sponsor a custom survey. The advantage of this approach is that the organization has the ability to design the survey, manage its administration, do its own data analysis, and customize its report specifically for its own use. Another advantage is that the organization is able to maximize its control over the transfer of data, thereby reducing the risk of an inappropriate disclosure of highly sensitive confidential information.

While choosing to conduct its own internal survey, an organization should contract with an outside consulting group or independent consultant to design the survey and process the data received in a confidential manner. Using an outside person or group relieves pressure on the organization and ensures compliance with Department of Justice antitrust guidelines.

External surveys have different options. National surveys are widely available through the U.S. Department of Labor and the Bureau of Labor Statistics. Many professional groups such as the Society of Human Resource Management (SHRM) and consulting firms conduct surveys of wage and job data for a wide range of professions and organizations.

Data Analysis

Organizations have an interest in survey data based on their market exposure, completion, their product or service, and employees. In order to be accurate, survey data must be verified and often aged, leveled, and factored for geography.

In the Trenches

Compensation Surveys: The Good, the Bad and Really?

Compensation surveys are essential tools for establishing the pay level of positions and staying competitive in the marketplace. In the "golden gilded age" of comp management (1990s to early 2000s), HR was delighted with the increased availability and access to market data, thanks to technology. Compensation information was enabling companies to balance their internal equity pay structures with what the local market was providing for high demand talent. The data was imperfect, but it was credible when HR would wave a ream of data to support their conclusions for talent bleeding (the loss of key and high potential employees). That was the *good*: ease of accessing data timely and directly. The cost savings were great as well because high-powered consultancy firms were no longer needed to gather information.

In more recent decades, focus of compensation surveys have shifted to calibrating pay levels primarily with the external market, and that in turn has created enormous pressure to obtain and ensure the data is accurate, timely, and "apple-to-apple" in terms of usefulness. Today there are literally thousands of published surveys that an HR professional can obtain for various job families, industries, geographical areas, and just about everything else you can sort data on. So there is a wealth of information at your fingertips, yet beware: *Just because you read it on the Internet, doesn't mean it's true.* And here comes *the bad*: only a fraction of companies participate in surveys. There are millions of

(Continued)

organizations, large and small, in the U.S. yet a very low percentage participate in compensation surveys. A survey that has 2,500 participants might sound great, yet 2,500 participants represent less than 1% of all companies that have more than 500 employees. What is most disturbing is that more companies use compensation survey data than contribute to the surveys as participants. Additionally, those companies participating are normally participating in multiple surveys, causing data to be two-dimensional.

Participation is the key to obtaining quality data and all HR pros have a responsibility for feeding the data that calibrates our economies. Data needs to be accurate, reliable, and timely for the critical needs of attracting or retaining of human capital. Just think what a mere 10% increase in participation would create—a more robust data source for decision makers to rely on in organizations. So participate, participate, participate!

Measurement Terms   The following are terms that are used to refine the accuracy of survey data.

- **Aging**   This is a technique used to make outdated data current, a phenomenon that regularly occurs with printed data as a result of the time lapse between when the data is collected, organized, printed, and published. An example of aging occurs when pay movement or increases average 1.5 percent a year. If you use a pay survey that is one year old, in order to be reasonably accurate, you would increase the survey data by 1.5 percent.

- **Leveling**   Pay surveys provide summary descriptions of each job surveyed. In many cases, this description is close but not an exact match with the organization's job. To accommodate this separation between the two jobs, a leveling technique is used. Leveling consists of adjusting the survey number by an appropriate percentage needed to achieve a match. As an example, an organization's Engineering I job description indicates an approximate 10 percent less scope of responsibility than described in the same job in a pay survey. Reducing the pay survey job data with a 10 percent reduction would be an appropriate technique to provide an accurate match.

- **Geography**   While many surveys are developed with a specifically described geographical location identified, in cases where this is not done, it would be appropriate to determine the percent difference in job value for a given location and factor that into the comparison.

Frequency Distribution and Tables   The following are techniques used to organize data in a logical manner for ease and accuracy of interpretation:

- **Frequency distribution**   This is a listing of grouped pay data from lowest to highest.

- **Frequency tables**   This is the number of workers in a particular job classification and their pay data.

Measures of Central Tendency   Another way to measure pay data involves the four standard measures of central tendency: mean (average), weighted average, median, and mode.

- **Mean (average)**   The arithmetic average or mean is the average value arrived at by giving equal weight to every participant's actual pay. This method is appropriate when the data to be determined is the average pay for a given job as opposed to actual pay levels applicable to that job. This figure is also known as the "unweighted average."

- **Weighted average**   This number provides an average result taking into account the number of participants and each participant's pay. This figure is also known as the "weighted average."

Based on the data shown in Table 9-4:

- The unweighted mean (average) pay is $37,500 ($150,000 ÷ 4 organizational participants).

- The weighted mean (weighted average) is $36,666.66 ($440,000 ÷ 12 participants).

- **Median**   This number is sometimes referred to in pay surveys as the "50th percentile." This is the middle number in a range. The median is calculated by averaging the two middle numbers in a range when the range data is sorted from lowest to highest.

- **Mode**   This is the most frequently appearing number ("wage" in a pay survey) in a range.

Table 9-4	Survey	Mean Pay	Number of Participants
Weighted and	A	$40,000	5
Unweighted Mean	B	$25,000	2
Calculation	C	$35,000	4
	D	$50,000	1
	Total	$150,000	12

Pay Structure

After an organization has determined its relative internal job values—i.e., job evaluation—and collected appropriate market survey data through pay surveys, work begins on developing the organization's pay structure, including creating pay grades and establishing pay ranges.

Pay Grades

Pay grades, or job groups, are the way an organization organizes jobs of similar values. The valuation is a result of the job evaluation process. Jobs, even though dissimilar in function, of the same or comparatively the same value, are paid within the same pay grade.

No fixed rules apply to creating pay grades; rather, the number of pay grades and their structure is more of a reflection of organizational structure and philosophy. Issues that should be considered include:

- The size and structure of the organization
- The "distance" between the lowest and the highest job in the organization
- The organization's pay increase and promotion policy
- The grouping of non-exempt and exempt jobs as well as job families, i.e., clerical, technical, professional, supervisory, and management jobs
- Creating sufficient grades to permit distinguishing difficulty levels but not so many that the difference between adjoining grades is insignificant

Well-structured pay grades enable management to develop a well-coordinated pay system rather than having to create a separate pay range for each job.

Pay Ranges

Pay ranges establish the upper and lower boundaries of each pay grade. Market data for a benchmark job (ideally, a "key" job that will link to market value) in each pay range helps to determine the range midpoint. The range spread reflects the equal dispersion of pay on either side of the midpoint to the lower and upper range boundary.

Quartiles and Percentiles

Quartiles and percentiles show dispersion of data throughout a range. These are commonly recognized reference points an organization uses to measure its position against the market as well as for internal compensation management purposes.

Range Spreads

The range spread is the dispersion of pay from the lowest boundary to the highest boundary of a pay range.

Range Spread Calculation

Range spread is calculated by subtracting the range minimum from the range maximum and dividing that figure by the range minimum. Range spread is expressed as a percentage.

$$\frac{\text{Maximum} - \text{Minimum}}{\text{Minimum}}$$

Example: The range spread for a pay range with a $30,000 minimum and a $45,000 maximum would be as follows:

$$\frac{\$45,000 - \$30,000}{\$30,000}$$
$$= 50\%$$

Typical range spreads in organizations are:

- Non-exempt jobs: 40%
- Exempt jobs: 50%
- Executive jobs: 60%

Generally, lower-level jobs have a narrow range between minimum and maximum pay ranges. Jobs at a lower level tend to be more skill-based, which provides for more movement opportunity than higher levels where jobs are more knowledge-based and progression is slower.

Ranges should overlap so that progression is steady within a pay grade; as a worker's pay increases with movement to a higher range quartile, the opportunity for managed movement is possible in a measured way.

There also should be a large enough distance between range midpoints so that pay compression between a lower pay grade and a high pay grade does not occur.

Broadbanding

Broadbanding is a recent concept that combines several pay grades or job classifications with narrow range spreads with a single band with a wider spread. Organizations usually adopt broadbanding as a way to simplify their pay levels and reduce management oversight requirements. As a result, broadbanding typically is more popular in large organizations than smaller ones.

While broadbanding has some advantages, it also has some disadvantages. In some cases, broadbanding does not work well with the organization's compensation philosophy. This is particularly true in organizations that focus on promotional opportunities. The reduction of pay grades as a result of broadbanding correspondingly reduces the number of opportunities for promotion.

Compa-ratios

Compa-ratios are indicators of how wages match, lead, or lag the midpoint, normally an indicator of market value. Compa-ratios are computed by dividing the worker's pay rate by the midpoint of the pay range.

The compa-ratio formula is: $\text{Compa-ratio} = \dfrac{\text{Pay rate}}{\text{Midpoint}}$

Compa-ratios less than 100 percent (usually expressed as a compa-ratio less than 1.00) mean the worker is paid less than the midpoint of the range. Compa-ratios above 100% (1.00) mean that wages exceed the midpoint.

Base Pay Systems

After an organization has analyzed, evaluated, and priced its jobs, as well as designed it pay structure, the next step is to determine a type of base pay system that will help attract, motivate, and retain employees. In most cases, employees receive some type of base pay, either as an hourly wage (paid to hourly employees) or a salary (a fixed wage that doesn't change regardless of the hours worked). Base pay system choices include: single or flat-rate systems, time-based step rate systems, performance-based merit pay systems, productivity-based systems, and person-based systems. Each of these systems is designed to best achieve the objectives of attracting, motivating, and retaining employees each under a different set of circumstances.

Single or Flat-Rate System

In the single, or flat-rate, system, each worker in the same job has the same rate of pay regardless of seniority or job performance. This pay system is most commonly found in elected public sector jobs or in a union setting. The single pay rate (or flat pay rate) usually is directly linked to an applicable market survey. This system is also used as a training rate under circumstances when the worker is being trained for a job.

Time-Based Step Rate System

The time-based step rate system bases the employee's pay rate on the length of time in the job. Pay increases are published in advance on the basis of time. Increases occur on a pre-determined schedule. This system has three variations, as described in the sections that follow.

Automatic Step Rate

In the automatic step rate system, the pay range is divided into several steps, each a pre-determined range apart. At the prescribed time interval, each employee with the required seniority receives a one-step pay increase. This system is common in public-sector jobs and in a union environment.

Step Rate with Performance Considerations

The step rate with performance considerations system is similar to the automatic system except that performance can influence the size or timing of the pay increase.

Combination Step Rate and Performance

In the combination step rate and performance system, employees receive step rate increases up to the established job rate. Above this level, increases are only granted for superior job performance. To work, this system requires a supporting performance appraisal program as well as good communication and understanding by the workers paid under this system.

Performance-Based Merit Pay System

The performance-based merit pay system is based on an employee's individual job performance. A performance-based pay system is often referred to as "merit pay" or "pay for performance." In this system, employees are typically hired at or near the minimum for their applicable pay range. Pay increases are normally awarded on an annual basis (or annualized if awarded on other than an annual basis) and influenced by the individual's overall job performance. A document identifying the percent pay increase linked to levels of performance and the individual's position in the applicable pay range is communicated to employees as an incentive to increase their performance, thereby earning a higher percentage increase. This document is known as "Merit Guidelines." A "Merit Guidelines" example is illustrated in Table 9-5.

In order to be effective, the merit pay system must be understood by employees affected by the system. In addition to the merit pay system, a clearly stated performance appraisal program is required to support the merit pay system. Key points that should be addressed in designing and implementing an effective merit pay system include those depicted in Table 9-6.

Productivity-Based System

In the productivity-based system, pay is determined by the employee's output. This system is mostly used on an assembly line in a manufacturing environment. The following subsections describe two types of productivity-based systems.

Performance Rating	1st Quartile	2nd Quartile	3rd Quartile	4th Quartile
Exceeds Performance Objectives	6–7%	5–6%	4–5%	3–4%
Meets Performance Objectives	4–5%	3–4%	2–3%	1–2%
Needs Improvement	2–3%	1–2%	0–1%	0%

Table 9-5 Merit Guidelines Example

Merit Pay System	Performance Appraisal Program
Merit pay figures within quartiles can be either a range or a single number depending on the experience of the raters.	Performance ratings should clearly link to documented pre-agreed performance objectives.
Use a range for experienced raters, a single number for inexperienced raters.	Performance ratings are for overall performance.
Use one standard (range) or the other (single number) for the entire program.	Not more than three performance levels should be used (as shown).
Gap between one performance level and the next should be at least 2 percent in order to be a significant incentive.	"Needs Improvement" ratings should be placed into a Performance Improvement Program with a defined period (usually not more than 90 days) to improve overall performance.

Table 9-6 Merit Pay and Performance Appraisal Key Points

Straight Piece Rate System

With the straight piece rate system, the employee receives a base rate of pay and is awarded additional compensation for the amount of output produced.

Differential Piece Rate System

In the differential piece rate system, the employee receives one rate of pay up to the production standard and a higher rate of pay when the standard is exceeded.

NOTE Both the straight piece system and the differential piece rate system focus on quantity rather than quality. As a result, other quality control programs may be required to ensure the required quality standard is met.

Person-Based System

In the person-based system, employee capabilities, rather than how the job is performed, determine the employee's pay. For example, two employees do the same work but one employee with a higher level of skill and experience receives more pay. There are three types of person-based systems, as described in the subsections that follow.

Knowledge-Based Systems

In the knowledge-based system, a person's pay is based on the level of knowledge he or she has in a particular field. This system is often used in the learned professions such as lawyers and doctors.

Skill-Based Systems

Employees paid in the skill-based system are paid for the number and depth of skills that they have that are applicable to their job. Heavy equipment operators are typically paid in this system.

Competency-Based Systems

In the competency-based system, pay is linked to the level at which an employee can perform in a recognized competency. In HR, a professional with specialty skills in organizational development or labor relations will typically be paid for his or her competency—for example, organizational development or labor relations, in the HR field.

Variations in Pay

Pay ranges must be periodically evaluated and adjusted to reflect organizational and market changes. Red circle rates, green circle rates, and cost of living adjustments are some of the techniques used to adjust to these changes.

Red Circle Rates

Organizations use red circle rates as a method to increase an employee's pay to a new rate higher than the maximum for the assigned pay range. This situation occurs more often in smaller organizations where promotional opportunities may be limited. When this happens, an employee's next pay raise indicated by the organization's merit guidelines might place the new pay level above the maximum for the applicable pay range.

An example of this is the accounting manager who is paid $95,000 per year, a point less than 5 percent from the top of the range. Based on job performance, the manager would be entitled to a 7 percent increase. The next promotion step is the CFO job. In this case, the company may decide to process the 7 percent increase as a red circle rate 2 percent above the range maximum for an accounting manager. Typically when this is done, the new pay level is frozen until the maximum of the pay range moves upward to exceed the accounting manager's pay level. This would usually happen when the comparative market numbers increase, thereby allowing a change to the pay range.

Green Circle Rates

Green circle rates occur when a new employee is hired at a pay rate lower than the minimum rate for the applicable grade. It can also happen when a "fast track" employee is promoted to a new job in a high pay grade under circumstances where the percentage pay increase needed to reach the new grade is excessive and might create an unwanted precedent. In this case, the pay increase may result in a pay level below the minimum level of the new pay grade, thus creating a "green circle rate."

Situations such as this should be avoided whenever possible and should be allowed only as a last resort because they can create serious morale issues and, even worse, may create an arguable case of pay discrimination. In any case, such actions should be carefully considered and justified in writing after all of the possible consequences are considered.

Cost of Living Adjustments (COLAs)

A cost of living adjustment is a pay increase given to all employees on the basis of market pressure, usually measured against the consumer price index (CPI), which is a measure of the price of goods and services in a given area over a period of time.

COLAs can be paid as a lump sum or over a period of time and usually are a negotiated practice in a unionized environment argued on the basis that they simply reflect the increased cost of living. This argument might be more persuasive during periods of high inflation.

Non-union employers typically resist the pressure to provide COLAs because, once started, they are difficult to stop, thereby diminishing the organization's ability to control its labor costs.

Types of Pay Increases

Pay increases differ depending on the circumstances and the purpose for which they are given. The following are typical pay increases.

General Pay Increases

In some limited circumstances, non-union employers may wish to provide a general pay increase to their employees without the precedent-setting basis of a COLA. A general pay increase is a pay increase given to all employees regardless of their job performance and not linked to market pressures. Usually, the only criteria is the desire to provide all employees a pay increase subject only to the ability to fund the increase.

Seniority Pay Increases

Whenever a pay increase is given based solely on length of service, it is considered a seniority pay increase. As with a general pay increase, it is simply a basis on which to award a pay increase. Seniority pay increases are common in a unionized setting. In a non-union setting, pay increases usually combine seniority with performance.

Lump Sum Increases

A lump sum increase can be either a standalone performance bonus or part of an annual pay increase. Because a lump sum increase is a single lump sum payment, it has some advantages that other pay increases don't have. Most other pay increases impact a series of wage and benefits actions such as base wage, overtime, shift differentials, sick leave, vacation pay, and holiday pay in that each increases in proportion to the size of the increase. This is because most pay increases are added to base pay and paid over a number of pay periods in a year; in other words, creating a proportional increase in all of these wage and benefits categories.

A lump sum increase is a single lump sum payment subject to applicable tax and withholding that is not added to the employee's base rate of pay because of its character as a single lump sum payment. This provides the full cash payment to the employee in a single lump sum payment.

NOTE In a red circle rate situation, the lump sum increase can be used for the amount that would otherwise exceed the range maximum without increasing the employee's base rate of pay beyond the range maximum.

Market-Based Increases

When employee retention is threatened because employee pay is not competitive with the market, employers can create market-based increases to adjust an employee's pay by better matching market levels.

NOTE Market-based pay increases are sometimes called "equity increases."

Pay Differentials

A pay differential is additional compensation paid to an employee as an incentive to accept what would normally be considered as adverse working conditions usually based on time, location, or situational conditions. The same pay differential is paid to all employees under the same circumstances or conditions. Pay differentials benefit the employer by incentivizing employees to accept work they might not otherwise accept; they benefit the employee as additional compensation for accepting the work.

Premium Pay

Some employers pay premium pay, i.e., overtime, at a higher rate than required by law, for working paid holidays or vacation days, for the sixth or seventh day of work in a single workweek, or after eight hours in a day. Premium pay for these working conditions may be company policy, required by a union contract, or required by state law, as it is in California.

NOTE As a matter of principle, the Fair Labor Standards Act (FLSA) recognizes that when state and federal law conflict, the entitlement that is most beneficial or protective for the employee prevails.

Hazard Pay

The hazard pay type of differential pay occurs when employees are called to work under adverse conditions either caused by the environment or due to the circumstances. Work generally considered putting an employee at risk for safety or health purposes would typically qualify for hazard pay differential.

Travel Pay

Hourly (non-exempt) employees typically receive travel pay for time traveling between one location and another under other than routine conditions. Under the Portal-to-Portal Act, normal commute time to and from work is not compensable time but time traveling from one work location to another normally qualifies for travel pay unless the time spent traveling is *de minimis*.

Labor Cost Differentials

Employers differentially structure their local compensation plans to match their competition. In areas where labor rates are high, without a locally differentiating compensation program, employers will be unable to compete for the best available talent thereby sacrificing productivity. In the opposite situation where local labor rates are low, without a locally deferential program, employers increase their labor costs over the local market thereby losing a competitive advantage.

Geographic-Based Differential Pay

Geographic-based differential pay is a type of differential pay that responds to geographic issues associated with where the employee works. Companies with locations in multiple regions of the United States have the challenge of customizing their compensation programs to be locally competitive. The result is a differentially structured pay program designed to respond to the local market in a way that is consistent with the company's strategic objectives.

Location-Based Differentials

Sometimes locations are undesirable because of their remoteness, a lack of amenities, climatic conditions, and other adverse conditions. To attract workers, in extreme cases employers will add a location-based differential to the employee's pay package.

Time-Based Differential Pay

Sometimes called "shift pay," generally, time-based differential pay rewards the employee who works hours normally considered undesirable such as a night shift or hours that are in addition to the employee's regular work schedule, i.e., overtime. Time-based differential pay may be a specified amount per hour or a percentage of the employee's regular rate of pay. Except for overtime, federal law does not legally require employers to pay a differential rate of pay, although state requirements may differ.

Overtime Pay

The Fair Labor Standards Act (FLSA) requires employers to pay non-exempt employees one and a half times their regular rate of pay when they work more than 40 hours in a single workweek.

Some employers pay more than the legally required time-and-a-half rate for overtime. The FLSA allows employers, at their discretion, to pay more than the FLSA requires; they may not pay less.

 NOTE A workweek is a fixed and regularly recurring period of 168 hours, or seven consecutive 24-hour periods.

Regular Rate of Pay

The FLSA requires employers to pay overtime based on an employee's regular rate of pay. Where an employee in a single workweek works at two or more different types of work for which different straight-time rates have been established, the regular rate for that week is the weighted average of such rates. That is, the earnings from all such rates are added together and this total is then divided by the total number of hours worked at all jobs. In addition, section 7(g)(2) of the FLSA allows, under specified conditions, the computation of overtime pay based on one and one-half times the hourly rate in effect when the overtime work is performed. The requirements for computing overtime pay pursuant to section 7(g)(2) are prescribed in 29 CFR 778.415 through 778.421.

Where non-cash payments are made to employees in the form of goods or facilities, the reasonable cost to the employer or fair value of such goods or facilities must be included in the regular rate.

Payroll

Payroll is a function that directly impacts compensation and thereby traditionally affects every employee in the organization. It has traditionally been treated as an administrative function responsible for issuing paychecks and maintaining payroll records. Today's payroll function is responsible for:

- Legal compliance (federal, state, and local)
- Ongoing periodic reporting
- Record generation and maintenance
- Control and security

Payroll integration, the cost of legally compliant payroll services, and the quality of services are all issues that influence the organization's approach to its payroll function. Payroll may be an in-house function, an outsourced function, or some combination of these approaches. In some cases, payroll responsibility may be an HR responsibility although, in most cases, payroll is part of the organization's finance and accounting function. In any case, payroll extensively interacts with HR and vice versa.

Most organizations rely on a combination of technology and automation in an effort to reduce direct payroll costs and the amount of transactional work involved. Employees expect their paychecks to be issued in the correct amount and on time. Their expectations are reinforced by a multitude of legal requirements associated with payroll.

Payroll Administration

Administering the payroll function is complex given the multitude of requirements that must be met, compliance with federal, state, and local legal requirements being chief among the requirements that must be met. Coupled with issuing paychecks, this administrative burden is significant.

Employers are required to keep a master file of employment records for the federal government in addition to an accurate master file to track their labor costs and maintain an organized pay process. This master file must contains information that includes:

- Personal data on each employee (including name, gender, birth date, and Social Security number

- Employment data (including date of hire, hours worked per day and per week, and employee's regular rate of pay)

- Tax and payroll data on each employee (including Form W-4 data, allowances claimed, marital status, time records, and Form W-2 for individual income tax purposes)

- Form 1099 for independent contractors who earn $600 or more for services they provide

- Payroll data for the organization, including Form 941, the employer's quarterly federal tax form with local wages subject to federal, state, and local income taxes; total income; Social Security and Medicare tax withheld; payroll ledgers, worksheets, reconciliation; copies of payroll tax deposit information; and Form W-3 (Transmittal of Wage and Tax Statements sent to the Social Security Administration)

Under the Fair Labor Standards Act (FLSA) and the Age Discrimination in Employment Act (ADEA), employers must retain payroll records for three years. States may have longer retention requirements. Employers may want to retain payroll records at least as long as the applicable state statute of limitations for contracts claims.

After an employee's termination of employment, payroll records should include a copy of the termination record as well as all wages, salaries, commissions, and any other compensation paid to the employee.

Payroll Systems

Most organizations use a computerized payroll system either outsourced or linked to an in-house server as part of an online or networked system. A customized system often includes integrated HRIS and payroll capabilities. This minimizes the chance for data processing error, eliminates redundancies, and ensures the HRIS and payroll systems are current and synchronized.

Other issues that should be considered include the following:

- The system's capability to service the organization's needs. Employees depend on the payroll system to receive timely and accurate paychecks; the organization needs a cost-efficient system that can reliably and dependably meet all of its payroll requirements.

- A good payroll system includes a series of checks and balances designed to accurately produce results with the capabilities to detect error, fraud, or any misuse of data.

- The HRIS and the payroll systems must be compatible. They must be able to share data and make changes to data so that records in one system are accurately and timely reflected in the other system.

- Outsourced payroll services are designed to provide the advantage of overall cost savings, better payroll expertise, accuracy, reliability, and accountability. Choosing a payroll vendor is an important decision that must be carefully made given the significance of the payroll function, and by extension, its link to the HRIS, both critically important to the organization.

Incentive Pay

▪ SPHR ▪ Incentive pay is pay designed to promote a higher level of job performance than otherwise included in the basic design of the job. Some incentive measures include: profits (organization-wide), organization performance, business unit/function/group rewards, and non-financial incentives such as customer satisfaction. Incentive pay plans are highly regulated; as such, legal and accounting expertise should be consulted.

Requirements

Organizational requirements include:

- **A stable base pay plan**   Must be fair and equitable with long-term stability. Staff must be compensated competitively. An incentive plan will not support a base compensation system that is internally or externally inequitable.

- **An existing strategic plan**   Long-term organizational goals, as expressed in the organization's strategic plan, must be clear, consistent, and measurable. There must be stability as measured through the organization's sales volume, expenses, profitability, and customer satisfaction.

- **Complete commitment**   A great deal of effort goes into creating an incentive plan. The plan must be accepted at all levels of management. Continued coaching and training are necessary for long-term stability. Learning must be reinforced by strong support and commitment to achieve desired results using measured output to evaluate performance.

Plan Criteria

The plan must meet the following criteria:

- **It must fit with other programs.** For example, individual sales reward programs must be compatible with larger team recognition and reward programs.

- **It must be in the employee's "line of sight."** Job performance measures should reflect the results the employee actually controls. For example, a laboratory technician's zero-defect completion of a prescribed number of test results within a specified period of time would be a "line of sight" accomplishment.

- **It must have a "sunset clause."** The incentive plan should be in effect for a specific time period with an identified end date for tracking and measurement purposes.

- **It must incorporate both short- and long-term perspectives.** It should be structured to reward short-term goals, i.e., increased production capacity, as well as long-term results, i.e., achieving a strategic growth objective. The short-term perspective may be easier to visualize and achieve but that may not encourage employees to think about long-term results.

Required Internal Processes

In addition to the plan criteria, an organization must consider its internal processes.

- **Good communication is required.** Incentive programs break down when there are barriers to good communication, such as a lack of teamwork, personal grievances, low morale, and other management failures. Good communication must be constant and ongoing. Management will need to share information relative to the organization's overall performance and how performance is rewarded. Employees need to understand their role in their organization's operations.

- **A reliable measurement system is required.** Both management and workers must be able to understand the results achieved and be committed to behaviors that will achieve an incentive plan's established goals.

Types of Incentive Programs

There is no "one size fits all" when it comes to incentive plans. In fact, an effective incentive plan is designed specifically to fit the culture of the organization it supports. Incentive plans can be broken down into three categories: individual programs, group programs, and organization programs.

Individual Incentive Programs

The objective of an individual incentive program is to improve job performance. As such, the individual incentive program must be available to all employees in a particular group. An individual incentive program must be clearly designed and implemented as an incentive separate from an individual's base pay. Individual incentive programs can be either cash-based or non-cash-based.

Cash Awards   Cash award programs reward performance with extra pay based on job performance. The rewards are usually lump sum rewards such as discretionary bonuses based on the judgment of a supervisor or manager, a performance-based bonus based on predetermined performance criteria, and formula-based bonuses based on a percentage of profits or other pre-established measurement.

Non-Cash Awards   Non-cash awards include prizes, gifts, recognition awards, and other similar non-cash items of value to the recipient. Sometimes these awards can be for length of service or contributions in addition to job performance.

NOTE   Although giving cash and non-cash awards appears to be pretty straightforward, in fact, it can be more complicated than circumstances suggest. Some awards have tax implications, so advice might be required from Accounting or your legal counsel as part of developing a cash or non-cash incentive program.

Group Incentive Programs

Incentive programs designed for groups of employees have the objective of rewarding job performance of a group considered necessary to accomplish a unit of work or when the desired result requires a team approach to the work. Group incentive programs can reward both short- and long-term work effort. Often, these programs include financial and non-financial measures as criteria for success. Group incentive programs include profit-sharing plans, gainsharing plans, and group performance incentives—for example, Employee Stock Ownership Plans (ESOPs).

Profit-Sharing Plans   Profit sharing refers to various incentive plans that provide direct or indirect payments to employees that depend on a company's profitability. These payments are in addition to the employees' regular salary and bonuses. In profit-sharing plans, the employer has the discretion to determine when and how much the company will pay into the plan. The contribution and any investment earnings accumulate in the plan on a tax-deferred basis. The IRS taxes these benefits only when employees receive distributions from the plan. A profit-sharing plan can be set up where all or some of the employee's profit sharing amount can be contributed to a retirement plan. These are often used in conjunction with 401(k) plans.

Gainsharing Plans   Gainsharing plans are similar to profit-sharing plans except that gainsharing plans measure the gain achieved from one performance period to the next while profit-sharing plans measure the profit to be shared from period to period. In a gainsharing plan, each member of the unit receives the same reward. Gainsharing measures usually apply to productivity terms while profit-sharing plan measures typically apply to profitability. Three types of gainsharing plans are the Scanlon Plan, the Rucker Plan, and the Improshare Plan.

- **The Scanlon Plan** The Scanlon Plan is the oldest and most widely used type of gainsharing plan. It's based on the historical ratio of labor cost to sales value of production. And, because it rewards labor savings, it is most appropriate for companies that have a "high touch labor" content. The distinctive characteristics of the Scanlon Plan are its philosophy of participative management, administration by a committee of employees and management, and its percentage method of payment. A distinguishing characteristic is that the organization does not have to be profitable for workers to receive an incentive.

- **The Rucker Plan** The Rucker Plan is based on the premise that the ratio of labor costs to production value is historically stable in manufacturing. The Rucker Plan tracks the value added to a product as a measure of productivity. In the Scanlon Plan, a ratio is calculated that expresses the value of production required for each dollar of the total wage cost.

- **Improshare Plan** Improshare measures change in the relationship between outputs and the time required to produce them. This plan uses past production records to establish base performance standards. A standard is developed that identifies the expected number of hours to produce something. Any savings between this standard and actual production are shared between the company and the workers. The organization and its employees share 50/50 in all productivity gains. It is minimally affected by changes in sales volume, technology and capital equipment, product mix, or price and wage increases. It's the easiest of the gainsharing plans to understand and install.

ESOPs (Employee Stock Ownership Plans)

An employee stock ownership plan (ESOP) is a retirement plan in which the company contributes its stock (or money to buy its stock) to the plan for the benefit of the company's employees. The plan maintains an account for each employee participating in the plan. Shares of stock vest over time before an employee is entitled to them. With an ESOP, you never buy or hold the stock directly while still employed with the company. If an employee is terminated, retires, becomes disabled or dies, the plan will distribute the shares of stock in the employee's account.[1]

Executive Incentives

Executives are the people who run the business. Executives form the highest level of management within their organization. In addition to their substantial management responsibilities within their organizations, they develop relationships with people outside their organization with the purpose of improving growth opportunities for their organizations. Their scope of activities and responsibilities impacts their compensation plans in two ways. First, their total compensation package includes their annual cash compensation plus the value of long-term incentives that usually accounts for the larger share of their total package. Second, their incentives are generally linked to the performance of the entire organization's profitability and, in some cases, other non-financial measures such as customer satisfaction and/or meeting certain other strategic objectives.

While there is no single compensation package designed for executives, their pay usually consists of a base salary that is "guaranteed," with other forms of variable (incentive) compensation dependent on performance factors.

Perquisites Special privileges for executives are referred to as "perks." These privileges include club memberships, company cars, reserved parking, and a host of other non-cash benefits. The 1973 Tax Act greatly diminished these perks but they remain a substantial element in an executive's compensation package.

Golden Parachutes These are provisions included in executive employment contracts that provide special payments or benefits to executives under certain adverse conditions such the loss of their position or if they are otherwise adversely impacted by organizational changes. Most often, these impacts are the result of an organizational merger in which there is a change of control that displaces a senior executive. These "golden parachutes" may provide for accelerated payments or early vesting in non-qualified retirement plan options, among other possibilities.

Long-Term Incentives

Long-term incentive plans reward employees for attaining results over a long measurement period. For this purpose, "long-term" generally means more than one year, and typically is between two and five years. Tax-deferred compensation plans, long-term cash plans, and certain stock-based plans are all considered long-term incentives.

The form of payment from a long-term incentive plan is typically cash or equity. An employer might choose one or the other based on the goals of the plan, the recipients of the awards, and the availability of cash or equity for payment.[2]

Incentive Stock Options

There are several varieties of stock options, all of which share some basic characteristics. A stock option is a right to purchase a share of stock in the future at a price determined at the grant (or based on a formula defined at the grant). Incentive Stock Options (ISOs) are a special subset of stock options, satisfying certain criteria promulgated by the Internal Revenue Service and discussed in Internal Revenue Code Section 422.

One of the primary restrictions is that an ISO can only be granted to an employee—ISOs cannot be granted to outside directors, independent contractors, consultants, or any other nonemployees. Also, the recipient must exercise the ISO within three months of terminating employment.

Employee Stock Purchase Plans (ESPP)

ESPP is a company-run program in which participating employees can purchase company shares at a discounted price. Employees contribute to the plan through payroll deductions, which build up between the offering date and the purchase date. At the purchase date, the company uses the accumulated funds to purchase shares in the company on behalf of the participating employees. The amount of the discount depends on the specific plan but can be as much as 15 percent lower than the market price.

Depending on when you sell the shares, the disposition will be classified as either qualified or not qualified. If the position is sold two years after the offering date and at least one year after the purchase date, the shares will fall under a qualified disposition. If the shares are sold within two years of the offering date or one year after the purchase date, the disposition will not be qualified. These positions will have different tax implications.[3]

Phantom Stock Plan

A Phantom Stock Plan is an employee benefit plan that gives selected employees (senior management) many of the benefits of stock ownership without actually giving them any company stock. This is sometimes referred to as "shadow stock."

Rather than getting physical stock, the employee receives "pretend" stock. Even though it's not real, the phantom stock follows the price movement of the company's actual stock, paying out any resulting profits.[4]

Restricted Stock Unit

Restricted stock unit is compensation offered by an employer to an employee in the form of company stock. The employee does not receive the stock immediately, but instead receives it according to a vesting plan and distribution schedule after achieving required performance milestones or upon remaining with the employer for a particular length of time. The restricted stock units (RSUs) are assigned a fair market value when they vest. Upon vesting, they are considered income, and a portion of the shares are withheld to pay income taxes. The employee receives the remaining shares and can sell them at any time.[4]

For example, suppose Madeline receives a job offer. Because the company thinks Madeline's skill set is particularly valuable and hopes she will remain a long-term employee, it offers part of her compensation as 500 RSUs, in addition to a generous salary and benefits. The company's stock is worth $40 per share, making the RSUs potentially worth an additional $20,000. To give Madeline an incentive to stay with the company and receive the 500 shares, it puts them on a five-year vesting schedule. After one year of employment, Madeline will receive 100 shares; after two years, another 100; and so on until she has received all 500 shares at the end of five years. Depending on how the company's stock performs, Madeline may actually receive more or less than $20,000.

Thus, the RSUs give Madeline an incentive not only to stay with the company long term, but to help it perform well so that her shares will become more valuable. In fact, Madeline decides to hold the shares until she receives all 500, at which point the company's stock is worth $50 and Madeline receives $25,000, minus the value of the shares that were withheld for income taxes and the amount due in capital gains taxes. However, if Madeline had left the company after 18 months, she would have received only the 100 shares that vested after year one. She would have forfeited the remaining 400 shares to the company.[5]

Performance Grants

Public companies can also benefit from linking stock-based compensation to organizational performance. If done properly, such an arrangement can qualify as performance-based compensation, which avoids the deduction limits that can be imposed under Code Section 162(m). Such arrangements can also motivate recipients to achieve goals that are valuable to the organization and its shareholders. The accounting consequences of such arrangements can be tricky, and care should be taken to get the views of the organization's accountants.[6]

Sales Personnel Incentive Programs

There are several ways to compensate personnel who are responsible for sales, depending on the circumstances surrounding the sales activities. Compensation usually is both *direct*, that is, paid by cash or by cash and incentives (in turn, incentives can be cash-driven—for example, bonuses and commissions), or *indirect*, that is, paid through perks and entitlements (for example, cars and expense accounts, club membership, and allowances).

Factors that influence the design of a salesperson's compensation plan include:

- The time involved servicing the account as compared to the time spent in the sale of goods or services.
- The ability to objectively measure the sales activity.
- The nature of the sales activity is difficult to distinguish from the activity spent providing support services.
- The degree and type of motivation associated with the sales activity.
- The significance of the sales cost involved in the transaction.
- The comparative market place practice.

Three types of compensation plans are most commonly used:

- Straight salary plans
- Straight commission plans
- Salary plus commission plans

Straight Salary Plans   Of the three types of plans, the straight salary plan is the least used but it more than likely will be found in situations where most of the time involved is spent servicing the account rather than selling the account. It is also more likely when sales costs would otherwise be higher than acceptable to management and finally when, by comparison, the marketplace is more likely to compensate sales on a straight salary basis.

Straight Commission Plans   This is the other extreme of the sales compensation spectrum. In this case, a person's entire salary is paid by commission. This most often occurs when the ultimate objective is the increase sales volume with less emphasis or need for service as well as when the marketplace approach is also to compensate by way of a straight commission plan.

In some cases, organizations that use a straight commission form of compensation will provide what is called a "draw" for novice or entry-level salespersonnel. Typically, the draw consists of a non-recoverable or guaranteed commission for a defined period of time, usually not more than one year. If, during this period, a salesperson does not earn a commission equal to or exceeding the draw, the salesperson does not owe the organization the difference. The period of time the draw is in place usually conforms with the organization's experience in developing the salesperson's selling capabilities to a point the individual is able to earn at least as much or more than the draw provides.

Salary Plus Commission Plans In a salary plus commission arrangement, a portion of the total salary is a fixed salary; the remainder is commission. This is the most popular form of sales compensation in that it incorporates parts of both the fixed salary, thus some stability with the individual's income flow, and the commission or the reward for sales success, thus the incentive for greater future success.

In the Trenches

The Total Rewards Proposition: When $15 per Hour Really Equals $30 per Hour
Larry Bienati, Ph.D., SPHR, CCP, Vice President, Organizational Development, The Cooper Companies, Inc.

When a human resource joins the organization, it is so important to clearly articulate the total rewards/compensation equation (salary + variable compensation + short term benefits + long term benefits + the delta factor). Too often, we focus on base pay, the next pay increase or top-end base compensation, if all performance expectations hold true, in an effort to attract, retain, and motivate that key employee. It is therefore important to promote the value proposition of compensation beyond the base salary. Whether a private, public, or not-for-profit sector organization, you are likely spending 30 percent to 60 percent of the total compensation dollar on what we call direct and indirect compensation. Direct compensation includes salary, bonuses, and other short term incentives. Indirect compensation includes short term and long term incentives like medical, dental, life, disability, sick leave, vacations, educational support, and other variable benefits like 401k offering/matching, profit sharing, pension plans, stock, and other perks. We have a fifth bucket called "the delta factor" or what I call the key differentiator of being a truly great workplace. This includes culture and quality of work-life opportunities that cannot always be measured in hard dollars, but have a profound impact in the retention and job satisfaction proposition. It is the extrinsic and intrinsic value proposition of being a great workplace with high levels of trust, pride, camaraderie, fairness, and sense of place. Not to mention the delicate balance of work-family-career and "give back" to the community you serve.

Enlightened HR/OD professionals who are viewed by their boards and senior management as trusted advisors, are true business partners, and have a respected seat at the c-suite table, believe that your most important organizational human assets come and go each day. Most importantly, these assets may constitute 70 percent of an organization's expense structure. Here is where the ROI and value proposition of enlightened total rewards practices can clearly impact the organization fiscal imperatives.

So, tell the story! Do the math! Set up the formula for your company on a simple Excel spreadsheet; see if your ERP system can offer this calculation, perhaps. Consider reminding your employees of their complete total rewards package on an annual basis each year. I would regularly produce, at the end of the fiscal year, a summary of all elements of total rewards equation, even including the protections offered by social security and other mandated state and federal benefits. When we celebrated another great year, we would present the total rewards package for that year (usually around the Holidays in most companies) so employees could truly appreciate the company's commitment to provide a fair, responsive, and protective compensation offering.

Compensation Administration

The employer's responsibilities administering its compensation practices are, for the most part, governed by the Fair Labor Standards Act (FLSA), commonly referred to as the Wage and Hour Law. The FLSA sets minimum wage standards and overtime pay requirements, and has created restrictions on the engagement of child labor in the workplace. The FLSA is administered by the Wage and Hour Division of the U.S. Department of Labor (DOL).

The DOL has issued a number of guidelines that explain how the FLSA should be interpreted and administered. This information is available on the Internet at www.dol. gove/esa/regs/compliance/whd/fairpay as well as in the following bulletins:

- Regulations, Part 541: Defining the Terms "Executive," "Administrative," Professional," and "Outside Salesman"

- Regulations, Part 778: Interpretive Bulletin on Overtime Compensation

- Interpretive Bulletin, Part 785: Hours Worked Under the Fair Labor Standards Act of 1938

- Child Labor Requirements in Nonagricultural Occupations Under the Fair Labor Standards Act

- Records to Be Kept by Employers Under the FLSA

HR practitioners should make it a point to carefully read and study these publications. Only the major topics will be summarized in this book.[7]

Exempt and Non-Exempt Status

Under the FLSA, most employees must be paid at least the federal minimum wage for all hours worked and overtime at time and a half the employee's regular rate of pay for all hours worked over 40 in a single workweek. Section 13(a) exempts bona fide executive, administrative, professional, outside sales employees, and computer professionals from FLSA's minimum wages and overtime payment requirements but to do this, these exempt employees generally must meet certain salary and job duties tests. Non-exempt employees generally are those who are covered by FLSA's minimum wage and overtime requirements.

Non-exempt employees are employees who are paid on the basis of time—that is, on an hourly basis. They include most manual workers such as technicians, blue collar workers, maintenance and constructions workers, technicians, laborers, and other semi-skilled workers. Job titles do not count. Job content, also called "job duties," are the sole criteria for determining the applicability of the FLSA's minimum wage and overtime requirements.

There are some limited exceptions to these general rules. As an example, certain types of farm workers, baby-sitters, and persons hired as companions for the sick or elderly are treated as exceptions to the general minimum wage and overtime requirements.[8]

Executive Exemption

To qualify for the executive exemption, *all* of the following tests must be met:

- The employee must be compensated on a salary basis at a rate of not less than $455 per week exclusive of board, lodging, or other facilities.

- The employee's primary duty, meaning the major or most important duty the person performs, must be managing the enterprise, or a recognized department or subdivision of the enterprise.

- The employee must customarily and regularly direct the work of two or more other full-time employees or their equivalent.

- The employee must have the authority to hire or fire other employees, or the employee's recommendations about the hiring or firing, advancement, promotion, or any other change of status of other employees must be given particular weight.

Management Generally, "management" includes, but is not limited to, activities such as interviewing, selecting, and training of employees; setting and adjusting their rates of pay and hours of work; directing the work of employees; maintaining production or sales records for use in supervision or control; appraising employees' productivity and efficiency for the purpose of recommending promotions or other changes in status; handling employee complaints and grievances; disciplining employees; planning the work; determining the techniques to be used; apportioning the work among the employees; determining the type of materials, supplies, machinery, equipment, or tools to be used or merchandise to be bought, stocked, and sold; controlling the flow and distribution of materials or merchandise and supplies; providing for the safety and security of the employees or the property; planning and controlling the budget; and monitoring or implementing legal compliance measures.

Administrative Exemption

To qualify for the administrative employee exception, *all* of the following tests must be met:

- The employee must be compensated on a salary basis at a rate of not less than $455 per week exclusive of board, lodging, or other facilities.

- The employee's primary duty is the performance of office or non-manual work directly related to the management or general business operations of the employer or the employer's customers.

- The employee's primary duty includes the exercise of discretion and independent judgment with respect to matters of significance.

Directly Related to Management or General Business Operations An employee's primary duty must be the performance of work directly related to the management or general business operations of the employer or the employer's customers. "Directly related to the management or general business operations" refers to the type of work performed by the employee. To meet this requirement, an employee must perform work directly related to assisting with the running or servicing of the business, as distinguished, for example, from working on a manufacturing production line or selling a product in a retail or service establishment.

Work directly related to management or general business operations includes, but is not limited to: work in functional areas such as tax; finance and accounting; budgeting; auditing; insurance; quality control; procurement; advertising; marketing; research; safety and health; human resources management; employee benefits; labor relations; public relations; government relations; computer network, Internet, and database administration; legal and regulatory compliance; and similar activities. Some of these activities may be performed by employees who also would qualify for another exemption.

An employee may qualify for the administrative exemption if the employee's primary duty is the performance of work directly related to the management or general business operations of the employer's customers. Thus, for example, employees acting as advisers or consultants to their employer's clients or customers (as tax experts or financial consultants, for example) may be exempt.

Discretion and Independent Judgment To qualify for the administrative exemption, an employee's primary duties must include the exercise of discretion and independent judgment with respect to matters of significance. In general, the exercise of discretion and independent judgment involves the comparison and the evaluation of possible courses of conduct, and acting or making a decision after the various possibilities have been considered. The term "matters of significance" refers to the level of importance or consequence of the work performed.

The phrase "discretion and independent judgment" must be applied in the light of all the facts involved in the particular employment situation in which the question arises. Factors to consider when determining whether an employee exercises discretion and independent judgment with respect to matters of significance include, but are not limited to: whether the employee has authority to formulate, affect, interpret, or implement management policies or operating practices; whether the employee carries out major assignments in conducting the operations of the business; whether the employee performs work that affects business operations to a substantial degree, even if the employee's assignments are related to operation of a particular segment of the business; whether the employee has authority to commit the employer in matters that have significant financial impact; whether the employee has authority to waive or deviate from established policies and procedures without prior approval; whether the employee has authority to negotiate and bind the company on significant matters; whether the employee provides consultation or expert advice to management; whether the employee is involved in planning long- or short-term business objectives; whether the employee investigates and resolves matters of significance on behalf of management; and whether the employee represents the company in handling complaints, arbitrating disputes, or resolving grievances.

The exercise of discretion and independent judgment implies that the employee has authority to make an independent choice, free from immediate direction or supervision. However, employees can exercise discretion and independent judgment even if their decisions or recommendations are reviewed at a higher level. Thus, the term "discretion and independent judgment" does not require that the decisions made by an employee have a finality that goes with unlimited authority and a complete absence of review. The decisions made as a result of the exercise of discretion and independent judgment may consist of recommendations for action rather than the actual taking of action. The fact that an employee's decision may be subject to review and that upon occasion the decisions are revised or reversed after review does not mean that the employee is not exercising discretion and independent judgment. For example, the policies formulated by the credit manager of a large corporation may be subject to review by higher company officials who may approve or disapprove these policies. The management consultant who has made a study of the operations of a business and who has drawn a proposed change in organization may have the plan reviewed or revised by superiors before it is submitted to the client.

An employer's volume of business may make it necessary to employ a number of employees to perform the same or similar work. The fact that many employees perform identical work or work of the same relative importance does not mean that the work of each such employee does not involve the exercise of discretion and independent judgment with respect to matters of significance.

The exercise of discretion and independent judgment must be more than the use of skill in applying well-established techniques, procedures, or specific standards described in manuals or other sources. The exercise of discretion and independent judgment also does not include clerical or secretarial work, recording or tabulating data, or performing other mechanical, repetitive, recurrent, or routine work. An employee who simply tabulates data is not exempt, even if labeled as a "statistician."

Educational Establishments The administrative exception also applies to salaried employees whose primary duty is to perform administrative functions directly related to academic instruction or training in an educational establishment such as superintendents of elementary or secondary school system; assistants responsible for matters such as curriculum development, instruction, and testing of students; the principal and any vice principals responsible for the operation of an elementary or secondary school; department heads in institutions of higher learning responsible for various subject matter departments; and other employees with similar responsibilities.

Professional Exemption

The professional exemption includes three types: learned, creative, and teaching. Each type is defined separately according to its own specific duties tests.

To qualify for the learned professional employee exemption, *all* of the following tests must be met:

- The employee must be compensated on a salary or fee basis (as defined in the regulations) at a rate of not less than $455 per week, exclusive of board, lodging or other facilities.

- The employee's primary duty must be the performance of work requiring advanced knowledge, defined as work that is predominantly intellectual in character and that includes work requiring the consistent exercise of discretion and judgment.

- The advanced knowledge must be in a field of science or learning.

- The advanced knowledge must be customarily acquired by a prolonged course of specialized intellectual instruction.

Learned Professional Employee

An exempt "learned" professional employee's primary duty must be the performance of work requiring advanced knowledge in a field of science or learning customarily acquired by a prolonged course of specialized intellectual instruction.

Work Requiring Advanced Knowledge This refers to work that is predominantly intellectual in character, and that includes work requiring the consistent exercise of discretion and judgment. Learned professional work is therefore distinguished from work involving routine mental, manual, mechanical, or physical work. A learned professional employee generally uses the advanced knowledge to analyze, interpret, or make deductions from varying facts or circumstances. Advanced knowledge cannot be attained at the high school level.

Field(s) of Science or Learning   Fields include law; medicine; theology; accounting; actuarial computation; engineering; architecture; teaching; various types of physical, chemical, and biological sciences; pharmacy, and other similar occupations that have a recognized professional status and can be distinguished from the mechanical arts or skilled trades where the knowledge could be of a fairly advanced type, but is not in a field of science or learning.

Customarily Acquired by a Prolonged Course of Specialized Intellectual Instruction   Restricts the learned professional exemption to professions where specialized academic training is a standard prerequisite for entrance into the profession. The best evidence of meeting this requirement is having the appropriate academic degree for the particular profession.

However, the word "customarily" means the exemption is available to employees in such professions who have substantially the same knowledge level and perform substantially the same work as the degreed employees, but who attained the advanced knowledge through a combination of work experience and intellectual instruction. Thus, for example, the learned professional exemption is available to the occasional lawyer who has not gone to law school, or the occasional chemist who does not possess a degree in chemistry. However, the learned professional exemption is not available for occupations that require only a four-year degree in any field or a two-year degree as a prerequisite for entrance into the field. The learned professional exemption is not available for occupations that customarily may be performed with knowledge acquired through an apprenticeship, or with training in the performance of routine mental, manual, mechanical or physical processes. The learned professional exemption also does not apply to occupations in which most employees acquire their skill by experience rather than by advanced specialized intellectual instruction.

Creative Professional Employee

A creative professional employee's primary duty must be the performance of work requiring invention, imagination, originality, or talent in a recognized field of artistic or creative endeavor.

To be exempt as a bona fide "creative" professional employee, *all* of the following tests must be met:

- The employee must be compensated on a salary basis at a rate of not less than $455 per week, exclusive of board, lodging, or other facilities.

- The employee's primary duty must be the performance of work requiring invention, imagination, originality, or talent in a recognized field of artistic or creative endeavor.

An exempt "creative" professional employee's primary duty must be the performance of work requiring invention, imagination, originality, or talent in a recognized field of artistic or creative endeavor, as opposed to routine mental, manual, mechanical or physical work. This requirement distinguishes the creative professions from work that primarily depends on intelligence, diligence, and accuracy.

Bona Fide Teacher Exemption

To be exempt as a bona fide teacher, all of the following tests must be met:

- The employee's primary duty must be teaching, tutoring, instructing, or lecturing in the activity of imparting knowledge.

- The employee must be employed and engaged in the teaching activity as a teacher in an "educational establishment" by which the employee is employed.

There is no minimum salary or "salary basis" requirement applied to teaching professionals. In addition, there is no minimum educational or academic degree requirement for bona fide teaching professionals in educational establishments.

Computer Employee Exemption

To be exempt as a bona fide "computer" employee, *all* of the following tests must be met:

- The employee must be compensated on a salary or fee basis at a rate of not less than $455 per week, or if paid on an hourly basis, at a rate not less than $27.63 per hour.

- The employee must be employed as a computer system analyst, computer programmer, software engineer, or other similarly skilled worker in the computer field performing the duties described below.

  - The application of systems analysis techniques and procedures, including consulting with users, to determine hardware, software or system functional specifications

  - The design, development, documentation, analysis, creation, testing, or modification of computer systems or programs, including prototypes, based on and related to user or system design specifications

  - The design, documentation, testing, creation, or modification of computer programs related to machine operating systems

  - A combination of the aforementioned duties, the performance of which requires the same level of skills

Outside Sales Employees

To be exempt as a bona fide "outside sales" employee, *all* of the following tests must be met:

- The employee's primary duty must be making sales, or obtaining orders or contracts for services or for the use of facilities for which a consideration will be paid by the client or customer.

- The employee must be customarily and regularly engaged away from the employer's place or places of business in performing his or her primary duty. "Primary duty" is defined as the principal, main, major, or most important duty that the employee performs. Determination of an employee's primary duty must be based on all the facts in each case with the major emphasis on the character of the employee's job as a whole. In determining the primary duty of an outside sales employee, work performed incidental to and in conjunction with the employee's own outside sales or solicitations, including incidental deliveries and collections, is considered exempt outside sales work. Other work that furthers the employee's own sales efforts is also considered exempt work— for example, writing sales reports, updating or revising the employee's sales or display catalogue, planning itineraries, and attending sales conferences.

The salary requirements of 29 CFR part 541 do not apply to the outside sales employee exemption.

Human Resources or Personnel Managers

Human resources managers who formulate, interpret, or implement employment policies and management consultants who study the operations of a business and propose changes in organization generally meet the duties requirements for the administrative exemption. Personnel clerks who "screen" applicants to obtain data regarding their minimum qualifications and fitness for employment generally do not meet the duties requirements for the administrative exemption. When the interviewing and screening functions are performed by the human resources manager or personnel manager who makes the hiring decision or makes recommendations for hiring from the pool of qualified applicants, such duties constitute exempt work, even though routine, because this work is directly and closely related to the employee's exempt functions as discussed in 29 CFR § 541.703.

BENEFITS

Strategic Objectives of Benefits

Benefit programs, as we discussed at the beginning of the chapter, also called "indirect compensation," are designed to promote organizational loyalty, reward continued employment, enable employees to live healthy lives, help them care for their families, and help provide for retirement benefits.

In addition to helping employees, benefits programs help employers:

- Attract and retain talent
- Increase the employee's loyalty and commitment to the organization
- Provide tax-advantaged health and welfare benefits

Benefits Needs Assessment

Employee benefits represent a significant financial investment on the part of the employer. To effectively meet its purpose, the employer's total benefits programs must be cost-effective, meet their stated purpose, must be affordable for both the employer and the employee, and must comply with local, state, and federal law. To accomplish these objectives, data must be collected and analyzed to determine whether the employer's benefits programs actually meet its objectives. This process is known as a benefits needs analysis.

A benefits needs analysis consists of several steps that include data collection and analysis culminating in a report called a "gap analysis." This process is as follows:

Reviewing the organization's overall culture and strategy. The results of this effort will determine the potential coverage and scope of its benefits programs.

Collecting and analyzing the employer's workforce demographics. This data is key to determining potential benefits needs.

Analyzing the utilization and costs of existing benefits plans and programs. The results of this data, coupled with the demographics data, will help determine the nature of coverage desired.

Determining potential benefits coverage and costs. This analysis will be an important factor for comparison with the demographics and benefits utilization data.

The final step is to compare the organizational needs and budget with employee needs and any existing benefits coverage. The end result is a gap analysis, a document that will indicate what a benefits package should and should not include.

Federal Legislation Impacting Benefits

Federal, state, and local government play a significant role in the management of compensation, including benefits programs. It is important to know and understand the impact that applicable laws, rules, and regulations have on employer benefits. (see FIgure 9-2). Laws that affect the tax treatment of benefits are listed in Figure 9-3.

- Employee Retirement Income Security Act (ERISA) (1974)

- Consolidated Omnibus Budget Reconciliation Act (COBRA) (1986)

- Older Worker's Benefit Protection Act (OWBPA) (1990)

- Family and Medical Leave Act (FMLA) (1993)

- Mental Health Parity Act (MHPA) (1996)

- Pension Protection Act (PPA) (2006)

- Retirement Equity Act (REI) (1984)

- Health Insurance Portability and Accountability Act (HIPAA) (1996)

- Unemployment Compensation Amendments (UCA) (1992)

- Uniformed Services Employment and Reemployment Rights Act (USERRA) (1994)

- Genetic Information Nondiscrimination Act (GINA) (2008)

- Patient Protection and Affordable Care Act (PPACA) (2010)

Figure 9-2   Key federal laws impacting benefits

- Revenue Act (1978)
- Omnibus Budget Reconciliation Act (OBRA) (1993)
- Tax Relief Act (TRA) (1997)
- Tax Reform Act (1986)
- Small Business Job Protection Act (SBJPA) (1996)
- Economic Growth and Tax Relief Reconciliation Act (EGTRRA) (2001)

Figure 9-3   Key federal laws that affect the tax treatment of benefits

Chapter 2 of this book addresses the provisions of all of the laws identified in Figures 9-2 and 9-3 and discusses their impact on employer benefits programs.

Other related federal legislation includes:

- Securities and Exchange Act
- Sarbanes-Oxley Act

Tax and Accounting Organizations with Benefits Oversight

Private and public tax and accounting organizations play a significant role in affecting employee benefits programs. These organizations include those discussed in the sections that follow.

U.S. Internal Revenue Service (IRS)

The IRS is the revenue service of the United States federal government. It is a bureau under the Department of the Treasury and is responsible for collecting taxes and for the interpretation and enforcement of the Internal Revenue Code. Its regulations effectively influence the types of benefits plans that employers can provide to their employees and the manner in which they fund and operate these plans.

Pension Benefit Guaranty Corporation (PBGC)

The PBGC is an independent agency of the United States Government that was created by the Employee Retirement Income Security Act of 1974 (ERISA). Its purpose is to encourage the continuation and maintenance of voluntary defined benefit pension plans, ensure the timely and uninterrupted payment of pension benefits to retirees, and keep pension insurance premiums at the lowest level necessary to carry out its operations. The PBGC is not funded by general tax revenues. Rather, its funds come from insurance premiums paid by sponsors of defined benefit plans—in some cases, assets held by pension plans it takes over, recoveries of unfunded pension liabilities, and investment income.

Financial Accounting Standards Board (FASB)

The FASB is a private, not-for-profit organization whose primary purpose is to develop generally accepted accounting principles (GAAP) in the public's interest within the United States. The Securities and Exchange Commission (SEC) designated the FASB as the organization responsible for setting accounting standards for public companies in the United States. In this role, the FASB-established standards impact the accounting practices of public companies and how they report their financial information to their shareholders.

Fiduciary Responsibilities

The Department of Labor ascribes the fiduciary responsibilities created by the Employee Retirement Income Security Act (ERISA) relative to those persons or entities who exercise discretionary control or authority over plan management or plan assets, have discretionary authority or responsibility for the administration of a plan, or provide investment advice to a plan for compensation or have any authority or responsibility to do so.

The primary responsibility of fiduciaries is to run the plan solely in the interest of participants and beneficiaries and for the exclusive purpose of providing benefits and paying plan expenses. Fiduciaries must act prudently and must diversify the plan's investments in order to minimize the risk of large losses. In addition, they must follow the terms of plan documents to the extent that the plan terms are consistent with ERISA. They also must avoid conflicts of interest. In other words, they may not engage in transactions on behalf of the plan that benefit parties related to the plan, such as other fiduciaries, services providers, or the plan sponsor.[9]

Government-Mandated Benefits

Some benefits are mandated by law. They must be provided and cannot be altered by the employer even when the employer may feel they are not necessary. Currently, federal law mandates Social Security/Medicare, healthcare under the Patient Protection and Affordable Care Act (PPACA), unemployment insurance, workers' compensation, COBRA, and FMLA. The PPACA, COBRA, and FMLA are described in detail in Chapter 2.

Social Security

Social Security originally was intended to provide retirement income for older workers. It has since expanded to include retirement, disability, death, and survivors' benefits. For tax purposes, the system is split into two programs, Social Security and Medicare. To qualify for Social Security, a person must earn a number of "quarters," usually 40 quarters, which takes at least ten years.

There is no age limit for Social Security. Employees who continue to work while receiving Social Security payments must also pay into it. The employer matches the employee's contributions; independent contractors and self-employed individuals pay both the employer's and the employee's share of the tax. The amount of monthly retirement income depends on the individual's average earnings on jobs covered by Social Security. Workers can begin to receive reduced benefits at age 62 but are entitled to full benefits if they wait until their retirement age, which is determined on a graduated scale.

Disability Benefits

Disability benefits are paid to workers if they have a medically determined physical or mental impairment that keeps them from working for at least five months and is expected to continue to at least one year or result in death. There is a five-month waiting period before monthly benefits start.

Survivor Benefits

Survivor benefits are paid monthly to eligible dependents who are:

- Surviving spouse age 60 or older (50 if disabled)
- Surviving spouse at any age caring for a child under age of 16 or disabled
- Unmarried children under age 18
- Disabled children of any age if disabled before age 22
- Dependent parents age 62 or older

Medicare

Medicare covers hospital insurance (Part A) and voluntary supplemental medical insurance (Part B) for people who reach age 65. If an employer provides health insurance coverage, the employer's health plan must be the primary healthcare plan for active employees. If the individual is retired, Medicare is the primary carrier and the employer's insurance is secondary. If the employer has less than 20 employees, Medicare can be primary for employees age 65 and older.

Medicare provides voluntary Part C (Medicare Advantage Plans). These plans allow an individual to participate in several optional healthcare delivery systems such as HMOs and PPOs, which offer extra coverage beyond Parts A and B and usually include prescription drug coverage.

Part D (prescription benefits) coverage is also optionally provided by private companies, but all Medicare plans must provide a minimum standard level of coverage. Benefits vary depending on the drug plan selected.

EEOC Ruling on Medicare

Effective December 26, 2007, an EEOC ruling allows employers to reduce health benefits for Medicare-eligible retirees in order to avoid paying premiums that are higher than those paid for retirees not covered by Medicare. If an employer provides retiree health benefits, the health insurance benefits received by Medicare-eligible retirees can be the same, or cost the same, as health insurance benefits received by younger retirees.

Unemployment Insurance (UI)

Unemployment insurance is a federally mandated program administered by the states that provides unemployment benefits to eligible workers who are unemployed through no fault of their own and who meet other eligibility requirements of applicable state law. UI benefits are designed to provide temporary financial assistance to unemployed workers. Each state administers its own unemployment insurance program within guidelines established by federal law. Eligibility for unemployment insurance, benefit amounts, and the length of time benefits are available are determined by state law. In the majority of states, benefit funding is based solely on a tax imposed on employers. The amount a person receives is based on the person's salary up to a monthly maximum amount.

Eligibility

To qualify for UI, individuals must meet requirements for wages earned or time worked during an established period of time referred to as the "base period." In most cases, the individual must be unemployed through no fault of his or her own; must be available and actively seeking work; cannot be terminated for misconduct; and must not be unemployed because of a labor dispute.

Individuals must file weekly or biweekly claims and respond to questions concerning their continuing unemployment. Any job offers or refusal of work must be reported for the period claimed.

Duration

Most states grant UI benefits for up to 26 weeks, but this is often extended during periods of high unemployment by Congress with the approval of the President.

Workers' Compensation

Workers' compensation is a type of insurance paid for by the employer that provides wage replacement income and medical care benefits to employees who suffer work-related injuries or illnesses in return for giving up the employee's right to sue his or her employer for negligence. Benefits are regulated by the states, not the federal government. Individual states prescribe the rules governing coverage, eligibility, types of benefits, and the funding of benefits.

Work-Related Disability

Workers' compensation defines a work-related disability as a physical condition that can result in an accident or illness and is caused, aggravated, precipitated, or accelerated by a work activity or environment. Workers' compensation only covers worker health problems that are identified as work-related disabilities, injuries, or illnesses.

Workers' compensation benefits include the following:

- Paid medical expenses and wage replacement benefits under certain circumstances
- Four types of workers' wage replacement benefits:

- **Income benefits** These benefits replace income that might be lost because of a work-related injury or illness. Income benefits can include temporary income benefits, impairment income benefits, supplemental income benefits, and lifetime income benefits.

- **Medical benefits** These benefits pay for necessary medical care to treat a work-related injury or illness.

- **Death benefits** These benefits replace a portion of lost family income for eligible family members of employees who are killed on the job.

- **Burial benefits** These benefits pay for some of the deceased employee's funeral expenses to the person who paid the expenses.

- Vocational rehabilitation or, in some cases, supplemental job displacement benefits

- Permanent and temporary partial or total disability benefits

- Survivor's benefits in cases of fatal work-injuries or illnesses

Healthcare Benefits

Health insurance is a major benefit to the average American worker. Although considered an essential part of a worker's benefits package, it was not a legally mandatory benefits program until the March 2010 enactment of the Patient Protection and Affordable Care Act (PPACA), also referred to as the "Affordable Care Act" (ACA) or "Obamacare." The goal of this law is to increase the quality and affordability of health coverage by expanding public and private insurance coverage and reducing the costs of healthcare for individuals and the government. The law includes mandates and subsidies, and creates new insurance exchanges to accomplish its goals. It makes health insurance coverage mandatory for individuals either through their employers or through newly created state health insurance exchanges.

The U.S. Supreme Court upheld the constitutionality of the ACA's individual mandate as an exercise of Congress's taxing power in 2012. The law and its implementation continues to face challenges in Congress and the federal courts as well as some state governments, certain advocacy groups, and private business associations.

Most employers offer one or more types of medical plans.

Fee-for-Service Plans

In the past, this was the traditional health plan sponsored by employers. In recent years, the fee-for-service plan has been largely replaced with various types of managed care plans. In a fee-for-service health plan, subscribers can go to any qualified physician, healthcare provider, hospital, or medical clinic and submit claims to the insurance company. Fees are generated on the basis of the service provided, thereby creating an incentive for the medical provider to provide more services.

Managed Care Plans

The concept behind the managed care plan is that this plan is structured to provide managed care to its subscribers. The core objective of a managed care plan is that the medical care a subscriber receives is medically necessary and provided in a cost-effective manner. All of the managed care plans typically offer basic medical coverage including hospitalization, outpatient services, doctor visits, and some forms of extended care.

Health Maintenance Organization (HMO)

The most common type of managed care plan is the Health Maintenance Organization (HMO) plan. The HMO plan is a capitated health care plan in which the health care provider is paid on a capitated basis, that is, on a "per person" basis rather than on the basis of the services provided. Members enroll by paying a monthly or annual fee. Members must use HMO healthcare providers and facilities in order for their expenses to be covered under their plan. HMO plans are relatively low-cost and often do away with claims and reimbursements when services are provided under their plan. Two types of HMOs include the individual practice association (IPA) where groups of healthcare providers in private practice also provide services through the HMO and staff model HMOs in which the healthcare providers are directly employed by the HMO. Kaiser Permanente is an HMO organized under the staff model concept.

Some other types of HMOs include those described in the material that follows.

Preferred Provider Organization (PPO)   A Preferred Provider Organization plan includes an in-network and an out-of-network option. PPO plans are one of the most popular types of plans in the health insurance market. PPO plans allow you to visit whatever in-network physician or healthcare provider you wish without first requiring a referral from a primary care physician. In-network services receive discounted copayments or deductibles. The out-of-network option provides access to the physicians and healthcare providers who are "out of network" but with higher copayments and deductibles. PPOs simply provide a wider range of medical choices and costs.

Point of Service (POS)   A Point of Service (POS) plan has some of the qualities of HMO and PPO plans with benefit levels varying depending on whether your care is received in or out of the health insurance company's network of providers. Like an HMO plan, the subscriber may be required to designate a primary care physician (PCP) who will then make referrals to network specialists when needed. Depending upon the plan, services rendered by the PCP are typically not subject to a deductible. Under the ACA requirements beginning 2014, preventive care benefits are included at no cost. Like a PPO plan, the subscriber may receive care from out-of-network providers but with greater out-of-pocket costs. Subscribers may also be responsible for copayments, coinsurance, and an annual deductible.

Prescription Drug Plans

Most non-Medicare prescription drug plans require a minimum copayment for prescriptions or a percentage of the cost subject to a minimum and ceiling. In some cases, plans may also require the use of generic-brand drugs or the use of formulary drugs. Some plans require subscribers to fill their prescriptions at specified pharmacies at a predetermined cost.

Dental Plans

Dental plan coverage is generally subject to a high adverse selection rate; that is, subscribers with dental issues are more likely to enroll in a dental plan than those who do not have dental issues. This affects the cost of coverage. To avoid the resulting cost issues, underwriting an employer-sponsored dental plan may require high enrollments, often with a cap on the benefits. Other approaches include a managed care form of coverage with coverage restricted only to network providers. Another approach is the indemnity plan style coverage in the form of reimbursements based on reasonable and customary charges regardless of the provider.

Vision Care Plans

Vision plans generally limit the frequency of coverage along with monetary cap on coverage. The majority of plans limit new lenses, frames, or contact lenses. In addition, most plans place a monetary cap on allowances for a standard set of lenses, frames, or contact lenses. Some plans provide discounts for laser vision correction surgery.

Healthcare Funding

Employers have some flexibility in how they fund their healthcare coverage, ranging from fully funded plans to self-funded plans.

Fully Funded Plans

In a fully funded plan, the employer pays the insurance carrier premiums that cover all of the costs associated with the level and type of coverage. This includes the insurance carrier's cost of coverage for medical charges, administrative costs, sales commissions, fringe costs, taxes and profits. On an annual basis, the carrier adjusts their premiums to coordinate with the employer's claims experience. In the fully funded plan, the carrier bears all of the risk; the carrier experiences either profits or losses based on its underwriting acumen. State insurance laws govern the terms and conditions within their state and vary from state to state.

Minimum Premium Plan

A minimum premium plan is a variation of a fully insured plan. This approach shifts some of the risk to the employer. When there are fewer claims, and therefore lower costs, in the previous year, the minimum premium plan passes a percentage of the savings to the employer. Conversely, when there are more claims, and therefore more costs, the employer potentially pays more.

Self-Funded Plans

When the employer has a self-funded health plan, the employer takes on the role of the insurance carrier and assumes all or most of the risk. Self-funded arrangements are subject to annual non-discrimination testing requirements to ensure the plan does not discriminate in favor of highly compensated employees either in eligibility for coverage or benefits. There are two different approaches to self-funded plans:

- **Administrative Services Only (ASO) plan**   In the ASO plan, all of the risk is assumed by the employer. The employer hires only the claims department of the insurance company for its claims services.
- **Third-Party Administrator (TPA) plan**   In the TPA plan as in the ASO plan, the employer assumes all of the risk. The employer hires an independent (not an insurance company's) claims department.

Because there is no insurance involved in an employer's self-funded benefits plan, state insurance laws cannot dictate the content and coverage of such plans because ERISA preempts state rights to regulate employee benefit plans except for the regulation of insurance.

Partially Self-Funded Plans

With partially self-funded plans, the employer purchases one or two types of stop-loss insurance coverage, either specific and/or aggregate stop-loss coverage:

- **Specific Stop-Loss Coverage**   Under this type of stop-loss coverage, the plan is protected against the risk of a major illness for one participant, or one family unit, covered by the plan.
- **Aggregate Stop-Loss Coverage**   Under this type of stop-loss coverage, the plan is protected against the risk of large total claims from all participants during the plan year.

Typically, partially self-funded plans utilize the administrative services of either an ASO or TPA as described previously.

Health Insurance Purchasing Cooperatives (HIPCs)

HIPCs act as purchasing agents for large group of employers. They use the size of the cooperative over the sized of the individual organizations to negotiate and purchase health insurance plans for their members. Their goal is to provide small organizations the advantage of their size in negotiating health plan contracts.

Healthcare Costs

All organizations are concerned with their ability to manage or control their healthcare costs. The following are some actions that can help with this effort:

- *Change the delivery system.* The type of healthcare delivery system has a major effect on costs. Managed care systems include HMOs and PPOs. HIPCs can help by negotiating better terms than might otherwise be possible with direct negotiations between the carrier and the organization.

- *Let employees choose.* Provide a benefits program with choices such as an HMO and a PPO or an indemnity plan. This is a way to avoid offering healthcare services that are not wanted or needed.

- *Redesign the programs.* Examine the balance between the employer share and the employee share of the premium. Changing the balance can also include:

  - Increasing deductibles and out-or-pocket requirements. Employers can mitigate shifting the burden to employees by allowing employees to pay these costs through pretax Section 125 healthcare spending accounts.

  - Requiring generic substitutions and/or mail-order drugs.

- *Promote prevention and wellness.* A number of programs can help:

  - Incentives for quitting smoking

  - On-site fitness facilities and/or discount memberships to off-site facilities

  - Health risk assessment programs

  - Encouraging healthy and safe behaviors—for example, promoting bicycling, and so on.

High-Deductible Health Plans

The objective of consumer-directed healthcare accounts is to allow employees to make more decisions about their healthcare while helping employer better control their costs. Health reimbursement accounts (HRAs) and health savings accounts (HSAs) are two types of consumer-directed healthcare programs. These programs help employers lower their costs and allow employees with set-aside money to pay for out-of-pocket medical and medical-related expenses. These plans are particularly attractive to younger healthy employees who don't want the financial burden of a health plan that does not match their needs but still want healthcare coverage for major injuries and illnesses.

Health Reimbursement Accounts

The HRA is a tax-advantaged benefit that allows both employees and employers to save on the cost of healthcare. HRA plans are employer-funded medical reimbursement plans. The employer sets aside a specific amount of pre-tax dollars for employees to pay for healthcare expenses on an annual basis. Based on the plan design, HRAs can generate significant savings in overall health benefits. The primary requirements for an

HRA are that (1) the plan must be funded solely by the employer and cannot be funded by salary reduction, and (2) the plan may provide benefits for substantiated medical expenses only. HRAs may be designed in many fashions to suit the specific needs of employer and employees alike. It is one of the most flexible types of employee benefits plans, making it very attractive to most employers.

Health Savings Accounts

The HSA is a tax-advantaged medical savings account available to taxpayers in the United States who are enrolled in a high-deductible health plan. The funds contributed to an account are not subject to federal income tax at the time of deposit. Unlike a flexible spending account (FSA), funds roll over and accumulate year to year if not spent. HSAs are owned by the individual, which differentiates them from company-owned health reimbursement accounts that are an alternate tax-deductible source of funds paired with either high-deductible or standard health plans. HSA funds may currently be used to pay for qualified medical expenses at any time without federal tax liability or penalty. However, over-the-counter medications cannot be paid with HSA dollars without a doctor's prescription. Withdrawals for non-medical expenses are treated very similarly to those in an individual retirement account (IRA) in that they may provide tax advantages if taken after retirement age and they incur penalties if taken earlier.

Section 125 Cafeteria (Flexible Benefit) Plans

A Cafeteria Plan (includes Premium Only Plans and Flexible Spending Accounts) is an employee benefits program designed to take advantage of Section 125 of the Internal Revenue Code. A Cafeteria Plan allows employees to pay certain qualified expenses (such as health insurance premiums) on a pre-tax basis, thereby reducing their total taxable income and increasing their spendable/take-home income. Funds set aside in Flexible Spending Accounts (FSAs) are not subject to federal, state, or Social Security taxes.

Premium Only Plan (POP)

Employers may deduct the employee's portion of the company-sponsored insurance premium directly from said employee's paycheck before taxes are deducted.

Flexible Spending Account (FSA)

In an FSA, employees may set aside a pre-established amount of money on a pre-tax basis per plan year. The employee can use the funds in the FSA to pay for eligible medical, dependent care, or transportation expenses.

Employers may add an FSA Plan as a key element in their overall benefit package. Because an FSA Plan offers a tax advantage, employers experience tax savings from reduced FICA, FUTA, SUTA, and workers' compensation taxes on participating employees. These tax savings reduce or eliminate altogether the various costs associated with offering the plan. Meanwhile, employee satisfaction is heightened because participating employees experience a "raise" at no additional cost to the employer.

An employee who participates in the FSA must place a certain dollar amount into the FSA each year. This "election" amount is automatically deducted from the employee's check (for that amount divided by the number of payroll periods). For example, an employee is paid 24 times a year, and elects to put $480 in the FSA. Thus, $20 is deducted pre-tax from each paycheck and is held in an account (by the plan administrator) to be reimbursed upon request.

Plan Year and Grace Period

The plan year for the Section 125 Plan is one full year (365 days) and generally begins on the first of a month. Many employers design their flexible spending plan to run on the same plan year as their insurance program. Short plan years are allowed in certain instances.

The grace period is a timeframe up to 75 days after the end of the official plan year during which employees may use up any funds remaining at the end of the plan year. For example, if the plan year runs from July 1 through June 30, the grace period for that plan may continue up to September 15. If an employee incurs an expense after June 30 but before September 15, he can utilize the remaining funds from the previous plan year and submit requests for reimbursement. In addition to the 75-day grace period, plan participants have an additional 90-day run-out period in which they can submit requests for reimbursement for expenses incurred during the dates of service within the plan year and grace period.

Uniform Coverage

Uniform coverage is an aspect of Section 125 that allows an employee to be reimbursed for qualified medical expenses that exceed their contributions to date. While this is a great benefit for the employee, it poses a potential risk to the employer. A case in point is when an employee terminates with a negative balance in her medical FSA. This risk should be offset because some other employees do not spend all of their FSA funds, so the risk is minimal.

This rule states that for the medical expense account, a participant may claim the full amount of her annual election even if she has contributed only a portion of the total. For example, Sue Summers decides to contribute $480 for the year to her FSA account. To accomplish this, $20 is deducted pre-tax from each of her 24 payrolls for the year. Her plan starts in January. In March, Sue experiences a medical expense that costs $400. To date, she has contributed only $20 on six payrolls, meaning she has only $120 actual dollars in her FSA account. However, due to the uniform coverage rule she can claim and be reimbursed for the full $400 because of the assumption that her biweekly contributions will continue and she will eventually contribute the $480 total. This honor system is a huge advantage for participants, and allows them to experience medical expenses at any time of the year with no worry about having the funds available at the time the expense is incurred.

Uniform coverage applies to the medical FSA only; it does not apply to a Dependent Care FSA.

NOTE With a Dependent Care FSA account, a participant's reimbursement may not exceed the balance in the FSA account at the time the claim was made.

The Use-It-Or-Lose-It Rule

This rule states that any funds remaining in the participating employee's FSA account at the end of the plan year will be forfeited to the employer. Although the rule is clear, many users of an FSA largely misunderstand the result of the rule: Loss of funds can be easily avoided.

Let's look at an example: Joe Smith chooses to participate in the FSA and elects to fund $500 for the year. After the plan year and grace period are complete, Joe finds that he spent only $400 of the original $500 he put away. He fears he has lost $100, but due to the taxes he saved on the $500 he has not. Let's say Joe is in the 28 percent tax bracket. By putting $500 away in his FSA, he saved $140 in taxes (money that was not taken out of his paycheck and given to the IRS). In sum, even if Joe leaves $100 in his FSA account, he has still saved $40! This vital key issue must be explained completely to potential FSA participants.

The maximum amount of salary reduction contributions that the participant is permitted to make under §125(i) of the Code is $2,500; this remains the same for 2014.

Cafeteria Plans are qualified, non-discriminatory benefit plans, meaning a discrimination test must be met based on the elections of the participants combined with any contribution by the employer.

Nondiscrimination Testing

Section 125 of the Internal Revenue Code requires that Cafeteria Plans be offered on a nondiscriminatory basis. To ensure compliance, the Internal Revenue Code sets forth testing requirements that must be satisfied. These testing requirements are in place to make certain that Cafeteria Plan benefits are available to all eligible employees under the same terms, and that the plan does not favor highly compensated employees, officers, and owners.

Full Cafeteria Plans

A full Cafeteria Benefits Plan allows employees to choose from a menu of eligible qualified benefits prior to the start of the plan year or coverage period. In these types of plans, employees typically are given credits that they can spend on a variety of qualified benefit items choosing not only between different benefits but also choosing items within a given benefit. As an example, an employee may choose to use his/her credits for additional disability coverage while purchasing a more conservative health option. In some cases, employees may cash out unused credits or buy additional benefits through pre-tax salary.

Common Benefits Provided to Employees

A number of benefits help employers to attract and retain employees. The following list provides a brief overview of tangible benefits that many employers provide:

- Disability benefits
- Life insurance
- Long-term care insurance
- Employee assistance programs (EAPs)
- Supplemental unemployment benefits (SUBs)
- Paid time off (PTO)
- Paid leaves

Disability Benefits

Employer disability plans normally cover three phases:

- **Employer sick leave** Sick leave provided by employer policies typically pay 100 percent of pay for a specified number of accrued days. Accrual is usually based on length of employment and subject to a maximum cap. Absences due to employee illness or injury and, in many cases, that of a family member are covered. Absences that exceed the average accrual rate may be covered by short-term disability.

- **Short-Term Disability (STD)** This coverage usually begins where sick leave ends. STD typically covers only a portion of lost income and may require a waiting period. In some cases, organizations may self-fund their STD. Typically, STD provides up to 50 to 70 percent of coverage of the employee's base salary up to six months.
  Five states have mandated short-term disability plans. They include: California, Hawaii, New Jersey, New York, and Rhode Island. In addition, Puerto Rico also has mandatory insurance requirements.

- **Long-Term Disability (LTD)** LTD coverage usually begins after short-term disability coverage ends. LTD is always underwritten by a commercial insurance company due to the risk associated with the coverage. When a disabled employee is also eligible for Social Security disability benefits, the LTD is often integrated with the Social Security coverage to avoid duplication of coverage. When employees go on LTD, their employment ends with their organization even though they are collecting LTD benefits.
  During their first two years of LTD coverage, individuals must be unable to perform their own occupation. After two years, a person must be unable to engage in any occupation or do any work to continue on LTD (unless their plan indicates otherwise).
  Benefits cease when a person returns to work or dies prior to normal retirement age. There are no income levels applicable to LTD coverage.

Life Insurance

Employees are concerned about care for their families if they were to die prematurely, leaving their families without adequate resources. Group term life insurance provides benefits that address this issue.

Group term life insurance provides a lump sum benefit to beneficiaries. The benefit may be in the form of a flat amount or a multiple of salary. Also, the amount may vary by length of service or position.

 NOTE Many employers keep the value of the group term life insurance to $50,000 because plans kept at that level or less are not taxable when nondiscriminatory. When plans are over $50,000, the amount over $50,000 is referred to as excess group-term life insurance and treated by the IRS as imputed income subject to tax. Imputed income is added to other income and appears on the employee's W-2 Form.

Long-Term Care (LTC) Insurance

Long-term care (LTC) insurance covers the cost of long-term care in a number of settings including care at home, in an assisted living facility, in a nursing home, or as an inpatient in a hospice. If LTC is offered, it must provide care for people who are chronically ill for at least 90 days. The premium payments are not counted as employee income and employers can deduct their part of the insurance premiums from their annual income tax liability.

Employee Assistance Programs (EAPs)

Employee assistance programs (EAPs) are employer-sponsored benefits that provide a number of services that help promote the physical, mental, and emotional wellness of individual employees who otherwise would be negatively impacted by health-related crises. EAPs help employees find professional resources to deal with their problems. Services are provided by licensed counselors typically through third-party organizations with a high degree of confidentiality for employees. Depending on the specific program, services can help employees meet personal goals, reduce stress and anxiety, and improve overall emotional and physical health.

Supplemental Unemployment Benefits (SUBs)

Supplemental unemployment benefits (SUBs) are unemployment benefits in addition to government benefits offered by some employers. SUBs are common in union environments. Under the Internal Revenue Code, SUBs may be exempt from federal income taxes for employers but not for employees.

Paid Time Off (PTO)

Many employers combine vacation and sick leave into a single program called "paid time off" or "PTO." PTO is a concept that allows employees to earn, typically by accrual over time, credits that the employee can then use whenever circumstances require that they be absent from work. PTO does not require justification for an absence, simply an approval in the event of a planned absence or the accrued balance to be used in an unplanned absence.

NOTE   In some states where PTO is offered, PTO accrual is treated in the same manner as vacation; that is, PTO is subject to the same rules that are applicable to vacation.

Paid Leaves

Many employers have found that paid time off as a reward for service provides the employee with relief from the ongoing demands of work as well as benefits the employer with increased morale and commitment. Types of paid leaves are described in the sections that follow.

Paid Holidays

While paid holidays are not legally required, employers find that both employers and employees benefit from them. The number of paid holidays vary from 6 to 12 a year, including New Year's Day, Memorial Day, Independence Day, Labor Day, Thanksgiving Day, and Christmas Day. Paid holidays are generally paid on the basis of the employer's schedule for a regular workday.

Paid Vacation

The standard vacation is based on an accrual system measured on an employee's length of service. State laws vary on the management of vacation accrual. Some states do not allow a "use-it-or-lose-it" policy, while others are silent on the subject. In some cases, vacation can be carried over from year to year with a provision for a reasonable cap. Many employers have a cash-out policy that allows an employee in states in which there is no rollover who hasn't taken his or her accrued vacation by the end of the year, to receive cash back for their unused accrued vacation. Generally, employees must receive advance approval to use their vacation so as not to disrupt the employer's work flow.

Sick Leave

Organizations that otherwise have paid vacation policies usually also have paid sick leave policies to provide for time off due to illness or injury. These sick leave programs are primarily intended for the benefit of the employee although in recent years, sick leave programs have often been expanded to cover an employee's time off to care for a family member. Some states mandate that a portion of the employee's sick leave accrual must be allowed for family care.

Sabbatical

Some professions or industries allow long-term employees to take a paid leave of absence as a way to complete a course of study, do research, or engage in other learned pursuits. This practice is particularly evident in the teaching profession although not restricted only to that profession. Some organizations allow its long-term employees with high-balance sick leave accounts to take extended unpaid time off with the opportunity to use a portion of their sick leave for paid time off during this absence.

Bereavement Leave

Most organizations have policies that provide for paid time off to attend a funeral of a family member. In some cases, this benefit is available to extended family members as well as close friends.

Personal (Floating) Days

Many organizations allow a limited number of paid days off for employees' personal needs. These are often referred to as "floating holidays" because when they are taken is determined by the employee. Typically, approval is required in advance. Because these paid days off are determined by the employee, some states apply the same rules to these days as they do to vacation or PTO.

Severance Packages

While not legally required, some organizations give employees who are terminated for a reason other than cause a severance package, which may include:

- Salary continuation for a specified period of time (for example, one week of pay for each year of service)

- Outplacement services such as resume assistance, interview preparation and placement counseling, testing, and job search assistance

- Retraining in some cases

- Paid benefits premium assistance for a limited period of time

Severance packages may have legal implications. As such, legal assistance should be sought whenever circumstances arise that include a potential severance package.

Less Common Benefits Provided to Employees

Employers have other benefits options less commonly provided to employees that can be considered. Such benefits should be formally published in an employee handbook as a way to ensure consistent and fair treatment of employees as well as for legal liability protection.

Childcare Services

Employers can provide a variety of childcare services to help working parents deal with the ongoing needs of pre-school or school-aged children:

- Supportive time-off policies
- Resource and referral services to identify available community services and childcare providers
- Direct financial assistance through a flexible benefit program (Section 125 Program)
- A flex-time program for working hours
- Work options such as job sharing and part-time work

Elder Care

Demographic changes often place family support pressures on employees and their elders as well as their children. Organization support services include:

- Supportive time-off policies
- Employer-sponsored group long-term care insurance
- Counseling assistance through an EAP
- Resource and referral services
- A flex-time program for working hours

Commuter Assistance

Most organizations have a significant number of employees who commute to work in their own car because the cost of public transit is either too expensive or not easily accessible to satisfy the employee's work requirements. Some organizational support services that can help include:

- Resource and referral services
- A flex-time program for working hours
- Mass transit cost assistance (tokens, transit passes, and so on)
- Van pooling or carpooling assistance
- Dedicated parking for employees at or near the employee's place of employment

Tuition Reimbursement

Many employers support employee education development by providing financial support to employees who undertake local educational courses related to their work or for general professional development purposes at recognized educational institutions. In some cases, employer tuition reimbursement programs also provide financial support for books and other ancillary supplies. In most cases, employers require a passing grade in order to qualify for tuition reimbursement support. There is an annual dollar limit on the amount of reimbursement eligible for income inclusion for tax purposes.

Prepaid Legal Insurance

Although not as popular as it was several years ago, some employers continue to provide prepaid legal insurance that covers the cost of routine legal services such as developing a will and assistance with real estate matters, divorces, and other basic legal assistance. This often is a relatively high-cost benefit that is utilized by a relative few employees, which may explain why this benefit is not widespread.

Benefits—Taxable and Non-Taxable

Employee benefits fall into two categories: taxable and non-taxable benefits. Both categories include direct compensation and indirect compensation (employer-paid coverage or reimbursements). Table 9-7 identifies some of the benefits we've discussed in this chapter in each category (the list is only generally indicative; it is not all-inclusive).

	Taxable Benefits	Non-Taxable Benefits
Direct Compensation	• Base pay • Differential pay • Severance pay • Paid time off	• Wages paid after death in a new year
Indirect Compensation	Employer paid or reimbursed: • Disability benefits when employer pays the premium • Life insurance when employee pays with pretax dollars • Gifts, prizes, and awards over certain dollar amounts • Personal use of a company vehicle • Sick pay	Employer paid or reimbursed: • Work-related expense reimbursements • Childcare (subject to limitations) • Company vehicle use (only work-related) • De minimis ($25 or less) • Group life insurance plans, $50,000 or less coverage • Educational expenses (subject to annual limits) • Medical, dental, health plans (employer contributions) • Employee-paid disability benefits when purchased with after-tax dollars

Table 9-7 Taxable and Non-Taxable Benefits

Evaluating and Communicating Compensation and Benefits Programs

HR's responsibility is to know whether an organization's compensation and benefits program is effective. Key questions that HR must be able to answer include:

- Is the system in legal compliance?

- Is the system compatible with the organization's mission and strategy?

- Does the system fit the organization's culture? Is it appropriate for its workers?

- Is the system internally equitable?

- Is the system externally competitive?

Measurements and Analysis

The following are measurements and analysis needed to determine whether an organization's compensation and benefits program is meeting its goals and objectives:

- Is the system legally compliant?
  - Does the system meet ERISA non-discrimination requirements?
  - Is there adverse impact on protected groups?
  - Are the organization's EEO and affirmative action objectives supported?
- Is the system compatible with the organization's mission and strategy?
  - Does it meet the organization's mission, goals, and objectives?
  - Does it help the organization to attract and retain employees?
  - Does it motivate employee performance?
- Does the system fit the culture? Is it appropriate for the workers?
  - Is the organization entitlement-oriented or contribution-oriented?
  - Does the system support the organization's orientation?
  - Does the system have programs that meet employee lifestyle needs?
- Is the system internally equitable?
  - Does the mix (fixed vs. variable, cash vs. benefits, retirement vs. health/welfare) fit?
  - Do the employees understand the system?
  - Do employees perceive the system to be fair and adequate?
  - What is the organization's turnover rate?
- Is the system externally competitive?
  - How does this system compare to the competition?
  - Are dollars spent generating a meaningful return?

Legally Required Communications

ERISA-required reporting and communicating requirements that must automatically be distributed to every employee include:

- **Summary Plan Description (SPD)**   Contains information on what the plan provides in layman terms. Distribution is required within 120 days after the plan's establishment or 90 days after eligibility. The SPD must be updated no less frequently than every five years.

- **Summary Annual Report (SAR)**   Contains financial information about the plan. Distribution is required within seven months after the end of the plan year.

- **Summary of Material Modifications (SMM)**   Required whenever any of the plan's features have been significantly changed or within 201 days after the end of the plan year.

Other Required Communications

Other required communications include the following:

- (Employers with 50+ employees) An FMLA policy statement in all employee handbooks
- (Employers with 20+ employees) General notification of federal (and state if applicable) COBRA rights
- Notice of special HIPAA enrollment rights and privacy rights

The preceding list is not all-inclusive. Due diligence is required so that all organizations understand the requirements of applicable laws, regulations, and instructions for any official forms or other official guidance.

In the Trenches

Employee Benefits: It's All About Strategy!

Fredi Foye-Helms, Vice President, Employee Benefits, EPIC

Managing employee benefit plans used to be routine and predictable. Employees assumed a comprehensive benefit package was a right of employment. Employers viewed employee benefit plans as an important tool to attract and retain employees, but for many, the benefits program was reviewed annually and the results were shared with employees at Open Enrollment. Once done, it was put to bed for another year and HR moved on to other priorities. Well, those days are gone. With health care costs rising and the burden of complying with numerous

(Continued)

provisions of the Affordable Care Act, benefit plans are front and center in HR strategy discussions, and the savvy HR professional needs to be ready for it.

We've all heard the statistics that report that employees spend less than 20 minutes a year on benefit decisions. We also understand that more frequent and relevant employee education about company-provided benefit plans will foster job satisfaction and influence employee loyalty. The biggest opportunity surrounding employee benefits continues to be well-crafted communications and a focus on basic strategies, such as:

- **Engage** Determine what communication method works best for your workforce. Use tactics that your group will respond to, based on their demographics, such as age, comfort with technology, work locations, language, and specifics of your firm or industry.

- **Educate** Make your communications simple and relevant. Include family members in the education effort. Provide education when and where they want it. Recorded webinars, videos, and podcasts are replacing in-person meetings in today's environment.

- **Innovate** What is your company's roadmap for employee benefits over the next three to four years? Assess the company priorities and lead toward that direction in your plan design and employee communications. Clarity of the long-term goal helps employees engage and begin taking the steps to reach that goal.

- **Measure** Measuring the impact of each benefit program will allow you to determine which benefits provide the most value to employees and the company, and this information will help you allocate future resources wisely, using the resulting data.

We all love choice and the benefits arena is no different. With the launch of the health insurance marketplace, emergence of public and private insurance exchanges, and increasing enrollment in high-deductible health plans, employees today have an increasing number of options for coverage. Recent surveys indicate that employees want more personalized benefits geared toward differing age groups. Employers and employees are being asked to become consumers of health care services and the technology and tools are advancing rapidly to support this ownership approach to health care services. Strategic thinking HR professionals will stay on top of emerging programs, tools, and resources.

It is a challenging time in employee benefits, but it is an exciting time that allows HR to empower employees to learn and take control of their health care and benefit decisions. The HR professional who uses creative tools and resources to communicate, engage, educate and innovate will help provide a more positive employee experience and in turn demonstrate HR's ability to develop strategic solutions and act as a valuable partner to support company goals.

Developing Employee Self-Service (ESS) Technologies

The communication requirements described in this section are influenced by the introduction of self-service technologies that are rapidly improving the communications abilities of organizations. Self-service technologies will continue to improve the ability of the organization to effectively implement its communications responsibilities. Employee self-service (ESS) applications will play a more active role in payroll and benefits by providing quick and easy access to information, which benefits the organization by:

- Increasing the accuracy of employee data
- Improving the timeliness of employee transactions
- Reducing HR costs associated with handling of traditional delivery channels

With increased benefits, ESS brings responsibilities:

- Application must be protected from hackers.
- Unauthorized internal and external access must be managed.
- Access to payroll data and benefits information must be protected.

HR can help promote the success of ESS technology by ensuring that employees:

- Understand the purpose of this technology, what functions are available, and how to apply the functions to meet their needs.
- Recognize the benefits of ESS technology when compared to traditional methods.
- Make the effort to use the technology to their advantage.

Compensation and Benefits— International Employees

SPHR Compensation and benefits are a critical element in an organization's strategic goals and plans. This principle is even more true when an organization is involved with international operations. The nature and complexity of international operations add to the complexity of the design features of international compensation and benefits as well as to the administration of international compensation and benefits plans. This section addresses some of the principles and issues international organizations face.

For the purposes of understanding types of employees involved in an organization's international operations, it is important to recognize the following international employees categories:

- **Expatriates** Traditionally applies to people who move from one country to another and are employed by an organization based in another country

- **Inpatriates** Describes employees brought in from another country to work in the headquarters country for a specified period of time

- **Repatriates** Refers to employees who have returned home from an international assignment

- **International assignee** An umbrella term that describes anyone who is assigned to an international location

Generally, organizations are reducing the number of long-term international assignments while increasing the number of local hire employees. In many cases, local nationals fill cross-border assignments on both short-term and permanent assignments.

This assignment pattern creates additional complexity in determining competitive terms and conditions of labor markets in other countries. The terms and conditions may vary widely from country to country based on local norms and customs related to each country's culture, driven by its history, laws, rules, and regulations. The following is a list of issues that HR must keep in mind as part of developing international compensation and benefits programs:

- **Standardization vs. localization** While strategies are typically standardized consistent with the organization's overall compensation and benefits strategy, specific practices tend to be localized to fit the context of the country, region, or local conditions.

- **Culture** Cultural differences that result from different local, regional, and national backgrounds add challenges to creating an understanding of applicable compensation and benefits programs. Benefits highly valued in one country may be almost meaningless in another. Differences are often the result of deeply entrenched beliefs, values, and attitudes.

- **Competitive labor market** The purpose of an effective compensation and benefits program is to attract and retain talent. The effectiveness of the program is mostly determined by the competitive demand for the talent. The competition for talent will vary from country to country, often driven by type of talent sought, geographic scope of available talent, the industries in which talent can be found, and a variety of compensation elements.

- **Collective bargaining, employee representation, and government mandates** In most parts of the world, employees are legally protected from actions that might impact their wages and employment conditions, although the extent of these protections vary widely from country to country. In some countries, unions play a powerful role, sometimes including provisions for management as well as workers. Work councils (not to be confused with unions) also offer worker protections.

- **Economic factors** Countries have a wide range of economic differences in terms of internal politics, the distribution of wealth, and rapidly changing events such as rates of inflation, currency valuation, and so on.

- **Taxation**   Tax regulations vary widely from country to country. While some countries have no income tax, others have income tax in excess of 50 percent. Benefits in some countries are taxable while in others they are not.

- **Laws and regulations**   There are significant differences in the legal protections from one country to the next: laws that affect work hours and compulsory time off, minimum wage, overtime, compulsory bonuses, employment at will, and acquired rights of employment.

Assignment Compensation Terms

Creating an international compensation plan is more complex than a domestic plan. Whereas a typical domestic compensation plan usually relies on pay level and ranges, the same cannot be effectively applied in an international situation. Because international assignments may involve high-cost locations as well as low-cost locations, the compensation and benefits portion of an effective compensation plan must be designed to respond to each international location's specific characteristics. In order to meet these characteristics as well as the objectives of both multi-national assignees and local hires, various approaches have been developed. The following examines some key concepts for international assignment lasting longer than one year and involving the relocation of the employee and his or her family to the host country. Common international assignment approaches include those discussed in the following sections.

Negotiation/Ad Hoc

Negotiation is typically used when the first few assignees are sent from headquarters to other countries and evolves to meet the needs of each individual assignee. Terms are negotiated on an ad hoc basis. The advantage of this approach is that it does not require long-term planning because its terms are negotiated on an individual basis. The disadvantage is inconsistency that develops over time.

Pure Localization

Of the different approaches, pure localization is the most straightforward. The assignee is paid exactly what local nationals in equivalent positions in the host country are paid. The advantage of this approach is that it is simple to communicate and administer. It works best when assignees are located from a low-salary country to a high-salary country. The disadvantage is that it is inappropriate for assignments from a high-salary country to a low-salary country. In some cases, allowances can help offset the disadvantage of an assignment from a high-salary country to a low-salary country.

Higher-of-Home-or-Host-Country

Higher-of-home-or-host-country is a variation of a localization strategy that basically keys on which location is the high-salary location and pays on that basis. It is simple to communicate. Its disadvantage is that it will usually require allowances and adjustments for differences in individual expenditures.

Home-Country-Based Balance Sheet

The employer in the home-country-based balance sheet approach pays a differential between home-country costs and assignment costs. In this approach, assignees maintain their home-country standard of living as they move from one country to another. This preserves an assignee's purchasing power at a fixed level; it eliminates the disincentive to repatriate due to a loss of purchasing power. A disadvantage is that it may create a perception of inequities among assignees of different nationalities working in the same host country.

Headquarters-Based Balance Sheet

The headquarters-based balance sheet is similar to the home-country-based balance sheet but calculates the compensation package only for the typical headquarters-based employees. It ensures that the same level of salary and allowances given to the headquarters country is given to assignees from other home countries. This approach maintains the purchasing power of assignees from the headquarters country. It is easy to communicate and administer. The disadvantage is that it often translates to high costs for the organization, especially for assignees from low-salary countries. This can make it difficult to repatriate assignees back to their home county.

Lump Sum

With a lump sum approach, the employer pays a lump sum instead of allowances and differentials. This provides maximum flexibility for the assignee. A disadvantage is that this approach may lead to the loss of certain tax advantages, particularly with host-country housing.

Cafeteria

With the cafeteria approach, the employer establishes several benefits options and offers these options to the employee subject to an overall limit. This provides a degree of flexibility for the assignee. A disadvantage is that some of the options may be inappropriate for some assignees from some countries.

International Benefits Variations

International benefits decisions can be a particular challenge for the international employer. Issues unique to international assignments include differences in what government taxes cover and what employees expect. The structure and administration of a benefits program is generally dictated by extensive but widely varying regulations in each country. Differences country to country and, in particular, differences between other countries and the United States significantly complicate the choice of benefits. For example, the governments of many countries provide healthcare coverage, but in the United States most health benefits have been employer-sponsored. This will begin to change, however, with the introduction of the Affordable Care Act healthcare provisions. The following are common country variations outside of the United States:

- **Government-provided benefits**   These benefits are administered and provided directly by the government, usually paid for through taxes.

- **Government-mandated benefits** These benefits are provided by employers by government mandate.

- **Benefits that are discretionary or market practice** Benefits are voluntarily provided by the employer but may not be entirely discretionary since the employer may be under the pressure of competitive practice.

Non-Salary International Benefits

Reflecting the wide range of different approaches to compensation and benefits, non-salary benefits also vary widely among countries.

- **Paid time off** Vacation and other paid time off often are determined by legislative mandate or collective bargaining. Generally, time off programs are strongly based in culture and tradition. Many countries have paid time off programs that reflect these influences and result in significant time off.

- **Healthcare** In many countries, healthcare is paid for through taxes or a form of social insurance. In some cases, healthcare is funded by employers, employees, general taxation, or some combination of these sources. In most cases, individuals are covered, at least partially, by some form of government-supported healthcare.

- **Disability** Generally, disability is treated differently depending on whether it is short- or long-term. The approach differs from country to country.

- **Life insurance** Generally, life insurance that is payable upon a person's death is covered by some form of social security. Some countries mandate that employers provide this life insurance although most employers voluntarily provide this benefit. Many countries allow an employee to purchase some form of supplemental coverage under their employee-sponsored group plan.

- **Social security** Social security benefits vary widely typically, reflecting the culture and political history of each country. In some countries, social security benefits are generous while other countries barely provide coverage. Beginning in the 1970s, the United States established a network of bilateral social security agreements that coordinate the U.S. Social Security program with comparable programs in other countries. These agreements, often referred to as "totalization agreements," have two objectives:

  - Eliminate dual social security taxation, a situation that occurs when a person works in another country and is forced to pay taxes in both the United States and the other country at the same time.

  - Help fill the benefit protection gaps of workers who have spent a part of their career overseas on international assignment and part of their career in the United States; in some cases, they are therefore not eligible for social security coverage in either nation.

- **Severance** Payments associated with terminations of employment, whether voluntary or involuntary, can be complex. Local laws may dictate the conditions under which an employee can be terminated and the amount of payment the employee is entitled to receive.

- **Retirement**   Retirement options vary country to country. In some cases, they are mandated by the government and often paid for with employee and employer contributions. Defined benefit plans are often used to provide retirement funds. Differing cultural expectations, local and country laws, and taxes create significant differences in how retirement is approached.

Chapter Review

This chapter examined how to develop, implement, administer, and evaluate compensation and benefits programs, two of the most visible elements of an organization's total rewards system. In this chapter, we examined direct compensation, that is, pay systems, and indirect compensation, that is, benefit and recognition programs. We began the chapter by examining the laws that affect compensation programs. Next, we looked at compensation and benefits as an intrinsic part of the organization's strategic direction as well as how HR can leverage compensation and benefits as a competitive advantage. This chapter also examined methods to determine internal and external job value followed by a review of the payroll function and its role in the management and administration of compensation and benefits. The remainder of this chapter focused on specific domestic and international compensation and benefits programs and their applications. Finally, this chapter reviewed the evaluation of the organization's compensation and benefits system and its associated communication requirements.

Questions

1. The purpose of a gap analysis is to
   - **A.** Determine which employees are underinsured
   - **B.** Revise benefits that are not meeting employee or organizational needs
   - **C.** Eliminate benefits that are too costly
   - **D.** Ensure that all employees receive the same benefits
2. According to COBRA, a company with 20 or more employees must offer
   - **A.** Health insurance to its employees
   - **B.** Continued medical insurance coverage to employees terminated for gross misconduct
   - **C.** COBRA benefits to workers if the company terminates its health plan
   - **D.** COBRA benefits to spouses of deceased workers

3. According to USERRA, employees called to active duty are entitled to

   A. Higher limits for salary deferral contributions

   B. Credited service for retirement plan purposes

   C. Lower copayments and deductibles for continued family benefits

   D. An early vesting schedule for retirement benefits

4. An employee elects a $500 annual deferment in his Section 125 Flexible Benefits Plan. His employer pays an FSA claim for $500 in March. In April, the employee terminates his employment after deferring only $290 to his plan. What happens in this situation?

   A. The employee must pay the company $290 for the amount in excess of his actual deferral.

   B. The employer may withhold $290 from the employee's final paycheck.

   C. The employee is entitled to the full reimbursement for $500.

   D. The employee becomes ineligible for the full FSA reimbursement.

5. A window manufacturer guarantees its installers a base wage plus an extra $25 for each job completed to specifications. The employer is using a

   A. Merit pay system

   B. Productivity-based pay system

   C. Competency-based system

   D. Flat-rate system

6. Under the factor comparison method, jobs are evaluated through the use of

   A. Pre-determined wage classes

   B. A wage/salary conversion table

   C. A scale based on compensable factors

   D. A comparison with market pricing

7. Which of the following laws covers both whistleblower protection and notice requirements for defined contribution plans?

   A. ERISA

   B. Sarbanes-Oxley Act

   C. False Claims Act

   D. Privacy Act

8. Which of the following is a common action taken in the United States to lower budgets that would most likely violate compensation laws in other countries?

   A. Reduce base salary levels

   B. Offer early retirement packages

    C. Delay or not fill open positions

    D. Downgrade job titles

9. To which of the following job evaluation methods does the paired comparison method belong?

    A. Ranking

    B. Job classification

    C. Point-factor

    D. Factor comparison

10. Which of the following is not a pay differential?

    A. Hazard pay

    B. Shift pay

    C. Base pay

    D. Overtime

11. If a leave under FMLA can be reasonably anticipated, how much notice must the employee give the employer?

    A. 7 days

    B. 14 days

    C. 30 days

    D. 90 days

12. Which of the following terms refers to collapsing multiple pay ranges into a single wide pay range?

    A. Wide banding

    B. Pay compression

    C. Green circle rates

    D. Broadbanding

13. This law requires an administrator of an employee benefit plan to furnish participants with a Summary Plan Description (SPD) describing their rights, benefits, and responsibilities under the plan.

    A. Health Insurance Portability and Accountability Act (HIPAA)

    B. Employee Retirement Income Security Act (ERISA)

    C. Family and Medical Leave Act (FMLA)

    D. Consolidated Omnibus Budget Reconciliation Act (COBRA)

14. Which of the following laws does not directly relate to a company's compensation or benefits programs?

    A. Equal Pay Act

    B. Fair Labor Standards Act

   C. Port-to-Portal Act

   D. Uniform Guidelines on Employee Selection Procedures

15. An organization establishes an ESOP by

   A. Deducting a small amount from the individual's pay for the purchase of stock

   B. Using stock as collateral to borrow capital from a financial institution

   C. Providing upper management with a bonus

   D. Having its profits distributed with favorable tax treatment

16. Social Security, COBRA, and Medicare are examples of

   A. Medical benefits

   B. Social benefits

   C. Government-sponsored benefits

   D. Legally mandated benefits

17. Employee benefits are indirect compensation given to employees for

   A. Loyalty

   B. Organizational membership

   C. Performance

   D. Organizational incentives

18. _____ is the right of employees to receive benefits from their retirement plans.

   A. Transference

   B. Portability

   C. Social Security

   D. Vesting

19. A statement of the qualifications necessary to perform a job is a

   A. Job specification

   B. Job analysis

   C. Job description

   D. Performance standard

20. Which job evaluation method is most difficult to use?

   A. Factor comparison method

   B. Ranking method

   C. Classification method

   D. Point-factor method

21. The simplest method of job evaluation is the

    A. Job ranking method

    B. Point-factor method

    C. Classification method

    D. Factor comparison method

22. A(n) _____ system is a productivity-based system in which an employee is paid for each unit of production.

    A. Incentive

    B. Merit

    C. Results-oriented

    D. Piece-rate

23. The Equal Pay Act prohibits wage discrimination on the basis of

    A. Race

    B. Sex

    C. Seniority

    D. Merit

24. A _____ job is one that is found in many organizations and performed by several individuals who have similar duties that are relatively stable and that require similar KSAs.

    A. Key

    B. Comparable

    C. Benchmark

    D. Red-circled

25. Under the Service Contracts Act, a company with a federal service contract exceeding $2,500 must pay

    A. The wage established by the contract

    B. Union wages

    C. 125 percent of the maximum wage

    D. The local prevailing wage

Answers

1. **B.** A gap analysis compares the organizational needs, the employee needs, and the existing set of benefits to determine what the organization's benefits package should and should not include.

2. **D.** COBRA provides up to 36 months' continuation of group health benefits in the event of a divorce or death of the employed spouse. None of the other choices are valid COBRA provisions.

3. **B.** USERRA gives employees on military leave the same seniority-based benefits, including retirement rights, as they would receive if they had not taken leave.

4. **C.** Flexible spending accounts are authorized under Section 125 (Cafeteria) plans. FSAs offer employees a pre-tax method to defer pay toward their group health plan costs as well as their out-of-pocket medical costs. FSA health care claims below the annual elected deferral must be paid by the employer when they are incurred even though the employee's FSA payroll deductions have not created a sufficient balance to cover the expense.

5. **B.** The employer is using an incentive program based on performance results, which is considered a productivity-based system. A merit-pay system does not address incentive pay. A competency-based system addresses capabilities, whereas a flat-rate system establishes a fixed rate of pay.

6. **C.** The factor comparison job evaluation method involves a set of compensable factors identified as determining the worth of jobs. Typically, the number of compensable factors is small. Next, benchmark jobs are identified. Benchmark jobs should be selected as having certain characteristics such as equitable pay and be distributed along a range. The jobs are then priced and the total pay for each job is divided into pay for each factor. This process establishes the rate of pay for each factor for each benchmark job. The other jobs in the organization are then compared with the benchmark jobs and rates of pay for each factor are summed to determine the rates of pay for each of the other jobs.

7. **B.** The Sarbanes-Oxley Act protects whistleblowers who expose security violations and also requires administrators of defined contribution plans to provide 30 days' notice of a blackout period.

8. **A.** Decreasing an employee's salary is illegal in most countries, particularly in Latin America and Europe. It is legal in the United States.

9. **A.** This is an example of ranking jobs. The paired comparison method involves plotting all of the jobs into a matrix. You then compare each job with every other job.

10. **C.** Hazard pay, shift pay, and overtime are all differentials. Base pay is the foundation of an employer's compensation program.

11. **C.** The FMLA allows employers to require 30 days' advance notice when the leave can be reasonably anticipated. The other choices are incorrect.

12. **D.** Broadbanding is a term that refers to pay ranges with a wide spread. This is often done to facilitate the management of pay levels within the pay range. A side effect of broadbanding is to reduce the opportunity for promotions due to a smaller number of ranges. That can adversely affect morale.

13. **B.** Among other things, ERISA requires plan administrators to furnish an SPD when a participant first becomes covered by a plan and then at regular intervals thereafter.

14. **D.** In 1978, the Civil Service Commission, the Department of Labor, the Department of Justice, and the Equal Opportunity Commission jointly adopted the Uniform Guidelines on Employee Selection Procedures to establish uniform standards for employers for the use of selection procedures and to address adverse impact, validation, and record-keeping requirements. The other choices are laws that directly relate to employers' compensation programs.

15. **B.** An Employee Stock Ownership Plan (ESOP) is an employee-owner method that provides a company's workforce with an ownership interest in the company. In an ESOP, companies provide their employees with stock ownership, often at no up-front cost to the employees. ESOP shares, however, are part of employees' remuneration for work performed. Shares are allocated to employees and may be held in an ESOP trust until the employee retires or leaves the company. The ESOP can borrow money to buy shares, with the company making tax-deductible contributions to the plan to enable it to repay the loan.

16. **C.** Social Security, COBRA, and Medicare are all government-sponsored benefits.

17. **B.** Employee benefits are indirect compensation given to employees for organizational membership. The other choices are incorrect.

18. **D.** Vesting is the absolute right to an asset that cannot be taken away by any third party, even though one may not yet possess the asset. The portion vested cannot be reclaimed by the employer, nor can it be used to satisfy the employer's debts. Any portion not vested may be forfeited under certain conditions, such as termination of employment.

19. **A.** Job descriptions describe the job and not the individual who fills the job. They are the result of job analysis within a given organization and are essential to the selection and evaluation of employees. A job specification is an analysis of the kind of person it takes to do the job—that is to say, it lists the qualifications.

20. **A.** The factor comparison method is a systematic and scientific method of job evaluation. It is the most complex method of the four recognized methods. Under this method, instead of ranking complete jobs, each job is ranked according to a series of factors. These factors include mental effort, physical effort, skill needed, responsibility, supervisory responsibility, working conditions, and other such factors. Pay will be assigned in this method by comparing the weights of the factors required for each job and divided among the factors weighted by importance. Wages are assigned to the job in comparison to its ranking on each job factor.

21. **A.** The simplest method of job evaluation is the ranking method. According to this method, jobs are arranged from highest to lowest, in order of their value or merit to the organization. Jobs can also be arranged according to the relative difficulty in performing them. The jobs are examined as a whole rather than on the basis of important factors in the job; the job at the top of the list has the highest value and obviously the job at the bottom of the list will have the lowest value. The ranking method is simple to understand and practice; it is best suited for a small organization. This kind of ranking is highly subjective in nature and may offend many employees.

22. **D.** The piece rate pay method compensates employees a set amount for each unit of work completed. For example, in a manufacturing setting, an employee receives a set amount for each item he produces, regardless of how fast or slow he works.

23. **B.** The Equal Pay Act requires that men and women be given equal pay for equal work in the same establishment. The jobs need not be identical, but they must be substantially equal. It is job content, not job titles, that determines whether jobs are substantially equal.

24. **C.** Benchmark jobs are positions that remain consistent across the industry in terms of salary, responsibilities, and seniority and can therefore be compared from organization to organization. Data is widely available on the key metrics of these jobs, including salary and career route.

25. **D.** The Service Contract Act requires contractors and subcontractors performing services on federal prime contracts in excess of $2,500 to pay service employees in various classes no less than the wage rates and fringe benefits found prevailing in the locality where work is performed.

Endnotes

1. "Overtime Pay Requirements of the FLSA," U.S. Department of Labor, Wage and Hour Division, Fact Sheet #23 (www.dol.gov/whd/regs/compliance/whdfs23 .pdf)

2. "ESOP (Employee Stock Ownership Plan) Facts," The National Center for Employee Ownership (NCEO) (www.esop.org/)

3. "Understanding and Using Long-Term Incentives," William H. Coleman and Keith E. Fortier, CCP, Salary.com, Inc.

4. "Employee Stock Purchase Plan – ESPP" (http://www.investopedia.com/)

5. "Phantom Stock Plan," http://www.investopedia.com/

6. "Restricted Stock Unit (RSU)," http://www.investopedia.com/

7. "Performance Grants," Society for Human Resource Management, 2013 SHRM Learning System, Module 4, Compensation and Benefits, Section 4-4, pp. 4–118

8. "Executive Administrative, Professional, Computer, and Outside Sales Exemptions - FLSA," U.S. Department of Labor Field Operations Manual, §13(a)(1)(29 U.S.C. §213(a)(1))

9. "Fiduciary Responsibilities," United States Department of Labor Website, http://www.dol.gov/, Health Plans and Benefits

List of Common
HR Acronyms

AAP Affirmative Action Plan

ACA Patient Protection and Affordable Care Act add (see also PPACA)?

ADA Americans with Disabilities Act

ADAAA Americans with Disabilities Act Amendments Act

ADEA Age Discrimination in Employment Act

ADR Alternative Dispute Resolution

AFL-CIO American Federation of Labor and Congress of Industrial Organizations

AI Appreciative Inquiry

AIDS Acquired Immune Deficiency Syndrome

ALJ Administrative Law Judge

ANSI American National Standards Institute

AP Accounts Payable

APA American Psychological Association

AR Accounts Receivable

ARRA American Recovery and Reinvestment Act

ASO Administrative Services Only Plan

B2B Business to Business

B2C Business to Consumer

BARS Behaviorally Anchored Rating Scale

BCP Business Continuity Plan

BFOQ Bona Fide Occupational Qualification

BLS Bureau of Labor Statistics

CBA Collective Bargaining Agreement

CBP Cafeteria Benefit Plan

CDC Centers for Disease Control

CEO Chief Executive Officer

CFO Chief Financial Officer

CFR Code of Federal Regulations

CHRO Chief Human Resources Officer

CO Compliance Officer

COBRA   Consolidated Omnibus Budget Reconciliation Act

COLA   Cost of Living Adjustment

CPA   Certified Public Accountant

CPH   Cost Per Hire

CPI   Consumer Price Index

CPM   Critical Path Method

CR   Corporate Responsibility

D&I   Diversity and Inclusion

DBA   Davis-Bacon Act

DMADV   Define, Measure, Analyze, Design, Verify

DMAIC   Define, Measure, Analyze, Improve, Control

DOL   U.S. Department of Labor

EAP   Employee Assistance Plan

ECPA   Electronic Communications Privacy Act

EE   Employee

EEO   Equal Employment Opportunity

EEOC   Equal Employment Opportunity Commission

EGTRRA   Economic Growth and Tax Relief Reconciliation Act

EI   Emotional Intelligence (see also *EQ*)

EO (or E.O.)   Executive Order

EPA   Equal Pay Act

EPLI   Employment Practices Liability Insurance

EQ   Emotional Intelligence (see also *EI*)

ER   Employer

ERISA   Employee Retirement Income Security Act

ESL   English as a Second Language

ESOP   Employee Stock Ownership Plan

ETA   U.S. Department of Labor, Employment and Training Administration

FACT   Fair and Accurate Credit Transactions Act

FAR   Federal Acquisition Regulations

FASB   Financial Accounting Standards Board

FCPA   Foreign Corrupt Practices Act

FCRA   Fair Credit Reporting Act

FES   Factor Evaluation System

FICA   Federal Insurance Contributions Act

FLRA   Federal Labor Relations Authority

FLSA   Fair Labor Standards Act

FMLA   Family and Medical Leave Act

FSA   Flexible Spending Accounts

FT   Full Time

FTE   Full Time Equivalent

FUTA   Federal Unemployment Tax Act

GATT   General Agreement on Tariffs and Trade

GDP   Gross Domestic Product

GINA   Genetic Information Nondiscrimination Act

GL   General Ledger

GS   General Schedule

HAS   Health Savings Account

HCE   Highly Compensated Employee

HCN   Home-Country Nationals

HHS   Department of Health and Human Services

HIPAA   Health Insurance Portability and Accountability Act

HIPC   Health Insurance Purchasing Cooperatives

HITECH   Health Information Technology for Economic and Clinical Health Act

HIV   Human Immunodeficiency Virus

HMO   Health Maintenance Organization

HR   Human Resources

HRA   Health Reimbursement Accounts

HRCI   Human Resources Certification Institute

HRCS   Human Resource Competency Study

HRD   Human Resources Department

HRIS   Human Resource Information System

HRM   Human Resource Management

ICE   U.S. Department of Homeland Security, Immigration and Customs Enforcement

IIPP   Injury and Illness Prevention Programs/Plans

ILO   International Labor Organization

INA   Immigration and Nationality Act

IRA   Individual Retirement Account

IRCA   Immigration Reform and Control Act

IRS   Internal Revenue Service

ISO   Incentive Stock Options

ISO   International Standards Organization

IT   Information Technology

JVA   Jobs for Veterans Act

KM   Knowledge Management

KSA   Knowledge, Skills, and Abilities

LMRA   Labor-Management Relations Act

LMRDA   Labor-Management Reporting and Disclosure Act

LMS   Learning Management System

LO   Learning Objectives

LOA   Leave of Absence

LTC   Long-Term Insurance Care

LTD   Long-Term Disability

M&A   Mergers and Acquisitions

MBO   Management by Objectives

MHPAEA   Mental Health Parity and Addiction Equity Act

MOU   Memorandum of Understanding

MSDS   Material Safety Data Sheets

MSHA   Mine Safety and Health Act

MSP   Managed Service Provider

MSPB   Merit Systems Protection Board

NIOSH   National Institute of Occupational Safety and Health

NLRA   National Labor Relations Act

NLRB   National Labor Relations Board

NMB   National Mediation Board

OBRA   Omnibus Budget Reconciliation Act

OD   Organizational Development

OFCCP   Office of Federal Contract Compliance Programs

OJT   On Job Training

OPM   Office of Personnel Management

OSHA   Occupational Safety and Health Act

OWBPA   Older Workers Benefit Protection Act

P&L   Profit and Loss

PBGC   Pension Benefit Guarantee Corporation

PCAOB   Public Company Accounting Oversight Board

PCN   Parent-Country Nationals

PDA   Pregnancy Discrimination Act

PEO   Professional Employer Organization

PERT   Project Evaluation and Review Techniques

PEST   Political, Economic, Social and Technological

PHR   Professional in Human Resources

PIP   Performance Improvement Program

PL (or P.L.)   Public Law

POP   Premium Only Plan

POS   Point of Service

PPA   Pension Protection Act

PPACA   Patient Protection and Affordable Care Act

PPE   Personal Protective Equipment

PPO   Preferred Provider Organization

PT   Part Time

PTO   Paid Time Off

QME   Qualified Medical Examiner

RCR   Recruiting Cost Ratio

REA   Retirement Equity Act

RFID   Radio Frequency Identification

RFQ   Request for Quotation

RFP   Request for Proposal

RIF   Reduction in Force

ROI   Return on Investment

RSU   Restricted Stock Unit

RYR   Recruitment Yield Ratio

SAR   Summary Annual Report

SBJPA   Small Business Job Protection Act
SCA   Service Contract Act
SCM   Supply Chain Management
SHRM   Society for Human Resource Management
SMM   Summary of Material Modifications
SNAP   Supplemental Nutrition Assistance Program (formerly known as the Food Stamp program)
SOX   Sarbanes-Oxley Act
SPD   Summary Plan Description
SPHR   Senior Professional in Human Resources
SSI   Supplemental Security Income
SSN   Social Security Number
STD   Short-Term Disability
STEEPLED   Social, Technological, Environmental, Economic, Political, Legal, Ethics and Demographics
SUB   Supplemental Unemployment Benefits
SUTA   State Unemployment Tax Act
SWOT   Strengths, Weaknesses, Opportunities and Threats
TANF   Temporary Assistance to Needy Families
TCN   Third-Country Nationals
TOC   Theory of Constraints
TPA   Third Party Administrator
TQM   Total Quality Management
UCA   Unemployment Compensation Amendments Act
UGESP   Uniform Guidelines on Employee Selection Procedures
UI   Unemployment Insurance
ULP   Unfair Labor Practice
URL   Uniform Resource Locator (Web Site Address)
USC   United States Code
USERRA   Uniformed Services Employment and Reemployment Rights Act
VEVRAA   Vietnam Era Veterans Readjustment Assistance Act
WARN   Worker Adjustment and Retraining Notification Act
WC   Workers' Compensation
WOTC   Work Opportunity Tax Credit
WPE   Workforce Planning and Employment

Federal Case Laws

Case Applications by Chapter

Chapter 4: Risk Management

Year	Citation	Decision
1991	*United Auto Workers v. Johnson Controls* (499 U.S. 187) www.law.cornell.edu/supct/html/89-1215.ZO.html	Supreme Court held that decisions about the welfare of future children must be left to the parents who conceive, bear, support, and raise them rather than to the employers who hire their parents.

Chapter 5: Workforce Planning and Employment

Year	Citation	Decision
1971	*Griggs v. Duke Power Co.* (401 U.S. 424) www.law.cornell.edu/supct/html/historics/USSC_CR_0401_0424_ZS.html	When an employer uses a neutral test or other selection device and then discovers it has a disproportionate impact on minorities or women, the test must be discarded unless it can be shown that it was required as a business necessity; this was the first Supreme Court recognition of adverse impact discrimination.
1971	*Phillips v. Martin Marietta Corp.* (400 U.S. 542) www.uiowa.edu/~prslaw/courses/gender/cases/martinpdf.pdf	Employers may not have different policies for men and women with small children of similar age.

Year	Citation	Decision
1973	*McDonnell Douglas Corp. v. Green* (411 U.S. 792) http://caselaw.lp.findlaw .com/cgi-bin/getcase .pl?court=us&vol=411&invol=792	In a hiring case, the charging party only has to show (1) The charging party is a member of a Title VII protected group; (2) He or she applied and was qualified for the position sought; (3) The job was not offered to him or her; (4) The employer continued to seek applicants with similar qualifications. Then the employer must show a legitimate business reason why the complaining party was not hired. The employee has a final chance to prove the employer's business reason was really pretext for discrimination. Establishes the criteria for disparate treatment discrimination.
1974	*Espinoza v. Farah Manufacturing Co.* (414 U.S. 86) https://bulk.resource.org/courts. gov/c/US/414/414.US.86.72-671 .html	Non-citizens are entitled to Title VII protection. Employers who require citizenship may violate Title VII if it results in discrimination based on national origin.
1974	*Corning Glass Works v. Brennan* (417 U.S. 188) http://supreme.justia.com/cases/ federal/us/417/188/	Pay discrimination cases under the Equal Pay Act require the employee to prove that there is unequal pay based on sex for substantially equal work.
1975	*Albermarle Paper v. Moody* (422 U.S. 405) http://supreme.justia.com/cases/ federal/us/422/405/	Requires employer to establish evidence that an employment test is related to the job content. Job analysis could be used to show that relationship, but performance evaluations of incumbents are specifically excluded.
1976	*Washington v. Davis* (426 U.S. 229) www.law.cornell.edu/supct/html/ historics/USSC_CR_0426_0229_ ZS.html	When an employment test is challenged under constitutional law, intent to discriminate must be established. Under Title VII there is no need to show intent, just the impact of test results.
1976	*McDonald v. Santa Fe Transportation Co.* (427 U.S. 273) http://supreme.justia.com/cases/ federal/us/427/273/case.html	Title VII prohibits racial discrimination against whites as well as blacks.
1977	*Hazelwood School District v. U.S.* (433 U.S. 299) http://caselaw.lp.findlaw .com/cgi-bin/getcase .pl?court=us&vol=433&invol=299	An employee can establish a *prima facie* case of class hiring discrimination through the presentation of statistical evidence by comparing the racial composition of an employer's workforce with the racial composition of the relevant labor market.
1977	*Trans World Airlines, Inc. v. Hardison* (432 U.S. 63) http://supreme.justia.com/cases/ federal/us/432/63/	Under Title VII, employers must reasonably accommodate an employee's religious needs unless doing so would create an undue hardship for the employer. The Court defines hardship as anything more than *de minimis* cost.

Year	Citation	Decision
1978	*Regents of University of California v. Bakke* (438 U.S. 265) http://caselaw.lp.findlaw .com/cgi-bin/getcase. pl?court=us&vol=438&invol=265	Medical school admission set asides (16 of 100 seats) were illegal if they discriminate against whites and there is no previous discrimination against minorities established.
1979	*United Steelworkers v. Weber* (443 U.S. 193) http://supreme.justia.com/cases/ federal/us/443/193/case.html	Affirmative action plans are permissible if they are temporary and intended to "eliminate a manifest racial imbalance."
1982	*Connecticut v. Teal* (457 U.S. 440) http://caselaw.lp.findlaw .com/cgi-bin/getcase. pl?court=us&vol=457&invol=440	An employer is liable for racial discrimination when any part of its selection process, such as an unvalidated examination or test, has a disparate impact even if the final result of the hiring process is racially balanced. In effect, the Court rejects the "bottom line defense" and makes clear that the fair employment laws protect the individual. Fair treatment to a group is not a defense to an individual claim of discrimination.
1984	*EEOC v. Shell Oil Co.* (466 U.S. 54) http://supreme.justia.com/cases/ federal/us/466/54/	The Supreme Court affirmed authority of EEOC Commissioners to initiate charges of discrimination through "Commissioner Charges."
1986	*Meritor Savings Bank v. Vinson* (477 U.S. 57) www.law.cornell.edu/supct/html/ historics/USSC_CR_0477_0057_ ZS.html	Defined "Hostile Environment Sexual Harassment" as a form of sex discrimination under Title VII. Further defined it as "unwelcome" advances of a sexual nature. Victim's failure to use employer's complaint process does not insulate the employer from liability.
1987	*Johnson v. Santa Clara County Transportation Agency* (480 U.S. 616) https://supreme.justia.com/cases/ federal/us/480/616/	Employer was justified in hiring a woman who scored 2 points less than a man because it had an affirmative action plan that was temporary, flexible, and designed to correct an imbalance of white males in the workforce.
1987	*School Board of Nassau v. Arline* (480 U.S. 273) http://supreme.justia.com/cases/ federal/us/480/273/case.html	A person with a contagious disease is covered by the *Rehabilitation Act* if they otherwise meet the definitions of "handicapped individual."
1988	*Watson v. Fort Worth Bank & Trust* (487 U.S. 977) http://supreme.justia.com/cases/ federal/us/487/977/case.html	In a unanimous opinion, the Supreme Court declared that disparate impact analysis can be applied to subjective or discretionary selection practices.
1989	*City of Richmond v. J. A. Croson Company* (488 U.S. 469) http://supreme.justia.com/cases/ federal/us/488/469/	Affirmative action programs can only be maintained by showing that the programs aim to eliminate the effects of past discrimination.

Year	Citation	Decision
1989	*Price Waterhouse v. Hopkins* (490 U.S. 288) http://caselaw.lp.findlaw .com/cgi-bin/getcase .pl?court=us&vol=490&invol=228	This decision relieved employers of liability if they would have made the same decision even if there had been no discrimination. Congress overturned the ruling providing that employers continue to have liability for injunctive relief, attorney fees, and costs even if they would have made the same decision in the absence of illegal discrimination.
1989	*Wards Cove Packing Co. v. Antonio* (490 U.S. 642) www.law.cornell.edu/supct/html/ historics/USSC_CR_0490_0642_ ZS.html	This decision made it more difficult for employees to prevail in employment discrimination cases. It was effectively overturned by Congress when it passed the Civil Rights Act of 1991.
1993	*Harris v. Forklift Systems Inc.* (510 U.S. 17) www.law.cornell.edu/supct/ html/92-1168.ZO.html	In a sexual harassment complaint, the employee does not have to prove concrete psychological harm to establish a Title VII violation.
1993	*St. Mary's Honor Center v. Hicks* (509 U.S. 502) www.law.cornell.edu/supct/ html/92-602.ZS.html	Title VII complaints require the employee to show that discrimination was the reason for a negative employment action.
1993	*Taxman v. Board of Education of Piscataway* (91 F.3d 1547, 3rd Cir.) http://caselaw.lp.findlaw .com/scripts/getcase. pl?navby=search&case=/ uscircs/3rd/961395p.html	Race in an affirmative action plan cannot be used to trammel the rights of people of other races.
1995	*McKennon v. Nashville Banner Publishing Co.* (513 U.S. 352) www.law.cornell.edu/supct/ html/93-1543.ZS.html	"After-acquired" evidence collected following a negative employment action cannot protect an employer from liability under Title VII or ADEA, even if the conduct would have justified terminating the employee.
1996	*O'Connor v. Consolidated Coin Caterers Corp.* (517 U.S. 308) www.law.cornell.edu/supct/ html/95-354.ZS.html	To show unlawful discrimination under the Age Discrimination in Employment Act, a discharged employee does not have to show that he or she was replaced by someone outside the protected age group (that is under age 40).
1997	*Robinson v. Shell Oil* (519 U.S. 337) www.law.cornell.edu/supct/ html/95-1376.ZS.html	Title VII prohibition against retaliation protects former as well as current employees.
1998	*Faragher v. City of Boca Raton* (524 U.S. 775) www.law.cornell.edu/supct/ html/97-282.ZO.html and *Ellerth v. Burlington Northern Industries* (524 U.S. 742) www.law.cornell.edu/supct/ html/97-569.ZS.html	Distinguished between supervisor harassment that results in tangible employment action and that which does not. When harassment results in tangible employment action, the employer is liable. Employers may avoid liability if they have a legitimate written complaint policy, it is clearly communicated to employees, and it offers alternatives to the immediate supervisor as the point of contact for making a complaint.

Year	Citation	Decision
1998	*Oncale v. Sundowner Offshore Service, Inc.* (523 U.S. 75) www.law.cornell.edu/supct/ html/96-568.ZO.html	Same-gender harassment is actionable under Title VII.
1998	*Bragdon v. Abbott* (524 U.S. 624) www.law.cornell.edu/supct/ html/97-156.ZS.html	An individual with asymptomatic HIV is an individual with a disability and therefore is protected by the ADA. Reproduction is a major life activity under the statute.
1999	*Kolstad v. American Dental Association* (527 U.S. 526) www.law.cornell.edu/supct/ html/98-208.ZO.html	Title VII punitive damages are limited to cases in which the employer has engaged in intentional discrimination and has done so "with malice or with reckless indifference…"
1999	*Gibson v. West* (527 U.S. 212) http://caselaw.lp.findlaw .com/scripts/getcase .pl?court=us&vol=527&invol=212	Endorses EEOC's position that it has the legal authority to require federal agencies to pay compensatory damages when EEOC has ruled during the administrative process that the federal agency has unlawfully discriminated in violation of Title VII.
2003	*Grutter v. Bollinger* (539 U.S. 306) http://supreme.justia.com/cases/ federal/us/539/306/case.html and *Gratz v. Bollinger* (539 U.S. 244) http://supreme.justia.com/cases/ federal/us/539/244/case.html	Diversity of a student body is a compelling state interest that can justify the use of race in university admissions as long as the admissions policy is "narrowly tailored" to achieve this goal. University of Michigan did not do so for its undergraduate program but the law school admissions program satisfied the standard.
2004	*General Dynamics Land Systems, Inc. v. Cline* (540 U.S. 581) www.law.cornell.edu/supct/ html/02-1080.ZS.html	ADEA does not protect younger workers, even those over 40, from workplace decisions that favor older workers.
2004	*Pennsylvania State Police v. Suders* (542 U.S. 129) www.law.cornell.edu/supct/ html/03-95.ZS.html	In the absence of a tangible employment action, employers may use the Ellerth/Faragher defense in a constructive discharge claim when supervisors are charged with harassment.
2005	*Smith v. Jackson, Mississippi* (544 U.S. 228) www.law.cornell.edu/supct/ html/03-1160.ZS.html	ADEA, like Title VII, offers recovery on a disparate impact theory.
2005	*Leonel v. American Airlines* (400 F.3d 702, 9th Circuit) http://cdn.ca9.uscourts. gov/datastore/ opinions/2005/04/27/0315890.pdf	To make a legitimate job offer under the ADA, an employer must have completed all nonmedical components of the application process or be able to demonstrate that it could not reasonably have done so before issuing the offer.

Year	Citation	Decision
2007	*Ledbetter v. Goodyear Tire & Rubber Co.* (550 U.S. 618) www.law.cornell.edu/supct/pdf/05-1074P.ZS	A claim of discrimination must be filed within 180 days of the first discriminatory employment act and the clock does not restart after each subsequent act (for example, issuance of a paycheck with lower pay than coworkers if based on sex). Congress overruled this decision with passage of the Lilly Ledbetter Fair Pay Act of 2009, which says the clock will restart each time another incident of discrimination occurs.
2009	*Ricci v. DeStefano* (No. 07-1428) www.supremecourt.gov/opinions/08pdf/07-1428.pdf	"…under Title VII, before an employer can engage in intentional discrimination for the asserted purpose of avoiding or remedying an unintentional disparate impact, the employer must have a strong basis in evidence to believe it will be subject to disparate-impact liability if it fails to take the race-conscious, discriminatory action."
2013	*Vance v. Ball State Univ.* (No. 11-556) www.supremecourt.gov/opinions/12pdf/11-556_11o2.pdf	Determined that an employee is a "supervisor" of another employee for purposes of liability under Title VII of the Civil Rights Act of 1964 only if he or she is empowered by the employer to take tangible employment actions against the other employee.
2013	*University of Texas Southwestern Medical Center. v. Nassar* (No. 12-484) www.law.cornell.edu/supremecourt/text/12-484	Retaliation claims brought under Title VII of the Civil Rights Act of 1964 must be proved according to principles of "but-for-causation," not the lesser causation test applicable to bias claims.

Chapter 6: Business Management and Strategy

There are no case laws that directly relate to this HRCI functional area.

Chapter 7: Employee and Labor Relations

Year	Citation	Decision
1988	*DeBartolo Corp. v. Gulf Coast Trades Council* (known as DeBartolo II) (485 U.S. 568) https://bulk.resource.org/courts.gov/c/US/485/485.US.568.86-1461.html	Supreme Court ruled that bannering, hand billing, or attention-getting actions outside an employer's property were permissible.
1992	*Electromation, Inc. v. NLRB* (Nos. 92-4129, 93-1169 7th Cir.) www.leagle.com/decision/199411 8335F3d1148_11017	NLRB held that action committees at Electromation were illegal "labor organizations" because management created and controlled the groups and used them to deal with employees on working conditions in violation of the NLRA.

Year	Citation	Decision
1993	*E. I. DuPont & Company v. NLRB* (311 NLRB 893)	Board concluded that DuPont's six safety committees and fitness committee were employer-dominated labor organizations and that DuPont dominated the formation and administration of one of them in violation of the NLRA.
1995	*NLRB v. Town & Country Electric* (516 U.S. 85) www.law.cornell.edu/supct/html/94-947.ZS.html	Supreme Court decision related to salting that held that a worker may be a company's "employee," within the terms of the National Labor Relations Act, even if, at the same time, a union pays that worker to help the union organize the company.
1995	*PepsiCo, Inc. v. Redmond* (No. 94-3942 7th Cir.) http://caselaw.findlaw.com/us-7th-circuit/1337323.html	Case in which district court applied inevitable disclosure doctrine even though there was no non-compete agreement in place. An employee who had left his position in marketing PepsiCo's All Sport sports drink to work for Quaker Oats Company and market Gatorade and Snapple drinks was enjoined from working for Quaker because he had detailed knowledge of PepsiCo's trade secrets pertaining to pricing, market strategy, and selling/delivery systems.
1998	*Wright v. Universal Maritime Service Corp.* (525 U.S. 70) http://supreme.justia.com/cases/federal/us/525/70/	Collective bargaining agreements must contain a clear and unmistakable waiver if it is to bar an individual's right to sue after an arbitration requirement.
2001	*Circuit City Stores v. Adams* (532 U.S. 105) www.law.cornell.edu/supct/html/99-1379.ZS.html	Ruled that a pre-hire employment application requiring that all employment disputes be settled by arbitration was enforceable under the Federal Arbitration Act.
2001	*Ronald Lesch v. Crown Cork and Seal Company* (334 NLRB 699) www.nlrb.gov/cases-decisions/board-decisions	NLRB decision that lifted some restrictions on the employer's use of employee participation committees.

Year	Citation	Decision
2002	*EEOC v. Waffle House* (534 U.S. 279) www.law.cornell.edu/supct/html/99-1823.ZS.html	Case in which Supreme Court ruled that even if there is a mandatory arbitration agreement in place, a relevant civil rights agency can still sue on behalf of the employee.
2002	*Phoenix Transit System v. NLRB* (337 NLRB 510) www.nlrb .gov/cases-decisions/board-decisions?volume=337&sort_by=case_nameSort&sort_order=ASC	NLRB ruling that struck down an employer rule prohibiting employees from discussing among themselves an employment complaint—in this instance, a complaint of sexual harassment—on the grounds that the prohibition was not limited in time and scope and interfered with a protected concerted activity.
2004	*NLRB v. Weingarten, Inc.* (420 U.S. 251, 254 1975) http://clear.uhwo.hawaii.edu/weindecis.html Overturned by *IBM Corp. v. NLRB* (341 NLRB No. 148, June 9, 2004) www.nacua.org/documents/IBM_Corp_and_KennethPaulSchult.pdf	On June 9, 2004, NLRB ruled by a 3–2 vote that employees who work in a nonunionized workplace are not entitled to have a coworker accompany them to an interview with their employer, even if the affected employee reasonably believes that the interview might result in discipline. This decision effectively reversed the July 2000 decision of the Clinton board, which had extended Weingarten rights to nonunion employees.
2007	*Toering Electric Company v. NLRB* (351 NLRB 225) www.nlrb .gov/cases-decisions/board-decisions?volume=351&sort_by=case_nameSort&sort_order=ASC	NLRB ruling that an applicant for employment must be genuinely interested in seeking to establish an employment relationship with the employer in order to be protected against hiring discrimination based on union affiliation or activity; creates greater obstacles for unions attempting salting campaigns.
2007	*Oil Capitol Sheet Metal, Inc. v. NLRB* (349 NLRB 1348) www .nlrb.gov/cases-decisions/board-decisions?volume=351&sort_by=case_nameSort&sort_order=ASC	NLRB decision that provides employers relief in salting cases by announcing a new evidentiary standard for determining the period of back pay; requires the union to provide evidence that supports the period of time it claims the salt would have been employed.
2007 and 2011	*Dana Corporation/ Metaldyne Corporation v. NLRB* (351 NLRB 434) www.nlrb.gov/cases-decisions/board-decisions?volume=351&sort_by=case_nameSort&sort_order=ASC	NLRB ruling that a recognition bar, which precludes a decertification election for 12 months after an employer recognizes a union, does not apply when the recognition is voluntary, based on a card check. Overruled in 2011 in *Lamons Gasket*, which restored the recognition bar for voluntary recognition but revised the prohibited time period from one year to a minimum of six months up to a year.

Year	Citation	Decision
2007	*Syracuse University v. NLRB* (350 NLRB 755) www.nlrb.gov/cases-decisions/board-decisions?volume=351&sort_by=case_nameSort&sort_order=ASC	NLRB found that an employee grievance panel did not violate the NLRA because the purpose of the panel was not to deal with management but to improve group decisions.
2010	*KenMor Electric Co., Inc. v. NLRB* (355 NLRB 173) www.nlrb.gov/cases-decisions/board-decisions?volume=351&sort_by=case_nameSort&sort_order=ASC	NLRB ruled that a system developed and operated by an association of electrical contractors violated the NLRA because it discriminated against individuals who were salts. The board held that an individual's right to be a salt is protected under the NLRA.
2011	*Staub v. Proctor* (131 U.S. 1186) http://supreme.justia.com/cases/federal/us/562/09-400/	Supreme Court applied the "cat's paw" principle to a wrongful discharge case, finding that an employer was culpable because the HR manager did not adequately investigate supervisors' charges against the fired employee.
2011	*AT&T Mobility v. Concepcion* (S.Ct. No. 09-893) www.supremecourt.gov/opinions/10pdf/09-893.pdf	Supreme Court ruled that some state statutes restricting the enforceability of arbitration agreements in a commercial context may be preempted by the Federal Arbitration Act.
2011	*Kepas v. Ebay* (131 S.Ct. 2160) www.ca10.uscourts.gov/opinions/09/09-4200.pdf	Supreme Court refused to review a lower court decision that held in an employment case that a cost provision was severable from the balance of an arbitration agreement. The cost provision was unenforceable, but the agreement to arbitrate was enforceable.
2011	*Specialty Healthcare and Rehabilitation Center of Mobile v. NLRB* (15-RC-008773) www.nlrb.gov/case/15-RC-008773	NLRB indicated that, in non-acute healthcare facilities, it will certify smaller units for bargaining unless the employer provides overwhelming proof of a community of interest.
2011	*UGL-UNICCO Service Company v. NLRB* (01-RC-022447) www.nlrb.gov/case/01-RC-022447	NLRB re-established the successor bar doctrine, allowing unions a window of six months to one year of presumed majority support after the transfer of ownership of a business.
2012	*D. R. Horton, Inc. v. NLRB* (12-CA-25764) www.cozen.com/cozendocs/outgoing/alerts/2012/labor_011012_link.pdf	NLRB ruled that requiring employees to agree to a class action waiver as a term and condition of employment violates Section 7 of the National Labor Relations Act.
2014	*Harris v. Quinn* (S.Ct. No. 11-681) http://www.supremecourt.gov/opinions/13pdf/11-681_j426.pdf	"The First Amendment prohibits the collection of an agency fee from [employees] who do not want to join or support the union." Essentially, this eliminates the Agency Shop.

Chapter 8: Human Resources Development

There are no case laws that directly relate to this HRCI functional area.

Chapter 9: Compensation and Benefits

Year	Citation	Decision
1987	*Leggett v. First National Bank of Oregon* (739 P.2d. 1083) http://or.findacase.com/research/wfrmDocViewer.aspx/xq/fac.19870722_0041873.OR.htm/qx	Employer invades privacy of employee when a company representative contacted the employee's psychologist (to whom the employee had been referred by an EAP—employee assistance program), inquiring about the employee's condition.
2000	*Erie County Retirees Association v. County of Erie* (2000 U.S. App. LEXIS 18317 3rd Cir. August 1, 2000) www.buypeba.org/publications/Eriecase.pdf	If an employee provides retiree health benefits, the health insurance benefits received by Medicare-eligible retirees cost the same as the health insurance benefits received by younger retirees.
2005	*IBP, Inc. v. Alvarez* (546 U.S. 21) www.law.cornell.edu/supct/html/03-1238.ZS.html	Time spent donning or doffing unique safety gear is compensable and the FLSA requires payment of affected employees for all the time spent walking between changing and production areas.
2008	*LaRue v. DeWolff* (No. 06-856, 450 F. 3d 570) www.law.cornell.edu/supct/cert/06-856	When retirement plan administrators breach their fiduciary duty to act as a prudent person would act in investment of retirement funds, the employee whose retirement account lost money can sue the plan administrators.
2009	*Kennedy v. Plan Administrators for Dupont Savings* (No. 07-636) www.supremecourt.gov/opinions/08pdf/07-636.pdf	Awarded retirement benefits to an ex-spouse even though she had agreed to disclaim such benefits, because the retiree had never changed beneficiary designation on the retirement plan. Points out the need for retirement plan administrators to pay attention to divorce decrees and qualified domestic relations orders.
2014	*Burwell v. Hobby Lobby Stores, Inc.* (S.Ct. No. 13-354) http://www.supremecourt.gov/opinions/13pdg/13-354_olp1.pdf	A closely held private corporation cannot be forced to pay for contraceptives as part of the Affordable Care Act if there is an objection based on religious beliefs of the business owners.

For Additional Study

Following is a list of course materials that can be helpful in your study for the PHR and SPHR exams, and for future reference as an HR Professional. Remember, all of the material in this chapter applies to more than one of the functional competency areas of the exams.

SHRM Code of Ethical and Professional Standards in Human Resource Management. Retrieved 2/7/2014 from www.shrm.org/about/pages/code-of-ethics.aspx.

"Models and Techniques of Manpower Demand and Supply Forecasting: A Strategic Human Resource Planning Model." Retrieved 2/7/2014 from http://corehr.wordpress.com/hr-planning/53-2/.

Becker, Brian E., Mark A. Huselid, and David Ulrich, *The HR Scorecard: Linking People, Strategy, and Performance*. Boston: Harvard Business School Press, 2001.

Benjamin, Steve. "A Closer Look at Needs Analysis and Needs Assessment: Whatever Happened to the Systems Approach?" *Performance Improvement* 28, no. 9, 12–16, Wiley Periodicals, Inc., 1989.

Bennett-Alexander, Dawn D., and Laura B. Pincus. *Employment Law for Business*. Chicago: Irwin Publishing, 1995.

Bliss, Wendy (Series Advisor). *The Essentials of Finance and Budgeting*. Boston: Harvard Business School Press and Alexandria, Virginia: Society for Human Resource Management, 2005.

Blosser, Fred. *Primer on Occupational Safety and Health*. Washington, D.C.: The Bureau of National Affairs, 1992.

Carrell, Michael R., and Christina Heavrin. *Collective Bargaining and Labor Relations*, 3rd ed. New York: Merrill, 1985.

Cherrington, David J. *The Management of Human Resources*, 4th ed. Englewood Cliffs, New Jersey: Prentice-Hall, 1995.

Cofey, Robert E., Curtis W. Cook, and Phillip L. Hunsaker. *Management and Organizational Behavior*. Boston: Austen Press, 1994.

DeLuca, Matthew J. *Handbook of Compensation Management*. Englewood Cliffs, New Jersey: Prentice-Hall, 1997.

Denisi, A., and R. Griffin. *HR*. Cengage Learning (January 1, 2011).

Doherty, Neil. *Integrated Risk Management: Techniques and Strategies*. McGraw-Hill (March 27, 2000).

Feldacker, Bruce. *Labor Guide to Labor Law*, 3rd ed. Englewood Cliffs, New Jersey: Prentice-Hall, 1990.

Fitz-Enz, Jac. *How to Measure Human Resource Management*. 2nd ed. New York: Mcgraw-Hill Book Company, 1995.

Grant, Phillip. *Multiple Use Job Descriptions: A Guide to Analysis, Preparation, and Applications for Human Resources Managers*. Praeger (January 20, 1989).

Hayes, John. *The Theory and Practice of Change Management*, Palgrave Macmillan (March 16, 2010).

Herzberg, Frederick. *The Motivation to Work*. Transaction Publishers (January 1, 1993).

Jackson Lewis. *Employer's Guide to Union Organizing Campaigns*. New York: Aspen Publishers, 2007.

Kahan, Seth. *Getting Change Right: How Leaders Transform Organizations from the Inside Out*. San Francsico: Jossey-Bass, 2010.

Kirkpatrick, Donald L. *How to Manage Change Effectively*. San Francisco: Jossey-Bass, 1985.

Knowles, Malcolm. *The Adult Learner: The Definitive Classic in Adult Education and Human Resource Development*. Butterworth-Heinemann (February 8, 2005).

Kushner, Gary. *Health Care Reform: The Patient Protection and Affordable Care Act of 2010*. SHRM/Kushner and Company, 2010.

Kutcher, David. "What Is a RFP, Where to Find RFPs, and Are RFPs Relevant?" *Confluent Forms*, May 13, 2013. Retrieved 2/7/2014 from www.confluentforms.com/2013/05/requests-for-proposals-rfp.html.

Lawler, Edward E., III. *Strategic Pay: Aligning Organnizational Strategies and Pay Systems*. San Francsico: Jossey-Bass, 1990.

Mantel Jr., S., J. Meredith, S. Shafer, and M. Sutton. *Project Management in Practice*. John Wiley & Sons (October 26, 2010).

Mathis, R., J. Jackson, and S. Valentine. *Human Resource Management*. Cengage Learning (August 5, 2013).

Maslow, Abraham H. *A Theory of Human Motivation*. Martino Fine Books (June 12, 2013).

McGregor, Douglas. *The Human Side of Enterprise* (annotated edition). McGraw-Hill (December 21, 2005).

Michaud, Patrick A. *Accident Prevention and OSHA Compliance*. Boca Raton, Florida: Lewis Publishers, 1995.

Milkovich, George T., Jerry M. Newman, and Carolyn Milkovich. *Compensation*, 7th ed. Boston: McGraw-Hill, 2002.

Porter, Michael E. *Competitive Strategy: Techniques for Analyzing Industries and Competitors*. New York: Free Press, 1980.

Richardson, Blake. *Records Management For Dummies*. For Dummies (October 16, 2012).

Rogers, Everett. *Diffusion of Innovations*. Free Press (August 16, 2003).

Scott, Mark, JD, CFE. "Managing Risks in Vendor Relationships." The Fraud Examiner. March 2012. Retrieved 2/7/2014 from www.acfe.com/fraud-examiner.aspx?id= 4294972428.

Tolbert, P., and R. Hall. *Organizations: Structures, Processes, and Outcomes*. Pearson (November 7, 2008).

Truesdell, William H. *Secrets of Affirmative Action Compliance*. Walnut Creek, California: Management Advantage, Inc., 2014.

Ulrich, David. *Delivering Results: A New Mandate for Human Resource Professionals*. Boston: Harvard Business Review, 1998.

About the CD-ROM

The CD-ROM included with this book comes complete with Total Tester customizable practice exam software loaded with simulated PHR and SPHR exam questions and a PDF copy of the book.

System Requirements

The software requires Windows XP or higher and 30MB of hard disk space for full installation, in addition to a current or prior major release of Chrome, Firefox, Internet Explorer, or Safari. To run, the screen resolution must be set to 1024 × 768 or higher. The PDF copy of the book requires Adobe Acrobat, Adobe Reader, or Adobe Digital Editions.

Total Tester Premium Practice Exam Software

Total Tester provides you with a simulation of the actual PHR and SPHR exams. You can also create custom exams from selected knowledge areas and further customize the number of questions and time allowed.

The exams can be taken in either Practice Mode or Exam Mode. Practice Mode provides an assistance window with hints, references to the book, explanations of the correct and incorrect answers, and the option to check your answer as you take the exam. Exam Mode provides a simulation of the actual exam. The number of questions, the types of questions, and the time allowed are intended to be an accurate representation of the exam environment. Both Practice Mode and Exam Mode provide an overall grade and a grade broken down by knowledge area.

To take an exam, launch the program and select either PHR or SPHR from the Installed Question Packs list. You can then select Practice Mode, Exam Mode, or Custom Mode. After making your selection, click Start Exam to begin.

Installing and Running Total Tester Premium Practice Exam Software

From the main screen, you can install Total Tester by clicking the Total Tester Practice Exams button. This will begin the installation process and place an icon on your desktop and in your Start menu. To run Total Tester, navigate to Start | (All) Programs | Total Seminars, or double-click the icon on your desktop.

To uninstall Total Tester, go to Start | Settings | Control Panel | Add/Remove Programs (XP) or Programs And Features (Vista/7/8), and then select the Total Tester program. Select Remove, and Windows will completely uninstall the software.

PDF Copy of the Book

The entire contents of the book are provided in PDF form on the CD-ROM. This file is viewable on your computer and many portable devices. Adobe Acrobat, Adobe Reader, or Adobe Digital Editions is required to view the file on your computer. A link to Adobe's website, where you can download and install Adobe Reader, has been included on the CD-ROM.

 NOTE For more information on Adobe Reader and to check for the most recent version of the software, visit Adobe's website at www.adobe.com and search for the free Adobe Reader or look for Adobe Reader on the product page. Adobe Digital Editions can also be downloaded from the Adobe website.

To view the PDF copy of the book on a portable device, copy the PDF file to your computer from the CD-ROM and then copy the file to your portable device using a USB or other connection. Adobe offers a mobile version of Adobe Reader, the Adobe Reader mobile app, which currently supports iOS and Android. For customers using Adobe Digital Editions and an iPad, you may have to download and install a separate reader program on your device. The Adobe website has a list of recommended applications, and McGraw-Hill Education recommends the Bluefire Reader.

Technical Support

Technical Support information is provided in the following sections by feature.

Total Seminars Technical Support

For questions regarding the Total Tester software or operation of the CD-ROM, visit www.totalsem.com or e-mail support@totalsem.com.

McGraw-Hill Education Content Support

For questions regarding the PDF copy of the book, e-mail techsolutions@mhedu.com or visit http://mhp.softwareassist.com.

For questions regarding book content, e-mail customer.service@mheducation.com. For customers outside the United States, e-mail international_cs@mheducation.com.

80% rule   The measurement known as a "rule of thumb" used to test for disparity in treatment during any type of employment selection decisions; also identified as Adverse Impact.

ADDIE   A five-step instructional design process: Analysis, Design, Development, Implementation, Evaluation.

Administrative exemption   Exemption from overtime payment based on several qualifying factors including minimum pay requirement, and exercise of discretion and independent judgment performing work directly related to management of general business operations.

Administrative services only plan   Health insurance programs in which all of the risk is assumed by the employer.

Adult learning   The process of learning associated with people who are over the age range of 18 and generally referred to as nontraditional learners; also identified as Andragogy.

Adverse impact   A legal category of illegal employment discrimination involving groups of workers and statistical proofs.

Adverse treatment   A legal category of illegal employment discrimination involving individual treatment or "pattern and practice" treatment of groups of workers.

Affirmative action   Use of special outreach and recruiting programs to ensure participation of qualified job candidates, vendors, or students in employment, employer purchasing programs, or college admissions.

Aggregate stop-loss coverage   The health plan is protected against the risk of large total claims from all participants during the plan year.

Aging   A technique used to make outdated data current.

Andragogy   The study of how adults learn.

Applicant tracking system   A method for retention of detailed information about job applicants either manual- or computer-based.

Assets   The properties an organization owns, tangible and intangible.

Automatic step rate   Division of the pay range into several steps that can be advanced by an employee when time-in-job has met the step requirement.

Average   Arithmetic average or mean arrived at by giving equal weight to every participant's actual pay; also, a number that is arrived at by adding quantities together and dividing the total by the number of quantities.

Back pay   Payment of salary or wages that should have been paid initially, usually as a form of remedy for a complaint of discrimination.

Background checks   Investigation of an individual's personal history including employment, educational, criminal, and financial.

Balance sheet   A statement of a business's financial position.

Balanced scorecard   A big picture view of an organization's performance as measured against goals in areas such as finance, customer base, processes, learning, human capital, and growth.

BARS   Behaviorally anchored rating scales.

Base-pay systems   Single or flat-rate systems, time-based step rate systems, performance-based merit pay systems, productivity-based systems, and person-based systems.

Bell curve   Used to describe the mathematical concept called "normal distribution."

Benefits needs assessment or analysis   Collection and analysis of data to determine whether the employer's benefits programs actually meet their objectives.

Bereavement leave   Paid or unpaid time off to attend funerals.

Bill   A proposal presented to a legislative body in the U.S. government to enact a law.

Boycott   A protest action that encourages the public to withhold business from an employer that is targeted by a union.

Branding   The process of conveying key organizational values and associations.

Broadbanding   Combination of several pay grades or job classifications with narrow range spreads and a single band into a wider spread.

Budgeting   Forecasting income and expenses by category and subcategory.

Business acumen   Knowledge and understanding of the financial, accounting, marketing, and operational functions of an organization.

Business concepts   An idea for producing goods or services that identifies the benefits that can be achieved for prospective customers or clients.

Business continuity   The ability to continue conducting business following an interruption of some sort.

Business ethics   Generally accepted norms and expectations for business management behavior.

Career development   A process involving individuals expanding their knowledge, skills, and abilities as they progress through their careers.

Career management   Planning, preparing, and implementing employee career paths.

Career planning   Activities and actions that individuals follow for a direction-specific career path.

Case studies   Simulation of a real-world problem that demands some application of skill or knowledge to resolve problems or issues.

Cash awards   Rewards for exceeding performance goals, a formula-based bonus based on a percentage of profits or other pre-established measurement.

Certification of a union   Formal recognition of a union as the exclusive bargaining representative of a group of employees.

Change management   Transitioning individuals, groups, teams, and institutions to a desired future state.

Change programs   Strategic approach to organizing and implementing specific changes (for example, policies or procedures) within an organization.

Child care services   Programs designed to help working parents deal with the ongoing needs of pre-school or school-aged children.

Code of conduct   An employment policy listing personal behaviors that are acceptable and required in the workplace.

Code of ethics   Principles of conduct that guide behavior expectations and decisions.

Cognitive learning   The refining of knowledge by adding new information thereby expanding prior knowledge.

Collective bargaining   A formal process of negotiating working conditions with an employer for a work group represented by a union.

Collective bargaining agreements   Union contracts for a represented group of employees and designated employers. A term usually used in the private sector.

Combination step-rate and performance   Employees receive step-rate increases up to the established job rate. Above this level, increases are only granted for superior job performance.

Communication skills   Verbal and written abilities that enable an individual to transmit and receive messages.

Commuter assistance   Employer assistance programs designed to help defray public transportation costs. associated with going to and from work.

Compa-ratios   An indicator of how wages match, lead, or lag the midpoint of a given pay range computed by dividing the worker's pay rate by the midpoint of the pay range.

Compensatory damages   A monetary equivalent awarded for pain, suffering, and emotional distress as a result of a legal proceeding.

Competencies   Measurable or observable knowledge, skills, abilities, and behaviors critical to successful job performance.

Competency-based system   Pay is linked to the level at which an employee can perform in a recognized competency.

Compliance evaluation   Formal audit by the Office of Federal Contract Compliance Programs (OFCCP) of a federal contractor subject to OFCCP oversight.

Computer employee exemption   Exemption from overtime payment based on several qualifying factors, including minimum pay requirement, job duties involving computer programming, software analysis, or software engineering.

Computer-based testing (CBT)   Testing delivery method via computer, in person at a testing center.

Construct validity   The degree to which a test measures what it claims to measure.

Consumer price index   The average of prices paid by consumers for goods and services.

Content validity   The extent a test measures all aspects of a given job.

Contract labor   Work performed under the terms of a legally enforceable contract.

Contract negotiation   The process of give and take related generally to content details and provisions of an employment contract such as a union agreement or Memorandum of Understanding (MOU).

Control chart   A chart that illustrates variation from normal in a situation over time.

Controlling   A management function involving monitoring the workplace and making adjustments to activities as required.

Cooperative learning   A strategy in which a small group of people working on solving a problem or completing a task in a way that each person's success is dependent on the group's success.

Copyright   A form of protection for authors or original works.

Core competency   A unique capability that is essential or fundamental to a particular job.

Corporate governance   The mechanisms, processes, and relations by which corporations are controlled and directed.

Corporate responsibility (CR)   Strategic goals achieved through local community relationships around social needs and issues.

Cost benefit analysis (CBA)   A business practice in which the costs and benefits of a particular situation are analyzed as part of the decision process.

Cost containment   Efforts or activities designed to reduce or slow down cost expenses and increases.

Cost of living adjustment   Pay increase given to all employees on the basis of market pressure, usually measured against the consumer price index (CPI).

Cost per hire   The measurement of dollar expense required to hire each new employee.

Credit report   Report obtained from one of the major credit reporting agencies that explains the individual's personal rating based on financial history.

Criterion-related validity   Empirical studies producing data that show the selection procedure(s) are predictive or significantly related with important elements of job performance.

Critical Path Method (CPM)   A sequence of activities in a project plan that must be completed on time for the project to be completed on the due date.

Cross-functional work team   A group of people from different functions working together to generate production or problem resolution.

Cultural blending   The blending of different cultural influences in the workforce.

Culture   Societal forces affecting the values, beliefs, and actions of a group of people.

Deauthorization of a union   Removal of "union security" from the contract. The union remains as the exclusive bargaining representative, and the collective bargaining agreement remains in effect, but employees are not forced to be members or pay dues to the union.

Decertification of a union   Removal of a union as the exclusive bargaining representative of the employees.

Defamation   Publication of something about an individual that the writer knows is untrue.

Demand analysis   Estimation of what customers, clients, or patrons will want in the future.

Demonstration   Showing students how something is done.

Dental plans   Medical insurance programs that cover some or all of the cost of dental services for subscribers.

Differential piece rate system   Employee receives one rate of pay up to the production standard and a higher rate of pay when the standard is exceeded.

Direct compensation   Base pay, commissions, bonuses, merit pay, piece rate, differential pay, cash award, profit sharing, gainsharing.

Directing   Managing or controlling people to willingly do what is wanted or needed.

Disaster recovery plans   A set of procedures used to protect and recover a business from a natural or other disaster that has impacted the organization or employer.

Discipline   Forms of punishment to assure obedience with policies.

Diversity and inclusion   The practice of embracing differences of race, culture, and background, and ensuring that everyone is a participant in workplace processes.

Diversity programs   Methods for recognizing and honoring various types of employee backgrounds.

Divestiture   The sale of an asset.

Dual-ladder   A system that enables a person to advance up either the management ladder or technical career development ladder in an organization.

Due diligence   The first step in mergers and acquisitions involving a broad scope of research and investigation.

Elder care   Programs to help employees deal with responsibilities for care of family elders.

E-learning   Internet-based training programs that can be instructor led or self paced.

Emotional intelligence (EQ or EI)   The ability of an individual to have understanding and sensitivity for another's emotions and control over their own.

Employee assistance programs   Employer-sponsored benefits that provide a number of services that help promote the physical, mental, and emotional wellness of individual employees who otherwise would be negatively impacted by health-related crises.

Employee complaints   Written or verbal statements of dissatisfaction from an employee that can involve charges of discrimination, lack of fairness, or other upset.

Employee engagement   Where employees are fully absorbed by and enthusiastic about their work and so take positive action to further the organization's reputation and interests.

Employee leasing   Contracting with a vendor who provides qualified workers for a specific period of time at a specific pay rate.

Employee relations programs   Methods for management of the employer-employee relationship.

Employee stock ownership plans   Retirement plans in which the company contributes its stock, or money to buy its stock, to the plan for the benefit of the company's employees.

Employee stock purchase plans   Programs allowing employees to purchase company stock at discounted prices.

Employee surveys   Tools used to gather opinions of employees about their employment experiences.

Employee-management committees Problem-solving groups of management and non-management employees focused on specific issues within the workplace.

Employer sick leave Paid leave for a specified number of hours or days absent from work due to medical conditions.

Employment affirmative action Programs required by federal regulations for some federal contractors to implement outreach and recruiting programs when the incumbent workforce is significantly less than computed availability.

Employment policies Rules by which the workplace will be managed.

Employment reference checks Verification of references, both personal and professional, provided by a job candidate on an application form or resume.

Employment testing Any tool or step used in the employment selection process. Commonly includes written tests, interviews, resume review, or skill demonstration.

Employment-at-will A legal doctrine that describes an employment relationship without a contract where either party can end the relationship at any time for any reason.

Environmental footprints The effect that a person, company, activity, etc. has on the environment.

Environmental scanning A process of studying the environment to pinpoint potential threats and opportunities.

Equal pay Providing equal compensation to jobs that have the same requirements, responsibilities, and working conditions regardless of the incumbent's gender.

Equity The difference between income and liabilities in a for-profit organization.

Ethics Principles and values that set expectations for behaviors in an organization.

Ethnocentric A policy calling for key management positions to be filled by expatriates.

Evacuation plan A written procedure for moving employees out of the work location to a safer location in case of fire or natural disaster.

Evaluation The ability to judge.

E-Verify A government database that employers access to confirm a match between a new employee's name and Social Security Number.

Executive coaching Coaching senior and executive-level management by a third party.

Executive exemption Exemption from overtime payment based on several qualifying factors, including supervision and minimum pay requirements.

Executive incentives   Variable compensation additives for executive employees that may include company stock or use of company facilities, such as vacation timeshares. These are usually variable based on the profitability of the company.

Exempt job   A job with content that is exempt from the FLSA requirement to pay overtime for work over 40 hours per week. Exemption can be based on several designated factors.

Exit interviews   Discussions with departing employees to explore how they feel about their experience as an employee and what recommendations they might have for the employer.

Expatriates   Employees working in a country other than that of their origin.

External coaching   Coaching that is provided by a third party or by a certified coach.

Extrinsic rewards   Rewards such as pay, benefits, incentive bonuses, promotions, time off, and so on.

Factor-comparison job evaluation   A process that involves each job by each compensable factor and then identifying dollar values for each level of each factor to develop an actual pay rate for the evaluated job.

Fast-track program   A career development program that identifies high potential leaders for rapid career growth and organizational knowledge.

Fee-for-service plans   Allows health plan members to go to any qualified physician, or other healthcare provider, hospital, or medical clinic and submit claims to the insurance company.

Fiduciary responsibilities   A legal and ethical relationship between two or more parties.

Final warning   Last step in the disciplinary process progression prior to removing the employee from the payroll.

Flat-rate or single system   Each worker in the same job has the same rate of pay regardless of seniority or job performance.

Flexible spending account   Allows employees to set aside a pre-established amount of money on a pre-tax basis per plan year for use in paying authorized medical expenses.

Floating holidays   Designated paid time off that can be used at any time during the year with the employer's approval.

Flow analysis   How processes operate and how flows of products, data, or other items go through these processes.

Forced Choice   An evaluation method in which the evaluator selects two of four statements that represent "most like" and "least like".

Frequency distribution   Listing of grouped pay data from lowest to highest.

Frequency tables   Number of workers in a particular job classification and their pay data.

Front pay   Payment of salary or wages that could have been earned had the individual continued to work on the job in question or had the person been employed for a future period of time.

Full-time   Employees who work a designated number of hours per week, usually in the 30- to 40-hour range.

Fully funded plans   Health insurance programs paid for entirely by the employer.

Functional work team   A group of people from the same function working together to generate production or resolve problems.

Gainsharing plans   Extra pay provided to individuals or groups of employees based on the gain in performance results in one measurement period over another period.

Gantt chart   A project planning tool that scopes and monitors the activities of a project, the time line, and accountability.

Gap analysis   Measurement of the difference between where you are and where you want to be.

General duty clause   A provision in OSHA regulations that imposes a duty on all subject employers to ensure a safe and healthy working environment for their employees.

General pay increases   A pay increase given to all employees regardless of their job performance and not linked to market pressures.

Geocentric   A staffing policy wishing to place the best person in the job regardless of their country of origin.

Geographic-based differential pay   Adjustment to base pay programs based on cost of living requirements in various geographic locations where employees work.

Geography   Adjustments to survey numbers based on geographic differences with original survey content.

Glass ceiling   A discriminatory practice that has prevented women and other protected class members from advancing to executive-level jobs.

Global Professional in Human Resources (GPHR)   A global competency-based credential validating the skills and knowledge of an HR professional who operates in a global marketplace.

Golden parachute   Provision in executive employment contracts that provides special payments or benefits to the executives under certain adverse conditions, such as the loss of their position.

Graphic organizers   Diagrams, maps, and drawings/webs as illustrations of learning materials.

Green circle rates   Pay at a rate lower than the minimum rate for the assigned pay range.

Green initiatives   Relationships around community and social issues.

Grievances   Formal employee complaints handled by a structured resolution process usually found in a union-represented workgroup.

Gross domestic product (GDP)   The total value of goods and services produced in a country.

Group incentive program   Pay to all individuals in a workgroup for achievement by the entire workgroup.

Group term life insurance   Provides lump sum benefit to beneficiaries on the death of an insured.

Halo effect   This occurs when an evaluator scores an employee high on all job categories because of performance in one area.

Harassment   Persecution, intimidation, pressure, or force applied to employees by supervisors, co-workers, or external individuals that interferes with the employee's ability to perform the job assignment.

Hazard pay   Additional pay for working under adverse conditions caused by environment or due to specific circumstances.

Health insurance purchasing cooperatives   Purchasing agents for large group of employers.

Health maintenance organization   Healthcare program where the insurer is paid on a per person (capitated) basis and offers healthcare services and staff at its facilities.

Health reimbursement accounts   Employer-funded medical reimbursement plans.

Health savings accounts   A tax-advantaged medical savings account available to taxpayers in the United States who are enrolled in a high-deductible health plan.

High-deductible health plans   These programs help employers lower their costs and allow employees with set-aside money to pay for out-of-pocket medical and medical-related expenses.

Histogram   A graphic representation of the distribution of a single type of measurement using rectangles.

Horn effect   This occurs when an employee receives a low rating in all areas due to one weakness influencing the evaluator.

Host-country nationals (HCN)   Employees originating in the country where a remote work location is being established.

HR business partner   HR staff that acts as an internal consultant to senior management.

HR Certification Institute (HRCI)   The certifying non-profit professional organization for the human resources profession.

HR professional certification   Status awarded to HR professionals by a recognized certifying agency after satisfying qualifying requirements.

HRCI Body of Knowledge (BOK)   The description of a set of concepts, tasks, responsibilities, and knowledge associated with HRCI credentialing.

HRIS   Human resources information system. Usually a computer-based collection of personal data for each employee.

Human capital   The value of the capabilities, knowledge, skills, experiences, and motivation of a workforce in an organization.

Human Resource Business Professional (HRBP)   A global, competency-based credential designed to validate generally accepted technical professional-level HR knowledge and skills.

Human Resource Management Professional (HRMP)   Credential for those with mastery of generally accepted HR principles in strategy, policy development, and service delivery.

Human resources development (HRD)   Systematically planned activities that help the organization's workforce meet the current and future job and skills needs.

Human resources management (HRM)   The direction of organizational systems to ensure that human talent is used effectively and efficiently to accomplish organizational goals.

Incentive pay   Pay designed to promote a higher level of job performance above the scope of the basic expectations of the job.

Incentive stock options   Awards of rights to purchase company stock in the future at a price determined at the time of the grant.

Indirect compensation   Social security, unemployment insurance, disability insurance, pensions, 401(k) and other similar programs, healthcare, vacations, sick leave, paid time off such as holidays.

Individual incentive program   An offer to individual employees in a workgroup to receive extra pay based on achievement of clearly defined objectives.

Injury and Illness Prevention Programs (IIPP)   A written workplace safety program conforming to the specifications of OSHA.

Inpatriates   Employees working at corporate headquarters who originated in a different country.

Instructional methods   Approaches to training that are either teacher-centered or learner-centered.

Internal coaching   Coaching by trained coaches who are employees in an organization, or by supervisors and other leaders.

Internal investigation   Gathering verbal and written information dealing with an issue that needs to be clarified.

Intrinsic rewards   Rewards such as meaningful and fulfilling work, autonomy, and positive feedback that lead to high levels of job satisfaction.

Investigation   A detailed search for facts involving records, witnesses, and other inputs.

Investigation file   A collection of documents related to complaints or charges of discrimination, policy violation, or criminal behavior assembled by an employer about an employee or event.

Involuntary separations   Individuals leaving the payroll for involuntary reasons, including such things as performance deficiencies, policy violations, or unauthorized absence.

Item Response Theory (IRT)   Method used to pre-equate the difficulty level of questions on an exam.

Job analysis   A process to identify and determine the particular job duties and requirements for a given job to fit into an employer's hierarchy of reporting relationships and compensation scales.

Job application   A form used to gather information significant to the employer about an individual who wants to be employed by this organization.

Job classification   Comparison of jobs to an outside scale with a predetermined number of grades or classifications.

Job description   A document that contains a summary of duties and responsibilities of a given job assignment, and a description of the physical and mental requirements of the job.

Job enlargement   Broadening the scope of a job by expanding the number of tasks.

Job enrichment   Increasing the depth of a job by adding responsibilities.

Job evaluation   A systematic determination of the relative worth of jobs in an organization.

Job evaluation method   Quantitative or non-quantitative programs allowing sorting or categorizing jobs based on their relative worth to the organization.

Job ranking   Comparison of jobs based on each job's measurable factors.

Job rotation   The process of shifting a person from job to job.

Job sharing   Two or more employees who work part-time in the same job to create one full-time equivalent person.

Judgmental forecasts   Projections based on subjective inputs.

Judgment-based forecasting   Simple estimates, the Delphi technique, focus group or panel estimates, or historically based estimates used in human resource management.

Knowledge   Facts and information gathered by an individual.

Knowledge management   The way an organization identifies knowledge in order to be competitive and for the design of succession plans.

Knowledge-based system   Pay that is based on the level of knowledge an employee has in a particular field.

K-W-L table   Display of what students know (K), what they want to know (W), and what they actually learned (L).

Labor cost differentials   Adjustment to pay structures based on local competitive comparisons.

Leadership concepts   The study of leadership styles and techniques.

Learning management system (LMS)   A comprehensive system that tracks training content, employee skill sets, training histories, and career development planning.

Learning objectives (LO)   Brief statements that define what will be expected to be learned.

Learning organization   Organizations that adapt to changes.

Lecture   An oral presentation intended to teach or present information.

Leniency errors   This occurs when ratings of all employees fall at the high end of the range.

Leveling   Adjustments to survey numbers by an appropriate percentage needed to achieve a match with specific jobs.

Liabilities   An organization's debts and other financial obligations.

Location-based differentials Adjustment to base pay programs based on work location remoteness, lack of amenities, climatic conditions, and other adverse conditions.

Lockout Employer action that prevents workers from entering the workplace to do their normal jobs.

Long-term care insurance Covers cost of long-term care at home, in an assisted living facility, in a nursing home, or as an inpatient in a hospice.

Long-term disability Begins where short-term disability ends. Covers some or all of employee's income for up to a specified period, usually from six months to age 65 or an alternative number of years.

Long-term incentives Rewards for attaining results over a long measurement period.

Lump sum increases Either a standalone performance bonus or part of an annual pay increase.

Managed care plans Insurance that provides plan subscribers with managed health care with the purpose of reducing costs and improving the quality of care.

Management by Objectives (MBO) A method of performance appraisal that specifies the specific performance goals that the employee and manager identify.

Management skills The abilities required to succeed at a management job. They include such skills as leadership, communication, decision making, behavior flexibility, organization, and planning.

Managerial estimates Projections based on managerial experience alone.

Mandatory bargaining issues Issues that must be discussed by employer and union when negotiating a contract of representation.

Market-based job evaluation Key jobs are measured and valued against the market and the remaining jobs are inserted into a hierarchy based on their whole-job comparison to the benchmark jobs.

Marketing The process of promoting the organization's products or services including research, sales, and advertising.

Mathematically based forecasting Staffing ratios, sales ratios, or regression analysis used in human resource management analysis of data elements.

Mean (average) Arithmetic average or mean arrived at by giving equal weight to every participant's actual pay.

Median The middle number in a range.

Medical file A collection of documents related to medical evaluations or status of an employee.

Memorandum of Understanding (MoU)   Union contracts for a represented group of employees and designated employers. A term usually used in the public sector.

Mentoring   A career relationship with an experienced individual with another who has less experience.

Mergers and acquisitions (M&A)   The joining together of two separate organizations (merger) or by acquiring of another organization (acquisition).

Minimum premium plans   Health insurance programs paid for in part by the employer and in part by the employee.

Mission statement   A statement describing what an organization does, who its customer/client base is, and how it will do its work.

Mode   The most frequently appearing number in a range.

Modified duty   Temporary alteration of job duties that can be performed by an employee who is medically restricted for a designated period of time.

Motivation concepts   Notions about what motivates individuals that have come about as a result of scientific studies.

Needs analysis   See *needs assessment*.

Needs assessment   Determining through analysis what gaps exist between a standard or an objective and existing capabilities.

Negligent hiring   A legal tort claim against an employer for injury to someone inside or outside the organization in a way that should have been predicted by the employer if a proper background check had been completed.

Negligent retention   A legal tort claim against an employer for keeping someone on the payroll who is known to be a danger to others inside or outside the organization.

Net assets   The difference between income and liabilities in a non-profit organization.

New employee orientation   The process of welcoming and orienting new workers into the organization.

Nominal group technique   Development of forecasts based on input from several groups of people.

Non-cash awards   Prizes, gifts, or recognition awards presented in recognition of service or production or other designated achievement.

Non-exempt job   A job with content that requires payment of overtime for work in excess of 40 hours per week under the FLSA.

Objective measurement   Impartial assessment of a result.

Objectives   Something aimed at end-result intentions.

Occupational categories   Groupings of job titles with similar levels of responsibility or skill requirements.

Occupational Safety and Health Administration (OSHA)   The federal agency within the Department of Labor that is responsible for safety in workplaces other than mines.

Offshoring   The relocation of functions or work to another country.

Oral employment contract   Verbal agreement involving promises of duration or conditions in the employment relationship.

Oral warning   Verbal notice that a rule or policy has been violated and further discipline will result if the behavior is repeated.

Organizational culture   The way an organization treats its employees, customers, and others.

Organizational development   The process of structured analysis and planning for strategic organizational accomplishment.

Organizational restructuring   Radical change to an organization's internal and external relationships.

Organizing   Union efforts to convince employees to support a union as the designated bargaining agent for a workgroup.

Orientation   A process or program introducing new employees to their jobs, organization, and facility.

Outplacement   A program that assists employees in finding jobs when their job is eliminated.

Outside sales exemption   Exemption from overtime payment based on several qualifying factors such as the primary duty being making sales or obtaining orders for products or services. Work must be customarily and regularly engaged away from the employer's place of business.

Outsourcing   Contracting for services with a third party rather than having them performed in the organization.

P2P   Person-to-person.

Paid holidays   Designated days each year that are awarded to employees as paid time off.

Paid leaves   Paid time off for a specific designated reason.

Paid sick leave   Accrued paid time off usually based on length of service.

Paid time off (PTO)   A bank of hours in which an employer pools sick days, vacation days, and personal days that employees can use as the need arises.

Paid vacation   Accrued paid time off usually based on length of service.

Parent-country nationals (PCN)   Employees sent from the home country to a remote country for a work assignment.

Partially self-funded plans   Health insurance programs where the employer purchases one or two types of stop-loss insurance coverage.

Part-time   Employees who work fewer than the number of hours required to be considered full-time.

Pass rates   The number of people shown as a percent, who were successful in passing an exam.

Pay differentials   Additional compensation paid to an employee as an incentive to accept what would normally be considered as adverse working conditions, usually based on time, location, or working conditions.

Pay grades   The way an organization organizes jobs of a similar value into job groups or pay grades as a result of the job evaluation process.

Pay ranges   Pay amounts constrained by the upper and lower boundaries of each pay grade.

Pay survey   Collections of data on prevailing market pay rates and information on starting wage rates, base pay, pay ranges, overtime pay, shift differentials, and incentive pay plans.

Payroll   The function of recordkeeping and computation of compensation for each employee that results in issuance of a check or electronic deposit and collection and deposit of payroll taxes and other withholdings.

Payroll administration   The act of managing the payroll function.

Payroll systems   Usually computerized software programs designed to accept work time data and generate paychecks or electronic deposits.

Percentiles   Distribution of data into percentage ranges, such as top 10 percent,

Performance appraisal   A process of evaluating how employees perform in their jobs.

Performance grants   Stock-based compensation that is linked to organizational performance.

Performance Improvement Program (PIP)   A written plan that a supervisor provides an underperforming employee that specifies performance results required by a specified date.

Performance management   The process used to identify, measure, communicate, develop, and reward employee performance.

Performance standards   Indicators of what a job is to accomplish and how it is to be performed.

Performance-based merit pay system   A system with pay determined based on individual job performance.

Permissible bargaining issues   Issues that may be discussed by employer and union during contract negotiations. They are neither required nor prohibited.

Perquisites   Special privileges for executives including club memberships, company cars, reserved parking, use of the company airplane, and other such benefits.

Personal protective equipment (PPE)   Equipment worn by employees as protection against injury or illness hazards on the job.

Person-based system   Employee capabilities rather than how the job is performed determine the employee's pay.

Personnel file   One or more sets of documents held by an employer that contain information about the employee's employment status, performance evaluations, disability accommodations, and so forth, collectively considered one personnel file.

Phantom stock plan   Employee benefit program giving selected senior management employees pretend stock rather than actual stock, with the same financial benefits over time.

Phased retirement   Partial retirement while continuing to work a reduced schedule.

PHR-CA   PHR credentials for experts in employment regulations and legal mandates specific to the state of California.

Picketing   Technique used by unions to announce to the public a problem with an employer over issues involving working conditions or benefits.

Plateau curve   A type of learning curve in which learning is fast at first, but then flattens out.

Point of service plan   A type of managed care plan that is a hybrid of HMO and PPO plans.

Point-factor job evaluation   An approach using specific compensable factors as reference points to measure relative job worth.

Policies   Statements describing how an organization is to be managed.

Polycentric   A condition that occurs when jobs at headquarters are filled with people from other countries and positions in remote countries are filled with people from the headquarters country.

Preferred provider organization   Healthcare program including an in-network and an out-of-network option for services.

Premium-only plans (sometimes called "POP plans")   Authorized under the IRS Code, Section 125, allows employer-sponsored premium payments to be paid by the employee on a pre-tax basis instead of after-tax.

Premium pay   Payment at rates greater than straight pay for working overtime, or other agreed condition.

Prepaid legal insurance   Employer financial support for cost of routine legal services such as developing a will, real estate matters, divorces, and other services.

Prescription drug plans   Medical insurance programs that cover some or all of the cost of prescription drugs for subscribers.

Procedures   Methods to be used in fulfilling organizational responsibilities and policies.

Process-flow analysis   A diagram of the steps involved in a process.

Productivity-based system   Pay is determined by the employee's production output.

Professional employer organization   Vendor who, as a co-employer, provides qualified workers to a client organization.

Professional exemption   Exemption from overtime payment based on several qualifying factors, including minimum pay requirement, advanced knowledge, or education and use of professional discretion and judgment.

Professional in Human Resources (PHR)   Credential that demonstrates mastery of the technical and operational aspects of HR practices and U.S. laws and regulations.

Profit & Loss statement (P&L)   A financial statement that summarizes the revenues, costs, and expenses incurred during a specific period of time.

Profit-sharing plans   Direct or indirect payments to employees that depend on the employer's profitability.

Program evaluation and review technique (PERT)   A project management tool used to organize, coordinate, and schedule tasks and people.

Progressive discipline   A system of penalties involving increasing sanctions that can be taken if unwanted behaviors reoccur.

Prohibited bargaining issues   Issues that may not be discussed by employer and union during contract negotiations. These are illegal issues under the NLRA.

Project hire An employee who is hired for the duration of a project. Once the project is completed, the employee is dismissed or laid off. See *term employee*.

Project management Guiding the implementation of a program from beginning to end.

Project management concepts The study of project management styles and techniques.

Project team A group of people with specific talent or experience brought together to resolve a problem or accomplish some other organizational goal.

Promotion Usually considered to be an increase in responsibility or compensation or both.

Proof of identity Document such as a passport or driver's license that contains a photo of the individual that proves that person's identity.

Proof of work authorization Document such as a Social Security Card or alien work registration authorization that proves the individual is authorized to work in the United States.

Punitive damages Translation of punishment into dollar amounts usually applied to employers who have done something egregious. The damages are intended to deter a defendant from engaging in conduct similar to that which was the basis of a lawsuit.

Qualitative analysis Research that explores the reasoning behind human behavior; often uses open-ended interviewing.

Quantitative analysis Research based on quantifiable data.

Quartiles Distribution of data into four quadrants: bottom quarter, lower-middle quarter, upper-middle quarter, and top quarter.

Range spreads Dispersion of pay from the lowest boundary to the highest boundary of a pay range.

Ratio analysis Comparison of current results or historic results at a specific point in time.

Reasonable accommodation Adjustment to a job condition or workplace that will allow an employee to perform the essential job duties.

Reasonable cause One possible determination from a state or federal enforcement agency concerning an investigation of a charge of illegal discrimination.

Recency error This occurs when an evaluator gives greater weight to recent events of performance.

Recognition Acknowledgment of accomplishments by individual employees.

Recordkeeping Documentation involving any aspect of employee management from discussions to personal employee information.

Red circle rates Pay at a rate higher than the maximum for the assigned pay range.

Regiocentric Orientation to culture in a specific region or collection of countries in regions such as Asia, South America, or Europe.

Regression analysis A statistical process of estimating the relationships among variables.

Rehire A former employee who is hired back onto the payroll.

Repatriates Employees who return to their home country following a work assignment in a different country.

Request for proposal (RFP) A written document asking for vendor input and suggestions along with cost estimates for any given work to be performed in the establishment.

Responsibility A required part of a job or organizational obligation.

Results measurement Methods for monitoring the amount of progress that has been accomplished toward a stated goal or objective.

Retention Measurement of the quantity of employees remaining with the employer over a given period of time.

Retiree An ex-employee who met the qualification requirements for retirement under the organization's definition or plan.

Return on investment (ROI) The calculation showing the value of expenditures versus the investment.

Return to work Clearance to return to active employment activities following an illness, injury, or other absence.

Risk management Identifies and manages potential liabilities that come from operating an employer organization.

Role-play Technique for simulating individual participation in real-life roles involving performance or action with regard to solving a problem.

Safety audit The process of evaluating the workplace for safety hazards and determining any needed corrective action.

Sales personnel incentive programs Bonuses or commissions based on predetermined formulas involving performance and time.

Scaffolding Teacher modeling skills and thinking for students, allowing students to take over those expressions based on the initial structure provided by the teacher.

Scatter diagram   A graphical tool that depicts the relationship among variables.

Seasonal employee   A worker hired for a specific seasonal surge in work levels, common in retail industry and also agriculture and other food processing businesses.

Section 125 cafeteria plans   Allows employees to pay certain qualified expenses on a pre-tax basis. See also *Premium-only Plans*

Self-directed team   A group of people with a specific assignment permitted to select its own leadership and direction to take toward the problem or task.

Self-funded plans   Health insurance programs where the employer assumes all of the risk as a self-insured entity.

Senior Professional in Human Resources (SPHR)   Credential for those who have mastered the strategic and policy-making aspects of HR management in the United States.

Seniority pay increases   A pay increase given based solely on length of service.

Severance package   Voluntary payment by some employers to laid-off employees. May include pay for designated number of workdays, job retraining, outplacement services, and/or paid benefits premium assistance.

Short-term disability   Begins where sick leave ends. Covers some or all of employee's income for up to a specified period, usually six months.

Simulations   Learning exercises designed to be as realistic as possible without the risk of a real-life circumstance.

Single or flat-rate system   Each worker in the same job has the same rate of pay regardless of seniority or job performance.

Six Sigma   A data-driven approach and method for eliminating defects.

Skill-based system   Pay is based on the number and depth of skills that an employee has applicable to their job.

SMART goal model   Model for creating goals that are: Specific, Measurable, Attainable/Achievable, Relevant/Realistic, and Timed.

Society of Human Resource Professionals (SHRM)   The world's largest HR membership organization devoted to human resource management. Representing more than 275,000 members in over 160 countries.

Solution analysis   Statistical comparison of various potential solutions.

Specific stop-loss coverage   The health plan is protected against the risk of a major illness for one participant, or one family unit, covered by the plan.

SPHR-CA SPHR credentials for experts in employment regulations and legal mandates specific to the state of California.

Standard deviation Scores in a set of data that spread out around an average.

Standards The yardstick by which amount and quality of output are measured.

State employment service The agency responsible for assisting citizens with job placement and unemployment benefits in each state.

Statistical forecasts Use of mathematical formulas to identify patterns and trends.

Step rate with performance considerations A system allowing performance to influence the size or timing of a pay increase along the step system.

Storytelling Use of multimedia technology such as PowerPoint to present interactive opportunities involving any subject.

Straight piece rate system Employee receives a base rate of pay and is awarded additional compensation for the amount of output produced.

Strategic business management That which formulates and produces HR objectives, programs, practices, and policies.

Strategic planning Identifying organizational objectives and determining what actions are required to reach those objectives.

Strategies Specific direction that outlines objectives to achieve long-term plans.

Strike Work stoppage resulting from a failed negotiation between employer and union.

Subject matter expert A person who is well versed in the content of a specific knowledge area.

Subjective measurement Assessment of a result using opinion or perception.

Substance abuse Personal use of alcohol or drugs in excess of amounts prescribed by a medical professional, or any use of illegal substances. Abuse generally results in an impairment of the individual's physical or mental capacities.

Succession planning Identification of future key job openings and individuals who will be ready to fill those jobs.

Supplemental unemployment benefits An unemployment benefit in addition to government benefits offered by some employers.

Supply analysis Strategic evaluation of job candidate sources, plant locations, and other factors.

Suspension Temporary hiatus of active employment, usually as a disciplinary step, that can be paid or unpaid.

SWOT analysis A process in strategic planning that looks at an organization's strengths, weaknesses, opportunities, and threats.

Talent management The management and integration of all HR activities and processes that align with the organization's goals and needs.

Talent retention The retention of key talent, those employees who are the strongest performers, have high potential, or are in critical jobs.

Task force A group of people assembled to address major organizational issues.

Teacher exemption Exemption from overtime payment based on several qualifying factors, including the primary duty of teaching in an educational establishment.

Teams A group of people focused on specific organizational issues.

Temp-to-lease Conversion of a temporary agency–provided employee to regular employee status in the client organization.

Term employee An employee who is hired for the duration of a project. Once the project is completed, the employee is dismissed or laid off. See *project hire*.

Termination End of the employment relationship.

Third party Someone other than the two primary parties involved in an interaction.

Third-country nationals (TCN) Employees who are moved from one remote location to another remote location for a work assignment.

Third-party administrator plan Health insurance programs in which the employer assumes all of the risk but hires an independent claims department.

Time-based differential pay Shift pay, which is generally time-based rewards for employees who work what are considered undesirable shifts such as night shifts.

Time-based step rate system Determining pay rate based on the length of time in the job.

Total quality management (TQM) A management system for achieving customer satisfaction using quantitative methods to improve processes.

Total rewards Financial inducements and rewards as well as non-financial inducements and rewards, such as the value of good job content and good working environment.

Trainability The readiness and motivation to learn.

Training The process whereby people acquire skills, knowledge, or capabilities to perform jobs.

Training effectiveness Measurement of what students are expected to be able to do at the end of the training course or module.

Training techniques Approaches to training including virtual, classroom, on-the-job, and one-on-one tutoring.

Transactional leadership A leadership style that focuses on rewards, or threat of discipline, in an effort to motivate employees.

Transfer Movement of current employee to a different job in a different part of the organization.

Transformational leadership A leadership style that motivates employees by inspiring them.

Travel pay Extra pay provided for travel time, either under legal requirement or by other agreement.

Trend analysis Comparison of historical results with current results to determine a trend.

Tuition reimbursement Employer financial support for employee continuing education efforts.

Turnover analysis Comparison of the reasons for employees leaving the workforce and the organizational problems that may be causing them.

Uniform Guidelines Federal regulations that specify how job selection tools must be validated.

Unpaid sick leave Accrued unpaid time off, usually based on length of service.

Validity The extent to which a test measures what it says it measures.

Values The principles or standards of behavior that are most important to either an individual or entity.

Veteran A former member of the U.S. military service in any branch.

Veto The action of canceling or postponing a decision or bill in the U.S. legislature.

Vision care plans Medical insurance programs that cover some or all of the cost of vision care (exams and corrective lenses) for subscribers.

Vision statement A statement that describes the desired future of an organization.

Voluntary separations Individuals leaving the payroll for voluntary reasons including such things as retirement, obtaining a different job, returning to full-time education, or personal reasons.

Weighted average An average result taking into account the number of participants and each participant's pay.

Workers' compensation   Program that provides medical care and compensates employees for part of lost earnings as a result of a work-related disability.

Workforce analysis   Assessment of the workforce and things that are influencing it.

Workforce planning and employment   The processes performed by an employer of recruiting, interviewing, staffing, ensuring equal employment opportunity, affirmative action orientating new employees, managing, retention, termination, and proper employee records.

Workplace violence   Personal behavior that ranges from shouting to hitting or worse taking place on an employer's premises.

Written employment contract   Written agreement involving promises of duration or conditions in the employment relationship.

Written warning   Written notice that a rule or policy has been violated and further discipline will result if the behavior is repeated.

Zero-based budgeting   A model of budgeting that is based on expenditures being justified for each budget year.

Zero-sum   A system in which the sum of the gains equals the sum of the losses.

INDEX

LICENSE AGREEMENT

THIS PRODUCT (THE "PRODUCT") CONTAINS PROPRIETARY SOFTWARE, DATA AND INFORMATION (INCLUDING DOCUMENTATION) OWNED BY McGRAW-HILL EDUCATION AND ITS LICENSORS. YOUR RIGHT TO USE THE PRODUCT IS GOVERNED BY THE TERMS AND CONDITIONS OF THIS AGREEMENT.

LICENSE: Throughout this License Agreement, "you" shall mean either the individual or the entity whose agent opens this package. You are granted a non-exclusive and non-transferable license to use the Product subject to the following terms:

(i) If you have licensed a single user version of the Product, the Product may only be used on a single computer (i.e., a single CPU). If you licensed and paid the fee applicable to a local area network or wide area network version of the Product, you are subject to the terms of the following subparagraph (ii).

(ii) If you have licensed a local area network version, you may use the Product on unlimited workstations located in one single building selected by you that is served by such local area network. If you have licensed a wide area network version, you may use the Product on unlimited workstations located in multiple buildings on the same site selected by you that is served by such wide area network; provided, however, that any building will not be considered located in the same site if it is more than five (5) miles away from any building included in such site. In addition, you may only use a local area or wide area network version of the Product on one single server. If you wish to use the Product on more than one server, you must obtain written authorization from McGraw-Hill Education and pay additional fees.

(iii) You may make one copy of the Product for back-up purposes only and you must maintain an accurate record as to the location of the back-up at all times.

COPYRIGHT; RESTRICTIONS ON USE AND TRANSFER: All rights (including copyright) in and to the Product are owned by McGraw-Hill Education and its licensors. You are the owner of the enclosed disc on which the Product is recorded. You may not use, copy, decompile, disassemble, reverse engineer, modify, reproduce, create derivative works, transmit, distribute, sublicense, store in a database or retrieval system of any kind, rent or transfer the Product, or any portion thereof, in any form or by any means (including electronically or otherwise) except as expressly provided for in this License Agreement. You must reproduce the copyright notices, trademark notices, legends and logos of McGraw-Hill Education and its licensors that appear on the Product on the back-up copy of the Product which you are permitted to make hereunder. All rights in the Product not expressly granted herein are reserved by McGraw-Hill Education and its licensors.

TERM: This License Agreement is effective until terminated. It will terminate if you fail to comply with any term or condition of this License Agreement. Upon termination, you are obligated to return to McGraw-Hill Education the Product together with all copies thereof and to purge all copies of the Product included in any and all servers and computer facilities.

DISCLAIMER OF WARRANTY: THE PRODUCT AND THE BACK-UP COPY ARE LICENSED "AS IS." McGRAW-HILL EDUCATION, ITS LICENSORS AND THE AUTHORS MAKE NO WARRANTIES, EXPRESS OR IMPLIED, AS TO THE RESULTS TO BE OBTAINED BY ANY PERSON OR ENTITY FROM USE OF THE PRODUCT, ANY INFORMATION OR DATA INCLUDED THEREIN AND/OR ANY TECHNICAL SUPPORT SERVICES PROVIDED HEREUNDER, IF ANY ("TECHNICAL SUPPORT SERVICES"). McGRAW-HILL EDUCATION, ITS LICENSORS AND THE AUTHORS MAKE NO EXPRESS OR IMPLIED WARRANTIES OF MERCHANTABILITY OR FITNESS FOR A PARTICULAR PURPOSE OR USE WITH RESPECT TO THE PRODUCT. McGRAW-HILL EDUCATION, ITS LICENSORS, AND THE AUTHORS MAKE NO GUARANTEE THAT YOU WILL PASS ANY CERTIFICATION EXAM WHATSOEVER BY USING THIS PRODUCT. NEITHER McGRAW-HILL EDUCATION, ANY OF ITS LICENSORS NOR THE AUTHORS WARRANT THAT THE FUNCTIONS CONTAINED IN THE PRODUCT WILL MEET YOUR REQUIREMENTS OR THAT THE OPERATION OF THE PRODUCT WILL BE UNINTERRUPTED OR ERROR FREE. YOU ASSUME THE ENTIRE RISK WITH RESPECT TO THE QUALITY AND PERFORMANCE OF THE PRODUCT.

LIMITED WARRANTY FOR DISC: To the original licensee only, McGraw-Hill Education warrants that the enclosed disc on which the Product is recorded is free from defects in materials and workmanship under normal use and service for a period of ninety (90) days from the date of purchase. In the event of a defect in the disc covered by the foregoing warranty, McGraw-Hill Education will replace the disc.

LIMITATION OF LIABILITY: NEITHER McGRAW-HILL EDUCATION, ITS LICENSORS NOR THE AUTHORS SHALL BE LIABLE FOR ANY INDIRECT, SPECIAL OR CONSEQUENTIAL DAMAGES, SUCH AS BUT NOT LIMITED TO, LOSS OF ANTICIPATED PROFITS OR BENEFITS, RESULTING FROM THE USE OR INABILITY TO USE THE PRODUCT EVEN IF ANY OF THEM HAS BEEN ADVISED OF THE POSSIBILITY OF SUCH DAMAGES. THIS LIMITATION OF LIABILITY SHALL APPLY TO ANY CLAIM OR CAUSE WHATSOEVER WHETHER SUCH CLAIM OR CAUSE ARISES IN CONTRACT, TORT, OR OTHERWISE. Some states do not allow the exclusion or limitation of indirect, special or consequential damages, so the above limitation may not apply to you.

U.S. GOVERNMENT RESTRICTED RIGHTS: Any software included in the Product is provided with restricted rights subject to subparagraphs (c), (1) and (2) of the Commercial Computer Software-Restricted Rights clause at 48 C.F.R. 52.227-19. The terms of this Agreement applicable to the use of the data in the Product are those under which the data are generally made available to the general public by McGraw-Hill Education. Except as provided herein, no reproduction, use, or disclosure rights are granted with respect to the data included in the Product and no right to modify or create derivative works from any such data is hereby granted.

GENERAL: This License Agreement constitutes the entire agreement between the parties relating to the Product. The terms of any Purchase Order shall have no effect on the terms of this License Agreement. Failure of McGraw-Hill Education to insist at any time on strict compliance with this License Agreement shall not constitute a waiver of any rights under this License Agreement. This License Agreement shall be construed and governed in accordance with the laws of the State of New York. If any provision of this License Agreement is held to be contrary to law, that provision will be enforced to the maximum extent permissible and the remaining provisions will remain in full force and effect.